society, crime, and criminal behavior

DON C. GIBBONS

Portland State University

FOURTH
EDITION

Prentice-Hall, Inc.
Englewood Cliffs, N.J. 07632

Library of Congress Cataloging in Publication Data

Gibbons, Don C.
 Society, crime, and criminal behavior.

 Previous eds. published as: Society, crime, and
criminal careers.
 Includes bibliographical references and index.
 1. Crime and criminals. I. Title.
HV6025.G46 1982   364   81-10723
ISBN 0-13-820118-8   AACR2

editorial production/supervision
 and interior design: **Barbara Kelly**
cover design: **Fred Charles, Ltd.**
cover photo researcher: **Anita Duncan**
manufacturing buyer: **John Hall**

Printed in the United States of America

10 9 8 7 6 5 4 3 2 1

ISBN 0-13-820118-8

Prentice-Hall International, Inc., *London*
Prentice-Hall of Australia Pty. Limited, *Sydney*
Prentice-Hall of Canada, Ltd., *Toronto*
Prentice-Hall of India Private Limited, *New Delhi*
Prentice-Hall of Japan, Inc., *Tokyo*
Prentice-Hall of Southeast Asia Pte. Ltd., *Singapore*
Whitehall Books Limited, *Wellington, New Zealand*

TWENTY-THREE

crime in america: the uncertain future   529

preface

A few central themes concerning lawbreaking in modern societies run throughout this book and provide coherence to it. Perhaps the most important is the emphasis upon the ubiquity of crime in contemporary American society. This book argues that criminality is found everywhere: on the streets, in corporate boardrooms, on university campuses, on Skid Row, on the highways, and in most other parts of the social landscape. At one time or another, most of us are touched by acts of lawbreaking, either as victims or as offenders.

There is abundant evidence on the ubiquity of crime presented in the pages of this book. The statistics and data summarize the experiences of individuals in this society. In my own case, in the years since this book first appeared in 1968, my house and car have been burglarized, my wife has twice had her purse stolen, and finally, my wallet was stolen from my coat pocket while I was in my office, busily typing a report to the federal Law Enforcement Assistance Administration!

This book also indicates that crime is the product of "criminogenic" features which are built into modern societies, that is, social conditions that are implicated both in conformity and lawbreaking. The student of social behavior can learn a great deal about social values and social structure from an examination of crime and reactions to it. For example, the criminological literature on organized crime is a rich source of information on ethnic status, ethnic succession, and upward mobility in American society. Organized crime has often been a major route of upward mobility for persons who have been on the receiving end of economic and social discrimination. Similarly, garden variety street crime reveals a good deal about the responses of persons mired in a situation of pervasive economic precariousness who are at the same time surrounded by highly visible signs of affluence. Some of the alienated members of the underclass turn to crime as a crude form of income redistribution.

This book argues that criminals are most often normal persons who are responding to economic pressures or other features of the social structure of complex societies, rather than flawed individuals whose lawbreaking can be accounted for by biological or psychological explanations. This text is an introduction to the criminological enterprise, that is, a branch of sociological inquiry devoted to the study of law-making, law-breaking, and social responses to violations of criminal laws. At the same time, biological forces or psychological pressures may play some part in certain kinds of criminality, thus these influences are also given some attention in the pages of this book.

The fourth edition of this text has been considerably revised. The title of the book has been altered slightly, for it now speaks of criminal behavior rather than criminal careers. Earlier versions of the book argued that offenders can be sorted into a number of relatively specific types or role-careers. However, recent evidence indicates that many lawbreakers can be assigned to categories of criminal type classifications only with great difficulty, if at all. Real-life offenders make up a heterogeneous collection of individuals. This edition stresses patterns of crime to a greater extent than earlier versions, with less attention to efforts to sort offenders into specific pigeon holes or categories.

This edition has been revised in other ways as well. Greater attention is given to radical-Marxist theories concerning criminal laws and criminality than in previous editions. A number of chapters have been relocated within the book. Finally, I have pruned out claims that seem unsupportable in the light of recent evidence. I have also attempted to bring all of the sections of the book up to date, by including most of the relevant theoretical developments and research studies that have appeared in the past few years.

I am grateful to the many professional colleagues who read and commented on either the complete manuscript or various chapters. Among these are: Stephen Cernkovich, Bowling Green State University; Gary Jensen, University of Arizona; Harold Finestone, University of Minnesota, and George Stine, Millersville State College.

A number of persons have contributed to this edition, including students and colleagues at Portland State University, as well as Ms. Barbara Kelly of Prentice-Hall, Inc. But, none of them are responsible for any deficiencies that are found in the book.

To Carlo Lastucci,
teacher, critic, and good friend

crime
in
modern
society

Crime is a topic of enduring interest to most Americans, as any quick perusal of the mass media in this society will show. Lawbreakers and police officers are among the most frequently encountered figures on television, while magazine articles, books, and movies dealing with criminality also enjoy much popularity.[1] But, most of this popular attention is focused upon "crime in the streets" and on what some have termed garden-variety crime—robberies, simple thefts, assaults, rapes, and a few other crude and forceful offenses. Corporate crime and other violations engaged in by socially powerful persons are less often noticed, and equally obscured as well are various mundane, low-level violations of the law that are common in complex societies.

Popular notions of the crime problem bear much similarity to nineteenth-century British stereotypes embraced by many who believed that crime was the work of "the dangerous classes."[2] In this view of things, malefactors are seen as depraved or alien, antisocial beings in a society in which most of us are law-abiding and upright in character. Lawbreakers are thought to be the products of unusual circumstances involving such things as biological quirks or disruptions of normal family life. Most laymen seem unimpressed by sociological arguments holding that offenders are often impelled toward criminality by forces which arise out of the social and economic order of modern societies.

Many Americans appear to have a love-hate relationship with lawbreaking, both fascinated by portrayals of crime in the mass media and at the same time fearful of the prospects of being robbed, burglarized, assaulted, or victimized in some other way. The apprehensiveness of citizens about crime in the streets has been amply documented. For example, opinion surveys undertaken in the past two decades have repeatedly shown that most people in the United States feel that crime is a worsening problem in their communities, although curiously many of them do feel safe near their homes, even when they live in high crime areas.[3] Most often Americans have attributed lawbreaking to the breakdown of moral standards or kindred factors, rather than to deleterious social conditions. Moreover, most have embraced repressive or punitive measures, rather than ameliorative steps, to curb crime.

Most popular beliefs about criminality in modern societies do not survive close examination. For one thing, it is by no means clear that American society is currently undergoing a crime wave of massive proportions, such that lawbreaking is increasing at an alarming rate. Although accurate American crime statistics spanning pre-twentieth-century periods are not available, there are historical accounts that suggest that lawlessness was exceedingly common at earlier points in American history.[4] Then, too, it would be well to acknowledge that apparent surges or waves of crime may actually reflect increased reporting of offenses or the proliferation of new laws, rather than changes in the levels of lawbreaking. One instructive report in this regard is a Portland, Oregon, victimization survey which indicated that the incidence of burglary declined in that city in 1973–1974 from the level observed in 1971–1972. At the same time, the proportion of burglary incidents reported to the police increased during this period, with the result that the official burglary rate increased, creating the erroneous impression that burglary was on the rise in Portland.[5] Some criminologists have argued that apparent increases in forcible rape and certain other crimes in recent years may similarly reflect increased crime reporting rather than actual changes in crime amounts.

Whatever the truth concerning crime waves, the fact remains that criminological research has amply documented sociologist Daniel Bell's claim that crime is an American way of life.[6] In modern American society crime is found everywhere, including on the streets, in college buildings, in corporate board rooms, in "Skid Row" alleys, and on the highways. In short, there are myriad forms and generous amounts of lawbreaking in modern societies; thus it is clearly not the case that criminality and criminals are relatively rare in the United States.

Citizen perspectives on crime causation are also fatally flawed.[7] While bizarre acts of criminality carried on by persons suffering from personality pathology are sometimes encountered, these make up only a very small part of the crime problem in modern societies. The lion's share of crime in America and elsewhere reflects societal conditions which operate as the root causes of this activity. For example, there is abundant evidence linking organized crime in our society to ethnic status, economic discrimination directed at certain ethnic groups, and pressures toward upward mobility that are experienced by nearly all citizens, conformists and lawbreakers alike. Also, organized crime is often related to efforts by lawmakers to legislate morality by forbidding people to gamble, drink, or to engage in other activities which many of them would like to pursue. Similarly, garden-variety street crime is usually carried on by persons who are mired in situations of economic precariousness but who are also surrounded by highly visible signs of affluence on the part of many of their more fortunate neighbors. Some of these alienated and resentful members who feel the sting of relative deprivation in an acquisitive society try to bring about income distribution at gunpoint or through other illegal means.

The discussion thus far has touched upon some major themes or broad contentions about crime. These themes stand as core propositions of the criminological perspective to which most sociological criminologists hold allegiance. Let us examine these perspectives in a bit more detail.

Although many of the facts concerning crime in modern society are in dispute, there is little question that lawbreaking is omnipresent in contemporary America. Masses of evidence are at hand which indicate that criminality is extremely common in this country and much more frequently encountered than in most other industrialized nations of the world. Although Chapter 5 will examine the existing data on crime in detail, a quick look at a handful of crime statistics will amply illustrate our point.

Consider some indicators of the pervasive nature of lawbreaking in America: According to statistics collected by the Federal Bureau of Investigation, there were 21,456 murder and nonnegligent manslaughter cases, 75,989 forcible rape incidents, 466,881 robberies, and 614,213 instances of aggravated assault reported to the police in the United States in 1979. Also, the police were informed of 3,299,484 burglaries, 6,577,518 larcenies, and 1,097,189 cases of car theft.[8] These figures indicate that 12,152,730 serious crimes were reported to the police in a single year, in a nation with a total population of 220,099,000 citizens.

However, these figures only begin to tell the story of crime in America. What about all those offenses that, for one reason or another, persons fail to report to the police? Some indication of the extent of "the dark figure of crime"—that is, unreported or undetected lawbreaking—is offered in Table 1, derived from the results of the National Crime Survey carried out by the U.S. Bureau of the Census in collaboration with the federal Law Enforcement Assistance Administration. In that survey, a national sample of individuals, households, and businesses representative of the country as a whole was interviewed about experience with crime during 1977. The results were then employed as the basis for estimates of the total number of victimizations that occurred in the United States in 1977. For the discussion here the most important observation from Table 1 is that, of a number of crimes surveyed, less than half were reported to the police. Thus it is clear that official statistics drastically understate the magnitude of crime in the nation.

These data reveal something about the extent of garden-variety crimes in the United States, but they provide only a partial accounting of lawbreaking. In particular, official crime statistics and citizens' reports of victimization reveal little about so-called white-collar criminal acts carried on by corporations and other business organizations. Although these latter kinds of lawbreaking are widespread and very costly in terms of harm inflicted upon the general public, they often are low-visibility offenses. They are much less frequently brought to our attention by the mass media than are dramatic instances of garden-variety crime. Then, too, business crimes often touch upon a diffuse collection of victims, many of whom are unaware that they have been victimized. It is for reasons of this sort that much white-collar lawbreaking goes unrecognized.

It takes only a bit of digging to unearth abundant evidence on white-collar crime.[9] For example, reports are available which document widespread criminal

table 1 estimated number of personal, household, and business victimizations, United States, 1977[a]

type of victimization	total	percent reported to the police	percent not reported to the police	percent unknown whether reported to the police
Personal victimizations				
rape and attempted rape	154,237	58	42	0
robbery	1,082,936	56	44	1
assault	4,663,827	44	55	1
personal larceny with contact	461,014	37	62	1
personal larceny without contact	16,469,154	24	74	1
Household victimizations				
burglary	6,766,010	49	50	1
larceny	9,415,533	25	74	0
vehicle theft	1,296,759	68	31	1
Business victimizations				
robbery	279,516	87	12	1
burglary	1,576,242	73	25	2

[a]Timothy J. Flanagan, Michael J. Hindelang, and Michael R. Gottfredson, eds., Sourcebook of Criminal Justice Statistics, 1979 (Washington, D.C.: Law Enforcement Assistance Administration, 1980), p. 328.

violations by major pharmaceutical manufacturers in the United States.[10] In one of these, Kurtz drew attention to a number of cases where laboratory test results which showed that new drugs had harmful side effects were tampered with or hidden from the Food and Drug Administration.[11] These drugs were then placed on the market and administered to patients, even though the offending companies were aware of their serious, negative side effects, such as blood disorders, liver damage, cataracts, or severe hair loss. Extremely lenient penalties were standard in these cases, which has been shown to be true of other corporate offenses as well. Kurtz argued that the Food and Drug Administration rarely goes beyond wrist-slapping of drug manufacturers because it is dominated by officials with ties to the organizations that it is supposed to police.

The crime problem in modern societies also involves a very large number of less dramatic but commonplace offenses such as traffic-law violations which one criminologist has termed "folk crimes."[12] These are violations of laws introduced to solve problems arising out of the increased complexity and division of labor in modern societies. Traffic-law violations, "chiseling" on unemployment compensation, and violations of regulatory statutes governing business and commerce are instances of folk crime. Folk crime also includes such low-visibility offenses as failure on the part of divorced spouses to provide child-support payments, violation of fish and game laws,[13] and vandalism in public parks,[14] all of which are quite widespread. Most folk crimes provoke only mild social responses, carry only a low degree of social stigma, and are often engaged in by persons of high social status. They are also dealt with in a variety of administrative ways; for example, traffic-law-violation cases are disposed of through special bureaus, bail forfeiture, and in other ways outside of courts. Although it is easy to minimize their significance, because such folk crimes make up a large part of modern-day criminality, they cannot be ignored or dismissed as "not really crimes."

That lawbreaking is frequent and widespread in American society is one claim which criminologists do not quarrel with. There is, however, a good deal of disagreement among them regarding the rates of criminality that are assumed to be associated with different groups in our society. In particular, opinions differ markedly as to whether crime is more frequent among blacks than whites. Some criminologists maintain that American blacks are more frequently involved in lawbreaking than are whites. But, in the view of many others, this seemingly excessive criminality reflects discriminatory law enforcement on the part of the police rather than inordinate involvement in criminality on the part of blacks. Then, too, those who assert that black citizens are more heavily implicated in crime base their arguments on statistics of reported garden-variety crimes and slur over the contrary evidence on unreported crime and white-collar criminality.

Criminological opinions are also divided on the question of social class and crime. Perhaps it is true, as conventional crime statistics suggest, that criminal acts are concentrated among those persons who are at the bottom of the economic heap in our society. Yet it may well be that these statistics are highly misleading, providing indicators of law-enforcement practices rather than the distribution of crime. If it were possible to assemble data on all of the forms of criminality that exist in our society, including garden-variety offenses, white-collar crime, and folk crime, it might be discovered that lawbreaking is actually distributed in some other way, perhaps as one of the broadly sketched crime distributions in Figure 1, which contrasts the "conventional" pattern (A) with four alternatives (B, C, D, and E).

In Figure 1, pattern A illustrates the view that crime rates are highest among groups on the bottom of the economic ladder. Pattern B places the highest rates of lawbreaking among groups at the top of the social-class structure. Pattern C represents the hypothesis of equal rates of crime across social-class groups, while D portrays crime rates as highest among middle-income citizens. Finally, pattern E presents a bimodal distribution of criminality, with highest rates among both the economically most advantaged and least advantaged in our society.

Many analysts in the United States have opted for the hypothesis that deviant behavior and criminality are most commonly encountered among the economically disadvantaged strata.[15] At the same time, there are other criminologists who find this argument unpersuasive. The latter group includes Marxist or radical criminologists who contend that it is members of a ruling class and other socially powerful citizens who are most involved in criminal acts in capitalist societies. Still other criminologists have reached conclusions on this issue that parallel pattern C in Figure 1, arguing that there is no significant link between social-class position and criminality.[16] For example, in a survey of residents of New Jersey, Oregon, and Iowa conducted by Charles Tittle and Wayne Villemez in 1972, persons were quizzed as to whether they had engaged in certain crimes.[17] Tittle and Villemez indicated that self-reported crimes were equally frequent among persons from different social-class groups. However, two of the six offenses about which the respondents were asked—"theft of something worth about $5" and "marijuana smoking"—were relatively petty ones. Responses to the questions about the remaining four offenses—"theft of something worth about $50," "illegal gambling," "income tax evasion," and "physically harming

Social
Class

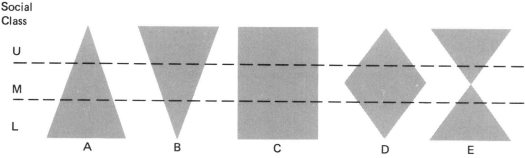

figure 1 *crime rates and social class*

another person"—probably need to be interpreted with caution. Conceivably, some individuals who admitted to tax evasion, gambling, and assault may have been reporting relatively serious offenses, while others might have been confessing to petty gambling such as church lotteries, small-scale tax evasion (such as failure to report income from tips), or minor acts of physical aggression. Quite different results might have turned up if a wider range of illegal acts had been the focus of attention and had the respondents been probed about the seriousness of the criminal acts to which they admitted.

The question of social-class linkages and criminality is a very large and complex one that will be addressed in detail at a number of points later in this book. However, it should be apparent from these brief remarks that as far as crime is concerned, the real world is rarely as clear and simple as public wisdom suggests.

the elastic boundaries of crime

Most citizens probably would not quarrel with the claim that crime levels often increase or decrease over time in particular societies. As we have already noted, many Americans believe that lawbreaking has mushroomed in this country during the past few decades. However, when citizens speculate about the expansion or contraction of criminality, they do so almost entirely in terms of the growth or decline of lawbreaking behavior. Laymen rarely show much awareness of the fact that crime is a social invention and an elastic social phenomenon, stretching or shrinking as new laws are added or old ones are expunged from the criminal statutes.

Historians of criminal law have provided a number of illustrations of the shifting definitions of crime that have characterized societies. For example, Jerome Hall traced the growth of modern property and theft laws back to the Carrier's Case in England in 1473, in which a person employed to carry a bale of goods from London to Southampton broke open the bale instead and absconded with the contents.[18] The decision arrived at by the court in this case established the legal precedent which gave rise to the plethora of property laws characteristic of modern industrialized societies. Thus today we have a large number of property criminals in considerable part because we have a vastly expanded list of property crimes.

Other studies have focused upon the historical proliferation of criminal laws in eighteenth-century England, including the flood of draconian legislation enacted then which increased crimes subject to capital punishment from 50 to over 200.[19] In a similar vein, William Nelson studied changes in criminal law and procedure in the Massachusetts Puritan colony from 1760 to 1830.[20] Nelson rummaged through court records to uncover the nature of law and prosecution during those years and discovered drastic changes in that system. In the pre-Revolutionary period, juries were empowered to determine law as well as fact. The laws functioned to enforce the Puritan morality of a tightly knit community. Blasphemy and other violations of Puritan morality were serious crimes. Property and contract law restrained people from pursuit of wealth and financial speculation. But that legal system became anachronistic in post-Revolutionary America when the emerging economy required new legislation that would reduce the restrictions on economic activity and on the pursuit of financial success. Ultimately, property and contract laws were revised to emphasize the protection of private property. Nelson concluded that the transformation of the Massachusetts legal system both mirrored the changing nature of the American social order and also helped to accelerate the growth of an entrepreneurial society.

Let us be clear on one point. The creation of criminal laws and procedures is a continuing process, as is the decriminalization of some activities resulting from certain laws being expunged. For example, in the period since the first juvenile court was created in the United States in 1899, the general drift has been in the direction of "widening of the nets" as juvenile courts have been awarded jurisdiction over more and more children. Expansion of juvenile-court control has resulted from the development of status-offender statutes which allow courts to deal with youngsters who have not violated the criminal law but who are judged to be immoral, wayward, ungovernable, or in some other way in need of court benevolence and protection. Thus juvenile courts are meant to operate therapeutically and effectively to rescue youngsters from a life of crime. However, in the past decade or so, much disillusionment with the juvenile court has set in, resulting in proposals that court jurisdiction be severely reduced, in part by deletion of status-offender provisions.[21]

Contemporary examples of the elastic boundaries of crime include the law-making activities of state legislatures, where new bills create "new" crimes year after year. Then, too, legislatures sometimes undertake wholesale revisions of criminal codes or criminal procedures. For example, the new criminal code enacted by the Oregon legislature in 1971 embodied a large number of changes, including deletion from the codes of adultery, lewd cohabitation, seduction, and private consensual acts of homosexuality between adults. The provisions regarding statutory rape now allow male defendants the defense that they were reasonably mistaken as to the age of the female. Also, possession of small amounts of marijuana for personal use was reduced to a "violation" carrying a maximum fine of $100. This revised criminal code also involved major changes in the penalty structure, such that many of the maximum punishments allowable for conviction of specific offenses were altered.

Pulling and tugging by different interest groups regarding the behaviors and activities that ought to be the law's business are also prominent features of modern societies. Social conflict over the appropriateness of various criminal statutes is probably more frequently encountered than is widespread societal consensus. As illustrative cases, one can point to the vigorous public debates that have been taking place in recent times over whether prostitution, homosexual acts among consenting adults, marijuana smoking, or various other activities ought to be decriminalized, that is, removed entirely from the compass of the criminal law.

Laymen rarely give much thought to the criminal laws that restrain them; instead, they are taken for granted. But, the brief commentary here concerning the growth and decline of statutes should indicate that we cannot ignore them if we are to comprehend the nature of crime in our society. Chapter 4 will devote a good deal of attention to theories regarding the social factors that give rise to criminal laws, as well as to a number of studies of specific pieces of criminal legislation that have been carried on by criminologists and legal historians.

crime as natural social behavior

What does it mean to say that crime is natural social behavior? There are several meanings to that claim, some having already been noted. To begin with, law-breaking can be regarded as normal social behavior in that the vast majority of acts of criminality are carried on by individuals who are free from severe forms of mental pathology. This is not to say that we can ignore completely the inner life of criminal actors, for there are some kinds of criminality in which person-ality disorders and aberrant mental processes do play a significant role. Even more important, it is extremely unlikely that explanatory accounts of criminal behavior can ignore the role of individual differences and psychological varia-tions among persons. We would be ill advised to assume that individuals are equally subject to criminogenic or crime-producing influences of one kind or another. Rather, we would do well to consider whether what determines if per-sons engage in crime or refrain from it is not due in part because some are particularly vulnerable to harmful social influences while others are insulated from these factors by virtue of their particular psychological characteristics. In short, probing into the contribution of psychogenic factors in criminality is a complex task (and one that will be taken up in detail in Chapter 8).

Another dimension of crime as normal behavior has already been noted, namely, that what constitutes crime is a matter of social definition, which changes from time to time. The boundaries of criminality expand and contract as new laws are created or old ones are jettisoned. Further, lawmaking is not random or capricious behavior; instead, it is activity that flows from various other social phenomena, one example being the sweeping changes in the social and economic structure of English society starting in the 15th century, which resulted in the proliferation of criminal laws designed to surround private prop-erty with the protections of the law. More recently, the growing complexity of business and financial operations in American society has resulted in the creation of such new offenses as credit-card fraud, computer crimes, and other delicts, or offenses. Chapter 4 will deal at length with the social analysis of lawmaking.

When sociologists speak of the normality of crime, they often have in mind the broad claim that lawbreaking arises out of root causes or criminogenic conditions that are part and parcel of the social structure of societies. Some of these crime-producing influences have already been noted, such as the moral crusades against alcohol with led to passing of the Volstead Act prohibiting alcohol and ultimately to the organized-crime networks which served as the illegal channel through which Americans continued to obtain liquor.

Many criminologists would also concur that garden-variety crime is often best viewed as a rational response by economically disadvantaged citizens to the economic precariousness which dominates their lives. For many of them, unsophisticated property crimes constitute a form of occupational "moonlighting" that is little different from other kinds of supplemental income activity, such as holding a second legitimate but low-paying job. In much the same way, sociological criminologists are quick to point to other ways in which the social structure of modern societies is implicated in the lawbreaking that is observed in those societies.

Although it is relatively easy to show broad agreement among many criminologists regarding social-structural influences that are involved in criminality, one should not assume that a full-blown sociological perspective on the causes of crime has been developed which nearly everyone can concur with. To the contrary, there are a good many vigorous disagreements among criminologists over issues of causation. For example, some have asserted that violence in American society can be linked to subcultures of violence, that is, social attitudes that support the use of interpersonal violence and which are shared by persons living in certain regions and areas of the country; other sociologists exhibit a good deal of skepticism about the existence of such subcultures. Along this same line, many criminologists attribute lawlessness to social and economic forces that are central to our society but at the same time believe that these conditions can be ameliorated through social reform. A smaller, noisier group of radical or Marxist criminologists asserts that lawbreaking arises out of economic and other forms of oppression in capitalist societies which cannot be changed through any steps short of revolution. A large part of this book is given over to the the examination of these discordant lines of argument regarding social-structural influences upon crime.

There is one other way in which it can be said that crime is natural or normal social behavior, namely, that social reactions to lawbreaking are related to a variety of basic characteristics of the societies within which they take place. For example, in one major study of the relationships between social structure and social reactions to crime, Georg Rusche and Otto Kirchheimer persuasively argued that major shifts in penal policies in European countries over the past several centuries have been closely linked to major alterations in economic conditions in those nations.[22] Closer to home, the facts show that offender-imprisonment rates are much higher in the United States than in European nations or most other countries of the world. These patterns probably reflect higher crime rates in this nation than elsewhere, but they are also related to broader social differences between the United States and many other countries. Then, too, there is abundant evidence indicating that the death penalty has much more frequently been visited upon convicted blacks than upon whites guilty of similar offenses, a clear indication of discriminatory handling of offenders which mirrors the pervasive racism in American society. Somewhat less dramatic but no less significant is the evidence pointing generally in our society to discriminatory enforcement of laws, such that blacks are often dealt with more severely by the police and courts than are whites. Numerous other examples showing linkages between social reactions to offenders and basic social conditions of American society could be offered in order to drive home the basic point—that police practices, the workings of courts, and penal responses to offenders are all matters that cry out for probing examination by sociologists and criminologists. In modern societies, formalized social-control mechanisms of one kind or another have been developed as major defenses against lawbreakers, persons thought to be mentally deranged, and various other nonconformists. One can learn much about American society through the study of its organs of social control.

summary

This introductory chapter has argued that criminality is an extremely complex matter, one which cannot be understood in terms of simple theories that offenders are the products of defective heredity, psychological aberrations, or a few abnormal or atypical features of society. In the same way, the control of crime is not likely to be accomplished through the application of simple panaceas. Instead, if we are to make sense of criminality and social responses to it, we must be prepared to grapple with some complex kinds of social phenomena. Criminological inquiry is serious business.

Thus far, only a few hints have been provided about the nature of the criminological enterprise as it is carried out by sociological criminologists. What is involved in thinking like a criminologist? More specifically, what are the central questions about crime and criminals that are raised by criminologists? What is the nature of causal analysis in criminology and other sciences of human behavior? What are the ingredients of the major explanatory theories advanced by criminologists? Finally, what are the intellectual roots of modern criminology? These are the major questions to which we will turn in Chapters 2 and 3.

notes

[1] The impact of mass-media coverage of crime and delinquency on citizens' views of these phenomena is discussed in Mark Fishman, "Crime Waves as Ideology," *Social Problems*, 25 (May 1978), 531–43; Mark Warr, "The Accuracy of Public Beliefs About Crime," *Social Forces*, 59 (December 1980), 456–70; Walter B. Miller, "Youth Gangs in the Urban Crisis Era," in *Delinquency, Crime, and Society*, James F. Short, Jr., ed., (Chicago: University of Chicago Press, 1976), pp. 91–128.

[2] J. J. Tobias, *Crime and Industrial Society in the 19th Century* (London: B. T. Batsford, 1967).

[3]For summaries of these studies, see Don C. Gibbons and Joseph F. Jones, *The Study of Deviance* (Englewood Cliffs, N. J.: Prentice-Hall, Inc., 1975), pp. 67–70; John E. Conklin, *The Impact of Crime* (New York: Macmillan, 1975); Timothy J. Flanagan, Michael J. Hindelang, and Michael R. Gottfredson, eds., *Sourcebook of Criminal Justice Statistics, 1979* (Washington, D. C.: Law Enforcement Assistance Administration, 1980), 247–326. Some individual studies are Jennie McIntyre, "Public Attitudes Toward Crime and Law Enforcement," *Annals of the American Academy of Political and Social Science*, 374 (November 1967), 34–46; John E. Conklin, "Dimensions of Community Response to the Crime Problem," *Social Problems*, 18 (Winter 1971), 373–85; Sarah L. Boggs, "Formal and Informal Crime Control: An Exploratory Study of Urban, Suburban and Rural Orientations," *Sociological Quarterly*, 12 (Summer 1971), 319–27; Don C. Gibbons, Joseph F. Jones, and Peter G. Garabedian, "Gauging Public Opinion About the Crime Problem," *Crime and Delinquency*, 18 (April 1972), 135–46.

[4]For example, see Paul Boyer, *Urban Masses and Moral Order in America, 1820–1920* (Cambridge: Harvard University Press, 1978).

[5]Anne L. Schneider, *Crime and Victimization in Portland: Analysis of Trends, 1971–74* (Eugene, Ore.: Oregon Research Institute, 1975).

[6]Daniel Bell, "Crime as an American Way of Life," *Antioch Review*, 13 (June 1953), 131–54.

[7]For one study on citizens' conceptions of criminal and delinquent acts, see Jack P. Gibbs and Maynard L. Erickson, "Conceptions of Criminal and Delinquent Acts," *Deviant Behavior*, 1 (October 1979), 71–100. Also see Russell A. Ward, "Typifications of Homosexuals," *Sociological Quarterly*, 20 (Summer 1979), 411–23.

[8]Federal Bureau of Investigation, U. S. Department of Justice, *Crime in the U. S.: Uniform Crime Reports, 1979* (Washington, D. C.: U. S. Government Printing Office, 1980), p. 40.

[9]For evidence on various forms of white-collar crime, see Edwin H. Sutherland, *White Collar Crime* (New York: The Dryden Press, 1949); Warren G. Magnuson and Jean Carper, *The Dark Side of the Marketplace* (Englewood Cliffs, N. J.: Prentice-Hall, Inc., 1968); David Caplovitz, *The Poor Pay More* (New York: Free Press, 1967); Gilbert Geis and Robert F. Meier, eds., *White-Collar Crime: Offenses in Business, Politics, and the Professions*, rev. ed. (New York: Free Press, 1977); John E. Conklin, *Illegal But Not Criminal: Business Crime in America* (Englewood Cliffs, N. J.: Prentice-Hall, Inc., 1977).

[10]Paul D. Rheingold, "The MER/29 Story—An Instance of Successful Mass Disaster Legislation," *California Law Review*, 56 (January 1958), 116–48; Howie Kurtz, "The Real Problem with the FDA," *Washington Monthly*, 9 (July/August 1977), 59–62.

[11]Kurtz, "The Real Problem with the FDA."

[12]H. Laurence Ross, "Traffic Law Violation: A Folk Crime," *Social Problems*, 8 (Winter 1960–1961), 231–41.

[13]Clayton A. Hartjen and Don C. Gibbons, "An Empirical Investigation of a Criminal Typology," *Sociology and Social Research*, 54 (October 1969), 56–63; Gibbons, "Crime in the Hinterland," *Criminology*, 10 (August 1972), 177–91.

[14]Joseph W. Bennett, *Vandals Wild* (Portland: Bennett Publishing Co., 1969).

[15]For one general review of the evidence on this claim, see John P. Hewitt, *Social Stratification and Deviant Behavior* (New York: Random House, 1970).

[16]Charles W. Tittle and Wayne J. Villemez, "Social Class and Criminality," *Social Forces*, 56 (December 1977), 474–502; Tittle, Villemez, and Douglas A. Smith, "The Myth of Social Class and Criminality," *American Sociological Review*, 43 (December 1978), 643–56. For detailed critiques of the conclusions of Tittle, Villemez, and Smith, see Donald Clelland and Timothy J. Carter, "The New Myth of Class and Crime," *Criminology*, 18 (November 1980), 319–36; John Braithwaite, "The Myth of Social Class and Criminality Reconsidered," *American Sociological Review*, 46 (February 1981), 36–57.

[17]Tittle and Villemez, "Social Class and Criminality."

[18]Jerome Hall, *Theft, Law and Society*, 2nd ed. (Indianapolis: Bobbs-Merrill, 1952).

[19]Douglas Hay, Peter Linebaugh, John G. Rule, E. P. Thompson, and Cal Winslow, *Albion's Fatal Tree: Crime and Society in Eighteenth Century England* (New York: Pantheon Books, 1975); E. P. Thompson, *Whigs and Hunters: The Origin of the Black Act* (New York: Pantheon Books, 1975); John Brewer, "An Ungovernable People: Law and Disorder in Stuart and Hanoverian England," *History Today*, 30 (January 1980), 18–27.

[20]William E. Nelson, *Americanization of the Common Law: The Impact of Legal Change on Massachusetts Society, 1760–1830* (Cambridge: Harvard University Press, 1975).

[21]These developments regarding juvenile courts are discussed at greater length in Don C. Gibbons, *Delinquent Behavior*, 3rd ed. (Englewood Cliffs, N. J.: Prentice-Hall, Inc., 1981), pp. 75–81.

[22]Georg Rusche and Otto Kirchheimer, *Punishment and Social Structure* (New York: Columbia University Press, 1939).

the
origins
of
criminology

Crime and crimelike acts have marred social life for all of recorded history. Over the long span of human existence, two general views of criminality have been advanced, the demonological and the naturalistic.[1] Demonological views entertain the belief that "other world" powers and spirits are at the root of criminality, while naturalistic theories hold that events and characteristics of the observable physical and material world are the active agents or forces producing crime. Criminology, defined as the scientific study of crime and social responses to it, is concerned with naturalistic explanations and observable evidence about lawbreaking.

Criminology arose in a number of European countries in the late 1700s. There, contributions to criminological study in Europe were made by physical scientists, medical doctors, and kindred researchers, as well as by sociologists and other social scientists. Because of the diverse backgrounds of those who probed into criminality in Europe, much of that early work had a biological cast to it that has been largely absent from modern American criminology.

This chapter offers a brief account of the development of criminological inquiry in Europe, while Chapter 3 will examine the nature of the contemporary criminological enterprise, particularly as it has taken shape in the United States.

the contributions of early criminology

Naturalistic, premodern criminology arose in the late 1700s. What can be learned from the pioneers in criminology who carried out the initial probings of criminality?[2] On one hand, perhaps not a great deal. Criminology's pioneering figures explored many blind alleys. Historical efforts were all too often fruitless meanderings into theoretical terrain which failed to account adequately for criminality. Thus, inquiry on lawbreaking, starting a century or so ago, has not been cumulative. Instead, current explanatory viewpoints are relatively unrelated to earlier theorizing about crime.

Concerning the discontinuity between past and present efforts in criminology, George Vold and Thomas Bernard have offered this assessment of one pervasive area of early inquiry, namely, the search for evidence that criminals represent a distinct physical type: "Physical type theories turn out to be a more-or-less sophisticated form of shadow-boxing with a much more subtle and difficult to get at problem, namely, that of the constitutional factor in human behavior."[3] Behind this evaluation of physical-type theories, and underlying the more sweeping negative judgment regarding historical endeavors as a whole, is the assertion that modern social science puts forth an image of man and society infinitely more complicated than implied in earlier arguments. Criminality and conformity are more complex phenomena than they were assumed to be by early investigators.

On the other hand, historical efforts in criminology have been of considerable value as indicators of theoretical veins that have been mined with negligible results. In this sense, although they ended in blind alleys, these earlier efforts have much significance for contemporary criminology. Moreover, although a good deal of discontinuity can be seen in criminological inquiry, it is also the case that some linkages between older lines of investigation and contemporary ones do exist. Accordingly, the person attempting to comprehend crime must begin with the writings of prior generations of criminologists.

Premodern criminology was not all of the same stripe. Instead, a number of "schools" of thought grew up, each centered around certain core ideas and major developers of them. Let us examine these schools, generally in the order that they arose. The brief accounts presented here will outline the contours of these earlier theories and will point out some linkages to modern theories as well.

the classical school

The classical school was centered around the writings of a number of European scholars in the late 1700s, particularly those of Cesare Beccaria in Italy (1738–94) and Jeremy Bentham in England (1748–1832).[4] The core concepts of the classical frame of reference were hedonism and free will. Vold and Bernard noted that all classical theorists accepted as valid, as did most of their lay contemporaries, certain beliefs about human behavior, including the existence of human will as a psychological reality. Prevailing opinions of the time agreed that all men, criminals included, act rationally and deliberately to avoid pain and encounter pleasure.[5] The conclusion from these premises was that the criminal makes a deliberate, rational, hedonistically oriented decision to engage in lawbreaking. If this is the case, to deter him or others from crime, a suitable amount and kind of punishment must swiftly and surely be administered to wrongdoers to counterbalance the pleasure they derive from criminal acts. In the works of some classical scholars, attempts were made to develop highly detailed scales or hedonistic calculi of punishment, in which specific amounts of pain were identified for each type of lawbreaking. In the criminal codes that grew out of classical writings, uniform punishments were decreed for particular violations of law, so the effect of these codes was to simply render judges into instruments for the application of the law. Codes were drafted in such a way as to limit severely the discretionary powers of judges in assigning penalties to offenders.

Early philosophers such as Bentham and Beccaria were not involved in the statement of criminological theories out of any fundamental or overriding interest in the explanation of crime. Instead, classical criminological theory represented a by-product of other concerns. Bentham, Beccaria, and others were social critics and reformers, interested in modifying the social-control practices of their own societies. They were distressed about the severe and barbaric punishments commonplace during the late 1700s. Similarly, they were appalled by the existence of tyrannical and capricious judges administering harsh and unfair punishments to offenders.[6] The classical perspective developed out of these conditions and a concern for their alleviation.

Initial attempts to devise specific, detailed, and strict codes following the themes of classical teachings encountered a number of difficulties in practice. As a result, exceptions to penalties were made and statutes were redrafted giving judges some latitude in the application of penalties. Similar revisions have continued up to the present. Such developments as the rise of the juvenile court and the separate, theoretically nonpunitive handling of juvenile lawbreakers—that is, the use of parole and probation—and other innovations have altered the strict form of classical theory and practice.

Nonetheless, the classical view has not passed from the scene, for the major outlines of Anglo-Saxon criminal law and procedure are still essentially consistent with classical arguments. Moreover, lawyers and citizens alike usually resist attempts to deviate from free-will premises and from relatively harsh and uniform penalties. For example, recent endeavors to widen the exclusionary operation of courts by freeing mentally disordered individuals from responsibility for their illegal acts represent one prominent case in which modern views on behavior have clashed with the surviving elements of the classical tradition. Finally, much clamoring for a return to punishment, fixed sentences, and other classical approaches to crime control has been heard in the United States in recent years.

the cartographic school

The cartographic or geographic school of criminology pursued the ecological facts of crime, that is, its members examined the distribution of forms and rates of criminality among spatial areas. Two of the best-known persons associated with the development of this orientation were Adolphe Quetelet in Belgium and A. M. Guerry in France. Alfred Lindesmith and Yale Levin have argued that the founding of modern criminology is erroneously attributed to Cesare Lombroso, for the cartographic scholars preceded Lombroso's work by 50 years.[7] Lindesmith and Levin listed many factual studies of crime and delinquency that followed an ecological approach. Also, the works of cartographic investigators had more in common with contemporary criminological efforts than did Lombroso's work.

The cartographic school arose out of the development of systems of social bookkeeping first established in European countries in the 1500s, such as the systematic recording of births and deaths.[8] Qualitative studies of crime began to occur in England and France around 1800. Guerry's ecological study of crime rates in France appeared in 1833, and Quetelet produced an elaborate analysis of crime and social conditions in France, Belgium, Luxembourg, and Holland in 1836.

These early endeavors were forerunners of a long line of studies that have continued to the present. One of these persistent interests has centered about the relationship, if any, between economic conditions and fluctuations in crime and delinquency. Literally hundreds of studies have appeared on this question.[9] (A subsequent section in this chapter, "Socialist Views: Crime and Economic Trends," discusses some of the major conclusions from this work.)

Another interest stemming from the cartographic school's beginnings is in regional variations in crime. For example, a study by Enrico Ferri in 1895 showed that homicide convictions varied widely from province to province in major European nations, and another study of major reported crimes in England observed that variations in crime rates were relatively stable among regions in that country.[10] More recently, a number of investigators have noted the existence of rural–urban and regional variations in crime rates in the United States.[11]

Studies of ecological variations in crime and delinquency rates in individual cities provide another modern version of cartographic interests.[12] For example, in a study in Seattle, Calvin Schmid examined 35,000 cases of offenses reported to the police and 30,000 arrests.[13] Schmid found that certain criminal acts were heavily concentrated in the central business district of the city, whereas others were more common in other parts of the city. Similarly, a variety of concentrations of criminal persons were found in different parts of the city. In general, illegal activities and criminal actors were most common in areas of low social cohesion, weak family life, low economic status, physical deterioration of property, high population mobility, and various forms of personal demoralization.

The difficulty with these investigations based on official data is that it is not clear whether they reveal the ecological distribution of criminality, the spatial patterning of police and judicial practices, or some blend of both. These studies may tell us more about law-enforcement policies and record keeping than they do about total crime.

the search for biological explanations

The central theme of biologically based viewpoints is familiar to laymen and criminologists alike. The belief that biological factors determine human behavior generally, and criminal behavior specifically, is of ancient origin. It has been phrased in a variety of ways and persists in the minds of many people today. Vold and Bernard have identified the core proposition of biological theories as follows: "Behind all physical type theories is the general idea of biological differences in behavior. All biological explanations rest on the basic logic that *structure determines function*. Individuals behave differently because of the fundamental fact that they are somehow structurally different" (emphasis in the original).[14]

LOMBROSO AND POSITIVISM

Let us begin with the writings of Cesare Lombroso (1836–1909). Given the benefit of hindsight, we might judge some of his ideas preposterous. The foundations of modern behavioral science contradict most of Lombroso's theories, such as the concept of *atavism* and the hypothesized criminal nature of prehistoric man. But at the time that he wrote, close on the heels of the appearance of Darwin's evolutionary teachings in *Descent of Man* (1871), the claim that criminals constitute evolutionary throwbacks seemed much more plausible. There is a sociology of knowledge; ideas develop out of particular social conditions in specific eras. So it is with criminological views, for they have been the natural product of social conditions and prevailing thought patterns in different historical periods.

Lombroso has often been a misunderstood pioneer figure. Although frequently described as the originator of the theory of atavism and of the criminal as a biological type, he receives far less recognition for his later, modified views on these subjects or for his key role in the development of the positivist approach to criminality.[15] Positivism emphasized crime as a natural phenomenon produced by a variety of factors (multiple causation), some of which were held to be biological and others environmental. Lombroso was the original spokesman for this viewpoint, which, in broad outlines, is the prevailing criminological opinion of today.

Lombroso's major claims centered about the notion that the criminal is of different physical type than the noncriminal. According to a frequently told tale, Lombroso, who was a physician, was once asked to perform an autopsy on a famous Italian brigand. In the course of this autopsy, he discovered a number of physical abnormalities in the brain of the criminal. He was struck by these observations, out of which he formulated the view that criminals are atavists, or genetic throwbacks to an earlier human species, *homo delinquens*. Lombroso supposed that modern man, *homo sapiens*, evolved out of this earlier, lower type of human. He assumed the earlier species to have various kinds of asocial behavior. Accordingly, a contemporary criminal is simply a biological reversion to this primitive form of man. These views were published in *The Criminal Man*, which went through five separate editions. In this book, Lombroso maintained that the degenerate and atavistic criminal type could be identified by a number of characteristics or stigmata, including facial asymmetry, eye defects and peculiarities, ears of unusual size, excessively long arms, and other physical peculiarities.

Lombroso held that although some offenders were throwbacks, others were not. In later editions of his book, a host of causal factors—in addition to that of reversion to an earlier biological type—were enumerated. In the most developed version of his thinking, he asserted that there were three major kinds of criminals: *born* criminals, *insane* criminals, and *criminaloids* (individuals of normal physical and psychological makeup who commit crimes in unusual circumstances). Less than half of the total population of offenders were asserted to be born criminals.

In the early 1900s, Charles Goring mounted a mortal assault upon Lombroso's physical-type theories.[16] Along with a number of collaborators he undertook a series of careful measurements of approximately 3,000 English convicts and of large numbers of noncriminals. Almost without exception Lombroso's hypothesized physical anomalies were no more common among the prisoners than the nondeviants. In Goring's words, "Our inevitable conclusion must be that *there is no such thing as a physical criminal type*" (emphasis in the original).[17] But it should also be noted that Goring did not reject the theory that crime is related to hereditary factors, for he argued that criminals were physically inferior to nonoffenders. He claimed that criminals were of smaller stature and body weight and of lower mental ability than noncriminals.

The two most famous followers of Lombroso were Enrico Ferri (1856–1928) and Raffaele Garofalo (1852–1934).[18] Ferri, a student under Lombroso, expanded the ideas of his teacher, claiming that social, economic, and political factors are involved in crime, as well as Lombroso's suggested biological causes. Ferri is also remembered for his fourfold classification of offenders as insane, born, and occasional criminals, and criminals by passion. Garofalo was a major Italian positivist who attempted to formulate a universal definition of "natural" crime, in which he held that the sociological conception of crime refers to acts that violate the sentiments of probity and pity.

HOOTON'S RESEARCH

After the initial enthusiasm for positivist perspectives, arguments on constitutional or physical type waned in influence. However, these claims were dramatically resurrected in the work of Harvard physical anthropologist Earnest A. Hooton.[19] His book, published in 1939, was the result of a 12-year study of over 13,000 prisoners, compared with a smaller number of civilian nonoffenders, on some hundred anthropometric measurements. Hooton concluded that "the primary cause of crime is biological inferiority."[20] Moreover, he claimed that biological inferiority was inherited, so that eugenic programs of sterilization represented the most effective solution to criminality.

Despite the impressive number of subjects in this research, sociologists, criminologists, and anthropologists greeted Hooton's work with hostility and criticism.[21] The major deficiencies in his research are clear.[22] His control groups of nonoffenders were markedly unrepresentative of noncriminal citizens as a whole, including an odd assortment of militiamen, municipal firemen, bathhouse patrons, and hospital outpatients. Some of the subgroups within the control sample differed more from one another than they did from the prisoners. A second defect was that many of the subsamples on which he based ethnic comparisons between convicts and civilians were extremely small. A third fault was that prisoners did not constitute a representative sample of criminals. There are good reasons for supposing that those offenders who fall into the hands of the police, and later into prison, might be in poorer physical shape than those who escape detection. Finally, Hooton had no explicit criterion of biological inferiority, thus any differences that turned up were interpreted as support for his thesis.

SOME OTHER LINES OF ACTIVITY

These activities of Lombroso and Hooton were among the most influential of their kind. However, criminological history shows some other biological directions as well. For example, the now-discredited phrenological arguments of Franz Joseph Gall (1758–1828) and John Gaspar Spurzheim (1776–1832) were at one time thought to represent powerful explanations of behavior generally and criminality specifically.[23] They argued that conformations of the skull reveal faculties or propensities to behavior which are the product of biological inheritance. Criminals were held to be deficient in some of the normal faculties influencing behavior.

A related line of analysis centered on the hypothesis that tendencies toward criminality are inherited.[24] As in the expression "like father, like son," so, in this view, criminal parents pass on to their offspring genetic tendencies toward lawbreaking. One kind of evidence brought forth to demonstrate the hereditary transmission of deviant tendencies concerned studies of identical (one egg) and fraternal (two egg) twins.[25] The logic is that environmental influences are controlled or constant for twins, so if hereditary influences are of importance in behavior, the one-egg twins should show concordance, or similar behavior. If one is a criminal, the other should also be a deviant. The two-egg twins, on the other hand, should show more discordant behavior, for they do not share the same hereditary backgrounds. Those investigators who have made such comparisons have turned up evidence of greater concordance of behavior among one-egg than two-egg twins, hence these analyses seemed to constitute proof of hereditary transmission. Yet the assessment of most biologists is that such a conclusion is not valid, in view of some serious defects in these studies. All of them were based on small samples. Identification of identical twins is fraught with possibilities of error because it rests on observations of external physical characteristics. Insofar as mistakes are made, they tend to be in the direction of misidentification of fraternal twins as identical, so that observations are biased in favor of the hereditary hypothesis. Also, environmental influences were not controlled in these comparisons, for identical twins may receive more comparable parental treatment than do two-egg twins. Consequently, whatever concordance of behavior that might have been observed could be attributable to environmental influences.

Following the arguments of Louis Berman and others in the 1920s on the relationships of glandular processes and personality, several persons attempted to devise theories showing that criminality is a result of endocrine malfunctioning.[26] For example, Max Schlapp and Edward Smith claimed that the explanation of criminality is in glandular imbalances.[27] However, careful research failed to support these claims. The general position of most endocrinologists at present is that we do not know nearly enough about endocrine functioning to be able to identify accurately personality consequences of endocrine patterns or connections of endocrine malfunction to criminality.

BODY TYPE, TEMPERAMENT, AND CRIMINALITY

When one of Shakespeare's characters uttered the warning, "Yon Cassius hath a lean and hungry look; he thinks too much. Such men are dangerous," he was expressing the ancient and widely popular thesis that man's physical structure explains his behavior. Hence, fat people are also jolly because corpulence produces a jovial temperament, and slim people are destined to be introverted. Such ideas have been extended to criminality, with the supposition that deviance is a function of physical structure. Versions of this thesis are found in the works of Ernst Kretschmer and William Sheldon.[28] Kretschmer argued in the 1920s that certain patterns of physical structure lead to particular temperament types and that, in turn, specific kinds of mental disorder and criminality are related to these somatic and personality structures. Kretschmer and others reported research findings that suggested a relationship between body type and patterns of criminality, but they failed to demonstrate the hypothesized temperament linkages to these patterns.[29]

A more recent version of the body-type and temperament argument is found in the work of Sheldon and associates.[30] Sheldon and his colleagues asserted that somatic structure can be classified in terms of the degree to which *endomorphic*, *mesomorphic*, or *ectomorphic* physical characteristics are most apparent in different individuals. Arguing that *viscerotonic*, *somatotonic*, or *cerebrotonic* temperament patterns tend to accompany certain of the body types, they developed scales for measuring these dimensions. Using this scale, individuals are scored on each component on a range from 1 to 7, with the highest score denoting predominance of that particular somatic pattern. Vold and Bernard summarized the characteristics of the physical and temperament patterns thus:[31]

physique	*temperament*
1. *Endomorphic*: relatively great development of digestive viscera; tendency to put on fat; soft roundness through various regions of the body; short tapering limbs; small bones; soft, smooth, velvety skin	1. *Viscerotonic*: general relaxation of body; a comfortable person; loves soft luxury; a "softie" but still essentially an extrovert
2. *Mesomorphic*: relative predominance of muscles, bone, and the motor-organs of the body; large trunk; heavy chest, large wrists and hands; if "lean," a hard rectangularity of outline; if "not lean," they fill out heavily	2. *Somatotonic*: active, dynamic person; walks, talks, gestures assertively; behaves aggressively
3. *Ectomorphic*: relative predominance of skin and its appendages which include the nervous system; lean, fragile, delicate body; small, delicate bones; droopy shoulders; small face, sharp nose, fine hair; relatively little body mass and relatively great surface areas	3. *Cerebrotonic*: an introvert; full of functional complaints, allergies, skin troubles, chronic fatigue, insomnia; sensitive to noise and distractions; shrinks from crowds

Although variations in individual physique do exist, we can hardly accept the hypothesized temperament relationships to body structure as correct. Sheldon's research failed to demonstrate the accuracy of that hypothesis. In one study of several hundred residents of a specialized rehabilitation home for boys, he claimed to have demonstrated links between delinquency and certain body types.[32] However, critics were not kind to Sheldon, pointing out that he employed a loose and atypical definition of delinquency, centered on "disappointingness" rather than involvement in illegal behavior. Because his methodological procedures were defective in other ways too, he failed to provide a convincing case for these hypotheses.[33] Two other studies of delinquents turned up evidence that delinquent boys tend toward mesomorphy and aggressiveness, but both have also been severely criticized as methodologically inadequate.[34]

feeblemindedness and crime

The most popular single theory of crime causation adhered to by laymen, and by many serious investigators as well, is that offenders are defective in some psychological fashion. In this view, the causes of crime and delinquency are "inside the person." An early version of this theme sought for the mainsprings of deviance in feeblemindedness, whereas later ideas centered on the search for mental abnormality in the form of psychotic symptoms in offenders. The modern variant of this orientation is concerned with the possibility that lawbreakers are responding to a variety of less sensational emotional problems.

At one time in the history of criminology, the thesis that criminality is the product of markedly low mentality was exceedingly popular. This theory claimed that general hereditary degeneracy, including feeblemindedness, leads to criminality because the physically and intellectually degenerate individual cannot cope with life circumstances in a normal and satisfactory way.

This argument grew out of a series of studies of families, disguised by such fictitious names as the Jukes, Kallikaks, and Nams,[35] which came to light in the late 1800s and early 1900s. In each of these accounts, presumably feebleminded ancestors produced a long family line of social misfits. The conclusion was that feeblemindedness is inherited and leads to social inadequacy, deviation, and criminality. Subsequent inquiry has, of course, indicated that the simple hereditary-transmission view of feeblemindedness is erroneous. The involvement of successive generations of individuals in deviant behavior is probably the result of *social* transmission.

In the early 1900s the development of intelligence tests led to the application of these measures to samples of offenders. Initial results seemed to confirm the picture of lawbreakers as uncommonly characterized by mental impairment. Thus, Henry Goddard reported results of different studies showing that a high percentage of the criminals investigated were feebleminded.[36] He concluded from these data: "It can no longer be denied that the greatest single cause of delinquency and crime is low-grade mentality, much of it within the limits of feeble-mindedness."[37]

These early studies of the intelligence of criminal persons were carried on without control-group comparisons and without accurate data on intelligence levels among law-abiding citizens. Instead, the average citizen was assumed to have attained a mental age of 16; that is, if tested, he or she would presumably respond correctly to all the questions which the test constructors regarded as appropriate for 16-year-old individuals. Measured against this standard, criminals seemed to be markedly deficient in intelligence. The error in these studies came to light with the publication of intelligence-test results from the World War I draft experience. The average mental age of draftees, presumably a representative sample of law-abiding citizens, was found to be 13.08, not 16! In short, citizens turned out to be less intelligent than had been supposed. When criminal samples were compared to the standard from the army testing, the offenders appeared to be no more defective than the draftees. Thus, Sutherland discovered that the average proportion of criminals diagnosed as feebleminded in some 350 studies surveyed was about 50 percent for the period 1910–1914 but only about 20 percent for the period 1925–1928.[38] Carl Murchison and Simon Tulchin each carried out systematic comparisons of prisoners and draftees showing negligible differences in intelligence between the two groups.[39]

Feeblemindedness and mental impairment as a significant cause of criminality did not survive the test of evidence. However, it is conceivable that offenders and nonoffenders do exhibit less pronounced differences in intelligence as measured by standard intelligence tests, with lawbreakers scoring somewhat lower on the average than nonoffenders. Indeed, we will encounter evidence to this effect in Chapter 8.

socialist views: crime and economic trends

Early socialist explanations of crime were an offshoot of Karl Marx's theories, published in the 1880s. According to socialist arguments, exploitation of workers in capitalistic societies leads to endemic poverty and misery. In turn, these conditions produce a variety of criminalistic responses, including alcoholism, prostitution, and larceny. The systems of criminal justice prevailing in capitalistic societies protect the exploitative interests of the owner class.[40] Thus, prevention of criminality demands social reorganization along socialist lines.

The most eminent contributor to socialist theories was Dutch sociologist Willem Bonger (1876–1940), who argued that the very nature of the capitalist economic system encourages *egoism*, that is, the relatively unrestrained pursuit of self-interest.[41] Egoism draws persons from all social ranks into criminality because their moral sensibilities are blunted. Those same individuals are motivated to engage in crime because of the economic precariousness they experience or due to other economic self-interests.

Much of Bonger's work should have a familiar ring to the modern sociology student. He anticipated a host of later sociological analyses of criminality in capitalistic societies, in which a variety of social and economic conditions have been held to be involved in the genesis of criminality.[42]

Socialist views of crime have reappeared in dramatic form in the writings of contemporary radical-Marxist criminologists. These observers have advanced a number of claims paralleling those found in Bonger's writings, but often couched in hyberbole and phrased in polemical terms. These contentions have often been long on radical rhetoric and short on logical cogency. Even so, modern radical-Marxist arguments demand our serious attention; thus we will examine them in detail in Chapter 7.

Studies of economic influences on crime have been numerous since Bonger's early works. In their summary of the principal findings of such inquiries, Sutherland and Cressey noted that one frequent conclusion is that lower-class groups have much higher crime rates than upper-class groups.[43] A great many investigations have been conducted of samples of arrested, convicted, or committed adult or juvenile offenders, all of which show that working-class groups are heavily overrepresented in the population of detected lawbreakers. Ecological studies of the distribution of crime and delinquency rates in cities have repeatedly pointed to the concentration of criminality in lower-class neighborhoods.[44] However, Sutherland and Cressey questioned the validity of the argument that lawbreaking is peculiarly lower class in distribution, on the same grounds as we challenged this conclusion in Chapter 1. Although certain juvenile and adult forms of crime, such as gang delinquency, do appear to be disproportionately the activity of working-class individuals, the same is not true of all forms of crime. If statistics on white-collar crime and a variety of other forms of underreported or unreported criminality are examined, the socioeconomic picture of illegal conduct becomes quite different.

Studies of fluctuations in crime rates and the business cycle have also been numerous since the days of Bonger.[45] A variety of theoretical and methodological inadequacies have flawed these investigations; however, taken as a whole they appear to show that the rate of *serious* crimes increases during times of depression, but that the *general* or *total* crime rate tends not to increase during those same periods of economic decline. These studies also suggest that property offenses accompanied by violence increase during depressions, whereas nonviolent property crimes do not. Drunkenness and crimes against persons do not show any consistent relationship to economic fluctuations, but rates of juvenile delinquency seem to increase during prosperity.

Vold and Bernard have raised a series of important questions about these generalizations. They noted that different assumptions regarding the time interval between the onset of economic changes and alterations in rates of criminality lead to drastically different conclusions from the same basic data.[46] They showed that in a study by Dorothy Swaine Thomas of crime rates and economic variations in England and Wales for the period 1857–1913, the correlation between economic conditions and criminality was -0.25 when the crime rates and economic measures for the same years were correlated.[47] However, the correlation between economic conditions for particular years and the crime rates observed *two years later* was $+0.18$. As they argued, we should assume that some time lag is required before economic and business changes have repercussions on the volume of lawbreaking.

The most sensible conclusion on this issue is that economic changes and business trends are imperfectly correlated with crime levels and trends. The total of criminal behavior is compounded out of many discrete forms of behavior, some of which are influenced by economic variations and others which are insensitive to such fluctuations. The causative factors in criminality are doubtless too many and too complex for the kinds of indices of economic fluctuations that are at hand to reflect or measure easily.[48]

summary

This brief and roughly chronological account of major episodes in the growth of premodern criminology has identified many of the major theoretical clues that have been investigated by earlier generations of criminologists. Many of these earlier viewpoints live on in altered form in contemporary efforts to account for criminality. For example, much of the biological criminology of past decades failed to reflect the complex interaction of hereditary and environmental influences in the unfolding of criminal and noncriminal behavior and was defective in other ways as well. However, the last word has not been heard on biological elements in deviance and criminality. There is a large and growing body of modern, biologically sophisticated theorizing and research currently underway which bids fair to contribute new insights on these old questions about biological contributions to criminality. This contemporary material will be examined in Chapter 8.

Here we conclude our brief look at the origins of criminology. In the next chapter attention turns to the development of the contemporary criminological enterprise. In particular, we will examine the major events in the maturation of American criminology. Chapter 3 will also identify the central questions or issues that monopolize the attention of criminologists as they go about their business. In short, this chapter will establish some markers or guideposts that will provide directions for our in-depth wanderings through theories and research findings in the remainder of this book.

notes

[1]George B. Vold and Thomas J. Bernard, *Theoretical Criminology*, 2nd ed. (New York: Oxford University Press, 1979), pp. 5–8. Vold and Bernard present a succinct summary and critique of a number of these historically important notions about crime. See also Stephen Schafer, *Theories in Criminology* (New York: Random House, 1969). The development of American sociological criminology is discussed in detail in Don C. Gibbons, *The Criminological Enterprise* (Englewood Cliffs, N.J.: Prentice-Hall, Inc., 1979).

[2]This term, "pioneers in criminology," is taken from a series of articles in the *Journal of Criminal Law, Criminology and Police Science* of some years ago in which the writings of a number of pioneers or early figures in criminology were examined. See, for example, Elio D. Monachesi, "Pioneers in Criminology: IX—Cesare Beccaria (1738–94)," *Journal of Criminal Law, Criminology and Police Science*, 46 (November–December 1955), 439–40.

[3]Vold and Bernard, *Theoretical Criminology*, p. 73.

[4]Ibid., pp. 18–34; see also Leon Radzinowicz, *A History of English Criminal Law and Its Administration from 1750*, vol. 1 (New York: Macmillan, 1948), for a detailed discussion of classical perspectives and the social conditions that gave rise to these notions.

[5]Vold and Bernard, *Theoretical Criminology*, pp. 20–21.

[6]Radzinowicz has enumerated these practices in great detail. See Radzinowicz, *A History of English Criminal Law*.

[7]Alfred Lindesmith and Yale Levin, "The Lombrosian Myth in Criminology," *American Journal of Sociology*, 42 (March 1937), 653–71; see also Levin and Lindesmith, "English Ecology and Criminology of the Past Century," *Journal of Criminal Law and Criminology*, 27 (March–April 1937), 801–16.

[8]For a summary of these developments, see Vold and Bernard, *Theoretical Criminology*, pp. 165–71.

[9]Many of these are summarized in Ibid., pp. 169–80.

[10]These studies and a number of others dealing with regional variations in crime are discussed in Edwin H. Sutherland and Donald R. Cressey, *Criminology*, 10th ed. (Philadelphia: Lippincott, 1978), pp. 178–82.

[11]For example, see Stuart Lottier, "Distribution of Criminal Offenses in Metropolitan Regions," *Journal of Criminal Law and Criminology*, 29 (May–June 1938), 37–50; Lottier, "Distribution of Criminal Offenses in Sectional Regions," *Journal of Criminal Law and Criminology*, 29 (September–October 1938), 329–44; Lyle W. Shannon, "The Spatial Distribution of Criminal Offenses by States," *Journal of Criminal Law, Criminology and Police Science*, 45 (September–October 1954), 264–73; also see Keith D. Harries, *The Geography of Crime and Justice* (New York: McGraw-Hill, 1974). This work consists of contemporary geographic analyses of crime rates and criminal-justice-system characteristics.

[12]See, as one example, Lyle W. Shannon, "Types and Patterns of Delinquency in a Middle-Sized City," *Journal of Research in Crime and Delinquency*, 1 (January 1964), 53–66.

[13]Calvin F. Schmid, "A Study of Homicides in Seattle," *Social Forces*, 4 (June 1926), 745–56; Schmid, "Urban Crime Areas, Part I," *American Sociological Review*, 25 (August 1960), 527–42; Schmid, "Urban Crime Areas, Part II," *American Sociological Review*, 25 (October 1960), 655–78.

[14]Vold and Bernard, *Theoretical Criminology*, p. 51.

[15]See Vold and Bernard's discussion of Lombroso for a detailed and balanced evaluation of his place in criminology, Ibid., pp. 35–40, 56–65.

[16]Charles Goring, *The English Convict: A Statistical Study* (London: His Majesty's Stationery Office, 1913).

[17]Ibid., p. 173.

[18]For a résumé of the works of Ferri and Garofalo, see Vold and Bernard, *Theoretical Criminology*, pp. 40–46.

[19]Earnest A. Hooton, *Crime and the Man* (Cambridge, Mass.: Harvard University Press, 1939).

[20]Ibid., p. 130.

[21]Some of these evaluations of Hooton's work are Robert K. Merton and M. F. Ashley Montague, "Crime and the Anthropologist," *American Anthropologist*, 42 (July–September 1941), 384–408; James S. Wallerstein and Clement J. Wyle, "Biological Inferiority as a Cause for Delinquency," *Nervous Child*, 6 (October 1947), 467–72; N. S. Timasheff, "The Revival of Criminal Anthropology," *University of Kansas Law Review*, 9 (February 1941), 91–100; William B. Tucker, "Is There Evidence of a Physical Basis for Criminal Behavior?" *Journal of Criminal Law and Criminology*, 31 (November–December 1940), 427–37.

[22]Vold and Bernard, *Theoretical Criminology*, pp. 63–65.

[23]Ibid., pp. 53–55.

[24]These arguments are summarized in Sutherland and Cressey, *Criminology*, pp. 119–23.

[25]A number of these studies are summarized and criticized in M. F. Ashley Montague, "The Biologist Looks at Crime," *Annals of the American Academy of Political and Social Science*, 217 (September 1941), 45–57.

[26]Louis Berman, *The Glands Regulating Personality* (New York: Macmillan, 1921); Berman, *New Creations in Human Beings* (New York: Doubleday, 1938).

[27]Max G. Schlapp and Edward H. Smith, *The New Criminology* (New York: Boni and Liveright, 1928).

[28]Summaries of Sheldon and Kretschmer's work can be found in Vold and Bernard, *Theoretical Criminology*, pp. 65–73.

[29]American research following Kretschmer's notions is found in George J. Mohr and Ralph H. Gundlach, "The Relation Between Physique and Performance," *Journal of Experimental Psychology*, 10 (April 1927), 117–57; and in Mohr and Gundlach, "A Further Study of the Relations Between Physique and Performance in Criminals," *Journal of Abnormal and Social Psychology*, 24 (April–June 1929), 91–103.

[30]William H. Sheldon, S. S. Stevens, and W. B. Tucker, *Varieties of Human Physique* (New York: Harper & Row, Pub., 1940); Sheldon and Stevens, *Varieties of Temperament* (New York: Harper & Row, Pub., 1942); Sheldon, Emil M. Hartl, and Eugene McDermott, *Varieties of Delinquent Youth* (New York: Harper & Row, Pub. 1949).

[31]Vold and Bernard, *Theoretical Criminology*, pp. 66–67.

[32]Sheldon, Hartl, and McDermott, *Varieties of Delinquent Youth*.

[33]Edwin H. Sutherland, "Critique of Sheldon's Varieties of Delinquent Youth," *American Sociologi-*

cal Review, 16 (February 1951), 10–13; S. L. Washburn, "Review of W. H. Sheldon's *Varieties of Delinquent Youth*," *American Anthropologist*, 53 (October–November 1951), 561–63.

34These studies are Sheldon Glueck and Eleanor Glueck, *Physique and Delinquency* (New York: Harper & Row, Pub., 1956); Juan B. Cortés and Florence M. Gatti, *Delinquency and Crime* (New York: Seminar Press, 1972). Criticisms of these studies are reviewed in Vold and Bernard, *Theoretical Criminology*, pp. 68–73.

35Richard L. Dugdale, *The Jukes* (New York: Putnam's, 1877); Henry H. Goddard, *The Kallikak Family* (New York: Macmillan, 1912); A. H. Estabrook, *The Jukes in 1915* (Washington, D.C.: Carnegie Institute, 1916); A. H. Estabrook and C. B. Davenport, *The Nam Family* (Lancaster, Pa.: New Era Publishing Co., 1912).

36Henry H. Goddard, *Feeblemindedness: Its Causes and Consequences* (New York: Macmillan, 1914).

37Henry H. Goddard, *Juvenile Delinquency* (New York: Dodd, Mead, 1921), p. 22.

38Edwin H. Sutherland, "Mental Deficiency and Crime," in *Social Attitudes*, ed. Kimball Young (New York: Holt, Rinehart & Winston, 1931), pp. 357–75.

39Carl Murchison, *Criminal Intelligence* (Worcester, Mass.: Clark University Press, 1939); see also Leslie D. Zeleny, "Feeblemindedness and Criminal Conduct," *American Journal of Sociology*, 38 (January 1933), 564–76.

40For a socialist interpretation of fluctuations in penal policies, see Georg Rusche and Otto Kirchheimer, *Punishment and Social Structure* (New York: Columbia University Press, 1939).

41 Willem Bonger, *Criminality and Economic Conditions* (Boston: Little, Brown, 1916).

42 See, for example, Donald R. Taft and Ralph W. England, Jr., *Criminology*, 4th ed. (New York: Macmillan, 1964), pp. 275–79; Robert K. Merton, *Social Theory and Social Structure*, rev. ed. (New York: Free Press, 1957), chaps. 4 and 5; Richard A. Cloward and Lloyd E. Ohlin, *Delinquency and Opportunity* (New York: Free Press, 1960).

43 Sutherland and Cressey, *Criminology*, pp. 228–32.

44Ibid., p. 234.

45 Many of these have been summarized in Thorsten Sellin, *Research Memorandum on Crime in the Depression* (New York: Social Science Research Council, 1937); see also Vold and Bernard, *Theoretical Criminology*, pp. 169–78; Sutherland and Cressey, *Criminology*, pp. 235–36.

46 Vold and Bernard, *Theoretical Criminology*, pp. 176–78.

47 Dorothy Swaine Thomas, *Social Aspects of the Business Cycle* (London: Routledge & Kegan Paul, 1925).

48 A study of crime trends and economic factors by Daniel Glaser and Kent Rice supported these interpretations. They found some support for the hypothesis that rates of juvenile delinquency are inversely correlated with unemployment, so that juvenile misconduct is most prominent during times of prosperity. On the other hand, criminality among adults between 18 and 35 years of age seemed to be most frequent during periods of widespread unemployment. Glaser and Rice interpreted these findings in terms of sociological theories that stress the demoralizing influences of unemployment on adults. Daniel Glaser and Kent Rice, "Crime, Age, and Employment," *American Sociological Review*, 24 (October 1959), 679–86.

contemporary criminology

THREE

What is criminology? Chapter 2 indicated that it has to do with the scientific study of crime and social responses to it. Sutherland and Cressey have observed that "criminology is the body of knowledge regarding juvenile delinquency and crime as social phenomena. It includes within its scope the processes of making laws, of breaking laws, and of reacting to the breaking of laws."[1] For the meantime these definitions are serviceable enough, although we will have more to say about the dimensions of criminological inquiry later in this chapter.

Chapter 2 indicated that criminology began in a number of European countries in the late 1700s. However, modern criminology is linked most directly to criminological endeavors that began in the United States from about 1880 onward with the fledgling discipline of sociology. Contemporary criminology shows relatively few connections to the premodern inquiry carried on in Europe in the nineteenth century.

Modern criminology as a scholarly enterprise is usually identified as a division of contemporary sociology, in that most of the persons who concentrate on criminological questions and who regard themselves as criminologists have been trained in sociology.[2] Also, most of the theoretical notions that now inform the work of criminologists throughout the world have been evolved by American sociological criminologists. Then, too, the largest share of research on lawbreaking has been produced by American criminological investigators. It is in this sense that it can be said that criminology is both an American development and an area of sociological inquiry.

But some qualifying comments are in order concerning the notion of criminology as a branch of American sociology. For one thing, criminological inquiry has also developed and remains very much alive in many countries outside the United States. In particular, a vigorous criminological enterprise exists in England, the Scandinavian countries, and a number of other Western European nations. It is true that American criminological concepts have diffused to other nations and have fueled much of the activity there. Even so, it would be a mistake to conclude that foreign criminological efforts are simply cheap copies of a made-in-America product.

An even more important point is that contributions to criminological knowledge have been made in considerable number by scholars and researchers from disciplines other than sociology. Biological investigators continue to probe about, looking for evidence of biological factors in lawbreaking. Similarly, psychologists and psychiatrists have had much to say about psychological factors and influences that allegedly differentiate offenders from noncriminals. A number of these modern biological and psychological arguments about crime causation will be examined in Chapter 8. Other contributions to the stockpile of criminological knowledge have been made by economists, political scientists, and representatives of other scholarly fields, so that sociologists cannot claim sole ownership of criminology.

Thinking about crime is a serious and complex business. Lawbreaking takes many forms, with causes that are multiple and intertwined. Responses to crime have varied markedly from one historical period to another, and, in addition, current practices in dealing with offenders differ from one place to another. As a result, criminology grapples with a number of difficult questions dealing with crime causation and responses to criminality.

During the developmental period from the turn of the century to the present, criminologists have put forth a large number of theories about crime and its control, many of which are rich and detailed. Then, too, a large body of research findings has accumulated. Many of these appear at first glance to point in different directions, hence they may seem more confusing than revealing. Much effort must be expended in order to make sense of and digest this store of empirical evidence. Finally, and most important, in order to think meaningfully about crime, one must do much more than master a grab bag of discrete bits and pieces of theory and factual evidence. Criminologists endeavor to make sense of all this material, sorting it out, evaluating it, and ordering it into a criminological perspective.

Criminology textbooks, therefore, must be more than weighty volumes filled with those above-mentioned bits and pieces of vaguely related knowledge. Much attention must be devoted to the articulation of "the big questions" of criminology. So it is with this book, for throughout its pages it strives to show the reader how to think like a criminologist.

the rise of contemporary criminology[3]

THE EARLY YEARS

We have already established that criminology in the United States is an offspring of American sociology, thus it is with the latter that we must begin in order to answer the question, When and where did contemporary criminology arise? As a number of observers have noted, early American sociology was largely a home-grown product, with few linkages to the works of such nineteenth-century European giants of sociology as Durkheim, Weber, Simmel, and Marx.[4] Further, early sociology was often moralistic, unsophisticated, and eclectic. Many of the early sociologists were reform-oriented persons, poorly trained in the new discipline, and often concerned with "the 3 Ds": the study of the defective, dependent, and delinquent classes. These early sociologists focused upon social problems of one sort or another and often viewed them as individualistic and pathological by-products of urbanization, industrialization, and other social evils. In short, early sociology was generally an ill-formed and unsophisticated discipline. No wonder, then, that early criminology also was relatively unimpressive.

One cannot isolate the exact date on which American criminology was born, but books dealing with crime and delinquency began to appear in some number before the turn of the century. These tomes contained a heavy stress on Lombrosian theories about inborn criminality and upon other evolutionary and biological beliefs. Social theories of crime were slow to sprout and take hold.

Some might argue that criminology was born with the appearance of the first full-length textbook by Maurice Parmelee in 1918, which was followed shortly by other volumes by sociologists.[5] Although some criminologists have argued that Parmelee's book was influential in moving criminology toward exploration of social causes and away from biological hypotheses, his book and most of the other early works largely contained a hodgepodge of ideas and arguments about causation, including much discussion of alleged biological influences upon lawbreaking.

CRIMINOLOGY 1930–1955

Modern criminology owes a much greater debt to Clifford Shaw, Henry D. McKay, Edwin H. Sutherland, and a few other criminologists who carved out its basic structure in the period from about 1930 onward.[6] Shaw and McKay were delinquency researchers who conducted studies of juvenile offenders in Chicago and elsewhere. They found that officially recorded cases of delinquency varied widely in city areas, with the highest rates in neighborhoods of rapid population change, poor housing, adult crime and mental disorders, and other signs of social dislocation. They also reported that most delinquents were psychologically normal youngsters who had become enmeshed in gang associations and other ties to antisocial persons in their neighborhoods. These observations led Shaw and McKay to conclude that delinquency and crime are produced by the social disorganization which is an endemic feature of modern urban communities. This general interpretation of crime causation became central to the views of most criminologists in this country.

Shaw and McKay are remembered most for their research findings which became building blocks in the criminology edifice. Edwin H. Sutherland, on the other hand, was the architect or master builder who sorted out the facts of crime and designed the criminological structure. His theoretical contributions were so numerous and so significant that it could be argued that he almost single-handedly fashioned the criminological enterprise.

Sutherland's contributions include his analysis of professional theft as a criminal behavior system.[7] Additionally, he did much of the pioneering work on white-collar crime, that is, violations of regulatory statutes by businesses and corporations.[8] He is most famous, however, for his theory of differential association, in which he argued that criminality is learned behavior. He also spelled out many of the factors that determine whether individuals learn criminal or noncriminal conduct norms and behavior.[9] Modern, complex, urban societies are characterized by societal complexity which Sutherland called *differential social organization.* In them, persons are bombarded by myriad social influences, some of which are of a crime-inducing variety, others of which encourage law-abiding conduct. We will take up this argument in Chapters 7 and 9 and will look at other contributions by Sutherland at various points in this book. I have offered a summary judgment about his impact upon criminology in another work:

The evidence is incontrovertible that Edwin Sutherland was the most important contributor to American criminology to have appeared to date. Indeed, there has been no other criminologist who even begins to approach his stature and importance. Moreover, it is extremely unlikely that anyone will emerge in future decades to challenge Sutherland's position in the annals of the field. Sutherland staked out many of the parameters of criminological inquiry and contributed most of the key concepts and hypotheses pursued by criminologists until recently.[10]

There were other important criminological developments during the period from about 1930 to 1955. For one, Robert Merton's anomie argument, attributing crime and other forms of deviance to defects in the American socioeconomic structure, quickly gained wide acceptance among sociologists.[11] Parallel arguments about crime that linked it to culture conflict, rapid social change, and various rents and tears in the social fabric were offered by a number of criminologists. These general themes enunciated by Shaw and McKay, Sutherland, Merton, and a few others formed the core ideas of mainstream criminology. By and large, criminological contributions in the past two or three decades have expanded upon these perspectives but have not altered them in any fundamental way.[12]

One of these elaborations upon mainstream criminology zeroed in upon unreported, "hidden" crime and delinquency, producing findings of considerable value regarding "the dark figure of crime." Another group of criminological workers devoted a good deal of energy to efforts to classify and categorize offenders into meaningful behavioral types. A third important body of theorizing centered upon gang delinquents and efforts to explain their behavior. A fourth group of theorists endeavored to account for juvenile delinquency with social-control theories that focused on juvenile offenders' poor self-concepts or weakened social ties.

Contemporary criminologists have not restricted themselves to crime causation. Some have poked and probed into the dark corners of prisons and other correctional organizations, turning up evidence that these agencies often function differently than their designers intended. Still others have examined punishment practices and related matters. Moreover, there are many other criminological topics and interests that do not fit neatly into any of the niches identified above. Criminology is a many splendored thing. Even so, this brief account indicates the flavor of mainstream criminology, which the remaining chapters will take up in detail.

Criminology is an emerging, developing enterprise rather than a fully explored area of inquiry. There are a great many questions for which criminologists have only incomplete answers, at best. Additionally, in recent years radical-Marxist theorists have been claiming that mainstream criminology is flawed in ways which render it incapable of accounting adequately for lawbreaking in contemporary America. Since we will scrutinize the radical challenge to mainstream viewpoints in Chapter 7, perhaps it is sufficient at this juncture to indicate that some of these critical observations are on the mark. There are some sweeping changes now taking place in modern societies that may make obsolete some of the criminological theories favored in the past.

criminology: major questions

Let us return to the nature of the criminological enterprise, by spelling out the major tasks that confront criminologists and other investigators as they go about poking into the facts of lawbreaking. Recall that Sutherland and Cressey identified three issues: the study of lawmaking, lawbreaking, and reactions to criminality. This list might be broadened a bit, to capture more fully the central questions around which criminological inquiry is focused. This expanded listing of key questions involves (1) the nature of crime and criminal behavior, (2) the origins of criminal laws, (3) the extent and distribution of criminality, (4) social structure and criminality, (5) the origins and development of criminal acts and careers, and (6) social reactions to crime.

THE NATURE OF CRIME AND CRIMINAL BEHAVIOR

How is crime different from sin, wickedness, deviance, or other forms of socially condemned behavior? Sociologists have not always been careful to spell out the boundaries of the phenomena they propose to study. Speaking on the general topic of deviant behavior, of which criminality is one form, Albert Cohen declared: "The most pressing problem in the field of social disorganization and deviant behavior is to define these terms. If we cannot agree on what we are talking about, we cannot agree on what is relevant, much less on what is important."[13] These comments by Cohen indicate that sociologists have not always been in agreement in their conceptualizations of deviance and conformity. Just as the first step in the analysis of deviance is defining the phenomenon of attention, the first stage in the study of criminality and criminals centers about clear specification of the scope and meaning of these labels. What do we mean by criminality? What is a criminal or a noncriminal? Who and what should we include or exclude from criminological scrutiny?

Not everyone agrees on the meaning of crime and criminals, for considerable controversy has raged in criminology over questions of this kind. Some authorities have suggested that the proper subject matter encompasses only those persons convicted in a criminal court of violations of law. Others have included within the population of criminals persons who have been arrested but not convicted. Still others study "white-collar criminals" who have violated criminal laws but have been processed informally or through civil courts. Probably the majority of students of criminality focus on individuals who have violated criminal laws, whether or not they have been apprehended.

From time to time in the past, some persons have come forth to urge that criminology concern itself with moral aberrance, parasitism, or some other form of crime defined in sociological rather than legal terms. Recently, a few radical sociologists have argued that criminologists and students of deviance should identify, as the proper subject for inquiry, violations of basic human rights and unethical acts of the socially powerful, whether or not these are included within criminal statutes.[14] The problem with these suggestions is that there is very little agreement among either the general public or sociologists as to what particular activities might rightly fall within these categories.

Parenthetically, while criminologists have been reluctant to depart from the confines of existing criminal statutes in identifying the phenomena to be studied, some of them have begun to ask whether particular acts that are now included within legal definitions of crime *should* be defined as crimes. Sociologists have begun to raise such questions and have joined citizens who are critical of the overreach of criminal law. Their principal complaint is that American society is *overcriminalized*—that is, criminal law reaches too far, covering socially harmless behavior such as marijuana use, homosexuality, gambling, or other "crimes without victims." These critics of criminal law suggest that we should decriminalize some kinds of behavior by removing the acts from the law books.

THE ORIGINS OF CRIMINAL LAWS

In the last analysis, society creates crime by singling out particular acts and labeling them "bad" and "criminal." By "society" is meant groups of persons who manage to get some act included within a set of statutes that declare certain behaviors criminal in form. Crime is not inherent in behavior; someone has to identify acts of one kind or another as criminal. For behavior to become criminalized, someone's concept of an act as criminal must get widespread adoption. Legislatures must pass a law that publicly asserts a defined crime.

The influence of social factors on conceptions of crime is evident in the fact that the number of acts regarded as crimes has steadily increased over the past several hundred years as lawmaking bodies have created more and more criminal statutes. Definitions of criminal acts differ from place to place. Within the United States marked variations in both the language and the content of criminal codes occur from one state to another, so that no uniform set of criminal laws exists in this country. Crime is not an unchanging, universal phenomenon, consistently the same in all places and at all times.

The processes of lawmaking constitute social behavior. Particular criminal laws have identifiable antecedents; reasons exist for the emergence of laws at some particular time or in some specific place. Moreover, statutes are created by specific persons whose actions can and should be made the subject of sociological attention. Lawmaking is a social process. But we know relatively little about the development of criminal laws and the variables that account for these origins, for this area of inquiry has been neglected until recently.[15] We shall examine a number of theories regarding the genesis of criminal laws, along with several pieces of research evidence on the development of theft laws, vagrancy statutes, and several other kinds of criminal laws in Chapter 4.

EXTENT AND DISTRIBUTION OF CRIMINALITY

Where should we begin in attempts to explain lawbreaking? An initial causal inquiry often begins with fact-gathering concerning the number, location, and social characteristics of offenders. Factual data are necessary prior to any attempt to explain criminality. A clear and detailed picture of the phenomenon to be studied is a prerequisite to causal inquiry.

If we were to employ a definition of criminality that restricted the term to persons convicted of criminal offenses in criminal courts, gathering the basic factual information would be a relatively simple task: we could glean the facts of crime from records of court proceedings. However, if we use a broader definition of crime, in which commission of illegal acts would be required for an individual to be termed a criminal but in which police apprehension or conviction in a court is not required, some complex data-gathering problems quickly arise.

We use the broader conception of criminality in this book; our purpose is to examine the actions of all persons who violate criminal laws, only a fraction of whom are apprehended and subsequently convicted of such offenses. As a result, we must assemble a picture of crime in American society that will clarify the size and characteristics of various components of the offender population. For example, we need to determine the proportion of all lawbreakers represented by individuals reported to the police. In addition, we want to discover whether some kinds of violators are more likely to be reported to the police than are others. Do variables such as social-class backgrounds, racial characteristics, and offender-victim relationships influence police-referral policies? These are complex questions, principally because the available data are often meager and of questionable accuracy.

SOCIAL STRUCTURE AND CRIMINALITY ("THE RATES QUESTION")

Discovery of the causes of crime and juvenile delinquency is the principal task of the criminologist-sociologist. His or her major aim is to develop a body of generalizations or propositions accounting for criminality. Although this task is many-faceted, two main components of the explanatory job exist.[16] The first has to do with the development of explanations for the *kinds and degree of criminality* observed in a society. The other centers about discovery of the processes involved in the *acquisition of criminal behavior patterns by specific individuals.* Concerning these two problems of analysis, Donald Cressey has commented:

. . . A theory explaining social behavior in general, or any specific kind of social behavior, should have two distinct but consistent aspects. First, there must be a statement that explains the statistical distribution of the behavior in time and space (epidemiology), and from which predictive statements about unknown statistical distributions can be derived. Second, there must be a statement that identifies, at least by implication, the process by which individuals come to exhibit the behavior in question, and from which can be derived predictive statements about the behavior of individuals.[17]

In this book, the first causal concern is identified as the issue of *social structure and criminality* or as "the rates question." The second is designated as *the origins and development of criminal acts and careers*, or as the "Why do they do it?" query.

What would a theory directed at social structure and crime look like? Consider a hypothetical example. Suppose that a study of lawbreaking patterns within a particular city shows that certain forms of adult property crime and certain kinds of juvenile delinquency are heavily concentrated in slum areas and uncommon elsewhere in the city. The focus of attention here would be on such questions as: "Why are these kinds of crime and delinquency so common in some areas and virtually nonexistent in others?" and "Does something within a community's social organization, such as different social-class patterns, result in these patterns of crime and delinquency?" These questions are primarily concerned with the explanation of *rates*. Some particular criminologist might come forward with hypotheses alleging that variations in neighborhood social structure and differences in expectations of material success in American society which exist between lower- and middle-class citizens are responsible for widely divergent rates of deviation. To test these claims, data would be needed to provide indices of neighborhood social organization, differential social-class values, and so on. In turn, these hypotheses would be confirmed or disproved to the degree that correlations were observed between crime rates and the measures of social organization. Insofar as those areas with high crime rates are also the most disorganized, and to the degree that low-crime neighborhoods are the most cohesive, these hypotheses would be verified.

Another illustrative case of social-structural analysis is found in comparative figures for the United States and certain European nations, which seem to indicate that American society is more troubled with criminality. According to a common sociological hypothesis, American society is more criminalistic or "criminogenic" than other societies because of the inordinate emphasis on material success and the disrespect for law and order in American values and beliefs. Although these claims have not been adequately tested and such research would be difficult to carry out, the kinds of evidence called for are relatively clear. Crime rates would have to be assembled to rank societies in terms of criminality, whereas indices of cultural values, attitudes toward materialism, law enforcement, and so on, would be required to test causal propositions.

In these examples of social-structural explanations, no mention was made of specific individuals and efforts to account for lawbreaking on the part of some of them and conformity on the part of others. Discovery of the process by which specific individuals acquire criminal attitudes and/or behavior patterns is an analytically separate issue.

THE ORIGINS AND DEVELOPMENT OF CRIMINAL ACTS AND CAREERS

The earlier example of different crime and delinquency rates in a specific city can be used to clarify the difference between this second question and the first dealing with social structure and rates. Suppose that we have noticed, in addition to the facts already specified, that juveniles in the high-delinquency area exhibit varied patterns of behavior. Some boys have high occupational aspirations, are highly motivated in school, and are nondelinquents. Other juveniles are "corner boys," not heavily involved in delinquency but also not enmeshed in patterns of "mobility striving" or achievement. They are unmotivated, conformist juveniles whose actions center about short-run hedonism. A third group is heavily caught up in delinquent activities; their major social role is that of "tough kid" and "delinquent." One criminological concern in this case is the discovery of factors that led the specific youths into several different behavioral pathways. One hypothesis might be that delinquent boys have more personality problems than conformist working-class boys. Perhaps the delinquents are from more lax or criminalistic families than are the nondelinquents; or, additionally, differential association in conformist or delinquent peer groups may be a factor of considerable importance.

Other examples of deviant socialization patterns and the development of criminal role patterns can be identified. Some attention has been given to the processes by which embezzlers manage to rationalize their deviant acts in advance of carrying them out. Other work has examined the variations in behavior among juveniles in high-delinquency areas. Finally, Sutherland's famous theory of differential association is centered on the origins of criminals acts and conduct definitions on the part of individuals.

It could be argued that truly adequate causal analysis should explain both variations in rates of criminalistic deviance and variations in involvement in criminality or law-abiding conduct on the part of individuals in particular neighborhoods, social classes, or other settings. Many specific instances of criminological theory and/or research are, in fact, jointly concerned with these two problems. Nevertheless, it makes sense to keep these two matters analytically separate.

Much of the ambiguity and confusion in contemporary theorizing and analysis of criminality is due to our failure to clearly specify the problem. For example, consider the psychiatric hypotheses which allege that offenders are pathological persons suffering from various psychological impairments. Are such claims intended to account for variations in rates of criminality, as among different social-class groups? Do they imply that much larger numbers of working-class individuals, criminals and conformists alike, suffer from personality problems as compared to members of other social classes? Such an inference follows if these hypotheses are put forth as an explanation of rate variations. On the other hand, psychiatric arguments that account for the development of deviant or nondeviant patterns on the part of certain individuals *within* a social-class group leave the matter of rate variations an open question. As an explanation of behavioral development, the personality-pathology framework is logically compatible, at least with a sociological explanation of rate variations that emphasizes such variables as differences in neighborhood organization. Conceivably, high crime rates might most commonly be found in social areas with community influences conducive to criminality, where, in addition, relatively large numbers of persons with personality problems are located and serve as candidates for criminality. Conversely, in neighborhoods more cohesive in character, individuals with personality aberrations may be prone to behavior of a noncriminal kind.

SOCIAL REACTIONS TO CRIME

Reactions to criminality in complex societies such as the United States take many forms. Some crimes are rarely reported to any social-control agency, such as the police. Other instances of deviation are reacted to with police arrest or court action in some cases but not in others, depending on such factors as the social-class backgrounds of offenders and the amount of incriminating evidence that can be accumulated against them. In addition, those violators who are processed in the social-control machinery to the point of court trial are subjected to a variety of subsequent experiences. Some are placed on probation, others incarcerated in jails, and still others sentenced to penal institutions.

Societal reactions to deviants are the consequence of a number of factors, some of which are only slightly understood at present. In any event, scrutiny of the elaborate pattern of social-control devices and experiences that law violators undergo as they are processed through this apparatus is a basic topic for the criminologist. Indeed, it might be argued that the workings of social-control patterns and structures should receive a major share of criminological attention. In modern societies, control, repression, or alteration of deviants has been formalized and turned over to several special occupational groups. As a result, the sociological analysis of social-control machinery ranks in importance with the study of social stratification, family behavior, or certain other core institutions in modern society. Elaborate social inventions for the control of deviants represent prominent social organizations in modern societies.

Societal reactions to offenders at any point in time reflect other characteristics of that social organization. Social definitions of crime and immorality change with alterations in the social order. Crime is not an immutable collection of universally forbidden acts.[18] Then, too, actions taken against law violators in different historical periods have changed over time, tending toward treatment or rehabilitation and away from punishment. Societal reactions are a part of the ongoing social structure. As social conditions change, reactions to deviants become altered. One task facing the criminologist is to develop generalizations to account for the historical trends observed in societal reactions.

causation and explanation in criminology[19]

Although criminologists pursue a number of separate interests concerning law-breaking, the causes of criminality have monopolized the attention of many. What is the nature of causal explanation in criminology and other social- or behavioral-science fields? Let us take a brief look at causal thinking and explanation.

Causal thinking is not restricted to social scientists, for we all go about posing causal questions. Few citizens are totally bewildered about the course of events and believe that "things just happen" by chance. Rather, most physical or social phenomena are presumed to be caused by something—those events which preceded them and which somehow produced them. Lung cancer is a case in point. Many would agree that the cause (or one of the causes) of lung cancer is smoking. Cigarettes cause cancer because their ingredients lead to physical changes in lung tissue, or, stated another way, cigarettes cause cancer because *if* an individual smokes them for an extended period of time *then* he or she will very likely end up with cancerous lungs.

Causal thinking in science bears some similarity to causal analysis on the part of laymen. In both cases, *relationships* are identified; one event or form of behavior is linked to another phenomenon which presumably led to it. Additionally, a *time sequence* is usually implied such that the cause of something rests in a factor which preceded it in time. Laymen and scientists alike deal in assertions of the relationship and time-sequence form—that is, "If X occurs, then Y will probably also occur." A criminological illustration would be: "If juveniles grow up in inner-city neighborhoods and associate with delinquent gangs, they will probably become involved in repetitive predatory crimes in adulthood." This example contains a third element that is common to the causal perspectives of laymen and scientists alike: *probabilistic thinking*. Here, the statement asserts that some event or phenomenon usually or frequently is followed by some other occurrence, but it does not contend that X always leads to Y. Most of us make allowances for unanticipated events, intervening variables, and unknown factors which intrude into explanations and predictions. Explanatory claims are usually couched in terms of greater or lesser certainty because, at any point in time, our knowledge of all the factors that enter into some phenomenon and the interactions among them is less than complete. A major goal of scientific inquiry is to make explanations increasingly more precise through a continuing process of theorizing and research activity, by which we move closer to complete causal accounts by successive approximations.

Although scientific and lay notions of causation show some similarities, they are not identical. The causal beliefs of laymen frequently involve notions that some single factor or experience nearly always lies behind some phenomenon to be explained, as for example, when crime is attributed to mental quirks or other single factors. Then, too, citizens sometimes contend that poverty is not a cause of crime because it does not always produce lawbreaking. By contrast, scientific explanations acknowledge that particular causal factors are not always linked to a single outcome, due to the operation of other, intervening factors. Returning to the case of smoking and lung cancer, although smoking has been shown to be associated with lung cancer, not all persons who smoke develop cancer or emphysema. Moreover, some individuals experience these disorders even though they have never smoked. The latter case indicates that respiratory problems and cancer may arise from more than one set of causal influences, including smog, industrial fumes, and kindred factors. The explanation for the less than perfect association between smoking and these physical ailments is that the effects of smoking are conditioned or mediated by other factors which differentiate between persons, such as variations in place of residence, physical vulnerability, and so on, as well as by the number of years one has smoked, the number of cigarettes consumed each day, and the like.

The situation is similar in criminology. For example, numerous investigators have identified various patterns of parent-child tension and family disorganization that operate in juvenile delinquency. At the same time, we know that some youthful offenders come from stable, warm family settings, while other youngsters who have experienced severely stressful family relationships nonetheless have been free from delinquent involvement. But none of this can be taken as evidence that family experiences are causally unimportant. Rather, these observations indicate the complex nature of causation, in which factors additional to family patterns are also implicated, thus mediating or influencing the part played by parent-child relationships. For example, the potentially deleterious impact of parent-child tensions may sometimes be balanced by warm relationships between youngsters and significant adults such as teachers or relatives. Also, some youths from stable family settings may be inducted into lawbreaking by their peers or by adults outside their family circle.

It is for reasons of this kind that many social scientists prefer to speak of *associations* or *relationships*, rather than of causes. These terms capture the complexity of etiological factors and processes in human behavior better than the latter term, in that it is difficult to disentangle it from oversimplified laymen's usages.

Causal explanation also involves the sorting out of spurious relationships from real ones. In the case of criminality, a spurious relationship would be one in which some factor appears to be importantly involved in lawbreaking when in actuality it is only incidentally related to the factors which actually lead to criminality. An example of a spurious "criminal" relationship might make this distinction clearer: Some investigators have reported that child molesters and certain other sex offenders often exhibit marked interest in religious activities. In prison, they are often the inmates who participate most frequently in religious services. One would be ill-advised to conclude that religious involvement is an important causal influence in the behavior of sex offenders. Rather, their involvement in prison religious programs and their sexual misconduct are probably both related to deep-seated feelings of inferiority and social isolation which they manifest. It is not likely that child molesters engage in law-violating acts due to religious reasons, nor would they be likely to desist in those activities by being persuaded to become less interested in religion. In order to alter the behavior of these offenders, the feelings of inferiority and other factors that have driven them to misconduct would have to be confronted.

Scientific perspectives on causation usually avoid the rigidly deterministic views that frequently pervade laymen's notions. Most social scientists, including criminologists, favor accounts of human behavior centered around what David Matza has termed "soft determinism."[20] This term draws attention to the possibility that, while humans are to a considerable degree constrained or influenced by social and environmental forces which surround them, they are also *reactive* individuals who are able to exercise some freedom or choice over their behavior. According to Matza ". . . human actions are not deprived of freedom because they are causally determined."[21]

The implication of soft determinism as a basic assumption behind causal theories is vast. If human behavior is reflexive, such that individuals are able to exert some independent influence over social-structural pressures, some degree of indeterminacy will probably always characterize causal accounts or explanations offered by social scientists. Some allowance will have to be made in those arguments for the operation of choice and freedom in human actions, with the result that perfect predictability of human behavior will never be achieved in scientific theories.

causation: basic perspectives

As we have seen, there are two kinds of causal questions: those which deal with rates of criminality and social structure and those which ask "Why do they do it?" Criminologists and other investigators have approached these questions in different ways and through explanatory perspectives that differ markedly. The commentary to this point has touched upon most of these orientations, which we can categorize as *biogenic, psychogenic, sociogenic,* and *typological* approaches. *Biogenic* hypotheses contend that the causation or genesis of criminality lies in biological factors and processes. *Psychogenic* theories maintain that lawbreaking is a response to various psychological pressures and personality problems that drive persons to lawbreaking. *Sociogenic* arguments assert that various aspects of social structure produce rates and patterns of criminality and that lawbreakers acquire their criminal motivations and behavior patterns through normal socialization experiences, such as differential association. These three orientations make up a family of causal perspectives, in that each involves different images of man, that is, distinct assumptions about the nature of human conduct.

The *typological* approach differs from the first three perspectives. Typological views emphasize the heterogeneity of criminality and advise us to spend less time in pursuit of theories of crime and criminal behavior and to spend more zeroing in on particular patterns or types of lawbreaking. As we shall see, some typological accounts of criminality have been offered by psychogenically oriented psychologists and psychiatrists, while others have been formulated by sociologists. It is in this sense that the typological view differs from the others, for it involves no commitment to any particular perspective or assumptions about human behavior.

The four above-mentioned causal groupings represent relatively distinct perspectives on criminality. At the same time, there are a number of specific biogenic, psychogenic, sociogenic, and typological arguments for each that must be scrutinized. Many of these are enumerated in Table 2. A look at Table 2 will quickly reiterate our earlier point that investigators from the biogenic and psychogenic approaches have had little to say about variations in crime rates. On the other hand, a host of theories regarding social-structural forces in criminality have stemmed from sociogenic sources.

Chapter 3 examined some premodern versions of biogenic theorizing. We will return to contemporary biological lines of inquiry in Chapter 8, taking up the biogenic arguments noted in Table 2. Chapter 8 also will examine a host of psychogenic theories and research studies. Chapters 6, 7, and 9 deal with sociogenic matters, the first two centering on social structure and criminality and the third dealing with the socialization processes through which criminal attitudes and behavior are acquired. Chapter 10 discusses typological views and asks whether criminals and criminal behavior can be sorted out into distinct types or patterns. Finally, Chapter 11 summarizes the current state of causal analysis, drawing the materials from the preceding chapters together into a synthesis of sorts.

Chapters 6 through 9 follow the causal division outlined earlier in this chapter, with two chapters concerned with social-structural theories being followed by two chapters focused on arguments intended to answer the "Why do they do it?" query. However, some readers may prefer to take up biogenic and psychogenic hypotheses first, before turning to contemporary sociological views concerning rates of criminality and processes through which lawbreaking behavior and criminal definitions are acquired.

table 2 causal perspectives in criminology

explanatory problem	basic approaches			typological
	biogenic	psychogenic	sociogenic	
Social structure and criminality ("rates question")	Biogenic theories have not paid attention to rates questions	Psychogenic arguments tend not to pay attention to rates questions	Anomie - - - - - - - Social disorganization - - - - - - - Differential social organization - - - - - - - Special theories (racism, sexism, etc.) - - - - - - - Pluralistic conflict and interest group theories - - - - - - - Radical-Marxist theory	Specific explanation for each type of criminality
The origins and development of criminal acts and careers ("Why do they do it?")	Body structure and temperament - - - - - - - Twin studies and heredity - - - - - - - Biopsychological theories - - - - - - - XYY chromosomal abnormality - - - - - - - Intelligence levels and criminality	Psychoanalytic theories - - - - - - - General emotional disturbances and lawbreaking - - - - - - - Psychopathy/ sociopathy	Labeling/social-reaction theories - - - - - - - Differential association - - - - - - - Social learning - - - - - - - Situational factors - - - - - - - Family factors and criminality	Specific explanation for each type of criminal

summary

This chapter began with an account of the rise of modern criminology. Like American sociology from which it took root, American criminology was initially a puny and unsophisticated product. But in the fifty or sixty years of its existence, it has grown into a complex, sophisticated intellectual enterprise. Additionally, it has become the model around which criminological inquiry has developed in other nations in the world.

It is no wonder that as scholars have come to devote sustained attention to lawbreaking, their explanations, perspectives, and research techniques have become increasingly richer and more variegated. Crime and responses to it in modern societies are complex phenomena which cannot be apprehended through simple theories and perspectives.

Modern criminologists have developed a body of formulations about lawbreaking and responses to it, along with research techniques for studying criminality, which, together with the scholars who employ them, make up the criminological enterprise. This introductory textbook introduces students to that enterprise. In short, this book demonstrates how to think like a criminologist, that is, how criminologists go about making sense of lawbreaking.

The criminological neophyte might well find some of the commentary in this chapter tedious, preferring instead to be introduced to some of the arcane crime techniques of professional safe burglars, to exposés about scandalous and illegal goings-on in corporate boardrooms, or to other lawbreaking tidbits which make criminology inherently interesting to most students. In some of the chapters to follow factual data of this kind will be scrutinized, for it is important to know what criminals do in the way of criminality, how convicts adjust to prison life, or how police officers go about their work. The central message of this chapter, however, is that the criminological beginner ought to start by becoming familiar with the thoughtways of criminology, in order to be able to make some sense of the vast collection of criminological facts.

Chapter 3 indicated that one basic topic for criminological attention has to do with identification of the scope of criminological inquiry by specifying the behavior that is to be studied as crime. A second chore centers about criminal laws and lawmaking processes. We need to identify the features which set criminal laws off from other rules and forms of social control, and we need to examine the social phenomena of lawmaking. It is to these topics that we turn in Chapter 4.

notes

[1] Edwin H. Sutherland and Donald R. Cressey, *Criminology*, 10th ed. (Philadelphia: Lippincott, 1978), p. 3.

[2] The development of American sociological criminology is discussed in detail in Don C. Gibbons, *The Criminological Enterprise* (Englewood Cliffs, N.J.: Prentice-Hall, Inc., 1979).

[3] This section is a much-abbreviated version of the analysis in Ibid.

[4]For example, see Anthony Oberschall, "The Institutionalization of American Sociology," in *The Establishment of Empirical Sociology*, Oberschall, ed. (New York: Harper & Row, Pub., 1972), pp. 187–251.

[5]Maurice F. Parmelee, *Criminology* (New York: Macmillan, 1918); Edwin H. Sutherland, *Criminology* (Philadelphia: Lippincott, 1924); Philip A. Parsons, *Crime and the Criminal* (New York: Knopf, 1926); John L. Gillin, *Criminology and Penology* (New York: Century, 1926).

[6]The contributions of Shaw, McKay, and Sutherland are discussed in detail in Gibbons, *The Criminological Enterprise*, pp. 38–76.

[7]Edwin H. Sutherland, *The Professional Thief* (Chicago: University of Chicago Press, 1937).

[8]Edwin H. Sutherland, *White Collar Crime* (New York: Dryden Press, 1949).

[9]The developmental process involved in the theory and the various versions of it advanced by Sutherland are discussed in Gibbons, *The Criminological Enterprise*, pp. 46–64.

[10]Ibid., p. 65.

[11]Robert K. Merton, *Social Theory and Social Structure*, rev. ed. (New York: Free Press, 1957), chaps. 4 and 5.

[12]The major criminological directions since 1955 are discussed in detail in Gibbons, *The Criminological Enterprise*, pp. 77–142.

[13]Albert K. Cohen, "The Study of Social Disorganization and Deviant Behavior," in *Sociology Today*, Robert K. Merton, Leonard Broom, and Leonard S. Cottrell, Jr., eds. (New York: Basic Books, 1959), p. 461; a more recent essay indicating that terminological and definitional confusion persists in the study of deviance is Don C. Gibbons and Joseph F. Jones, *The Study of Deviance* (Englewood Cliffs, N.J.: Prentice-Hall, Inc., 1975).

[14]Alexander Liazos, "The Poverty of the Sociology of Deviance: Nuts, Sluts, and Preverts," *Social Problems*, 20 (Summer 1972), 103–20; Herman and Julia Schwendinger, "Defenders of Order or Guardians of Human Rights?" *Issues in Criminology*, 5 (Summer 1970), 123–37.

[15]Clarence R. Jeffery, "The Structure of American Criminological Thinking," *Journal of Criminal Law, Criminology and Police Science*, 46 (January–February 1956), 658–72.

[16]These two explanatory problems have been discussed in detail in Cohen, "Social Disorganization and Deviant Behavior," pp. 461–84.

[17]Donald R. Cressey, "Epidemiology and Individual Conduct: A Case from Criminology," *Pacific Sociological Review*, 3 (Fall 1960), 47.

[18]On this point, see Kai T. Erikson, *Wayward Puritans* (New York: John Wiley, 1966).

[19]This section has been adapted from Don C. Gibbons, *Delinquent Behavior*, 3rd ed. (Englewood Cliffs, N.J.: Prentice-Hall, Inc., 1981), pp. 95–104.

[20]David Matza, *Delinquency and Drift* (New York: John Wiley, 1964), pp. 1–32.

[21]Ibid., p. 9.

crime
and
the
criminal
law

Now that we have established a firm historical and theoretical base, we can begin to explore in depth criminality in modern societies. But where shall we start? Chapter 3 noted that there are two concerns that arise for criminologists early in their work. First, there is the choice of a definition of crime and criminal behavior that is to guide inquiry. Crime can be, and usually is, conceptualized legalistically, but it is also possible to devise various sociological definitions of criminality that pay little or no attention to criminal statutes.

A second related task, but one which is important in its own right, is to acquire some understanding of criminal law as distinct from other social norms. How can we tell when we are faced with instances of the criminal law, rather than other rules? And, from what sources do criminal laws arise? Are they legislative responses to broad demands from the general public, or, instead, are criminal laws most often created for the benefit of particular powerful interest groups?

Concerning the definitional task, unless criminologists can first agree on the nature and scope of the phenomena they are to study, little or no progress can be made in the understanding of crime and criminal behavior. Whatever final decision the investigator of criminality makes regarding the appropriate phenomena to be probed, his or her starting point must necessarily be with the criminal law, which ". . . may be broadly conceived as that body of law which defines criminal offenses, establishes procedures for the apprehension, charging, and trial of suspected offenders, and which fixes penalties and modes of treatment applicable to convicted offenders."[1] If the criminologist proposes to zero in on a body of subject matter different from that contained in the criminal statutes, he or she must defend that departure from convention.

This chapter takes up some major features of criminal law that differentiate it from other forms of social control or bodies of normative proscriptions. It is also concerned with the sociology of criminal law, and explores the origins of criminal law in detail. A variety of theories are presented that attempt to account for the development of legal norms, along with several investigations of the social sources of certain criminal laws. Criminologists also are curious about the extent to which social sentiments support criminal laws; hence, we shall look at several studies that illuminate this question. Finally, the last portion of the chapter grapples with the issue of whether we should take a legalistic or some other viewpoint regarding crime. Should "antisocial" persons be the focus of attention? Should we study all norm violations, or should we restrict attention to violations of criminal laws?

elements of criminal law

LAW AND SOCIAL CONTROL

Criminal laws are only one of a number of devices intended to accomplish the goal of social control. The term *social control* designates those social arrangements that have been developed in response to deviance and lawbreaking. These social control measures are intended to promote predictability of behavior and social regularity, although they often fail to bring about those ends. Social control stands in contrast to *personal control*, which refers to those mechanisms inside the actor that constrain behavior. The latter consist of internalized or introjected norms, along with such internal or psychological mechanisms of control as feelings of guilt. A major share of the predictability of human behavior is the result of personal control rather than external coercion. In turn, a central task of the socialization process centers about the inculcation of mechanisms of personal control. Personal and social control are not entirely independent phenomena, but social control develops to take care of behavioral instances in which personal control has broken down. In brief, social control is brought into play when the individual fails to be "his own policeman"—when he or she fails to curtail deviant impulses.

The forms of social control are varied; criminal laws comprise only one kind of social control. It is apparently true that "all organized societies display, even if in rudimentary form, a body of rules, norms or customs tending to protect the security of individual interests and the survival of the group as a whole."[2] Negative sanctions or penalties are imposed on those who violate norms, whereas positive sanctions such as praise or recognition are bestowed on exemplary persons. These positive and negative sanctions are forms of social control. Some social controls are formal or official, while others are informal or unofficial in character, such as gossip or ridicule. Some official apparatus established for that purpose exercises formal controls. In the case of criminal laws, enforcement and implementation rest with an elaborate machinery of police agencies, judicial, and correctional structures.

Karl Llewellyn and E. Adamson Hoebel identified the distinctive features of law as a form of social control.[3] They noted that laws are a part of the normative structure of a society; that is, they constitute one set of definitions of obligatory or forbidden actions. Laws involve sanctions, so they are accompanied by penalties or punishments invoked in instances in which they are disobeyed. A third characteristic of laws is that in cases of conflict with other interests, laws must be followed, even in violation of other norms. Laws must prevail over other injunctions. Finally, laws are part of a larger legal system, which includes a relatively explicit underlying rationale or philosophy, a set of procedures for applying and enforcing laws, and a body of recognized officials delegated the responsibility of carrying out legal procedures. Each of these characteristics must be present for a normative system to be considered legal.

Most of us are rarely touched directly by the criminal law, but we all grow up surrounded by it, take it as a basic feature of modern life, and rarely if ever ask questions about it. In short, we take the existence of the criminal law for granted—as a natural part of our environment, like the air we breathe or the ground upon which we walk. However, the formalization of bodies of law, including criminal statutes, is a relatively recent development. For many centuries, human beings restrained themselves and others from certain actions by various informal procedures and through unwritten, informal norms, often called *folkways* and *mores* by sociologists. Moreover, the accretion of modern law made up of formalized norms and sanctions has been uneven throughout the world. Law has flourished in urbanized, Western nations, while in some contemporary non-Western societies laws are still relatively undeveloped and traditional informal controls are still dominant.[4]

The modern criminal law of England and the United States grew out of the English common law of crimes. This body of law originated in decisions of judges, which by the middle of the thirteenth century were applied throughout the English realm and were thus "common" to it.[5]

English common law unfolded slowly over several hundred years, during which England changed from a collection of independent, warring fiefdoms, each with local customs and traditions and ruled by local barons, into a united kingdom. The common law originally consisted of a largely unwritten collection of laws and customs of different parts of England that were declared to be the law of the land by King Edward the Confessor (1003–1066). However, when William the Conqueror took the throne of England in 1066, he encountered a nation that was still closer to anarchy than to statehood. One of his first acts was to declare the entire populace to be under his control and leadership, in short, to exert kingship over the realm. The king's judges embarked upon the task of translating unwritten common law into a set of legal rules, mainly through judicial decisions rather than legislated statutes. It is these decisions that are usually referred to as the common law. These common-law principles continue to be invoked as guides to judicial decision making through the principle of *stare decisis*, which means to look to past cases and abide by the decisions reached in them.

As a result of his efforts to unify the nation under his leadership, William the Conqueror inaugurated a long period of turmoil in England. He separated lay and ecclesiastic courts in an effort to wrest power away from the Church. He also came into conflict with the local barons when he declared that it was solely his responsibility to maintain the "the King's peace" throughout the land. However, by the time of death of Henry II in 1189, the struggles between the king, the Church, and the landed gentry had been won by the crown. And, by then, most of the procedural and substantive elements upon which modern English and American criminal law have been built had emerged.

C. Ray Jeffery has provided an account of the transformation of England from tribalism to feudalism and, ultimately, to nationalism, a transition which took place over the eight centuries from A.D. 400 to 1200.[6] During this evolution, the *land-tie* replaced the *blood-tie* as the basis for social order. Jeffery observed that:

During the tribal period there was a fusion of institutional functions in the kinship unit. This body was the political, economic, family, religious, and ecological unit. By 1200 separate institutions existed in these several areas. Political authority was now in the hands of landlords. By the time of Henry II the king emerged as the supreme landlord in this feudal hierarchy. Economic organization shifted from a hunting, fishing, and pastoral economy, where the kinship group was the economic unit, to an agricultural economy, where the feudal manor was the economic unit. Each man occupied land belonging to his lord, rather than to his kin, and he was attached to this land through a personal-legal relationship known as the tenure system. Status was now based on this tenure system. Feudalism was based on a division of men into two classes: military and agricultural. Religion was now controlled by a professional hierarchy of priests and bishops who acted as both church officials and landlords. Christianity was an important aspect of the feudal system. The conjugal family did not perform the many functions performed by the tribal family. This shift from an institutional family to a companionship family is a familiar theme in sociological literature today.

A new social structure emerged in England, and as a result of these changes a new legal system came into existence. During the tribal period the legal system was in the hands of the tribal group, and justice was based on the blood-feud. As tribalism gave way to feudalism, the feud was replaced by a system of compensations. Justice passed into the hands of the landlords. There was no separation of lay and ecclesiastical courts until the time of William. State law and crime came into existence during the time of Henry II as a result of this separation of State and Church, and as a result of the emergence of a central authority in England which replaced the authority of the feudal lords. Henry replaced feudal lords with state justice by means of justices in eyre, the king's peace, a system of royal courts, and a system of royal writs. Common law emerged as the law of the Crown available to all men. The myth that the common law of England is the law of the Anglo-Saxons is without historical foundation. The family was no longer involved in law and justice. The State was the offended social unit, and the State was the proper prosecutor in every case of crime. Justice was now the sole prerogative of the State. "Custom passes into law." This shift occurred historically when a political community separate from the kinship group emerged as a part of the social organization.[7]

This brief account of the rise of Anglo-American criminal law indicates that laws are social phenomena which have roots in the social and economic conditions of nations from which they emerge. Laws do not arise simply by chance. As social and economic features change, so do the legal rules that govern the conduct of the members of societies. We will return to this topic later in this chapter, where our concern will be with the various theories that have been concocted to account for criminal statutes, along with the research that can be marshalled on the origins of laws.

Broadly speaking, criminal laws prohibit or compel instances of conduct held to be important for the welfare of society or the state. Criminal laws exist in contradistinction to civil laws, which are a body of legal rules governing the conduct of individual persons in their private lives. The wrongs identified by civil law are considered to be private ones rather than wrongs against the state. A tort is a violation of civil law, or an offense against an individual. The injured individual must set the court machinery in operation, and he is the recipient of redress from the offender. But a crime is a violation of criminal law and an offense against the state. The state acts as the plaintiff, initiates the action against the offender, and exacts the punishment assigned the offender.

Parenthetically, this distinction between crimes and torts is not clear-cut. There are a number of injuries that are treated as torts when, in fact, they could also be dealt with as crimes. For example, citizens may bring civil action against an industry for pollution violations or the state may issue an injunction against some practice which is also defined in criminal law as illegal. Broadly speaking, the social power of the offending party or parties tends to be a major determinant of whether a civil or criminal action is instituted.

Edwin Sutherland and Donald Cressey have identified the essential characteristics of criminal law as *politicality, specificity, uniformity*, and *penal sanction*.[8] These components are identified in legal theory; in other words, these elements of criminal law would be present in a completely rational, ideal system of criminal statutes. The law in practice can and does depart from these characteristics. Also, the differences between criminal laws and other bodies of conduct regulations are sometimes less clear-cut than these categories imply.

Politicality means that the criminal laws originate through the actions of the state rather than some private organization or group. In modern America, those rules promulgated by legislatures of the state and its subdivisions constitute criminal laws. Regulations of labor unions, social fraternities, college faculties, and so on, are not criminal statutes even though they often show some similarity to the rules created by legislative processes.

Specificity means that criminal statutes provide strict definitions of the particular acts that constitute crimes. In turn, those acts not clearly and unmistakably included in descriptions of crimes within the statutes are not to be labeled as crimes. However, in practice, specificity is a matter of degree, for some laws are relatively broad and general in language, such as those defining vagrancy and disorderly conduct, or omnibus clauses in definitions of juvenile delinquency, which list "immorality" and "ungovernability" as forms of delinquent behavior. Societies have sometimes adopted broadly worded statutes that depart markedly from the principle of specificity. Thus, in Nazi Germany, the German Act of 1935 provided that persons could be tried for acts not forbidden by law but which violated "the sound feelings of the people." Similarly, the Soviet penal code adopted in 1926 penalized any "socially dangerous" behavior.[9]

Uniformity as a feature of criminal laws refers to the effort to specify crimes and invoke sanctions against offenders evenhandedly. Criminal laws do not allow some categories of individuals to be dealt with differently from other groups that have committed similar law violations. Instead, criminal liability is supposed to be uniform for all, irrespective of social background or social status. However, uniformity breaks down in practice at several points. Law-enforcement processes are not always uniformly administered, and judicial decisions are not always free from theoretically extraneous or irrelevant considerations of background variations or social influence.

Penal sanction means that penalties are specified for violation of the statutes. Laws declare that certain acts are forbidden or required and that violators of the law will be punished in some way.

The foregoing elements of criminal codes are essentially *external* characteristics: they indicate the outward ingredients of the criminal law. Political bodies create criminal statutes, which involve penalties when they are violated. Legal scholars have also identified the *differentiae of crime*, those elements of behavior that must occur for certain actions to be brought within the criminal law.[10] The differentiae of crime are those characteristics of the behavior of an individual that must be present for the behavior to constitute criminal conduct.

The first requirement is that the behavior constitute a "harm." The act must result in visible, external consequences detrimental to social interests. Insofar as an act is held to result in injuries only to the parties immediately concerned in the act, that behavior does not qualify as a crime. Private injuries are civil offenses, not criminal acts.

To be identified as a crime, an act must legally be forbidden. In other words, antisocial conduct is not criminal until it has specifically been proscribed in the body of criminal law. In the proceedings against a person, careful attention is usually paid to the question of whether an act has explicitly been forbidden. It is not enough that the behavior in question be reasonably similar to actions proscribed by law. Instead, the instance at hand must clearly fit within an existing category of forbidden conduct. Moreover, an elaborate appeal system has been contrived as a safeguard against misapplication of laws, so detailed scrutiny is often given to alleged acts of unlawful conduct. Accused persons are sometimes able to secure their release from criminal prosecution by showing that their actions fell outside the legal rules.

In addition to the foregoing, "conduct" must occur for a crime to take place. Intentional behavioral events, resulting in some harmful consequence, must have taken place. For instance, to convict an individual of murder, it must be proven that the person actually pulled the trigger of a gun or behaved in some other way that led directly to the death of the victim. It is not enough to show by a chain of circumstantial reasoning that a particular harmful consequence *probably* ensued from some illegal actions of a suspect. To convict an alleged offender of murder, more would be required than simply a demonstration that the suspect owned the weapon used to kill a person; someone else might have used the gun and committed the murder.

A fourth and critical element in crime is that of *mens rea*, literally "evil mind" or "guilty mind." *Mens rea* refers to *intent* rather than to *motivation*. To demonstrate *mens rea*, it must be shown that an actor intended or calculated to behave in a manner defined as illegal. Thus, for example, an individual is guilty of arson if he or she deliberately sets a fire in a dwelling, with the result that the house burns to the ground. If a fire occurs as a result of an accidental action by the actor, it would not qualify as arson.

A guilty individual may have engaged in a line of conduct or formed criminal intent out of various reasons or motives, but these reasons or motives are not directly relevant to the question of *mens rea*. For example, a person who, out of feelings of compassion, deliberately kills an invalid spouse suffering from an incurable and painful disease is equally as guilty of a crime as a professional killer who murders someone in cold blood and for pay. *Mens rea* would be present in both cases. Of course, the penalty handed out to each of these murderers may be considerably different, and the professional killer might receive a decidedly more punitive sentence than the other murderer. Variations in sentences that are a function of social-background differences among offenders, differences in motivation, and so on, are commonplace in the workings of the legal machinery. However, the basic point remains that good motives are not taken into account in the determination of whether a crime has occurred, at least in legal theory.

Mens rea is basic to the plea of insanity as extenuating in criminal-court trials. In brief, the claim that an individual was insane at the time that a harmful act took place, if successfully sustained, relieves that person of culpability of a criminal act. The actor is held to be guiltless because of an incapacity to form criminal intent, from the absence of *mens rea*.

A fusion of *mens rea* and conduct or a simultaneous occurrence of the two is also a necessary element of crime. For example, a crime has not taken place in the instance of an intended but abortive attempt by A to murder B, followed by a later event in which B dies through the unintended negligence of A, who has left a gas stove turned on but unlighted, resulting in B's death from gas poisoning.

A causal relationship between someone's voluntary misconduct and the legally forbidden harm is also required. In other words, it must be shown that the harm was a direct consequence of the misconduct rather than an indirect one or a result of some other antecedent events. An obvious illustration of the causal connection would be a homicide in which a drunken driver runs over a pedestrian having the right-of-way in a crosswalk, and the pedestrian dies immediately after being hit by the car. A not-so-clear instance might be a drug addict who received medical care in a hospital and recovers from a drug overdose, but who then succumbs to another disease contracted while in the hospital. In the latter case, the drug dealer who supplied the drugs could plead not guilty of homicide by reason of a lack of causal connection between his illegal acts and the death of the victim. The drug dealer would be guilty of illegally selling narcotics but not of the death of his customer.

The final element of crime is that the forbidden act must carry a legally prescribed punishment. The voluntary conduct of the violator must be punishable by law.

Criminal law in practice shows discrepancies from these criteria of crimes.

In particular, *mens rea* is not required in the so-called strict liability offenses. That is, with certain kinds of offenses the intent of the actor is not considered, so that certain actions and consequences constitute crimes even though the perpetrator did not intend harmful consequences. Statutory rape and "contributing to the delinquency of a minor" are cases in point, as are certain automobile violations. In the instance of contributing to the delinquency of a minor, an individual can be held liable for law violation for a number of acts carried on with a minor female (or male) in which no criminal conduct was intended. Similarly, in most states a person can be convicted and punished for statutory rape if he has sexual intercourse with a minor female, even though he went through elaborate efforts to determine her age and was completely convinced that the girl was above the age of consent. In these cases, it is enough that the person engaged in some line of conduct; intentions are legally irrelevant.

criminal law revision

As we have already seen, criminal law has a history. For example, over the past hundred years, property law has been expanded in a number of ways to take account of the needs of changing social conditions. A recent example is credit-card fraud. These statutes were developed in response to the problems created by the rapid diffusion of credit cards as an alternative to retail purchases by means of cash or checks.

Criticism of the criminal law, calling for statutory revisions of one kind or another, is a constant phenomenon in the United States. One recurring complaint has been that the various state criminal and penal codes are varied and inconsistent, with differing statutory definitions of particular crimes and also with criminal penalties that differ markedly from one jurisdiction to another. For instance, the dividing line between petty and grand larceny is specified as $50 in some states, $75 in others, and $100 in still others. Along the same line, statutory definitions of sexual offenses sometimes punishable as misdemeanors are dealt with as felonies in other jurisdictions. Frequently, the same criminal offense calls for quite different maximum prison terms in individual states. In short, American criminal law does not exist; rather, a large number of state penal codes bear some loose relationship to one another.

Another criticism of American criminal statutes centers upon the allegation that the law is often employed inappropriately as a means for dealing with behavior that is not socially harmful. A considerable number of critics have argued that use of criminal law as a means of controlling "personal vices" such as marijuana use or homosexuality is improper and unwise.

Herbert Packer contended that criminal sanction is too widely employed in American society. Hence, he offered the following criteria for the use of criminal laws and penalties to control behavior.[11]

1. The conduct is prominent in most people's view of socially threatening behavior and is not condoned by any significant segment of society.

2. Subjecting the conduct to criminal sanction is not inconsistent with the goals of punishment.

3. Suppressing it will not inhibit socially desirable conduct.

4. The conduct may be dealt with through evenhanded and nondiscriminatory enforcement.

5. Controlling the conduct through the criminal process will not expose that process to severe qualitative or quantitative strains.

6. No reasonable alternatives to the criminal sanction for dealing with the conduct exist.

Applying these criteria to existing criminal statutes, Packer recommended that a number of acts, including certain moral offenses, should be "decriminalized" by expunging the relevant laws from the statute books. Edwin Schur has expressed similar views. He argued that existing laws concerning "crimes without victims" represent good candidates for repeal.[12] Crimes without victims are those offenses in which both parties to the offense are voluntary participants and in which no clear danger to the public welfare can be perceived in the conduct. Schur discussed drug addiction, homosexuality, and abortion as cases in point, along with certain other victimless crimes.[13]

The most ambitious attempt to impose order upon the chaos of criminal codes in the United States is found in the work of The American Law Institute, culminating in the drafting of the Model Penal Code in 1962.[14] Among the many problems tackled in that model code was the definition of specific crimes, along with the removal of certain offenses from the scope of the criminal law.[15] The model code retained forcible rape and forcible deviate sexual intercourse as criminal offenses, but it erased consensual homosexual acts from the statutes.

This recommendation was paralleled in England in the proposals of the Wolfenden Report, named for the jurist, Sir John Wolfenden, who presided over the work of the governmental commission.[16] That report urged that consensual acts of homosexuality between adults be removed from the criminal law, along with prohibitions against prostitution. The decriminalization of homosexuality was accomplished in Great Britain in 1966.

The Model Penal Code also tackled the thorny issue of criminal responsibility and the insanity defense, which has a long and stormy history.[17] Until recently, the most common standard for determining responsibility for criminal acts has been the M'Naghten rule, formulated in 1843. This rule arose out of an English homicide case, in which M'Naghten killed Drummond, the secretary to Sir Robert Peel. A principle emerged from this trial: for a person to be declared insane and not responsible for a criminal act, it must be shown that "at the time of the committing of the act, the party accused was laboring under such a defect of reason, from disease of the mind, as to not know the nature and quality of the act he was doing; or, if he did know it, that he did not know he was doing what was wrong."[18]

Critics of the M'Naghten standard argue that the rule pays too much attention to intellectual capacity and ignores emotional states. According to this view, a person may know in some cognitive sense what he is doing at the same time that he is incapable of controlling his behavior. Then, too, the M'Naghten rule can only be applied to markedly disordered persons, so that many psychotic individuals end up being dealt with as criminals rather than mentally ill persons. Psychiatrists have often voiced harsh objections to the M'Naghten ruling on the grounds that it calls upon them to make judgments about a legal state, "insanity," even though their knowledge and expertise center about a quite different phenomenon, mental illness.

A few states have adopted a second rule, the "irresistible impulse" test, along with the M'Naghten standard, in which persons are held not responsible for criminal acts which have resulted from the inability of the mind to control the will due to some uncontrollable impulse.

An alternative standard was formulated in *Durham* v. *United States* in the Court of Appeals for the District of Columbia. The ruling in that case was that "an accused is not criminally responsible if his unlawful act was the product of mental disease or defect."[19] However, that standard has not become widely adopted. Critics of the Durham rule have noted that it does not define mental disease or defect and thus opens the door to the possibility that relatively minor or innocuous disorders of personality might be offered as grounds for avoiding criminal responsibility. Then, too, no standard is provided for indicating the degree of causal linkage between the mental state and the lawbreaking conduct which is required. How directly must the psychological factors be tied to the criminal conduct?

The American Law Institute formulated a standard for criminal responsibility more in keeping with modern thought on criminal motivation and psychopathological states—a standard that at the same time avoids some of the looseness and fuzziness of the Durham standard. The Model Penal Code stated: "A person is not responsible for criminal conduct if at the time of such conduct as a result of mental disease or defect he lacks substantial capacity either to appreciate the criminality [wrongfulness] of his conduct or to conform his conduct to the requirements of the law."[20] The model code specifically excludes mental disease or defects that include abnormality manifested only by repeated criminality or by other antisocial conduct.

Although the M'Naghten rule has suffered a barrage of attacks, and even though many authorities favor the American Law Institute standard, the former has persisted as the most widely used test of mental responsibility.

The Model Penal Code also sought to bring order into the matter of penalties, sentencing, and corrections. The code identified three degrees of felonies, each carrying specified minimum and maximum sentences.[21] First-degree felonies have minimum prison sentences of not less than one year or more than ten years with a maximum period of life imprisonment. Second-degree and third-degree felonies have lesser minimum and maximum terms. The model code also provided for "extended terms" of imprisonment for the three grades of felonies when the individuals involved in them meet certain criteria such as chronic recidivism or habitual criminality. For example, a ten-to-twenty-year minimum extended sentence was provided for Class I felonies meeting the criteria. Finally, the model code established a number of procedural rules for due process for offenders in the postconviction stage of corrections. For example, provisions are made for lawyers to represent probationers at probation revocation hearings, ensuring that the rights of the individual will be upheld.

Since 1962, and the appearance of the Model Penal Code, over 30 states have embarked on reform efforts directed at revision of their criminal codes. For example, the new criminal code enacted by the Oregon legislature in 1971 embodied a number of the suggestions of the model code.[22] In the set of statutes, adultery, lewd cohabitation, seduction, and private consensual acts of homosexuality between adults were removed from the codes. The provisions regarding statutory rape now allow the individual to offer as a defense that he was reasonably mistaken as to the age of the female. Also, the model-code standard for criminal responsibility was incorporated in place of the M'Naghten test. The statutory definitions of assault and murder were also revised in the direction suggested in the model code.

The processes of statutory modification show no signs of abating. In recent years, statutes dealing with simple possession of marijuana have been modified, making this act a "violation" subject to a small fine instead of a criminal act involving a major penalty. Similarly, in the case of juvenile delinquency statutes, a good deal of agitation has recently centered upon status offenses such as ungovernability, immorality, and waywardness.[23] In the view of many critics, these ought to be dealt with outside of the framework of the juvenile court. Finally, the death penalty has been reinstated and put back into use in a number of states. In short, lawmaking and law revision are continuing social processes.

the social sources of criminal law

THE PROBLEM

As we have seen, modern criminal law in England and the United States has a thousand-year history, dating back to William the Conqueror. We also noted that criminal laws do not encompass all antisocial or socially harmful acts, at the same time that they include some behaviors that many would claim are not antisocial or social harms, such as homosexual acts between consenting partners or the use of various drugs. Moreover, contemporary criminal codes contain many more acts specified as illegal than the criminal laws of a century or two ago. Lawmaking is a continuous process and exists as a response to social influences operating in societies at various points in time.

Although the making of criminal laws represents a fundamental social process to which criminologists ought to attend, American criminology has emphasized the study of criminal behavior, rather than crime and lawmaking.[24] Chambliss has commented on the need to pay attention to the social processes leading to the creation of criminal laws:

Crime is a political phenomenon. What gets defined as criminal or delinquent behavior is the result of a political process within which rules are formed which prohibit or require people to behave in certain ways. It is this process which must be understood as it bears on the definition of behavior as criminal if we are to proceed to the study of criminal *behavior*. Thus to ask "why is it that some acts get defined as criminal while others do not" is the starting point for all systematic study of crime and criminal behavior. Nothing is inherently criminal, it is only the response that makes it so. If we are to explain crime, we must first explain the social forces that cause some acts to be defined as criminal while other acts are not [emphasis in the original].[25]

What are the social factors that have produced criminal laws of one kind or another? Let us first examine the theories that have been advanced by sociologists and legal scholars to account for the emergence of criminal statutes, after which we will take up the evidence bearing upon these theories.

CRIMINAL LAWS AND THE MORES

According to one line of argument, as Western societies grew in size, complexity, and impersonality over the past several centuries, folkways and mores became inadequate for the task of maintaining social stability. Consequently, legal institutions developed to support the more traditional forms of control. In this view, lawmaking is the behavior of desperate citizens trying to reverse the deterioration of informal norms. Joseph Eaton's study of social changes among the Hutterites is a microcosmic illustration of this development. The Hutterites, a contemporary North American religious sect, practiced an Anabaptist faith coupled with a socialist economy.[26] As this group was drawn into more intense contacts with the surrounding social organization of non-Hutterites, many unwritten customs of the group were challenged. In response to these perceived breakdowns, the elders of the sect formalized previously informal norms and created specific punishment for rule violations.

A number of arguments have been offered by sociologists, all revolving around this thesis that criminal laws grew up to replace, buttress, or shore up decaying informal norms. In the classical view, criminal norms were seen as originating in torts or private wrongs, from which the state eventually came to redefine some private injuries as social ones. However, the process by which private harms were converted into public or social ones has largely been left unspecified. A second view on the origin of criminal laws asserts that they are an attempt to codify the mores and develop a coherent supportive rationale for the body of formalized mores. A third contention regarding custom and law is that the latter grows up in response to perceived shortcomings in the mores or their implementation. All of these theories imply that criminal laws reflect broad cultural consensus on basic interests and values within societies. That is, criminal laws are taken as a crude index of the core interests held in common by large segments of the population.

SOCIAL CONFLICT AND INTEREST-GROUP THEORIES

The claim that laws grew out of early societal mores may be relevant to at least some laws that have developed in the past, but it does not qualify as an adequate explanation of most lawmaking in modern societies. It is extremely difficult to speak meaningfully of mores and customs in contemporary complex societies. Accordingly, a competing perspective on the origins of criminal laws has gained a large number of supporters, holding that laws grew out of special interests of particular groups in the population. This view stresses cultural differences, value clashes, social conflict, and differences in social power said to characterize complex societies. Criminal norms are alleged to mirror these conflicts of interest between different power groups, so that the laws symbolize the victory of one faction over another. For example, according to this view, the claim that modern property laws in Western, capitalistic societies exist for the benefit of all citizens is a fiction disguising the fact that these statutes provide the means by which the wealthy are able to maintain exploitative relationships over the "have-nots."

William Chambliss and Robert Seidman have articulated an interest-group theory of the origins of criminal laws in modern societies.[27] They rejected those formulations that stress natural law, in which criminal codes are thought to represent legal innovations that arise as solutions to problems of social integration in complex societies. Instead, they argued: "Every detailed study of the emergence of legal norms has consistently shown the immense importance of interest-group activity, *not 'the public interest,'* as the critical variable in determining the content of legislation" (emphasis in the original).[28] In another discussion, they claimed:

Deviancy is not a moral question; it is a political question. No act, nor any set of acts, can be defined as inherently "beyond the pale" of "community tolerance." Rather, there are in effect an infinite number and variety of acts occurring in any society which may or may not be defined and treated as criminal. Which acts are so designated depends on the interest of the persons with sufficient political power and influence to manage to have their views prevail. Once it has been established that certain acts are to be designated as deviant, then how the laws are implemented will likewise reflect the political power of the various affected groups.[29]

Chambliss and Seidman's thesis that interest-group activity is a critical factor behind much legislative action in modern societies is on the mark.[30] However, this argument is not yet a detailed theory about lawmaking. The range and variety of competing interest groups involved in the social processes of law creation have yet to be spelled out. Additionally, because interest-group formulations contain very few details regarding the dynamics of rule making, there is still much to be learned about the processes through which the values of competing interest groups become incorporated in criminal statutes.[31]

RADICAL-MARXIST THEORIES

Many of the claims about criminal laws derived from social-conflict or interest-group theory have implied that power to bring about legislation is diffuse and shared by various collectivities—that is, that a multiplicity of shifting interest groups help create law. However, during the past decade or so, the radical-Marxist wing within criminology has vigorously advocated a markedly less equivocal theory, holding that criminal laws arise to serve the interests of the ruling class.[32] For example, Richard Quinney declared: "The state is organized to serve the interests of the dominant economic class, the capitalist ruling class. Criminal law is an instrument of the state and ruling class to maintain and perpetuate the existing social and economic order."[33] Similarly, Chambliss has asserted: "Acts are defined as criminal because it is in the interests of the ruling class to so define them."[34]

Critics have not been kind to this argument.[35] Those who have taken issue with it contend that radical theorizing about the origins of criminal laws overlooks the large number of laws that are supported by societal consensus and which serve general interests, rather than solely those of a ruling class. Then, too, the ruling-class element of Marxist theories has been challenged. Many have contended that political power is wielded in modern societies by a plethora of influential groups rather than a single, monolithic ruling class. Indeed, many of the critics of radical theorizing have denied that any single ruling class even exists in American society. Still others have drawn attention to criminal legislation which seems to restrict, rather than to increase, the powers of corporate capitalists. These objections to Marxist theorizing about the origins of laws all come together to form a complex picture of criminal laws, class relations, and social power in modern societies.

One indication of the real-life complexity with which theories of lawmaking must contend is found in Peter Manning's analysis of the 1829 Metropolitan Police Act in England. This act created the first full-time, paid police force in the world. Manning took issue with those who attribute this legislation to a single motive—protection of the capitalist elite from "the dangerous classes." He observed:

Closer attention to historical facts and additional investigation would have revealed, however, that the origins of the civil police in England can be attributed to a variety of "factors" or "causes," some in combination with each other. For example, there are at least five distinct arguments with supporting evidence which can be formulated to explain the "interests" which "lay behind" the conceptualization and passage of the Metropolitan

Police Act of 1829. They may be enumerated in a very brief form. (1) A Marxist *interest* theory seeing the elites as key backers of the police idea as a means of attempting repression of the working classes; (2) a *reformist* conception or interpretation which links elites, scholar-intellectuals, and administrators in a broadly conceived effort to reform the penal code, judicial structure and function, and law enforcement organization and practice; (3) a *"middle-class"* "growth of respectability" argument which claims that elites, bourgeoisie and working-class "tories" or loyalists united to create mechanisms to control social disorder in burgeoning cities; (4) a view which saw the development of the police as a logical outgrowth of the *utter failure of the army* to control domestic disorders—a pragmatic bargain struck between the elites, the army, and rural landed gentry; (5) a *counterrevolutionary* explanation which portrays large segments of the population, supported in their beliefs by Methodism and responding to Jacobin sentiments and activities of urban artisans and labourers, as working through mob action and demands upon politicians to seek to repress democratic or revolutionary strivings. Each of these views is defensible: a repressive elite argument; a responsible elite argument; a modernisation argument; a pragmatic centered argument; and a counterrevolutionary anti-Jacobin argument; but none adopts the rigid simplicity of the crude interest theory implied by Quinney and others.[36]

Unfortunately, criminal laws and their social roots have not been studied in great number by criminologists. However, some findings are at hand concerning the rise of particular criminal laws. These research results, taken together, add credence to the argument here which stressed the complexity of rule-making processes.

SOME STUDIES OF CRIMINAL LAWS

In the opening chapter, attention was directed at the elastic boundaries of crime and at lawmaking as a social process. That discussion made passing reference to some historical investigations of the origins of criminal laws, including Nelson's inquiry regarding changes in criminal law and procedure in the Massachusetts Puritan Colony from 1760 to 1830.[37] That study indicated that in the pre-Revolutionary War period, the Puritans were most concerned about blasphemy, adultery, and other violations of Puritan morality. But, the emerging post-Revolutionary economy of the new nation ultimately brought about marked changes in the legal system in Massachusetts. These changes were part of the broader movement toward an entrepreneurial society.

A number of the inquiries into the social origins of criminal laws deal with lawmaking in England. As one case in point, William Chambliss examined the origins of vagrancy laws in England and the United States and the shifts in their nature since their creation.[38] The first vagrancy statute, enacted in England in 1349, made the giving of alms to any unemployed person of sound mind and body a crime. This law was the indirect result of the Black Death, which struck England about 1348 and had the effect of decimating the English labor force. Half of the English population is estimated to have died during the plague epidemic. As a result, the supply of cheap labor was severely reduced precisely at a time when serfdom was beginning to break down and peasants began to flee from the manors. Landowners had begun to experience great difficulties in the maintenance of their holdings. According to Chambliss, "It was under these conditions that we find the first vagrancy statutes emerging. There is little question but that these statutes were designed for one express purpose: to force laborers (whether personally free or unfree) to accept employment at a low wage in order to insure the landowner an adequate supply of labor at a price he could afford to pay."[39] In effect, the vagrancy laws attempted to sustain conditions of serfdom after the breakdown of the serf-manor system had already begun.

For most of the period after their enactment in 1349 to the sixteenth century, vagrancy laws remained a dormant statutory device because the conditions that spurred their development had disappeared. However, about 1530 the statutes were revised in language and restored to use. The new phraseology focused attention on criminals rather than on unemployed persons. In effect, these revamped vagrancy codes were intended to provide the control of persons suspected of being robbers or other criminals but not yet apprehended for some specific violation of law. Chambliss accounted for these changes as a social response to the growth of commerce and industry in England. The large number of foreign merchants abroad in that country in the sixteenth century were subject to frequent attacks by robbers. The same concern for the regulation and protection of commerce and merchants in England provided the source of early statutes identifying theft as a crime.

Further elaborations and changes in vagrancy laws occurred over the past several hundred years. However, the general trend was to broaden the range of kinds of individuals who come within the definition of vagrant. A mechanism was devised that provided police agencies with broad powers to "clear the streets" of various "suspicious" and "undesirable" persons. Accordingly, vagrancy laws served as a means of controlling the denizens of such city areas as Skid Row. As Chambliss noted, the individual states in the United States borrowed the eighteenth-century English vagrancy laws substantially in toto, so that the laws in both countries are relatively similar.

Chambliss argued that the creation of vagrancy laws, and the subsequent changes in these statutes and their interpretation or implementation, represent one case consistent with the interest-group theory regarding the origin of criminal codes. The vagrancy statutes were contrived and later altered to protect the interests of such specific groups as landowners and merchants.

A second, influential study of the development of law was Jerome Hall's investigation of the growth of modern theft laws.[40] Hall traced the growth of property and theft statutes to the Carrier's Case of 1473. In that case, a defendant had been charged with a felony because he failed to carry out properly an assignment from a merchant. The carrier had been hired to carry certain bales to Southampton, England, but instead had absconded with them, broken them open, and taken the contents. In the ensuing deliberations, some of the judges argued that no felony had been committed and that the carrier could not steal what he already had in his possession. This line of argument was in accord with decisions previously rendered in the most common kinds of property crimes occurring up to this point, thefts of cattle, in which trespassing was an essential element. There the taking of property meant literally the physical removal of it. No such act had occurred in the Carrier's Case. Nonetheless, the defendant was ultimately found guilty on the grounds that he had broken open and taken the contents of the bales. Although he had possession of the bales, he did not have possession of their contents. Hall asserted that this case laid the foundation for an emerging distinction between *custody* of goods and *possession* of them, which was to become the basis for succeeding elaborations of theft law. In short, Hall's study showed that the judiciary revised existing legal rules to solve a social-control problem posed by the carrier and his actions.[41]

According to Hall, the following social conditions gave rise to the creation of new legislative interpretations beginning with the Carrier's Case:

> With the growth of manufacturing in the fifteenth century came marked changes in the manorial system and numerous departures from its mediaeval form. Came also the decay of serfdom and the rise of a new class of tenants whose rights were gradually recognized by the courts. But most important of all is the fact that during this period the older feudal relationships gave way before a rising middle class which owed its influence to the development of a rapidly expanding industry and trade. For example, in the middle of the fourteenth century there were only 169 important merchants, but at the beginning of the sixteenth century there were more than 3,000 merchants engaged in foreign trade alone. . . .
>
> The great forces of an emerging modern world, represented in the above phenomena, necessitated the elimination of a formula which had outgrown its usefulness. A new set of major institutions required a new rule. The law, lagging behind the needs of the times, was brought into more harmonious relationship with the other institutions by the decision rendered in the Carrier's Case.[42]

The remainder of Hall's analysis was concerned with subsequent elaborations of modern theft law up to the present. The major conclusion drawn from the Carrier's Case, which germinated this process, was that new laws governing property rights emerged correlative with the emergence of commerce and industrialization in the Western world. Thus, Hall and Chambliss both showed the linkages between certain laws, the Industrial Revolution, and the growth of the marketplace.

The vast changes in England that began in the 1300s and 1400s when that nation moved from agrarian feudalism to premodern capitalism continued into succeeding centuries. Those societal alterations led, in turn, to further elaborations and alterations in criminal law.

A group of English social historians has thrown light upon these interrelated changes in a series of studies of law and social order in eighteenth-century England.[43] They found that between 1688 and 1820 the number of capital offenses increased from about 50 to over 200 in that country. Almost all of these crimes concerned offenses against property.

These investigators parted company with historical accounts that picture eighteenth-century England as a tranquil, harmonious nation in which lawmaking reflected societal consensus and represented codification of informal mores. They argued instead that hangings, whippings, and other draconian punishments were the legal instruments of terror which enforced the emerging sharp definitions of property rights. The English ruling class—the monarchy, aristocracy, gentry, and the great merchants—through their control of the state, passed act after act to protect their property from theft or malicious damage. The proliferation of laws concerning private property and the severe punishments for their violation were part of a larger sweep of events in which England was emerging as a major trade, commercial, and industrial power. The newly enacted criminal laws were designed to enhance the wealth and powers of the propertied classes in that society.

Class conflict and class struggle between the propertied classes and the have-nots in eighteenth-century England turned up repeatedly in these studies. For example, Cal Winslow indicated that smuggling was widespread although forbidden by the new laws. Smuggling was often a means by which the rural poor were able to maintain themselves in an otherwise harsh and mean environment. More importantly, the common people viewed smuggling as a "right" in accordance with custom and tradition.[44] In much the same way, those who engaged in ship wrecking and plundering along the English coastline often regarded these activities as customary rights. Concerning wrecking and plundering, Rule reported: "Much evidence suggests that wreckers believed themselves to have a perfect right to the property which they appropriated."[45] Much the same was true of poaching and game-law violations.[46] The majority of persons in rural England in the eighteenth century apparently regarded these laws as unjust, for they saw themselves as having as much right to the game and the forests and fields as the landowners. Finally, the unlawful sending of anonymous, threatening letters appeared to be a form of social and individual protest by those who were the underclass victims of an emerging capitalist society.

E. P. Thompson's separate study of the infamous Black Act of 1723 provided parallel findings.[47] The Black Act was "an astonishing example of legislative-overkill," for it created over fifty capital offenses having to do with seemingly innocuous offenses such as killing or stealing deer, poaching of hares or fish, damaging fish ponds, maiming cattle, or cutting down trees.[48] Although it has often been assumed that this legislation was a response to an overwhelming emergency in the form of a rural crime wave, Thompson indicated that poaching and related offenses were equally common in earlier and later times. The emergency that led to the Black Act was instead "the repeated public humiliation of the authorities; the simultaneous attacks upon royal and private property; the sense of a confederated movement which was enlarging its social demands. . . . It was this displacement of authority, and not the ancient offense of deer-stealing, which constituted, in the eyes of the Government, an emergency."[49] Here, again, class conflict emerged as the underlying force producing legislation.

Those who practiced deer stalking and the like were engaged in class insub-
ordination and agrarian protest, resisting the enclosure of forest lands and other
actions by the new moneyed men that were eroding their customary rights to
the forests and farmlands.

Although terror was an instrument employed by the ruling class, it was used
sparingly. Many were arrested and convicted of capital offenses, but relatively
few persons were actually hanged. Compared to earlier periods, the eighteenth-
century criminal laws resulted in few executions, with many convicted offenders
receiving royal pardons or mitigated sentences such as transportation to Australia or other English colonies. A number of factors accounted for this state of
affairs, but a major one centered about the criminal law as an ideology or belief
system that legitimated class power. The criminal law was central to the maintenance of obedience, deference, and respect for the status quo in a society
which could not call upon religious or military authority or an organized police
force. In order to legitimate the system of class relations which the law was
designed to protect, terror had to be tempered with discretion and mercy so
that the mass of citizens would willingly embrace the rule of law.

Leon Radzinowicz's study of changes (1750–1833) in English law, police systems, and criminal policy was concerned with the shift in English criminal law
away from the situation when capital offenses were numerous and executions
commonplace (even for what would now be regarded as petty offenses) and toward a reduction in the number of capital crimes and lawful executions. According to Radzinowicz, many factors impeded the development of a more rational
and humane system of correctional control.

. . . among the effects of the Industrial Revolution was the emergence of great urban
agglomerations and industrial regions, the formation of a large and mobile class of wage
earners, the disintegration of some of the ancient orders of society, and the rapid accumulation of wealth by some sections of the community coinciding with the spread of
poverty and economic instability, the evils of which were accentuated by the lack of a
protective social policy. . . . England was in a state of transition and it is a truism that in
such periods of social tension the Legislature becomes overridingly preoccupied with the
strengthening of the State against the danger of an anticipated wave of lawlessness, inclined to lay stress on the deterrent function of criminal law and to oppose any attempt
to change the established system of criminal justice, particularly if it would entail relax-
ation of severity.[50]

Radzinowicz's analysis traced the emergence of a more equitable, humane,
and less punitive system of legislation and correctional machinery from the writings of Beccaria and Jeremy Bentham. From an earlier pattern of conflicting,
overlapping police systems in which officers were employed part-time, his study
showed the growth of modern metropolitan police systems during the latter part
of the eighteenth century.[51] To a marked degree, the legislative, penal, and law-
enforcement reforms that Radzinowicz studied laid the foundation for contemporary systems of criminal processing.

A more recent inquiry into the social factors implicated in criminal statutes is Edwin Sutherland's work concerning sexual psychopath laws.[52] The first of these originated in Illinois in 1938, followed in rapid succession by sexual psychopath laws in other states. In nearly every case, their enactment followed a few dramatic, well-publicized sexual attacks, so these laws represented a legislative reflex action. Sutherland pointed out that these laws are hopelessly ambiguous, usually defining a sexual psychopath as someone who has demonstrated an inability to control his sexual urges. These statutes are based on a number of faulty or erroneous assumptions, not the least of which is the belief that a clinical entity, the sexual psychopath, exists in identifiable form. This particular legislative action was an attempt to deal with a behavioral problem through legislation, in advance of the requisite knowledge of the basic dimensions of the problem. For all these reasons, sexual psychopath laws are essentially inoperable.

Joseph Gusfield's inquiry into the social background of the Volstead Act bore on the interest-group theory regarding origins of criminal laws.[53] That legislation, designed to enforce the Eighteenth Amendment of the United States Constitution, was passed in 1919 and repealed in 1933. The law banned the sale of beverages containing more than one-half of one percent alcohol. Organized crime and gangsterism arose to satisfy widespread public clamoring for alcoholic beverages; private citizens often made their own "bathtub gin"; and the Volstead Act was disobeyed on a grand scale.

What kind of explanation can account for legislation as unpopular as the Volstead Act? Gusfield maintained that this law was a symbolic reaffirmation of more basic interests of one segment of the population—native, white, rural, Protestant Americans—who perceived their values as under attack by foreign-born groups within the population. By getting this statute adopted, the group hoped to assert the dominance of their values over these "alien" ones. According to Gusfield:

Prohibition was an effort to establish the legal norm against drinking in the United States. It was an attempt to succeed in coercive reform. But in what sense can a legal norm, which is probably unenforceable, be the goal of a reform movement? If the drinking behavior which the movement sought to end occurred in communities in which the Temperance advocates were unlikely to live and the laws were not likely to be enforced, what was the rationale for the movement? We have shown that Prohibition had become a symbol of cultural domination or loss. If the Prohibitionists won, it was also a victory of the rural, Protestant American over the secular, urban, and non-Protestant immigrant. It was the triumph of respectability over its opposite. It quieted the fear that the abstainer's culture was not really the criterion by which respectability was judged in the dominant areas of the total society.[54]

Anthony Platt's analysis of the rise of the juvenile court in the United States turned up findings somewhat similar to Gusfield's.[55] Platt noted that the creation in 1899 of the juvenile court was the culmination of a long series of correctional developments aimed at the severe handling of youthful offenders. In addition, he observed that the motives of many of those who sponsored the juvenile-court movement were less positive and therapeutic than has sometimes been supposed, for many of the advocates of the court saw it as a device through which idle and deviant urban youths could be coerced into life styles of working-class conformity.

Still another piece of evidence regarding the backgrounds of particular laws comes from Howard Becker's study of the development of criminal norms to repress the use of marijuana.[56] Becker noted that the Marijuana Tax Act of 1937 had forerunners in earlier criminal statutes designed to suppress the pursuit of vices and ecstatic experiences, such as the Volstead Act (alcohol) and the Harrison Act (opium and derivatives). The Narcotics Bureau of the Treasury Department was unconcerned with marijuana in its earlier years, arguing instead that the regulation of opiates was the real problem. However, in the several years before 1937, the Narcotics Bureau came to redefine the matter of marijuana use as a serious problem. As a consequence, this agency acted in the role of moral entrepreneur, in which it attempted to create a new definition of marijuana use as a social danger. For example, the bureau provided information to mass-media systems on the dangers of marijuana, including "atrocity stories" which detailed the gruesome features of marijuana smoking. Finally, in 1937, the Marijuana Tax Act was passed, ostensibly as a taxation measure but with the real purpose of preventing persons from smoking marijuana. One revealing sidelight on this legislation is that this bill encountered strenuous objections from users of hempseed oil and the birdseed industry, which held that hemp seeds constituted a vital ingredient in various birdseed mixtures. These objections stalled the bill temporarily but were finally satisfied through changes in the act which exempted hemp seeds from control. This modification highlights interest-group involvement in the passage of criminal laws.

A final study showing the involvement of a number of interest groups in law enactment (and enforcement) is Pamela Roby's investigation of the 1965 revision of prostitution statutes within the New York State Penal Code.[57] The revised code reduced prostitution from a criminal offense to a "violation" subject only to a maximum 15-day jail sentence, and additionally declared that persons who patronize prostitutes are guilty of a violation. According to Roby, a number of different interest groups contended with each other during the period in which criminal-code revision was going on, with civil libertarian and welfare groups winning out over business and police organizations during the law-enactment stage. Subsequently, however, police and businessmen succeeded in getting enforcement policies adopted in which patrons of prostitutes were rarely arrested. Roby's study suggested that the scope of interest-group arguments needs to be expanded to reflect the fluctuating involvement and influence of varied interest groups in lawmaking activities.

There is no single or simple conclusion which can sum up all of these inquiries. Taken together, these findings indicate that to declare that all criminal laws arise directly from the ruling elite's control of the lawmaking processes and that those laws serve ruling-class interests alone will not provide the ultimate key to the sources of criminal law. There are myriad social interests behind criminal legislation. Some statutes are of benefit principally to socially powerful groups, but others protect much broader social interests. On this same point, the interested groups and parties that have agitated for the passage of particular criminal laws are numerous and varied, rather than congealing into a single ruling elite. Finally, we are still critically lacking in detailed studies of contemporary criminal lawmaking as it goes on in state legislatures. There is much that is yet to be learned about law creation in modern societies.

criminal law and social sentiments

A criminal statute may be born out of relatively widely shared social sentiments, or it may have only a narrow base of public support. Criminal laws that once received general approval may fall into disfavor as they become out of tune with social values. In the same way, court actions sometimes accord with citizen preferences and at other times do not. In this sense, criminal laws and correctional practices mirror social values, but sometimes in a distorted manner. In the extreme case, when laws or practices depart too far from public preferences, pressures for revisions or modifications in laws develop. We have not given much attention to social sentiments toward the law and its implementation, but some studies do illuminate these concerns.[58]

First, let us consider some evidence concerning social attitudes about deviant or criminal conduct across different nations. Robert Edgerton has gathered a mass of cross-cultural evidence which indicated that behaviors such as theft and refusal to share, suicide, violent acts, sexual misconduct, generational conflict, the use of psychoactive drugs, mental retardation, and mental illness are all encountered relatively often in societies throughout the world.[59] He also indicated that these forms of behavior tend to be looked upon with disfavor by most of the members of the societies in which they occur.

Somewhat related findings have been reported by Graeme Newman, resulting from a study conducted in 1973 in India, Indonesia, Italy, Yugoslavia, Iran, and the United States.[60] In Newman's research, citizens in those six countries were asked whether they thought that any of ten different kinds of behavior ought to be illegal. These activities included robbery, incest, failure to render aid to a person in danger, and abortion. Additionally, the respondents were quizzed about individual or factory pollution, homosexuality, nonviolent political protest, embezzlement of government funds, and drug use. In all six nations, over three-fourths of the respondents indicated that robbery, pollution, embezzlement, and drug use ought to be the law's business. The most tolerant attitudes toward incest, homosexuality, and failure to render aid were found among Americans.

Arnold Rose and Arthur Prell conducted a study of lay attitudes toward forms of lawbreaking and the punishments thought to be appropriate to them. Thirteen minor felonies in California state law, carrying nearly equal minimum and maximum penalties, were selected for analysis.[61] College students were asked to choose the most serious offenses among these crimes, which included childbeating, assault with a deadly weapon, and issuing fictitious checks. A pronounced rank order of judgments was found, in which childbeating and assault with a deadly weapon were held to be the most serious offenses, whereas unlawful manufacture, sale, or possession of weapons was judged to be least serious. These opinions about crimes seemed unrelated to the sentencing policies of the California courts, in that inmates in a California prison who had been convicted of childbeating received considerably shorter sentences than did those involved in crimes judged as less important.

In another study, San Francisco citizens indicated the degree of punishment they deemed appropriate for a wide range of crimes.[62] The criminal acts were described in detail, so as to elicit responses to run-of-the-mill or usual instances of these offenses. The respondents selected the disposition they thought most fitting from among choices ranging from no penalty to execution.

The severest penalties were selected for murder, robbery, rape, and certain other garden-variety crimes. Also, a good many persons offered some penalty other than the ones included in the questionnaire for certain offenses. Nearly all of those for rape, narcotics use, child molesting, and exhibitionism centered about psychiatric care for persons involved in that conduct. The penalty choices on the questionnaire were treated as a crude scale, with a score of 8 given to execution, a score of 1 to "other," a score of 0 to no penalty, and scores of from 7 to 2 for intervening choices. Mean scores on offenses for the total sample and for males and females in the samples are shown in Table 3.

The rank order of scores in Table 3 indicates that the harshest penalties were chosen for five offenses included within the FBI classification of index offenses (serious crimes); hence, criminal acts that are highly visible and often involve coercive attacks on property are the ones citizens would have punished heavily. These crimes often do result in long prison sentences for the perpetrators. However, the citizens also deemed quite serious several offenses that tend to receive relatively lenient penalties. Over half elected sentences of a year or more in prison for embezzlers and antitrust violators.[63]

Citizen judgments about various crimes were also the focus of a study conducted in Baltimore in 1972, in which laymen were asked to rank 140 different offenses in terms of seriousness.[64] In general, a high degree of consensus existed among these citizens, with crimes against persons being given the highest seriousness rating, followed by property offenses, and misdemeanors being regarded as least serious. Moreover, various sample subgroups defined by race, educational attainment, and sex did not differ much in their responses to the various offenses. These several studies of citizen perceptions of crime seriousness all convey much the same message, namely, that there is a large measure of agreement within the general population concerning the relative seriousness of different offenses.

There are some additional studies of this kind. Elizabeth Rooney and Don

Gibbons questioned a group of San Francisco residents about the policies they felt should be pursued in cases of abortion, homosexuality, and drug addiction.[65] The respondents agreed generally that the laws regarding abortion should be liberalized. For example, 79 percent held that women should be allowed to obtain therapeutic (legal) abortions if they have contracted German measles early in their pregnancy, whereas 83.6 percent agreed that a pregnancy resulting from rape or incest should be allowable grounds for an abortion. At the time of the study, in California and in over half of the other states, the only condition under which an abortion could legally be carried out was if the pregnancy imperiled the life of the woman. Obviously, those abortion laws had not kept pace with changing social values. Legislators came under increased pressure to liberalize abortion statutes as this gap between what the law permits and what people are willing to tolerate grew. Indeed, California statutes were modified early in 1967, while in 1973, a Supreme Court ruling struck down criminal statutes prohibiting abortions.

The citizens in this research investigation were much less sympathetic to proposed reforms in the laws that would ignore voluntary acts of homosexuality. Instead, they generally opted for policies that treat consenting homosexual conduct as criminal. Finally, most respondents were antagonistic to any changes in statutes that would result in drug users being dealt with outside the framework of the criminal law.

Some reports are also available concerning public opinion of the juvenile justice system. In one of these, William Lentz surveyed a sample of Wisconsin adults concerning attitudes toward juvenile control.[66] Most citizens favored swift

table 3   mean penalty scores, total sample and by sex

offense	total sample	males	females
Murder, second degree	6.6	6.6	6.5
Robbery	6.3	6.3	6.5
Manslaughter	6.3	6.2	6.7
Burglary	6.2	6.2	6.2
Rape	6.0	6.0	5.8
Embezzlement	5.3	5.3	5.6
Antitrust	4.6	4.6	4.5
Auto theft	4.2	4.2	4.4
Child molesting	4.3	4.1	4.5
Check forgery	3.7	3.6	4.1
Narcotics	3.9	3.8	3.9
Assault	3.4	3.4	3.5
Misrepresentation in advertising	3.2	3.4	2.8
Draft evasion	3.0	3.2	2.6
Marijuana	2.8	2.8	2.8
Exhibitionism	2.9	2.9	3.0
Drunk driving	2.9	2.9	2.9
Tax evasion	1.9	2.0	1.7
Statutory rape	2.1	2.2	1.9
Homosexuality	1.9	1.9	1.9

and impartial justice toward juveniles; many felt that punishment should fit the crime; over half advocated publishing the names of juvenile offenders; most favored probation in place of institutional commitment; and many asserted that juvenile offenders are "ill" and in need of expert treatment.

A second study, by Howard Parker, dealt with citizen views of the juvenile court in four Washington state communities.[67] Many of the respondents claimed that the juvenile court was not tough enough in its dealings with offenders. But, when these same persons were asked to indicate what they would have done in the way of punishment to actual offenders, their penalty choices were similar or less severe than the ones actually handed out by juvenile courts.

criminology, crime, and criminals

LEGAL VERSUS "SOCIOLOGICAL" CRIME

Legally, crime consists of violation of certain conduct norms possessing a specified character. Similarly, a criminal, from a legalistic viewpoint, is an individual who has behaved in ways that diverge from the prohibitions or injunctions in the criminal law.

Obviously, criminal law in any country has changed over time so that it does not represent a body of stable behavioral norms. Similarly, in a single nation such as the United States, variations exist from one jurisdiction to another in both the content and the language of criminal codes. In short, what is crime in one area may not have been crime at an earlier time or in another place. Because criminal codes are far from entirely capricious in character, much of the criminal law of Western societies is concerned with the regulation or repression of many common forms of behavior. Still, the lack of consistency in statutes has led some students of crime to suggest that criminology should abandon legalistic definitions of its field of inquiry in favor of some other universal and unchanging units of study.

Jeffery summarized a number of these sociological approaches to crime, which avoid legalistic definitions of the phenomena of study in favor of conduct norms and the violation of them.[68] Similarly, Herbert Bloch and Gilbert Geis commented on approaches to criminology that would substitute the study of such phenomena as moral aberrance, parasitism, or deviancy for the investigation of legally defined crime.[69] The rationale for these proposals is that criminology should be concerned with antisocial conduct, whether or not it happens to be included within the criminal law. According to this view, criminology would be directed at a uniform body of subject matter rather than at a mixture of behavior haphazardly singled out by criminal laws, which at the same time ignore other forms of sociological crime. Bloch and Geis quite properly criticized these concepts of moral aberrance, parasitism, or deviancy as little more than figures of speech devoid of specific meaning. To substitute these concepts for a legalistic definition of crime would mean that criminology would be mired in even more terminological and definitional confusion than would result from use of a legalistic criterion.

Thorsten Sellin's work concerning conduct norms was a well-known attempt to devise a substitute for a legalistic definition of crime.[70] Sellin suggested that criminology should study the violation of such norms and declared: "These facts lead to the inescapable conclusion that the study of conduct norms would afford a sounder basis for the development of scientific categories than a study of crime as defined in the criminal law. Such study would involve the isolation and classification of norms into universal categories, transcending political and other boundaries, a necessity imposed by the logic of science."[71]

At first glance, these recommendations appear to solve the difficulties imposed by legal definitions of crime. However, the study of conduct norms is still only in its infancy; we are a distance away from any sort of inventory of conduct norms, even within the United States. The development of cross-cultural listings of conduct standards is an even more distant goal, however laudable it might be as an end to pursue. Moreover, even if such inventories of conduct definitions were available, they would not accomplish the results Sellin foresaw. In their critique of Sellin, Sutherland and Cressey identified the shortcomings of social norms as the unit of study. They argued: "In this respect crime is like all other social phenomena, and the possibility of a science of criminal behavior is similar to the possibility of a science of any other behavior. Social science has no stable unit, for all social sciences are dealing with phenomena which involve group evaluations."[72] Conduct norms are no more stable, universal, or unchanging than legal norms, and they are a good deal more ephemeral in character. Conduct norms vary over time and from place to place, so that we gain little (and perhaps lose much) by employing them rather than legal norms in the definitions of the boundaries of inquiry.

A final remark on the variability of criminal codes, and hence of crime, is that this variability presents the investigator with a problem for investigation rather than with an obstacle to be avoided by redefinition of the field. Criminal laws do vary through time and from place to place, but the study of social origins and influences in criminal law should be a major subject of sociological attention. As part of this inquiry, the sociologist of law should attempt to pinpoint the factors responsible for particular statutory variations in criminal law.

WHO IS THE CRIMINAL?

Efforts to articulate a sociologically meaningful conception of the criminal have accompanied the search for extralegal definitions of crime. Indeed, the conduct norm position on crime contains obvious parallel views on criminals so that the latter group is comprised of all violators of social norms. However, the controversy over the proper meaning of criminal has been more complex than simply a quarrel as to whether norm violators are to be considered criminals.

From a legalistic standpoint a criminal is some individual who has violated a criminal law. But some people find this definition objectionable. Ernest Burgess advanced one of these counterpositions. He declared: "A criminal is a person who regards himself as a criminal and is so regarded by society. He is the product of the criminal-making process."[73] Burgess made these remarks in conjunction with a discussion of Frank Hartung's study of violations of rationing regulations in Detroit during World War II. Burgess claimed that such activities were not "sociologically" classifiable as criminal, even though they violated criminal laws.

Burgess's claims were not well thought-out. If we followed his recommendations, many prison inmates would be excluded from study on the grounds that they do not define themselves as criminals! Additionally, the notion of condemnation of crime by society implies that we can discern uniform societal reactions. Criminals are the product of the criminal-making process, so that we should identify as criminals only those persons who have violated criminal laws. But the varied self-definitions of offenders and the divergent societal reactions to criminal acts represent phenomena to be studied rather than criteria for assigning boundaries to the field of study. Criminologists should be attentive to variations in self-image on the part of different law violators. Similarly, variations in societal reactions to different kinds of criminality form an important topic for investigation. But to identify these as critical items for inquiry is different from including them as definitional criteria, as did Burgess.

The position of this book on the question of who is or is not a criminal is close to that of Paul Tappan. In one essay on the question "Who is the Criminal?" he offered some trenchant criticism of views that equate the study of criminals with the study of violators of conduct norms.[74] He also attacked the use of the label "white-collar crime" to cover myriad instances of antisocial or sharp business practices and other occupational behavior not specifically included within some body of criminal statutes. In another place, Tappan offered a definition of crime (and, implicitly, of criminals) with which we agree: "What then is the legal definition of crime as it has been employed in practice not only in our courts of law, but in criminology as well? *Crime is an intentional act or omission in violation of criminal law (statutory and case law), committed without defense or justification, and sanctioned by the state as a felony or misdemeanor*" (emphasis in the original).[75] Tappan did not demand that the terms *crime* and *criminal* be restricted to acts that have resulted in court conviction or to persons adjudged as criminals by a court. In an earlier essay, he did argue that the legal tag of criminal be restricted to persons so adjudicated, apparently to emphasize that the legal status of criminal is different from that of noncriminal, in that the former carries a number of penalties with it, such as loss of civil rights and restrictions upon movement, which are not imposed on non-adjudicated offenders.[76] Acquisition of the legal status of criminal also results in social stigma in addition to the penalties and deprivations authorized in the criminal law. Thus, to be a criminal is to acquire a negative public identity of more than slight importance.[77]

The demand that we keep clearly in mind the special legal status occupied by individuals who have been adjudged to be criminals has much merit. We should not use the term *criminal* indiscriminately, without distinguishing between those who occupy the legal status as a result of being processed through a court and those who have escaped detection or prosecution. At the same time, we should reject the demand, sometimes insistently put forward, that criminologists study only persons legally identified as criminals. Criminology should be concerned with the study of criminalistic *behavior*. Differentials in the correctional process do exist: some offenders do not become reported whereas others are reported to the police; some reported offenders are apprehended and others are not; some are prosecuted whereas others are not; or some receive penalties not handed out to others. Such differentials depend on a number of variables, including differences in the kinds of criminal behavior that occur, differences in police policies from one area to another, and variations in social background among offenders. The criminologist must take, as his or her primary data, lawbreaking behavior, or, in Sutherland's words, "behavior which would raise a reasonable expectancy of conviction if tried in a criminal court or substitute agency."[78] Differential experiences of criminal deviants are important topics for the criminologist's concern, but he or she should not restrict attention to adjudged offenders.

If we adopt a legalistic conception of crime, we must attend to all instances of behavior fitting that definition. Hence, we need to examine a number of forms of lawbreaking now given scant attention. As H. Laurence Ross noted, modern societies have given rise to a large number of folk crimes and other mundane offenses that merit sociological attention.[79] These offenses make up a large proportion of modern-day criminality, so they cannot be ignored or dismissed as not really crime.

summary

This chapter began with a discussion of criminal law as one form of social control. Although laymen sometimes profess the belief that deviant impulses are held in check principally by criminal statutes and legal prohibitions, the truth of the matter is that conformity is brought about largely through informal social and personal controls. The criminal laws represent emergency measures to be activated when other controls break down.

This chapter also took note of the formal properties of criminal codes identified in legal theory: politicality, specificity, uniformity, and penal sanction. These are the identifying marks of criminal statutes which, taken together, distinguish criminal laws from other rules and behavior standards. Our discussion also examined the differentiae of crime, that is, those elements that must be observed for some line of behavior to constitute a form of criminal action. Crime involves a "harm" or social injury which is legally forbidden and which carries a legally prescribed punishment. Further, in order for a person to be convicted of a crime, it must be demonstrated that conduct occurred, accompanied by intent or *mens rea*.

Criminal laws are not immutable. The broad trend in modern Western societies has been in the direction of expansion of the criminal law to encompass an ever-widening array of behavior. Also, lawmaking processes are revealed in criminal-law-revision endeavors in the United States and in the efforts to decriminalize some currently prohibited forms of conduct.

A diverse collection of theories regarding the social origins of criminal laws has been advanced, with some contending that the statutes grow out of the mores and others arguing that they are the product of social conflict and the clash of competing interest groups. However, conflict theories come closest to accounting for the development of most criminal laws. That conclusion was drawn, in part, from a number of specific inquiries that have been conducted regarding particular statutes.

This chapter also discussed current knowledge regarding citizen perspectives on the criminal law. Some studies have probed the attitudes and beliefs of laymen regarding crime, criminal laws, and punishment, with most of them showing that citizens have only some hazy understanding of crime and responses to it. At the same time, there are a number of questions about citizen views on the law which ought to be the focus of future criminological research.

This chapter concluded with the contention that the criminal codes define the parameters of criminological inquiry. Criminal laws specify the boundaries of the category of offenders. This group includes those who breach the law; they are the primary concern of criminology. However, one segment of this group is made up of criminals—in other words, offenders who have been apprehended and processed through the legal machinery.

notes

[1]*Encyclopaedia Britannica*, vol. 6 (Chicago Encyclopaedia Britannica, Inc., 1965), p. 762. Edwin M. Schur, among others, has pointed out that, until recently, the sociological study of law and legal institutions has been a neglected area of inquiry in sociology. See Edwin M. Schur, *Law and Society* (New York: Random House, 1968), pp. 5–16. Schur's book is a useful, brief introduction to the sociological study of law. For other indications of the central concerns in the study of law and legal institutions, particularly criminal law and its implementation, as well as samples of sociological inquiry regarding legal processes, see Ronald L. Akers and Richard Hawkins, eds., *Law and Control in Society* (Englewood Cliffs, N.J.: Prentice-Hall, Inc., 1975); Richard D. Schwartz and Jerome H. Skolnick, eds., *Society and Legal Order* (New York: Basic Books, 1970); William J. Chambliss, ed., *Criminal Law in Action* (Santa Barbara: Hamilton Publishing Co., 1975).

[2]*Encyclopaedia Britannica*, p. 762.

[3]Karl N. Llewellyn and E. Adamson Hoebel, *The Cheyenne Way* (Norman, Okla.: University of Oklahoma Press, 1941).

[4]For a relatively brief but comprehensive discussion of modern criminal law and its emergence in the twelfth century, see Clayton A. Hartjen, *Crime and Criminalization*, 2nd ed. (New York: Holt, Rinehart & Winston, 1978), pp. 19–41.

[5]The emergence of English common law is discussed in detail in F. T. Plucknett, *A Concise History of the Common Law* (London: Butterworth, 1948).

[6]C. Ray Jeffery, "The Development of Crime in Early English Society," *Journal of Criminal Law, Criminology and Police Science*, 47 (March–April 1957), 647–66.

[7]Ibid., p. 666.

[8]Edwin H. Sutherland and Donald R. Cressey, *Criminology*, 10th ed. (Philadelphia: Lippincott, 1978), pp. 5–8.

[9]Jerome Hall, *General Principles of Criminal Law* (Indianapolis: Bobbs-Merrill, 1947), p. 42.

[10]Sutherland and Cressey, *Criminology*, pp. 12–17; Hall, *General Principles of Criminal Law*, pp. 19–20.

[11]Herbert L. Packer, *The Limits of the Criminal Sanction* (Stanford, Calif.: Stanford University Press, 1968), p. 297; also see Gilbert Geis, *Not the Law's Business?* (Rockville, Md.: National Institute of Mental Health, 1972).

[12]Edwin M. Schur, *Crimes Without Victims* (Englewood Cliffs, N.J.: Prentice-Hall, Inc., 1965); also see Schur and Hugo Adam Bedau, *Victimless Crimes* (Englewood Cliffs, N.J.: Prentice-Hall, Inc., 1974). Although the concept of crimes without victims has become a popular one, it would be well to keep in mind that some so-called victimless offenses are ones about which a good deal of public controversy can be observed. In particular, there are a good many persons who view abortion as immoral under nearly all circumstances. Similarly, many citizens would prefer to have homosexual acts forbidden by criminal laws.

[13]For a study of public attitudes toward laws relating to victimless crimes, see Elizabeth A. Rooney and Don C. Gibbons, "Social Reactions to 'Crimes Without Victims,' " *Social Problems*, 13 (Spring 1966), 400–410.

[14]The American Law Institute, *Model Penal Code* (Philadelphia: The American Law Institute, 1962).

[15]Ibid., pp. 123–241.

[16]Departmental Committee on Homosexual Offenses and Prostitution, *Report* (London: Her Majesty's Stationery Office, 1957).

[17]An excellent summary of this story can be found in Paul W. Tappan, *Crime, Justice and Correction* (New York: McGraw-Hill, 1960), pp. 401–11.

[18]Ibid., p. 403.

[19]Ibid., pp. 403–4.

[20]The American Law Institute, *Model Penal Code*, p. 66.

[21]Ibid., pp. 91–100.

[22]Criminal Law Revision Commission, *Oregon Revised Statutes* (Salem, Ore.: Criminal Law Revision Commission, 1971).

[23]Status-offender clauses and the criticisms of them are discussed in Don C. Gibbons, *Delinquent Behavior*, 3rd ed. (Englewood Cliffs, N.J.: Prentice-Hall, Inc., 1981), pp. 19–23.

[24]Clarence R. Jeffery, "The Structure of American Criminological Thinking," *Journal of Criminal Law, Criminology and Police Science*, 46 (January–February 1956), 658–72.

[25]William J. Chambliss, "The State, the Law, and the Definition of Behavior as Criminal or Delinquent," in *Handbook of Criminology*, Daniel Glaser, ed. (Chicago: Rand McNally, 1974), p. 39.

[26]Joseph W. Eaton, "Controlled Acculturation: A Survival Technique of the Hutterites," *American Sociological Review*, 17 (June 1952), 331–40.

[27]William J. Chambliss and Robert B. Seidman, *Law, Order, and Power* (Reading, Mass.: Addison-Wesley Publishing Co., 1971), pp. 56–74. Conflict and interest-group theories in criminology are discussed in detail in Don C. Gibbons, *The Criminological Enterprise* (Englewood Cliffs, N.J.: Prentice-Hall, Inc., 1979), pp. 156–62.

[28]Chambliss and Seidman, *Law, Order, and Power*, p. 73.

[29]Ibid., p. 67.

[30]A third view of lawmaking holds that enactment of law is a somewhat irrational, emotional response to social problems. This hypothesis is encountered in the frequent claim of foreign visitors to the United States that citizens of this nation place undue and somewhat unthinking faith in the power of legislation to eradicate social problems. Thus, Americans are sometimes said to pass laws first and only later to make effective efforts to understand and solve problems against which they have already legislated.

[31]Beginning attempts at theorizing are found in Chambliss and Seidman, *Law, Order, and Power*. Also see Stuart L. Hills, *Crime, Power, and Morality* (Scranton, Pa.: Chandler Publishing Co., 1971).

[32]Radical-Marxist criminology is discussed in detail in Gibbons, *The Criminological Enterprise*, pp. 165–93. For a detailed critique of radical criminology, see Richard F. Sparks, "A Critique of Marxist Criminology," in *Crime and Justice: An Annual Review*, Norval Morris and Michael Tonry, eds. (Chicago: University of Chicago Press, 1980), pp. 159–210; David Shichor, "The New Criminology: Some Critical Issues," *British Journal of Criminology*, 20 (January 1980), 1–19.

[33]Richard Quinney, *Critique of Legal Order* (Boston: Little, Brown, 1974), p. 16.

[34]William J. Chambliss, "Toward a Political Economy of Crime," *Theory and Society*, 2 (Summer 1975), 152.

[35]For example, see David F. Greenberg, "On One-Dimensional Criminology," *Theory and Society*, 3 (1976), 610–21; Gibbons, *The Criminological Enterprise*, pp. 188–93; Paul Rock, "The Sociology of Deviance and Conceptions of Moral Order," *British Journal of Criminology*, 14 (April 1974),139–49.

[36]Peter K. Manning, "Deviance and Dogma," *British Journal of Criminology*, 15 (January 1975), 14.

[37]William E. Nelson, *Americanization of the Common Law: The Impact of Legal Change on Massachusetts Society, 1760–1830* (Cambridge: Harvard University Press, 1975).

[38]William J. Chambliss, "A Sociological Analysis of the Law of Vagrancy," *Social Problems*, 12 (Summer 1964), 67–77.

[39]Ibid., p. 69.

[40]Jerome Hall, *Theft, Law and Society*, 2nd ed. (Indianapolis: Bobbs-Merrill, 1952).

[41]Ibid., pp. 4–33.

[42]Reprinted from *Theft, Law and Society* by Jerome Hall, Copyright 1935, 1952, by the Bobbs-Merrill Co., Inc. Reprinted by permission. All rights reserved.

[43]Douglas Hay, Peter Linebaugh, John G. Rule, E. P. Thompson, and Cal Winslow, *Albion's Fatal Tree: Crime and Society in Eighteenth-Century England* (New York: Pantheon Books, 1975); see particularly Douglas Hay, "Property, Authority, and the Criminal Law," pp. 17–63; E. P. Thompson, *Whigs and Hunters: The Origins of the Black Act* (New York: Pantheon Books, 1975).

[44]Cal Winslow, "Sussex Smugglers," in Hay, et al., *Albion's Fatal Tree*, pp. 119–66.

[45]John G. Rule, "Wrecking and Coastal Plunder," in Hay, et al., *Albion's Fatal Tree*, p. 176. Modern examples of local customs favoring the plundering of wrecked boats and ships can be found in coastal communities along the West Coast of the United States, indicating that this is not an archaic illustration of the clash of laws and customs.

[46]Douglas Hay, "Poaching and the Game Laws on Cannock Chase," in Hay, et al., *Albion's Fatal Tree*, pp. 189–254.

[47]Thompson, *Whigs and Hunters*. The Black Act was so named after the practice of poachers of "blacking" their faces and employing disguises in order to stalk deer.

[48]Ibid., p. 196.

[49]Ibid., pp. 190–91.

[50]Leon Radzinowicz, *A History of English Criminal Law and Its Administration from 1750*, 3 vols. (New York: Macmillan, 1948–1957), pp. 351–52.

[51]Ibid., vol. 3, "Cross-Currents in the Movement for Reform of the Police."

[52]Edwin H. Sutherland, "The Sexual Psychopath Laws," *Journal of Criminal Law and Criminology*, 40 (January–February 1950), 543–54; Sutherland, "The Diffusion of Sexual Psychopath Laws," *American Journal of Sociology*, 56 (September 1950), 142–48.

[53]Joseph R. Gusfield, *Symbolic Crusade* (Urbana, Ill.: University of Illinois Press, 1963).

[54]Ibid., p. 110.

[55]Anthony M. Platt, *The Child Savers* (Chicago: University of Chicago Press, 1969). A revised, Marxist interpretation of the rise of the juvenile court has been presented in Platt, "The Triumph of Benevolence: The Origins of the Juvenile Justice System in the United States," in *Criminal Justice in America*, Richard Quinney, ed. (Boston: Little, Brown, 1974), pp. 356–89. For a critique of this argument, based on a research study of Canadian juvenile courts, see John Hagan and Jeffrey Leon, "Rediscovering Delinquency: Social History, Political Ideology, and the Sociology of Law," *American Sociological Review*, 42 (August 1977), 587–98. Other discussions of the origins of the juvenile court include J. Lawrence Schultz, "The Cycle of Juvenile Court History," *Crime and Delinquency*, 19 (October 1973), 457–76; Robert M. Mennel, *Thorns and Thistles: Juvenile Delinquency in the United States, 1825–1940* (Hanover, N.H.: University Press of New England, 1973); Steven L. Schlossman, *Love and the American Delinquent* (Chicago: University of Chicago Press, 1977).

[56]Howard S. Becker, *Outsiders* (New York: Free Press, 1963), pp. 121–46; see also Troy Duster, *The Legislation of Morality* (New York: Free Press, 1970). Duster pointed out in some detail how moral outrage directed at drug addicts resulted *from* legislation, rather than providing the original impetus for lawmaking.

[57]Pamela A. Roby, "Politics and Criminal Law: Revision of the New York State Penal Law on Prostitution," *Social Problems*, 17 (Summer 1969), 83–109.

[58]These studies, including those summarized here, are enumerated and discussed in Don C. Gibbons and Joseph F. Jones, *The Study of Deviance* (Englewood Cliffs, N.J.: Prentice-Hall, Inc., 1975), pp. 68–81. For a compendium of opinion-survey results on public attitudes toward crimes and criminal-justice related topics, see Timothy J. Flanagan, Michael J. Hindelang, and Michael R. Gottfredson, eds., *Sourcebook of Criminal Justice Statistics, 1979* (Washington, D.C.: Law Enforcement Assistance Administration, 1980), pp. 247–326.

[59]Robert B. Edgerton, *Deviance: A Cross-Cultural Perspective* (Menlo Park, Cal.: Cummings Publishing Co., 1976).

[60]Graeme Newman, *Comparative Deviance: Perception and Law in Six Cultures* (New York: Elsevier North-Holland, 1976).

[61]Arnold M. Rose and Arthur E. Prell, "Does the Punishment Fit the Crime? A Study in Social Valuation," *American Journal of Sociology*, 61 (November 1955), 247–59. In a somewhat related study, carried on in the San Francisco area, a number of citizens were asked to complete a questionnaire inquiring about the knowledge they had about criminality, corrections, and kindred matters. The principle of "out of sight, out of mind" described the responses, for most of the persons knew about a few flamboyant or bizarre cases of criminality, but few had any detailed knowledge of the workings of the law-enforcement, judicial, or correctional systems. See Don C. Gibbons, "Who Knows What About Correction?" *Crime and Delinquency*, 9 (April 1963), 137–44. Some recent evidence on public awareness of crimes and penalties that are associated with particular offenses can be found in Jack P. Gibbs and Maynard Erickson, "Conceptions of Criminal and Delinquent Acts," *Deviant Behavior*, 1 (October 1979), 71–100; Kirk R. Williams, Gibbs, and Erickson, "Public Knowledge of Statutory Penalties: The Extent and Basis of Accurate Perception," *Pacific Sociological Review*, 23 (January 1980), 105–28.

[62]Don C. Gibbons, "Crime and Punishment: A Study in Social Attitudes," *Social Forces*, 45 (June 1969), 391–97.

[63]The level of public support is unclear for a good many cases of criminal law and practice. White-collar crime is a case in point, for the character of citizen sentiments regarding business crimes is open to conjecture and speculation. Some light was shed on this question through Donald Newman's investigation concerning violations of the Federal Food, Drug and Cosmetic Act, revised 1938. He asked about 175 adults to indicate the degree of punishment they thought appropriate for cases of product misbranding and food adulteration selected from the files of a federal district attorney. He then compared these choices with the sentences actually imposed. About 78 percent of the citizens felt that the penalties should be more severe than the actual court decisions. However, nearly all respondents selected punishments within the maximum allowable by law. Thus, public disapproval was centered on the administration of food and drug laws rather than upon the laws themselves. Finally, the penalties the citizens chose were not as severe as those imposed on such run-of-the-mill offenders as thieves and burglars. See Donald J. Newman, "Public Attitudes Toward a Form of

White Collar Crime," *Social Problems*, 4 (January 1957), 228–32.

[64]Peter H. Rossi, Emily Waite, Christine E. Bose, and Richard E. Berk, "The Seriousness of Crimes: Normative Structure and Individual Differences," *American Sociological Review*, 39 (April 1974), 224–37.

[65]Rooney and Gibbons, "Social Reactions to 'Crimes Without Victims.' "

[66]William P. Lentz, "Social Status and Attitudes Toward Delinquency Control," *Journal of Research in Crime and Delinquency*, 3 (July 1966), 147–54.

[67]Howard Parker, "Juvenile Court Actions and Public Response," in *Becoming Delinquent*, Peter G. Garabedian and Don C. Gibbons, eds. (Chicago: Aldine, 1970), pp. 252–65.

[68]Jeffery, "The Structure of American Criminological Thinking," pp. 660–63.

[69]Herbert A. Bloch and Gilbert Geis, *Man, Crime, and Society*, 2nd ed. (New York: Random House, 1970), pp. 18–21. More recent proposals along this line have been made by Herman and Julia Schwendinger, "Defenders of Order or Guardians of Human Rights?" *Issues in Criminology*, 5 (Summer 1970), 123–37. They would have criminologists center their attention upon violations of human rights rather than upon more narrowly defined violations of existing criminal statutes. The basic problem with the Schwendinger recommendation is that there is precious little agreement on what constitutes basic human rights.

[70]Thorsten Sellin, *Culture Conflict and Crime* (New York: Social Science Research Council, 1938).

[71]Ibid., p. 30.

[72]Sutherland and Cressey, *Criminology*, p. 23.

[73]Ernest W. Burgess, "Comment" on Frank E. Hartung, "White-Collar Offenses in the Wholesale Meat Industry in Detroit," *American Journal of Sociology*, 56 (July 1950), 32–33; see also Hartung, "White-Collar Offenses," *American Journal of Sociology*, 56 (July 1950), 25–32; "Rejoinder," *American Journal of Sociology*, 56 (July 1950), 33–34; Burgess, "Concluding Comment," *American Journal of Sociology*, 56 (July 1950), 34.

[74]Paul W. Tappan, "Who is the Criminal?" *American Sociological Review*, 12 (February 1947), 96–103.

[75]Paul W. Tappan, *Crime, Justice and Correction* (New York: McGraw-Hill, 1960), p. 10.

[76]Tappan, "Who is the Criminal?" pp. 100–103.

[77]One revealing study of the stigmatizing consequences of being convicted of a criminal offense (and even of being acquitted of a crime!) can be found in Richard D. Schwartz and Jerome H. Skolnick, "Two Studies of Legal Stigma," in *The Other Side*, Howard S. Becker, ed. (New York: Free Press, 1964), pp. 103–17.

[78]Edwin H. Sutherland, "White-Collar Criminality," *American Sociological Review*, 5 (February 1940), 6.

[79]H. Laurence Ross, "Traffic Law Violation: A Folk Crime," *Social Problems*, 8 (Winter 1960–1961), 231–41; see also Clayton A. Hartjen and Don C. Gibbons, "An Empirical Investigation of a Criminal Typology," *Sociology and Social Research*, 54 (October 1969), 56–63; Gibbons, "Crime in the Hinterland," *Criminology*, 10 (August 1972), 177–91.

extent
and
distribution
of crime

FIVE

The first order of business in the study and understanding of criminality is the fact-gathering task. We want to identify the number of offenders in society, the various forms their offenses take, their social characteristics, and other features of lawbreaking and lawbreakers. Or, if we cannot count all the crimes that occur and the criminals who carry them out, we want to develop some relatively accurate estimates of offenses and offenders.

However, gathering facts on lawbreaking is inevitably frustrating and unsatisfactory. For one thing, the agencies that process known violators have often been more interested in distorting their statistics than in reporting them accurately. The most basic problem, however, confronting persons who amass statistical facts on criminality is that most lawbreakers take pains to keep their violations secret. Estimates of the extent of illegal behavior must be made from data on those offenses known to the authorities. This is a small and biased sample of total crime, and gauging the relationship between the two is exceedingly difficult.

Criminologists often speak of "the dark figure of crime," referring to undetected and unreported offenses and offenders. Although there are ways through which we can guess at this figure's dimensions, short of getting all citizens to truthfully report on the crimes they have committed we can never be overly comfortable with conjectures about the total amount of crime in the United States. Obviously, surveys among the general public asking people to confess to crimes are never likely to be markedly successful. Persons who have escaped detection for serious crimes are not likely to blurt out confessions to criminological researchers!

sources and problems of criminological data

SOURCES OF INFORMATION

Criminological investigators have sometimes endeavored to discover the extent of American criminality through citizen self-reports. In these studies, which we will return to later in this chapter, the researchers have asked citizens to acknowledge the illegal acts that they have performed. These studies have been employed frequently with samples of juveniles. However, the more common index used to estimate the magnitude of crime in society has been constructed from statistics concerning crimes reported to the police, persons arrested, and other reports of this sort.

Official figures and reports are of several kinds. Beginning in 1940, the Children's Bureau of the U.S. Department of Health and Human Services began publishing estimates of the number of delinquency cases in juvenile courts each year. More recently, juvenile-court-data collection has been the responsibility of the National Institute of Juvenile Justice and Delinquency Prevention of the Law Enforcement Assistance Administration. The Law Enforcement Assistance Administration also compiles figures regarding the number of individuals incarcerated in prisons each year. These data are reported in *National Prisoner Statistics*. Additionally, the National Office of Vital Statistics collects information on homicides through the records of coroners in the United States, reporting this information in *Vital Statistics in the United States*. A number of state agencies also gather and publish data on criminality, as do local police departments and correctional agencies.

The Federal Bureau of Investigation gathers the most widely used data on American criminality, which are reported annually in *Crime in the United States*. Statistics include crimes known to the police for eight major offenses, which comprise the bureau's Crime Index.[1] Reports from police agencies in the United States are collated to provide Crime Index information about nearly 98 percent of the total population. In addition to figures on index crimes known to the police, the FBI also gathers and publishes information regarding arrests for nonindex crime.[2]

PROBLEMS OF OFFICIAL DATA

Crime statistics are among the most unreliable and questionable social facts, as a number of authorities have pointed out. For one thing, crimes known to the police constitute only a fraction of all offenses. Moreover, the ratio of known illegal acts to committed criminal acts varies from offense to offense. Variations in legal codes from one jurisdiction to another reduce the possibility of meaningful statistical comparisons between areas and communities. Sutherland and Cressey noted that police agencies have not always reported statistics honestly. They cited the case of New York City, where in 1966 the Police Commissioner found that less than a fourth of the auto theft and rape cases known to the department were properly recorded, as compared with 54 percent of the known larcenies and 96 percent of the burglaries reported to the department.[3]

The report of the President's Commission on Law Enforcement and Administration of Justice provided some additional evidence on police tampering with statistics. The report discussed an instance in Philadelphia in 1953, in which the police reported 28,560 index crimes, negligent manslaughter offenses, and cases of larceny under 50 dollars. This figure represented an increase of 70 percent over that for 1951, but the sudden jump was a result of modifications in reporting procedures rather than an increase in crime. An even more dramatic case of reporting problems came from Chicago, which from 1935 to 1950 reported many more burglaries and robberies than did New York City, even though it had only about one-half the population of New York City.[4]

The President's Commission report discussed in some detail the factors implicated in variations in crime-reporting practices. The commission suggested that relatively more offenses are now being subjected to official attention, so they turn up in official statistics more often than was formerly the case.[5] The changing expectations of slum-area citizens may have made them less tolerant of lawbreaking and more likely to complain to the police. In turn, the professionalization of police agencies may make them more likely to take official actions against offenders rather than to handle violators informally.[6] Citizens may be quicker to inform the police of thefts than they once were, because of the belief that theft-insurance policies require that offenses be reported to law-enforcement authorities. On the other hand, the commission argued that police manipulation of crime statistics continues to create problems in the interpretation of official data. According to the commission report:

The reporting problem arises at least in part from the tendency of some cities, noted in 1931 by the Wickersham Commission, to "use these reports in order to advertise their freedom from crime as compared with other municipalities." This tendency has apparently not yet been fully overcome. It sometimes arises from political pressure outside the police department and sometimes from the desire of the police to appear to be doing a good job of keeping the crime rate down. Defective or inefficient recording practices may also prevent crimes reported by citizens from becoming a part of the record.[7]

Those who would generalize about the total population of offenders on the basis of official statistics have usually taken a pessimistic view toward these data. For example, Sutherland and Cressey argued:

Ordinarily, a statistical index, such as a "cost of living index," is a compilation of fluctuations in a sample of items taken from the whole; the relationship to the whole is known, and the index serves as a convenient shortcut to a sufficient approximation of variation in the whole. But in crime statistics the rate as indicated by any set of figures cannot be a sample, for the whole cannot be specified. Both the true rate and the relationship between the true rate and any "index" of this rate are capricious "dark figures" which vary with changes in police policies, court policies, and public opinion. The variations in this "dark figure" in crime statistics make it almost foolhardy to attempt a comparison of crime rates of various cities, and it is hazardous even to compare national rates or the rates of a given city or state in a given year with the rates of the same jurisdiction in a different year. International comparisons are even more difficult.[8]

Some investigators have argued that official statistics should be studied for what they reveal about the processes and procedures of official labeling agencies in the correctional apparatus.[9] In this view, the official statistics may be a defective and biased representation of true crime, but they are accurate indicators of the workings of official agencies, which go about isolating and labeling some individuals as deviants and lawbreakers. In other words, the real deviants and criminals in modern societies are those individuals enforcement and control organizations have identified as such. Similarly, this argument holds that sociologists should concentrate on the activities of these agencies, including the business of how they go about identifying and processing their clientele.

Jerome Skolnick has provided an illustration of sociological analysis of statistics making. He pointed out that the clearance rate concerning offenses the police solve is subject to a good deal of manipulation. Of the offenses reported to them, police officers can classify a number as unfounded, thereby increasing the percentage of offenses cleared. Also, clearance of a case may mean that the police have arrested someone, or it may mean that the officers have persuaded an offender apprehended for another crime to "cop out" to a series of hitherto unsolved cases. [10]

The suggestion that the sociologist treat crime and delinquency statistics as primary sociological phenomena for study has considerable merit. However, criminologists must also continue to grapple with the problem of gauging the extent of total crime from the data on offenses known to authorities. In short, the study of statistics making should go hand in hand with efforts to assess the magnitude of criminal acts, including those known to agencies and those unreported and undetected.

Another problem with crime statistics, even if they are carefully and consistently amassed, is that they are often misused. Most crime statistics are presented in terms of rates for the *total* population rather than computed for the population groups most usually involved in lawbreaking. In a situation where the component group of young individuals is increasing disproportionately in the general population, we expect an increase in total crime, in that young persons are most frequently involved in crime. But in this case, the crime *rates* for young persons might not be increasing; that is, the amount of crime among youthful individuals might simply be increasing at the same pace as the increase in the size of this population group. However, when crime rates are calculated in terms of the total population, a misleading impression could emerge, suggesting that the extent of lawbreaking is outstripping the growth of the population. [11]

Other students of crime data have suggested that crime patterns would be more realistically portrayed if statistics on offenses were related to changes in the supply of victims of various kinds. For example, Leroy Gould has observed that although rates for auto thefts and bank robberies computed on the basis of population have been increasing in recent decades, the rates of occurrence of these offenses in terms of units of property available to be stolen have decreased. [12] In other words, the number of auto thefts and bank robberies has not increased as markedly as has the number of registered motor vehicles or the cash in banks available to be stolen. Although these kinds of rate computations are unfamiliar ones to laymen, they are, perhaps, more accurate indicators of the seriousness of crime than are conventional rates.

some dimensions of known crime and criminals

THE EXTENT OF KNOWN CRIME

As indicated earlier, the FBI Crime Index is made up of eight major crimes; the FBI collects information regarding the number of these offenses known to the police. These eight crimes were chosen to compose the Crime Index because they are types of criminality likely to be reported to the police when they occur. Table 4 shows the number of these index crimes reported in 1979.

The President's Commission on Law Enforcement and Administration of Justice has provided further evidence regarding the nature and extent of serious crimes in the United States. The commission's report indicated that a survey of 297 robberies in Washington, D.C. showed that injury was inflicted upon the victims in about one-fourth of the cases. Injuries were caused to victims in large proportions of other cases, too. The commission concluded that the chances of serious personal attack of any American in a given year was about 1 in 550. In the view of the commission, the risk of personal attack was high enough to warrant concern on the part of all Americans.[13]

As previously mentioned, the FBI collects nationwide statistics on arrests—rather than crimes known to the police—for nonindex crimes. These data are difficult to match, in that the ratios between crimes known to the police and arrests vary. About 90 percent of known larcenies are solved by arrests. The FBI indicated that in 1979, 73 percent of all known murders and nonnegligent manslaughter cases were cleared by arrest. Forcible rapes were cleared in 48 percent of the cases; 59 percent of the aggravated assaults were cleared, as were

table 4   index of serious crimes, 1979[a]

offense	number known to the police
Total	12,152,730
Murder and nonnegligent manslaughter	21,456
Forcible rape	75,989
Robbery	466,881
Aggravated assault	614,213
Burglary	3,299,484
Larceny-theft	6,577,518
Motor-vehicle theft	1,097,189
Arson	not available

[a]Federal Bureau of Investigation, U.S. Department of Justice, *Crime in the United States: Uniform Crime Reports,* 1979 (Washington, D.C.: U.S. Government Printing Office, 1980).

25 percent of the robberies, 15 percent of the burglaries, 14 percent of the car thefts, and 19 percent of the larcenies.[14]

FBI statistics on nonindex crimes far outnumber index offenses. Table 5 shows the numbers and rates of arrests for the ten most frequent offenses in the United States in 1979. As we can see, drunkenness arrests and other peace-keeping matters occupy much of the time and attention of the police.

Another category of criminal acts not discussed in FBI reports concerns federal crimes. In 1978, cases were filed in U.S. district courts numbering 34,624, including 25,200 felony offenses. Of the total filings, 1,377 involved robberies, while 4,637 were fraud cases. Forgery and counterfeiting cases numbered 3,818, while there were also 3,745 drug cases, 1,734 immigration-law violations, and 1,888 federal-statute offenses. The latter included civil-rights violations, food-and-drug-law violations, migratory-bird-law violations, and a number of other federal-statute violations.[15] These figures suggest that federal crimes are relatively few in number. However, we shall see in Chapter 14 that white-collar violations of federal regulatory statutes are much more frequent than revealed in these data.

SPATIAL DISTRIBUTION OF CRIME

Crime rates vary markedly from one state to another. The rates for index crimes known to the police in 1979 show that Nevada had the highest murder and nonnegligent manslaughter rate, 17.5 per 100,000 population. Georgia, Louisiana, Texas, and Alabama had high rates, and North Dakota, Vermont, South Dakota, Iowa, and Minnesota had the lowest rates. Aggravated assaults were most frequent in the states of South Carolina, Florida, Maryland, and New Mexico, whereas the lowest rates were in North Dakota and Hawaii. Alaska had the highest rate of forcible rape, followed by Nevada, California, Colorado, and Florida; low rates were observed in North Dakota, Maine, and Iowa. New York, Nevada, California, and Maryland led the nation in robberies, while larceny rates were highest in Arizona, Hawaii, Florida, and Colorado.[16]

table 5 number of persons arrested for the ten most frequent offenses, 1979[a]

offense	number
Driving under the influence	1,324,800
Larceny-theft	1,181,500
Drunkenness	1,172,700
Disorderly conduct	765,500
Drug-abuse violations	558,600
Burglary	503,600
Other Assaults	485,500
Aggravated assault	276,000
Fraud	261,900

[a]Federal Bureau of Investigation, *Crime in the United States,* p. 188.

Crime rates also vary considerably within urban areas. Table 6 shows rates for index crimes for the 15 largest standard metropolitan areas in 1979. Los Angeles had the highest rates for two of the seven offenses, but generally the rates are not consistently higher in one community than another. Most apparent from Table 6, crime rates for the index crimes are of quite different magnitudes within the 15 areas so that, for example, robbery rates range from 164.9 to 926.7 per 100,000 population.

How do crime rates for standard metropolitan statistical areas compare with those for other portions of the United States? Index-crime rates are shown in Table 7 for standard metropolitan areas, other cities, and rural parts of the country.

In that the majority of the American population lives in metropolitan areas, we should not be surprised to find that most crimes occur there. But Table 7 also indicates that the *relative* occurrence of crime is less in rural areas; metropolitan areas show high rates of crime, as well as large numbers of offenses. The pronounced contrast of rates is for robbery, burglary, larceny, and auto theft. The high rates of property crime in urban areas are probably explained in terms of the loosened social bonds, lack of legitimate opportunities, and other concomitants of urbanization. We shall have more to say about differential social organization in cities and its link to criminality in later chapters.

AGE VARIATIONS

In 1979, persons under 25 years of age were involved in criminality far out of proportion to their numbers in the population. Persons under 25 were involved in 57 percent of the arrests reported by the police. Conventional crime is heavily concentrated within this group, although variations from crime to crime exist in the contribution by young persons. Table 8 shows the arrest figures for 1979 by age.

Table 8 indicates that persons under 25 years of age accounted for 57.0 percent of all arrests. However, these individuals were particularly implicated in those serious property crimes occurring most frequently and causing the most concern to the community. Thus, persons under 25 years of age carried out 74.4 percent of the robberies, 83.0 percent of the burglaries, and 82.4 percent of the auto thefts. Persons over 25 years of age were most frequently involved in fraud, embezzlement, gambling, drunkenness, vagrancy, and offenses against the family.

SEX VARIATIONS

One of the most striking features of known crime in the United States is that it is mainly the work of males. In 1979, males were responsible for 89.8 percent of the violent offenses and 78.2 percent of the property crimes among index

table 6   crime rates, standard metropolitan areas, 1979ª (rates per 100,000 population)

	murder, nonnegligent manslaughter	forcible rape	robbery	aggravated assault	burglary	larceny-theft	motor-vehicle theft
Baltimore	13.7	43.1	470.3	561.0	1,652.2	3,705.6	570.2
Boston	4.7	25.8	290.4	327.3	1,619.7	2,608.4	1,419.1
Chicago	14.3	34.0	263.1	257.4	1,193.2	3,150.4	727.1
Dallas–Ft. Worth	18.3	60.2	262.3	353.2	2,245.1	4,258.4	590.3
Detroit	13.8	51.9	351.5	369.2	1,623.5	3,413.6	953.1
Houston	30.0	68.3	394.4	180.8	2,450.0	2,967.1	1,144.5
Los Angeles	20.0	71.3	529.2	584.7	2,387.8	3,156.7	1,056.7
Minneapolis	3.2	31.7	164.9	156.2	1,457.5	3,398.9	456.0
Newark	9.9	40.3	484.5	322.0	1,736.6	2,973.3	978.5
New York	19.8	44.5	926.7	506.0	2,916.9	3,012.0	1,079.5
Philadelphia	10.6	32.1	257.5	228.6	1,219.5	2,330.3	559.9
Pittsburgh	5.2	25.6	171.3	160.4	847.8	1,508.1	563.1
St. Louis	16.0	44.3	319.5	341.7	1,727.8	2,883.2	576.7
San Francisco	11.0	56.0	426.1	369.2	2,199.9	4,424.1	731.7
Washington	9.3	45.3	390.6	247.7	1,540.4	3,879.5	475.4

ªFederal Bureau of Investigation, *Crime in the United States*, pp. 60–86.

table 7   crime rates, metropolitan areas, other cities, and rural areas, 1979ª (rates per 100,000 population)

	total	murder, nonnegligent manslaughter	forcible rape	robbery	aggravated assault	burglary	larceny-theft	motor-vehicle theft
U.S. total	5,521.5	9.7	34.5	212.1	279.1	1,499.1	2,988.4	498.5
Standard metropolitan areas	6,313.1	10.9	41.1	276.2	312.5	1,708.8	3,353.1	610.6
Other cities	4,948.6	5.7	18.3	57.9	248.0	1,134.4	3,218.0	266.3
Rural areas	2,167.5	7.4	15.1	22.1	142.8	770.8	1,072.2	137.1

ªFederal Bureau of Investigation, *Crime in the United States*, p. 38.

offenses.[17] Males made up 86.3 percent of the arrests for murder and nonnegligent homicide, 99.2 percent of those for forcible rape, and 92.6 percent of those for robbery. Aggravated assault arrests involved males in 87.6 percent of the cases, as did 93.7 percent of the burglaries, 69.7 percent of the larcenies, 91.1 percent of the auto thefts, and 88.7 percent of the arson arrests.

Women are not equally involved in all forms of crime. In 1979, females accounted for 67.5 percent of the prostitution arrests, 40.4 percent of the arrests for fraud, 25.3 percent of those for embezzlement, as well as 58.4 percent of those for runaway activity (an offense restricted to juveniles).

What is the explanation for the disproportionate contribution of males to criminality? The usual answer offered by sociologists is that socialization into the female role in American society deters women from lawbreaking. In this view,

table 8   total arrests of persons under 25 years of age, 1979[a]

offense charged	total	number of persons arrested under 25	percentage under 25
Total	9,506,347	5,421,875	57.0
Murder and nonnegligent manslaughter	18,264	8,073	44.2
Forcible rape	29,164	16,270	55.8
Robbery	130,753	97,248	74.4
Aggravated assault	256,597	128,030	49.9
Burglary	468,085	388,696	83.0
Larceny-theft	1,098,398	780,189	71.0
Motor-vehicle theft	143,654	118,323	82.4
Arson	18,387	13,459	73.2
Other assaults	451,475	238,043	52.7
Forgery and counterfeiting	70,977	38,533	54.3
Fraud	243,461	87,071	35.8
Embezzlement	7,882	3,710	47.1
Stolen property: buying, receiving, etc.	107,621	76,867	71.4
Vandalism	239,246	196,344	82.1
Weapons: carrying, possessing, etc.	152,731	81,009	53.0
Prostitution and commercial vice	83,088	51,605	62.1
Sex offenses (except forcible rape and prostitution)	62,633	29,861	47.7
Drug-abuse violations	519,377	373,953	72.0
Gambling	50,974	11,437	22.4
Offenses against family and children	53,321	19,186	36.0
Driving under the influence	1,231,665	417,746	33.9
Liquor laws	386,957	324,079	83.8
Drunkenness	1,090,233	345,591	31.7
Disorderly conduct	711,730	417,918	58.7
Vagrancy	34,622	18,896	54.5
All other offenses (except traffic)	1,595,864	896,399	56.2
Suspicion	18,135	12,326	68.0
Curfew and loitering-law violations	78,147	78,147	100.0
Runaways	152,866	152,866	100.0

[a]Federal Bureau of Investigation, *Crime in the United States,* p. 198. The arrest figures in this table are from 11,758 police agencies, representing a 1979 estimated population of 204,622,000.

the social learning involved in feminine role acquisition, along with restrictions upon opportunities for crime embodied in female sex roles, have precluded women from widespread involvement in criminality. However, during the past decade or so, women have begun to move closer toward parity with men in terms of crime incidence, reflecting the growing social equality of females and other trends.[18] We shall return to this topic in detail in Chapter 17, which is devoted to an examination of criminality among women.

RACIAL VARIATIONS

The major concern of those curious about racial characteristics of lawbreakers centers about the extent of black involvement in criminality. In 1980, black citizens constituted about 11 percent of the American population. They represent the major racial group other than Caucasians in the United States.

Blacks are apparently strongly overrepresented in crime. Table 9 shows the distribution of blacks among persons arrested in 1979. Blacks comprised 56.9 percent of persons arrested for robbery, 47.7 percent of those apprehended for murder and nonnegligent manslaughter, 47.7 percent of those arrested for forcible rape, and 28.7 percent of those involved in burglary. Table 9 also indicates that blacks were much less frequently involved in certain patterns of criminality, including liquor-law violations, drunkenness, sex offenses other than forcible rape, fraud, and embezzlement. In general, the high crime pattern for blacks is composed largely of crude, unskilled personal assaults or property crimes.

These arrest statistics suggest two factors that may account for these patterns. First, blacks are overrepresented in criminality in part through differential law enforcement. That is, these arrest figures reflect the policies of the police, who sometimes deal officially with offenses by blacks that would be handled informally or ignored entirely if they were committed by whites. Gambling and prostitution arrests are cases in point, for the police enforce the laws against these activities differentially against blacks. In particular, the police often harass black streetwalkers but allow white prostitutes to conduct their criminal activities.

The crime-producing experiences to which many blacks are subjected in American society also explain the figures in Table 9. If racial characteristics per se influence criminality, we would expect to find crime rates for different offenses to be relatively uniform. Instead, black and white rates are quite varied.

Support for this argument can be found in a study by Edward Green in Ypsilanti, Michigan.[19] He analyzed black and white arrest patterns for select years before 1942 and 1965 in that city and endeavored to uncover the effects of age, sex, and socioeconomic trends on these rates. He found that black crime had increased markedly since 1942, but this increase was largely the result of the growth of the total black population. Over this twenty-year time period, black crime rates actually *declined*. Green accounted for the excess of black over white arrest rates in terms of the economically disadvantaged position of blacks, including high unemployment and unskilled jobs, and in terms of the handicaps stemming from migration from the rural South. In short, he argued that socio-economic factors, not racial background, explained higher crimes rates among blacks.[20]

VICTIMIZATION STUDIES

The President's Commission report contained considerable information on the topic of victims, a matter that has received little attention in the past.[21] Victimization surveys are of importance in two ways. First, they illuminate the victim side of the offender-victim relationship, indicating the characteristics of individ-

table 9   arrests by race, 1979[a]

offense charged	total	black	black percentage of total
Total	9,467,502	2,342,664	24.7
Murder and nonnegligent manslaughter	18,238	8,693	47.7
Forcible rape	29,068	13,870	47.7
Robbery	130,585	74,275	56.9
Aggravated assault	255,987	94,624	37.0
Burglary—breaking and entering	464,099	133,011	28.7
Larceny-theft	1,093,998	330,325	30.2
Motor-vehicle theft	143,197	38,905	27.2
Arson	18,304	3,513	19.2
Other assaults	444,893	144,324	32.2
Forgery and counterfeiting	70,486	22,630	32.1
Fraud	241,731	75,037	31.0
Embezzlement	7,873	1,862	23.7
Stolen property: buying, receiving, etc.	106,727	34,253	32.1
Vandalism	237,595	36,805	15.5
Weapons: carrying, possessing, etc.	152,096	54,964	36.1
Prostitution and commercial vice	83,035	43,706	52.6
Sex offenses (except forcible rape and prostitution)	62,371	12,607	20.2
Narcotic drug laws	516,142	112,748	21.8
Gambling	50,840	34,540	67.9
Offenses against family and children	53,042	18,739	35.3
Driving under the influence	1,224,126	151,168	12.3
Liquor laws	385,709	25,338	6.6
Drunkenness	1,089,965	181,483	16.7
Disorderly conduct	709,888	210,678	29.7
Vagrancy	34,613	12,291	35.5
All other offenses (except traffic)	1,590,936	430,490	27.1
Suspicion	17,903	5,557	31.0
Curfew and loitering-law violations	78,067	16,907	21.7
Runaways	151,988	19,321	12.7

[a]Federal Bureau of Investigation, *Crime in the United States,* p. 200. The arrest figures in this table are from 11,589 police agencies, representing a 1979 estimated population of 204,363,000.

uals who are most likely to have offenses committed against them, the interpersonal or social dynamics of criminal incidents, and other facts of that sort. Second, surveys of victimization provide valuable information regarding the total extent of criminality, in that they uncover instances of crime that have not been reported to the police as well as violations known to the authorities.

One of the early victimization studies was a survey that the National Opinion Research Center undertook for the President's Commission. That study asked a representative sample of 10,000 American citizens whether they had been the victims of a crime in the previous year. Although the results showed a mixed pattern, low-income persons were the most frequent targets of rape, robbery, and burglary. Other observations of the President's Commission noted that nonwhites were victimized relatively more often than were whites by all index crimes except grand larceny. Men were the victims of crime about three times more frequently than women.[22]

More recent victimization studies have been conducted by the Law Enforcement Assistance Administration (LEAA) in collaboration with the United States Bureau of the Census. These agencies are jointly involved in the National Crime Survey, a yearly sampling of households and commercial establishments in the United States. These surveys question individuals about personal offenses of rape, robbery, assault, and personal larceny; in addition, findings are gathered regarding household violations involving burglary, household larceny, and motor-vehicle theft. Also, commercial establishments are interviewed about instances of burglary and robbery.

The findings from the national-panel surveys are consistent with the earlier ones reported by the President's Commission. Some of these results are shown in Tables 10, 11, and 12. Table 10 contains findings parallel to those in Table 7, in that highest rates of victimization and of offenses reported to the police are found in core cities of standard metropolitan areas. Table 11 indicates the estimated number of personal and household victimizations in 1977 and business victimizations in 1976, along with the portions of these victimizations that were reported to the police. Most of the offenses shown in Table 11 were two or three times more frequent than are crimes known to the police and reported to the FBI. The data in Table 11 lend convincing support to the argument that crime is truly ubiquitous in American society.

Table 12 lists estimated rates of victimization for whites and blacks and other races, and also for income groups within these racial categories. By and large, these estimates indicate that black citizens are more likely to suffer robberies and aggravated assaults than are whites. Then, too, persons with family incomes under $10,000 per year are more frequently the victims of robbery and personal larceny with contact than are individuals with larger incomes. In short, garden-variety crimes are commonly directed at economically disadvantaged persons, rather than being instances of "Robin Hood" crime aimed at affluent members of society.

table 10 personal and household victimization, by extent of urbanization, 1977[a] (rates per 100,000 population)

type of victimization	core cities within Standard Metropolitan Statistical Areas	areas within Standard Metropolitan Statistical Areas, but outside of core cities	areas outside Standard Metropolitan Statistical Areas	Total
Personal victimizations				
Rape	116	95	56	89
Robbery	1,193	496	261	622
Assault	3,413	2,779	1,892	2,679
Personal larceny with contact	499	208	122	265
Personal larceny without contact	10,796	10,510	6,958	9,462
Household victimizations				
Burglary	11,150	8,682	6,835	8,856
Larceny	14,090	13,576	9,123	12,324
Vehicle theft	2,440	1,831	817	1,697

[a]Timothy J. Flanagan, Michael J. Hindelang, and Michael R. Gottfredson, eds., Sourcebook of Criminal Justice Statistics, 1979 (Washington, D. C.: Law Enforcement Assistance Administration, 1980), p. 342.

table 11 personal and household victimizations, 1977, and business victimizations, 1976*

type of victimization	total		reported to police		not reported to police		don't know whether reported to police	
	number	percent	number	percent	number	percent	number	percent
Personal victimizations:								
Rape and attempted rape	154,237	100	90,136	58	64,102	42	0	0
Robbery	1,082,936	100	601,225	56	472,283	44	9,428	1
Robbery and attempted robbery with injury	386,405	100	255,540	66	128,312	33	2,553	1
Serious assault	214,670	100	161,568	75	51,881	24	1,221	1
Minor assault	171,735	100	93,972	55	76,431	45	1,332	1
Robbery without injury	412,505	100	262,747	64	145,858	35	3,901	1
Attempted robbery without injury	284,026	100	82,938	29	193,113	70	2,975	1
Assault	4,663,827	100	2,030,438	44	2,580,808	55	52,582	1
Aggravated assault	1,737,774	100	894,680	51	817,292	47	25,802	1
With injury	541,411	100	330,569	61	202,278	37	8,564	2
Attempted assault with weapon	1,196,363	100	564,111	47	615,014	51	17,239	1
Simple assault	2,926,053	100	1,135,758	39	1,763,516	60	26,779	1
With injury	755,780	100	357,946	47	387,258	51	10,576	1
Attempted assault without weapon	2,170,273	100	777,812	36	1,376,257	63	16,203	1
Personal larceny with contact	461,014	100	171,292	37	287,147	62	2,574	1
Purse snatching	87,937	100	54,719	62	31,955	36	1,263	1
Attempted purse snatching	46,687	100	7,740	17	38,947	83	0	0
Pocket picking	326,390	100	108,834	33	216,246	66	1,311	0
Personal larceny without contact	16,469,154	100	4,031,783	24	12,263,379	74	173,992	1
Household victimizations:								
Burglary	6,766,010	100	3,300,528	49	3,416,342	50	49,141	1
Forcible entry	2,300,292	100	1,667,565	72	614,080	27	18,647	1
Unlawful entry without force	2,962,705	100	1,157,587	39	1,791,089	60	14,029	0
Attempted forcible entry	1,503,013	100	475,376	32	1,011,172	67	16,465	1
Larceny	9,415,533	100	2,392,239	25	6,989,661	74	33,633	0
Under $50	5,443,697	100	780,261	14	4,652,680	85	10,756	0
$50 or more	2,851,831	100	1,352,220	47	1,480,338	52	19,273	1
Amount not ascertained	410,196	100	72,063	18	335,788	82	2,345	1
Attempted	709,808	100	187,695	26	520,854	73	1,259	0
Vehicle theft	1,296,759	100	887,620	68	398,715	31	10,424	1
Completed	797,671	100	706,777	89	85,826	11	5,067	1
Attempted	499,089	100	180,843	36	312,889	63	5,357	1
Business victimizations:								
Robbery	279,516	100	243,980	87	32,763	12	2,773	1
Burglary	1,576,242	100	1,148,424	73	400,731	25	27,087	2

*Flanagan, Hindelang, and Gottfredson, Sourcebook of Criminal Justice Statistics, p. 328.

table 12   estimated rates of personal victimization, by race and family income of victim, 1977[a]

type of victimization and race of victim	family income						
	under $3,000	$3,000 to $7,499	$7,500 to $9,999	$10,000 to $14,999	$15,000 to $24,999	$25,000 or more	not ascertained
Base							
White	7,589,945	25,265,459	13,469,635	33,124,985	39,596,131	17,697,391	15,643,404
Black and other races	2,757,595	6,493,760	2,217,505	3,663,548	3,043,745	1,124,476	2,374,895
Rape and attempted rape							
White	185	159	105	53	57	62	86
Black and other races	159	120	221	39	0	B	110
Robbery							
White	1,106	657	683	513	437	373	454
Black and other races	2,096	1,205	1,409	959	1,011	B	971
Robbery and attempted robbery with injury							
White	354	262	242	181	135	111	159
Black and other races	1,138	481	553	288	385	B	230
Serious assault							
White	155	133	152	96	54	76	76
Black and other races	842	274	373	251	302	B	106
Minor assault							
White	200	129	90	85	81	36	84
Black and other races	295	208	180	37	83	B	125
Robbery without injury							
White	506	203	271	189	166	144	172
Black and other races	761	489	598	329	414	B	423
Attempted robbery without injury							
White	245	193	170	143	136	118	122
Black and other races	197	235	258	342	212	B	318
Assault							
White	4,225	3,115	2,539	2,672	2,548	2,409	1,979
Black and other races	2,824	2,829	3,495	2,250	2,176	B	2,951
Aggravated assault							
White	1,634	1,156	849	935	877	845	781
Black and other races	1,403	1,489	1,462	1,032	1,049	B	1,321

With injury							
White	523	380	294	321	258	254	222
Black and other races	498	547	314	151	133	B	369
Attempted assault with weapon							
White	1,111	776	555	614	619	591	560
Black and other races	905	942	1,148	881	916	B	952
Simple assault							
White	2,592	1,959	1,691	1,737	1,671	1,564	1,198
Black and other races	1,421	1,340	2,033	1,219	1,127	B	1,629
With injury							
White	697	491	478	443	429	377	281
Black and other races	492	448	415	228	314	B	678
Attempted assault without weapon							
White	1,895	1,468	1,213	1,294	1,241	1,186	917
Black and other races	929	892	1,618	991	813	B	952
Personal larceny with contact							
White	404	253	265	152	170	208	335
Black and other races	627	653	749	604	323	B	595
Purse snatching							
White	115	46	39	24	20	7	108
Black and other races	141	153	142	0	111	B	275
Attempted purse snatching							
White	20	54	38	8	10	15	41
Black and other races	44	0	139	139	48	B	0
Pocket picking							
White	270	152	187	121	141	186	186
Black and other races	442	500	467	465	164	B	320
Personal larceny without contact							
White	9,761	7,811	8,357	9,365	10,562	12,840	7,859
Black and other races	6,029	6,682	9,216	10,742	11,477	B	7,280

ªFlanagan, Hindelang, and Gottfredson, *Sourcebook of Criminal Justice Statistics*, p. 359.

the economic costs of crime

The President's Commission report included some estimates of the economic costs of crime.[23] According to the commission, in 1967, crimes against persons cost about $815,000,000 per year through losses of earnings, hospitalization, and so on. Crimes against property resulted in annual costs to the public of around $3,932,000,000. Index crimes contributed only about $600,000,000 in economic costs to this figure, unreported commercial thefts were thought to cost about $1,400,000,000 annually, and embezzlement resulted in losses of about $200,000,000 per year. Frauds were estimated to involve economic losses of around $1,350,000,000 yearly, forgeries cost $82,000,000, and arson and vandalism resulted in losses of about $300,000,000. Clearly, such garden-variety property offenses as larceny and burglary were economically less costly than a variety of "white-collar" and "hidden" crimes. Also, it is clear that the costs of crime would be considerably higher if current estimates were available.

The President's Commission set the annual cost of crimes involving illegal goods and services, such as prostitution, gambling, and other forms of organized crime, at $8,075,000,000. The cost of law-enforcement and criminal-justice operations was estimated to be about $4,212,000,000 annually, composed of $2,792,000,000 in police expenses, $261,000,000 in court costs, $125,000,000 in prosecution and defense-counsel expenses, and $1,034,000,000 for the operation of correctional services.

More recent figures are available concerning the costs of operating the various parts of the criminal-justice machinery in the United States, provided by the LEAA and the U.S. Census. Table 13 indicates the levels of expenditure for criminal-justice services in 1977. According to Table 13, over 21 billion dollars was spent on all criminal-justice activities, with $13,027,249,000 of that sum constituting local government costs for criminal-justice activities, largely in the form of police protection. By contrast, the largest share of state funds was spent on the operation of correctional agencies.

The figures in Table 13 suggest that a dramatically sudden decline of crime in the United States would have major consequences, some of which might be disruptive. The reduction of crime would alter the economic workings of society and probably produce revenue that could be used for more positive ends. But a major drop in criminality would also result in employment dislocations, rendering many social-control agents idle. In this sense at least, crime is functional in American society in that it produces employment opportunities in some quantity.

"hidden" criminality

The crime information examined to this point was derived mainly from offenses known to the police or from arrest data, supplemented by evidence from victimization studies. Most of this information indicated that garden-variety lawbreak-

table 13 expenditures for criminal justice activities, by type of activity and level of government, 1977 (dollar amounts in thousands)[a]

level of government	total	police protection	judicial	legal services and prosecution	public defense	corrections	other criminal justice
All government	$21,573,756	$11,864,875	$2,638,251	$1,225,344	$403,754	$4,934,067	$507,465
Federal	3,601,647	1,771,922	289,626	185,604	140,452	338,400	875,643
State	6,689,474	1,963,975	735,829	314,472	90,393	2,974,890	609,915
Local	13,027,249	8,304,366	1,707,783	745,585	185,151	1,814,539	269,825

[a]Flanagan, Hindelang, and Gottfredson, Sourcebook of Criminal Justice Statistics, p. 5.

ing is most often the work of persons from lower-income backgrounds and is directed at others who are similarly disadvantaged. But what if we cast our nets more broadly, scooping up cases of unreported criminality in the world of business or other acts of lawbreaking that are not likely to turn up in police reports or victimization studies? Would we find that criminality is markedly more widespread? More important, would we discover that unreported or hidden lawbreaking is common among population groups that are underrepresented in the group of known law violators? Are middle-class citizens frequently engaged in acts of illegality, which they keep from the eyes of the police?

Most of the work on these questions has concerned juvenile delinquency. For some time, delinquency researchers have been interested in the juvenile lawbreaking of children who live in comfortable, middle-class neighborhoods.[24] For example, Austin Porterfield elicited reports from college students about the misbehavior they had been involved in prior to entry into college. He found that nearly all of them had been active in delinquency, although virtually none had become known to the police or courts.[25] This study was quite crude, but a group of investigators, starting with F. Ivan Nye and James Short, have improved the methods of gaining self-reports about delinquency.[26]

The studies of hidden delinquency add up to a broad picture of the undetected deviations of youngsters. Most of these children admit that they have been engaged in at least one or another delinquent act, but most misbehavior they report tends to be relatively harmless. Also, when youngsters from different social-class levels have been compared concerning involvement in *relatively petty acts of delinquency*, no relationship between delinquency and social status has been observed; that is, petty juvenile offenders are found in about the same number at all social-class levels.[27]

On the other hand, the evidence indicates that official delinquents come disproportionately from lower-income backgrounds. Some have taken the findings on petty hidden delinquency and economic status and have jumped to the conclusion that social class is unrelated to delinquent involvement. They have argued that certain juveniles find their way into juvenile court or training schools because the police discriminate against low-status persons rather than because they are more delinquent than hidden offenders.

Such a conclusion does not survive close scrutiny. A number of research investigations have shown that institutionalized delinquents have been engaged in all the relatively petty acts high school students have admitted, but also in more serious and repetitive offenses to which hidden delinquents do not admit.[28]

Investigations of unreported adult criminality have been few. James Wallerstein and Clement Wyle asked a cross-section of the adult population to report the acts of law violation in which they had engaged.[29] Most respondents admitted one or more deviant acts that had gone unreported. Many of these incidents appeared to be relatively harmless and of little concern to the police. For instance, one woman reported an assault, by which she meant that she had thrown an ashtray at a suitor. Such cases suggest the need for caution lest we draw the conclusion that nearly all citizens are involved in criminality.

This caveat applies equally well to a more recent survey reported by Charles Tittle and Wayne Villemez.[30] That survey, conducted among citizens in New Jersey, Oregon, and Iowa in 1972, quizzed persons as to whether they had engaged in certain crimes. Tittle and Villemez concluded that self-reported crimes were equally frequent among persons from different social-class strata. However, some of the offenses such as theft of something worth about five dollars or marijuana smoking were relatively petty ones, while in the case of the other items, it is likely that a number of individuals who admitted these crimes had been involved in minor forms of income-tax evasion, assaultive conduct, and the like. Quite different results might have turned up if a wider collection of illegal acts had been surveyed or had the respondents been quizzed further about the nature of their confessed crimes.

Tittle, Villemez, and Douglas Smith have also reviewed the results of 35 studies containing evidence on the question of social class and criminality.[31] They argued that these investigations indicate only a slight negative association between socioeconomic status and lawbreaking and also that the relationship is lower in self-report studies than in those based on official statistics. They concluded that, on balance, the belief that social class and criminality are related is a myth.

At the very least, the Tittle et al. conclusion is unconvincing. For one thing, most of the research investigations on which they drew were studies of unreported delinquency, rather than adult criminality. Additionally, their case rested on evidence of the kind contained in the Tittle and Villemez study, in which a truncated scale of offenses, consisting principally of relatively petty acts of lawbreaking, had been used in investigating unreported lawbreaking. Homicides, aggravated assaults, forcible rapes, and other serious felonies have not been included in self-report instruments, for reasons that are relatively apparent. Finally, Tittle et al. did not include studies and evidence on white-collar criminality within their survey. Had they done so, they might have reached a different conclusion about social class and criminality.

The commentary in Chapter 1 took note of a number of hypotheses that might be advanced concerning crime and social class. These different possibilities are shown in Figure 2 (which, for the reader's convenience, repeats Figure 1 from Chapter 1).

Which of these diagrams comes closest to capturing the linkages between social class and crime of various kinds in the United States? This question borders on being unanswerable, since ever accumulating detailed evidence on many forms of undetected criminality remains impossible. Tittle et al. argued for diagram C, contending that there is no social class patterning in lawbreaking. But, in this book we claim that diagram E is the more accurate one. Crime in American society is distributed *bimodally*.

Garden-variety criminality is most frequently directed at low-income, inner-

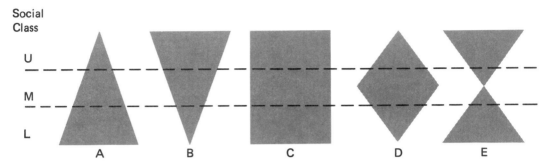

Social
Class

U

M

L

A   B   C   D   E

figure 2 crime rates and social class

city residents. Those who commit these crimes are also most commonly from the bottom of the economic pyramid. Yet there is another side to the crime picture. When embezzlement and other employee crimes, along with white-collar offenses by businesses and corporations, are examined, it becomes clear that lawbreaking is frequent both at the top and the bottom of the economic heap in the United States. We shall examine the existing data concerning white-collar crime in detail in Chapter 14.

trends in crime

In contemporary America it is fashionable to assume that lawlessness is at an unparalleled high point. But hard evidence that conclusively demonstrates this hypothesized upsurge of criminality is hard to come by. Even inadequate statistics of the sort discussed in this chapter have been gathered for only a short time, so long-term trends cannot be identified. However, some evidence suggests that America prior to the twentieth century may have been more lawless than it is now.[32]

Crime trends can be studied for relatively short periods in the immediate past, and these data do suggest that criminality has been growing at an accelerated pace in the past few decades. Figure 3, taken from the President's Commission report, shows the trend in index property crimes known to the police between 1933 and 1965. This chart indicates that these crimes increased between 1960 and 1965 at a much more pronounced rate than they grew over the longer period since 1933. This same pattern of more prominent increases in recent years was observed for index crimes of violence as well, although the rates for property crimes grew most prominently: the 1960 to 1965 increase in violent crimes was 25 percent, whereas the increase in property offenses was 36 percent.[33] Nonindex violations also increased prominently during the period from 1960 to 1965.

The trends revealed in Figure 3 have continued since 1965. Table 14 indicates the index-crime rate for the United States from 1970 to 1979, while Table

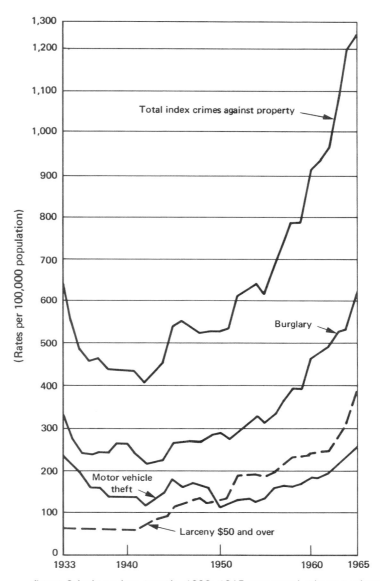

figure 3 index crime trends, 1933–1965; reported crimes against property *(the president's commission on law enforcement and administration of justice, the challenge of crime in a free society, p. 23.)*

15 shows the percent change in numbers and rates of index crimes from 1970 to 1979. Although the index-crime rate decreased somewhat between 1971 and 1972 and between 1976 and 1977, the general trend has been in the direction of a continuing growth of crime in this country. Table 15 indicates that while the

table 14   index crime rate, 1970–1979 (rate per 100,000 population)[a]

1970	3,984.5	1975	5,281.7
1971	4,164.7	1976	5,226.4
1972	3,961.4	1977	5,055.1
1973	4,154.4	1978	5,109.3
1974	4,850.4	1979	5,521.5

[a]Federal Bureau of Investigation, *Crime in the United States,* p. 41.

numbers and rates for all index crimes increased from 1970 to 1979, the most pronounced increases were for forcible rape and aggravated assault. Regarding forcible rape, some of this increase may be due to increased reporting, rather than to growth in the actual number of rapes. In much the same way, there are several interpretations that can be offered for some of the other changes in crime revealed in Table 15. One would do well to treat statistics of this kind gingerly, in the light of the many problems that plague crime statistics. Even so, these data make it difficult to argue that no real increase in crime has taken place in the United States in the last few decades.

summary

This chapter began with a strong warning about the inadequacies of crime statistics. Accurate social-bookkeeping data on criminality are almost completely lacking. But even so, the available data can be utilized in order to identify the gross outlines of lawbreaking in American society. This chapter identified some major dimensions of known crime in the United States. In addition, we have explored

table 15   percent change in numbers and rates of index crimes, 1970–1979[a]

| | percent change over 1970 | |
	number of crimes	rate per 100,000 population
Crime Index Total	+ 50.1	+38.6
Violent crimes	+ 59.5	+47.3
Property crimes	+ 49.1	+37.7
Murder	+ 34.1	+22.8
Forcible rape	+100.0	+84.5
Robbery	+ 33.4	+23.2
Aggravated assault	+ 83.4	+69.4
Burglary	+ 49.6	+38.2
Larceny-theft	+ 55.7	+43.7
Motor-vehicle theft	+ 18.2	+ 9.1
Arson	——	——

[a]Federal Bureau of Investigation, *Crime in the United States,* p. 37.

some aspects of hidden violations. We have seen that criminality is extremely widespread and costly, and we have observed that lawbreaking is patterned in a variety of ways so that it is more common in some areas than others. It is also apparent that some individuals, such as those who are male, young, black, or from low-income backgrounds, are more likely to be apprehended as criminals than are other persons. These materials provide the beginnings to a study of crime causation, to which our attention now turns.

notes

[1] Until 1978, the crime index included seven offenses: murder and nonnegligent manslaughter, forcible rape, robbery, aggravated assault, burglary, larceny-theft and motor-vehicle theft. By congressional mandate, arson was added in late 1978 as the eighth index offense.

[2] For history and critique of the *Uniform Crime Reports*, see Marvin E. Wolfgang, "Uniform Crime Reports: A Critical Appraisal," *University of Pennsylvania Law Review*, 111 (April 1963), 708–38; see also Paul Ward, " 'Careers in Crime': The F.B.I. Story," *Journal of Research in Crime and Delinquency*, 7 (July 1970), 207–18; Leroy C. Gould, "Crime and Its Impact in an Affluent Society," in *Crime and Justice in American Society*, Jack D. Douglas, ed. (Indianapolis: Bobbs-Merrill, 1971), pp. 81–118.

[3] Edwin H. Sutherland and Donald R. Cressey, *Criminology*, 9th ed. (Philadelphia: Lippincott, 1974), p.29.

[4] The President's Commission on Law Enforcement and Administration of Justice, *The Challenge of Crime in a Free Society*, (Washington, D.C.: U.S. Government Printing Office, 1967), pp. 24–27.

[5] As an actual case in point, a victimization survey in Portland, Oregon, indicated that the incidence of burglary declined in 1973–74 from the level observed in 1971–72. At the same time, the proportion of burglary incidents reported to the police increased from 50 percent to 71 percent during this period. As a consequence, the official burglary rate increased, but this increase was due to an increase in reporting rather than to actual burglaries. See Anne L. Schneider, *Crime and Victimization in Portland: Analysis of Trends, 1971–1974* (Eugene, Ore.: Oregon Research Institute, 1975).

[6] Wilson reported precisely this difference for two juvenile operations in separate police departments. In one the juvenile officers were well-trained, and in the other the officers were untrained in juvenile work. In the professionalized department, more juveniles were processed officially than in the less professional force. Wilson argued that the professional training of the officers made them more likely to be strict with the offenders than were the untrained officers. Also, in the professionalized department, the juvenile bureau was centered at headquarters rather than dispersed in precincts. The effect of this arrangement was to encourage police officers to take official action. See James Q. Wilson, "The Police and the Delinquent in Two Cities," in *Controlling Delinquents*, Stanton Wheeler, ed. (New York: John Wiley, 1967), pp. 9–30.

[7] The President's Commission on Law Enforcement and Administration of Justice. *The Challenge of Crime in a Free Society*, p. 27. Another report on widespread police manipulation of statistics is David Seidman and Michael Couzens, "Getting the Crime Rate Down: Political Pressure and Crime Reporting," *Law and Society Review*, 8 (Spring 1974), 457–93. These authors discussed the *reactivity* of archival measures such as police arrest statistics, indicating that those who gather these data often come under pressure to manipulate and distort them. Also, they presented evidence from Washington, D.C., and other cities, pointing to police downgrading of crimes reported to them. Downgrading refers to misclassification of offenses as less serious ones in order to create a false impression that serious crimes have been reduced.

[8] Edwin H. Sutherland and Donald R. Cressey, *Criminology*, 10th ed. (Philadelphia: Lippincott, 1978), pp. 29–30.

[9] John I. Kitsuse and Aaron V. Cicourel, "A Note on the Uses of Official Statistics," *Social Problems*, 11 (Fall 1963), 131–39.

[10]Jerome H. Skolnick, *Justice Without Trial* (New York: John Wiley, 1966), pp. 164–81.

[11]One case in point is found in Roland Chilton and Adele Spielberger, "Is Delinquency Increasing? Age Structure and the Crime Rate," *Social Forces,* 17 (March 1971), 487–93. These investigators indicated that most of the increase in juvenile court cases in Florida between 1958 and 1967 was attributable to changes in the age structure of that state. Also see Philip Sagi and Charles Wellford, "Age Composition and Patterns of Change in Criminal Statistics," *Journal of Criminal Law, Criminology and Police Science,* 59 (March 1968), 29–36.

[12]Gould, "Crime and Its Impact in an Affluent Society"; Gould, "The Changing Structure of Property Crime in an Affluent Society," *Social Forces,* 48 (September 1969), 50–59.

[13]The President's Commission on Law Enforcement and Administration of Justice, *The Challenge of Crime in a Free Society,* pp. 38–43.

[14]Federal Bureau of Investigation, U.S. Department of Justice, *Crime in the United States: Uniform Crime Reports, 1979* (Washington, D.C.: U.S. Government Printing Office, 1980), p. 178.

[15]Timothy J. Flanagan, Michael J. Hindelang, and Michael R. Gottfredson, eds., *Sourcebook of Criminal Justice Statistics, 1979* (Washington, D.C.: Law Enforcement Assistance Administration, 1980), p. 542.

[16]Federal Bureau of Investigation, *Crime in the United States,* pp. 48–59.

[17]Ibid., p. 199.

[18]Freda M. Adler, *Sisters in Crime* (New York: McGraw-Hill, 1975).

[19]Edward Green, "Race, Social Status, and Criminal Arrest," *American Sociological Review,* 35 (June 1970), 476–90.

[20]See Charles E. Reasons and Jack L. Kuykendall, eds., *Race, Crime, and Justice* (Pacific Palisades, Calif.: Goodyear Publishing Co., 1972).

[21]The President's Commission on Law Enforcement and Administration of Justice, *The Challenge of Crime in a Free Society,* p. 20.

[22]Ibid., p. 39.

[23]The President's Commission on Law Enforcement and Administration of Justice, *The Challenge of Crime in a Free Society,* pp. 31–35.

[24]These studies are summarized in Don C. Gibbons, *Delinquent Behavior,* 3rd ed. (Englewood Cliffs, N.J.: Prentice-Hall, Inc., 1981), pp. 37–54.

[25]Austin L. Porterfield, "Delinquency and Its Outcome in Court and College," *American Journal of Sociology,* 44 (November 1943), 199–208.

[26]F. Ivan Nye and James F. Short, Jr., "Scaling Delinquent Behavior," *American Sociological Review,* 22 (June 1957), 326–31; Short and Nye, "Extent of Unrecorded Juvenile Delinquency, Tentative Conclusions," *Journal of Criminal Law, Criminology and Police Science,* 49 (November–December 1958), 296–302; Nye, *Family Relationships and Delinquent Behavior* (New York: John Wiley, 1958); Harwin L. Voss, "Socio-Economic Status and Reported Delinquent Behavior," *Social Problems,* 13 (Winter 1966), 314–24; Ronald L. Akers, "Socio-Economic Status and Delinquent Behavior: A Retest," *Journal of Research in Crime and Delinquency,* 1 (January 1964), 38–46; John P. Clark and Eugene P. Wenninger, "Socio-Economic Class and Area as Correlates of Illegal Behavior Among Juveniles," *American Sociological Review,* 27 (December 1962), 826–34; Robert A. Dentler and Lawrence J. Monroe, "Social Correlates of Early Adolescent Theft," *American Sociological Review,* 26 (October 1961), 733–43; William R. Arnold, "Continuities in Research: Scaling Delinquent Behavior," *Social Problems,* 13 (Summer 1965), 59–66; Nancy Barton Wise, "Juvenile Delinquency Among Middle-Class Girls," in *Middle-Class Juvenile Delinquency,* Edmund W. Vaz, ed. (New York: Harper & Row, 1967), pp. 179–88; Nils Christie, Johs. Andanaes, and Sigurd Skirbekk, "A Study of Self-Reported Crime," *Scandinavian Studies in Criminology,* 1 (1965), 86–116.

[27]Dentler and Monroe, "Social Correlates of Early Adolescent Theft"; Clark and Wenninger, "Socio-Economic Class and Areas as Correlates of Illegal Behavior Among Juveniles"; Akers, "Socio-Economic Status and Delinquent Behavior"; Arnold, "Continuities in Research"; Voss, "Socio-Economic Status and Reported Delinquent Behavior."

[28]Short and Nye, "Extent of Unrecorded Juvenile Delinquency;" Maynard L. Erikson and LaMar T. Empey, "Court Records, Undetected Delinquency, and Decision-Making," *Journal of Criminal Law, Criminology and Police Science,* 54 (December 1963), 456–69; Martin Gold, "Undetected De-

linquent Behavior," *Journal of Research in Crime and Delinquency*, 3 (January 1966), 27–46. For a detailed discussion of the issue of discrepancies between self-report and official measures of delinquency, see Michael J. Hindelang, Travis Hirschi, and Joseph G. Weis, "Correlates of Delinquency: The Illusion of Discrepancy Between Self-Report and Official Measures," *American Sociological Review*, 44 (December 1975), 995–1014. These authors argue that the apparent discrepancies using these two measures of delinquency arise because different behavior domains are tapped by these measures. Official reports deal mainly with "hard core," serious offenders, while self-report measures center upon less serious forms of delinquency.

[29]James S. Wallerstein and Clement Wyle, "Our Law-Abiding Lawbreakers," *Probation*, 25 (April 1947), 107–12.

[30]Charles W. Tittle and Wayne J. Villemez, "Social Class and Criminality," *Social Forces*, 56 (December 1977), 474–502.

[31]Charles W. Tittle, Wayne J. Villemez, and Douglas A. Smith, "The Myth of Social Class and Criminality: An Empirical Assessment of the Empirical Evidence," *American Sociological Review*, 43 (October 1978), 643–56. For detailed critiques of this review, see Donald Clelland and Timothy J. Carter, "The New Myth of Class and Crime," *Criminology*, 18 (November 1980), 319–36; John Braithwaite, "*The Myth of Social Class and Criminality* Reconsidered," *American Sociological Review*, 46 (February 1981), 36–57.

[32]Daniel Bell, "Crime as an American Way of Life," *Antioch Review*, 13 (June 1953), 131–54; The President's Commission on Law Enforcement and Administration of Justice, *The Challenge of Crime in a Free Society*, pp. 22–23.

[33]The President's Commission on Law Enforcement and Administration of Justice, *The Challenge of Crime in a Free Society*, pp. 23–24.

social structure and criminality: mainstream perspectives

Chapter 3 indicated that criminologists often zero in upon crime rates and patterns of criminality, rather than upon the lawbreaking or conformist behavior of particular individuals. Moreover, if we ask virtually any criminologist-sociologist to account for crime, his or her answer is likely to be much the same, namely that certain root causes or criminogenic influences in the social order are responsible for it. It could hardly be otherwise, given that sociologists center their attention upon social structure or social groups and their influence upon individuals. The study of social order is the stuff of sociology as a discipline. Basic to "the sociological imagination" is the assumption that social structure, cultural values, and social processes largely determine the kinds of behavior, whether socially approved or not, exhibited by individuals in different societies. Accordingly, it should come as no surprise to find that criminologists have constructed a number of accounts of the criminogenic features of our own or other societies to which lawbreaking has been attributed.

Chapter 3 commented on the development of criminological thought in American sociology.[1] It is difficult to decide precisely when sociological theorizing about criminality began.[2] However, a good case can be made for dating the development of American criminology from 1918, when Maurice Parmelee's *Criminology* was published, for this was the first comprehensive criminology textbook written in this country.[3] His book was followed by Sutherland's textbook in 1924 and by a number of books thereafter.[4] Most of the pioneers in American criminology took the criminal law as a given and as the codification of morality. Criminals were seen as morally defective members of the "criminal classes." Causal analysis asked how moral weaklings were produced; and etiological hypotheses pointed in the direction of hereditary taint, aberrant family life, or other specific conditions thought to produce defective or amoral persons. Societal defects were either ignored or downplayed.

American criminologists in succeeding decades gradually began to ask complex social questions about the nature of crime and criminals and to offer elaborate sociological accounts of the factors and influences that lead to criminal-law violations. The result is that there is now in existence a *mainstream* sociological perspective on crime causation which is shared by most contemporary criminologists.

One core assumption of mainstream criminology is that most lawbreaking is produced by imperfections, rents and tears, and other structural defects in modern societies. This thesis is expressed in claims that American society and other modern nations are "criminogenic," that is, they contain forms of social structure that engender or produce criminality.

In mainstream criminological analysis, the social order or societal structure is seen as relatively viable. While many contemporary criminologists are quick to concede that social-structural defects play a major role in crime causation, they view these as eradicable through social repair. However, the criminogenic influences which produce criminality are exceedingly pervasive and intimately bound up with the core institutions of modern society. The task of uncovering etiological factors in lawbreaking requires a penetrating examination of many central features of American society.

The contemporary criminologist often projects a cynical or pessimistic stance, growing out of his or her awareness that crime causation is exceedingly complex and extraordinarily difficult to uncover. Then, too, many contemporary criminologists are not markedly optimistic about the prospects for amelioration of crime, given its intricate interweaving in the fabric of society. Finally, the sociologist observes that social organizations often operate in ways quite different from those shown in organizational charts. Many correctional agencies show marked resistance to restructuring along rehabilitative lines. Not infrequently, mainstream criminologists are skeptical about the perfectibility of the criminal-justice and correctional machinery, but they do assume that this apparatus will continue to creak along, doing at least a minimally acceptable job of containing criminality.

Although it makes sense to speak of mainstream criminology as a theoretical entity, it also is clear enough that there is no single position on crime causation that is shared by all criminologists. Instead, there are a number of specific lines of sociological theorizing about criminality which are broadly similar, but which also differ in conceptual details. Mainstream sociological arguments fall into two groupings: those dealing with rates of criminality and social-structural factors that account for them, and those dealing with the processes through which individuals acquire criminal attitudes, norms, and behavior patterns. Chapter 6 examines social-structural arguments, while Chapter 9 takes up a variety of theories of the second kind.[5]

There are a number of ways in which contemporary social-structural theories can be classified. The following sections of this chapter first examine a number of theoretical statements having to do with deviant conduct and criminality. Most contemporary views regarding deviance represent elaborations upon the pioneering works of Emile Durkheim, so we shall begin with his writings and follow with Robert Merton's subsequent elaborations. Following that discussion, attention will turn to theories centered about social disorganization and differential social organization.

These arguments are all general ones that speak of crime in broad terms, with little or no concern for differences between major forms of lawbreaking such as violence, predatory crimes, organized crime, or white-collar criminality. However, some social-structural formulations have been centered upon racial or sexual factors in crime or upon particular patterns of illegal conduct. The latter part of this chapter touches upon some of these more specific or narrow social-structural theories.

Jumping ahead of our story for the moment, we will see that most main-stream theories of crime causation leave much to be desired in terms of clarity and logical structure. Even more important, mainstream formulations have been vigorously lambasted by radical-Marxist criminologists in recent years. The central message of radical critiques is that mainstream theories are critically flawed because they ignore the central role played in criminality by class relations and by the political economy of advanced capitalist nations. Chapter 7 will examine these claims in detail.

theories of deviant behavior

DURKHEIM'S CONTRIBUTIONS[6]

French sociologist Emile Durkheim (1858–1917) was one of the first to insist on the normality of criminality.[7] He maintained that the normal and the pathological are not intrinsically different forms of behavior but rather are labels standing for social distinctions men impose upon behavior. Moreover, Durkheim asserted that it is neither possible nor desirable for a society to repress criminality completely. To do so would be to create a situation inimical to innovation and desirable social changes. In this sense, criminality is functional or desirable behavior.

Why is criminality a natural and inevitable feature of social life? Durkheim pointed out that crimes are matters of social definition. Members of a society condemn behavioral deviations that depart markedly from prevailing norms, singling these out as crimes. The criminal serves as an identifying sign of the limits of permissible behavior. If these major violations of normative sentiments could be repressed, men would become sensitive to the less marked deviations they now overlook, and these acts would then be regarded as crimes. In turn, if these were repressed, even slighter deviations would be elevated to the status of crimes, and so on, in an unending process of crime definition. These increasingly intolerable demands for conformity, which would then be imposed on individuals not now thought of as criminal, would be detrimental to social progress, for "to make progress, individual originality must be able to express itself. In order that the originality of the idealist whose dreams transcend his century may find expression, it is necessary that the originality of the criminal, which is below the level of his time, shall also be possible. One does not occur without the other."[8]

Durkheim's most important contribution to the study of deviant behavior was the theory of *anomie*, originally developed as an explanation of suicide.[9] According to Durkheim, the social needs or desires of humans are potentially insatiable, so collective order (social organization) is necessary as an external regulating force to define and control the goal-seeking of men. If the collective order is disrupted or disturbed, human aspirations may increase to the point of outdistancing all possibilities of fulfillment. At this point, when traditional rules have lost their authority over behavior, a state of deregulation, normlessness, or anomie is said to exist. Durkheim claimed that the regulatory functions of the collective order most commonly break down at the occurrence of sudden depression, sudden prosperity, or rapid technological change, when persons are misled into aspiring to goals extremely difficult if not impossible to achieve. Sudden depressions have this effect because individuals cannot adapt readily to a reduced state of existence. Sudden prosperity is conducive to anomie because it lures some individuals into supposing that they can attain seemingly limitless wealth and achievement. Much the same effect stems from rapid technological change, which instills in some persons imagination of boundless possibilities of achievement. According to Durkheim, these conditions engender pressures toward suicide, particularly in Western industrialized societies.[10]

Durkheim was not concerned about criminality in the theory of anomie. However, Robert K. Merton modified and elaborated on Durkheim's original thesis in a widely noted contemporary theory of deviant behavior which included specific applications to criminal conduct.[11]

MERTON AND ANOMIE THEORY

American sociologist Robert K. Merton developed a rich body of elaborations on Durkheim's original notions regarding the breakdown of regulatory norms and deviant behavior. In turn, others have added to Merton's work in important ways. The resulting body of ideas has served as the most influential formulation on the sociology of deviance over the past 25 years, as attested to by the copious citations in sociological textbooks. Merton has continuously enunciated the sociologist's operating premise that "some unknown but substantial proportion of deviant behavior does not represent impulses of individuals breaking through social controls, but, on the contrary, represents socially induced deviations— deviations which the culture and the social organization conjoin to produce."[12] His work sketched out the details of the processes by which societally generated deviance may come about.

In his analysis, Merton distinguished between two major elements of social and cultural structures: the culturally defined goals human beings are enjoined to pursue, and the social structure that regulates and controls the acceptable modes or means for the pursuit of goals and interests. He noted that goals and institutionalized norms may vary independently of each other, sometimes leading to malintegrated states, one extreme being the instance of excessive stress on goals with little concern for prescribed means. In this case, a condition of "anything goes" prevails, with only considerations of technical expedience governing goal-striving behavior. Merton cited the example of unethical and illegal activities in college athletics, particularly football, in which institutionalized norms have been weakened in favor of excessive concern with certain goals—winning games and profits. The other polar case of goals/means malintegration involves undue emphasis on ritualistic conformity to norms. Between these two extremes are relatively stable societies, with a rough balance between goals and norms.[13]

Merton maintained that contemporary American society is anomic, for it represents the polar type in which success goals are emphasized without equivalent emphasis on institutionalized conduct norms. Merton asserted:

The emphasis upon this set of culture goals is imperfectly integrated with organization of our society, which, as matter of objective and generally recognizable fact, does not provide equal access to those goals for all members of the society. On the contrary, there are heavily graded degrees of access to this, in terms not only of class and ethnic origins, but also in terms of less immediately visible differentials.

Given the composite emphasis of this uniform cultural value of success being enjoined upon all irrespective of origins, and given the fact of a social organization which entails differentials in the availability of this goal, pressure is exerted upon certain classes of individuals to engage in deviant behavior, particularly those classes or strata or groups which have the least direct access to the goal.[14]

Merton's thesis was that the cultural system of American society encourages all citizens to strive for success goals by means of certain normatively regulated or approved forms of behavior. Yet, at the same time, opportunities to reach these goals through socially approved means are unequally distributed. For example, persons at the lower end of the income scale are often precluded from attending college and are thereby shut off from access to socially desirable and well-paying jobs. According to Merton, "It is only when a system of cultural values extols, virtually above all else, certain *common* success-goals for the population at large while the social structure rigorously restricts or completely closes access to approved modes of reaching these goals, *for a considerable part of the same population*, that deviant behavior ensues on a large scale" (emphasis in the original).[15] Merton identified five modes of adaptation to the situation of disjunction: *conformity, innovation, ritualism, retreatism,* and *rebellion.* Innovation is of particular interest to the criminologist, for it refers to cases in which individuals continue to aspire to approved goals, but by means of deviant or illegal techniques. In accounting for the adaptations or directions different individuals take, Merton strongly emphasized variations in class-linked patterns of socialization, arguing that innovative responses are most common among relatively imperfectly socialized persons.

Richard A. Cloward had an important role in the further development of anomie theory. He directed attention to the fact of differentials in *illegitimate* opportunities as well as in legitimate opportunity structures.[16] He pointed out that the forms of deviant behavior are conditional *both* on the goals/means disjunction *and* on the opportunities to engage in deviant conduct. Just as the pros-

pects for achievement of cultural goals through institutionalized means are unequally distributed, so are the opportunities for various kinds of careers in
deviant conduct. For example, the use of drugs depends in part on contacts with
suppliers of illicit narcotics. Similarly, development of a career as a professional
criminal is partially contingent on contact with individuals who will induct the
person into this kind of deviant pattern.

Cloward has also been involved in two major applications of anomie theory
to specific instances of deviant conduct. In the first, he studied a military prison
in which the captors encouraged the prisoners to strive for restoration to active
duty through certain approved forms of conduct summed up in the injunction,
"Do your own time." However, the inmates soon came to understand that the
goal put forth by the administrators was a deception, for only 6 percent of the
prisoners were actually restored to active duty, and even those individuals were
given this status for reasons different from those the officials presented. Cloward
observed that this situation led some to conformist adaptations, whereas other
prisoners followed the pattern of ritualism or passive noncooperation.[17] The Cloward prison report stands as a microcosmic illustration of the societal pattern
described by Merton.

The other application of anomie theory is found in the explanation of gang
or subcultural delinquency by Cloward and Lloyd Ohlin.[18] The essentials of that
theory are as follows: lower-class boys share a common American value commitment to success, measured largely in material terms. But unlike middle-class
youths, they do not have access to legitimate means to attain these success goals.
If they do have access, they perceive their chances of success as limited. Thus,
for many lower-class boys, a severe gap exists between aspiration levels and
expectations. The goals/means disjunction generates pressures to engage in deviant behavior. In turn, the particular deviant adaptation that develops is a function of opportunity structures for delinquent behavior, at least in part. Some
lower-class areas are characterized by integration of criminalistic and conformist
patterns of social organization, whereas others are lacking in stable criminalistic
patterns. In the organized, criminalistic area, criminalistic gang subcultures develop in which boys are involved in instrumental acts of theft and in careers that
often eventually lead to adult criminal behavior. In areas lacking in criminalistic
traditions, gang delinquency tends to take the form of subcultural conflict behavior, in which gang fighting predominates. Finally, some boys, failures in both
the legitimate and illegitimate opportunity arenas, engage in retreatist behavior
and become drug users.

The Mertonian formulation is an elegant, plausible, and appealing one. Ruth
Kornhauser summarized it nicely when she asserted: "The charm of Merton's
strain model consists one-third of its apparent simplicity, one-third in its seem-
ing plausibility, and one-third in its virtual mandate to range sociologists
squarely behind the poor."[19] But, even though the anomie perspective has enjoyed wide popularity, some sociologists have noted a number of points at which

elaboration of the argument is in order. For example, Albert Cohen has argued that the theory is incomplete, for it does not adequately account for the particular kinds of deviance engaged in by different persons, it does not capture the twists and turns taken by many individuals as they drift or blunder into nonconformity, and it says little about group or collective responses to deviance-producing situations.[20]

A number of critics of the anomie perspective have gone much further, subjecting it to a barrage of harsh criticism.[21] For example, Jonathan Turner is one of many who have pointed to its discursive and ambiguous nature, which renders it largely untestable.[22] He also indicated that the formulation fails to spell out the conditions under which one or another adaptation or response to anomie is likely to occur. Parallel complaints were registered by Marvin Scott and Roy Turner, for among other things, they indicated that Merton made no attempt to ascertain the range and variety of real-life forms of nonconformity which might be accounted for by this theory. They also contended that Merton's version of anomie bears little resemblance to the state of affairs described as anomic by Durkheim, in that in the former, anomie centers around a relatively permanent societal condition involving disjunction, while in Durkheim's view, anomie arises during periods of rapid social change and social dislocation.[23]

One of the most telling attacks upon Merton's claims was made by Edwin Lemert, who contended that Merton was guilty of reification when speaking of societal values, for only individuals or groups can properly be said to be carriers of social values.[24] Stated differently, "society" is an abstraction or term which summarizes modal tendencies in the way of behavior of groups and individuals. There is no such thing as a society which exhibits values in any real sense. An even more fundamental point raised by Lemert was that American society is more accurately characterized by value diversity, value pluralism, and conflicts of values among different groups than it is by an overarching set of values shared by most citizens throughout the nation. He pointed to regional and other subcultural groups who are carriers of goals and behavioral standards that often clash with each other and with the criminal laws. Lemert offered a number of examples of value pluralism, such as violation of fish-and game laws by Indians or "moonshining" (illegal production of beverage alcohol) in which deviance arises out of the pursuit of traditional values by some group which has had alien standards imposed upon it. The imagery conjured up by Lemert's discussion is of a society characterized by discordant values existing side by side, with many individuals being pulled and tugged by the behavioral expectations of competing reference groups to which they belong.

Finally, Ruth Kornhauser has focused a cold analytic eye upon the anomie argument and has judged it to be fatally flawed.[25] She drew attention to a host of ambiguities and logical inconsistencies in the theory, as for example, the fact that there is no need to invoke anomie or disjunction to account for deviance on the part of lower-class individuals if, as Merton argued, those persons are weakly socialized. Poorly socialized persons would be likely to take deviant short cuts to goals even if they were not suffering from lack of legitimate opportunities for success, for they would not be restrained by an internalized policeman, that is, moral norms to which they hold allegiance. Kornhauser's assessment of the anomie formulation was a bleak one: "In conclusion, Merton's conception of cultural imbalance is neither viable nor true; it should be pruned from the causal structure of strain theory."[26]

What shall we conclude from this cacophony of praise and criticism directed at the anomie argument? The inescapable conclusion is that the critics have had much the better of it in this exchange. There is little question that Merton put forth an abstract explanatory metaphor, rather than a tightly reasoned, unambiguous set of propositions about deviance. The critics are surely correct in indicting him for failing to spell out the scope of the argument and linking the categories of adaptation to the social labels for deviance familiar in everyday life, such as "bums," "hoods," "winos," "robbers," "pimps," "hustlers," or "crazies."

When we turn our attention to the real world, we quickly discover that it is full of deviants whose activities fall outside the scope of the anomie formulation. Although there is a ring of plausibility to claims that armed robbers are engaged in innovation, gaining material success by illegitimate means, anomie notions can be applied to forcible rape, other assaultive conduct, and myriad other forms of deviance and criminality only with great difficulty, if at all. In short, the anomie argument is an incomplete theory of deviance, at best.

The critics are also on the mark in judging Merton's schema to be inadequate, even when applied to patterns of deviance and lawbreaking to which it seems to have some plausible connection. Put another way, in its present form, the anomie interpretation fails to provide a clear and accurate account of the processes and factors that are involved in deviant activities of any kind.

Does this mean that feelings of frustration over failure to achieve economic goals, which is at the heart of the Mertonian formulation, must be jettisoned from the conceptual cargo of criminology? Goals/means disjunction and anomie are members of a large family of kindred notions such as relative deprivation, economic precariousness, and the like, that have been embraced by criminologists as major explanatory factors, particularly for property crimes carried on by predatory offenders. Should a moratorium be declared on such concepts?

Although there are few if any criminologists and sociologists who embrace the assertion that poverty directly causes crime—or other simpleminded claims about the influence of class and economic influences in lawbreaking—most do regard those factors as major ones in criminality. Moreover, assumptions about the potency of economic factors are buttressed by a wide variety of supporting evidence. What all of the data at hand suggest is that, following Kornhauser's recommendation, Merton's particular conceptualization of the economic-strain–criminality hypothesis ought to be abandoned in favor of some yet-to-be-developed accounts which are free from the flaws that plague the Merton statement. These formulations would continue to place economic influences at center stage.

mainstream theories of criminality

As we have seen, nearly all sociological criminologists follow some basic assumption about criminality: that it is normal in all societies and that lawbreaking is the product of various organizational features of particular nations. Further, most hold that crime rates vary from country to country because of organizational or structural variations. Within a society, specific individuals become criminals or noncriminals as a consequence of their positions in that social system. Most sociologists also agree that the more immediate causes of criminality are found in value patterns, normative systems, conflicting patterns of conduct standards, social-class influences of various kinds, family and peer-group influences, and so forth. Let us examine some versions of this criminogenic-society perspective.

SOCIAL DISORGANIZATION AND CRIME

The concept of social disorganization has had an important place in sociology, particularly in the 1940s and 1950s. The usual definition of social disorganization is a breakdown or disruption in the bonds of relationship, coordination, teamwork, and morale among groups of interrelated persons so as to impair the functions of the society or smaller social organization.[27] The United States and other Western nations have been diagnosed as in various stages of disorganization, and their apparent high crime rates and rates of deviation of other kinds have been linked to that diagnosis.

Analyses of criminality from a social-disorganization viewpoint have often begun by studying systems without serious manifestations of social disorganization, taking them as benchmarks or standards against which to measure the extent of disorganization in industrialized societies. Thus, the antithesis of modern, urban, criminalistic societies is the folk society.

Robert Redfield cited the following elements in describing the folk society: (1) small size, (2) isolation from surrounding cultures, (3) nonliterate population, (4) dependence on folk knowledge, (5) little unconventional behavior, (6) homogeneity of personality types, (7) complex kinship relations, (8) dependence on folkways, and (9) use of informal social controls rather than formal codes of law to control personal behavior.[28] Little nonconforming behavior exists in them because culturally prescribed aspirations and socially structured ways of realizing them are in tune. Little personal insecurity or confusion is engendered, and only slight motivation toward deviant behavior is evident.

The concept of folk society represents an ideal which various cultures resemble in greater or lesser degree. Robert Faris described the characteristics of successful social organizations, as opposed to modern, relatively disorganized systems, in much the same terms: high morale, little personal deviation, and a predominance of integrated customs and folk knowledge, along with informal controls.[29] Both Redfield and Faris found the closest approximations of folk so-cieties mainly in the underdeveloped, agrarian nations of the world. American society probably never approached the ideal of a folk society, but it has become even more unlike that societal organization with each passing decade.

Part of the foregoing argument is that in such a well-organized, consistent society, little personal inconsistency of behavior would be found. In comparison with urban society, personal deviation is uncommon. But we should not suppose that men and women are uniformly molded into one image even in folk societies or that deviations from conventional roles are virtually nonexistent. Nicholas Demerath has reviewed studies of the distribution of schizophrenia among pre-literates and maintained that the early reports by Elsworth Faris and others of an almost total absence of mental disorder are questionable, in light of the de-fective research methods on which those reports were based. Demerath indi-cated that studies have discovered instances of mental disorder of various kinds among primitives. He also suggested that although the data are inadequate for any firm conclusions regarding the relative incidence of mental disorder in one society or another, mental disorder is quite rare in truly primitive groups but increases with the process of acculturation. As a formerly isolated folk group undergoes contact with other societies, certain persons react to culture conflict and marginality of status, with a resulting increase of serious mental aberrations.[30]

A study of a modern counterpart of the folk society, the Hutterites of North America, revealed that mental disorders were not unheard of there. The Hut-terites are an Anabaptist religious sect who live a simple rural life, with a har-monious social organization and considerable economic security. A number of Hutterites had shown symptoms of mental disorder at some point in their lives, so although the authors of study concluded that mental pathology was relatively rare among them, even a well-organized society does not completely prevent deviant behavior.[31]

In contrast to the folk society, the United States and other urbanized nations are complex, dynamic, materialistic, impersonal, and characterized by other fea-tures conducive to widespread crime and other kinds of deviant behavior. Ac-cording to Faris:

The essential feature in the social disorganization that underlies criminality appears to be the partial failure of the normal mechanisms of social control. In a modern secular civili-zation this control is not as strong as in isolated and homogeneous primitive or peasant societies, or as in such religious societies as those of rural Quebec or the early Shaker or Mormon communities. In cities, and particularly in urban slums, the weakening of family and neighborhood controls may be so extreme as to constitute complete failure. In such a situation children who have not already acquired life-organizations based on habits of conventional behavior are, though not inevitably delinquent, at least easily subject to the positive influences of the boy gangs, "fences," and the organized rewards of underworld criminal organizations. . . .

General confusion of standards in our changing contemporary society is also a factor in the encouragement of criminal behavior. The underworld organization of professional criminals is provided with important support by the noncriminal citizen who vigorously insists upon his right to consume prohibited beverages or drugs, to engage in illegal gambling, to purchase goods in evasion of rationing and price regulations, and the like. "Rights" of different kinds and of different origins have come into conflict, and no unified code is accepted by the mass of the population. In this confusion it becomes easy to make and to rationalize moral decisions on the basis of individual interest.[32]

Unfortunately, the concept of social disorganization is itself disorganized. Merton has provided one of the clearest definitions of this concept: "Social disorganization refers to inadequacies or failures in a social system of interrelated statuses and roles such that the collective purposes and individual objectives of its members are less fully realized than they could be in an *alternative workable system*" (emphasis added).[33] Application of this definition to real-life situations would require that collective purposes and individual objectives of members of a society be readily apparent to different sociologists. But many would argue that the purposes and objectives are problematic and by no means obvious. The question of alternative workable systems would provoke considerable controversy among different observers. To classify American society as disorganized, using this definition, we must entertain some picture of a more harmonious and attainable system. Although such an alternative image of organization compatible with the major value orientations of Americans might be conjured up, its outlines are certainly not clearly visible to all.

Critics of social disorganization notions have also suggested that applications to real-life situations have often been tautological, the same behavior to be explained by disorganization being used to demonstrate the existence of that state of affairs. Also, few specific propositions to account for forms of pathological behavior have been derived from the general theory of social disorganization.[34] Over the life history of social-disorganization formulations, the major objection has been that the notions are judgmental. Nearly all sociologists agree that modern industrialized societies represent an amalgam of competing value patterns and normative systems, of different social strata with varied life styles, and of subcultures and contracultures of one kind or another. The diversified, pluralistic character of modern societies is not at issue. But, many of the conditions considered as examples of disorganization or unorganization represent, instead, alternative systems of organization yielding satisfactions to the individuals who are their constituents.[35] For these reasons, the drift of thinking in recent decades has been away from disorganization views and toward stress on complexity and differential social organization.

CULTURE CONFLICT AND CRIME

Although those who have spoken of social disorganization have fallen silent, due to the now-plain deficiencies of that viewpoint, this broad theme has kept reappearing in slightly different form. The criminogenic culture thesis has not disappeared, rather, it has simply been recycled. For example, Thorsten Sellin advanced these ideas many years ago in the argument that crime is caused by culture conflict.[36] He was particularly impressed by the part presumably played in crime by the clash of cultural values resulting from the immigration and mobility widespread in America in the 1800s and early 1900s. Similarly, Donald Taft and Ralph England articulated another version of the root-causes perspective, arguing that value conflicts, impersonality, individualism, disrespect for law and order, exploitativeness, and other ingredients central to the American way of life make widespread criminality an inevitable by-product of that cultural system.[37] All of these theoretical statements were limned with broad strokes, so that while they are reasonably plausible, none of them tell us much about the ways in which these criminogenic conditions actually enter into particular forms of lawbreaking or precisely how they operate to cause criminality.

DIFFERENTIAL SOCIAL ORGANIZATION

Edwin Sutherland stands out in the development of American criminology, largely because of his theory of differential association which contends that persons learn criminal-conduct definitions and behavior patterns through the same basic learning process by which others acquire noncriminal roles. However, Sutherland and Donald Cressey were also attentive to the other side of the coin, namely, the social-structural question of why criminal norms and criminal activities are widely available to be learned in the first place. Their answer was a relatively well-developed version of the criminogenic-culture thesis, which they termed a theory of "differential social organization."[38]

The differential-social-organization argument flows along the following lines. First, Sutherland and Cressey put forth a folk-culture view holding that in nonliterate and peasant societies the social influences which surround persons are relatively uniform, harmonious, and consistent. Societies of that kind, exemplified by nineteenth-century China, exhibit little crime.

But, according to Sutherland and Cressey, complex, modern societies show differential social organization, that is, normative conflict stemming from social pluralism. The social heterogeneity of modern societies leads to normative incongruence in which the influences that play upon persons are often relatively inharmonious and inconsistent. For example, the same individual who is an upstanding, respected member of his local church may also be engaged in "sharp" business practices in the sale of used cars because of the economic pressures experienced by automobile dealers. It is this state of affairs that is designated as differential social organization. And, it is in societies that are characterized by differential social organization that opportunities and pressures leading to the learning of criminal norms are widespread.

What is responsible for the shift of societies from the folk-society pattern to one of differential social organization? Sutherland and Cressey indicated that these changes took place over a long time period, starting with the breakdown of the feudal order in Europe, including the destruction of a system of fixed social classes and mutual responsibilities which restrained most persons from acts of misconduct. The Industrial Revolution led to capitalism and inordinate cultural emphasis upon individualism and acquisitiveness. Personal wealth became the standard by which all people were measured. According to Sutherland and Cressey, in complex industrial societies and in the United States in particular, a cultural system which argues that upward mobility and achievement are open to all coexists with a social structure which sets severe limits upon the life chances of many citizens, so that many individuals are systematically deprived of economic opportunities because of racial and other barriers. Those who feel the sting of relative deprivation most sharply become candidates for deviance and lawbreaking. The reader will doubtless note the closeness of this view to Merton's anomie formulation.

In their elaboration of this theory, Sutherland and Cressey also drew attention to the existence of different subcultures and social groups with varying social values; these have arisen at different locations in the social structure of modern societies. It is this fact of regional and other kinds of social pluralism which goes some distance toward accounting for the varied patterns of crime that are observed in different parts of American communities, different regions, and so on. Finally, Sutherland and Cressey argued that modern societies are characterized by marked forms of spatial and social mobility, in which individuals are often cut off from dense social ties, whether of family, kinship groups, or other social collectivities. As a consequence, the informal social ties and controls which keep most persons in simple societies from straying from the path of conformity have become attenuated, thus allowing individuals to more easily drift into lawbreaking.

special theories of crime

The theoretical contentions examined up to this point are all general ones, in that they endeavor to make sense of crime without attending in detail to the features that set garden-variety, predatory property crime off from violent offenses, organized crime, white-collar lawbreaking, or other major forms of criminality. Then, too, these general theories usually incorporate into their fabric a number of broad influences such as mobility, economic frustration, and the like. However, criminologists have also crafted a number of more specific or special theories of crime, dealing in detail with some particular societal condition such as sexism or racism, or with a particular form of lawbreaking. Let us examine a sampling of these special theories.

RACISM AND CRIME

As Chapter 5 indicated, blacks in the United States have considerably higher rates of arrest for major crimes than do whites, particularly for such offenses as homicide, forcible rape, aggravated assault, robbery, weapons charges, prostitution, and gambling. How do we explain this apparent excessive criminality among blacks?

One line of sociological exposition holds that some significant portion of black offenders are victims of *differential law enforcement*. A number of studies, such as those by Nathan Goldman,[39] Irving Piliavin and Scott Briar,[40] and Theodore Ferdinand and Elmer Luchterhand,[41] demonstrate that police often deal with black youths more harshly than with white youngsters. Other crime differentials between blacks and whites also probably reflect unequal enforcement of law. Prostitution and gambling arrests are cases in point; a good deal of commonsense observation suggests that the police differentially enforce the laws against blacks involved in these forms of lawbreaking. In addition, blacks are frequently the targets of gratuitous physical force used against them by the police.

Arguments that stress unequal application of the law do not deny that black citizens are involved in criminality but, rather, point out that arrest rates and other measures of involvement in lawbreaking are inflated for blacks because of racism, manifested in discriminatory operation of the police, courts, and correctional agencies.

Let us assume, as most authorities do, that even after we allow for differential law enforcement, American blacks do have higher rates of involvement in many kinds of crimes than do whites. If so, how do we explain this excess?[42] Certainly not in terms of the patently false theory that black crime is racially determined. This contention holds that blacks are members of a biologically primitive race, innately inclined toward crime. Because they cannot exercise control over their emotions, they engage in crimes of violence; because they lack moral commitment to property rights, they are uninhibited from engaging in property offenses. Views of this kind hardly square with observations that most American blacks show mixed racial heritage and are not members of a biologically pure type, that crime rates vary among different black social-class groups, or that crime rates are much lower among African blacks than among American blacks.

Those who reject biological explanations usually lean toward some theory holding that various forms of social and economic discrimination in American society are indirectly bound up in black criminality and represent the root causes of it. In the most dramatic expression of this argument, black crime is the product of endemic racism and oppression in American society.

What does it mean to say that United States is a racist society? How does racial oppression lead to crime? These are extremely broad questions, but their answers lie in the following historical directions.

To begin with, oppression of blacks began with enslavement of Africans by Europeans in the fifteenth century. The first black slaves were brought to America in 1619. By the time of the Revolutionary War, several hundred thousand black slaves were in America.[43]

Black slaves in the United States were dealt with as property rather than as

humans. Slavemasters deliberately broke up black families, creating family instability among blacks which has persisted up the present. As Andrew Billingsley
observed:

> In short, there was the absence, in the United States, of societal support and protection
> for the Negro family as a physical, psychological, social, or economic unit. This crippled
> the development, not only of individual slaves, but of families, and hence of the whole
> society of Negro people. The consequences of these conditions wrought for generations
> of Negroes under the slave system were direct and insidious. The consequences for suc-
> ceeding and even modern generations of Negroes are, perhaps, less direct, but no less
> insidious.[44]

After slavery, various attempts were made to maintain blacks under conditions of oppression and to exclude them from the mainstream of society. In the
South, the "separate but equal" system of schools and other social institutions
worked to keep blacks mired in rural poverty and inferior social status. Individuals who dared to fight against this system ran the risk of reprisals, such as a
visit from Ku Klux Klan night riders. Intimidation, including the lynching of
Southern blacks, has been a continuing part of the postslavery experience, persisting even up to the present.[45] For example, between 1961 and 1965, 150
incidents of major violence were directed at blacks in Mississippi. During the
summer of 1965 in that state alone, 35 shootings, 30 bombings, 35 church burn-
ings, 80 beatings, and at least 6 murders were related to civil-rights activities.[46]

Racism outside the South took other, more subtle but pervasive forms.
Some authorities have characterized this situation as one of colonization.[47] Robert Blauner argued:

> There appear to be four basic components of the colonization complex. . . . Colonization
> begins with a forced, involuntary entry. Second, there is an impact on the culture and
> social organization of the colonized people which is more than just a result of such "nat-
> ural" processes as contact and acculturation. The colonizing power carries out a policy
> which constrains, transforms, or destroys indigenous values, orientations, and ways of
> life. Third, colonization involves a relationship by which members of the colonized group
> tend to be administered by representatives of the dominant power. . . . a final funda-
> mental of colonization is racism . . . by which a group seen as inferior or different in
> terms of alleged biological characteristics is exploited, controlled, and oppressed socially
> and psychologically by a superordinate group.[48]

Exploitation and oppression of American blacks outside the South has been
manifested in a variety of ways. Blacks have been the victims of systematic discrimination in employment. Because of low incomes and discriminatory housing
policies, blacks have received inferior educations in ghetto schools, which ill-
equip them for success-striving and upward mobility. Finally, the sting of relative deprivation suffered by contemporary blacks is probably more deeply felt
because of the general affluence of American society, which has intensified the
deprived condition of blacks.[49]

These conditions of racism and exploitation provide the warrant for speaking of criminogenic influences within black society. The basic argument is plausible enough: these conditions exert massive pressures on blacks to engage in lawbreaking. Economic pressures are the cause of property crimes among blacks; while crimes of violence are the outgrowth of neighborhood conditions of disorder and weak social ties among black citizens. In a broad and general way, this theory of racism and black crime is correct. Also, if this formulation captures the root causes of black crime, those causes are ultimately attributed to racial oppression and other defects of the encompassing society within which American blacks live. Black crime is a consequence of white racism.

The problem with this theorizing is that it is incomplete. We ultimately want to know more about the causes of lawbreaking among black citizens. How do these conditions of discrimination and oppression get "inside the heads" of black offenders, so to speak? What are the more specific dynamics lying behind different forms of criminality in which blacks engage? We shall take up such questions in detail in succeeding chapters, where we begin to examine the causal processes operating in particular forms of criminality.

OTHER SPECIAL THEORIES

Modern criminology includes a number of other special theories dealing with particular criminogenic factors or with specific forms of criminality. Most of these special formulations turn up in the chapters ahead that deal with major patterns of crime. It might be useful, however, to make brief mention now of two specialized versions of the criminogenic-society thesis.

The first variant of the root-causes argument centers about predatory property crime, particularly the relatively crude and unsophisticated versions of it. The offenders who engage in that form of lawbreaking are often thought to be the products of long-term exposure to criminalistic influences in inner-city neighborhoods, thus many of them are gang delinquents grown up. Economic precariousness and feelings of relative deprivation, along with deleterious social conditions that are said to surround inner-city residents, are assigned major importance in most theories endeavoring to account for predatory offenders. Arguments of this kind will be examined in detail in Chapter 12, where attention turns to predatory property crime.

The second variant centers about the subcultures-of-violence thesis, which holds that homicides and assaults are often carried out by individuals who show allegiance to such a subculture. Proponents of this perspective argue that subcultures of violence are social collectivities that share attitudes and norms, that view outside individuals with suspicion as potential assailants, and in which interpersonal violence receives social approval as a dispute-settling technique. Also, theoretically, violent subcultures are centered in certain regions of the South, in inner-city neighborhoods in major metropolitan communities, and in certain other social and ecological niches in American society.

We will return to the subcultures-of-violence thesis in Chapter 13, where the validity of this argument as an explanation of homicides and assaults will be probed. Chapter 13 will also take up a closely related thesis, namely, that forcible rape and certain other sexual offenses are also influenced by subcultural values. Applied to forcible rape, this argument holds that sexual assaults are most frequently carried out by persons who have grown up in social circumstances in which many young males look upon sexual activity in aggressive terms and hold females in low esteem, hence they are less restrained from sexual assaults than persons who have not come into contact with these subcultural viewpoints.

Other specific theories of criminality have been developed to account for business or white-collar crime and also for organized crime involving racketeering, vice, and other activities. These kinds of lawbreaking and the explanatory accounts developed around them are the subjects of Chapters 14 and 15. Additionally, criminologists have devoted attention to various kinds of relatively petty, low-visibility "folk crimes" in American society and to explanations for that kind of conduct, although criminological concern has not been commensurate with the magnitude and importance of this activity. Hypotheses and evidence about folk crime are the focus of Chapter 16. Finally, in recent years, there has been a resurgence of criminological interest in female criminality, with some authorities arguing that crime rates and crime patterns among women have changed markedly in the recent past. Chapter 17 will examine these arguments and the supporting evidence that can be marshalled concerning them.

summary

At this point, the task of scrutinizing sociological theories identifying criminogenic conditions or the root causes of crime is half-complete, for in this chapter we have already explored many such lawbreaking and social-structure concepts which are accepted by the majority of contemporary criminologists.

The commentary in this chapter indicated that most social-structural theories are sketchy and relative ambiguous. Certain of them, and the anomie argument in particular, are hopelessly flawed. Although research evidence can be assembled which seems broadly consistent with some of the other formulations, it is difficult to visualize a crucial or definitive empirical test of them.

Even though mainstream criminological arguments do not measure up when judged according to advanced scientific standards, it is possible to arrive at some tentative conclusions about the validity of these perspectives. Some critics of mainstream formulations have contended that these theories are, at the least, incomplete, because they do not attend to some new forms of criminality that are emerging in American society, including acts of social protest involving destruction of property, vandalism, and the like; hedonistic activities taking a criminal form; and certain other new kinds of crime.[50] However, the most serious and sustained attacks have come from a small group of radical-Marxist criminologists. These critics have argued that mainstream theories are markedly defective, if not completely in error, because they disguise or obfuscate the criminogenic features of advanced capitalism which drive persons to lawbreaking through economic oppression. Although mainstream theorists pirouette around the margins of this causal complex, they never penetrate to the center of these ideas. Stated another way, the radical-Marxist complaint is that mainstream viewpoints blur the factor of economic oppression sufficiently that most of us fail to perceive the ways in which the political-economic structure of advanced capitalism engenders lawbreaking.

Whatever the merits of these charges against mainstream criminology, it cannot be argued that radical-Marxist theorists have developed full-blown, mature alternative perspectives on criminality. As we shall see in Chapter 7, many of the radical diagnoses of the criminogenic features of American society are sketchy, overdrawn, and filled with hyperbole. Even so, these are claims that must be taken seriously and it is to them that we now turn.

notes

¹The development of American criminology is dealt with in detail in Don C. Gibbons, *The Criminological Enterprise* (Englewood Cliffs, N.J.: Prentice-Hall, Inc., 1979). Also see Gibbons and Peter G. Garabedian, "Conservative, Liberal, and Radical Criminology: Some Trends and Observations," in *The Criminologist: Crime and the Criminal*, Charles E. Reasons, ed. (Pacific Palisades, Calif.: Goodyear Publishing Co., 1974), pp. 51–65; and Travis Hirschi and David Rudisill, "The Great American Search: Causes of Crime, 1876–1976," *Annals of the American Academy of Political and Social Science*, 423 (January 1976), 14–22.

²Charles Richmond Henderson's *Introduction to the Study of the Dependent, Neglected, and Delinquent Classes* (Boston: D.C. Heath, 1893) may provide one date (1893) for the beginnings of sociological interest in criminality.

³Maurice F. Parmelee, *Criminology* (New York: Macmillan, 1918).

⁴Edwin H. Sutherland, *Criminology* (Philadelphia: Lippincott, 1924).

⁵Varieties of mainstream criminological thought are discussed in Gresham M. Sykes, "The Future of Criminality," *American Behavioral Scientist*, 15 (February 1972), 409–19. Also see Gibbons, *The Criminological Enterprise*.

⁶Emile Durkheim, *Suicide*, trans. J. A. Spaulding and George Simpson (New York: Free Press, 1951); Durkheim, *The Rules of Sociological Method*, George E. G. Catlin, ed. (Chicago: University of Chicago Press, 1938). For excerpts from Durkheim's work relevant to the discussion here, see Lewis A. Coser and Bernard Rosenberg, eds., *Sociological Theory: A Book of Readings*, 2nd ed. (New York: Macmillan, 1964), pp. 539–48.

⁷Durkheim, *The Rules of Sociological Method*, pp. 65–75.

⁸Coser and Rosenberg, *Sociological Theory*, p. 588. For a somewhat related theme, holding that punishment of crime is functional for the affirmation of social solidarity, see George Herbert Mead, "The Psychology of Punitive Justice," *American Journal of Sociology*, 23 (March 1918), 585–92. For elaborations of this theme regarding functional consequences of deviance, see Lewis A. Coser, "Some Functions of Deviant Behavior and Normative Flexibility," *American Journal of Sociology*, 68 (September 1962), 172–81. But also see Travis Hirschi, "Procedural Rules and the Study of Deviance," *Social Problems*, 21 (Fall 1973), 161–63, for some critical observations on the claims advanced by Coser and others relative to the alleged social functions of deviance.

[9]Durkheim, *Suicide*, pp. 247–57.

[10]For some important discussions of Durkheim's theory, see Marvin E. Olsen, "Durkheim's Two Concepts of Anomie," *Sociological Quarterly*, 6 (Winter 1965), 37–44; A. R. Mawson, "Durkheim and Contemporary Social Pathology," *British Journal of Sociology*, 21 (September 1970), 298–311; John Horton, "The Dehumanization of Anomie and Alienation: A Problem in the Ideology of Sociology," *British Journal of Sociology*, 15 (December 1964), 283–300.

[11]Robert K. Merton, *Social Theory and Social Structure*, rev. ed. (New York: Free Press, 1957), pp. 131–94; Merton, "Social Conformity, Deviation, and Opportunity Structures: A Comment on the Contributions of Dubin and Cloward," *American Sociological Review*, 24 (April 1959), 177–89; Merton, "The Social-Cultural Environment and Anomie," in *New Perspectives for Research on Juvenile Delinquency*, Helen L. Witmer and Ruth Kotinsky, eds. (Washington, D.C.: U.S. Department of Health, Education and Welfare, 1955), pp. 24–50; Merton, "Anomie, Anomia, and Social Interaction: Contexts of Deviant Behavior," in *Anomie and Deviant Behavior*, Marshall B. Clinard, ed. (New York: Free Press, 1964), pp. 213–42.

[12]Merton, "The Social-Cultural Environment and Anomie," p. 29.

[13]Merton, *Social Theory and Social Structure*, pp. 131–36.

[14]Merton, "The Social-Cultural Environment and Anomie," p. 30.

[15]Merton, *Social Theory and Social Structure*, p. 146.

[16]Richard A. Cloward, "Illegitimate Means, Anomie, and Deviant Behavior," *American Sociological Review*, 24 (April 1959), 164–76.

[17]Witmer and Kotinsky, *New Perspectives for Research on Juvenile Delinquency*, pp. 80–92.

[18]Richard A. Cloward and Lloyd E. Ohlin, *Delinquency and Opportunity* (New York: Free Press, 1960). For an inventory of empirical and theoretical studies of anomie, see Stephen Cole and Harriet Zuckerman, "Appendix: Inventory of Empirical and Theoretical Studies of Anomie," in Clinard, *Anomie and Deviant Behavior*, pp. 243–313.

[19]Ruth Rosner Kornhauser, *Social Sources of Delinquency* (Chicago: University of Chicago Press, 1978), p. 143.

[20]Albert K. Cohen, "The Sociology of the Deviant Act: Anomie and Beyond," *American Sociological Review*, 30 (February 1965), 5–14.

[21]Criticisms of the anomie argument are summarized in Don C. Gibbons and Joseph F. Jones, *The Study of Deviance* (Englewood Cliffs, N.J.: Prentice-Hall, Inc., 1965), pp. 70–72.

[22]Jonathan H. Turner, *The Structure of Sociological Theory*, rev. ed. (Homewood, Ill.: Dorsey Press, 1978), pp. 83–91.

[23]Marvin B. Scott and Roy Turner, "Weber and the Anomic Theory of Deviance," *Sociological Quarterly*, 6 (Summer 1965), 233–40.

[24]Edwin M. Lemert, *Human Deviance, Social Problems, and Social Control*, 2nd ed. (Englewood Cliffs, N.J.: Prentice-Hall, Inc., 1972), pp. 26–61. Also see Jack D. Douglas, "Deviance and Order in a Pluralistic Society," in *Theoretical Sociology*, John C. McKinney and Edward A. Tiryakian, eds. (New York: Prentice-Hall, Inc., 1970), pp. 367–401.

[25]Kornhauser, Social *Sources of Delinquency*, pp. 143–80.

[26]Ibid., p. 165.

[27]Robert E. L. Faris, *Social Disorganization*, 2nd ed. (New York: The Ronald Press, 1955), pp. 3–83.

[28]Robert Redfield, "The Folk Society," *American Journal of Sociology*, 52 (January 1947), 293–308. For a detailed critique of the folk/urban argument, see Horace Miner, "The Folk-Urban Continuum," *American Sociological Review*, 17 (October 1952), 529–37.

[29]Faris, *Social Disorganization*, pp. 3–33.

[30]Nicholas J. Demerath, "Schizophrenia Among Primitives," *American Journal of Psychiatry*, 98 (March 1942), 703–7. For a large body of evidence indicating that deviance is not uncommon in simple societies, see Robert B. Edgerton, *Deviance: A Cross-Cultural Perspective* (Menlo Park, Cal.: Cummings Publishing Co., 1976).

[31]Joseph W. Eaton and Robert J. Weil, "The Mental Health of the Hutterites," in *Mental Health and Mental Disorder*, Arnold Rose, ed. (New York: W. W. Norton & Co., 1955); see also Herbert

Goldhamer and Andrew W. Marshall, *Psychoses and Civilization* (New York: Free Press, 1953).

[32]Faris, *Social Disorganization*, p. 246.

[33]Robert K. Merton, "Social Problems and Sociological Theory," in *Contemporary Social Problems*, 3rd ed., Merton and Robert Nisbet, eds. (New York: Harcourt Brace Jovanovich, 1971), pp. 819–20.

[34]Edwin M. Lemert, *Social Pathology* (New York: McGraw-Hill, 1951), pp. 7–10.

[35]As one case illustrating the functional utility of crime, see Daniel Bell, "Crime as an American Way of Life," *Antioch Review*, 13 (June 1953), 131–54.

[36]Thorsten Sellin, *Culture Conflict and Crime* (New York: Social Science Research Council, 1938).

[37]Donald R. Taft and Ralph W. England, Jr., *Criminology*, 4th ed. (New York: Macmillan, 1964), pp. 277–79.

[38]Edwin H. Sutherland and Donald R. Cressey, *Criminology*, 10th ed. (Philadelphia: Lippincott, 1978), pp. 99–117.

[39]Nathan Goldman, *The Differential Selection of Juvenile Offenders for Court Appearance* (New York: National Council on Crime and Delinquency, 1963).

[40]Irving Piliavin and Scott Briar, "Police Encounters with Juveniles," *American Journal of Sociology*, 70 (September 1964), 206–14.

[41]Theodore N. Ferdinand and Elmer G. Luchterhand, "Inner-City Youth, the Police, the Juvenile Court, and Justice," *Social Problems*, 17 (Spring 1970), 510–27; also see Terence P. Thornberry, "Race, Socioeconomic Status and Sentencing in the Juvenile Justice System," *Journal of Criminal Law and Criminology*, 64 (March 1973), 90–98.

[42]For a review of theories and evidence on racial variations in crime, see Sutherland and Cressey, *Criminology*, pp. 137–55. Also see John A. Davis, "Blacks, Crime, and American Culture," *Annals of the American Academy of Political and Social Science*, 423 (January 1976), 89–98.

[43]A lesser-known fact of history is that a runaway black slave, Crispus Attucks, was the first person killed in the Boston massacre of 1770, an important incident leading up to the Revolutionary War.

[44]Andrew Billingsley, *Black Families in White America* (Englewood Cliffs, N.J.: Prentice-Hall, Inc., 1968), pp. 68–69. For a theory attributing delinquency to family instability among blacks, see Walter B. Miller, "Lower Class Culture as a Generating Milieu of Gang Delinquency," *Journal of Social Issues*, 14, no. 3 (1958), 5–19.

[45]One famous and dramatic case of discriminatory justice directed at Southern blacks was the Scottsboro incident. See Haywood Patterson and Earl Conrad, *Scottsboro Boy* (New York: Doubleday, 1950).

[46]U.S. Commission on Civil Rights, *Law Enforcement: A Report on Equal Protection in the South* (Washington, D.C.: U.S. Government Printing Office, 1965).

[47]Robert Blauner, "Internal Colonialism and Ghetto Revolt," *Social Problems*, 16 (Spring 1969), 393–408. For one application of this argument to black crime, see Robert Staples, "White Racism, Black Crime, and American Justice: An Application of the Colonial Model to Explain Crime," *Phylon*, 36 (March 1975), 14–22.

[48]Blauner, "Internal Colonialism and Ghetto Revolt," p. 396.

[49]Jackson Toby, "The Prospects for Reducing Delinquency Rates in Industrial Societies," *Federal Probation*, 27 (December 1963), 23–25.

[50]Gresham M. Sykes, "The Future of Criminality," *American Behavioral Scientist*, 15 (February 1972), 409–19.

social
structure
and criminality:
new directions

It was philosopher Thomas Kuhn who, a number of years ago, argued that scientific fields move ahead, not by slow, steady, incremental steps, but by major breakthroughs followed by periods of "normal science."[1] According to Kuhn, scientific revolutions come about when new *paradigms* are developed which put facts in a startling new light, so that major new discoveries flow from paradigm revolutions. The notion of paradigms refers to broad theoretical perspectives or ways of looking at the world that are characteristic of particular scientific fields.

In the past decade or so, a number of sociologists have taken to speaking of sociological paradigms, paradigm shifts, and of sociology as a multiparadigmatic field characterized by lack of consensus on its basic views of the world. While there is more than a little doubt about the applicability of Kuhn's notion of scientific paradigm to fields such as sociology, characterized as they are by extremely fuzzy and vague theorizing, there is little question that sociological orientations do wax and wane in importance, often quite independently of any hard evidence that might be brought to bear upon them. So, too, it is with criminology, for the explanatory schemes that have been in vogue at different times in the history of this field of study have varied.

The most recent candidate as the new criminological paradigm has been called variously "Marxist," "radical," "critical," "conflict," and "new" criminology. These terms have often been used interchangeably, which might imply that there is a single new criminological perspective which is meant to replace the mainstream viewpoints reviewed in the previous chapter.

However, the newer orientations in criminology are not all identical. Instead, some formulations stressing social conflict as the major force behind lawmaking and lawbreaking preceded modern radical-Marxist views and differ importantly from the latter, although the dividing point between social-conflict arguments and radical-Marxist theories is not always clear and distinct.

Our focus in this chapter will first be upon conflict and interest-group theories, followed by an extended examination of the major claims of radical-Marxist criminology.[2] This order of presentation makes sense because general conflict theories developed earlier than did radical-Marxist viewpoints. The reader may recall that we have already encountered one facet of these newer views in Chapter 4, where we took up interest-group and radical claims about the social origins of criminal laws.

Although the concern of this chapter is with contemporary criminological theories, it would be well to note that, contrary to some of the claims made by radical criminologists, the pioneers of American criminology were not totally oblivious to the role of social conflict in the creation of laws and lawbreakers. Comments in this direction appeared in Parmelee's 1918 book, in Sellin's extended discussion of culture conflict and crime, and in some of Sutherland's writings. A relatively well-developed version of conflict theory was contained in Vold's 1958 volume.[3]

Why have conflict views become more prominent in the past decade or so? How can we account for the radicalization of criminology, in which a sizable number of criminologists have turned to radical-Marxist perspectives? In brief, the answer is that these trends mirror the increase of social conflict in the real world, at least in part. We live in a changing world which mainstream theories of crime causation often seem to misrepresent.

conflict and interest-group theories in criminology[4]

Conflict and interest-group theories have emphasized lawmaking and enforcement activities more than social-structural sources of criminality. These arguments attribute lawmaking and crime to a relatively diffuse and pluralistic pattern of conflicting interest-group activities and phenomena in American society, rather than to a monolithic political-economic structure dominated by a national ruling class. For example, Stuart Hills has argued:

In a rapidly changing pluralistic society such as the United States, however—with its racial, religious, ethnic, and class diversity; its sharply competing economic and political interest groups; its conflicting life styles and value orientations among different subcultures; and its frequent recourse to the criminal law to regulate and prohibit a wide variety of behavior—the interest-group perspective would seem more useful in understanding the enactment and selective enforcement of law involving marijuana use, organized crime, and white-collar crime.[5]

Austin Turk is a major conflict theorist who regards the search for answers to the question "Why do they do it?" as a relatively futile one and has argued that "nothing and no one is intrinsically criminal; criminality is a definition applied by individuals with the power to do so, according to illegal and extralegal, as well as legal criteria."[6] Lawbreaking cannot be distinguished from conformity, except for the reactions of authorities who have applied criminal status to some people. The implications of this perspective are far-reaching.

Turk had much to say about social order in modern societies, arguing that the prevailing situation is one of conflict among different groups who all seek to gain social and material advantages over each other. These conflicts are kept under control in part through legal norms and patterns of norm enforcement which the *authorities* (those in dominant social positions) impose on the *subjects* (those in relatively powerless groups). Successful authority-subject relations are predicated on the submission of the relatively powerless to the authorities, rather than being maintained by coercion. Accordingly, "lawbreaking is taken to be an indicator of the failure or lack of authority; it is a measure of the extent to which rulers and ruled, decision-makers and decision-acceptors, are not bound together in a perfectly stable relationship."[7]

Turk dealt at length with the conditions under which cultural and social differences between authorities and subjects are likely to result in conflict and under which criminalization will likely occur. "Criminalization" is the assignment of criminal status to people through the norm-enforcement mechanisms of arrest and trial.

Turk's argument was abstract and relatively silent on a number of important issues. For example, at one point he indicated that how authorities come to be authorities is irrelevant. But, as we shall see later in this chapter, this is a fundamental question on which mainstream and radical criminologists disagree. Radical theorists argue that effective power in American society is monopolized by members of a corporate ruling class, which is a very different view from that espoused by mainstream criminologists, including conflict theorists such as Turk who opt for a pluralistic conception of interest groups and power relationships in modern society.

A second perspective on crime, law, and social control has been put forth by William Chambliss and Robert Seidman.[8] They contended that criminal laws in complex societies reflect value antagonisms and value pluralism, in which the interests of the socially powerful are most likely to become incorporated into criminal statutes. They argued, too, that criminal laws and other legal norms are most frequently applied to those who lack social power. They took note of the role of value conflicts in the work of legislatures, arguing that lawmaking is most often a response of the demands of socially powerful groups, thus: "Deviancy is not a moral question; it is a political question."[9]

A final example of conflict theory is found in Richard Quinney's propositions regarding the social reality of crime.

1. Crime is a definition of human conduct that is created by authorized agents in a politically organized society.
2. Criminal definitions describe behaviors that conflict with the interests of the segments of society that have the power to shape public policy.
3. Criminal definitions are applied by the segments of society that have the power to shape the enforcement and administration of criminal law.
4. Behavior patterns are structured in segmentally organized society in relation to criminal definitions, and within this context persons engage in actions that have relative probabilities of being defined as criminal.
5. Conceptions of crime are constructed and diffused in the segments of society by various means of communication.
6. The social reality of crime is constructed by the formulation and application of criminal definitions, the development of behavior patterns related to criminal definitions, and the construction of criminal conceptions.[10]

The most fundamental criticism directed at Quinney's views has also been leveled at other conflict theorists, namely, that their models describe pluralistic conceptions of social conflicts, interest groups, and social structure. Consider Quinney's remarks on the institutional orders within which interests operate:

> For our use, these may be called: (1) the *political*, which regulates the distribution of power and authority in a society; (2) the *economic*, which regulates the production and distribution of goods and services; (3) the *religious*, which regulates the relationship of man to a conception of the supernatural; (4) the *kinship*, which regulates sexual relations, family patterns, and the procreation and rearing of children; (5) the *educational*, which regulates the formal training of the society's members; and (6) the *public*, which regulates the protection and maintenance of the community and its citizens. Each segment of society has its own orientation to these orders. Some, because of their authority position in the interest structure, are able to have their interests represented in public policy.[11]

Arguments of this kind fail to acknowledge the overpowering significance of class relationships growing out of productive arrangements in societies, which lead to monopolization of effective power by a ruling class rather than myriad interest groups.[12]

Some of those who have espoused conflict views have been unwavering in support of these themes, but Chambliss and Quinney have since modified their perspectives, rejecting pluralistic views of social order in favor of Marxist arguments stressing class relations and ruling-class domination. Let us turn to their views and those of other radical-Marxist theorists.

radical-marxist theories in criminology

THE ORIGINS OF RADICAL CRIMINOLOGY

Although conflict-oriented views in criminology that stress the pluralistic nature of American society have existed at least in rudimentary form for some time, only within the past 15 years has a thoroughly radical, Marxist version of criminological thought emerged. For the most part, this new brand of theorizing has been an American and English invention, for there is little in the way of contemporary Marxist criminology elsewhere.[13]

What produced the radicalization of criminologists and criminological thought? Why have Marxist views of crime captured the attention of many criminologists, particularly relatively young ones? Is it because existing explanatory paradigms have persistently failed to deal with new empirical facts that have come to light? The new facts behind the emergence of radical criminology have arisen from the world of social events outside the discipline of sociology, not from criminological research studies that have turned up puzzling results.

One report on radical criminology asserted that it "appeared on the crest of the final surges of social protest by women, blacks, the poor, students, and many others whose rage has scoured American institutions throughout the previous decade."[14] The first murmurings of radical criminology appeared in radical and New Left publications such as *The Berkeley Barb* and were linked to the Vietnam War and the political turmoil that it generated, to black militancy, and to the development of youth contracultures. Sykes likewise attributed its rise to the war in Vietnam and growing citizen cynicism regarding the government, the development of a youth counterculture, widespread brutality and illegality in police responses to political dissidents and the Black Panthers, and growing evidence of the ubiquity of white-collar crime carried on with impunity by upper-class individuals.[15]

Interpretations of the precise linkage of these events to radical criminology vary somewhat, but most observers agree that the role of the state in the oppression of the citizenry through the criminal law and a variety of other devices has been exposed by these tumultuous happenings. Also, the overriding importance of corporate capitalism and class relationships in criminality has been revealed with great clarity, producing a crisis in mainstream criminology.

VARIETIES OF RADICAL CRIMINOLOGY

What are the central features of radical-Marxist criminology? Let us approach this question in roundabout fashion, by first examining an unintended caricature of mainstream criminology by Anthony Platt.[16] To begin with, Platt charged mainstream criminologists with blind acceptance of the state's definition of crime, taking legal codes as given and lending support to the corrective or rehabilitative thrust of social-control efforts directed at garden-variety offenders. According to Platt, they deliberately avoid the study of behavior forms that are not currently defined as crime, such as imperialism, exploitation, racism, and sexism. Platt also charged that they ignore violations of the criminal law that are not typically prosecuted, such as tax evasion, price fixing, consumer fraud, and police violence.

Platt also contended that mainstream or liberal criminology "supports the extension of state capitalism and gradualist programs of amelioration, while rejecting radical and violent forms of social and political change."[17] Mainstream criminologists were also held to be at fault for rejecting macrocosmic theory and historical analysis. The consequence, according to Platt, is:

[that] the liberal emphasis on pragmatism, short-range solutions and amelioration reveals an attitude of cynicism and defeatism concerning human potentiality and the possibility of far-ranging changes in society. This focus serves to exclude or underestimate the possibility of a radically different society in which cooperation replaces competition, where human values take precedence over property values, where exploitation, racism and sexism are eliminated, and where basic human needs are fulfilled. Liberal cynicism serves to reinforce the malevolent view that radical change is utopian and visionary, thereby helping to impede the development of revolutionary social and political movements.[18]

According to radical-Marxist criminologists, the perspectives which they recommend would go far toward remedying these alleged defects of mainstream criminology. Let us turn to a detailed examination of the new criminology, that is, radical-Marxist arguments.

There is no single Marxist perspective which all radical criminologists embrace, but it is possible to describe a set of broad views with which most are in general agreement. One of those claims is that crime arises out of the economic oppression of the working-class masses by the capitalist ruling class. Underclass individuals steal from others because of the precarious existence they lead or engage in acts of violence because of the social degradation and disorder surrounding them. The ruling class is directly responsible for criminal laws which are enacted to protect their interests and which are detrimental to the interests of the working class. Most citizens conform to the criminal laws, many of which are designed to protect private property, because they are misled into believing that the laws are intended to protect them. Those persons who engage in lawbreaking are dealt with by the police and the courts, which are instruments of ruling-class domination. Finally, in order to significantly reduce the extent of criminality, sweeping changes in the political-economic structure of modern corporate-capitalist societies would be required.

Economist David Gordon offered a moderate version of radical criminological thought which argued that nearly all crimes in capitalist societies represent rational responses to the organization of capitalist institutions.[19] Crimes constitute attempts by offenders to survive in a situation of *economic precariousness* generated by the social order. Further, he argued that many of the important differences among particular kinds of lawbreaking, such as garden-variety property violations, organized crime, or white-collar offenses, are related to the class structure of corporate societies and to the class biases of the state. Gordon also articulated a functional argument contending that imprisonment of blacks and other minority persons serves to keep them out of the job market and also operates to prevent them from organizing with others to attempt to change the economic system that oppresses them.

Gordon drew on a variety of sources to support his contentions about crime in the United States. Some might object that this supporting evidence is weak, anecdotal, and inconclusive, while others might take issue with his claim that a manifest function of prisons is to remove blacks from the job market and prevent them from organizing with others to engage in revolutionary actions. Further, since Gordon meant his piece to be primarily a provocative essay and not a tightly structured theoretical exposition, he was relatively silent on a number of points. For example, it is unclear how rape and a number of other relatively common offenses would be interpreted within this framework. Also, he had little to say about why some ghetto residents go about "income redistribution" through armed robbery while others avoid these criminal activities.

Many of the themes voiced by Gordon were not marked departures from the viewpoints contained in mainstream criminology. Indeed, Gordon's argument was radical mainly because of its conclusion that significant reductions in crime and fundamental reform in the criminal-justice system can only be achieved insofar as the capitalist system in the United States undergoes radical changes in the direction of socialism.

Another venture into radical theorizing was by Raymond Michalowski and Edward Bohlander, centering around social control rather than crime causation.[20] They argued for a conflict model of criminal law and its enforcement, contending that the legal basis of the state is created by those who occupy positions of social power and is used to maintain this power differential. They held that the criminal law is an instrument of repression through which certain individuals and groups in society are thwarted from achieving their organic interests, that is, fulfillment of their basic goals such as health, happiness, and a sense of personal worth.

Who are those who enjoy positions of social power and whose interests are incorporated into the criminal law? According to Michalowski and Bohlander, in a modern capitalist society this power group is comprised of the owners, controllers, and managers of the means of production. They viewed the law and the criminal-justice system as a device through which the corporate ruling class attempts to shape society in its own image. However, they conceded that the relationship between power and the administration of justice is not always clear. Advocates for the underclasses and disadvantaged can sometimes force compromises in the law, while, on other occasions, the ruling class may sponsor reforms that seemingly run counter to its own best interests. While these concessions are probably in order, Michalowski and Bohlander did not indicate the circumstances under which each of these outcomes is most likely.[21]

If the legal order in the United States serves the interests of the capitalist ruling class and is utilized for the repression of the economically and politically disadvantaged classes, how is it that the underclasses lend their support to the laws and the criminal-justice machinery? Why do working-class citizens tolerate the crimes that are carried on with relative impunity by corporations? Why does there appear to be social consensus regarding the legal order, in the face of ruling-class oppression? Michalowski and Bohlander's answer, in brief, was that the power-holding groups control the social definition of crime.

The powerful class shapes a definition of crime which supports their capitalist interests by insuring that the bulk of offenses from which individuals will acquire the meaning of crime bear no resemblance to the harmful acts of corporate profiteers, and that the majority of offenders—by the example of whom we learn to identify who is the criminal—bear no resemblance to members of the capitalist ruling class.[22]

Steven Spitzer has also outlined a Marxist theory of deviance.[23] He provided an account of the processes of deviance production, examining the development and changes in societal definitions of deviance, the sorting processes that produce problem behaviors and problem populations, and the development and operation of control systems at different points in history. His discussion dealt with a variety of forms of deviance and was not restricted to criminality, although like much of the other deviance literature, many of the illustrative cases were drawn from the world of lawbreaking.

Spitzer's Marxian argument about deviance production held that the capitalist mode of production forms the foundation of American society, that this productive system contains fundamental contradictions that are products of capitalism, and that the social and political superstructure serves to preserve the power position of capitalists and corporate managers.

Problem populations arise in capitalist societies that are composed of persons who threaten the social relations of production. Spitzer asserted that these are groups that disturb, hinder, or call into question:

1. The capitalist modes of appropriating the product of human labor (e.g., when the poor "steal" from the rich)
2. The social conditions under which capitalist production takes place (e.g., those who refuse or are unable to perform wage labor)
3. Patterns of distribution and consumption in capitalist society (e.g., those who use drugs for escape and transcendence rather than sociability and adjustment)
4. The process of socialization for productive and nonproductive roles (e.g., youth who refuse to be schooled or those who deny the validity of "family life")
5. The ideology which supports the functioning of capitalist society (e.g., proponents of alternative forms of social organization).[24]

The problem with this inventory of potential problem populations is that it is so broad and general as to provide a place for nearly everyone. It is not entirely helpful to learn that nearly everyone *might* become a target of the control machinery under unspecified circumstances.

Spitzer dealt at length with the production in capitalist societies of a relative surplus population from which recruits to deviance, or problem populations, are drawn. Many are from segments of black society which have become economically redundant as a result of the growth of technology and mass production in America. As a result, they are economically marginal, faced with chronic underemployment, or, in many cases, permanent unemployment. Problem groups create grave problems for capitalist societies, because they must be maintained through funds that could otherwise be used for capital investment. Moreover, surplus populations constitute potential recruits to political organizations that may endeavor to overthrow the capitalist system.

Other contradictions of capitalism create problem populations. For example, Spitzer argued that mass education in the United States was originally developed in order to provide a means by which the young would first be withheld from the labor market and then later assimilated into wage-laborer niches in the economy. But mass education may also provide the underclass with insights into the oppressive and alienating character of capitalist institutions, thereby creating individuals who become hostile to the status quo and who may become mobilized to challenge it.[25]

Spitzer also commented on the conditions under which problem groups are likely to be responded to as deviants. He distinguished between problem groups who constitute "social junk" and those that are "social dynamite." Skid Row alcoholics illustrate the first category, as they are relatively passive persons who have opted out of the economic order but who pose no threat to the ruling class. Social dynamite, by contrast, refers to groups who are widely believed by the authorities to be activists and revolutionaries and who are consequently likely to be dealt with much more harshly. Illegal attacks on such groups have been made by the police, but these attacks have often been ignored owing to the public fears that surround certain putatively revolutionary groups.

Still another explication of Marxist criminality theory has been put forth by William Chambliss, who, as we have seen, was at an earlier time an exponent of a pluralistic-conflict point of view. Chambliss enumerated nine propositions said to be derived from Marxist theory.

A. On the content and operation of criminal law
  1. Acts are defined as criminal because it is in the interests of the ruling class to so define them.
  2. Members of the ruling class will be able to violate the laws with impunity while members of the subject classes will be punished.
  3. As capitalist societies industrialize and the gap between the bourgeoisie and the proletariat widens, penal law will expand in an effort to coerce the proletariat into submission.
B. On the consequences of crime for society
  1. Crime reduces surplus labor by creating employment not only for the criminals but for law enforcers, locksmiths, welfare workers, professors of criminology, and a horde of people who live off the fact that crime exists.
  2. Crime diverts the lower classes' attention from the exploitation they experience and directs it toward other members of their own class rather than toward the capitalist class or the economic system.
  3. Crime is a reality which exists only as it is created by those in the society whose interests are served by its presence.
C. On the etiology of criminal behavior
  1. Criminal and noncriminal behavior stem from people acting rationally in ways that are compatible with their class position. Crime is a reaction to the life conditions of a person's social class.
  2. Crime varies from society to society depending on the political and economic structures of society.
  3. Socialist societies should have much lower rates of crime because the less intense class struggle should reduce the forces leading to and the functions of crime.[26]

Chambliss's discussion did not provide convincing support for these propositions. For example, he took note of some studies of the origins of criminal laws, which he contended were evidence that laws serve ruling-class interests. He concluded:

In all of these studies there is substantial support for the Marxian theory. The single most important force behind criminal law creation is doubtless the economic interest and political power of those classes which either (1) own or control the resources of the society, or (2) occupy positions of authority in the state bureaucracies. It is also the case that conflicts generated by the class structure of a society act as an important force for legal innovation. These conflicts may manifest themselves in an incensed group of moral entrepreneurs (such as Gusfield's lower middle class, or the efforts of groups such as the ACLU, NAACP, or Policemen's Benevolent Society) which manage to persuade courts or legislators to create new laws. Or the conflict may manifest itself in open riots, rebellions or revolutions which force new criminal law legislation.[27]

We examined these same studies in Chapter 4. Taken together, they suggest that some statutes reflect societal support, many of them foster the goals of specific interest groups, and some directly serve the interests of the most powerful groups in American society. But it is debatable that the goals of the Women's Christian Temperance Union, the NAACP, the ACLU, or the Policemen's Benevolent Society, which are promoted by some laws, are identical with "the interests of the ruling class" about which Chambliss spoke.

Other questions arise about this sketchy Marxist perspective offered by Chambliss. At one point, he asserted: "Class differences in rates of criminal activity are probably negligible. What difference there is would be a difference in the type of criminal act, not in the prevalence of criminality."[28] The data examined in Chapter 5 do not square with this claim. Many criminologists agree that a number of kinds of criminality represent reactions to the life circumstances faced by persons at different class levels. Gordon's claims about the role of economic precariousness in different forms of lawbreaking is another version of this theme. But, while this argument is plausible when applied to burglary, robbery, and the like, its relevance to rape, assault, homicide, and a variety of other crimes is not so evident. In this regard, Chambliss's theorizing is similar to much of the radical-Marxist work to date, in that many of these newer formulations have been sketchy, anecdotal, and relatively unfinished.

This brief review of contributions to radical criminology would not be complete without mention of the work of Richard Quinney, who has been the most prolific and prominent spokesman for radical criminology in the United States. In his *Critique of Legal Order*, published in 1974, he enunciated a set of propositions about crime.

1. American society is based on an advanced capitalist economy.
2. The state is organized to serve the interests of the dominant economic class, the capitalist ruling class.
3. Criminal law is an instrument of the State and ruling class to maintain and perpetuate the existing social and economic order.
4. Crime control in capitalist society is accomplished through a variety of institutions and agencies established and administered by a governmental elite, representing ruling class interests, for the purpose of establishing a domestic order.
5. The contradictions of advanced capitalism—the disjunction between essence and ex-

istence—require that the subordinate classes remain oppressed by whatever means necessary, especially through the coercion and violence of the legal system.

6. Only with the collapse of capitalist society and the creation of a new society, based on socialist principles, will there be a solution to the crime problem.[29]

The Marxist perspective contained in these six claims was extremely sketchy. Quinney stressed the domination exercised in the United States by a ruling class made up of a small, monolithic collectivity of corporation heads who engage in malevolent schemes to oppress the entire citizenry, with particular focus on the underdogs in American society: blacks and other minorities, and working-class groups.

Quinney's book contained a number of questionable claims, including the argument that the Law Enforcement Assistance Administration is a tool of the ruling class engaged in funding counterinsurgency research. Such a description is, at best, misleading, for it fails to describe the confused history or the complexity, internal contradictions, and other organizational features of that agency.[30]

In a later book, *Class, State, and Crime*, Quinney confronted some of the criticisms and objections of those who rejected radical criminology.[31] In it, he expanded on many of the themes already encountered in the writings of Spitzer, Gordon, and others. He contended that the productive relationships of capitalism produce a relative surplus population, some of the members of which turn to crime as an adaptive response to their predicament. In this view, the basic relations of production are the foundations on which the superstructure of social relations and social institutions is created. More directly relevant to crime, capitalist production involves fundamental contradictions, particularly those centered on a growing army of relative surplus individuals and alienated laborers, which generate recruits to crime and potential participants in class struggle and revolutionary action.

In one section of this book, Quinney outlined a Marxist typology of crime.[32] Two broad categories were identified—crimes of domination and crimes of accommodation and resistance—along with a number of subtypes.

A. Crimes of domination
   1. Crimes of control
   2. Crimes of government
   3. Crimes of economic domination
B. Crimes of accommodation and resistance
   1. Predatory crime
   2. Personal crimes
   3. Crimes of resistance

Crimes of control include such things as illegal police violence and other violations carried on by agents of legal control. Crimes of the government have to do with such matters as the Watergate crimes, along with illegal acts carried on by the FBI, CIA, and other agencies. Crimes of economic domination in-

clude white-collar offenses, organized crime, and social injuries. The latter refers to phenomena that fall outside the existing statutes, having to do with violations of basic human rights. Taken together, the crimes of domination are
those offenses engaged in with relative impunity by the authorities and members of the ruling class.

By contrast, crimes of accommodation and resistance are violations carried
on by underdogs—members of the lower class. Predatory crimes are responses
to the economic deprivation suffered by those at the bottom of the economic
heap, while personal crimes arise "in immediate situations that are themselves
the result of more basic accommodations to capitalism."[33] Crimes of resistance
involve various deliberate and calculated threats to the state, in the form of
revolutionary acts.

Quinney attempted to deal in some detail with class relations in capitalist
America, moving beyond gross assertions about the machinations of the ruling
class. He argued that although advanced capitalism continues to be characterized by a basic class division between the owners of property and the laboring
class, it has also given rise to a number of *fractions* or subgroups within the two
basic classes. Finally, Quinney elaborated on some of the central problems of
the modern state as it attempts two simultaneous maneuvers: (1) to provide
governmental support for capital accumulation, through regulating and supporting financial affairs and industrial development, including the utilization of tax
revenues and other governmental funds to buttress the economy; and (2) to
manage the growing problems of capitalism through the welfare state. The modern capitalist state faces an insoluble problem generated by the inexorable expansion of the relative surplus population which requires increased state management through welfare and other maintenance and control programs, on the
one hand, and the unwillingness and/or inability of the capitalist economy to
provide the requisite funding, on the other.[34]

CRITICISMS OF RADICAL-MARXIST CRIMINOLOGY

There has been no great rush of clamoring mainstream criminologists to embrace radical-Marxist views and to renounce allegiance to older viewpoints.
Rather, radical contentions have been subjected to a vigorous barrage of criticism, much of it centering around the complaints hinted at in previous sections
of this chapter.[35] In one way or another, many of the critics of radical theorizing
have charged that these new perspectives advance a distorted, overly simple
picture of crime and societal structure.

One critic, Robert Meier, declared that there is little that is really new in
"the new criminology."[36] He claimed that, rather than evolving new insights
into lawbreaking and responses to it, radical criminologists have taken many
established viewpoints from mainstream criminological thought and rephrased
them in political or ideological terms. He charged that radical criminology con-

tains elements drawn from the social-pathology tradition, as well as mainstream criminology, functionalism, and labeling arguments.

Where the older social-pathology notions dealt with alleged defects of individuals, the new criminology stresses the political pathology of capitalism. The new criminology also parallels the Chicago tradition fostered by Shaw and McKay in the 1930s, in that both are concerned with normative conflict. Moreover, the Chicago researchers also examined the repressive operations of the criminal-justice system. Meier noted that Sutherland's studies of white-collar crime implied the need for a redefinition of crime. Finally, radical criminology is functionalist insofar as it implies that the criminal-justice machinery operates to maintain the privileges of the ruling class.

Paul Hirst and Stephen Mugford, among others, have charged that contemporary Marxist criminology is not drawn in any direct fashion from the writings of Marx, who in fact had little to say about criminality or criminals. Thus, radical criminology presents a distorted version of Marxist thought.[37] But others have enumerated a number of connections between the writings of Marx and radical criminologists.[38]

One of the major complaints by critics of Marxist criminology is a counterclaim to the radical charge that mainstream criminology is involved in "mystification" of the real world, through promulgation of consensus views of the criminal law that disguise the role of the ruling class in criminal lawmaking and its implementation. Radical criminologists have often claimed that they are involved in demystification, that is, the stripping away of these false accounts of the real world offered by mainstream criminologists. According to many radical theorists, they are "telling it like it is." However, radicals are even more guilty of mystification through the portrayals they have offered of a monolithic ruling class that determines which acts are to be criminalized. These accounts oversimplify the nature of social power and class relations in modern societies, they fail to acknowledge that many criminal statutes are the product of myriad forces and interests, and they overlook the large number of laws that are supported by societal consensus.

Consider the ruling class imagery in radical theorizing, which is a linchpin of this argument. Many critics have castigated Marxist criminologists for their crude conspiratorial characterizations of a monolithic ruling elite, which are devoid of specifics that reveal either the composition of this ruling group or the nature of the social power exercised by that shadowy group. (Radical portrayals of the ruling class have a good deal in common with organized-crime, ruling-class stereotypes about the Mafia or Cosa Nostra, in that both claim that immense influence is wielded by a small, centralized collection of powerful figures.)

This dialogue on the shortcomings of ruling-class hypotheses in criminology is part of a larger quarrel in sociology regarding social power and influence in modern societies.[39] On the one side of the debate are ranged the pluralistic theorists who argue that social power is exercised in a varying and shifting fashion by a multiplicity of groups who compete for influence in modern communi- ties. According to this perspective, no single group occupies a position of power sufficient to dominate in almost all decisions of major importance.[40]

The competing elitist view of social power owes much to the writings of C. Wright Mills, who articulated this thesis at a time when pluralistic notions reigned almost unchallenged.[41] He contended that a power elite, made up of corporate officials, governmental figures, and military leaders, exercises nearly all of the real power in American society.

Radical criminologists and other adherents of ruling-class notions often in- voke Mills's name, and they also place much weight upon the more recent writ- ings of William Domhoff, who has endeavored to outline the contours of political power in the United States.[42] Domhoff has probed the social backgrounds of those who occupy positions of putative leadership and has reported that most come from similar, privileged backgrounds:

> We conclude that income, wealth, and institutional leadership of what Baltzell calls the "American business aristocracy" are more than sufficient to earn it the designation "gov- erning class." As Sweezy would say, this "ruling class" is based upon the national corpo- rate economy and the institutions that economy nourishes. It manifests itself through what the late C. Wright Mills called the power elite.[43]

Those who disagree with these conclusions have argued that Domhoff and others have failed to provide clear evidence that the reputedly powerful do ac- tually enjoy a monopoly on social power in American society. Although a small cadre of socially advantaged individuals may indeed occupy a number of seem- ingly strategic decision-making positions, it is conceivable that they may not actually control the processes of influence. In particular, it may be that powerful elites drawn from the ranks of corporations may share influence with represen- tatives of the state who also command a good deal of political power, which they sometimes employ in ways that run counter to the interests of the ruling class. Then, too, even if it could be demonstrated that a ruling elite exists, it does not necessarily follow that such a group will always act to maximize its own interests to the detriment of other competing groups, or that it will always be successful in overpowering the opposition of other groups.

Radical criminologists would do well to examine recent discussions of class power and state power in the United States. For example, Roberta Ash Garner has argued that the conspiratorial view of a small, powerful elite clique running the nation is an entirely too crude characterization of power relationships.[44] Her portrayal of ruling-class–state linkages was a more finely grained one, calling attention to a variety of direct and indirect organizational linkages between the managers of the corporate economy and the government. State support for corporate-class interests often comes about even though specific organizational links between capitalist elites and state officials have not been forged. She lik- ened the situation to that of a luxury cruise ship, in which the passengers (rulers) and the crew (the state) all move in the same direction, even though they do not directly collaborate in running the ship.

The crew is committed to smooth sailing for several reasons. At its upper levels, the crew's officers have a tradition of service to passengers, a love of the sea that is shared with the passengers, a sense of accomplishment at running a tight ship, and a substantial remuneration. At the bottom levels, pay is less, but it is the major incentive because the sailors must make a living. The crew does not openly question its passengers' desires to enjoy the cruise and arrive at a certain destination.[45]

Although critics have uncovered a number of defects in ruling-class theory, their strongest attacks have focused on the oversimplified conceptualization of social structure and of the moral order contained in radical theorizing regarding the nature and origins of criminal laws. We have already encountered some of these negative evaluations in Chapter 4. For example, Paul Rock has complained that "although there are exceptions, it is most difficult to discover in the writings on deviance a description of legislation and rule-making which embodies more than an anthropomorphic conspiracy theory."[46] Much the same assessment of radical and conflict hypotheses about the criminal-law origins has been made by Peter Manning.[47] Also, some parallel objections to radical criminology and its views of the criminal law have been offered by David Greenberg, who charged that radical criminologists have ignored the existence of substantial consensus among members of the general public concerning many categories of crime.[48] Greenberg also judged the radical views of social power and class relations to be immature. "Powerful groups are generally portrayed as operating virtually without constraint, never as being forced to make concessions to challenging groups or as being forced to act contrary to short-run interests so as to maintain legitimacy by responding to the expectations of a public."[49]

One of the most searching and comprehensive evaluations of conflict theories of law, including radical-Marxist claims, has been offered by S. D. Stein, who was particularly harsh in his evaluation of ruling-class hypotheses and arguments.[50] For one thing, the conclusion that laws are enacted to serve ruling-class interests, he pointed out, is based on a very small and unrepresentative sample of empirical investigations of the origins of statutes. We examined a large share of that collection of studies in Chapter 4. Drawing on the activities of the British Parliament in modern times, he noted that that lawmaking group enacts nearly a hundred major criminal statutes per year, many of which seem to be only slightly related, if at all, to ruling-class interests. A much larger number of lesser laws is created each year, and it is quite unlikely that all of them can be attributed to ruling-class influences.

Stein echoed the views of other critics of radical theorizing in his comments concerning the paucity of evidence joining elite groups and law enactment. Nearly all radical and conflict theories are circular in reasoning because they fail to demonstrate the relative power of different groups, independent of the laws that are supposed to be accounted for by power differentials. Stated differently, the superior power of a specific socioeconomic group is usually demonstrated by showing that some law serves the interests of that group.

A third problem with radical hypotheses, according to Stein, is that their exponents are forced to take refuge in various tortured or specious arguments in order to explain away the existence of many laws which clearly seem inimical to the interests of the ruling class. Still another difficulty encountered with radical theories is that all slur over the rich diversity of legislation that exists from one society to another, thus the legal rules are assumed to be much the same from one capitalist society to another. However, Stein offered a number of examples—such as variations in divorce laws between England, New Zealand, Australia, Canada, and the United States, and variations in personal-injury-compensation laws from one country to another—that are inadequately recognized in existing radical arguments about laws and interest groups.

Why do the substantive legal rules show considerable variability from one nation to another? According to Stein, it is because of major differences among lawmaking bodies in different countries, as well as variations in the political, economic, social, and legal institutions from one nation to another. For example, members of Parliament are in a lawmaking body that differs markedly from the United States Congress or state legislatures, with the result that those who serve in the latter are markedly more subject to pressure and influence from their constituents.

In Stein's view, conflict theories regarding lawmaking are flawed because "instead of relying on models which link together a series of inter-related propositions, each of which relates a number of different variables, many sociologists have felt justified in making sweeping generalizations about this subject matter, on the basis of the acceptance of a single hypothesis."[51] His recommendation was for "a more broadly based, socio-structural, comparative approach to these problems, one which focuses attention on the ways in which major institutional structures systematically favour the adoption or rejection of particular legislative policies."[52]

There are other bases for describing radical-Marxist criminology as one-dimensional.[53] For one, radical theorists have often gone about charging that the police in America, in particular, serve as the repressive instrument of the ruling class. This interpretation has sometimes taken a highly dramatic form, as for example, when Balkan, Berger, and Schmidt asserted that the Chicago police murdered Black Panther leader Fred Hampton "in cold-blood" on December 4, 1969.[54] In fact, State Attorney Hanrahan and the police involved in this incident were acquitted of these charges!

Whatever the truth of this allegation by Balkan, et al. concerning the Chicago police, it is clear that the police do *sometimes* engage in activities that serve the interests of socially powerful groups in our society.[55] Moreover, some of the tactics sometimes employed by the police are blatantly illegal. Equally important, however, is the fact that the police also engage in peace-keeping activities and a variety of other tasks that have little or nothing to do with suppression of dissent or with other repressive actions, however broadly defined. For example, the police in Portland, Oregon, respond to a large number of requests for general assistance from citizens and are involved in many other activities additional to enforcement of the criminal law. One frequent call for assistance is termed by the police, "standby for moveout." When a female has been threatened by her spouse or boyfriend, police officers are ready to aid her in moving out of the household and to thwart violent acts. Any account that omits consideration of the vast amount of peace-keeping by the police in modern America is highly one-sided and flawed.

Radical-Marxist theorists have yet to squarely confront another obdurate fact, namely, that increased criminality appears to be a concomitant of modernization, industrialization, and growing social complexity, and one which applies equally to all societies moving in these directions and not merely to capitalist nations. Contrary to some radical criminological writings, there is no dearth of crime in Russia or other modern socialist nations.[56] The forms or relative amounts of lawbreaking may differ among societies with differing political-economic systems of organization. For example, organized crime is a much more endemic feature of American society than it is in either capitalist or socialist nations in Europe. Nonetheless, the basic point remains that existing radical theorizing has as yet failed to adequately confront these obstinate facts about lawbreaking, which cannot be accommodated within one-dimensional theories.

summary

This chapter has concluded a two-part survey of social-structural theories of criminality. However, unlike a novel or story, what has been provided in Chapters 6 and 7 is an account with a beginning and a middle, but with no clear ending. We saw in Chapter 6 that mainstream theories about lawbreaking are vague, sketchy, and flawed in other ways, thus it cannot be said that we are now equipped with a valid and comprehensive account of the criminogenic features of modern societies. Chapter 7 similarly has shown that the conflict and radical-Marxist theories that have arisen in the past few decades are also deficient in a number of ways.

Although radical-Marxist arguments are vulnerable to criticism—centering on their failure to capture the complexity and richness of social organization, social processes, and criminality—this newer brand of theorizing has stimulated renewed attention to the central role of economic and political relationships in crime in modern societies. Sparks was on the mark in suggesting that this development has been salutary, because it urges criminologists to distance themselves from microscopic analyses of marijuana use, behavior in topless bars and nudist camps, and kindred studies, many of which are trivial.[57]

There is much more work that is required if we are to identify with precision the contributions that political and economic factors make to criminality. Regarding economic forces, it is unlikely either that these are inconsequential or that the relationship between economic forces and lawbreaking is simple, direct, and powerful. Instead, there is evidence that adverse economic conditions, particularly unemployment and inflation, are moderately correlated with various forms of deviant behavior, including crime, mental illness, alcoholism, and suicide.[58] For example, Levine has reported a relatively high correlation between robbery rates in the 26 largest cities in the United States in 1970 and the proportion of the 16- to 20-year-old, out-of-school, out-of-work males in those cities.[59] Other investigators have argued that economic factors, including feelings of relative deprivation, are entangled with other influences that loom large in crime causation.[60]

As criminologists continue their efforts to formulate social-structural theories of crime, they probably will increasingly turn their attention toward arguments that zero in on particular forms of criminality and away from broad perspectives that downplay or ignore variations in criminal conduct. Much of the critical commentary in Chapters 6 and 7 suggests that social-structural theories have been imprecise, in considerable part, because they have slurred over important differences between such forms of criminality as garden-variety, predatory property crime; violent crimes; organized criminality; white-collar lawbreaking; and mundane, folk crimes. It may be that when criminologists begin to develop a family of social-structural formulations, each member of which is specific to a particular variant of criminality, marked progress may be made in the understanding of the social sources of crime. This is a point which will recur throughout the rest of this book and which is given detailed attention in Chapters 10 and 11.

notes

[1] Thomas S. Kuhn, *The Structure of Scientific Revolutions* (Chicago: University of Chicago Press, 1952).

[2] A large share of the commentary in this chapter has been adapted from Don C. Gibbons, *The Criminological Enterprise* (Englewood Cliffs, N.J.: Prentice-Hall, Inc., 1979), pp. 156–94.

[3] Maurice F. Parmelee, *Criminology* (New York: Macmillan, 1918), pp. 32–36; Thorsten Sellin, *Culture Conflict and Crime* (New York: Social Science Research Council, 1938); Albert K. Cohen, Alfred Lindesmith, and Karl Schuessler, eds., *The Sutherland Papers* (Bloomington, Ind.: Indiana University Press, 1956), pp. 103–104; George B. Vold, *Theoretical Criminology* (New York: Oxford University Press, 1958), pp. 203–61.

[4] The rise of conflict theories in criminology was part of a larger development, in which sociologists rediscovered social conflict in the 1950s. T. B. Bottomore has pointed out that mainstream sociologists in the 1930s and 1940s most frequently embraced social-systems theories and equilibrium models of society, which treated social conflict as temporary and aberrant in nature. See Bottomore, "Sociological Theory and the Study of Social Conflict," in *Theoretical Sociology*, John C. McKinney and Edward A. Tiryakian, eds., (New York: Prentice-Hall, Inc., 1970), pp. 137–53. Bottomore contended that Simmel, Cooley, Small, and many other early figures in sociology had much to say about social conflict. According to Bottomore, the revival of interest in social conflict came about in large measure as a result of World War II—and the international tensions that have continued since then—of racial conflict in the United States, and of other real-world events that have impinged upon sociological perspectives. For another useful discussion of the general background within which conflict theories in criminology reside, see William J. Chambliss, ed., *Sociological Readings in the Conflict Perspective* (Reading, Mass.: Addison-Wesley, 1973), pp. 1–38.

[5] Stuart L. Hills, *Crime, Power, and Morality* (Scranton, Pa.: Chandler Publishing Co., 1971), p. 6; also see John F. Galliher and James L. McCartney, *Criminology: Power, Crime, and Criminal Law* (Homewood, Ill.: Dorsey Press, 1977).

[6] Austin T. Turk, *Criminality and Legal Order* (Chicago: Rand McNally, 1969), p. 10.

[7] Ibid., p. 48.

[8] William B. Chambliss and Robert B. Seidman, *Law, Order, and Power* (Reading, Mass.: Addison-Wesley, 1971).

[9] Ibid., p. 4.

[10] Richard Quinney, *The Social Reality of Crime* (Boston: Little, Brown, 1970), pp. 15–23. Some critics of these views of Quinney have pointed out that they oversimplify the real world and also that some of these statements are definitions, not propositions or empirical claims. See Jack P. Gibbs and Maynard L. Erickson, "Major Developments in the Sociological Study of Deviance," in *Annual Review of Sociology*, Alex Inkeles, James Coleman, and Neil Smelser, eds. (Palo Alto: Annual Reviews, 1975), pp. 21–42. Also see Peter K. Manning, "Deviance and Dogma," *British Journal of Criminology*, 15 (January 1975), pp. 1–20.

[11] Quinney, *The Social Reality of Crime*, p. 38.

[12] For one critique centering largely on pluralistic conflict theory, see Eugene Doleschal and Nora Klapmuts, "Toward a New Criminology," *Crime and Delinquency Literature*, 5 (December 1973), 607–26. The term, "new criminology," first appeared in Ian Taylor, Paul Walton, and Jock Young, *The New Criminology* (London: Routledge & Kegan Paul, 1973). Doleschal and Klapmuts were on the mark in their characterization of shifts in criminological thinking that have occurred during the past two or three decades. However, they described a revised rather than a new criminology. The theoretical shift in the direction of pluralistic conceptions of society and conflict theory has been gradual rather than abrupt, which is also true of the growth of labeling viewpoints. But, even more important, what these commentators had in mind as the new criminology is a blander version of theorizing than the radical or Marxist viewpoints. Also see Gresham M. Sykes, "The Rise of Critical Criminology," *Journal of Criminal Law and Criminology*, 65 (June 1974), 206–13.

[13] The development of Marxist criminology, particularly in England, is discussed in Richard F. Sparks, "A Critique of Marxist Criminology," in *Crime and Justice: An Annual Review of Research*, Norval Morris and Michael Tonry, eds., (Chicago: University of Chicago Press, 1980), pp. 159–210. Also see Erich Buchholz, Richard Hartmann, John Lekschas, and Gerhard Stiller, *Socialist Criminology*, translated by Ewald Osers (Lexington, Mass.: Lexington Books, 1974). This volume was produced by East German scholars and presents a socialist interpretation of crime, both in capitalist and socialist countries. Criminality in socialist nations was attributed to various "survivals" and "relics" of capitalism.

[14] Editorial, *Crime and Social Justice*, 1 (Spring–Summer 1974), p. 1.

[15] Sykes, "The Rise of Critical Criminology," pp. 210–12.

[16] Anthony M. Platt, "Prospects for a Radical Criminology in the United States," *Crime and Social Justice*, 1 (Spring–Summer 1974), 2–10.

[17] Ibid., p. 3.

[18] Ibid., p. 4.

[19] David M. Gordon, "Class and the Economics of Crime," *Review of Radical Political Economics*, 3 (Summer 1971), 51–75. For another work which parallels Gordon's views, see Barry Krisberg, *Crime and Privilege: Toward a New Criminology* (Englewood Cliffs, N.J.: Prentice-Hall, Inc., 1975).

[20] Raymond J. Michalowski and Edward W. Bohlander, "Repression and Criminal Justice in Capitalist America," *Sociological Inquiry*, 46 (1976), 95–106.

[21] A parallel and similarly imprecise argument about criminal laws and ruling-class interests is John R. Hepburn, "Social Control and the Legal Order: Legitimate Repression in a Capitalist State," *Contemporary Crises*, 1 (January 1977), 77–90.

[22] Michalowski and Bohlander, "Repression and Criminal Justice in Capitalist America," p. 104.

[23] Steven Spitzer, "Toward a Marxian Theory of Deviance," *Social Problems*, 22 (5:1975), 638–51.

[24] Ibid., p. 642.

[25] For some elaborations upon this theme, see David F. Greenberg, "Delinquency and the Age Structure of Society," *Contemporary Crises*, 1 (April 1977), 189–223.

[26]William Chambliss, "Toward a Political Economy of Crime," *Theory and Society*, 2 (Summer 1975), 152–53.

[27]Ibid., p. 154.

[28]Ibid., p. 166.

[29]Richard Quinney, *Critique of Legal Order* (Boston: Little, Brown, 1974), p. 16.

[30]A good deal of the published commentary on LEAA, much of it quite critical of that agency, is reviewed in Don C. Gibbons, Joseph L. Thimm, Florence Yospe, and Gerald F. Blake, Jr., *Criminal Justice Planning* (Englewood Cliffs, N.J.: Prentice-Hall, Inc., 1977), pp. 12–27.

[31]Richard Quinney, *Class, State, and Crime: On the Theory and Practice of Criminal Justice* (New York: McKay, 1977). For a Marxist deviance-criminology text that parallels Quinney's analysis, see Sheila Balkan, Ronald J. Berger, and Janet Schmidt, *Crime and Deviance in America: A Critical Approach* (New York: Wadsworth, 1980).

[32]Quinney, *Class, State, and Crime*, pp. 43–62.

[33]Ibid., p. 54.

[34]Quinney's commentary on these matters is in the direction of such works as Charles H. Anderson, *The Political Economy of Social Class* (Englewood Cliffs, N.J.: Prentice-Hall, Inc., 1974); and James O'Connor, *The Fiscal Crisis of the State* (New York: St. Martin's Press, 1973).

[35]For a review of much of this criticism and a listing of many of these critiques, see Gibbons, *The Criminological Enterprise*, pp. 186–93. Also see David Shichor, "The New Criminology: Some Critical Issues," *British Journal of Criminology*, 20 (January 1980), 1–19; Sparks, "A Critique of Marxist Criminology"; James A. Inciardi, ed., *Radical Criminology: The Coming Crises* (Beverly Hills, Cal.: Sage Publications, Inc., 1980).

[36]Robert F. Meier, "The New Criminology: Continuity in Criminological Theory," *Journal of Criminal Law and Criminology*, 67 (December 1976), 461–69.

[37]Paul Q. Hirst, "Marx and Engels on Law, Crime, and Morality," *Economy and Society*, 1 (February 1972), 28–56; Stephen K. Mugford, "Marxism and Criminology: A Comment on the Symposium on 'The New Criminology,'" *Sociological Quarterly*, 15 (Autumn 1974), 591–96. Also see Zenon Bankowski, Geoff Mungham, and Peter Young, "Radical Criminology or Radical Criminologist?" *Contemporary Crises*, 1 (January 1977), 37–51; Piers Beirne, "Empiricism and the Critique of Marxism on Law and Crime," *Social Problems*, 26 (April 1979), 373–85.

[38]Ian Taylor and Paul Walton, "Radical Deviancy Theory and Marxism: A Reply to Paul Q. Hirst's 'Marx and Engels on Law, Crime, and Morality,'" in *Critical Criminology*, Taylor, Walton, and Jock Young, eds. (London: Routledge & Kegan Paul, 1975), pp. 233–37; David F. Greenberg, ed., *Crime and Capitalism* (Palo Alto: Mayfield Publishing Co., 1980).

[39]This debate is reviewed in William J. Chambliss and Thomas E. Ryther, *Sociology* (New York: McGraw-Hill, 1975); Anderson, *The Political Economy of Social Class*, pp. 216–33.

[40]For example, see Robert Dahl, *Who Governs? Democracy and Power in an American City* (New Haven, Conn.: Yale University Press, 1961); and Nelson W. Polsby, *Community Power and Political Theory* (New Haven, Conn.: Yale University Press, 1963).

[41]C. Wright Mills, *The Power Elite* (New York: Oxford University Press, 1956).

[42]G. William Domhoff, *Who Rules America?* (Englewood Cliffs, N.J.: Prentice-Hall, Inc., 1967); Domhoff, *The Higher Circles: The Governing Class in America* (New York: Random House, 1970); Domhoff, *The Bohemian Grove and Other Retreats: A Study in Ruling Class Cohesiveness* (New York: Harper & Row, Pub., 1974).

[43]Domhoff, *Who Rules America?* p. 156.

[44]Roberta Ash Garner, *Social Change* (Chicago: Rand McNally, 1977), pp. 252–59. For an important illustration of class and state power and the clash between the two, see Stephen D. Krasner, "A Statist Interpretation of American Oil Policy Toward the Middle East," *Political Science Quarterly*, 94 (Spring 1979), 77–96.

[45]Garner, *Social Change*, p. 258.

[46]Paul Rock, "The Sociology of Deviancy and Conceptions of Moral Order," *British Journal of Criminology*, 14 (April 1974), 139–49.

[47]Peter K. Manning, "Deviance and Dogma," *British Journal of Criminology*, 15 (January 1975), 1–20.

[48]David F. Greenberg, "On One-Dimension Criminology," *Theory and Society*, 3 (1976), 610–21. Also see Andrew Hopkins, "On the Sociology of Criminal Law," *Social Problems*, 22 (5:1975), 608–19.
The radical rejoinder to this point raised by Greenberg and others is that substantial public consensus on laws does not disprove the radical argument about the ruling-class origins of laws. Through the control of the media and educational institutions, ruling groups manage to manipulate public sentiments and create public support for laws that are inimical to the interests of most citizens. A more damaging case against ruling-class arguments would come from evidence showing that certain laws run counter to the interests of ruling-class groups.

[49]Greenberg, "On One-Dimensional Criminology," p. 612. One not entirely successful attempt to answer these charges that radical criminology is unable to explain laws that seem not to favor ruling-class interests has been made by Hepburn, "Social Control and the Legal Order."

[50]S. D. Stein, "The Sociology of Law: Some Comments on Theoretical Paradigms and Case Studies," *British Journal of Criminology*, 20 (April 1980), 99–122. Also see John Hagan, "The Legislation of Crime and Delinquency: A Review of Theory, Method, and Research," *Law and Society Review*, 14 (Spring 1980), 603–28.

[51]Stein, "The Sociology of Law," p. 119.

[52]Ibid., p. 120.

[53]Greenberg, "On One-Dimensional Criminology:"

[54]Balkan, Berger, Schmidt, *Crime and Deviance in America*, pp. 96–97.

[55]Sidney L. Harring, "Policing a Class Society: The Expansion of the Urban Police in the Late Nineteenth and Early Twentieth Centuries," in Greenberg, *Crime and Capitalism*, pp. 292–313: Samuel Walker, *A Critical History of Police Reform* (Lexington, Mass.: Lexington Books, 1977).

[56]Walter D. Connor, "Juvenile Delinquency in the U.S.S.R.: Some Quantitative and Qualitative Indicators," *American Sociological Review*, 35 (April 1970), 288–97; Mark G. Field, "Alcoholism, Crime, and Delinquency in Soviet Society," *Social Problems*, 3 (October 1955), 100–109; Valery Chalidze, *Criminal Russia: Essays on Crime in the Soviet Union*, translated by P. S. Falla (New York: Random House, 1977).

[57]Sparks, "A Critique of Marxist Criminology."

[58]M. Harvey Brenner, "Estimating the Social Costs of National Economic Policy: Implications for Mental and Physical Health and Criminal Aggression," paper no. 5 prepared for the Joint Economic Commission, Congress of the United States (Washington, D.C.: U.S. Government Printing Office, 1976); Brenner, "Effects of the Economy on Criminal Behavior and the Administration of Criminal Justice in the United States, Canada, England and Wales and Scotland," in *Economic Crises and Crime* (Rome: United Nations Social Defense Institute, 1976).

[59]James P. Levine, "The Ineffectiveness of Adding Police to Prevent Crime," *Public Policy*, 23 (Fall 1975), p. 136.

[60]Llad Phillips, Harold L. Votey, Jr., and Darold Maxwell, "Crime, Youth, and the Labor Market," *Journal of Political Economy*, 80 (May–June 1972), 491–503; Sheldon Danziger and David Wheeler, "The Economics of Crime: Punishment or Income Redistribution," *Review of Social Economy*, 33 (October 1975), 113–30.

explaining criminal behavior: biogenic and psychogenic approaches

EIGHT

It is now at last time in our scrutiny of the criminological enterprise to take up the question: "Why do they do it?" What are the processes through which persons become entangled in lawbreaking? This query was also identified in Chapter 3 as dealing with the origins and development of criminal acts and careers, because it is concerned with discovery of the processes and experiences that lead specific individuals into criminal conduct. Chapter 3 also indicated that answers to this question are of several kinds: biogenic, psychogenic, and sociogenic.

The biogenic and psychogenic approaches are what Albert K. Cohen has called "kinds of people" theories, for they assume that explanations of crime and other forms of deviance reduce down to the question: "What sort of person would do this sort of thing?"[1] The biogenic answer is that individuals engage in criminality, at least in part, due to biological characteristics that differentiate them from nonoffenders. The layman's version of this might be that misbehaving persons are somehow "born that way." Psychogenic theories, on the other hand, assert that lawbreakers are impelled into criminal acts due to flaws in their psyches or other psychological aberrations not found among noncriminals.

The third approach, sociogenic explanations, assumes that law violators are biologically and psychologically normal individuals who learn criminal attitudes and behavior patterns from others, or who drift or blunder into misconduct through situational stresses and pressures. Chapter 8 is concerned with biogenic and psychogenic theories and research evidence, while Chapter 9 takes up sociogenic accounts of the processes of becoming a criminal.

contemporary biogenic explanations of crime

EARLY WORK

Chapter 2 provided a fairly detailed account of biological explanations of criminality that have been pursued in the past, starting with the work of Lombroso in the 1800s. We saw that Lombroso and those who followed him, such as Hooton, tried to ferret out evidence that criminals are physically inferior compared to nonoffenders but failed to produce that evidence. Further, the investigations of fraternal and identical twins, designed to show that criminality is inherited, turned out to be a blind alley from which nothing was produced. Then, also, investigators who have tried to demonstrate that criminality is linked to body structure and temperament patterns failed to provide convincing evidence supporting that thesis, as was also true of those early researchers who searched for indications that crime is due to feeblemindedness.

Most of the investigations on biological hypotheses in criminality were clearly defective, even when considered apart from their inadequate research methodology. Nearly all the biogenic works proceeded on the basis of faulty assumptions, one of which was that "nature" and "nurture" (heredity and environment) can be separated from each other and studied in isolation. Another erroneous presupposition was that criminality is a constant, unchanging kind of behavior. For crime, in fact, varies from place to place and from time to time. Therefore, if biological forces are involved in criminality, hypotheses to discover them will have to be sufficiently sophisticated to determine how such culturally and temporally variable phenomena could be transmitted genetically.[2]

The many years of biogenic exploration of criminality have not produced valid generalizations about biological factors in deviance. For this reason—and equally because biogenic hypotheses run counter to the theoretical preferences of sociological criminologists—biological hypotheses have been out of popularity with that group.

MODERN BIOSOCIAL VIEWS

While most of the biogenic theorizing and research inquiry until recently has been markedly defective in one way or another, it would be an error to conclude, as some have done, that biological hypotheses can safely be ignored in the search for etiological understanding. A careful reading of the evidence suggests, instead, that the last word may not have been heard on biological forces in human behavior and that this question remains open for further examination.

Recent admonitions by sociologists regarding the need to "bring beasts back in"[3] have been followed by new efforts to uncover biosocial processes in human behavior.[4] Modern work on biogenic factors stresses the *biosocial* nature of human behavior. Contemporary arguments about biological factors in human behavior, including deviant conduct, are much more in tune with current thinking in such fields as biology and human genetics where it is argued that human behavior is influenced by *interactions* between biological and genetic factors, on the one hand, and social experiences, on the other. The crude biological determinism of an earlier generation of criminologists has been supplanted by biosocial hypotheses which recognize the interplay of biological and environmental factors.

The current state of biological thinking research in criminality has been described by Saleem Shah and Loren Roth:[5] "Recent advances in the biological sciences have led to a veritable explosion of knowledge concerning the variety of biological factors influencing human behavior. Advances in experimental behavior genetics, human population genetics, the biochemistry of the nervous system, experimental and clinical endocrinology and neurophysiology, and many related developments now permit more sophisticated understanding of the complexities of nature-nurture interactions as they influence the growth, development, and functioning of the human organism."[6]

Shah and Roth charged that contemporary criminologists have given short shrift to this emerging literature on biological influences. For example, they reported that in one analysis of violence, Marvin Wolfgang and Franco Ferracuti took note of electroencephalographic (EEG) evidence of brain abnormalities among many violent offenders.[7] However, these same authors went on to assert that because the relationship of EEG abnormalities and violence is never invariable or total, and since these inner characteristics do not by themselves explain aggressive behavior, they are of no causal significance in violence.[8] Shah and Roth were critical of this line of reasoning, arguing:

The implication is given by Wolfgang and Ferracuti that biological contributions are expected to provide "invariable or total" explanations "by themselves" in order for criminologists to give them serious consideration. The obvious fact is, however, that if we used similar criteria for accepting the importance of sociological and psychological factors, we would undoubtedly have to dismiss most of these variables since they rarely—if ever—demonstrate *invariable* relationships with, nor do they provide *total explanations* for, complex phenomena, such as aggression and crime. (emphasis in the original)[9]

In their comments on the role of biogenic factors in behavior, Shah and Roth outlined a position on hereditary and environmental influences in human conduct that agrees with modern biological knowledge. They examined the nature-nurture question in detail, noting that *genotype* refers to the totality of factors that make up the genetic complement of an organism, while *phenotype* designates the totality of that which can be observed about the organism. The phenotype is not inherited; instead, it evolves as a product of the interactions between the genotype and the environment. Human traits or characteristics develop out of the interaction between genotypes and varying environments. In other words, genetic endowment fixes a range within which human behavioral patterns can develop, rather than leading directly to particular traits, characteristics, or behavior. If this is the case, all behavior, criminal or otherwise, must be understood as involving interactions between organisms and particular environments.[10]

As another illustration of this basic point, consider the investigations of bodily structure among delinquents by Sheldon and Eleanor Glueck.[11] They noted that mesomorphs, that is, boys with athletic, muscular body types, were found more frequently among offenders than among nonoffenders. Mesomorphic structure characterized 60.1 percent of the lawbreakers but only 30.7 percent of the nondelinquents they studied. These findings were the result of careful measurement, thus there is little question about their accuracy. What if a number of research efforts were to turn up consistent evidence of mesomorphy among delinquents? What conclusions would be in order? A reasonable interpretation would be that a process of social selection joined to biological differences, rather than biological determinism, would explain such results. In other words, recruits to delinquent conduct may be drawn from the group of more agile, physically fit boys, just as Little League baseball or Pop Warner football players tend toward mesomorphy. Fat delinquents and fat ballplayers might be uncommon because social behavior involved in these cases puts fat, skinny, or sickly boys at a disadvantage. But while social selection might be involved in these instances, an equally important conclusion would be that *biological differences are the bases on which this selection operates*. Even though social selection could be invoked to account for mesomorphic delinquents and mesomorphic football players, the biological element in this sorting process would not vanish as a consequence. Stated differently, social scientists would be compelled to take cognizance of an important biological factor in this instance.

RECENT EVIDENCE

Several reviews of the current evidence on biological factors in crime and delinquency are available. On the basis of a relatively uncritical survey of a number of studies of chemical imbalances of the brain and behavior disorders of one kind or another, Leonard Hippchen concluded that "our present emphasis on sociological and psychological factors as explanations for crime is too limited and that our theory needs to be amended to accommodate these new discoveries in biochemistry."[12]

Shah and Roth assembled a large body of research evidence dealing with the contributions of a variety of biological variables to criminality.[13] They surveyed the findings regarding the effect of brain tumors and other disorders of the limbic system, a term which designates certain portions of the central nervous system. Additionally, they dealt with evidence on crime, epilepsy, and endocrine abnormalities. They also examined a body of findings regarding neurological dysfunction produced by prenatal and postnatal experiences of infants, as well as data concerning lesser forms of brain dysfunction in children and adolescents. Studies of hypothesized biological factors in psychopathy, evidence on chromosomal abnormalities, and recent studies on physique, temperament, and behavior, were also reviewed. One thing was clear from their discussion, namely that criminologists can ill afford to engage in cavalier dismissals of biological influences in criminality.

Sarnoff Mednick has also reviewed a number of studies of biological factors, including those that he has conducted.[14] He surveyed a number of investigations of criminality among identical (monozygotic) and fraternal (dizygotic) twins which suggest that concordance, or similarity, of behavior is greater for the former than the latter. These findings lend some support to biogenic hypotheses, for it can be argued that environment is controlled for twins, thus allowing comparison of persons who share the same genetic pattern with those who differ in this regard. However, Mednick also conceded the point often made by critics of these inquiries, namely, that identical twins may often undergo more similar social-environmental experiences than do fraternal twins, which would account for the greater concordance among them.[15]

Mednick also presented data from studies of adopted children which allow some assessment of biological and environmental contributions to lawbreaking. These data appear to indicate that criminal adoptees more often have criminal natural-parents than they do criminal adoptive-relatives. However, Mednick was cautious in his interpretation of these findings, for he did indicate that there are a number of methodological problems surrounding them. His conclusion was a judicious one: "There is no suggestion in these findings that biological factors predestine criminality in some inevitable, fateful manner. Rather, they suggest that there must be some biosocial interaction at work."[16]

Mednick was also of the opinion that offenders frequently exhibit autonomic nervous system functioning that differentiates them from nonoffenders. In particular, they show lower fear reactions such as increased heart and pulse rate, increased respiratory rate, sweating, and skin conductivity. The hypothesized link between autonomic nervous system functioning and criminality is that those who manifest slow or low fear reactions will be difficult to socialize, thus they will be more prone to lawbreaking. Mednick outlined the argument in the following way: "(1) Child A contemplates aggressive action. (2) Because of previous punishment he suffers fear. (3) He inhibits the aggressive response. What happens to his anticipatory fear? (4) It will begin to dissipate, to be reduced. We know that fear-reduction is the most powerful, naturally occurring reinforcement that psychologists have discovered."[17]

The study of biogenic factors in criminality is fraught with difficulty, largely because of the problem of separating out biological factors from social or environmental forces which might account for findings that appear supportive of biological hypotheses. In the case of autonomic nervous system functioning, Vold and Bernard have drawn attention to alternative interpretations of the results reported by Mednick and others, concluding that "it is possible that differences in autonomic nervous system functioning may be caused by, rather than the cause of, differences in personality."[18]

EYSENCK'S BIOPSYCHOLOGICAL THEORY

Mednick's arguments about autonomic nervous system functioning are closely related to the views of British psychologist Hans Eysenck that deal with extroversion and criminality.[19] In the initial version of this theory, Eysenck offered the following argument:

[A] psychological theory was adumbrated to the effect that (1) propensity to crime is universal, but is held in check in most cases by a given person's "conscience"; (2) this "conscience" was essentially a generalized set of conditioned responses built up during childhood and adolescence according to the rules of Pavlovian conditioning; (3) this "conscience" might be expected to be underdeveloped *either* through failure of social and family conditions to provide the proper means of developing it, *or* through innate weakness in the person concerned of the mechanism involved in the elaboration of conditioned responses. It was further postulated that (4) extraverted persons tended, under certain conditions, to condition less well than introverted ones, thus making them *ceteris paribus* more likely to behave in an anti-social fashion, and that (5) high degrees of anxiety or neuroticism tended to act as a drive strongly reinforcing the extraverted or introverted tendencies favoring or disfavoring anti-social conduct. From this chain of argument, each of which was supported by experimental evidence (of admittedly unequal value), it was deduced that anti-social conduct, particularly crime, would be found more frequently in people whose personality placed them in the high extraversion/high neuroticism quadrant, and a number of experimental studies were quoted to support this deduction.[20]

The thrust of this viewpoint is that individuals refrain from lawbreaking to the extent that they are adequately conditioned and acquire an internalized conscience. In some cases, inadequate conditioning and tendencies toward criminality and deviance develop when parental failures in socialization occur. Additionally, extraverted individuals are said to be difficult to condition to conformity due to autonomic system functioning, so that their behavior has roots in biological factors.

Eysenck's arguments go well beyond the crude biological determinism involved in most of the earlier biogenic theorizing reviewed in Chapter 2. At the same time, his formulations and research procedures have received a good deal of criticism, charging him with computational errors, biased sampling procedures, employing scales of questionable validity, and other failings.[21]

The research evidence regarding the claims of Eysenck is far from clear-cut. In one study, Hans Eysenck and Sybil Eysenck argued that psychoticism is related to criminality, along with extraversion and neuroticism. However, when they gathered observations on unmatched groups of prison inmates, working-class nonprisoners, university students, and industrial apprentices, they found that the apprentices scored highest on extraversion and also that the prison inmates were not markedly more neurotic than the members of the other groups. The convicts did have higher scores on psychoticism than the other groups.[22] Along this same line, M. S. Hoghughi and A. R. Forrest reviewed a number of studies of boys in English training schools and public-school control-group cases and reported that, contrary to Eysenck's contentions, the young offenders were more introverted than the nonoffenders, rather than tending toward extraversion.[23] They also argued that biologically based formulations of this kind fail to speak to the question of discontinuity and drift in delinquent careers, in which offenders frequently withdraw from misbehavior even though they have not been resocialized or treated. If criminality is the product of autonomic nervous system characteristics and extraversion, how are these alterations in deviant patterns to be explained? Eysenck was silent on this question.

There are others who have argued that Eysenck's claims have not been given a fair test. P. K. Burgess has offered the hypothesis that criminality should be particularly frequent on the part of individuals who score high on both the extraversion and neuroticism dimensions and claims that the methodology used in earlier studies has been defective.[24] Burgess reported findings indicating that high-extraversion–high-neuroticism cases are likely to be involved in deviance, but, at the same time, he noted that this pattern of characteristics is present in only a small portion of the offender population.[25]

THE XYY CHROMOSOMAL PATTERN AND CRIMINALITY

One biologically related hypothesis which caught the public eye—and was widely thought to be the key to unlocking the mysteries of criminality—was the XYY, or extra-chromosome, argument. This theory holds that certain kinds of criminals are inordinately drawn from that group of males in the population who have this chromosomal abnormality.[26] Much of the interest in this notion derived from a few spectacular cases, such as the mass murders and sexual assaults committed by Richard Speck in Chicago in 1966. Examination of Speck initially indicated that he had the XYY chromosomal pattern, although this diagnosis later turned out to be incorrect.[27]

What is involved in chromosomal patterning and behavior? Richard Fox summarized the matter as follows:

In general terms, chromosomes are threads of complex molecules (DNA) containing the genetic material which transmits hereditary messages from generation to generation of both plant and animal life. These messages direct the development of the offspring after fertilization. The number of chromosomes to be found in each plant or animal cell varies according to species. There are, for instance, two chromosomes in each cell of a simple worm, fourteen in the garden pea, and forty-six in man. There is an exception to the general rule that each normal human cell has 46 chromosomes. The female ovum and male sperm cells respectively contain only 23 chromosomes but, on uniting at conception, they pool their chromosomes so that the fertilized ovum contains 46 chromosomes. These are arranged in 23 pairs. As the fertilized ovum grows by division into a new individual, each of the 46 chromosomes also divides so that eventually each normal cell (other than sperm and ovum) contains the same number of chromosomes. Of the 23 pairs of chromosomes in each cell one pair contains genes which determine, among other features, the primary sexual characteristics of the individual. In woman this single pair of chromosomes are of similar size and are called X chromosomes or, in the biologists' shorthand, XX. In the male this pair of chromosomes are unequal in size; one of the pair is an X chromosome and is larger than the other which is called the Y chromosome. In the biologists' shorthand, the male's sex chromosomes are described as XY. The primary biological characteristics of masculinity are determined by the Y chromosome. From this it becomes obvious that the sperm of the father, not the ovum of the mother, determines the sex of the new individual. The character of the male sperm cell, X or Y, that fertilizes the ovum determines the sex of the child. If the sperm contains a Y chromosome the child will be male; if the sperm contains an X chromosome the child is normally female. If this process fails to operate effectively individuals may be born with either too few or too many chromosomes. Numerous chromosomal abnormalities are recognized. The XXY or Klinefelter Syndrome is one in which the person is usually found to be outwardly male but sterile, somewhat mentally retarded and suffering from some breast enlargement. This anomaly (which occurs in approximately one out of every 400–500 male births) has been linked with antisocial behavior, especially alcoholism and homosexuality, but as yet few findings of importance have been published. XXYY males have also been discovered. These persons generally exhibit the same physical features as XXY males but the view has been expressed that the additional Y chromosome may have a deleterious effect on the development of their personality and, as a consequence, on their behavior. It is, however, the XYY male who is presently of special interest to criminologists.[28]

The XYY chromosome hypothesis is of relatively recent origin, for the first male with this pattern was not discovered until 1961. Additionally, that individual was *not* abnormal but, instead, was normal in behavior and of average physical structure and intelligence. Shortly after the discovery of this male, several dramatic cases of criminality came to light in Australia, France, and the United States, involving males with the chromosomal abnormality.

As Fox noted, some authorities have contended that persons with an extra Y chromosome tend toward tall stature, long arms, severe acne, mental retardation, severe mental illness, and pronounced aggressive antisocial behavior of long duration. Clearly, if such a pattern were established, biological endowment would be linked to criminality.

Fox also reviewed a series of studies showing that the XYY pattern is found in only about 0.15 percent of newborn male infants in the United States, Scotland, and Canada. It appeared in about 3 percent of the males in a Scottish maximum-security mental hospital where offenders were incarcerated, and it was also found to be more frequent in some other samples of offenders.[29] Fox concluded: "It cannot be denied that there is evidence that gross chromosomal abnormalities are found in a small but unexpected number of males who become institutionalized for criminal or abnormal psychiatric behavior; but the stage at which it is meaningful to talk of an XYY syndrome . . . has certainly not been reached."[30] Parallel results came out of a study among a large sample of Danish men which found that the XYY pattern was quite rare in the general population. Those males who did show this chromosomal pattern had higher crime rates than men of normal chromosomal type, but the XYY offenders did not turn out to be involved in aggressive crimes.[31]

The evidence at hand only indicates that somewhat larger numbers of incarcerated deviants than normal members of the population have the XYY pattern (although some males who show the XYY pattern are not abnormal or criminal). Regarding violent bizarre antisocial tendencies on the part of such individuals, the existing data indicate that "contrary to expectations generated by popular reports and mass media, the studies done thus far are largely in agreement and demonstrate rather conclusively that males of the XYY type are not predictably aggressive. If anything, as a group they are somewhat less aggressive than comparable XY's."[32] Existing evidence does not support notions that physical, neurological, and physiological abnormalities characterize XYY individuals.[33] Fox and several others also suggested that the apparent tendency for XYY persons to be relatively tall may be implicated in a social way in criminality; courts and psychiatrists may be biased in directing them toward mental hospitals and prisons because their great build and height present a frightening picture.

In summary, the XYY pattern is rare enough in the population that it cannot be a major factor in lawbreaking. Additionally, identified offenders who show this pattern seem not to be violent and aggressive individuals, contrary to popular views. Finally, how the XYY pattern produces deviant behavior, if indeed it does have this effect, remains unclear. Fox, as well as Theodore Sarbin and Jeffrey Miller, concluded that this argument about XYY chromosomes is a modern version of demonism, in which fruitless attempts are made to locate the causes of crime in internal defects within the offender rather than in the operation of social and cultural factors.

INTELLIGENCE LEVELS AND DELINQUENCY

This review of biogenic endeavors would be incomplete without at least some mention of recent work on the issue of the relationship, if any, between intelligence and delinquency. Recall that Chapter 2 devoted some attention to the premodern versions of this line of argument, which claimed that adult and juvenile offenders are frequently drawn from the feebleminded segment of the general population. Advocates of that proposition were not able to produce evidence supporting it. However, this general hypothesis has been resurrected in a much-modified form in recent claims that delinquents tend to exhibit somewhat lower intelligence-test scores than nondelinquents. This modern contention does not argue that offenders are intellectually impaired or that they show other gross differences in intelligence.

Robert Gordon carried out one inquiry that related to intelligence levels of delinquents and nondelinquents.[34] He assembled a number of studies that provided data on the prevalence of delinquency in different communities, that is, the portion of all youths who become involved in juvenile misconduct before reaching age 18. He reported that delinquency rates for white youths are relatively stable for cities over about 40,000 population, as are rates for black youngsters, although the latter show greater involvement in lawbreaking than do the former. Gordon offered the interpretation that delinquency is most often engaged in by youths with lower intelligence scores than nonoffenders, and that racial variations in intelligence are responsible for higher rates among black youths.

In another essay, Hirschi and Hindelang contributed to the renewed dialogue on biologically related factors in lawbreaking through their detailed review of the research evidence on delinquency and intelligence.[35] They showed that intelligence is strongly related to delinquency, probably because of its effects on school performance. Youths with lower IQs who do poorly in school become engaged in juvenile misconduct. Intelligence apparently is an important variable that differentiates juvenile offenders—particularly officially processed youths—from nondelinquents, in spite of much sociological wisdom to the contrary. What is less clear regarding these findings is the extent to which measured intelligence is itself a social product arising from subcultural variations in learning environments and other social factors of that kind, rather than an index of innate intelligence. The debate on that question is a continuing and heated one.

SUMMING UP

What shall we make of this mass of material on biogenic factors in criminality? It is difficult to disagree with Shah and Roth in their judgment that sociologists and criminologists have been premature in dismissing biologically related hypotheses from causal analysis.[36] The recent research findings growing out of modern theories cannot be dismissed out of hand. Although only equivocal conclusions are in order, the research results to date demand that an open mind be maintained on the issue of biological correlates of lawbreaking.

psychogenic explanations of crime

Chapter 3 noted that the psychogenic approach is devoted predominately to the identification of social-psychological factors that result in lawbreaking by particular actors. The central hypothesis is that the critical causal factors center around personality problems to which criminality is a response. Regarding delinquent behavior, August Aichhorn, a pioneering figure in the development of this perspective, declared: "There must be something in the child himself which the environment brings out in the form of delinquency."[37] According to this view criminals and delinquents behave as they do because they are in some way "sick" or "maladjusted." Aichhorn's statement also indicated a second premise of the psychogenic perspective: the environment may act as a precipitating but never as a primary force in causation. However, as we shall see in later sections of this chapter, different psychogenic statements accord varying weight to the influences of environmental pressures. Thus, psychogenic arguments have given varying amounts of attention to environmental versus social factors.

Psychiatric formulations are nearly always mute regarding *rates* of deviance. They pay little or no attention to the differential rates of criminality among the different social classes or among other segments of the population, even though official data regarding conventional criminality, to which psychogenic propositions are usually applied, suggest that this kind of illegality is heavily concentrated in lower-class groups, minority groups, and so forth. How are psychogenic claims, emphasizing personality problems of offenders, to be reconciled with these observations?

Four possible arguments that might explain this apparent contradiction are: (1) personality problems are not class concentrated. Thus, personality pathologies might lead to criminality under certain environmental stresses but result in other reponses in different environmental settings. It may be that middle-class individuals solve their emotional tensions in noncriminal ways, while severe conditions of social deprivation impel emotionally upset individuals toward criminality. That is, in less stressful social circumstances emotional tensions may be discharged in noncriminal ways, while under more stressful conditions the reverse may operate. (2) Personality problems, again, are common at all social-class levels. Further, these personality dynamics lead to criminality as a common response at all class levels. However, differential law-enforcement practices result in lower-status individuals becoming officially designated as offenders and middle-class persons remaining "hidden" criminals. (3) Both personality problems and criminality are concentrated in lower-class groups, so that middle-class persons are both noncriminal in behavior and well adjusted in terms of mental health.[38] And (4), conventional offenders do not commonly exhibit personality problems at all.

The psychogenic perspective, largely the product of psychiatrists, has been a major theme in etiological analysis, with a large number of articles and books presenting causal theories and research in these terms. This approach has been the dominant influence in the development of individual-treatment theories and processes. The rise of the rehabilitative orientation in correctional institutions centered, for the most part, around the growth of theories arguing that offenders are emotionally "sick." Prison programs, probation services, guidance clinics, juvenile courts, and other treatment agencies have considered the lawbreaker as an emotionally disturbed person in need of psychotherapeutic treatment, almost to the exclusion of any other tactic.[39]

The remainder of this chapter will summarize the basic outlines of the psychogenic perspective. This is no small job, so we need a sorting scheme if we are to come to grips with the many versions of psychogenic theory and research efforts.

FORMS OF PSYCHOGENIC ANALYSIS

First, let us consider the now defunct concern with the hypothesis that criminals are to be explained as sufferers from psychoses or some other marked pattern of mental disorder. This early idea failed to pass the test of evidence. The major portion of this chapter examines a number of contemporary psychogenic perspectives which, in one form or another, advance the thesis that offenders respond to relatively subtle psychological forces rather than to some kind of gross pathology. The *psychoanalytic* position is one of these variants growing out of the psychoanalytic theory developed by Sigmund Freud and extended to crime and delinquency by Aichhorn, Friedlander, and others. In addition, a host of more *general arguments* regarding misbehavior and personality problems do not stem directly from psychoanalytic thought, such as the work of Healy and Bronner, Hewitt and Jenkins, the Gluecks, and many others. A third argument is that criminal deviance is the product of *psychopathic* or *sociopathic* personality structures.

In the following material, psychogenic statements regarding both criminals and delinquents will be noted. There are several reasons for discussing psychiatric claims about juvenile delinquents. Many of the most detailed versions of psychiatric viewpoints have been concerned with delinquents. Many psychogenic arguments imply that they hold for adult and juvenile lawbreakers alike. Finally, separation of adult from youthful offenders is often an arbitrary distinction, in that many juvenile delinquents eventually become adult criminals. If personality problems and emotional tensions are involved in juvenile misconduct, they are also indirectly implicated in the causation of adult criminality.

The concluding part of this chapter articulates some psychogenic considerations that we must attend to in the development of etiological theory. Certain psychological formulations are essential elements of crime causation and we cannot overlook them if we are to explain criminality. In some kinds of criminal behavior, emotional tensions play a highly significant causal role. However, as will become clear, a number of improvements are needed in psychogenic theory and research before psychogenic formulations can be combined with sociogenic views.

mental disorder and crime

Following the death of the feeblemindedness theory of criminality, the idea grew that criminality is often attributable to serious forms of mental disorder or impairment. In the early enthusiasm for this view, large proportions of offenders were diagnosed as suffering from mental pathology. Thus, 99.5 percent of the inmates at the Pontiac Reformatory in Illinois, during the period from 1919 to 1929, were classified as psychiatrically abnormal, and most were diagnosed as "psychopathic."[40] Bernard Glueck's study of Sing Sing inmates classified 12 percent of the prisoners as mentally diseased or deteriorated, along with 19 percent as "psychopathic personalities."[41] At the same time, a summary of surveys of the incidence of mental disorders among offenders, carried out before 1931, showed wide variations from one jurisdiction to another in the prevalence and forms of pathology reported.[42] This early work revealed more about the biases and preconceptions of the psychiatrists and other diagnosticians than it did about the actual characteristics of offenders.

After the first enthusiasm for the psychopathological hypothesis, inquiries into the extent of psychotic disorders and other gross forms of pathology among criminals involved estimates that these conditions are not much more common in offenders than among law-abiding citizens. One investigation of the psychiatric clinic of the Court of General Sessions in New York between 1932 and 1935 involved nearly 10,000 felons, of whom only 1.5 percent were diagnosed as psychotic, 6.9 percent as psychoneurotic, 6.9 percent as psychopathic, and 2.4 percent as feebleminded.[43] Stated differently, 82.3 percent of the individuals passing through that court were diagnosed as "normal," although they were regarded as exhibiting mild forms of personality maladjustment. A similar report by Paul Schilder for the same court in 1937 indicated substantially the same thing, classifying 83.8 percent of the offenders as "normal."[44] H. Warren Dunham's study of over 500 males committed to the Illinois Security Hospital as criminally insane reached parallel conclusions.[45] According to Dunham, schizophrenia is a negligible factor in the causation of crime, although when criminal behavior and mental disorder occur together in the same person, schizophrenia is more often involved than are other kinds of disturbance. In turn, schizophrenic disorders are most common in cases of crimes against persons. Results parallel to these were found in another investigation by M. H. Erickson.[46]

By now we might conclude that few criminals are psychotics. These are two different and independent forms of deviance. As this psychopathological theory has proved untenable, interest has shifted toward the hypothesis that offenders are responding to more subtle forms of pathology. One of these modern, currently popular views is the psychoanalytic, to which we now turn.

psychoanalytic theories

The psychoanalytic perspective has proven to be one of the most influential of nineteenth- and twentieth-century theories of human behavior. Psychoanalytic thought originated in the writings of Sigmund Freud (1856–1939),[47] but his original arguments were elaborated and revised by himself and a host of other psychiatrists.[48] The basic thesis has been changed considerably over time. What follows is a brief version of psychoanalytic theory, in the direction of Freud's original views, that has been dominant in the explanation of criminal and delinquent behavior.

Three propositions are at the heart of psychoanalytic thought. First, behavior is largely the product of unconscious psychological-biological forces (*drives* or *instincts*) which are not directly perceived or understood by the actor. Second, functional-behavior disorders, including criminality, arise out of conflicts related to these basic drives. These behavioral pathologies may be the result of the repression of instinctual energy, which presses for recognition in disguised form, or they may be the product of inadequate socialization so that normal control over impulses is lacking. Third, to modify undesirable behaviors, the person must be guided toward insight into the unconscious roots of his or her responses so he or she can develop control over such impulses. Through psychoanalysis or some variant, a skilled psychoanalyst or therapist uncovers the basis of behavior through dream analysis, free associations, and other observations that point to unconscious motivational factors.

According to Freudians, human personality is made up of a trio of provinces or components. Newborn infants enter the world with an energy reservoir of instinctive, biological drives which are uncontaminated by external reality and undifferentiated in terms of object at birth. This component of personality is the *Id*, or instinctual forces, a major but not exclusive part of which centers around sexual drives in a broadly defined sense. At this point, the human organism is prepared to behave only in terms of the *pleasure principle*, toward the discharge of instinctual energy or tension whenever it arises.

However, soon after birth the *Ego* begins to develop. The autistic, self-absorbed infant begins to acquire an awareness of self as distinct from the surrounding environment and begins to adapt his or her drives to the requirements of reality. Expression of instinctual drives may have to be temporarily postponed owing to unavailability of a suitable outlet or the wishes of other persons in the immediate environment. The Ego represents that outgrowth of the Id which adapts the instinctual urges to one another and to the demands of reality. As such, the Ego operates as the executive of personality. Under the influence of the external world, one part of the Id undergoes a special development to act as intermediary between the Id and the world of reality. This is the Ego, which determines whether an instinct shall be allowed to obtain satisfaction or be suppressed. The Ego reaches such decisions in terms of the *reality principle:* the Ego attempts to allow or postpone instinctual gratification so as to minimize pain. Initially, the Id and the Ego are not in conflict, for the Ego works under the guidance of the reality principle to get satisfactions for the Id.

The third component of personality, which develops out of the Ego in childhood, is the *Superego*. The Superego is the last part of the personality to be formed and consists in large part of morality or conscience. The Superego is formed out of the Ego from introjected standards and expectations of parents and other authority figures. In essence, the Superego represents the norms, values, and ideals of the society which the actor internalizes as his own. It functions to "police" the person by laying down rules and punishing him or her for failure to behave properly. This psychic punishment consists of guilt feelings and anxiety. The Superego limits the expression of instinctual energy, not in accordance with the reality principle but with the perfectionist standards of parents and authority figures.

In a well-balanced personality, these three components work in relative harmony. But in neurotic individuals and other abnormal cases, some imbalance and disharmony occurs. Superego may become dominant, so that a too-powerful and rigid Superego may create guilt feelings about repressed instinctual drives. Or repressed instinctual energy may press for recognition in disguised form, leading to bizarre behavior quite different from surface appearances. In particular, manifestations of the sexual instinct may appear in these forms. Still another possibility is that the Superego may not be sufficiently well developed and that antisocial behavior results as a consequence of poorly controlled instincts.

Applications of psychoanalytic notions to criminality grew directly out of the general theory. The earliest important application of psychoanalytic thought to the explanation of criminal behavior was the work of August Aichhorn, an Austrian psychiatrist and director of a correctional institution in that country in the early 1900s.[49] Out of his experience, he began applying Freudian theory to the analysis of behavior problems of the boys in his institution. His book, *Wayward Youth*, which presented his line of reasoning, became the parent of a long line of psychoanalytic treatises on crime and delinquency.

Aichhorn's writings described several kinds of delinquents. Some were alleged to be similar to neurotic individuals; others were aggressive and lacking in Superego development. Some were said to have little capacity for repressing their instinctual drives; others were believed to have strong, distorted cravings for affection.[50]

A plethora of psychoanalytic writings regarding crime and delinquency has emerged in the past several decades.[51] For example, Kate Freidlander devoted an entire book to the exposition of this subject.[52] She agreed with Aichhorn that delinquents are persons expressing antisocial impulses repressed in normal persons. Unfavorable environments play a part in lawbreaking, but only as a precipitating cause that calls out antisocial impulses from within the person.[53] She also argued that the difference between neurotic and criminalistic persons is that the former are characterized by overly strict Superegos, whereas the latter show weak and defective Superegos stemming from early parental deprivations in childhood.[54]

David Abrahamsen is another prominent psychoanalytic theorist.[55] Although he conceded that environmental and social factors play some part in the causation, he dismissed these as having only a precipitating, never primary, role in etiology. His theory of causation is indicated in these remarks: "In general, we may say that the causes of a child's delinquent behavior may be traced to his parents, particularly to his mother's emotional attitude toward his early instinctual manifestations, which may be partly caused by her own personality makeup or by other elements from his environment. In addition, his antisocial attitude is also accentuated by the particular way his Ego and Superego [conscience] develop."[56]

Psychoanalytic formulations and applications to criminality have not escaped criticism.[57] Many persons have pointed to the vague, obscure language and circular reasoning that render many of the central propositions within the theory untestable (e.g., claims about the unconscious mind and other notions of that kind).

Another group of criticisms dealt with the substantive content of the theory, that is, the claims about human behavior contained in psychoanalytic thought. Here are some of the most frequent and telling:

1. The theory is erroneous because it assumes biological motivation, particularly instincts. Evidence indicates that instincts or drives do not exist and that human behavior is not the product of biological forces.

2. The argument is defective because it stresses the impact of experiences of infancy and early childhood, particularly weaning, toilet training, and so on, for personality development. The data do not bear out such influences of early and harsh toilet training, and other experiences, on later personality formation.[58]

3. The theory is flawed because it minimizes the influence of social factors on human behavior. Personality patterns develop out of variations in socialization experiences among cultures, and within a particular society, so that the influences of culture and social structure represent more than simply precipitating forces in their effects. However, variations exist among psychoanalysts regarding the role assigned to cultural variables in personality development; in addition, the fact that psychoanalysts do not pay much attention to cultural variables does not by itself invalidate psychoanalytic arguments.

4. The theory overemphasizes sexual aspects of behavior and motivation. The supposition that most human behavior is linked, directly or indirectly, to erotic sources of motivation is erroneous. In particular, the Freudian claims regarding infantile sexuality are open to serious question.[59]

The argument of this book is that psychoanalytic views should be rejected in favor of alternative theories that make better sense of the facts of lawbreaking. Irrational elements may sometimes enter into acts of criminality, and some offenders might sometimes be only dimly aware of or totally oblivious to the reasons for their actions. In this sense, lawbreaking is "unconsciously" motivated. However, the particular claims about unconscious mainsprings of human action found in psychoanalytic theories of criminality are erroneous. Most important, a major portion of the criminal population involves persons whose behavior has nothing to do with unconscious elements of personality or personality aberrations of any kind—who are instead normal, well-socialized individuals.

emotional problems and criminality

Since roughly 1900 psychiatrists and others have written much about emotional disturbances and criminality, a great deal of which is independent of orthodox Freudian interpretations. The emotional dynamics they have identified are of many kinds, and they have alleged that the genesis of these problems involves a large variety of background situations, particularly parent-child tensions and distorted relationships. This view owes something to the psychoanalytic position, but it does not strictly follow Freudian theory.

SOME EARLY STUDIES

Cyril Burt's allegation that 85 percent of the delinquents he studied were emotionally impaired was an early example of the general-personality-problems view.[60] Probably the most influential of the older studies was the research of William Healy and Augusta Bronner, who compared 105 delinquents with 105 of their nondelinquent siblings in New Haven, Boston, and Detroit. After examining these children, Healy and Bronner concluded:". . . it finally appears that no less than 90 percent of the delinquents gave clear evidence of being or having been unhappy and discontented in their life circumstances or extremely emotionally disturbed because of emotion-provoking situations or experiences. In great contradistinction we found similar evidence of inner stress at the most in only 13 percent of the controls."[61]

These were impressive findings indeed. Nevertheless, this investigation received critical attention as well as acclaim.[62] The critics pointed out that the differences between the delinquents and nonoffenders were probably exaggerated, because the staff members who reported on personality characteristics of the subjects were psychiatrists and psychiatric social workers, predisposed to the view that the major causal variable in delinquency is emotional disturbance. Also, the clinical assessments were obtained by subjective methods, no attempt being made to conceal the identities of the subjects prior to the psychiatric examinations. Knowledge of the delinquent–nondelinquent status of the subjects may have colored these judgments. Moreover, the psychiatric workers were conducting a treatment program with the offenders and were in frequent contact with them. The question arises: If they had spent an equivalent amount of time with the nonoffenders, would they have observed emotional problems originally overlooked? The critics built such a damaging case against the Healy and Bronner investigation that its findings cannot be accepted as valid. At best, other research results only partially support these psychogenic contentions.

Advocates of psychogenic arguments must contend with the findings of Karl Schuessler and Donald Cressey, who reviewed a large number of studies of personality characteristics of delinquents and criminals. They concluded: ". . . of 113 such comparisons, 42 percent showed differences in favor of the noncriminal, while the remainder were indeterminate. The doubtful validity of many of the obtained differences, as well as the lack of consistency in the combined results makes it impossible to conclude from these data that criminality and personality elements are associated."[63] More recently, Gordon Waldo and Simon Dinitz updated Schuessler and Cressey's survey and reviewed a series of studies done since 1950.[64] They too found no clear psychological factors associated with criminality.

Hakeem reviewed data from surveys of emotional disturbance among cases from an adolescent's court, a psychiatric clinic attached to a juvenile court, and a juvenile correctional institution.[65] The findings showed a diversity of diagnostic decisions in each of the studies. One set of diagnostic labels categorized a number of offenders as suffering from psychoneurosis or neurotic character disturbances; in two other studies this category did not appear. Immaturity and mental conflict appeared in one report but not in the others. In addition, in comparable diagnostic groups in the three investigations, the separate tabulations contained diverse proportions of offenders. Hakeem concluded that the results probably revealed more about the biases of the psychiatrists than about the characteristics of offenders. In addition, a number of the diagnostic categories in these three studies were of dubious validity. For example, in one, the diagnosis "conduct disorders" was used to classify about one-third of the cases. But were any identifiable characteristics of offenders used to recognize conduct disorders apart from the facts of involvement in delinquency? Quite likely, a tautological classification was involved: the delinquent activity of the juvenile was used to indicate the existence of a conduct disorder.

One report Hakeem cited was the Gluecks' investigation in *Unraveling Juvenile Delinquency*.[66] The delinquents and controls in that research were subjected to a psychiatric interview and Rorschach tests, a projective instrument designed to measure basic personality traits. The Gluecks reported: "Considering first those traits in which the delinquents as a group significantly exceed the nondelinquents, we observed that they are to a much greater degree socially assertive, defiant and ambivalent to authority; they are more resentful of others, and far more hostile, suspicious and destructive; the goals of their drives are to a much greater extent receptive (Oral) and destructive-sadistic; they are more impulsive and vivacious, and decidedly more extroversive in their behavior trends."[67] A number of characteristics identified through the Rorschach test as more common among offenders are not clearly signs of maladjustment. Assertiveness, impulsiveness, and vivacity could indicate that the delinquents are better adjusted than the nondelinquents.

Psychiatric diagnoses of the offenders and nondelinquent controls brought out several points.[68] First, the differences between the two groups were not pronounced; about half of both groups showed no conspicuous mental pathology. Second, the delinquents classified as showing mental deviations exhibited a variety of disorders, whereas the disturbed nonoffenders were predominantly neurotic or showed neurotic trends. This finding ran counter to many psychogenic arguments in the criminological literature, which suggest that delinquency is a form of neurotic, acting-out behavior.

OTHER STUDIES

Another body of data on the psychogenic thesis came from studies using the Minnesota Multiphasic Personality Inventory (MMPI).[69] The MMPI includes eight scales in which certain responses to questions in each scale are indicative of particular personality patterns. For example, persons with high scale points on the Pa, paranoia scale, of the MMPI give responses similar to those of individuals clinically diagnosed as suffering from paranoia.

One piece of research using this inventory involved its application to over 4,000 Minneapolis ninth-grade pupils during 1948. In 1950, the same children were traced through the Hennepin County Juvenile Court and the Minneapolis

Police Department to determine which had acquired records of delinquency. Of the boys, 22.2 percent had become delinquent, and 7.6 percent of the girls had become known to the court or the police. In analyzing the responses of delinquents and nonoffenders, the researchers found such results as these: 27.7 percent of the boys with high Pd (psychopathic deviate) scale points were delinquent, as were 25.4 percent with high Pa (paranoia) scale points. Of the boys with "Invalid" responses indicating uncooperativeness, lying, and so on, 37.5 percent were delinquent. Thus, delinquent boys tend to show disproportionate numbers in some of the scale areas of the MMPI, and substantially similar results were obtained with girls.

Starke Hathaway and Elio Monachesi were modest in the claims they made on the basis of these data. In the main, they argued only that the inventory possesses some discriminatory power. Nevertheless, critics have noted the problems of interpretation involved in the variability of results and have pointed out that a number of social factors correlate more highly with delinquency than do MMPI scores.[70]

One sophisticated piece of work on personality characteristics of offenders concerned the Jesness Inventory.[71] This instrument, developed in the California correctional system, involves eight scales and a delinquency prediction score. The eight scales measure defensiveness, value orientation, neuroticism, authority attitude, family orientation, psychoticism, delinquency orientation, and emotional immaturity.

The data produced from studies of official delinquents (training-school inmates) and nondelinquents, using this instrument, indicated that delinquents and nondelinquents did *not* differ significantly on defensiveness, value orientation, neuroticism, or family orientation. The two groups did vary on authority attitude, with delinquents exhibiting the greater hostility toward authority figures. They also differed on psychoticism, as the offenders were more suspicious and distrustful of other persons. Additionally, they varied on delinquency orientation and emotional immaturity. Compared to the nonoffenders, institutionalized delinquents were more concerned about being normal, exhibited more marked feelings of isolation, were less mature, lacked insight, and tended to deny that they had problems.

John Conger and Wilbur Miller's study dealt with tenth-grade students in Denver schools in 1956.[72] Youths who had appeared in juvenile court were identified as a subgroup among the students. Both delinquents and nondelinquents were studied retrospectively so that school records and teachers' ratings of the youths were examined. Conger and Miller found that teachers had viewed the delinquent youths as less well adjusted than the nonoffenders as early as the third grade. Additionally, personality tests administered to the two groups indicated that the delinquents were more immature, egocentric, impulsive, inconsiderate, and hostile than the nondelinquents.

A final case of psychogenic theorizing is the Interpersonal Maturity Levels (I-Levels) system developed in the juvenile correctional system in California.[73]

The I-Levels argument is that there are seven stages or levels of interpersonal maturity, through which persons move as they become socialized. Not all individuals reach the higher levels of interpersonal competence or maturity, remaining fixated at a lower level of development. According to the I-Levels formulation, delinquents are generally at lower or less developed levels of maturity than are nondelinquents. The I-Levels scheme further classifies juvenile lawbreakers into nine subtypes within three main interpersonal maturity levels, such as "immature conformist" or "neurotic, acting out." For each diagnostic type, the scheme specifies different patterns of treatment, carried on by different kinds of treatment agents.

The I-Levels theory is a complex formulation in tune with the common view that lawbreakers engage in deviant conduct because of flawed personality structure. However, practitioners have experienced difficulty in sorting real-life offenders into the diagnostic categories. More important, no firm evidence demonstrates that delinquents actually are less interpersonally mature than nonoffenders.

VOICES OF DISSENT

The popularity of the view that virtually all crime and delinquency is the product of emotional disturbances has not diminished significantly, despite considerable evidence that this claim does violence to the facts. At the same time, some psychiatrists have voiced doubts about the validity of psychiatric assertions.

A sophisticated psychiatric dissent from simple psychogenic notions is found in the work of Richard L. Jenkins.[74] His arguments are doubly impressive because many of them are solidly anchored in a foundation of objective research rather than based on clinical impressions. Jenkins and several collaborators conducted a series of research investigations of delinquent types, out of which Jenkins advanced two common forms of misbehavior—adaptive and maladaptive delinquency.[75] Jenkins claimed that delinquent misconduct is not a form of neurotic behavior, for neuroticism involves a high level of inhibition, sense of duty, and introjected standards and strict superego control, whereas delinquency is frequently the direct opposite of such a pattern. According to Jenkins, most offenders are less neurotic than nonoffenders. In addition, only the maladaptive or unsocialized delinquent offender has a disturbed personality. The aggressive delinquent is poorly socialized, lacking in internalized controls, antagonistic toward his peers, and generally maladjusted. The more frequently encountered adaptive, or pseudosocial, violator is usually the product of lower-class slum areas and is reasonably well socialized among his peers and parents. He has weakened inhibitions; his loyalty and group identification do not extend to the wider community beyond his local area and immediate peers. He engages in violations against the community with relatively little guilt or concern. From the perspective of agents of law enforcement and social control, such behavior may be regarded as abnormal, but in terms of the adaptive offender's immediate situation, his activities are rational and goal directed. His social adjustment, from this perspective, does not justify the judgment that he is maladjusted.

psychopathy and criminality

According to a popular hypothesis, many delinquents and criminals exhibit a form of mental pathology termed psychopathic personality (or sociopathic personality). The term *psychopath* usually refers to a pattern characterized by egocentricity, asocial behavior, insensitivity to others, hostility, and so on. Actually, the designation is only one of a number of synonymous terms used at different times, including psychopathic personality, constitutional psychopathic inferiority, moral imbecility, semantic dementia, sociopathy, and moral mania.

What is a psychopath? The answer varies from one respondent to another. Hervey Cleckley provided one definition. He listed six general symptoms:

1. The psychopath is free from neurosis, psychosis, or mental defectiveness. He knows the consequences of his behavior but seems to have no inner feeling for what he verbalizes so rationally.
2. The psychopath is habitually unable to adjust his social relations satisfactorily.
3. Punishment does not deter him; instead, he seeks it out.
4. He lacks motivation, or, if motivated, the motivation is not congruent with his behavior.
5. The psychopath expresses normal affective responses but shows a total lack of concern and callous indifference to others.
6. He has poor judgment and does not learn from experience, as is evident from his pathological lying, repeated crime, and other antisocial acts.[76]

Harrison Gough offered another list of signs of the psychopath, which included overevaluation of immediate goals, unconcern for the rights and privileges of others, and impulsive behavior. Other characteristics of the psychopath were poorly loyalty and social attachments, poor planning and judgment, no distress over his or her maladjustment, and projection of blame to others. Finally, Gough listed as common psychopathic patterns meaningless lying, lack of responsibility, and emotional poverty.[77] In both Cleckley's and Gough's descriptions, a picture emerged of a poorly socialized, indifferent, and uncooperative person.

Attempts to account for the genesis of psychopathic personalities have taken several directions. Some authorities have held that these persons are the product of genetic factors. However, the most common hypothesis is that the disorder stems from some defect of family relationships.[78]

If it exists, such a personality pattern might bear more than a slight relationship to criminality, for persons showing these traits might be less subject to the demands of society because they lack inner controls and are insensitive to contemporary conduct norms. However, if we are to make any use of the concept of psychopathic personality, we must first develop some way to recognize psychopaths. But this task is difficult because the concept has not been defined satisfactorily. Note that Gough's and Cleckley's definitions indicate a general and unspecific symptomology. Yet these are two of the clearer statements in the literature of psychopathy.

According to Paul Preu: "The term 'psychopathic personality' as commonly understood is useless in psychiatric research. It is a diagnosis of convenience arrived at by a process of exclusion. It does not refer to a specific behavior entity. It serves as a scrapbasket to which is relegated a group of otherwise unclassified personality disorders and problems . . . delinquency of one kind or another constitutes the most frequently utilized symptomatic basis for the diagnosis of psychopathic personality."[79] The term can be used in this way, but if it is to be a synonym for criminality, it cannot be used to explain that same behavior. Other observers have reached much the same conclusion as Preu in indicating that, in practical application, the concept has no stable referent and constitutes a psychiatric wastebasket.

PSYCHOPATHY AND CRIMINALITY

The results of investigations on psychopathy and criminality have been extremely confusing. Sutherland and Cressey reviewed the evidence and concluded that no relationship has been shown to exist. They noted that one psychiatrist at the Illinois State Penitentiary classified 98 percent of the inmates as psychopaths, but in a similar institution with different psychiatrists, only 5 percent of the prisoners were so diagnosed. Such variations tell us more about psychiatrists than they do about prisoners.[80] Other criminologists have reached similar conclusions about the uselessness of the psychopathy notion.[81]

In a rather remarkable piece of research on psychopathy, Lee Robins traced the adult adjustments of 54 child-guidance-clinic patients in St. Louis 30 years after they had appeared in the clinic.[82] She also conducted a follow-up study of 100 normal school children in adulthood. Most of the guidance-clinic juveniles had been sent by the juvenile court, for over 70 percent had been referred for "antisocial conduct," such as runaway behavior, truancy, and theft. The remarkable feature of this study was that the investigators managed to obtain interviews concerning 82 percent of those individuals who had lived to age 25, either from the individuals themselves or from their relatives.

The clinic patients who had been referred for neurotic symptoms exhibited satisfactory adult adjustments closely resembling those of the control subjects. However, the antisocial juveniles showed adult careers filled with frequent arrests for criminality and drunkenness, numerous divorces, occupational instability, psychiatric problems, and dependency on social agencies. For example, 44 percent of the male antisocial patients had been arrested for a major crime, but only 3 percent of the controls had serious criminal records. In short, the clinic subjects exhibited generally messed-up adult lives.

A major part of this research concerned the detailed study of sociopathic personality among the subjects in terms of adult behavior patterns. To be judged a sociopath, an individual had to show symptoms of maladjustment within at least five of nineteen life areas. That is, he had to show some combination of poor work history, financial dependency, drug use, sexual misconduct, and so on. The final determination that a subject was sociopathic rested with the psychiatrists, who made clinical judgments from interview material. In all, 22 percent of the clinic subjects and 2 percent of the controls were designated as sociopaths.

Those skeptical about the sociopath concept will remain unimpressed by this study. Robins asserted that some kind of "disease" or personality entity was behind the symptoms that produces sociopaths, but no convincing evidence of this elusive entity appeared in the report. Instead, the sociopathic argument was tautological in form. Although this study emphatically showed that many youngsters who get into juvenile courts and guidance clinics live fairly disordered lives as adults, making a career out of failure, little evidence in this research indicated that these individuals were pathological personalities. Indeed, some findings tended to undermine the sociopath concept. For example, the data suggested that antisocial children who avoided the juvenile court or a training school were less likely to become sociopaths than those who had been through these agencies. Does the crude machinery of these organizations, rather than sociopathy, contribute to adult misfortune and botched lives? About a third of the sociopaths were judged to have given up much of their deviant activity by the time of the follow-up investigation. If sociopaths are supposed to be especially intractable, what happened to these sociopaths?

It is difficult to escape the conclusion that psychopathy or sociopathy has often been a pejorative label hung upon certain lawbreakers because of their nonconformist behavior, rather than a psychiatric diagnosis pointing to some kind of psychological impairment on their part. Stated another way, these terms have been used tautologically, with individuals being identified as psychopaths or sociopaths because of their involvement in criminality, drug addiction, or some other troublesome behavior, followed by "explanations" that account for the behavior on the basis of psychopathy.

However, not all of the research has been of this kind. We will find in Chapter 13 that some more careful studies have been conducted on the developmental backgrounds of offenders who often exhibit extreme forms of aggressive conduct and who often get labeled as psychopaths or sociopaths. Additionally, Harrison Gough's work on the relationship between criminality and psychopathy demands our attention. It is to that work which we now turn.

GOUGH'S CONTRIBUTION

Gough's work represents a singularly novel and fruitful approach to questions about psychopathy.[83] In a 1948 essay, he identified the major attitudes and characteristics of psychopathic personality and developed a role-taking theory to account for emergence of this syndrome. Briefly stated, the psychopath cannot look on himself as an object or identify with another's point of view (role-taking ability). Thus, the psychopath does not experience social emotions such as embarrassment, contrition, identification, or loyalty. When other persons look at the psychopath, they see him as asocial because he does not play the social game by the conventional rules. He is a "lone wolf," not a "team player."[84]

In subsequent elaborations of his views, Gough explicitly conceptualized psychopathy as a continuum rather than as dichotomous. Instead of viewing psychopathy as a clinical entity clearly marked off from normal individuals, he argued for a socialization continuum. Thus, a representative sample of the population at large would show personality patterns ranging from the exemplary citizen at one extreme, through persons with negative and positive traits, to the markedly asocial individual at the other extreme. In turn, these variations are the product of variations in the role-taking experiences of persons. Finally, Gough argued that correlations should be found when variations in socialization among persons are matched up with social-behavior categories in which these persons are placed. We should expect relatively asocial individuals to be disproportionately criminals and other deviants, and well-socialized persons to occupy social positions of trust and repute. However, he noted: ". . . discrepancies are of course to be expected in individual instances between the sociological baseline and the psychological measurement, if for no other reason than that the culture will occasionaly make mistakes, in putting some men in prisons and others in positions of trust and responsibility."[85]

Gough developed measuring techniques to investigate this theory. His California Personality Inventory includes a number of scales to measure particular personality dimensions. One of these, the Socialization (So) Scale, was developed from the psychopathy theory. The following samples represent the kinds of items in this scale:

1.   Before I do something I try to consider how my friends will react to it.
2.   I often think about how I look and what impression I am making on others.
3.   I would rather go without something than ask for a favor.
4.   I find it easy to drop or "break with" a friend.

Taken together, the 54 items in the scale provide indices of role-taking deficiencies, insensitivity to the effects of one's behavior on others, resentment against family, feelings of despondency and alienation, and poor scholastic achievement and rebelliousness.[86] These characteristics differentiate relatively asocial persons from relatively well-socialized individuals.

Gough tested a number of samples of citizens on the So Scale, ranging from "best citizens" in a high school, through various occupational groups, to known delinquents and prison inmates. These groups exhibit clear differences in mean or average scores. Mean scores indicate average number of positive or "socialized" responses members of the different groups made. A group of "best citizens" in high school had a score of 39.44, a group of college students had a score of 37.41, and a collection of Selective Service inductees showed a mean score of 32.83. Various groups of deviants showed mean scores lower than any of the above: county-jail inmates turned up with a score of 29.27, California prison inmates had a mean of 27.76, and a group of inmates in a federal reformatory showed a score of 26.23.[87]

These variations between offenders and nonoffenders have been established in other research studies as well.[88] One case is the work of Walter Reckless and associates, which examined the factors that "insulate" some boys who live in high-delinquency areas from delinquent involvement. The potential offenders and nondelinquents in these studies differed in terms of So Scale responses in the expected direction.

Gough's research and companion studies that use Gough's techniques have much promise for the study of personality problems and criminality. One major implication of Gough's work is that the search for personality variations will only succeed insofar as the measuring instruments are specifically related to some explicit hypothesis under investigation.

the future of psychogenic hypotheses

What can be made of this mass of psychogenic material? What are we to conclude from these theories and research findings? We have seen that hypotheses that characterize offenders as suffering from such gross pathologies as psychoses are demonstrably false. The extent of psychotic disorders among criminals is no greater than among nonoffenders; indeed, psychoses may be less common among offenders. We have also clearly rejected conventional psychoanalytic formulations about criminality. These theories of behavior are hopelessly ambiguous, making rigorous scientific tests of the propositions of psychoanalytic thought impossible. Moreover, psychoanalytic hypotheses about criminality, even when liberally interpreted, are inconsistent with the facts. Most offenders are responding to observable motives different from those suggested by psychoanalysts.

Some instances of criminal deviation may represent the expression of dimly perceived motivational elements different from surface ones. For example, some arson cases may be related to certain sexual tensions on the part of the actor. But the motivational pattern and the social background from which it arose differ in important ways from the representations of psychoanalytic theory. More important, the vast majority of offenders are guided in their conduct by observable motivational pressures of which they are at least dimly aware and which are relatively utilitarian in character.

Conventional notions about psychopaths are worthless. As used in analyses of lawbreakers, psychopathy formulations are nothing more than a deceptive form of name calling. However, Gough's unique treatment of psychopathy is meritorious, and the research resulting from his views has produced noteworthy findings. Along related lines, most studies of general emotional problems have turned up negative or inconclusive results. Offenders do not differ from non-offenders in many of the personality dimensions studied. At the same time, certain inquiries into personality dimensions of law violators, such as the research of Hewitt and Jenkins, the Gluecks, Jesness, and Conger and Miller, have reported positive evidence. To dismiss the possibility that certain forms of personality structure do bear a relationship to criminality would be premature.

We need to emphasize one major point regarding the results of the studies of the Gluecks, Jesness, Gough, and others: that *prison inmates, training school wards,* or other samples of *incarcerated* offenders turn out to differ from seemingly noncriminal or nondeliquent individuals, particularly in terms of hostility, negativism, and antagonism toward authority figures, should cause little surprise. Indeed, observation of only trifling differences would be surprising, for the experience of incarceration is unlikely to have neutral effects on the self-images and attitudes of prisoners. A common technique for warding off self-condemnatory feelings stemming from the experience of being segregated in an institution with other "bad" people might be to project blame and hostility on "the system" instead of on one's self. A frequent outcome of the experience of "doing time" may be some deterioration of the person's self-image as he or she takes on some of the offensive identity that society attributes to him or her. In the same way, other experiences with the social control machinery, such as placement on probation, may serve to create attitudinal and self-concept changes in individuals who go through this social apparatus. In short, some psychological characteristics observed in offenders, which differentiate them from nonoffenders, may be the *result* of involvement in deviance rather than a cause of their misbehavior. The usual argument is that emotional factors produce deviance, but the reverse is not so often considered.

Even if the social-psychological concomitants of deviant behavior are the product of deviance in some cases, the question still remains: Do predispositional patterns of personality structure contribute to at least some kinds of criminality? Such relationships may exist but they are much more subtle in character than present psychogenic theories suggest. To search for marked variations in emotional adjustment between a sample of officially designated criminals and another sample of presumed noncriminals is probably futile.

To begin with, the event of acquiring the official label or identity of criminal, or of avoiding such labeling, is often fortuitous. A great many lawbreakers have avoided apprehension, conviction, and detention.[89] Accordingly, comparison of prison inmates, probationers, or some similar group against noncriminals involves a contaminated sample. Even if we could find some way, using new investigative techniques, to obtain pure samples of criminals and noncriminals, we still should not expect marked personality variations between the two groups. The reason is that criminality is compounded of a mixed bag of behavioral forms having little in common other than a shared label. Good reasons exist for supposing that a great many normal individuals make their way into the criminal group. Some are accidental offenders with no great involvement in lawbreaking, for whom criminality is an isolated and atypical behavioral episode. Others are persons whose deviant behavior represents a response to organizational strains of some sort rather than to internal states of affairs. The white-collar criminal involved in law violations in the course of business activities is a case in point.

The noncriminal group includes normal individuals and others who are not so well adjusted, some of whom may exhibit personality patterns similar to those observed among some group of criminals. For example, some individuals may show excessive dependence. Some may be naïve check forgers; others may be noncriminals but involved in alcoholism; and still others may be caught up in yet another pattern of adjustment. These varied outcomes in behavior may result from variations in "career contingencies" or in life experiences, which divert some individuals into one line of behavior and others along another pathway.[90] Most behavior patterns are the combined product of such personality elements as attitudes and self-images, as these interact with, or are conditioned by, differential social experiences. This is as true for deviant as it is for nondeviant roles. It may take an "addiction-prone" personality pattern and an opportunity structure of learning experiences with drugs, contacts with drug suppliers, and so forth for an individual to become caught up in the role of drug addict. In the same way, variations in social experience may affect individuals who share certain personality elements in common in such a way to lead variously to deviant and nondeviant outcomes. On this matter of personality considerations, Alex Inkeles has argued:

Sociologists have traditionally explained the fact that most people fulfill their major social obligations by referring to the system of sanctions imposed on those who fail to meet, and the rewards granted to those who do meet, the expectations of society. Performance is thus seen as largely dependent on factors "outside" the person. The only thing that need be posited as "inside," in this view, is the general desire to avoid punishment and to gain rewards. Important as such "drives" may be, they do not seem sufficient to explain the differences in the way people perform their assigned social roles. While accepting the crucial importance of the objective factors which determine social behavior, we must recognize that recruitment into occupational and other status-positions, and the quality of performance in the roles people are thus assigned, may, to an important degree, be influenced by personal qualities in individuals. It may be assumed, further, that this happens on a sufficiently large scale to be a crucial factor in determining the functioning of any social system. To the degree that this is true, to predict the functioning of a particular institution, of a small- or large-scale system, we need to know not only the system of status-positions but also the distribution of personality characteristics in the population at large and among those playing important roles in the system.[91]

Inkeles stressed the role of personality configurations as they affect the ways persons become allocated to positions in the social order. That emphasis is well placed, although the conditioning effects of differential opportunities on the role-allocation processes should not be minimized.

If the foregoing remarks are on the mark, new directions are called for regarding psychogenic hypotheses. More attention is required to explicate hypotheses that spell out the *specific* personality ingredients assumed to accompany some specific pattern of criminality. The theorist will have to indicate the factors that act on personality configurations to produce deviant or nondeviant outcomes.

Edwin Lemert's research on dependency as a predispositional factor in alcoholism provides an appropriate example.[92] Lemert investigated the specific hypothesis that alcoholic individuals are frequently dependent in character prior to the onset of alcoholism. He discovered evidence of several kinds favoring this contention in a sizable proportion of the cases examined. The criminological significance of this study is that a related, intuitively derived hunch frequently advanced by correctional agents is that naïve check forgers are dependent individuals. Perhaps a personality configuration of dependency leads, under different circumstances, to alcoholism or to check forgery.

One final observation is that a number of improvements in criminological theory are required before we can conduct a completely definitive assessment of psychogenic factors. Some innovations in research procedure are also necessary.[93] For one thing, the search for psychogenic correlates of offender behavior calls for construction of research instruments specific to the hypotheses under study. Too often in the past, researchers have proceeded in vacuum-cleaner fashion to administer indiscriminately a variety of personality tests to samples of offenders and nonoffenders, in an attempt to discover significant differences between the two groups. Probably a great many of the personality measures bear no relationship to critical personality variations. For example, there is no reason to suppose that a scale measuring masculinity–femininity would differentiate between some group of offenders and another group of law-abiding citizens or between types of lawbreakers, because masculinity–femininity is a personality dimension uncorrelated with criminality. In order to confirm specific psychogenic hypotheses, the instruments used must be suitable to the formulation under investigation. In a number of instances, we may need to contrive instruments because appropriate ones do not exist.

Attempts to investigate psychogenic hypotheses will continue to be flawed insofar as we fail to expand the samples studied so as to cover offenders-in-fact. Stated another way, researchers will need to follow the example of investigators of "hidden delinquency" by extending inquiry to representative cross-sections of the population and devising means to identify individuals as criminals or noncriminals without relying on official labels. We need to study uncontaminated samples of offenders and nondeviants.[94]

A final modification in research calls for longitudinal studies of lawbreakers. Whenever research focuses on samples of individuals at some fixed point in time after they have progressed some distance through the social-control machinery, observed differences between them and nonoffenders under investigation could be the result of correctional experiences rather than evidence of etiologically significant variations. The most conclusive demonstration that certain personality variables influence future behavior would be one in which the persons studied were followed chronologically from a point in time before the onset of deviant careers. Although that kind of research would be costly and time-consuming, individuals can be studied retrospectively so as to assess the likelihood that observed personality configurations did, in fact, precede the deviant behavior now under observation. At any rate, however accomplished, research will have to become more sensitive to untangling the process that generates criminality.

summary

This chapter has reviewed a considerable quantity of biogenic and psychogenic theorizing and research data, all devoted to the search for evidence of biological and psychological malfunctioning as the mainspring from which criminality flows.

The discussion of biological factors in lawbreaking ended inconclusively, in that there is some indication that yet-to-be-discovered biogenic variables do play some part in criminality. Concerning psychological forces, the commentary indicated that little convincing evidence has been produced by those who have asserted that delinquents and criminals are characterized by psychologicl problems and emotional distortions of one kind or another. At the same time, sociological characterizations that portray individuals as no more than robotlike role-players lacking in unique psychological dispositions and characteristics are surely overdrawn. The search for psychological correlates of criminality is to be encouraged.

A substantial part of this chapter was devoted to the direction in which probing for psychological correlates of lawbreaking might proceed. Most of the work done to this point has been flawed as the result of inattention to variations among offenders, so that investigators have studied mixed collections of offenders rather than check forgers or other specific offender groups. Also, many of these studies have been a-theoretical and have employed inappropriate psychological measures. Some basic revisions in theory and innovations in research design are needed if the role of psychological elements in lawbreaking is to be fully revealed. Among other things, those arguments must be meshed with those views that focus on social and cultural influences. But, all of these tasks must be pursued if criminological analysis is to be complete.

notes

1Albert K. Cohen, *Deviance and Control* (Englewood Cliffs, N.J.: Prentice-Hall, Inc., 1966), pp. 41–45. Also see Don C. Gibbons and Joseph F. Jones, *The Study of Deviance* (Englewood Cliffs, N.J.: Prentice-Hall, Inc., 1975), pp. 114–19.

2For an incisive critique of theories seeking to find the causes of crime in genetically inherited traits, see Richard R. Korn and Lloyd W. McCorkle, *Criminology and Penology* (New York: Holt, Rinehart & Winston, 1959), pp. 199–204.

[3]Pierre L. Van den Berghe, "Bringing Beasts Back In: Toward a Biosocial Theory of Aggression," *American Sociological Review*, 39 (December 1974), 777–88.

[4]Edward C. Wilson, *Sociobiology: The New Synthesis* (Cambridge: Harvard University Press, 1975).

[5]Saleem A. Shah and Loren H. Roth, "Biological and Psychophysiological Factors in Criminality," in *Handbook of Criminology*, Daniel Glaser, ed. (Chicago: Rand McNally, 1974), pp. 101–73.

[6]Ibid., p. 101.

[7]Marvin E. Wolfgang and Franco Ferracuti, *The Subculture of Violence* (New York: Barnes & Noble, 1967).

[8]Ibid., p. 143.

[9]Shah and Roth, "Biological and Psychophysiological Factors in Criminality," p. 102.

[10]Ibid., pp. 102–107.

[11] Sheldon and Eleanor Glueck, *Physique and Delinquency* (New York: Harper & Row, Pub., 1956).

[12]Leonard J. Hippchen, "Contributions of Biochemical Research to Criminological Theory," in *Theory in Criminology: Contemporary Views*, Robert F. Meier, ed. (Beverly Hills, Calif.: Sage Publications, 1977), p. 57.

[13]Shah and Roth, "Biological and Psychophysiological Factors in Criminality."

[14]Sarnoff A. Mednick, "Primary Prevention of Juvenile Delinquency," in *Critical Issues in Juvenile Delinquency*, David Shichor and Delos H. Kelly, eds. (Lexington, Mass.: Lexington Books, 1980), pp. 263–77. Also see Mednick and Karl O. Christiansen, eds., *Biosocial Bases of Criminal Behavior* (New York: Gardner Press, Inc., 1977).

[15]One recent twin study found that when monozygotic and dizygotic twins who had the same environmental backgrounds were compared, the two groups were closely similar in concordance of behavior, thus undermining the biological conclusions from twin studies. See Odd Steffen Dalgard and Einar Kringlen, "A Norwegian Twin Study of Criminality," *British Journal of Criminology*, 16 (July 1976), 213–32.

[16]Mednick, "Primary Prevention of Juvenile Delinquency," p. 269.

[17]Ibid., p. 274.

[18]George B. Vold and Thomas J. Bernard, *Theoretical Criminology*, 2nd ed. (New York: Oxford University Press, 1979), p. 122. See their extended discussion, pp. 35–123, for a detailed examination and critique of various early and contemporary versions of biological theorizing and research.

[19]Hans J. Eysenck, *Crime and Personality* (London: Granada Press, 1970).

[20]Sybil B. G. Eysenck and H. J. Eysenck, "Crime and Personality: An Empirical Study of the Three-Factor Theory," *British Journal of Criminology*, 10 (July 1970), 225–39.

[21]Ian Taylor, Paul Walton, and Jock Young, *The New Criminology* (London: Routledge and Kegan Paul, 1973), pp. 47–61; Richard Christie, "Some Abuses of Psychology," *Psychological Bulletin*, 53 (1956), 439–51.

[22]Eysenck and Eysenck, "Crime and Personality."

[23]M. S. Hoghughi and A. R. Forrest, "Eysenck's Theory of Criminality," *British Journal of Criminology*, 10 (July 1970), 240–54.

[24]P. K. Burgess, "Eysenck's Theory of Criminality: A New Approach," *British Journal of Criminology*, 12 (January 1972), 74–82.

[25]Somewhat parallel findings were reported in Michael J. Hindelang and Joseph G. Weis, "Personality and Self-Reported Delinquency: An Application of Cluster Analysis," *Criminology*, 10 (November 1972), 268–94.

[26]This theory and the evidence concerning it are summarized in Shah and Roth, "Biological and Psychophysiological Factors in Criminality," pp. 134–39; Richard G. Fox, "The XYY Offender: A Modern Myth?" *Journal of Criminal Law, Criminology and Police Science*, 62 (March 1971), 59–73; Theodore R. Sarbin and Jeffrey E. Miller, "Demonism Revisited: The XYY Chromosomal Abnormality," *Issues in Criminology*, 5 (Summer 1970), 195–207; Vold and Bernard, *Theoretical Criminology*, pp. 116–19.

[27]Shah and Roth, "Biological and Psychophysiological Factors in Criminality," p. 135.

[28]Fox, "The XYY Offender," p. 61.

[29]Ibid., pp. 62–73.

[30]Ibid., p. 66.

[31]Herman A. Witkin, Sarnoff A. Mednick, Fini Schulsinger, Eskild Bakkestrøm, Karl O. Christiansen, Donald R. Goodenough, Kurt Hirschhorn, Claes Lunsteen, David R. Owen, John Philip, Donald B. Rubin, and Martha Stocking, "Criminality in XYY and XXY Men," *Science*, 193 (August 13, 1976), 547–55.

[32]Fox, "The XYY Offender," pp. 72–73.

[33]Ibid., p. 370; Shah and Roth, "Biological and Psychophysiological Factors in Criminality," pp. 134–39.

[34]Robert Gordon, "Prevalence: The Rare Datum in Delinquency Measurement and Its Implication for the Theory of Delinquency," in *The Juvenile Justice System*, Malcolm W. Klein, ed. (Beverly Hills, Calif.: Sage Publications, 1976), pp. 201–84.

[35]Travis Hirschi and Michael J. Hindelang, "Intelligence and Delinquency: A Revisionist Review," *American Sociological Review*, 42 (August 1977), 571–87.

[36]Shah and Roth, "Biological and Psychophysiological Factors in Criminality," pp. 153–54.

[37]August Aichhorn, *Wayward Youth* (New York: Meridian Books, 1955), p. 30.

[38]Several studies have been conducted on the issue of class linkages and mental disorder, with results that are not entirely clear. See August B. Hollingshead and Frederick C. Redlich, *Social Class and Mental Illness* (New York: John Wiley, 1958); Leo Srole, Thomas S. Langner, Stanley T. Michael, Marvin K. Opler, and Thomas A. C. Rennie, *Mental Health in the Metropolis* (New York: McGraw-Hill, 1962).

[39]For an analysis of the theoretical foundations of correctional treatment, see Don C. Gibbons, *Changing the Lawbreaker* (Englewood Cliffs, N.J.: Prentice-Hall, Inc., 1965). For two versions of psychiatric argument concerning causes and treatment of crime, see Karl Menninger, *The Crime of Punishment* (New York: Viking, 1968); Seymour L. Halleck, *Psychiatry and the Dilemmas of Crime* (New York: Harper & Row, Pub., 1967).

[40]Paul W. Tappan, *Crime, Justice and Correction* (New York: McGraw-Hill, 1960), p. 117. Tappan summarized a relatively large body of related studies of criminality and mental disorder in *Crime, Justice and Correction*, pp. 117–19.

[41]Bernard Glueck, "Concerning Prisoners," *Mental Hygiene*, 2 (April 1918), 177–218.

[42]Morris Ploscowe, *Some Causative Factors in Criminality*, vol. 1 of the Reports of the National Commission on Law Observance and Enforcement (Washington, D.C.: U.S. Government Printing Office, 1931).

[43]Walter Bromberg and Charles B. Thompson, "The Relation of Psychosis, Mental Defect and Personality Types to Crime," *Journal of Criminal Law and Criminology*, 28 (May–June 1937), 70–89; see also Walter Bromberg, *Crime and the Mind* (Philadelphia: Lippincott, 1948).

[44]Paul Schilder, "The Cure of Criminals and Prevention of Crime," *Journal of Criminal Psychopathology*, 2 (October 1940), p. 152.

[45]H. Warren Dunham, "The Schizophrene and Criminal Behavior," *American Sociological Review*, 4 (June 1939), 352–61.

[46]M. H. Erickson, "Criminality in a Group of Male Psychiatric Patients," *Mental Hygiene*, 22 (July 1938), 459–76.

[47]Sigmund Freud, *The Ego and the Id*, trans. Joan Riviere (London: Hogarth Press, 1927); Freud, *A General Introduction to Psychoanalysis* (New York: Boni & Liveright, 1920); Freud, *Civilization and its Discontents*, trans. and ed. A. A. Brill (New York: The Modern Library 1938); A. A. Brill, *Freud's Contribution to Psychiatry* (New York: W. W. Norton and Co., Inc. 1944); Patrick Mullahy, *Oedipus: Myth and Complex* (New York: Hermitage Press, 1952); Bartlett H. Stoodley, *The Concepts of Sigmund Freud* (New York: Free Press, 1959). For a relatively brief but lucid and careful summary of psychoanalytic thought, see Calvin S. Hall and Gardner Lindzey, "Psychoanalytic Theory and its Application in the Social Sciences," *Handbook of Social Psychology*, Gardner Lindzey, ed. (Reading, Mass.: Addison-Wesley, 1954), pp. 143–80.

[48]For a summary of the various schools of psychoanalytic thought, see Ruth S. Monroe, *Schools of Psychoanalytic Thought* (New York: Dryden Press, 1955).

[49]Aichhorn, *Wayward Youth*, passim.

[50]Ibid., p. 115.

[51]Prominent examples of psychoanalytic writings on criminality include David Abrahamsen, *Crime and the Human Mind* (New York: Columbia University Press, 1945); Abrahamsen, *Who Are the Guilty?* (New York: Holt, Rinehart & Winston, 1952); Abrahamsen, *The Psychology of Crime* (New York: Columbia University Press, 1960); Franz Alexander and William Healy, *Roots of Crime* (New York: Knopf, 1935); Alexander and Hugo Staub, *The Criminal, the Judge, and the Public*, rev. ed. (New York: Free Press 1956); Lucien Bovet, *Psychiatric Aspects of Juvenile Delinquency* (Geneva: World Health Organization, 1951); Kate Friedlander, *The Psychoanalytic Approach to Juvenile Delinquency* (London: Routledge & Kegan Paul, 1947); Benjamin Karpman, *The Individual Criminal* (Washington: Nervous and Mental Disease Publishing Co., 1935); Robert M. Lindner, *Rebel Without a Cause* (New York: Grune & Stratton, 1944); Lindner, *Stone Walls and Men* (New York: Odyssey Press, 1946); William A. White, *Crimes and Criminals* (New York: Farrar & Rinehart, 1933); Gregory Zilboorg, *The Psychology of the Criminal Act and Punishment* (New York: Harcourt Brace Jovanovich, 1954).

[52]Friedlander, *The Psychoanalytic Approach to Juvenile Delinquency*, passim.

[53]Ibid., pp. 7–10.

[54]Ibid., pp. 116–17.

[55]Abrahamsen, *Crime and the Human Mind*, passim.

[56]Abrahamsen, *Who Are the Guilty?*, p. 27.

[57]For a discussion of some of these criticisms, see Vold and Bernard, *Theoretical Criminology*, pp. 131–38; Michael Hakeem, "A Critique of the Psychiatric Approach," in *Juvenile Delinquency*, Joseph S. Roucek, ed. (New York: Philosophical Library, 1958), pp. 79–112; Hakeem, "A Critique of the Psychiatric Approach to Crime and Correction," *Law and Contemporary Problems*, 23 (Autumn 1958), 650–82.

[58]This evidence is contained in Harold Orlansky, "Infant Care and Personality," *Psychological Bulletin*, 46 (January 1949), 1–48; Robert R. Sears, *Survey of Objective Studies of Psychoanalytic Concepts* (New York: Social Science Research Council, 1943); William H. Sewell, "Infant Training and the Personality of the Child," *American Journal of Sociology*, 58 (September 1952), 150–59.

[59]Robert E. L. Faris, *Social Psychology* (New York: The Ronald Press, 1952), pp. 25–26.

[60]Cyril Burt, *The Young Delinquent* (London: University of London Press, 1938).

[61]William Healy and Augusta F. Bronner, *New Light on Delinquency and its Treatment* (New Haven, Conn.: Yale University Press, 1936), p. 122.

[62]Hakeem, "A Critique of the Psychiatric Approach," pp. 89–95.

[63]Karl F. Schuessler and Donald R. Cressey, "Personality Characteristics of Criminals," *American Journal of Sociology*, 55 (March 1950), 476–84.

[64]Gordon P. Waldo and Simon Dinitz, "Personality Attributes of the Criminal: An Analysis of Research Studies, 1950–1965," *Journal of Research in Crime and Delinquency*, 4 (July 1967), 185–202. For another review of this research, see D. J. Tennenbaum, "Research Studies of Personality and Criminality: A Summary and Implications of the Literature," *Journal of Criminal Justice*, 5 (3:1977), 1–19.

[65]Hakeem, "A Critique of the Psychiatric Approach," pp. 86–89. Studies of psychological characteristics of delinquents are also summarized in Don C. Gibbons, *Delinquent Behavior*, 3rd ed. (Englewood Cliffs, N.J.: Prentice-Hall, Inc., 1981), pp. 108–23; Herbert C. Quay, *Juvenile Delinquency* (Princeton, N.J.: D. Van Nostrand Co., 1965), pp. 139–69.

[66]Sheldon Glueck and Eleanor Glueck, *Unraveling Juvenile Delinquency* (Cambridge, Mass.: Harvard University Press, 1951).

[67]Ibid., p. 240.

[68]Ibid., p. 239–43.

[69]Starke Hathaway and Elio D. Monachesi, eds., *Analyzing and Predicting Juvenile Delinquency with the Minnesota Multiphasic Personality Inventory* (Minneapolis: University of Minnesota Press, 1953); Hathaway and Monachesi, "The Minnesota Multiphasic Personality Inventory in the Study of Juvenile Delinquents," *American Sociological Review*, 17 (December 1952), 704–10; Hathaway and Monachesi, *Adolescent Personality and Behavior—MMPI Patterns* (Minneapolis: University of Minnesota Press, 1963); Dora F. Capwell, "Personality Patterns of Adolescent Girls: II. Delinquents and Nondelinquents," *Journal of Applied Psychology*, 29 (August 1945), 289–97; Elio D. Monachesi, "Some Personality Characteristics of Delinquents and Non-delinquents," *Journal of Criminal Law and*

Criminology 38 (January–February 1948), 487–500; Monachesi, "Personality Characteristics and So-cio-Economic Status of Delinquents and Non-delinquents," *Journal of Criminal Law and Criminology*, 40 (January–February 1950), 570–83; Monachesi, "Personality Characteristics of Institutional-ized and Noninstitutionalized Male Delinquents," *Journal of Criminal Law and Criminology*, 41 (July–August 1950), 167–79; Thomas E. Hannum and Roy E. Warman, "The MMPI Characteristics of Incarcerated Females," *Journal of Research in Crime and Delinquency*, 1 (July 1964), 119–26. Also see Edwin I. Megargee, Martin J. Bohn, Jr., James E. Meyer, Jr., and Frances Sink, *Classi-fying Criminal Offenders: A New System Based on the MMPI* (Beverly Hills, Calif.: Sage Publica-tions, 1979).

[70]Clarence C. Schrag, review of Hathaway and Monachesi, "Analyzing and Predicting Delinquency with the Minnesota Multiphasic Personality Inventory," *American Sociological Review*, 19 (August 1954), 490–91; Sethard Fisher, "The M.M.P.I.: Assessing a Famous Personality Test," *American Behavioral Scientist*, 6 (October 1962), 21–22. Fisher's main point was that the M.M.P.I. is funda-mentally inappropriate in the study of deviant roles. Instead, research needs to look for role-specific patterns of social-psychological characteristics.

[71]Carl F. Jesness, *The Jesness Inventory: Development and Validation*, Research Report No. 29 (Sac-ramento: California Youth Authority, 1962). See also Jesness, *Redevelopment and Revalidation of the Jesness Inventory*, Research Report No. 35 (Sacramento: California Youth Authority, 1963). The 1963 report presented somewhat different findings from application of the Jesness Inventory to additional samples. However, the outlines of the Jesness Inventory results from this later study of delinquents and nondelinquents were not materially altered from those of the 1962 report, discussed here.

[72]John Janeway Conger and Wilbur C. Miller, *Personality, Social Class, and Delinquency* (New York: John Wiley, 1966).

[73]For a detailed critique of the I-levels argument, see Don C. Gibbons, "Differential Treatment of Delinquents and Interpersonal Maturity Levels Theory: A Critique," *Social Science Review*, 44 (March 1970), 22–33; see also Gibbons, *Delinquent Behavior*, pp. 115–18; Jerome Beker and Doris S. Heyman, "A Critical Appraisal of the California Differential Treatment Typology of Adolescent Offenders," *Criminology*, 10 (May 1972), 3–59; "Special Issue on I-Level," *California Youth Author-ity Quarterly*, 22 (Fall 1969); Edgar W. Butler and Stuart N. Adams, "Typologies of Delinquent Girls: Some Alternative Approaches," *Social Forces*, 44 (March 1966), 401–7; Roy L. Austin, "Con-struct Validity of I-Level Classification," *Criminal Justice and Behavior*, 2 (June 1975), 113–29.

[74]H. Hart, Richard L. Jenkins, Sidney Axelrad, and P. Sperling, "Multiple Factor Analysis of Traits of Delinquent Boys," *Journal of Social Psychology*, 17 (May 1943), 191–201; Richard L. Jenkins and Sylvia Glickman, "Common Syndromes in Child Psychiatry," *American Journal of Orthopsychiatry*, 16 (April 1946), 244–61; Jenkins and Glickman, "Patterns of Personality Organization Among Delin-quents," *Nervous Child*, 6 (July 1947), 329–39; Lester E. Hewitt and Richard L. Jenkins, *Funda-mental Patterns of Maladjustment: The Dynamics of Their Origin* (Springfield: State of Illinois Printer, 1947); Jenkins and Hewitt, "Types of Personality Structure Encountered in Child Guidance Clinics," *American Journal of Orthopsychiatry*, 14 (January 1944), 84–94.

[75]Richard L. Jenkins, "Adaptive and Maladaptive Delinquency," *Nervous Child*, 2 (October 1955), 9–11; Jenkins, "Motivation and Frustration in Delinquency," *American Journal of Orthopsychiatry*, 27 (July 1957), 528–37; Jenkins, *Breaking Patterns of Defeat* (Philadelphia: Lippincott, 1954).

[76]Hervey Cleckley, *The Mask of Sanity* (St. Louis: C. V. Mosby, 1941); Cleckley, "Psychopathic Personality," in *Encyclopedia of Criminology*, Vernon C. Branham and Samuel B. Kutash, eds. (New York: Philosophical Library, 1949), pp. 413–16; Cleckley, "The Psychopath, A Problem for Society," *Federal Probation*, 10 (October–December 1946), 22–26; see also Ben Karpman, "A Yardstick for Measuring Psychopathy," *Federal Probation*, 10 (October–December 1946), 26–31.

[77]Harrison G. Gough, "A Sociological Theory of Psychopathy," *American Journal of Sociology*, 53 (March 1948), 359–66.

[78]Harry R. Lipton, "The Psychopath," *Journal of Criminal Law, Criminology and Police Science*, 40 (January–February 1950), 584–96. For a general summary of the psychopath literature and hypoth-esized causes, see William McCord and Joan McCord, *Psychopathy and Delinquency* (New York: Grune & Stratton, 1956).

[79]Paul W. Preu, "The Concept of Psychopathic Personality," in *Personality and the Behavior Disor-ders*, vol. 2, J. McV. Hunt, ed. (New York: The Ronald Press, 1944), pp. 922–37.

[80]Edwin H. Sutherland and Donald R. Cressey, *Criminology*, 10th ed. (Philadelphia: Lippincott, 1978), p. 162.

[81]Hakeem, "A Critique of the Psychiatric Approach," p. 111. In his evaluation of McCord and McCord, *Psychopathy and Delinquency*, Hakeem argued that the authors missed the important point that the concept of psychopath is useless for etiological explanation.

[82]Lee N. Robins, *Deviant Children Grown Up* (Baltimore: Williams & Wilkins, 1966).

[83]Gough, "A Sociological Theory of Psychopathy"; Gough and Donald R. Peterson, "The Identification and Measurement of Predispositional Factors in Crime and Delinquency," *Journal of Consulting Psychology*, 16 (June 1952), 207–12; Gough, "Theory and Measurement of Socialization," *Journal of Consulting Psychology*, 24 (February 1960), 23–30.

[84]Gough, "A Sociological Theory of Psychopathy," *passim*.

[85]Gough, "Theory and Measurement of Socialization," p. 23.

[86]Gough and Peterson, "The Identification and Measurement of Predispositional Factors in Crime and Delinquency," p. 209.

[87]Gough, "Theory and Measurement of Socialization," p. 25.

[88]Walter C. Reckless, Simon Dinitz, and Barbara Kay, "The Self Component in Potential Delinquency and Potential Non-delinquency," *American Sociological Review*, 22 (October 1957), 566–70; Reckless, Dinitz, and Ellen Murray, "The 'Good' Boy in a High Delinquency Area," *Journal of Criminal Law, Criminology and Police Science*, 48 (May–June 1957), 18–25.

[89]For a discussion of this point, see Austin T. Turk, "Prospects for Theories of Criminal Behavior," *Journal of Criminal Law, Criminology and Police Science*, 55 (December 1964), 454–61.

[90]Howard S. Becker, *Outsiders* (New York: Free Press, 1963).

[91]Alex Inkeles, *What Is Sociology? An Introduction to the Discipline and Profession*, © 1964. Reprinted by permission of Prentice-Hall, Inc., Englewood Cliffs, N.J., p. 57. For commentary on this general issue of psychological elements in behavior, see chap. 4, pp. 47–61.

[92]Edwin M. Lemert, "Dependency in Married Alcoholics," *Quarterly Journal of Studies on Alcohol*, 23 (December 1962), 590–609.

[93]For some commentary related to this point, see Richard Quinney, "A Conception of Man and Society for Criminology," *Sociological Quarterly*, 6 (Spring 1965), 115–27.

[94]One example of psychogenic research on offenders "at large" is Michael J. Hindelang, "The Relationship of Self-Reported Delinquency to Scales of the CPI and MMPI," *Journal of Criminal Law, Criminology and Police Science*, 63 (March 1972), 75–81. Hindelang found that those youths who reported engaging in a wide range of delinquent activities were more likely than other youngsters to show unfavorable scores on portions of the California Personality Inventory and the MMPI.

explaining criminal behavior: sociogenic approaches

Why do they do it? How do individuals become drawn into lawbreaking? Chapter 8 indicated that, contrary to widely held views among the general public, most offenders are not biologically flawed or persons driven by aberrant psychological pressures. Instead, most crime is the work of relatively normal individuals who are responding to social pressures and influences of one kind or another.

However, more is required of an explanation. How is it that many relatively normal persons refrain from lawbreaking, while others embark upon criminal misconduct? A variety of answers to this question have been offered by sociologists. These *sociogenic* theories regarding the processes of becoming an offender, the subject of this chapter, break down into three major hypotheses which will be discussed in turn, and into a variety of less formal explanations which will be examined in a fourth section.

First, we will consider the theory usually referred to as the *labeling* or *social-interactionist argument* concerning deviance. Labeling theorists zero in on the processes by which individuals become engaged in deviant conduct, for example, mental disorder, homosexuality, and especially criminality. Further, these theories stress the part played by social audiences and their responses to the norm-violations of individuals. Ideally, the study of criminal acts and careers should be part of the exploration of deviant behavior, thus general propositions about deviant conduct would account for specific types of deviance such as criminality. However, no completely adequate, comprehensive theory of deviance has yet been developed. Instead, labeling or social-interactional viewpoints have only been partly sketched out by sociologists. Even so, they contain a number of concepts that are useful in making sense out of criminal behavior.

Second, criminologists have often argued that criminality is the product of the same general learning process through which conformist conduct is acquired. According to this view, lawbreakers and noncriminals differ in terms of attitudes and behavior that have been learned, but not in terms of the mechanisms by which they acquired these motives and behavior patterns. Considerable attention will be paid in this chapter to learning arguments in criminology.

Third, a less frequently entertained hypothesis is that the acts of lawbreakers are often the result of situational inducements instead of motives that differentiate them from nonoffenders. Even so, because situational factors merit a good deal of attention, they also are examined in this chapter.

Finally, the last section of this chapter takes up some relatively well-defined views that have been put forth regarding particular factors or sets of variables thought to play a major role in the development of criminal or delinquent behavior. For example, certain patterns of family structure, such as broken or unhappy homes, have often been singled out in attempts to specify criminal-producing processes. Other notions have assigned etiological importance to the influences of mass media and a host of other specific variables.

social-interactional and labeling theories of deviance[1]

Chapter 6 examined theories centering about the social-structural forces that produce criminality and deviance, with the anomie formulation singled out for considerable attention. In these theories, deviance is thought to represent behavioral departures from a common value system. Since they assume that central cultural values are relatively few in number and generally shared by citizens throughout the society, these theories have paid little attention to reactions to deviance. Instead, the implicit assumption is that societal responses are of little significance or interest to sociologists.

A new and different orientation about deviant behavior has sprung up in the past decade or so, most commonly designated as the social-interactional or labeling view. Although it would be misleading to claim that any single theoretical position can be identified as labeling theory, a sizable body of sociologists do share a set of common themes or viewpoints.[2] A generous supply of critical commentary has developed regarding this perspective as well.[3]

What are the central arguments of labeling theory? To begin with, the theorists of this persuasion remind us that deviance is problematic and a matter of social definition, in that the violated standards or norms are not universal or unchanging. Then, too, deviance is the result of social judgments that a social audience imposes on persons. Becker's view on this point is frequently cited:

Social groups create deviance by making the rules whose infraction constitutes deviance, and by applying those rules to particular people and labeling them as outsiders. From this point of view, deviance is *not* a quality of the act the person commits, but rather a consequence of the application by others of rules and sanctions to an "offender." The deviant is one to whom that label has been applied; deviant behavior is behavior that people so label.[4]

Statements such as Becker's are sometimes taken to mean that only those persons involved in nonconformity and subjected to specific labeling or defining experiences are deviants. On the other hand, many sociologists often speak of secret deviants, who have not been publicly identified, or of primary deviance, which has not received a societal reaction. But all agree that nonconformists singled out by the police, mental-health personnel, or other social audiences face adjustment problems centering about spoiled identity not encountered by "hidden" deviants. This proposition is at the center of the labeling orientation.

A second common theme in labeling views is that *deviance arises out of diverse sources* or circumstances. These theorists do not agree that some small core of cultural values and unequally available opportunity structures can account for the varied forms deviance takes in complex societies. Instead, they stress the value pluralism of modern societies and underscore the significance of subcultural normative patterns in nonconformity. Deviant acts often develop in situations where individuals are pulled and tugged by competing interests and values. Whatever the circumstances producing norm violation, they cannot be covered by some all-embracing theory such as anomie.

These theorists differ among one another on the importance of examining the causes of initial acts of norm violation and on whether such causes can be discovered at all. Some have given slight attention to the question of initial causation, apparently because they assume that it is not possible to specify the many circumstances out of which these events flow. Others have put forth value-pluralism and risk-taking hypotheses designed to suggest the range of conditions producing deviance and have commented upon the origins of deviant acts in considerable detail. In either case, labeling formulations have paid relatively little attention to rates of deviance and social-structural factors producing them. In short, the labeling perspective has developed as a distinct alternative to social-structural or anomie arguments. Few attempts have been made by sociologists to develop detailed formulations that deal both with causal analysis of deviance rates and with processes operating in individual deviant activities and careers. Nanette Davis has commented that the labeling theory, "as practiced, has been largely astructural, ahistorical, and noncomparative, and tends to promote a sociology of the segmental, the exotic, and the bizarre."[5]

Labelers agree that deviant behavior should be examined as a *social process*, in which the acts of nonconforming individuals are bound up with the responses of others to those deviations. Labelers draw attention to *careers*, in which persons who become caught up in nonconformity exhibit changes in behavior and self-concept patterns over time. In turn, careers arise and unfold in response to social reactions directed at the deviant person.

In many examples that labelers discuss, the actors often deny or disavow initial deviant acts so that their acts are "normalized." That is, for a time at least, the person defines his or her misbehavior as unimportant or as alien to his or her real self. But social reactions directed at the person ultimately undermine this claim to normality. At some point, the person is driven toward an altered social identity as a deviant or, less frequently, away from involvement in norm violation.

Labeling theorists single out organizations and agencies that function seemingly to rehabilitate the deviant or in other ways to draw him or her back into conformity. They contend that various people-changing organizations often produce results quite different from their intentions, for they seal off opportunities for the deviant to withdraw from deviance. These agencies stigmatize the person and create other social impediments that stand in the way of rehabilitation. Labeling theorists are generally pessimistic about training schools, prisons, mental hospitals, and other such institutions, for they suspect that these places often aggravate the problems of the deviant.

To date, labeling views have been long on theory and short on empirical evidence. The labeling orientation stands as a set of plausible contentions about deviance rather than as a well-documented collection of empirical generalizations. For example, the labeling perspective on mental disorder does not seem to bear a close relationship to empirical facts currently at hand.[6] Along a similar line, we shall see in later chapters that the evidence regarding the operations of correctional organizations is less clear than labeling arguments imply.

Although labeling theories are designed to account for a variety of forms of deviance, many illustrative cases on which these arguments draw for support have to do with criminality and delinquency. We shall touch on these in the following pages. However, let us now examine certain labeling arguments in more detail.

LEMERT'S VIEWS

Edwin Lemert's work represents a seminal version of labeling theory. Lemert has written extensively on the processes by which persons are singled out as deviants, and by which the life careers of some become organized or individuated around deviant statuses.[7] Lemert's work is social-psychological in character in that he emphasized deviant individuals and their immediate social interactions with others, rather than rates of deviance and the larger social structures producing these rates. Lemert's viewpoint was based on the assumption that "behavioral deviations are a function of culture conflict which is expressed through social organization."[8] Lemert rejected structural-functional arguments, such as anomie, in favor of value pluralism, which emphasizes subcultural values and value conflicts as the sources of deviance.[9]

Lemert's writings distinguished between several contexts within which deviant conduct can arise. He suggested the categories of *individual*, *situational*, and *systematic* deviation to stand for these varied sources of origin.[10] Individual deviation emanates from psychic pressures "within the skin," so to speak, whereas situational deviation is conduct that develops as a function of situational stresses or pressures. Acts of situational deviation are relatively independent of psychic pressures among actors so that different individuals placed in the same stressful setting would be expected to respond in similar deviant ways. Systematic deviation refers to collective or organized forms of norm violation.

There are instances of deviation that approximate these limiting cases. For example, some kinds of sexual deviation can be explained only as the consequence of the wholly idiosyncratic motives of the offender. On the other hand, it is possible to point to nearly pure illustrations of situational deviation, including the prison guard caught up in conflicting role expectations making deviant acts unavoidable for him, the aircraft worker compelled to use deviant work practices to solve technological problems created by ill-fitting airplane assembly sections,[11] or individuals implicated in situations of catastrophic financial stress such that theft appears the only problem-solving pattern of activity open to them.

As Lemert would acknowledge, individual and situational deviation represent polar extremes on a causal continuum. Many occurrences of deviant conduct arise as the joint product of pressures of social situations and factors from the inner life of the individual. In many real-life cases, the etiological task is evaluation of the relative contribution that each motivational source makes to the behavioral product under examination. This job is often at the heart of satisfactory explanation; many areas of deviant behavior need theoretical models that clarify and assign specific weights to these two factors. Take the case of deviant police conduct as illustrative of the problem. In explaining these acts, the sociologist would probably have to examine variations in ethical standards, personality structure, and so on, among police recruits, for these individuals probably vary in relevant ways at the time they enter into the social system of the police department. Police officers vary in terms of involvement in deviant acts, partly as a result of personality differences they bring with them into police work. But, the sociologist would also need to examine the normative system of the organization to assess the part played in deviance by *organizational tolerance* for being "on the take" (petty graft), employing violence in contacts with citizens, and other infringements.

The issue in the above illustration revolves around the extent to which psychogenic or sociogenic factors enter into acts of deviant conduct. We shall have occasion to return to this central issue later. For example, it appears that embezzlement is most likely to occur when certain kinds of personalities are collected in particular kinds of organizational structures. Similarly, there are other kinds of criminality in which psychological and social factors both play a part.

Lemert employed the term *systematic deviation* to refer to patterns of deviant behavior that take on the coloring of subcultures or behavior systems. He asserted: "When such communication [between deviants] carries specific content, when rapport develops between deviants and common rationalizations make their appearance, the unique and situational forms of deviation are converted to organized or systematic deviation."[12] Systematic or organized deviance results from deviant conduct that was individual or situational in origin. Lemert indicated that systematic deviation is most likely to occur in situations where society makes survival as a deviant person problematic for the individual unless he or she can become absorbed into some kind of protective social system. Accordingly, the existence of homosexual subcultures in American society is, at least in part, a consequence of the harassment and hostility the identified homosexual encounters in the United States. One point Lemert made is that most deviant subcultures follow a limited or circumscribed set of deviant mores, for most values of the members are those of the dominant culture.[13] Hence, drug addicts, homosexuals, or other social outcasts tend to hold allegiance to most conventional values of society, with a few specific deviant beliefs and conduct.

Much of Lemert's emphasis was on *processual* aspects of deviant behavior, in which he showed that deviant careers often undergo marked changes over time. In the past, the usual model of explanation was of a simple stimulus-response kind, endeavoring to discover some set of influences that antedated the deviant behavior under study, often with a considerable time span separating the causal factors and present behavior. Little attention was paid to changes in deviant careers, which flow out of differential experiences the deviant undergoes in his or her life history.

In Lemert's theorizing, initial acts of deviant behavior are frequently instances of "risk taking," representing tentative flirtations with forbidden behavior patterns.[14] Whatever the reasons for these actions, many become subjected to societal reactions. Someone observes the acts and makes them the focus of concern. In this view, societal reactions may influence the subsequent career experiences of the deviant more than anything else that has occurred prior to his or her involvement in disapproved conduct. Lemert noted that societal definitions and reactions in complex societies are often heavily *putative*, so that beliefs become attached to deviant persons which have no foundation in their actual behavior. The "drug fiend" mythology, which holds that addicts are generally depraved and immoral, is a case in point.[15]

Lemert introduced a major distinction between *primary* and *secondary* deviation.[16] Primary deviation represents that state of affairs in which an individual engages in norm-violating conduct he or she regards as alien to his or her true self. Secondary deviation, on the other hand, involves cases in which the person reorganizes his or her social-psychological characteristics around the deviant role. On this point, Lemert declared: "The deviant individuals must react symbolically to their own behavior aberrations and fix them in their socio-psychological patterns. The deviations remain primary deviations or symptomatic and situational as long as they are rationalized or otherwise dealt with as functions of a socially acceptable role."[17]

Sometimes primary deviation becomes secondary; in other cases it remains primary. Secondary deviation most often arises out of repeated acts of norm violation and the experience of societal reactions. A feedback process often takes place in which repetition of misconduct or deviation triggers societal reactions, which then stimulate further deviant acts. According to Lemert:

The sequence of interaction leading to secondary deviation is roughly as follows: (1) primary deviation; (2) social penalties; (3) further primary deviation; (4) stronger penalties and rejections; (5) further deviation, perhaps with hostilities and resentments beginning to focus upon those doing the penalizing; (6) crisis reached in the tolerance quotient, expressed in formal action by the community stigmatizing of the deviant; (7) strengthening of the deviant conduct as a reaction to the stigmatizing and penalties; (8) ultimate acceptance of deviant social status and efforts at adjustment on the basis of the associated role.[18]

Lemert has applied these theoretical notions to a number of forms of misconduct and pathological behavior. Development of deviant status results in a variety of limitations being imposed on the social participation of the deviant, thus his or her economic activities, mobility experiences, and so on, become markedly circumscribed as he or she progresses in deviant conduct. Lemert applied these insights to alcoholic persons,[19] the development of paranoid social patterns,[20] and the genesis of certain forms of criminality.[21]

LABELING THEORY AND CRIMINOLOGICAL ANALYSIS

Like many other sociological formulations, there is more than a slight bit of conceptual flabbiness, ambiguity, and the like to the labeling perspective. Even more important, labeling arguments sometimes distort the real world, characterizing deviance and social processes in exaggerated or misleading ways. For example, Charles Wellford has examined the theoretical and research literature bearing upon the key propositions of the labeling argument.[22] He argued that, contrary to one key claim of this viewpoint, certain forms of misbehavior are consistently prohibited across different societies.[23] Also, he contended that there is little evidence that the social characteristics of labeled deviants are the major determinants of their fates in the correctional machinery. Instead, most officially identified offenders get into the hands of the authorities because of actual law-breaking in which they have engaged, and that the major determinant of subsequent decisions about them is offense seriousness.

Wellford also concluded that the contention that labeling experiences drive individuals further into repetitive criminality is without firm empirical support. It has not yet been established that labeling processes do lead to self-concept and attitudinal changes on the part of stigmatized offenders. Furthermore, even if these societal reactions do sometimes have such consequences, the varying social circumstances in which labeled deviants find themselves are also importantly involved in the behavioral paths they subsequently pursue.

On the whole, the existing evidence lends relatively little support to the sweeping claims that have sometimes been advanced about the allegedly harmful effects on offenders of correctional intervention efforts and about other contentions of the labeling perspective. Although labeling insights are important, we need to be on guard against the plausible but facile and exaggerated contentions that have sometimes been put forth by labeling theorists. On the other hand, some of the core concepts that have been developed by these theorists promise to be of value to criminologists. Some, such as the distinction between primary and secondary forms of deviation and the notion of situational deviance, will turn up in the pages to follow, when attention turns to the more detailed scrutiny of particular forms of criminal conduct.

differential association and other learning theories

Few sociologists have played a more dominant role in their field than Edwin H. Sutherland (1883–1950). Sutherland's best-known endeavors are a study of professional theft as a behavior system,[24] the development of the "white-collar-crime" concept along with research studies of this activity,[25] and his theory of differential association, which he attempted to apply to various kinds of criminality.[26] No other major contributions to the sociological study of adult criminal behavior have been made in the three decades since Sutherland's death, which serves as a testimonial to his signal place in criminology.

Sutherland's theory of differential association is the most well-developed of his causal arguments, but, as we have seen, he also addressed the question of crime rates and social structure. His theory of differential social organization, discussed in Chapter 6, attempted to spell out the societal conditions under which differential association, or the learning of criminal attitudes and conduct, is likely to occur.

The theory of differential association emerged over an extended period of development. As Sutherland reported the gestation of this theory, his first ideas on criminological theory began to take shape around 1921, but not until 1947 did he develop the mature version of differential-association theory.[27] His aim in evolving the differential-association perspective was stated in this passage: "I reached the general conclusion that a concrete condition cannot be a cause of crime, and that the only way to get a causal explanation of criminal behavior is by extracting from the varying concrete conditions things that are universally associated with crime."[28] In Sutherland's view, differential association is universally linked to criminal action.

Sutherland's arguments on crime causation were built from a foundation of notions on differential social organization, which we examined in Chapter 6. In his words: "Cultural conflict in this sense is the basic principle in the explanation of crime."[29] The social and economic changes involved in industrialization of the Western world are believed to have generated a pervasive individualism and other conditions conducive to criminality. The social influences persons encounter through their lifetimes are inharmonious and inconsistent, so that many individuals become involved in contacts with carriers of criminalistic norms and become criminals as a consequence. This process is known as "differential association."

SUTHERLAND'S THEORY OF DIFFERENTIAL ASSOCIATION

The elements of Sutherland's differential-association theory as stated in 1947 and in subsequent editions of *Criminology* are:

1. *Criminal behavior is learned.* Negatively, this means that criminal behavior is not inherited, as such; also, the person who is not already trained in crime does not invent criminal behavior, just as a person does not make mechanical inventions unless he has had training in mechanics.
2. *Criminal behavior is learned in interaction with other persons in a process of communication.* This communication is verbal in many respects but includes also "the communication of gestures."

3. *The principal part of the learning of criminal behavior occurs within intimate personal groups.* Negatively, this means that the impersonal agencies of communication, such as movies and newspapers, play a relatively unimportant part in the genesis of criminal behavior.

4. *When criminal behavior is learned, the learning includes (a) techniques of committing the crime, which are sometimes very complicated, sometimes very simple; (b) the specific direction of motives, drives, rationalizations, and attitudes.*

5. *The specific direction of motives and drives is learned from definitions of the legal codes as favorable or unfavorable.* In some societies an individual is surrounded by persons who invariably define the legal codes as rules to be observed, while in others he is surrounded by persons whose definitions are favorable to the violation of the legal codes. In our American society these definitions are almost always mixed, with the consequence that we have culture conflict in relation to the legal codes.

6. *A person becomes delinquent because of an excess of definitions favorable to violation of law over definitions unfavorable to violation of law.* This is the principle of differential association. It refers to both criminal and anticriminal associations and has to do with counteracting forces. When persons become criminal, they do so because of contacts with criminal patterns and also because of isolation from anticriminal patterns. Any person inevitably assimilates the surrounding culture unless other patterns are in conflict; a Southerner does not pronounce "r" because other Southerners do not pronounce "r." Negatively, this proposition of differential association means that associations which are neutral so far as crime is concerned have little or no effect on the genesis of criminal behavior. Much of the experience of a person is neutral in this sense, e.g., learning to brush one's teeth. This behavior has no negative or positive effect on criminal behavior except as it may be related to associations which are concerned with the legal codes. This neutral behavior is important especially as an occupier of the time of a child so that he is not in contact with criminal behavior during the time he is so engaged in the neutral behavior.

7. *Differential associations may vary in frequency, duration, priority, and intensity.* This means that associations with criminal behavior and also associations with anticriminal behavior vary in those respects. "Frequency" and "duration" as modalities of associations are obvious and need no explanation. "Priority" is assumed to be important in the sense that lawful behavior developed in early childhood may persist throughout life, and also that delinquent behavior developed in early childhood may persist throughout life. This tendency, however, has not been adequately demonstrated, and priority seems to be important principally through its selective influence. "Intensity" is not precisely defined but it has to do with such things as the prestige of the source of a criminal or anticriminal pattern and with emotional reactions related to the associations. In a precise description of the criminal behavior of a person these modalities would be stated in quantitative form and a mathematical ratio be reached. A formula in this sense has not been developed, and the development of such a formula would be extremely difficult.

8. *The process of learning criminal behavior by association with criminal and anticriminal patterns involves all of the mechanisms that are involved in any other learning.* Negatively, this means that the learning of criminal behavior is not restricted to the process of imitation. A person who is seduced, for instance, learns criminal behavior by association, but this process would not ordinarily be described as imitation.

9. *While criminal behavior is an expression of general needs and values, it is not explained by those general needs and values since noncriminal behavior is an expression of the same needs and values.* Thieves generally steal in order to secure money, but likewise honest laborers work in order to secure money. The attempts by many

scholars to explain criminal behavior by general drives and values, such as the happiness principle, striving for social status, the money motive, or frustration, have been and must continue to be futile since they explain lawful behavior as completely as they explain criminal behavior. They are similar to respiration, which is necessary for any behavior but which does not differentiate criminal from noncriminal behavior.[30]

The essence of Sutherland's argument was that criminal behavior is enacted by individuals who have acquired a number of sentiments in favor of law violation, sufficient to outweigh their prosocial or anticriminal conduct definitions. In turn, different persons get their prosocial and procriminal conduct standards through associations with others in their social invironment. In general, contacts or associations with the greatest impact on persons are frequent, lengthy , early in point of origin, and most intense or meaningful. Sutherland suggested: "It is not necessary, at this level of explanation, to explain why a person has the associations he has; this certainly involves a complex of many things."[31] However, he maintained that differential social organization characteristic of modern societies is responsible, in general terms, for the varied associational ties of different persons.

Sutherland's formulation has dominated criminology for two reasons. First, it is the major effort by a sociologist to state a theory regarding criminality in which a set of general propositions is enunciated to explain the occurrence (or nonoccurrence) of criminal conduct. The differential-association argument stands in contrast to multiple-factor orientations, for the latter are no more than descriptive inventories of a list of specific variables bearing some association to criminality, with few if any linkages indicated between them. Second, differential-association claims are stated in terms of a small group of core concepts and arguments to which all sociologists owe allegiance. The sociological perspective advances an image of humans as the products of social experiences, which provide them with the definitions or standards of conduct and beliefs that stimulate and sustain their activities. Moreover, the sociological view is that the primary groups to which individuals belong (Sutherland's "intimate personal groups") exert the strongest influence. The sociologist sees man as driven by a "motor" the social process has placed inside him. No wonder that Sutherland's formulation won wide acceptance, for it is stated in the terminology of sociology. It includes no alien language from the psychologist's or psychiatrist's bag of words.

CRITICISMS OF THE THEORY

For all its merits, the theory of differential association is not without faults. As is true of most sociological exposition, the theory lacks clarity and precision. The problem is not that the claims are false but rather that they are overly ambiguous; they are plausible but essentially untestable. For example, what are we to make of the contention that persons become criminal owing to an excess of definitions favorable to law violation over prosocial sentiments? Perhaps the sheer *number* of conduct definitions of one kind or another is the major determinant of conduct, with criminality resulting whenever the ratio of an individual's criminalistic attitudes to law-abiding ones becomes two to one, or some other ratio. But, some conduct definitions could be more compelling than others, so a few criminalistic attitudes could, under certain circumstances, overpower a large number of conformist preferences. If we cannot agree as to which of these interpretations is correct and if we cannot spell out more adequately the relationship suggested by the theory, we cannot definitively test the argument.

The same point holds for other parts of Sutherland's statement. Are "associations" to be interpreted as identifiable, physical group contacts in which individuals are enmeshed? The passages from *Criminology* indicate that group associations of the individual are the important forces in behavior. However, some persons have interpreted Sutherland's statements to mean that associations are collectivities to which persons orient their conduct—their reference groups—so that some individuals are in differential association with social units other than those with which they are in physical contact.[32] But let us retain the interpretation of associations that Sutherland apparently intended. What kinds of associations are "intense" ones? The commonsense ring to the notion of intensity enables us to agree that somehow certain groups to which we belong are more important to us than are others. Yet it is quite another thing to operationalize the concept of intensity by settling on empirical indicators that measure the intensity of different group associations.

These are some of the objections that have been leveled at Sutherland's differential-association theory. The dialogue of criticisms and rejoinders has been so massive as to testify to the seminal role of Sutherland's conceptualization in the development of criminological theory. Whatever the final evaluation of this framework, it has served criminology well in the role of an intellectual "pump primer."

Donald Cressey has prepared a detailed and incisive account of the differential-association controversy.[33] According to Cressey, allegations of defects in the differential-association theory fall into two groups; those based on misinterpretations of the language of the theory or on ambiguities contained in it, and those directed at substantive claims in the argument.

One erroneous interpretation holds that the theory suggests persons who associate with criminals become criminals in turn. But close examination of the argument shows that Sutherland maintained that criminality ensues from an excess of criminal associations over noncriminal ones. Another incorrect interpretation asserts that the theory says that criminality results from involvements with criminal persons, while the formulation actually refers to criminal *patterns*, many of which are carried and communicated by persons who are not gangsters or robbers. Other objections have been raised that the theory does not specify why individuals have the associations they have, even though Sutherland did give much attention to this question at other points in his work. Still another class of erroneous judgments stems from incorrect notions about the role of theoretical frameworks.[34]

Concerning substantive criticisms, Cressey noted that criminologists have asserted that the theory fails to account for certain forms of criminality, but often without identifying the exceptional cases thought to be outside the boundaries of differential association. Differential association has been said not to apply to rural offenders, violators of World War II OPA regulations, naïve check forgers, and certain other types of lawbreakers subjected to research investigation.[35]

Differential-association theory has also been criticized for ignoring "personality traits" or "psychological variables." As Cressey made clear, Sutherland wrestled at length with this objection. Sutherland believed that even if some personality traits are associated with forms of criminality (as distinct from being the *result* of deviant careers), so that some kinds of offenders are uncommonly "aggressive," "introverted," or "anxious," differential association still determines which individuals with the personality patterns become criminal and which do not. This rejoinder is reasonable as far as it goes. Still, we are left with the major task of specifying linkages between offender patterns and personality constellations, as well as isolating and explaining ingredients of the processes by which individuals of some type get selectively recruited and channeled by social experience along different behavioral paths. This is major, unfinished theoretical business for criminology, but Sutherland cannot be held accountable for a failure to solve this question.

Another problem with the theory centers about its failure to spell out the effects that experiences of the person at different age periods have on his or her behavior at any time. Some early life experiences may affect the *meaning* of later ones. They become influential in conditioning subsequent events, with persons who have encountered them reacting to certain adult associations and definitions significantly. At the same time, adult life events may have a neutral or insignificant impact on persons who have experienced a divergent set of earlier life happenings.[36] These possibilities resemble the statistician's notion of *stochastic processes*, in which the effects of any present experience or variable depend on an earlier happening in the life histories of the subjects under examination. Further, the probabilities of future events are likely to vary among individuals, as they encounter variations in experiences that have not yet taken place. Concepts such as "sequential models," "careers," and "career contingencies," capture this theme.

The theory is also said to be defective because the ratio of learned behavior patterns used to explain criminality cannot be precisely studied in specific cases. Cressey offered a number of examples in which researchers have been unable to measure accurately definitions favorable, or unfavorable, to violation of law.[37] Finally, a number of critics have claimed that the learning process for acquiring criminality or law-abiding behavior is more complex than the theory indicates. For example, it does not allow for the possibility that some individuals contrive their criminality apart from contact with criminal associations.[38]

We can find no better summary evaluation of the dialogue on differential association than Cressey's. He concluded:

On the other hand, it also seems safe to conclude that differential association is not a precise statement of the process by which one becomes a criminal. The idea that criminality is a consequence of an excess of intimate associations with criminal behavior patterns is valuable because, for example, it negates assertions that deviation from norms is simply a product of being emotionally insecure or living in a broken home, and then indicates in a general way why only some emotionally insecure persons and only some persons from broken homes commit crimes . . . . Yet the statement of the differential association process is not precise enough to stimulate rigorous empirical test, and it therefore has not been proved or disproved.

Differential-association theory has proven to be a highly valuable point of view around which many facts of criminality can be organized.[39] However, there are a number of ambiguous points in it that need to be cleared up. Furthermore, it is likely that the theory applies more clearly to some kinds of lawbreaking than it does to others. Perhaps some forms of criminality arise out of some process akin to differential association while others do not. The latter may be produced by situational pressures, psychological factors, or other forces that are not captured in the differential-association formulation. Contemporary criminology needs causal arguments that reflect the complex character of social interaction as it is played out in real life.

LEARNING THEORIES: REVISIONS AND ELABORATIONS

During the past two decades, several efforts have been made to revise differential-association theory and make it more serviceable. S. Kirson Weinberg suggested that a dynamic view of human personality must be incorporated into the theory.[40] Clarence Jeffery criticized the argument on the grounds that it is not stated in terms of modern learning theory.[41] Melvin DeFleur and Richard Quinney restated Sutherland's views in the language of set theory, putting the formulation into a tightly logical form.[42] They turned up several points of ambiguity in the original theory. DeFleur and Quinney's most import conclusion was that a testable version of differential-association theory would have to be linked to an adequate classification of criminal role patterns because there are probably a number of forms of differential association that are related to different criminal patterns. In short, DeFleur and Quinney argued that differential association is a label for an assortment of factors or experiences implicated in different forms of lawbreaking.

The most significant restructuring of differential-association theory has been carried out by persons who have restated it in modern learning-theory terms.[43] The most important such endeavor is Ronald Aker's revision using the conceptual language of modern behavioral-reinforcement theory.[44] Akers has provided a brief summary of that revised version of differential-association theory:

The primary learning mechanism in social behavior is operant (instrumental) conditioning in which behavior is shaped by the stimuli which follow, or are consequences of the behavior. Social behavior is acquired both through direct conditioning and through *imi-*

tation or modelling of others' behavior. Behavior is strengthened through reward (positive reinforcement) and avoidance of punishment (negative reinforcement) or weakened by aversive stimuli (positive punishment) and loss of reward (negative punishment). Whether deviant or conforming behavior is acquired and persists depends on past and present rewards or punishments for the behavior and the rewards and punishments attached to alternative behavior—*differential reinforcement*. In addition, people learn in interaction with significant groups in their lives evaluative *definitions* (norms, attitudes, orientations) of the behavior as good or bad. These definitions are themselves verbal and cognitive behavior which can be directly reinforced and also act as cue (discriminative) stimuli for other behavior. The more individuals define the behavior as good (positive definition) or at least justified (negative definition), the more likely they are to engage in it (emphasis in the original).[45]

Akers also observed that reinforcers can sometimes be nonsocial ones, such as direct physiological effects of drugs or alcohol, but the major reinforcers come from group associations because it is in primary group settings such as the family and peer-friendship groups that effective reinforcement or punishment of alternative lines of behavior are experienced.

Although some of the language in the Akers argument is unfamiliar to laymen and also to many sociologists, this set of claims parallels the major contentions originally advanced by Sutherland. Aker's reformulation has been utilized, for the most part, as a *post factum* interpretation for making sense of a wide variety of forms of deviant conduct. However, Akers and his associates have subjected this argument to research evaluation, in which they investigated adolescent drinking and drug behavior.[46] That study involved a self-report questionnaire administered to over 3,000 male and female junior and senior high-school students in seven communities in three midwestern states. Some of the questionnaire items gathered information on drug and alcohol use or abstention, while others were designed to get at imitation, differential association, conduct definitions, and differential reinforcement—key concepts in reinforcement-learning theory. The results indicated that each of these ingredients of social learning was to some extent involved in drug or alcohol use or nonuse, but the single most important factor was differential association with peers who either engaged in alcohol and/or drug use or who refrained from these activities.

situational factors in criminality[47]

Differential-association theory provides an answer to the question: How does someone come to be the kind of person who commits a crime? It asserts that offenders learn definitions favoring violations of law from their social associations. According to this framework, without motivation, deviation does not occur. But the differential-association theory may be inaccurate for many lawbreakers. Differential association may be an answer to a defective question that assumes motivation to criminality must be inside individuals who engage in criminal conduct. Many offenders may not be any more motivated to engage in criminality than nonoffenders. Their lawbreaking behavior may arise out of some combination of situational pressures and circumstances, along with opportunities for criminality, which are totally *outside the person*. Perhaps criminological attention should shift somewhat away from person-oriented perspectives toward more concern with criminogenic situations. Many offenders may be virtually indistinguishable from other citizens at the point of initial involvement in deviance, so traditional views of causal relationships may not hold for many contemporary criminals.

Ironically, Sutherland offered a major alternative perspective on etiology as well as differential-association notions. He noted that differential association was a specific case of *historical* or *genetic* views of causation, which he contrasted to *mechanistic* or *situational* perspectives.[48] By "genetic" he did *not* mean hereditarily acquired, rather, in this usage, the genetic approach looks for factors operating in the earlier life history of the criminal or delinquent that can be linked to his or her lawbreaking. On the other hand, the mechanistic-situational-dynamic view examines processes occurring at or near the moment of the criminal event. A situational perspective assumes that the causal process operating in some instance of criminality grew out of events closely tied in location and time to the deviant act.

Sutherland gave scant attention to *situational* or *mechanistic causation*. He declared: "The objective situation is important to criminality largely to the extent that it provides an opportunity for a criminal act."[49] In his view, different persons will define the same objective situation differently; for some, the situation is conducive to criminality, but for others, it is not. Thus, only individuals motivated to engage in criminality will do so when confronted by particular situations. An historical explanation is required to explain how criminals define current situations. Hence the image that emerges of the offender is of a person different, at least in social-psychological terms, from the nonoffender.

Sutherland probably overstated the matter by assuming that the earlier life experiences of offenders, extending over a lengthy time period, are always implicated in criminality. Contrary to his assumption, a long-term developmental process may not always operate with situational elements to create current lawbreaking. In many cases, criminality may be a response to nothing more temporal than the provocations and attractions bound up in the immediate circumstances out of which deviant acts arise.

Clearly, for some instances of criminality, historical or developmental factors are quite powerful and situational elements are of minor significance, such as certain types of deviant sexual conduct involving exhibitionism, voyeurism, or pronounced sexually aggressive acts. Concerning these forms of conduct, John Gagnon and William Simon asserted: "In these cases, the causal nexus of the behavior appears to exist in the family and personality structures of the individual and is linked to the contingencies of his biography rather than those of social structure.[50] Aggressive lawbreaking often labeled "psychopathic" appears to be another form of criminality arising out of historical-developmental factors, in this case, severe and early parental rejection.

However, one can isolate other patterns of offender behavior composed primarily of situational elements, so probing about for historical factors is unwarranted. As one case, consider the report in *Tally's Corner*, that the incidence of burglary and other property crimes increases markedly during the winter in Washington, D.C., when black construction workers are laid off and turn to criminality to eke out a living.[51] Little in that report suggested that criminality is a preferred pattern of behavior, that these persons are favorable to law violation, or that their lawbreaking is the outgrowth of a lengthy genetic process of differential socialization. Along the same line, Leroy Gould showed that the upsurge of car theft and bank robberies over the past several decades has been directly related to the growing abundance of these "victims."[52] Then, too, George Camp argued that bank robberies are usually the work of desperate men, representing a last resort designed to solve some perceived crisis in the life of the robber.[53] They are not the acts of criminalistic gangs of "heavies" who make a career of carefully planned heists or whose lawbreaking has causal antecedents located in criminalistic associations that occurred years earlier.

Drunken driving and manslaughter may be other situational patterns of offender behavior. Then, too, Mary Cameron showed that "snitches" or amateur shoplifters are peripheral criminals rather than vocational offenders.[54] They do not think of themselves, prior to arrest, as thieves, and no clear-cut historical-developmental process emerged in the backgrounds of these offenders.

Another case of situational factors is found in Lemert's report on naïve check forgery, which he contended is an outgrowth of the process of "risk-taking."[55] Risk-taking was defined in the following terms: "This concept refers to situations in which persons who are caught in a network of conflicting claims or values choose not deviant alternatives but rather behavioral situations which carry risks of deviation. Deviation then becomes merely one possible outcome of their actions, but it is not inevitable."[56] The individual who writes a check while drinking, hoping to get to the bank with funds to cover it before it reaches the bank, illustrates this process. Close examination of other kinds of criminality might show risk-taking elements as well.

Some forms of criminal behavior involve a heavy component of genetic-historical causation, whereas situational elements may loom large in others. However, in a good many instances, genetic factors and situational contingencies are both significant. For example, acts of murder appear to be most frequent among individuals who have grown up in a subculture of violence, who have been subjected to a number of disorganizing social influences over an extended period of time, and who look on others as potential assailants. At the same time, not all individuals who share these experiences commit acts of homicide. Those who engage in murder often do so within situations of marital discord or tavern fights, in which a number of provocative moves and countermoves of interactional partners culminate in acts of homicide.[57] However, one should not assume that all participants in these short-lived events intended them to have this criminal outcome, even a minute or so before the killing actually occurred.

This example of homicide is a criminological application of the "value-added" framework employed by Neil Smelser[58] and John Lofland and Rodney Stark[59] in the analysis of collective behavior and social movements. According to Smelser, the value-added process refers to a series of stages or events in which each must occur according to a particular pattern for a certain outcome to be produced. He noted: "Every stage in the value-added process, therefore, is a necessary condition for the appropriate and effective addition of value in the next stage. The sufficient condition for the final production, moreover, is the combination of *every* necessary condition, according to a definite pattern" (emphasis in the original).[60]

A value-added conception of homicide would assert that the experience of growing up in a subcultural setting where violence is a common theme is a precondition for violent acts, but that specific instances of aggression and homicide do not occur until other events take place, such as a marital dispute while drinking. Value-added ideas can also be applied to forcible rape. The research evidence indicates that forcible rapists are often working-class males who come from social situations in which exploitative and aggressive themes regarding females are commonplace.[61] But only a small number of those males who regard sexual intercourse as something to be done *to* rather than *with* a female, or who express similar attitudes, become involved in forcible rape. An important factor in the value-added process, increasing the likelihood that forcible rape will occur, may be the situational one of sexually provocative interaction between a male and female during an evening of drinking.

A value-added analysis of criminality involves a considerably different view of the relationship between historical-genetic and situational factors than the one emphasized by Sutherland. He argued that proximate situational influences were unimportant in criminality compared to conduct definitions acquired from developmental processes. However, the preceding commentary argued that situational influences may often be the crucial, final element in a value-added process that results in lawbreaking. Without the situational correlates, the necessary and sufficient causes of at least some kinds of criminality fail to occur.

Much is to be said for the exploration of such familiar notions as criminogenic culture from a value-added position that looks for links between historical and situational factors. For example, definitions favorable to law violation in the form of tolerant sentiments toward petty theft are widespread in American society and much less common in many other nations, so persons in this country do learn these attitudes from some kind of long-term socialization experience. These acquired conduct definitions account partly for cross-cultural variations in crime rates, even though additional factors must be identified to uncover the complete causal pattern producing criminally deviant acts on the part of specific individuals.

Quite probably criminology has paid inordinate attention to motivational formulations and developmental processes and given insufficient weight to situational factors in criminality. More concern should be given to identification of those cases in which one or another or both of these sets of influences are operating, to explication of the relationships between these factors, and to determination of the relative weights assigned to these factors in particular cases of criminality.

Some sense of the directions to be explored is contained in the preceding pages. Situational elements are probably involved in a good many nontrivial instances of criminality, not just when the speeding motorist responds in a lawbreaking fashion to the inducements of the moment. Thus, prisons may contain many persons who became enmeshed in criminality more out of adverse situations than out of differential learning. Along this line is Bruce Jackson's account of the life style of a contemporary Texas "character" (criminal argot for a police character, that is, an offender well known to law-enforcement agencies).[62] This thief was a safe-robber from an upper-middle-class background who drifted into deviance after becoming detached from familial ties, rather than being inducted into crime through some kind of associational learning. Once involved in the thief life, he discovered that he enjoyed stealing and the "wine, women, and song" life style that accompanied it. Another instructive case is Gilbert Geis's analysis of the occupational cross-pressures under which participants in the heavy electrical equipment antitrust cases of 1961 found themselves. Situational inducements to law violation appeared to have more to do with this behavior than did any kind of learning of antisocial sentiments through differential association.[63]

Examples illustrating the need for attention to situational elements in lawbreaking could be multiplied. However, systematic attention to etiological theory rather than the simple addition of illustrations is required.

family factors and other particularistic hypotheses

Theoretical formulations about single factors or causal patterns in criminality have enjoyed a good measure of popularity. The most important of these assigns a crucial etiological role to intrafamily experiences. A great many psychiatrists, psychologists, and sociologists generally agree that the family is critical in the genesis of patterns of lawbreaking. Beyond this consensus, however, a variety of interpretations of the precise significance attached to home factors exists. Some people claim that the family variable is *the* crucial one; others take a much more cautious position, arguing that it is only one of a number of important considerations and not always the most critical.

The rationale behind heavy emphasis on home factors in criminality is easily stated. Take first the matter of delinquency and the role of parental family processes in it. In almost every society, the family has the most intense and consistent contact with children from infantile dependence through at least the preadolescent stage of life. Even in American society, where other social structures invade childrearing, no other social institution has the same degree of control over the socialization process as does the family. Thus, primary group interaction within family settings probably greatly influences the behavior of all young-sters, delinquent or nondelinquent. As a consequence, much interest has centered on relationships among home conditions, childrearing practices, and delinquent conduct.

The family is an important force in adult criminality, but for somewhat different reasons. Some forms of adult lawbreaking may result from distortions and pathologies in the offender's childhood experiences in his or her family. But nearly all adult persons eventually leave the parental family situation and move into a marriage, where they become engaged in the creation and maintenance of a new family system. At any point in time, most adult Americans are either married or in transition between marriages. The family is the major anchorage point for most adults; given that an individual is in a stable family unit, his or her behavior is likely to be conventional. On the other hand, since disruptions of marital relationships often seem implicated in a host of forms of aberrant, deviant, or otherwise unusual behavior, some kinds of criminality may represent responses to distorted family relationships. Father–daughter incest, acts of victim-precipitated homicide carried out on marital partners, and exhibitionism are instances wherein family variables may be importantly involved.

As far as investigations of the role of family dynamics in criminality are concerned, the bulk of research has concentrated on juvenile delinquents. Sutherland and Cressey have summarized the generalizations involving home conditions and delinquency. Delinquents tend to come from homes characterized by one or more of the following conditions: other members of the family are criminal, delinquent, or alcoholic; one or both parents are absent from the home through divorce, desertion, or death; the home is marked by a lack of parental control; home uncongeniality is evidenced by such things as domination by one member, favoritism, oversolicitude, overseverity, neglect, or jealousy; racial or religious differences in conventions and standards; foster home or institutional home situations; and economic pressures stemming from unemployment or insufficient income.[64]

The Gluecks' study of 500 delinquents and 500 nonoffenders was a major source of data regarding home factors.[65] They reported that 49.8 percent of the delinquents but only 28.8 percent of the nonoffenders were from broken homes.[66] Moreover, 60.4 percent of the delinquents and 34.2 percent of the nondelinquents had at some time prior to the study lived in a home broken by separation, divorce, death, or prolonged absence of one parent.[67] The offenders were more commonly from homes in which the parents had a history of serious physical ailments, mental retardation, emotional disturbance, drunkenness, or criminality.

The social climate of the delinquents' homes was wretched in other ways, too. The parents of the delinquents were not good managers of income, were relatively poor planners of home routine, and exhibited less self-respect than parents of the nonoffenders. The same parents were less ambitious, had poorer conduct standards, and poorer conjugal relations. The mothers of the delinquents gave poor supervision to their children, and the parents showed less cohesiveness than did those of nondelinquents.[68] Marked differences were seen between parental affection exhibited toward delinquent children as compared to nondelinquents.[69] The parents of the offenders were also more frequently lax, overstrict, or erratic in disciplining their children than were the parents of the nondelinquents.[70]

From this amalgam of factors, the Gluecks concluded that defective family patterns represent the major causal dimension in delinquency. It would be hard to ignore this generalization, given these supportive findings. However, other variables, such as peer-group relationships, could loom equally large in the etiology of delinquency, as other findings of the Gluecks tended to indicate. Second, different family relationships among delinquents might be observed if the focus of attention were to shift away from working-class, gang delinquents to other juvenile offenders. The evidence from studies of middle-class offenders and certain other kinds of adolescent lawbreakers points to a different constellation of parent–child relationships.

Broken homes have received a great deal of emphasis, with much research directed toward discovering the relationship between this factor and juvenile misconduct. Estimates of the proportion of broken homes among official delinquents vary from one study to another, but in general they range from 30 to 60 percent of the offenders, with lesser numbers of broken homes for nondelinquents.[71]

One contrary piece of evidence on broken homes came from an early study by Clifford Shaw and Henry McKay, who compared the incidence of broken homes among Chicago schoolboys and male juvenile delinquents.[72] They found that the broken-home rate of offenders was 42.5 percent as compared to 36.1 percent for the nondelinquents, an insignificant difference. However, Jackson Toby has shown that evaluation of broken homes as inconsequential in delinquency is valid for older male delinquents but not for male preadolescents or female offenders.[73] He indicated that the Shaw and McKay study did not include girls, and other research shows that female delinquents do come from broken homes in considerable numbers.[74] Furthermore, he showed that the difference in broken homes between preadolescent delinquents and nondelinquents is rather marked; the broken home does have some causal impact on both girls and preadolescent boys.

The role of family factors in crime and delinquency is probably variable, depending on the form of lawbreaking that is the focus of attention. Several instances of research have generally confirmed this contention.[75] The influence of family patterns on delinquent and criminal conduct cannot be denied. However, to argue that family variables always have primacy over other factors would be to draw a caricature of real life. Claims that some particular family pattern is found in all forms of criminality are erroneous. Parental influences vary in significance in different types of criminality, just as parental factors or marital relationships important in one type of deviance are not significant in another. The place of family factors in the causation of various forms of criminal conduct will be explored in the chapters ahead.

By now, most of the major general and specific theories on criminality have been covered. Some other particularistic, single-factor arguments have been made in addition to those previously enumerated. For example, some attention has been given to the role of mass media in criminality, parallel to the common form of this contention popular with the general public. However, most of these specific claims are concerned with delinquents rather than with adult criminals.

Evaluation of single-variable contentions should be fully apparent. Insofar as single variables have merit, it is only as components of more complex, multivariate formulations. Single causal variables operate in a complex interrelationship with many others, and the criminologist's theoretical task is to identify these groups of variables.

summary

This chapter began with a brief look at theories regarding the onset and development of patterns of deviant behavior, with particular attention given to labeling formulations about deviance. Arguments about the genesis of criminality represent a special case or particular variant of more general propositions about deviant conduct.

Labeling theorists put forth claims which argue that deviance arises out of myriad circumstances, or as some have put it, deviance is polygenetic. Also, many theorists lay considerable emphasis upon situational factors and deviance-provoking circumstances rather than upon psychological motivations in attempts to account for nonconformity of various kinds. Another major focus centers about the study of process elements in deviance, with much attention given to shifts and turns which deviant patterns take as they unfold. The various deviant pathways are thought to be heavily influenced by social reactions directed at norm violators, so that experiences such as being arrested or dealt with in a mental hospital are viewed as significant career contingencies.

These insights can be applied fruitfully to the study of criminality. They suggest that criminologists ought to pay more attention to situational elements in criminal etiology. The latter part of this chapter took up the question of situational factors in criminality, concluding that there are a number of situational hypotheses that remain to be investigated.

This chapter also examined Sutherland's theory of differential association at some length, for that argument has been the single most influential attempt by a sociologist to articulate a theory of criminal etiology taking a social learning form. Although this formulation has played a signal role in the development of American criminology, the argument contains some major ambiguities in it, such that it is provocative but essentially untestable.

This chapter has concluded the comprehensive probing into the body of existing theoretical formulations on criminality. The time has now come for a close look at a different orientation, which directs attention to patterns of crime and criminal behavior and away from general formulations of the kind considered in this chapter.

notes

[1]For a critical examination of deviance theory, including certain aspects of social-psychological and other approaches to deviance, see Don C. Gibbons and Joseph F. Jones, *The Study of Deviance* (Englewood Cliffs, N.J.: Prentice-Hall, Inc., 1975); Gibbons, *The Criminological Enterprise* (Englewood Cliffs, N.J.: Prentice-Hall, Inc., 1979), pp. 143–55.

[2]For some of the major works that have advanced this perspective, see Edwin M. Lemert, *Human Deviance, Social Problems, and Social Control*, 2nd ed. (Englewood Cliffs, N.J.: Prentice-Hall, Inc., 1972); Lemert, *Social Pathology* (New York: McGraw-Hall, 1951); Lemert, "Beyond Mead: The Societal Reaction to Deviance," *Social Problems*, 21 (April 1974), 457–68; Howard S. Becker, *Outsiders* (New York: Free Press, 1963); Jack D. Douglas, "Deviance and Order in Pluralistic Society," in *Theoretical Sociology*, John C. McKinney and Edward A. Tiryakian, eds. (New York: Prentice-Hall, Inc., 1970); Douglas, *American Social Order* (New York: Free Press, 1971); Douglas, ed., *Deviance and Respectability* (New York: Basic Books, 1970); Kai T. Erikson, "Notes on the Sociology of Deviance," *Social Problems*, 9 (Spring 1962), 307–14; John I. Kitsuse, "Societal Reaction to Deviant Behavior: Problems of Theory and Method," in *The Other Side*, Howard S. Becker, ed. (New York: Free Press, 1964), pp. 87–102; John Lofland, *Deviance and Identity* (Englewood Cliffs, N. J.: Prentice-Hall, Inc., 1969); David Matza, *Becoming Deviant* (Englewood Cliffs, N.J.: Prentice-Hall, Inc., 1969); Edwin M. Schur, *Labeling Deviant Behavior* (New York: Harper & Row, Pub., 1971); Eliot Freidson, "Disability as Social Deviance," in *Sociology and Rehabilitation*, Marvin B. Sussman, ed. (Washington, D.C.: American Sociological Association, 1965), pp. 71–99; Robert A. Scott and Jack D. Douglas, eds., *Theoretical Perspectives on Deviance* (New York: Basic Books, 1972); Earl Rubington and Martin S. Weinberg, *Deviance: The Interactional Perspective*, 2nd ed. (New York: Macmillan, 1973); Erich Goode, *Deviant Behavior* (Englewood Cliffs, N.J.: Prentice-Hall, Inc., 1978).

[3]These include David J. Bordua, "Deviant Behavior and Social Control," *Annals of the American Academy of Political and Social Science*, 369 (January 1969), 149–63; Ronald L. Akers, "Problems in the Sociology of Deviance: Social Definitions and Behavior," *Social Forces*, 46 (June 1968), 455–65; Jack P. Gibbs, "Conceptions of Deviant Behavior: The Old and the New," *Pacific Sociological Review*, 9 (Spring 1966), 9–14; Gibbs, "Issues in Defining Deviance," in *Theoretical Perspectives on Deviance*, Scott and Douglas, eds., pp. 39–68; Gibbs and Maynard L. Erickson, "Major Developments in the Sociological Study of Deviance," in *Annual Review of Sociology*, Alex Inkeles, James Coleman, and Neil Smelser, eds. (Palo Alto: Annual Reviews, 1975), pp. 21–42; Edwin M. Schur, "Reactions to Deviance: A Critical Assessment," *American Journal of Sociology*, 75 (November 1969), 309–22; Nanette J. Davis, *Sociological Constructions of Deviance*, 2nd ed. (Dubuque, Iowa: Wm. C. Brown Co., 1980), pp. 197–234; Peter K. Manning, "Survey Essay: On Deviance," *Contemporary Sociology*, 2 (March 1973), 123–28; Manning, "Deviance and Dogma," *British Journal of Criminology*, 15 (January 1975), 1–20; Milton Mankoff, "Societal Reaction and Career·Deviance: A Critical Analysis," *Sociological Quarterly*, 12 (Spring 1971), 204–18; Ian Taylor, Paul Walton, and Jock Young, *The New Criminology* (London: Routledge & Kegan Paul, 1973), pp. 139–71; Paul G. Schervish, "The Labeling Perspective: Its Bias and Potential in the Study of Political Deviance," *The American Sociologist*, 8 (May 1973), 47–57; John I. Kitsuse, "Deviance, Deviant Behavior, and Deviants: Some Conceptual Problems," in *Introduction to Deviance*, William J. Filstead, ed., (Chicago: Markham Publishing Co., 1972), pp. 233–43; Paul Rock, "The Sociology of Deviance and Conceptions of Moral Order," *British Journal of Criminology*, 14 (April 1974), 139–49. These critiques are discussed in detail in Gibbons and Jones, *The Study of Deviance*, pp. 130–33.

[4]Becker, *The Other Side*, p. 9.

[5]Nanette J. Davis, "Labeling Theory in Deviance Research: A Critique and Reconsideration," *Sociological Quarterly*, 13 (Autumn 1972), p. 453.

[6]The labeling view of mental illness is most explicit in Thomas J. Scheff, *Being Mentally Ill* (Chicago: Aldine, 1966). For an evaluation of the empirical adequacy of this argument, see Walter R. Gove, "Societal Reaction as an Explanation of Mental Illness: An Evaluation," *American Sociological Review*, 35 (October 1970), 873–84. For a detailed examination of the evidence regarding the effects of social responses upon alcoholics, homosexuals, mentally retarded, mentally ill, and offenders, see Gibbons and Jones, *The Study of Deviance*, pp. 144–81.

[7]Lemert, *Social Pathology*; Lemert, *Human Deviance, Social Problems, and Social Control*. We should note that Lemert's writings on deviance date back to 1951, long before most other labeling theorists were active. One forerunner of modern labeling views was Frank Tannenbaum, *Crime and the Community* (Lexington, Mass.: Ginn, 1938), pp. 19–21. In that work, Tannenbaum drew attention to "dramatization of evil," which was his term for the societal reaction experiences that drive the deviant further into misconduct.

[8]Lemert, *Social Pathology*, p. 23.

[9]Lemert, *Human Deviance, Social Problems, and Social Control*, pp. 26–61.

[10]Lemert, *Social Pathology*, p. 23.

[11]Joseph Bensman and Israel Gerver, "Crime and Punishment in the Factory: The Function of Deviancy in Maintaining the Social System," *American Sociological Review*, 28 (August 1963), 588–98.

[12]Lemert, *Social Pathology*, p. 44.

[13]Ibid, pp. 48–50.

[14]Lemert, *Human Deviance, Social Problems, and Social Control*, pp. 38–40.

[15]Lemert, *Social Pathology*, pp. 55–57.

[16]Lemert, *Human Deviance, Social Problems, and Social Control*, pp. 62–92.

[17]Lemert, *Social Pathology*, p. 75.

[18]Ibid., p. 77.

[19]Lemert, "Dependency in Married Alcoholics," *Quarterly Journal of Studies on Alcohol*, 23 (December 1962), 590–609.

[20]Lemert, "Paranoia and the Dynamics of Exclusion," *Sociometry*, 25 (March 1962), 2–20.

[21]Lemert, "The Behavior of the Systematic Check Forger," *Social Problems*, 6 (Fall 1958), 141–49; Lemert, "An Isolation and Closure Theory of Naïve Check Forgery," *Journal of Criminal Law, Criminology and Police Science*, 44 (September–October 1953), 296–307. Becker's views parallel those of Lemert. See Becker, *The Other Side*. He pointed out that no automatic, fixed, and invariant relationship exists between behavioral acts and societal reactions to conduct as deviant. Becker also stressed the temporal patterning of deviant behavior, suggesting that sociologists need to pay attention to *sequential models of deviance*, that is, orderly changes in the actions of the deviant over time. He offered the concepts of *deviant careers* and *career contingencies* as explanatory tools. A career contingency is a factor that results in the movement of a career incumbent from one position to another in a career pattern. Another major insight in Becker's work centers on the distinction between *master* and *subordinate* statuses, in which he argued that a particular deviant status, such as that of "hood," "crazy," or "hustler," may become superordinate over the individual's other statuses, coloring all of his or her social relationships.

[22]Charles Wellford, "Labeling Theory and Criminology: An Assessment," *Social Problems*, 22 (February 1975), 332–45.

[23]Robert B. Edgerton, *Deviance: A Cross-Cultural Perspective* (Menlo Park, Calif.: Cummings Publishing Co., 1976); Graeme Newman, *Comparative Deviance: Perception and Law in Six Cultures* (New York: Elsevier/North-Holland, 1967).

[24]Edwin H. Sutherland, *The Professional Thief* (Chicago: University of Chicago Press, 1937).

[25]Edwin H. Sutherland, *White Collar Crime* (New York: Dryden Press, 1949).

[26]Edwin H. Sutherland and Donald R. Cressey, *Criminology*, 10th ed. (Philadelphia: Lippincott, 1978), pp. 80–83. See also Albert K. Cohen, Alfred Lindesmith, and Karl Schuessler, eds., *The Sutherland Papers* (Bloomington: Indiana University Press, 1956) for a résumé of a large number of other papers and studies by Sutherland. For other useful comments on differential-association theory, see Donald R. Cressey, "Epidemiology and Individual Conduct: A Case from Criminology," *Pacific Sociological Review*, 3 (Fall 1960), 47–58.

[27]The development of the theory is discussed in detail in Gibbons, *The Criminological Enterprise*, pp. 46–61.

[28]Cohen, Lindesmith, and Schuessler, *The Sutherland Papers*, p. 19.

[29]Ibid., p. 20.

[30]Sutherland and Cressey, *Criminology*, pp. 80–83.

[31]Ibid., p. 82.

[32]Daniel Glaser, "Criminality Theories and Behavioral Images," *American Journal of Sociology*, 61 (March 1956), 433–44.

[33]Cressey, "Epidemiology and Individual Conduct."

[34]Ibid., pp. 48–50.

[35]Ibid., p. 51.

[36]Ibid., p. 53.

[37]Ibid., passim.

[38]Ibid., pp. 53–54.

[39]Ibid., p. 57.

[40]S. Kirson Weinberg, "Personality and Method in the Differential Association Theory. Comments on 'A Reformulation of Sutherland's Differential Association Theory and a Strategy for Empirical Verification,'" *Journal of Research in Crime and Delinquency*, 3 (July 1966), 165–72.

[41]C. R. Jeffery, "Criminal Behavior and Learning Theory," *Journal of Criminal Law, Criminology and Police Science*, 56 (September 1965), 294–300.

[42]Melvin DeFleur and Richard Quinney, "A Reformulation of Sutherland's Differential Association Theory and a Strategy for Empirical Verification," *Journal of Research in Crime and Delinquency*, 3 (January 1966), 1–22; also see Donald R. Cressey, "The Language of Set Theory and Differential Association," *Journal of Research in Crime and Delinquency*, 3 (January 1966), 22–26.

[43]Robert L. Burgess and Ronald L. Akers, "A Differential Association–Reinforcement Theory of Criminal Behavior," *Social Problems*, 14 (Fall 1966), 128–47; Reed Adams, "Differential Association and Learning Principles Revisited," *Social Problems*, 20 (Spring 1973), 458–69.

[44]Ronald L. Akers, *Deviant Behavior: A Social Learning Approach*, 2nd ed. (New York: Wadsworth, 1977); Akers, Marvin D. Krohn, Lonn Lanza-Kaduce, and Marcia Radosevich, "Social Learning and Deviant Behavior: A Specific Test of a General Theory," *American Sociological Review*, 44 (March 1978), 636–55.

[45]Akers, Krohn, Lanza-Kaduce, and Radosevich, "Social Learning and Deviant Behavior," pp. 637–38.

[46]Ibid.

[47]This section is an abridged version of Don C. Gibbons, "Observations on the Study of Crime Causation," *American Journal of Sociology*, 77 (September 1971), 262–78.

[48]Sutherland and Cressey, *Criminology*, pp. 79–80.

[49]Ibid., p. 80.

[50]John H. Gagnon and William Simon, eds., *Sexual Deviance* (New York: Harper & Row, Pub., 1967), p. 9.

[51]Elliot Liebow, *Tally's Corner* (Boston: Little, Brown, 1967), pp. 29–71.

[52]Leroy Gould, "The Changing Structure of Property Crime in an Affluent Society," *Social Forces*, 48 (September 1969), 50–59.

[53]George M. Camp. "Nothing to Lose: A Study of Bank Robbery in America," (Ph.D. diss., Yale University, 1967).

[54]Mary Owen Cameron, *The Booster and the Snitch* (New York: Free Press, 1964).

[55]Lemert, *Human Deviance, Social Problems, and Social Control*, pp. 137–49.

[56]Ibid., pp. 38–39.

[57]Marvin E. Wolfgang. *Patterns of Criminal Homicide* (Philadelphia: University of Pennsylvania Press, 1958).

[58]Neil J. Smelser, *Theory of Collective Behavior* (New York: Free Press, 1963).

[59]John Lofland and Rodney Stark, "Becoming a World-Saver: A Theory of Conversion to a Deviant Perspective," *American Sociological Review*, 30 (December 1965), 862–75.

[60]Smelser, *Collective Behavior*, pp. 13–14.

[61]Menachem Amir, "Forcible Rape," *Federal Probation*, 31 (March 1967), 51–58. For a study that examined situational factors in forcible rape, see Lorne Gibson, Rick Linden, and Stuart Johnson, "A Situational Theory of Rape," *Canadian Journal of Criminology*, 22 (January 1980), 51–65.

[62]Bruce Jackson, *A Thief's Primer* (New York: Macmillan, 1969).

[63]Gilbert Geis, *White Collar Criminal* (New York: Atherton Press, 1968), pp. 103–18.

[64]Sutherland and Cressey, *Criminology*, p. 212. Also see Don C. Gibbons, *Delinquent Behavior*, 3rd ed. (Englewood Cliffs, N.J.: Prentice-Hall, Inc., 1981), passim; Gary F. Jensen and Dean G. Rojek, *Delinquency* (Lexington, Mass.: D.C. Heath, 1980), pp. 192–225.

[65]Sheldon Glueck and Eleanor Glueck, *Unraveling Juvenile Delinquency* (Cambridge, Mass.: Harvard University Press, 1951).

[66]Ibid., p. 88.

[67]Ibid., p. 122.

[68]Ibid., pp. 108–16.

[69]Ibid., pp. 125–26.

[70]Ibid., p. 131.

[71]For a discussion of these estimates, see Harry M. Shulman, "The Family and Juvenile Delinquency," *The Annals of the American Academy of Political and Social Science*, 261 (January 1949), 21–31; P. M. Smith, "Broken Homes and Juvenile Delinquency," *Sociology and Social Research*, 39 (May–June 1955), 307–11. For a more recent discussion of the evidence on broken homes and other home factors as causal influences in delinquency, see Jensen and Rojek, *Delinquency*, pp. 192–225; Susan K. Datesman and Frank R. Scarpitti, "Female Delinquency and Broken Homes: A Reassessment," *Criminology*, 13 (May 1975), 33–55.

[72]Clifford Shaw and Henry D. McKay, "Social Factors in Juvenile Delinquency," *Report on the Causes of Crime*, National Commission on Law Observance and Enforcement, vol. 2 (Washington, D.C.: U.S. Government Printing Office, 1937), pp. 261–84.

[73]Jackson Toby, "The Differential Impact of Family Disorganization," *American Sociological Review*, 22 (October 1957), 505–12.

[74]See, for example, Don C. Gibbons and Manzer J. Griswold, "Sex Differences Among Juvenile Court Referrals," *Sociology and Social Research*, 42 (November–December 1957), 106–10; William Wattenberg and Frank Saunders, "Sex Differences Among Juvenile Offenders," *Sociology and Social Research*, 39 (September–October 1954), 24–31.

[75]Richard L. Jenkins and Lester E. Hewitt, "Types of Personality Structure Encountered in Child Guidance Clinics," *American Journal of Orthopsychiatry*, 14 (January 1944), 84–94. Albert J. Reiss, Jr., "Social Correlates of Psychological Types of Delinquency," *American Sociological Review*, 17 (December 1952), 710–18.

patterns
of crime
and criminal
behavior

The compass of criminology is extremely broad, taking in hundreds of acts committed or omitted in violation of criminal laws. No adult citizen needs a criminological education to appreciate the fact that the criminal statutes define a very large number of acts as illegal, for all of us in complex societies grow up with some grasp of this fundamental fact of life. Then, too, few if any adults are unaware of the great variation among these prohibited acts, which range from violations of fish-and-game codes, such as "chumming" for fish; to burglary, robbery, and other crude predatory crimes; or to white-collar offenses among businesses and corporations; and finally, to organized-crime activities such as loan sharking, control of illegal gambling, and the like. We all are aware that the reach of the criminal law is long, extending to myriad forms of misconduct.

Although most citizens are aware of the variability of crime, this is not to say that their perceptions accurately reflect the real world of criminality in all its details. In American society, many adults acquire much of their knowledge and many of their beliefs about the world from their television sets. It should come as no surprise then to find that many of them have little awareness of the unskilled, mundane, crude criminal activities that are engaged in by garden-variety offenders, for these rarely receive media attention. Similarly, when television programs project distorted, stereotypical images of organized crime and many other kinds of lawbreaking, unsophisticated television viewers are likely to view crime in much the same way.[1]

One observation criminological evidence provides is that individual instances of particular kinds of lawbreaking tend to closely resemble other instances of the same crime; that is, rape, robbery, burglary, and other offenses usually occur in much the same way from one case to another. For example, most but not all homicides develop spontaneously, without premeditation, from disputes among persons who are acquainted with each other. Similarly, a large share of all car thefts in the United States represent "joyriding" by juveniles, who steal a car for recreational purposes without intending to permanently deprive the owner of his or her automobile. These stolen cars are usually recovered by the police, relatively undamaged and fairly near the locale from which they were stolen.

That "same-type" crimes follow a pattern is reflected in the notion of "normal crimes"; those who staff criminal-justice agencies—the public defender's office, the prosecutor's office, and other places in the criminal-justice system—use this term to acknowledge that individual instances of different offenses often closely parallel each other.[2] These criminal-justice functionaries voice claims that burglary, for example, often takes place in a relatively standardized or "normal" manner or that most car thefts are the work of amateur "joyriders."

There is another side to these typifications of normal crimes that needs to be emphasized. Some criminal acts are not identified as normal or "run-of-the-mill" offenses because they depart in important ways from the commonly encountered form. For example, many car thefts are joyriding episodes, but large numbers of automobiles are also stolen each year by professional car-stripping gangs who carry on a lucrative illegal business, dismantling stolen cars and selling the parts. Burglary is another illustration, in that among citizens, burglars and burglaries are viewed as pretty much alike. However, the police officer speaks of "cat burglars" and "regular burglars," applying the "cat burglar" label to persons who burglarize dwelling units while the occupants are on the premises. These individuals differ in criminal techniques from "regular burglars," who take special pains to make sure that no one is at home during the time they are engaged in their crimes. In the police officer's view, "cat burglars" or "hot prowlers" are "weirdos" who get "kicks" from their crimes, unlike the utilitarian, businesslike, run-of-the-mill burglars. Along the same line, forcible rape must be distinguished from less frequently encountered cases of violent sexual assaults in which the victims are severely abused, mutilated, and often killed by the offender. In short, although particular crimes are patterned rather than being collections of unique, idiosyncratic acts, it is not the case that there is only a single form taken by these crimes.

Consider some of the research evidence on the patterning of different crimes. In one investigation conducted in Boston, Thomas Reppetto reported that burglaries in that city were commonly carried out by young nonwhite males.[3] These offenders, most of whom were relatively unskilled, most commonly chose as targets single-family homes. Burglary rates were highest in low-income neighborhoods, although within those areas, more affluent lower-income persons were most often victimized. Also, high-burglary-rate areas were ones with large numbers of persons under 18 years of age residing in them. Parallel results have turned up in other studies of burglary as well.[4]

A group of homicide studies add up to much the same picture of violence in different cities.[5] Summarizing them, it can be said that: (1) criminal homicides are most common in physically deteriorated, inner-city neighborhoods; (2) homicide rates are considerably higher among blacks than among whites; (3) the parties to the crime are most often family members or acquaintances, rather than strangers, and (4) premeditation and planning are absent from most cases of murder.

Although the criminological literature provides evidence on the nature of many kinds of criminality, that literature is spotty and incomplete in its coverage of lawbreaking. There are a number of forms of crime about which criminological knowledge is deficient and in which criminologists disagree about the facts concerning them. For example, we will discover in Chapter 14 that there are a number of unsettled issues concerning organizational, or white-collar, crime in the United States. In particular, there is much that is yet to be learned about the internal dynamics of business organizations and the processes through which corporation officials become engaged in violations of statutes that are designed to regulate the conduct of business affairs. Also, there is marked disagreement among different authorities on the extent to which organized crime in the United States is a criminal conspiracy controlled by a nationwide organized-crime ruling class. Some researchers have claimed that organized crime consists of a loose confederation of regionally based crime groups, while others have heatedly argued for the national-conspiracy view.

Other examples of data gaps can be offered. For example, there is currently much debate among criminologists concerning the extent to which female crime is both increasing rapidly and changing in the direction of more violent, aggressive, "masculine" patterns of conduct. Thus it would be an error to claim that all answers to the query, "What do offenders do?," have been provided by research.

Not surprisingly, in the light of these facts regarding the variability and patterning of criminality, large numbers of criminologists have arrived at the conclusion that efforts to develop broad theories that explain crime or criminal behavior are doomed to failure. Common sense suggests that we are likely to find little in common between such diverse forms of crime as homicide, fish-and-game-law offenses, and white-collar offenses other than that these are all violations of criminal statutes. This thesis has already surfaced at a number of points earlier in this text, where it has been argued that anomie theory, the differential-association formulation, or psychogenic accounts of causation may be more relevant to some kinds of criminality than to others.

Criminology textbooks usually reflect the heterogeneous nature of crime, in that most of them include chapters devoted to property crime, crimes of violence, victimless crimes, political crime, and other patterns of lawbreaking.[6] This structuring of criminological analysis is another admission of the fruitlessness of searches for overarching theories that will satisfactorily account for crime in its manifold forms.

This textbook is organized around the argument that criminological efforts must pay attention to the rich and diverse forms in which crime is encountered in modern societies. Chapter 12 brings together a large sampling of research evidence and theorizing about garden-variety predatory crime, while Chapter 13 takes up crimes of violence: homicide, assault, and sexual offenses. Chapter 14 explores the evidence concerning white-collar crime, Chapter 15 is devoted to an in-depth probing of organized crime in America, and Chapter 16 takes up a number of "folk crimes" and "vices," or victimless crimes. Finally, Chapter 17 explores crime among women, including arguments holding that female crime has increased dramatically in recent years.

crime patterns and offender types

Two different strategies can be employed when attempting to organize the facts of criminality: a *crime-centered* or a *criminal-centered* approach. In the first strategy, the investigator would endeavor to sort criminal acts into relatively distinct types, such as residential burglary, strong-armed robbery, antitrust violations, and so on. The crime-centered investigator would also emphasize the collection of information about the correlates of crime patterns, including data on the social areas in which these activities are most common, the social backgrounds of offenders and victims, temporal variations in the occurrence of the offenses, and kindred facts. This form of analysis would be designed to produce explanations or accounts of the causal processes that operate to produce different kinds of lawbreaking.

By contrast, a criminal-centered or person-centered perspective focuses on individual offenders rather than individual forms of crime and tries to identify relatively distinct types of criminals (or delinquents) and the causal backgrounds out of which they come. For example, some investigators have conducted crime-centered studies of robbery, in which different kinds of robbery incidents were categorized,[7] while other criminologists have zeroed in upon types of "robbers" as criminal actors.[8] This latter tactic assumes that persons can be identified who specialize in acts of robbery and who avoid entanglement in other kinds of crime. In turn, the criminologist's expectation is that offenders who fall into one or another of these criminal types will show common etiological backgrounds.

In actual practice, some criminologists have taken both approaches at the same time, studying both patterns of crime and types of offenders. However, crime-centered efforts have been a good deal less common than have inquiries into offender types. Many of the offender classifications that have been advanced have revolved around criminal activities, with persons being sorted into such pigeon holes as professional thieves, robbers, naïve check forgers, or child molesters. However, a variety of lawbreaker classifications in terms of psychological characteristics have also been developed. Typological or classificatory efforts have been numerous and varied in form.

the development of offender typologies[9]

In the period following World War II, considerable criminological interest centered on offender typologies. A number of scholars argued that lawbreakers are so heterogeneous that they must be sorted into some meaningful behavioral types if their criminality is to be understood. According to this view, offender typologies are required in order that: (1) progress can be made on the explanation of criminality, and (2) effective treatment of offenders can be developed.

The causal argument is that no single theory can be uncovered to account for such diverse types of lawbreakers as embezzlers, forcible rapists, arsonists, gang delinquents, aggressive delinquents, female offenders, and so forth. Separate but perhaps interrelated causal theories must be developed for each distinct offender type. The closeness of this perspective to a medical model of specific syndromes or disorders, each arising out of a different disease pattern or set of causal factors, is readily apparent.

The case for typologies and diagnostic classifications in correctional treatment closely parallels the etiological argument. The basic claim is that "different strokes for different folks" are in order, that is, differential treatment must be developed in which various tactics such as psychotherapy, group counseling, reality therapy, behavior modification, or other stratagems would be matched with particular offender types. The treatment would be tailored to the offender, thereby bringing about more effective rehabilitation than is now achieved.[10]

How shall we go about classifying offenders? Most sociological classification schemes represent ways of sorting out and categorizing persons or social phenomena which are imposed upon the facts of social life, rather than being drawn from direct observations. Stated differently, offender "types" such as the naïve check forger or white-collar criminal are identified by criminologists. Too often, however, the real-life lawbreakers who are thought to fit within these types are blissfully unaware they are members of such a pattern. Corporation executives and forgers do not go about declaring themselves to be white-collar criminals or forgers!

Criminals or delinquents might be classified or typed in almost an infinite number of ways, but these taxonomies may not all be equally significant. For example, one scheme for sorting offenders would be on the basis of specific instant offenses, that is, by the crime for which they were most recently convicted. However, the widely used "plea-copping" process, in which persons plead guilty to reduced charges, means that legal categories often do not accurately reflect the offense the person actually committed. Even more important, legal-offense categories often fail to reflect significant dimensions or aspects of the social behavior that has been the subject of social-control-agency attention. The legal category of rape includes varied patterns of deviant activity; some rape involves extreme violence and the totally unwilling participation of the victim, whereas these elements are missing in other cases.

Still another problem with legal-offense categories is that in many cases offenders do not consistently commit only a single deviant act; a person labeled a burglar today may become a larcenist tomorrow. Finally, it is doubtful that legal classifications identify theoretically meaningful types. There is little reason to suppose that persons characterized as burglars or as some other legal-offense type are the products of a uniform etiological process.

The criminological enterprise requires much more than the reporting skills of a trained journalist. Criminologists endeavor to go well beyond the recording of commonsense observations about the real world. When they attempt to sort offenders into meaningful behavioral types, they invent conceptual schemes or new ways of looking at the facts of lawbreaking which are not part of the thoughtways of real-life offenders or their victims. Violators can be classified in many different ways: offense, hair color, race, urban-rural residence, and so on. When criminologists settle upon one scheme from the many that might be employed, they hope that they have chosen a system that will allow them to place offenders into clear-cut categories that also are causally significant. Let us examine some of the offender typologies that have been put forth by criminologists to see how clear, unambiguous, useful, and meaningful these have been.

typological directions in criminology[11]

Typological statements, enumerating a number of relatively distinct categories into which most offenders allegedly can be placed, have appeared in a number of criminology textbooks. In one of these, Marshall Clinard and Richard Quinney produced a classification made up of nine types: violent personal crime, occasional property crime, organized crime, political crime, public-order crime, conventional crime, occupational crime, corporate crime, and professional crime.[12] They also discussed a number of dimensions along which these patterns are assumed to vary, such as the criminal career of the offender or the societal reaction to his or her criminal conduct. However, because they lumped together within some of these nine types several specific forms of criminality of varying "seriousness"—for example, the category of political crime included everything from political protest to espionage—some important differences among lawbreakers tended to get slurred over. Furthermore, the Clinard and Quinney scheme was ambiguous, for although it employed crime-pattern labels, their discussion of these nine categories was centered around types of criminals such as violent offenders or corporate offenders. Although the Clinard and Quinney typology is of considerable use in classroom settings, allowing instructors to direct the attention of students to some important dimensions along which lawbreaking varies, it is likely that considerable difficulty would be encountered in attempts to sort actual offenders into their patterns.

Another of these comprehensive typologies was authored by Daniel Glaser.[13] He identified ten criminal patterns, including "adolescent recapitulators," "subcultural assaulters," "vocational predators," "crisis-vacillation predators," and "addicted performers." Glaser's typology was based on what he termed "offense descriptive" variables and "career commitment" variables. Offense-descriptive variables were those which separate predatory from nonpredatory offenses, personal from property crimes, and so forth, while career-commitment variables had to do with recidivism, criminal-group contacts maintained by offenders, and other factors of that sort. Glaser employed these variables to identify adolescent recapitulators as "adults who periodically repeat the pattern of delinquency begun in adolescence—or even in childhood,"[14] while subcultural assaulters were defined as individuals who "live in a subculture emphasizing violence as a value more than does the rest of our society."[15]

There is little question that many offenders do resemble more or less closely the offender profiles sketched out by Glaser. However, he also offered some pithy observations that pointed up some of the problems with offender classifications. He acknowledged that many lawbreakers exhibit great diversity rather than specialization in the offenses they commit, making it very difficult to sort them into criminal career types. According to Glaser, "the difficulty arises from the fact that a large variety of offenses are found in most separate criminal careers, and the combinations occur in all possible proportions."[16] We would also do well to keep in mind some other remarks by Glaser:

In the real world, the gradations and mixtures of characteristics in people are so extensive that most of our categories must be given very arbitrary boundaries if everyone in a cross-section of the population is to be placed in one empirical type or another. Most real people just do not fall neatly into uniform patterns. Therefore, we formulate explanations in terms of idealizations, we revise them on the basis of research on empirical types, and in the practical world we qualify most explanations for separate cases to meet the variations we encounter beyond what any set of type labels denote.[17]

Criminologists who have formulated comprehensive typologies of lawbreakers have often pointed to a number of research studies of specific offender types as supporting evidence for classificatory ventures. For example, in one empirical investigation by Julian Roebuck, based on a sample of 1,155 inmates in the District of Columbia Reformatory, he sorted prisoners into such categories as "Negro armed robbers," "Negro drug addicts," and "Negro 'short con' men."[18] His typology was based on legal categories of offense behavior studied within the framework of criminal careers. He sorted prison inmates into classes on the basis of their overall crime record as revealed in official records. Roebuck identified 13 patterns of criminal careers in all.

After he constructed this typology, Roebuck went on to compare single types with the balance of the offender group. For example, black armed robbers were compared with the rest of the inmates to uncover significant differences between the robbers and the other prisoners. In the main, the robbers were from more disorganized home backgrounds and more deteriorated and criminalistic areas of urban communities than were the other prisoners. They were also characterized by short-run hedonism, that is, having no long-term plans and having relatively spontaneous and uncommitted attitudes.

These reports comprise part of the intellectual capital out of which a general criminal typology might be evolved. Nonetheless, this research had some problems, among which was the ethnic orientation of this typological system. Ethnic background is probably not an important variable for identifying homogeneous types of offenders. There is little reason to suppose that most black armed robbers or other kinds of criminals are much different from their white counterparts.

The list of studies of specific-offender patterns is a large one, but additional to the Roebuck investigations, we should mention here Conklin's research on robbers,[19] as well as Lemert's studies of naïve forgers and systematic forgers.[20] Comprehensive offender typologies have not been constructed out of thin air, for there is a body of evidence that provides a measure of support to this direction.

the role-career perspective

OFFENDER PATTERNS

One of the most detailed and comprehensive typological formulations in the criminological literature has been developed over a number of years by the author. Let us examine this role-career typological portrayal in some detail, along with a variety of evidence bearing upon it. That examination should tell us a good deal about the strengths and limitations of typological ventures in criminological analysis.

The role-career typology rests upon the assumption that the behavior of individuals can be meaningfully examined as a pattern of social roles. Social roles represent how persons interact with others in terms of various statuses or positions within social systems. Statuses are "jobs" in a social division of labor, involving normative expectations or rules that the person occupying that status is expected to follow in pursuit of some interactional end or objective. The task of professor in an academic institution is an example of a status, for it involves expectations that any particular teacher will behave in specified ways toward students, colleagues, and the general public. The actual performance activity of a specific professor represents role behavior within this particular status.

The relevance of status and role concepts is easy to see when applied to such professions as school superintendent, physician, and a variety of other occupational or social positions. However, status and role analysis may not be so quickly perceived as relevant to such deviant patterns as homosexuality, drug addiction, political radicalism, or criminality. Even though criminal and delinquent statuses often involve expectations that persons in these positions will behave in ways frowned upon by some social groups, criminalistic behavior can, nonetheless, be tackled within a status-role perspective. Actually, many statuses and roles in addition to the criminalistic are negatively defined by some group or groups.[21] Moreover, negative evaluation of criminal or delinquent statuses is relative to particular group standards. Within associations of offenders, deviant statuses are frequently evaluated positively; the "old-time box man" (skilled safe-cracker) is admired by his criminal peers. Similarly, many "tough" prisoners in institutions are highly esteemed by other inmates, many narcotic users are fondly regarded by other drug users, and so forth.

Criminal categories constitute only one set of the many statuses and roles in which persons may find themselves. However, in many cases criminality may well become what Becker termed a *master status*, that is, the separate social niches occupied by the offender become heavily colored by his or her involvement in lawbreaking.[22] As one example, the occupational activities of the male exconvict are often so greatly influenced by his "parolee" identity that he finds the task of obtaining a job exceedingly difficult, which may create further distortions in the exconvict's marital role and other facets of his life as well; thus, to be a criminal is to be the occupant of a highly significant status.[23]

Description of offender roles includes the social context within which behavior occurs, for the concept of role is relatively meaningless when divorced from the network of role expectations of others. Thus, in addition to indicating that an offender engages in role activity taking the form of burglary, we also need to ask about the social circumstances of that behavior. Were the criminal acts carried on in isolation? Or did the behavior take place within the structure of a group of participating role players (other burglars)? Or, finally, is the activity of the person part of a pattern of responses within a deviant subculture in which other individuals encourage deviant acts?

Some criminal roles, such as embezzlement, are enacted secretly, because nonembezzlement is defined as the appropriate behavior within the system of action in which such offenses occur. Other kinds of criminality represent role activities that associates of the offender evaluate positively, even though the larger social organization may define the acts negatively. Some forms of criminality grow out of situations in which the victim was an interactional partner of the offender—for example, murder of one's spouse, or rape. In other instances, the victim has had no prior contact with the lawbreaker; and in still other situations no specific victim can be identified—for example, in white-collar crime, shoplifting, and kindred other offenses. All of these matters need to be attended to in a sociological description of criminality.

We can identify two basic components of offender roles: *behavioral acts* and *role conceptions* (self-image patterns and role-related attitudes). This distinction is illustrated in everyday life when predictions are made about the future conduct of an individual. For example, knowledge that a person has committed an assault is not sufficient evidence on which to predict that episodes of violence will occur in the future. Confidence in such a prediction is enhanced with the observation that the assaultive individual defines himself as a "tough guy" and regards other persons as "mean" and not to be trusted. Quite a different estimate would be in order with observations that the assaulter acted under conditions of severe personal stress and now regrets his actions.

This distinction between role behavior and role conceptions is closely parallel to Lemert's notions of *primary* and *secondary* deviation.[24] Lemert noted that deviant behavior is often primary in character, for the person views the behavior as atypical on his or her part and lacks a self-image as a deviant. Some deviant roles become secondary in form because the actor ultimately integrates the aberrant activity into his or her total personality organization. In this process, the person eventually undergoes a measure of personality reorganization in which deviant behavior becomes a role verbalized by such self-reference statements as: "I am a hype" or "I am a thief" or "I am a lush." [25] Although primary deviation precedes secondary deviation, the latter does not always follow from involvement in primary deviance. One obvious illustration of this point, at least in degree, is the "square John" inmate in prison who persistently alleges that he is not a "real criminal." [26]

Offender roles can also be analyzed in longitudinal terms as *role-careers*. Many nondeviant roles, such as occupational ones, continue over extremely long periods and involve a series of behavioral changes as particular social situations alter. A medical career illustrates this point nicely, for this career originates when a person makes an initial decision to become a doctor and undertakes activity to implement this choice. Medical school is a further episode in the medical career, and professional employment as a physician a still further involvement. Medical-role incumbents display behavior patterns that are somewhat different at each stage. They also exhibit role conceptions that are not identical in each of these periods. [27] Nonetheless, these varied behavior patterns and role conceptions are parts of a long-term career, for they "hang together" in obvious ways. In these cumulative events, advanced stages of occupational involvement are built on experiences occurring in earlier parts of the occupational history.

Although the notion of careers is most familiar in occupational analysis, other roles, including deviant ones, can be analyzed in this manner. The alcoholism career, extending over several decades during which the drinker becomes progressively more involved in deviant drinking, as well as in other altered social relationships flowing out of his alcoholism, comes to mind as one illustration of a complex deviant-career pattern. Also, the collection of life experiences beginning with petty delinquent episodes of gang members in slum areas stands as an example of an offender career. With advancing age, this career line leads into more systematic involvement in utilitarian thefts, and still later it culminates in a sustained pattern of adult episodes of property crimes interrupted by periodic prison terms. The career finally terminates when the offender withdraws (or "retires") from active participation in criminality in middle age, as he comes to evaluate continued lawbreaking as too fraught with such hardships as long penal commitments. [28]

Some delinquent patterns lead to adult criminal careers, whereas other patterns are terminal and do not culminate in adult criminality. In turn, some criminal careers begin with juvenile-delinquent behavior, whereas other forms of adult lawbreaking develop in adulthood and do not result from prior delinquent conduct. On this matter, one major argument is that a role-career perspective promises to untangle the web of relationships between juvenile and adult criminality. The durable saying that "the delinquent of today is the criminal of tomorrow" is frequently false, for although some delinquents become adult of-fenders, others do not.

Some role-careers involve more changes in component episodes of the pat-tern that do others. For example, many adult predatory offenders begin their lawbreaking with minor offenses in early adolescence. These frequently lead to more serious forms of delinquency with advancing age, which in turn result in repeated police contacts, commitment to juvenile institutions, "graduation" into adult forms of crime, and more contacts with law-enforcement agencies and cor-rectional institutions. Over this lengthy developmental sequence, the social-psy-chological characteristics of offenders also change. The degree of hostility toward police officers and correctional agents the adult criminal exhibits is likely to be considerably greater than the enmity demonstrated at an earlier age. The same point holds for other changes in self-image, attitudes, and kindred other characteristics.

This point of view regarding role-careers provided the foundation for a ty-pological analysis of lawbreakers based on the description of criminal role-ca-reers according to the patterns of illegal role behavior they exhibit and also in terms of the social context of their deviant acts. Offenders were also classified along two other dimensions: self-image patterns and role-related attitudes. Fi-nally, observations about temporal changes in deviant roles were provided in a summary of the characteristics of the role type. In all, twenty offender types were spelled out in this typology:

1. Professional thieves
2. Professional "heavy" criminals
3. Semiprofessional property offenders
4. Naïve check forgers
5. Automobile thieves—"joyriders"
6. Property offenders, "one-time losers"
7. Embezzlers
8. White-collar criminals
9. Professional "fringe violators"
10. Personal offenders, "one-time losers"
11. Psychopathic assaultists
12. Statutory rapists
13. Aggressive rapists
14. Violent sex offenders
15. Nonviolent sex offenders
16. Incest offenders
17. Male homosexuals
18. Opiate addicts
19. Skid Row alcoholics
20. Amateur shoplifters

In this typology, an offender would be labeled a "naïve check forger," for example, if he or she showed the pattern of criminal behavior and the social-psychological characteristics specified in the typology.

TYPOLOGIES AND CAUSATION

Basically, the role-career scheme asserts that "this is the way offenders are—these are the ways they behave." Additionally, the typological sketches include comments about the background characteristics of offender types, organized within four broad categories: social-class origins, family-background patterns, peer-group associations, and contacts with defining agencies.

The immediate social circumstances in which persons are enmeshed are part of larger patterns of social organization. Individuals are situated in particular neighborhoods and social-class locations, as well as being members of family and peer associations. Another elementary fact is that the development of a specific person's role behavior is a function of the processes of socialization: the complex processes of social interaction through which an individual learns habits, skills, beliefs, and standards of conduct. Not all interaction is equally important to the individual, so his or her self-conception, attitudes, and behavioral motives are most likely to be the product of primary-group interaction. Family and peer group associations are two kinds of primary groups, and the great attention social psychologists give to interactional processes within these groups is not accidental.

Although class-linked behavior patterns do exist, the behavior of individual members of particular social classes varies quite markedly because of differences in the interactional processes in particular primary groups. This general argument provides the rationale for singling out social-class, family, and peer relationships as major background variables.

What about the causal consequences of contacts with defining agencies? Defining agencies are official and semiofficial agencies responsible for detecting, apprehending, punishing, and rehabilitating offenders. Some offenders may be driven further into criminality as a result of employment difficulties and other problems they encounter because of their social stigma. In other cases, including amateur female shoplifters ("snitches"), contacts with defining agencies or kindred groups may have positive effects. In a study in Chicago, Mary Owen Cameron found that women shoplifters rarely repeated the act after store personnel had apprehended them and compelled them to admit that they were "thieves" and "criminals." Apparently, the painful social-psychological trauma involved in admitting their deviance served to deter these persons from further shoplifting.[29]

Contacts with defining agencies could be positive, so as to deflect the offender away from further misconduct. Or they could be harmful, driving the lawbreaker into further violations in response to his or her changed social identity. A third possibility is that such experiences could be of neutral significance, neither deterring nor harmfully affecting the individual. Bits of empirical evidence seem to indicate that each of these possibilities does occur. Further, according to the role-career claims, these effects also vary from one offender type to another.

The structure of this role-career argument about offender types is portrayed in Figure 4, which presents a diagram which suggests that particular offender types show specific backgrounds in common. In short, the role-career scheme consists of a collection of claims, arguing that there are types or groups of offenders who behave similarly and that those groupings of lawbreakers exhibit common backgrounds that distinguish them from other offender types.

The complete set of twenty offender-types descriptions will not be presented here.[30] However, it will be useful to examine one sample from the set, so that the reader can grasp the basics of the role-career argument. The following section presents the definitional and background dimensions for the *semi-professional property criminal role-career*. The format shown is standard for all offender-type descriptions.

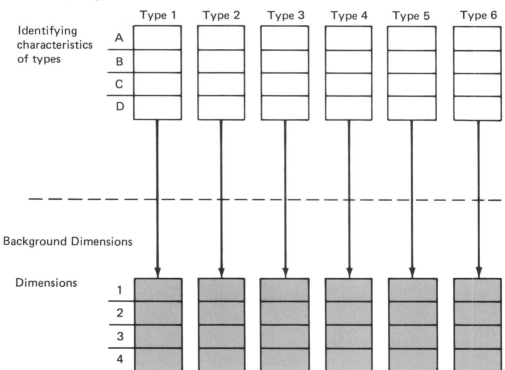

figure 4 the structure of typological arguments

the semiprofessional property criminal role-career[31]

definitional dimensions

Offense behavior: Semiprofessional property offenders engage in strong-arm robberies, holdups, burglaries, larcenies, and similar direct assaults upon personal or private property. They employ crime skills which are relatively simple and uncomplicated. For example, strong-arm robbery does not involve much detailed planning and careful execution of the crime, but rather application of crude physical force in order to relieve a victim of his money. This is referred to as semiprofessional crime, because even though technical skill is not characteristic of these offenders, most of them attempt to carry on crime as an occupation.

Interactional setting. Many of the offenses of the semiprofessional offender are two-person affairs involving an offender and a victim, for example, strong-arm robbery and liquor-store and gas-station stickups. On occasion, semiprofessionals operate in collections of several crime partners, as in instances of burglary and safe-robbery. In either event, the criminal act tends to be direct and unsophisticated, a complex interactional pattern rarely being involved.

Self-concept. Semiprofessional property offenders view themselves as criminals. Additionally, the semiprofessional sees himself as an individual who has few alternatives to criminal behavior and as a victim of a corrupt society in which everyone has a "racket." Thus the semiprofessional is relieved from any sense of guilt regarding his criminality by deflecting blame onto "the system."

Attitudes. The attitudes of the semiprofessional offender toward the police tend to be hostile and antagonistic. Doubtless, this is in considerable part a function of the large number of contacts with police agents experienced by this offender. Semiprofessionals also look down on conventional occupations as a way of life, holding that "only slobs work." They frequently show a diffuse set of bitter and resentful attitudes toward not only the police and correctional agents, but also their parents, social agencies, and schools.

Role-career. Semiprofessional property offenders represent the more usual outcome of patterns of predatory gang delinquency, as contrasted to the professional "heavy" adult outcome. That is, most adult semiprofessional offenders exhibit juvenile backgrounds of predatory gang behavior, and many juvenile-gang offenders continue in criminality as semiprofessionals. As an adult, the semiprofessional rapidly accumulates an extensive "rap sheet," or record of crimes and institutional commitments. Because of the low degree of skill involved in the criminality of the semiprofessionals, the risks of apprehension, conviction, and incarceration are high. Many semiprofessionals spend a considerable part of their early adult years in penal institutions, where they are likely to be identified as "right guys," or antiadministration inmates. It does not appear that conventional treatment efforts are successful in deflecting many of these persons away from continuation in crime. On the other hand, many of them ultimately do withdraw from crime careers upon reaching early middle age.

background dimensions

Social class. Semiprofessionals are from working-class social origins. Most of them are from inner-city neighborhoods characterized by physical deterioration and other slum conditions.

Family backgrounds. Semiprofessionals usually are from relatively large families in which one or more of the family members are also involved in lawbreaking. Although parental supervision of children in these families is often relatively lax and informal, the family backgrounds of semiprofessionals are not usually ones in which marked family tension or conflict is apparent.

Peer-group associations. Semiprofessionals experience a rich set of peer-group associations with gang offenders. However, semi-professionals have usually been restricted in their interactional experiences to associations with other relatively unskilled offenders, so they have not had opportunities to learn the more esoteric or complex crime skills. In addition, semiprofessional offenders usually interact as adults with kindred types of individuals, rather than with professional criminals. That is, the noncriminal endeavors of these persons as they act out their general social roles take place within collectivities of noncriminal citizens or semiprofessional offenders.

Contact with defining agencies. Semiprofessionals experience repeated agency contacts, particularly as juveniles, appearing in juvenile courts and training schools. Adult semiprofessional offenders spend major portions of their lives in penal institutions. Many are recidivists who enter, leave, and reenter prisons, so they are treatment failures. It appears that many of them become progressively more hostile in attitude and fixed in behavior as they undergo these recurrent prison commitments. Contacts with defining agencies play a contributory role in the development of their deviant careers.

typologies and the real world

It is easy to see why typologies have had much appeal for many criminologists. If we could sort lawbreakers into some relatively small number of distinct behavioral types, we might then be able to throw considerably more light upon the causes of crime than is possible with general theories purporting to apply to all criminal behavior. But, how valid are typologies? How closely do offenders fit within the types? How comprehensive are the typologies? Can most real-life lawbreakers be assigned to one or another type, or, instead, are there large numbers of them who are not described within existing classification schemes? In particular, how accurate are the role-career profiles described in the preceding section?

These questions need not remain unanswered, for there is a body of evidence that can be brought to bear upon them. Some of the data relate specifically to the role-career argument, while others are tangentially linked to it and other typological claims.

One instructive case regarding offender typologies comes from the reports of Clarence Schrag regarding inmate types in the prison community.[32] According to Schrag, prisoners exhibit patterns of social-role behavior identified in inmate language or argot by the labels "square John," "right guy," "ding," "outlaw," and "politician." These roles are structured around loyalty attachments to other prisoners; thus, the "right guy" is a loyal member of the inmate subculture, while the "square John" is an alien in that system. Gresham Sykes reported that similar inmate role types existed in the prison that he studied.[33]

If distinct social-role types exist among prison inmates, this may be an indication of social roles among criminals at large. Perhaps "right guys" and other inmate types are persons who also exhibit particular criminal patterns outside the walls as well.

Schrag's observations were relatively impressionistic ones, which also was true of Sykes's comments on inmate argot roles. Some indication of the loose fit between typological characterizations and the real world can be found in a study that Peter Garabedian conducted in the same prison where Schrag had done his research.[34] Garabedian identified incumbents of prisoner social roles through inmate responses to a series of questionnaire items. Although about two-thirds of the convicts did fall into the Schrag types, about one-third were unclassifiable. Moreover, although the social correlates such as prior-offense records, participation in prison programs, and attitudes toward the penitentiary said to be associated with the role types were observed, many of the associations were much less striking than implied in some of the writings on prisoner types. This study seemed to demonstrate that social types exist at the same time that it indicated that the Schrag typological scheme implied considerably more regularity of inmate behavior than actually exists.

An even more damaging body of evidence came from a study by Robert Leger, in which he employed a number of different techniques in order to uncover inmate social types.[35] Leger used the attitudinal items from Garabedian's questionnaire that were intended to identify "right guys" and other types, but in addition, he quizzed inmates as to which social type, if any, they belonged. Further, he obtain judgments from guards as to which convicts were members of particular types. Finally, he sorted prisoners into social types in terms of the social backgrounds that are supposed to characterize the different types. Unfortunately for the advocates of typological approaches, Leger found very little agreement among these techniques, with very few prisoners being consistently identified as "square Johns" or some other type.

When investigators begin to examine some specific type of offender in detail, or when they try to develop a sorting scheme to be used in practice, one common occurrence is the proliferation of subtypes as they attempt to capture the variability of behavior encountered among actual offenders. For example, in one project in a federal probation office—in which the present offenses of probationers, along with their ages, prior records, and scores on a personality inventory were used as the bases for classifying them—54 possible types of offenders were noted.[36] Moreover, probationers were found in all of these categories.

On this same point, Charles McCaghy found it necessary to sort child molesters into six types,[37] while John Conklin contended that there are four types of robbers: professional, opportunist, addicted to drugs, and alcoholic robbers.[38]

Conklin's typology of robbers warrants special mention, for it turned out that the opportunist robber "may commit such other forms of theft as larceny and shoplifting frequently, but he robs infrequently."[39] Further, Conklin indicated that addict and alcoholic robbers also engaged in criminal acts additional to robbery, thus it appears that the criminal type "robber" may be more fiction than fact!

Supporters of typologies which include such types as "robbers" must also contend with a study conducted among 49 "armed robbers" in a California prison.[40] These persons had been identified as robbers because their current prison sentence was for that crime. The average age of these convicts was 39, thus most of them had been criminally active for some time. When these offenders were asked to report how many times since becoming involved in lawbreaking they had committed any of nine specific crimes, they confessed to 10,505 offenses, or an average of 214 per offender! These were obviously not novices in crime! An even more striking finding was that these individuals admitted collectively to 3,620 drug sales, 2,331 burglaries, 1,492 automobile thefts, 995 forgeries, 993 grand thefts, and 855 instances of robbery. How, then, can they be validly categorized as "armed robbers"?

Two studies have been conducted specifically on the role-career scheme. One of these investigations took place in a California county probation department.[41] In that study, a group of probation officers attempted to classify probationers, sorting them into the categories specified in the role-career typology. Employing abridged typological profiles of offenders, groups of three officers acting as independent judges read case files of probationers in order to determine to which type, if any, each person belonged.

Slightly less than half of the probationers fell within a type in the typology, even when relatively relaxed classificatory rules were used. Subsequently, Clayton Hartjen sifted through the records of the cases that had not been assigned to the typology. Using offense records, he managed to place most of these individuals into seven types, such as "nonsupport offenders" or "petty property offenders." However, these ad hoc types did not differ markedly from each other in terms of commitment to deviance, social backgrounds, or other variables. Hartjen concluded that most of these offenders were involved in "folk crime," which was Laurence Ross's term for forms of lawbreaking arising out of laws introduced to solve problems related to the increased complexity of modern society.[42] Such offenses draw little public attention and involve little social stigma.

James McKenna also carried out an investigation of the role-career typology.[43] Inmates in a state correctional institution were classified into offender types through examination of their arrest records, with 87 percent of them being placed in twelve offender types. McKenna then sought to determine whether the combination of characteristics said to differentiate role-career incumbents actually occured among offenders. Only in one of the twelve types did the definitional dimension pattern emerge, while all the other types showed basic disagreements between the typological claims and the empirical observations. In other words, prisoners who had been assigned to one type or another in terms of offense patterns often showed a good deal of similarity to members of other offense types in terms of attitudes, self-concept patterns, and interactional setting. As a result, McKenna's findings indicated that many real-life offenders cannot be assigned with much precision to the categories of the role-career typology.

offender typologies: an assessment

Considerable pessimism is in order concerning classification systems which assign criminal offenders to a relatively small number of distinct types. A number of the typological schemes that have been put forth are relatively fuzzy and ambiguous, rendering them difficult if not impossible to verify through research efforts. By contrast, the role-career perspective and typology has the advantage of being relatively clear and explicit. But, as we have seen, the degree of patterning of offense behavior and other definitional configurations assumed in that typology (and in others noted in this discussion) appear not to exist in the real world of criminality. Stated another way, there are some lawbreakers who closely resemble the sketches of "naïve check forgers," "semiprofessional property criminals," or "aggressive rapists" that appear in offender typologies. However, they are mixed in with a much larger number of offenders who defy classification into some distinct type category.

Typological systems that sort offenders into relatively homogeneous types do have heuristic value, alerting us to broad groupings of lawbreakers that make up the criminal population. However, they put forth an oversimplified characterization of the real world of criminality and criminals. Many offenders are "situational-casual" criminals who are involved in various forms of short-run criminality, such that they do not fall into any clear-cut type, syndrome, or role-career. Additionally, many lawbreakers exhibit relatively unique combinations of criminal conduct, attitudinal patterns, and other characteristics, such that we are able to sort them into some general categories only with considerable difficulty.

Behavioral diversity rather than offense specialization characterizes many offenders. Then, too, many lawbreakers engage in flirtations with criminality; they get drawn into misconduct for a variety of reasons, and many of them manage to withdraw from criminal activity. Moreover, many of these miscreants who do not exhibit narrowly specialized, long-term criminal careers probably have become involved in lawbreaking due to "risk-taking" processes and situational pressures, drifting into crime rather than being socialized into a full-blown criminal role through some process akin to differential association.

summary

This chapter has been concerned with the strengths and limitations of typological approaches to crime and criminal behavior. The basic arguments in favor of classifactory endeavors are clear and straightforward. Offender typologies have been advocated as a way of gaining a more detailed and accurate grasp of causal processes. Classifications can take either a crime-centered or a criminal-centered direction, but to date, the majority of these schemes have been of the second kind. The basic arguments in support of typological efforts are clear enough. However, it turns out that there are many lawbreakers who defy pigeonholing in any typology.

In the chapters ahead, a good deal of attention will be paid to major crime patterns or broad groupings of lawbreaking activities. Garden-variety predatory property crime is one general form to be examined, along with homicides, assaults, and sexual crimes as another pattern. Additionally, separate chapters are devoted to organizational and occupational crime, including "white-collar" offenses, as well as to organize crime. Finally, "vices" and "folk crime" are singled out for attention, as is female lawbreaking. These discussions of crime patterns will take note of any offender patterns that can be identified but will avoid the extreme forms of typological claims that do violence to the behavioral richness of the real world.

notes

[1]For a review of studies of citizen perceptions of crime and other forms of deviance, see Don C. Gibbons and Joseph F. Jones, *The Study of Deviance* (Englewood Cliffs, N.J.: Prentice-Hall, Inc. 1975), pp. 66–81. Also see Russell A. Ward, "Typifications of Homosexuals," *Sociological Quarterly*, 20 (Summer 1979), 411–23.

[2]David Sudnow, "Normal Crimes: Sociological Features of the Penal Code in a Public Defender Office," *Social Problems*, 12 (Winter 1965), 255–76.

[3]Thomas A. Reppetto, *Residential Crime* (Cambridge, Mass.: Ballinger Publishing Co., 1974).

[4]Irvin Waller and Norman Okihiro, *Burglary: The Victim and the Public* (Toronto: The University of Toronto Press, 1978); Harry A. Scarr, Joan L. Pinsky, and Deborah S. Wyatt, *Patterns of Burglary* (Washington, D.C.: Law Enforcement Assistance Administration, 1973).

[5]Marvin E. Wolfgang, *Patterns of Criminal Homicide* (Philadelphia: University of Pennsylvania Press, 1958); Robert C. Bensing and Oliver Schroeder, Jr., *Homicide in an Urban Community* (Springfield, Ill.: Chas C Thomas, 1960); Henry A. Bullock, "Urban Homicide in Theory and Fact," *Journal of Criminal Law, Criminology and Police Science*, 45 (January–February 1955), 565–75; Alex D. Pokorny, "A Comparison of Homicides in Two Cities," *Journal of Criminal Law, Criminology and Police Science*, 56 (December 1965), 479–87. For research findings on two relatively distinct types of homicide, see M. Dwayne Smith and Robert Nash Parker, "Type of Homicide and Variation in Regional Rates," *Social Forces*, 59 (September 1980), 136–47.

[6]For example, see Gresham M. Sykes, *Criminology* (New York: Harcourt Brace Jovanovich, 1978), pp. 85–233; Hugh D. Barlow, *Introduction to Criminology* (Boston: Little, Brown, 1978), pp. 105–371.

[7]F. H. McClintock and Evelyn Gibson, *Robbery in London* (London: Macmillan Ltd., 1961).

[8]John F. Conklin, *Robbery and the Criminal Justice System* (Philadelphia: Lippincott, 1972), pp. 59–78.

[9]Typological arguments are reviewed in detail in Don C. Gibbons, "Offender Typologies—Two Decades Later," *British Journal of Criminology*, 15 (April 1975), 140–56; Gibbons, *The Criminological Enterprise* (Englewood Cliffs, N.J.: Prentice-Hall, Inc., 1979), pp, 85–92. For an earlier, detailed version of a causal and diagnostic typological argument, see Gibbons, *Changing the Lawbreaker* (Englewood Cliffs, N.J.: Prentice-Hall, Inc., 1965).

[10]One prominent version of this argument for differential treatment structured around an offender typology is the Interpersonal Maturity Levels system developed in California and discussed briefly in Chapter 8.

[11]Some general essays on offender typologies include Albert Morris, "The Comprehensive Classification of Adult Offenders," *Journal of Criminal Law, Criminology and Police Science*, 56 (June 1965), 197–202; Edwin D. Driver, "A Critique of Typologies in Criminology," *Sociological Quarterly*, 9 (Summer 1968), 356–73.

[12]Marshall B. Clinard and Richard Quinney, *Criminal Behavior Systems*, 2nd ed. (New York: Holt, Rinehart, & Winston, 1973).

[13]Daniel Glaser, *Adult Crime and Social Policy* (Englewood Cliffs, N.J.: Prentice-Hall, Inc., 1972), pp. 28–66.

[14]Ibid., p. 28.

[15]Ibid., p. 32.

[16]Ibid., p. 18.

[17]Ibid., p. 14.

[18]Julian B. Roebuck and Mervyn L. Cadwallader, "The Negro Armed Robber as a Criminal Type: The Construction and Application of a Typology," *Pacific Sociological Review*, 4 (Spring 1961), 21–26; Roebuck, "The Negro Drug Addict as an Offender Type," *Journal of Criminal Law, Criminology and Police Science*, 53 (March 1962), 36–43; Roebuck and Ronald Johnson, "The Negro Drinker and Assaulter as a Criminal Type," *Crime and Delinquency*, 8 (January 1962), 21–33; Roebuck and Johnson, "The Jack-of-all Trades Offender," *Crime and Delinquency*, 8 (April 1962), 172–81; Roebuck, "The Negro Numbers Man as a Criminal Type: The Construction and Application of a Typology," *Journal of Criminal Law, Criminology and Police Science*, 54 (March 1963), 48–60; Roebuck and Johnson, "The 'Short Con' Man," *Crime and Delinquency*, 10 (July 1964), 235–48; Roebuck, *Criminal Typology* (Springfield, Ill.: Chas C Thomas, 1966).

[19]Conklin, *Robbery and the Criminal Justice System.*

[20]Edwin M. Lemert, "The Behavior of the Systematic Check Forger," *Social Problems*, 6 (Fall 1958), 141–49; Lemert, "An Isolation and Closure Theory of Naïve Check Forgery", *Journal of Criminal Law, Criminology and Police Science*, 44 (September–October 1953), 296–307. This chapter has not considered a large number of efforts to develop typologies of juvenile delinquents. See Theodore N. Ferdinand, *Typologies of Delinquency* (New York: Random House, 1966); National Clearinghouse for Mental Health Information, *Typological Approaches and Delinquency Control: A Status Report* (Washington, D.C.: U.S. Department of Health, Education and Welfare, 1967); John W. Kinch, "Continuities in the Study of Delinquent Types," *Journal of Criminal Law, Criminology and Police Science*, 53 (September 1962), 323–28; Kinch, "Self-Conceptions of Types of Delinquents," *Sociological Inquiry*, 32 (Spring 1962), 228–34; Sethard Fisher, "Varieties of Juvenile Delinquency," *British Journal of Criminology*, 2 (January 1962), 251–61; Richard L. Jenkins and Sylvia Glickman, "Patterns of Personality Organization Among Delinquents," *Nervous Child*, 6 (July 1947), 329–39; Lester E. Hewitt and Jenkins, *Fundamental Patterns of Maladjustment, The Dynamics of Their Origin* (Springfield: Illinois State Printer, 1947); Jenkins and Hewitt, "Types of Personality Structure Encountered in Child Guidance Clinics," *American Journal of Orthopsychiatry*, 14 (January 1944), 84–94; Albert J. Reiss, Jr., "Social Correlates of Psychological Types of Delinquency," *American Sociological Review*, 17 (December 1952), 710–18.

[21]Two studies ot deviant roles other than criminal ones are Thomas J. Scheff, *Being Mentally Ill* (Chicago: Aldine, 1966); Robert B. Edgerton, *The Cloak of Competence* (Berkeley: University of California Press, 1967).

[22]Howard S. Becker, *Outsiders* (New York: Free Press, 1963), pp. 31–34.

[23]For a revealing investigation of this matter, see Richard D. Schwartz and Jerome H. Skolnick, "Two Studies of Legal Stigma," in *The Other Side*, Howard S. Becker, ed. (New York: Free Press, 1964), pp. 103–17. Another incisive analysis of the role problems of parolees is John Irwin, *The Felon* (Englewood Cliffs, N.J.: Prentice-Hall, Inc., 1970). His discussion centered about the desires of the parolee to find a postprison noncriminal role that involves a measure of dignity to him.

[24]Edwin M. Lemert, *Social Pathology* (New York: McGraw-Hill, 1951), pp. 73–98; see also Becker's discussion of the concept of "commitment" in Howard S. Becker, *Sociological Work* (Chicago: Aldine, 1970), pp. 261–87; Albert K. Cohen, *Deviance and Control* (Englewood Cliffs, N.J.: Prentice-Hall, Inc., 1966), pp. 97–101.

[25]For an excellent illustrative case of secondary deviation, centered about a criminal identity, see Bruce Jackson, *A Thief's Primer* (New York: Macmillan, 1969); see also Henry Williamson, *Hustler!* (New York: Doubleday, 1965).

[26]The matter of self-concept variations among offenders has not received the research attention it deserves. The most systematic body of data on this topic is found in the work of Reckless and associates, dealing with favorable self-concept as an "insulator" against delinquency. For example, see Walter C. Reckless, Simon Dinitz, and Ellen Murray, "Self-Concept as an Insulator Against Delinquency," *American Sociological Review*, 21 (December 1956), 744–56. This research is summarized in Don C. Gibbons, *Delinquent Behavior*, 3rd ed. (Englewood Cliffs, N.J.: Prentice-Hall, Inc., 1981), pp. 136–40. For a discussion of self-concept notions in the study of deviance, see L. Edward Wells, "Theories of Deviance and the Self-Concept," *Social Psychology*, 41 (December 1978), 189–204.

[27]Howard S. Becker, Blanche Geer, Everett C. Hughes, and Anselm L. Strauss, *Boys in White* (Chicago: University of Chicago Press, 1961).

[28]In some criminal roles, an isolated illegal act intruding into an otherwise exemplary life history represents role performance, whereas in other criminal roles, involvement in sustained deviance continues over several decades, as in the case of professional criminals. In the first instance, it would be well to identify this case as one involving a deviant act, reserving the career label for the second pattern of recurrent lawbreaking. Although in some ways persons who commit one fugitive act of lawbreaking hardly qualify as criminals, many do acquire a public identity as violators. Some end up in penal institutions and other correctional settings, or they encounter other societal reactions directed at them as "bad persons," so their personal acts of deviance do make a difference. Many persons found in arrest tabulations have been involved in relatively petty acts of lawbreaking. Quite probably, many of these individuals have been involved in brief escapades of criminality. For evidence on this point, see Don C. Gibbons, "Crime in the Hinterland," *Criminology*, 10 (August 1972), 177–91.

[29]Mary Owen Cameron, *The Booster and the Snitch* (New York: Free Press, 1964).

[30]The complete set of typological characterizations of adult offenders and of juvenile delinquent types as well is presented in Gibbons, *Changing the Lawbreaker*.

[31]Gibbons, *Changing the Lawbreaker*, pp. 104–6.

[32]Clarence C. Schrag, "A Preliminary Criminal Typology," *Pacific Sociological Review*, 4 (Spring 1961), 11–16; Schrag, "Some Foundations for a Theory of Correction," in *The Prison*, Donald R. Cressey, ed., (New York: Holt, Rinehart & Winston, 1961).

[33]Gresham M. Sykes, *The Society of Captives* (Princeton, N.J.: Princeton University Press, 1958), pp. 84–108.

[34]Peter G. Garabedian, "Social Roles in a Correctional Community," *Journal of Criminal Law, Criminology and Police Science*, 55 (September 1964), pp. 338–47; Garabedian, "Social Roles and Processes of Socialization in the Prison Community," *Social Problems*, 11 (Fall 1963), 139–52.

[35]Robert G. Leger, "Research Findings and Theory as a Function of Operationalization of Variables: A Comparison of Four Techniques for the Construct, 'Inmate Type,'" *Sociology and Social Research*, 63 (January 1979), 346–65. Also see Eric D. Poole, Robert M. Regoli, and Charles W. Thomas, "The Measurement of Inmate Social Roles: An Assessment," *Journal of Criminal Law and Criminology*, 71 (Fall 1980), 317–24.

[36]William P. Adams, Paul M. Chandler, and M. G. Neithercutt, "The San Francisco Project: A Critique," *Federal Probation*, 35 (December 1971), 45–53.

[37]Charles H. McCaghy, "Child Molesters: A Study of Their Careers as Deviants," in *Criminal Behavior Systems*, Marshall B. Clinard and Richard Quinney, eds., (New York: Holt, Rinehart & Winston, 1967), pp. 75–88.

[38] Conklin, *Robbery and the Criminal Justice System*, pp. 59–78.

[39]Ibid., p. 68.

[40]Joan Petersilia, Peter W. Greenwood, and Marvin L. Lavin, *Criminal Careers of Habitual Felons* (Washington, D.C.: Law Enforcement Assistance Administration, 1978).

[41]Clayton A. Hartjen and Don C. Gibbons, "An Empirical Investigation of a Criminal Typology," *Sociology and Social Research*, 54 (October 1969), 56–62.

[42]H. Laurence Ross, "Traffic Law Violation: A Folk Crime," *Social Problems*, 9 (Winter 1961), 231–41.

[43]James J. McKenna, *An Empirical Testing of a Typology of Adult Criminal Behavior* (Ph.D. diss., University of Notre Dame, 1972).

causal
analysis:
summing up

The preceding five chapters have presented a bewildering array of theories and research data concerning the causes of criminality and criminal behavior. We might well ask at this point: "What does it all mean?" This brief chapter presents a reprise of these discussions, with an assessment of some of the major dimensions of causation as they have emerged from the preceding chapters.

Figure 5 offers a representation of some of the major forces in the development of lawbreaking behavior, focusing on the actions of individuals. Although we often try to account for patterns of criminality or crime rates involving collections of individuals, the behavior of particular criminal persons is the ultimate unit we attempt to explain. Individual offenders added together make up rates of burglary, rape, or other kinds of misconduct.

In brief, Figure 5 indicates that lawbreaking is related to a variety of *basic factors*, centering about major ingredients of social structure, including cultural values, social-class patterns, racism, and other aspects of the collective order. These root causes of criminality affect nearly all citizens within a particular society to some degree, although criminogenic features have more impact on some citizens than others. A number of *intervening variables* mediate or influence these basic forces. These forces differentiate members of society and partially determine the different lines of activity they pursue. For example, family-interaction patterns vary among even those who grow up in the same social-class group and, in turn, shape to some extent the social roles these individuals play.

Figure 5 also shows that *precipitating factors*, which are the immediate sources of criminality, join basic factors and intervening variables. One set of precipitating influences includes attitudes and motives favorable to law violation, but other precipitators of lawbreaking exist as well.

Criminality takes many forms, thus various combinations of basic factors, intervening influences, and precipitating factors can be identified and linked to these different forms of lawbreaking. In this sense, multiple causation lies behind criminality.

The causal process outlined in Figure 5 also indicates that various *career contingencies* which occur to persons who engage in initial or primary acts of criminal conduct exert considerable influence on the subsequent course they take. Correctional experiences, difficulties in employment that arise out of "ex-con" status, and kindred other experiences play a major role in deflecting some offenders out of lawbreaking or in preventing others from withdrawing from criminality.

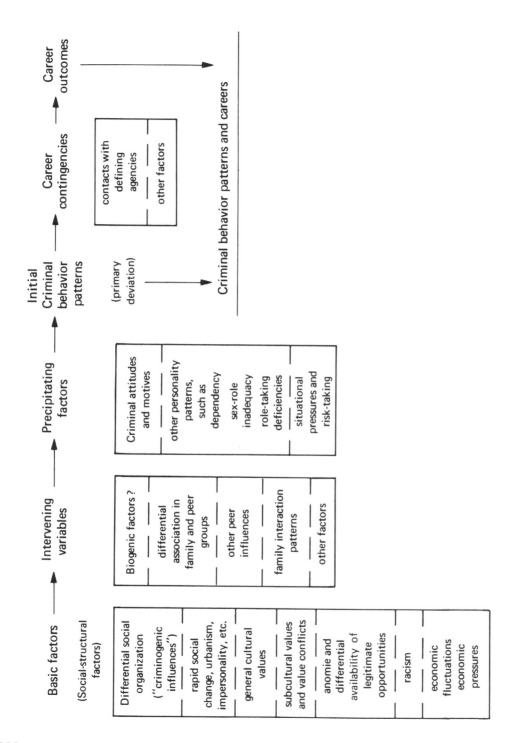

figure 5 causal processes in criminality

The preceding five chapters have already discussed particular basic factors, intervening variables, precipitating factors, career contingencies, and criminal-behavior patterns at some length. However, let us take a closer look at the argument and categories illustrated in Figure 5.

basic factors—social-structural variables

DIFFERENTIAL SOCIAL ORGANIZATION

We agree, as do nearly all criminologists, with Sutherland and Cressey's contention that "crime is rooted in the social organization and is an expression of that social organization."[1] *Differential social organization* is a general or summary label for a variety of social-structural factors generating criminality (criminogenic influences). Concerning differential social organization, Sutherland and Cressey declared:

This condition of normative conflict is ordinarily considered "social disorganization" or "unorganization," because the social pressures for conformity on the part of the person are not uniform or harmonious. . . . Actually, the social conditions in which the influences on the person are relatively inharmonious and inconsistent are themselves a kind of social organization. Such social organization is characteristic of all except the earliest societies and the most isolated contemporary societies, although there are wide variations in the degree of heterogeneity and in the pervasiveness of the normative inconsistencies.[2]

Normative conflict takes many forms. In American society, some societal pressures toward lawbreaking revolve around the unavailability of legitimate opportunities for the achievement of common success values. Unequal access to law-abiding routes to upward mobility and material success is particularly pronounced for some groups within society. Earlier, we examined this component as racism in American society.

Other social-structural influences have to do with subcultural value patterns that encourage lawbreaking. Some theorists have spoken of a subculture of violence in the United States, in which the group members are extremely suspicious of one another and prone to use physical aggression in interpersonal interaction. Along the same line, others have claimed that subcultural attitudes toward sexuality and physical force have much to do with the social-class concentration of forcible rape among working-class groups. As we have already noted, some observers have identified this situation of value conflicts and subcultural value patterns as constituting value pluralism.

According to another claim about the criminogenic impact of growing social complexity, impersonality and loose social bonds among citizens characterize modern societies; hence, persons are less inhibited from criminality as a result.[3]

Differential social organization in the contemporary United States is usually attributed to historical processes centering about rapid social change, stress on material success, the growing scale of modern social structure, pronounced urbanism, population heterogeneity flowing out of mass movements of foreign-born into the country in earlier periods, and other such occurrences. For example, many people have claimed that contemporary American lawlessness grew out of frontier traditions in which violence predominated as a means of settling disputes. Others have linked some of the current problems of criminality to traditional American values that stress individual freedom and that developed with the founding of the nation.

Knowledge is a relative matter. Some might argue that criminology is a puny discipline, for criminologists have not yet pinpointed all of the social-structural forces that contribute to criminality in modern societies. For example, there is abundant reason to suspect that the endemic racism of American society has a good deal to do with much of the lawbreaking observed in it, even though criminologists are not yet able to spell out in great detail precisely how racism operates to produce criminality. Then, too, the contributions, if any, of the political-economic structure of corporate capitalist societies, which have been hinted at by radical criminologists, have yet to be isolated. Chapter 7 indicated that radical-Marxist theories developed to date largely have been crude, overly general formulations filled with hyperbole.

However, on the other side of the coin criminological knowledge is more developed than first appearances might suggest. Criminologists have made considerable progress in isolating many of the basic forces that lie behind lawbreaking. In the chapters ahead, devoted to more detailed consideration of crime patterns, a good deal of additional material on these basic forces will be presented.

intervening variables

The number of variables intervening between basic social-structural processes and the occurrence of criminal acts must be large indeed. Figure 5 only hints at some of these factors. One collection of intervening influences centers about opportunities for lawbreaking actions. For example, an employee who works on an assembly line would be hard pressed to embezzle any of the firm's funds, no matter how motivated he or she might be to do so. Similarly, middle-class citizens have less chance to satisfy any curiosity they might have about narcotics than do individuals who frequent the "Tenderloin" area of the community, where opportunities to pursue various "vices" are much more available.

ARE THERE BIOGENIC INFLUENCES IN CRIMINALITY?

Our earlier perusal of the literature on biological factors in criminal behavior failed to turn up any evidence to support hypotheses of that sort. Theoretical and methodological inadequacies of one kind or another have flawed much of the criminological work in that area. The most recent of these arguments, concerning XYY chromosomal abnormality, is unconvincing. From the material in Chapter 8, one might conclude that no biological influences exist in criminality. But that conclusion is not warranted. All that can be said about biological arguments is that, to date, no proof of these hypothesized relationships have been uncovered. Conceivably, future investigations might turn up evidence supporting biological assertions. In addition, modern biological inquiry into crime involves sophisticated theoretical models more in tune with modern biological thought, in which environmental and biological *interaction* is stressed. It is too early to tell what the yield from this work will be, but an open mind is in order on this issue.

DIFFERENTIAL ASSOCIATION

Chapter 8 included a detailed examination of differential-association theory. That discussion acknowledged the crucial role that theoretical argument played in the development of modern criminology. Also, some processes similar to those Sutherland described as differential association are probably involved in some forms of criminal conduct and absent in others. Some kinds of lawbreaking are the outgrowth of lengthy episodes of differential association with carriers of criminal norms. On the other hand, in some forms of criminal deviance, association with criminalistic individuals is not implicated. In short, differential association is a label for one extremely important set of intervening variables, although other intervening factors exist as well.

OTHER PEER- AND FAMILY-INTERACTION PATTERNS

Chapter 9 acknowledged the impact of various kinds of family interaction patterns on criminality. Particular kinds of lawbreaking are related to distorted parent–child relationships, as in the case of incest; parent–child tensions, as involved in some forms of juvenile delinquency; and husband–wife disharmony, as in homicide and assault. In general, social and cultural forces have their effects on individuals only as they are mediated through the groups in which persons interact.

precipitating factors

CRIMINAL ATTITUDES, MOTIVES, AND PERSONALITY PATTERNS

According to the traditional criminological view, lawbreaking is the result of a causal process in which the social experiences persons encounter produce criminal attitudes and motives, which in turn lead them to engage in deviant acts.

The discussion of differential-association theory conceded that this kind of etiological process probably is accurate for many offenders. In some criminal acts and careers, the actors have acquired criminalistic attitudes out of protracted involvement in differential association, broadly defined.

At the same time, some kinds of lawbreaking arise out of other precipitating factors, some of which involve personality patterns or attributes that differentiate offenders from nonoffenders. The evidence examined in Chapter 7 failed to support the claim that most forms of criminality involve personality pathology. But those data did not by any means rule out the possibility that personality deviations are implicated as precipitating elements in some specific instances of offender behavior. We would be hard pressed to ignore such a hypothesis when considering the violent sex offender or "psychopathic" assaultist.

Psychological patterns are involved as precipitating factors in many instances of criminal behavior, in addition to those involving personality pathology. For example, the hypothesis that certain check forgers are drawn into this behavior because of an overly dependent personality structure is worthy of further examination.

SITUATIONAL PRESSURES AND RISK-TAKING

Chapter 9 devoted much discussion to situational pressures as precipitating forces in lawbreaking. Traditional criminological views of lawbreaking have tended to stress social-structural factors and intervening variables, along with criminal attitudes and motives, as the necessary combination of elements for criminality to occur. The offender has been viewed as different from the nonoffender because of the former's motivation to engage in lawbreaking. Situational factors have been assigned a minor role in traditional criminological perspectives. A strong case exists for heavier emphasis upon risk-taking processes and situational influences in criminality. There is considerable evidence now at hand indicating that many persons drift into misconduct or in some other way unwittingly become involved in it. Indeed, it could hardly be otherwise, in view of the large number of criminal laws which impinge upon persons and the crosscurrents of conflicting group affiliations and other pressures experienced by individuals in complex, modern societies.

A word or two is in order regarding the prediction of criminal behavior on the basis of basic factors, intervening variables, and precipitating factors. The remarks on causal thinking in Chapter 3 pointed out that for many citizens, prediction or explanation only exists when unequivocal statements can be made to the effect that one event always follows the occurrence of another. Thus economic precariousness is sometimes denied as a cause of crime because not all persons who suffer economic pressures engage in lawbreaking. But, if the members of modern societies are buffeted about by conflicting pressures, discordant group loyalties, and the like, social influences that contribute to lawbreaking are not likely to have uniform effects upon all the persons who experience them.

Instead, criminogenic factors that turn some individuals in the direction of criminality may be nullified or countered by prosocial influences in other instances.

Another fact to be kept clearly in mind is that human actors are not like billiard balls that merely respond to external pressures that impinge upon them. They are self-aware, thinking organisms who are able to anticipate and reflect upon social experiences that they encounter, with the result that *reactivity* characterizes them. It is for this reason as well that predictions of criminality or other forms of behavior will probably always be couched in probabilistic terms.

criminal behavior, career contingencies, and career outcomes

Forces leading up to or producing initial or primary acts of lawbreaking may not determine the course that criminal involvement takes. In many cases, experiences with police or correctional agencies may play a major part in career outcomes. In some instances, these contingencies may deter the lawbreaker from more than a single flirtation with deviance. In other cases, the person may become further entangled in misbehavior, partly as a consequence of his or her experiences with correctional processes.

In actuality, relatively little is known about the impact of imprisonment on specific offenders or about other experiences of that kind. Although there are numerous essays about prisons as "crime schools," hard evidence concerning the effects of the penitentiary on particular offender careers is not abundant. The same is true of other correctional structures and processes.

summary

This brief chapter has outlined a broad synthesis of the etiological elements identified in earlier chapters. The commentary in this chapter and the preceding ones is a general theoretical exposition on crime causation. We turn now to a more detailed examination of particular forms of criminal conduct. Chapter 12 begins this task.

notes

[1] Edwin H. Sutherland and Donald R. Cressey, *Criminology*, 10th ed. (Philadelphia: Lippincott, 1978), p. 83.

[2] Ibid., p. 101.

[3] For some evidence on this point, see Erwin O. Smigel, "Public Attitudes Toward Stealing as Related to the Size of the Victim Organization," in *Crimes Against Bureaucracy*, Smigel and H. Laurence Ross, eds. (New York: Van Nostrand Reinhold, 1970), pp. 15–28; see also Smigel, "Public Attitudes Toward 'Chiseling' with Reference to Unemployment Compensation," in ibid., pp. 29–45.

garden-variety predatory crime

It is fitting that the discussion of major forms of crime and of the criminals who carry them out should begin with garden-variety predator offenders. Predators, according to the dictionary, live by plundering or robbing others. The term, garden-variety draws attention to the fact that the majority of citizens have their most frequent and most direct experiences with relatively crude larcenies, burglaries, robberies, automobile thefts, and other predatory acts. Although many citizens are actually victimized in subtle but more serious and costly ways by white-collar crimes, frauds, and borderline criminal acts encountered in the marketplace, their recognizable experiences are most frequently with garden-variety predatory crimes.

Robbery is included in the collection of property crimes considered in this chapter, even though it is also often classified as a crime of violence or personal offense. Robbery is appropriately designated a property crime, first, because many robberies are accomplished without actual force or violence being used against the victim. More important, while force and threats of force are sometimes employed by robbers, these are essentially incidental to the real purpose of the crime, namely, to relieve the victim of money or other personal property.

In the imagery of crime carried about in the heads of many laymen, garden-variety predatory crimes are attributed to "criminals" who are members of "the dangerous classes," set apart from law-abiding citizens. The belief that a distinct group of ruthless, full-time predators exists in our midst who are responsible for most crimes against property is one that bears much similarity to the perceptions of the eighteenth- and nineteenth-century English; they saw criminality as being part of a shadowy, underworld populated by the likes of Bill Sykes, Jonathan Wild, and other members of the dangerous classes.[1]

Although such beliefs may have had some validity in eighteenth- and nineteenth-century England, they markedly distort the phenomenon of crime in modern societies. One of the major points of this chapter is that predatory crime is commonplace in American society, with the great bulk of it being accomplished by individuals who are amateurs in criminality, who are relatively uncommitted to lawbreaking or procrime sentiments, and who live in the midst of other citizens who refrain from predatory crimes.

crime as work²

Criminologists have often invoked conceptual language from the sociology of work when dealing with predatory offenders, speaking of professional criminals, semiprofessional property offenders, vocational predators, and other groupings of lawbreakers who labor at crime as an illicit occupation. Then, too, much has been said about the learning processes through which crime skills are acquired, about careers in crime, and about other notions that are familiar from the world of work. In recent years, occupational perspectives on predatory crime have become prominent within the criminal-justice system as well, as prosecuting attorneys in a number of jurisdictions have established special programs for prosecuting "career criminals."

There is a good deal to be said in favor of an occupational perspective on predatory lawbreaking. This way of looking at criminality draws attention to the fact that garden-variety property crimes are often carried out by individuals who differ little in mental-health terms from those who refrain from criminality. Moreover, it is possible to single out some predatory offenders as professional criminals, in that they do exhibit a long period of training, complex occupational skills, and a shared set of occupationally oriented attitudes—elements usually regarded as central to professional status.³ There are other offenders for whom the label of semiprofessional property criminal would be appropriate, in that they are engaged more or less full-time in criminality as a livelihood.

However, occupational concepts in criminology should be used cautiously. Many predatory crimes that occur in the real world are isolated, one-time law-breaking acts by individuals who lead generally law-abiding lives. It makes little sense to speak of crime as an occupation in such instances. Even more important, there are other offenders who become involved in repetitive acts of criminality, but who also work at least intermittently at conventional jobs. For these individuals, crime is a form of "moonlighting," not a full-time occupation or career.

Some predatory criminals are inducted into a criminal occupation relatively early in their lives, and to them the notion of a criminal career can be meaningfully applied. But for many predatory offenders, involvement in criminal occupations or part-time lawbreaking unfolds in ways that parallel the drift of many young adults into occupational niches. There is much blundering about, experimentation, and short-term employment in an array of relatively low-paying jobs before new recruits to the labor pool finally settle upon a particular occupation to be pursued over a longer period. In much the same way, many violators engage in a good deal of experimentation with criminality. Finally, many of these unskilled criminals drift out of criminal involvement entirely.

varieties of predatory crime

The preceding remarks suggest there are some relatively distinct forms of predatory crime and of groupings of offenders who commit them that can be singled out for attention. Some forms of property crime bear many earmarks of professionalism, while others are crude and unsophisticated forays against the property of others. Let us examine some of these constellations of crime forms and collections of offenders.

PROFESSIONAL THEFT AS A WAY OF LIFE

Professional theft is a term that is usually employed in connection with the non-violent, complicated crimes of a colorful group of offenders who call themselves "grifters," "boosters," "carnies," or other argot terms and whom sociologists call "professional thieves." Professional thieves engage in a variety of nonviolent and frequently complex forms of property crime, usually involving some element of the "con" or manipulation of the victim or victims. They exhibit a long period of training, complex occupational skills, and a shared set of occupationally oriented attitudes, which is the warrant for terming them professionals.

Much of the evidence on professional theft deals with the criminal activity in which grifters engage.[4] Police officers have compiled lengthy collections of case material on the *modus operandi* of thieves,[5] and several sociologists have also spent some of their energy cataloguing the details of professional grifting.[6] What emerges from all of these accounts is a picture of criminality that demonstrates the esoteric and complex nature of grifting as a kind of crime.

Considerably less is known about the backgrounds from which professional thieves derive than is apparent about the criminality in which they engage. Thieves are often recruited from occupations in which contact with underworld figures is fairly common and, in addition, grifters may often be drawn from a cohort of individuals with particular personality patterns. On this first point, Sutherland's report on professional offenders indicated that many of these persons were originally active in occupational pursuits peripheral to criminalistic ones.[7]

Psychiatrist Richard L. Jenkins contended that thieves show a "budding grifter" personality structure.[8] He suggested that "budding grifters" are specialists in deceit who have developed interpersonal betrayal into a fine art. Rather than experiencing guilt over their devious activities, they exhibit a professional pride in their workmanship and may feel chagrin and humiliation in instances where their manipulative endeavors go awry.

According to Jenkins, elements or experiences that may contribute to the development of "budding grifter" personalities include:

1. Experiences (as of unusual hardship) during the formative period which put a high premium upon material success.
2. Early experiences which force a close self-protective attention to the emotional reactions of intermittently or constantly hostile adults.
3. Early experiences which tend toward the development of distrust and the expectation of betrayal.
4. Attitudes on the part of those emotionally important to the child which sanction unreliability, or which laud deceit or betrayal as an adaptation and means of getting on in the world. In some instances this involves definite teaching or coaching in the art of betrayal.
5. Early and repetitive gain from the use of deceit.
6. Attitudes and experiences which lead to the development of verbal facility, social charm and ingratiating ways.[9]

Social settings likely to culminate in learning of deceit and reward for its practice include disharmony and marital tension between the parents of the child. In this situation, the parents compete for the allegiance of the child, attempting to win his or her loyalty and alienate the child from the other marital partner. The "budding grifter" learns to turn this situation to advantage by playing one parent against the other.

These claims represent a series of clinical hunches, not hard facts from careful research. Moreover, the hypothesis advanced in this case was broad, holding that the "grifter" personalities these experiences generate subsequently make their way into a variety of social circumstances. Jenkins did not argue that all or most of them become professional criminals, thus one might expect to find "budding grifters" at work on used-car lots, selling vacuum cleaners or aluminum siding, or in countless other settings where manipulative skills can be employed.[10]

Although facts are hard to come by, it is clear that professional theft has always been a relatively uncommon form of criminality in American society. Moreover, grifting has generally been on the decline for decades. Certain forms of grifting in particular have become nearly obsolete, as a consequence of certain broad changes that have occurred in societal conditions in the United States. For one, the practice of the "big con" has waned as a result of changes in banking procedures, the growing sophistication of "marks," and other trends of that sort. Carnival grifting is a declining form of illegality because of the disappearance of the carnival as a feature of small-town life in this country. Certain other forms of grifting have survived to the present: "boosting" (shoplifting) and certain "short con" games such as "the pigeon drop" persist as forms of professional theft. But even these surviving patterns are probably infrequent in comparison to the garden-variety forms of lawbreaking.

What is the significance of professional theft? Two points stand out in any evaluation of the criminological salience of grifting. First, professional theft is an extreme illustration of the extent to which a pattern of deviant conduct may become elaborated into a complex interactional pattern, behavior system, or subculture, in which the members are bound together by a variety of social ties in addition to their involvement in criminal acts. Moreover, these deviant actors are players in a complex social system in which they exist together with a variety of "noncriminals," including police officers, tipsters, fences, cab drivers, and other related types. Professional theft is deviant conduct transmitted from generation to generation; much of the content of activity originated well before the birthdates of contemporary thieves.

The second observation to be made about criminality, stemming from the study of grifting, has to do with the interconnections of illegality to other features of organized social life. For example, Edwin Schur suggested that professional theft cannot be understood apart from consideration of basic values of American society, which encourage or condone swindles, frauds, "sharp" business practices, and unethical conduct of various kinds.[11] The United States exhibits a cultural climate in which profit motives, salesmanship, and "something for nothing" interests stand out. The professional thief turns this situation of tolerance for devious conduct to his advantage. Grifters claim that in England grifting is difficult if not impossible because of the lesser emphasis on risk-taking, acquisitive actions in that nation. In the same way, they frequently assert the impossibility of "conning" or victimizing an honest man; the mark must have "larceny in his soul" to be swindled. In short, professional thieves point up the impossibility of sustaining the clear distinctions between the "good guys" and the "bad guys" in American society. The law violator is no less a product of society than the moral, upright citizen, and both of them have much more in common than they are likely to acknowledge.

PROFESSIONAL "HEAVY" CRIME

Criminologists have often singled out professional "heavy" criminals, who engage in larcenies, robberies, and burglaries, from semiprofessional and "one-time-loser" property criminals, who also commit larcenies and related offenses, largely in terms of the criminal expertise they demonstrate. To be a "heavy" criminal, in the argot of offenders, means to be involved in lawbreaking acts where violence and threats of violence are employed as crime techniques. These crimes stand in contrast to professional theft or grifting, where chicanery is a basic crime skill.

However, the distinction between professional "heavy" crime and less sophisticated activities is actually one of degree rather than kind. Also, the dividing line between professional and semiprofessional offenders is somewhat arbitrary. On the whole, professional "heavies" reap large sums of money from their illegal activities and work at this occupation full-time. Semiprofessionals tend to be relatively unskilled, poorly paid for their criminal endeavors, and work at crime in many cases on a part-time basis. Some offenders fall clearly into one or another of these types, but many criminals might be difficult to categorize in that technical skill, amount of profit from crime, and involvement in criminality are matters of degree rather than of different qualitative attributes of offenders.[12]

Numerous descriptions of professional "heavy" crime are in existence, including several in the form of the life stories of professional criminals.[13] One useful account of professional crime is the famous Brink's robbery that occurred in Boston in 1950. The following excerpt from the Federal Bureau of Investigation report of the Brink's robbery clearly communicates the flavor of professional crime:

The Brink's robbery was the product of a combined thought and criminal experience of men who had known one another for many years. The gang spent more than a year in planning the robbery and they started a systematic study of the Brink's organization after it moved to its present site on Prince Street in Boston.

Before the robbery was carried out, all the participants were well acquainted with the Brink's premises. Each had surreptitiously entered the building on several occasions after the Brink's employees had left for the day and they made a study of Brink's schedules and shipments.

The planning for the robbery included several "trial runs" in which the gang members practiced their approach to the building in a truck and their flight over the "getaway" route. The gang abandoned plans to carry out the robbery several times when conditions were not favorable.

During these occasions one gang member was stationed on the roof of a building on Prince Street overlooking Brink's. He signaled the others with a flashlight. The last of these "false" approaches took place on the evening before the robbery.

During the early evening of January 17, 1950, members of the gang met in the Roxbury section of Boston and entered the rear of a Ford stake-body truck which had been stolen in Boston in November, 1949, to be used in the robbery.

Including the driver, this truck carried nine members of the gang to the scene of the robbery. During the trip from Roxbury seven of the men donned Navy-type peacoats and chauffeur's caps. Each of the seven also was given a pistol and Halloween-type mask. Each had gloves and wore either crepe-sole shoes or rubbers so their footsteps would be muffled.

As the men approached the Brink's building, they looked for a signal from the "lookout" on the roof of a Prince Street building. The "lookout" previously had arrived in a stolen Ford sedan.

After receiving the "go ahead" signal, seven members of the gang left the truck and walked through a playground which led to the Prince Street entrance to Brink's. Using the side-door key they had previously obtained, the men quickly entered and donned the masks.

Other keys in their possession enabled them to proceed to the second floor, where they took five Brink's employees by surprise. The seven robbers ordered the employees to lie face down on the floor, tied their hands behind them, and placed adhesive tape over their mouths. Before fleeing with the loot, the seven armed men attempted to open a metal box containing the payroll of the General Electric Co., but they had brought no tools and were unsuccessful.

Immediately upon leaving, the gang loaded the loot into the stolen truck. As the truck sped away with nine members of the gang, the "lookout" departed in the stolen sedan.

The truck was unloaded at the home of one of the participants in Roxbury that same evening. Some members of the gang made a preliminary effort to count the loot, but they quickly dispersed to establish alibis for themselves.

On the night of the robbery, approximately $380,000 of the loot was removed from the house in Roxbury for security reasons. Additionally, the equipment used in the robbery was taken by a gang member for disposal. On January 18, 1950, another gang member took the remainder of the loot from the house; and several weeks later it was divided among the eleven men.

In addition to the cash and securities, the robbers took four pistols from Brink's. One of these was recovered by a Somerville, Mass., police officer on February 5, 1950. It had been found by a group of boys near the Mystic River in Somerville.

Descriptions of the truck used in the robbery were obtained from persons in the vicinity of the crime scene. Pieces of an identical truck were found at a dump in Stoughton, Mass., March 14, 1950. This truck has been cut up with an acetylene torch.

During the F.B.I.'s six-year investigation thousands of possible suspects were eliminated. Thousands of other persons, possible witnesses and individuals who could furnish background information concerning matters arising in various phases of the investigation were interviewed. Circulars concerning a $100,000 reward offered by Brink's were distributed to all parts of the country and no tip was overlooked.[14]

In many of its details, this illustration parallels the *modus operandi* of the "heist" described by former robber Everett DeBaun.[15]

SEMIPROFESSIONAL AND UNSKILLED PREDATORY CRIME

Professional crime is the stuff of which movies such as *The Sting, The Asphalt Jungle*, and *Topkapi* are made; in them, a band of extraordinarily skilled criminals makes off with a huge haul through an extremely complex and well-planned burglary or robbery. But it is not the perpetrators of this kind of lawbreaking that loom large in the population of offenders; instead, it is semiprofessional and novice, "one-time losers" who contribute most heavily to garden-variety crime. The label "semiprofessional" is used to direct attention to relatively unskilled violators who engage sporadically in predatory acts. Many of these persons are of average intelligence, are from socially and economically deprived neighborhoods, and have been involved in numerous contacts with the police, juvenile authorities, and custodial institutions. Semiprofessional crime is usually crude and unsophisticated, lacking in planning, and carried on by offenders acting alone. Not surprisingly, semiprofessional predators rarely obtain "big scores," that is, large payoffs from criminal activity.

Persons fitting the semiprofessional-property-offender characterization turn up in some number in prisons and other correctional settings. But, not all predatory crime is the work of individuals who engage in crime full- or part-time and who are recidivists. Often many "one-time losers"—novices in lawbreaking—are found in probation caseloads, diversion programs, and other places to which putatively amateur offenders are sent.[16]

The writing and passing of "bum checks" is an extremely costly and widespread form of American crime. The significance of checks in modern society is indicated by Herbert Bloch and Gilbert Geis, who reported that over 90 percent of the money transactions in the United States at present take place by means of checks rather than through cash transferrals.[17] Professional criminals are constantly attempting to obtain money through fraudulent-check passing, for forgery and check passing are relatively easy in a cultural situation where check transactions are normal activities arousing little suspicion. Professional forgers engage in check passing as a livelihood and exhibit complicated and well-developed crime skills.[18] They manufacture and pass checks in bunches, frequently in an elaborate fashion involving the printing of authentic-looking payroll checks from a nonexistent company. Professional forgers often pass fictitious checks made to look legitimate through the use of a stolen check-printer. Professional check passing is a form of "grifting," a variant of professional theft.

However, as a part of growing up, nearly every adult citizen learns to handle his or her affairs through checking accounts. The amateur offender in need of emergency funds has acquired simple skills that can be turned toward forgery. These persons who write checks upon their own bank accounts, who are unskilled at crime, and who are not involved in other forms of lawbreaking, are designated at *naïve check forgers*.

The analysis of crime statistics for the United States in Chapter 5 documented the widespread nature of forgery, much of which is amateurish in form. But, there is good reason to suspect that these known cases are a small fraction of all check violations. Many instances of behavior that qualify technically as forgery probably go unreported because they are suspected of being accidental. Persons do fairly commonly write checks that "bounce" unintentionally because they have miscalculated the amount of money in their checking accounts. As a result, the line between mistakes and willful misconduct is hazy. Deliberate or intentional forgers have this defense available to employ against aggrieved merchants. They can assert that "NSF" checks were accidental miscalculations and businessmen may well find themselves forced to honor this explanation for fear of alienating customers. Offended merchants may also be deterred from responding to a forger's misconduct as crime out of feelings of identification and sympathy for the actor, particularly if the forger is a person of middle-class position and a long-standing customer. Finally, merchants may be loath to report such cases to authorities for fear of getting entangled in time-consuming court appearances and also out of anticipation that they will then be unable to gain recompense for financial losses suffered.

One bit of evidence of the differential handling of forgers came in interviews with the manager of a suburban chain drugstore in the San Francisco area who disclosed that large numbers of check forgers victimized this establishment each week, even though it took elaborate steps to prevent such incidents.[19] Nearly all the checks that "bounced" and were returned to the store by banks were handled informally. The drugstore endeavored to collect its losses from the check passers and in many cases succeeded in doing so. But the store did not always manage to recoup its losses; the manager reported that "chiselers" who pass bad checks for small amounts frequently refused to make good on them. They based their actions on the assumption that the store would not be willing to go through the cumbersome, time-consuming steps required to prosecute. These forgers were usually correct in this assumption, for the management rarely engaged in formal actions against check passers. Cases that were prosecuted normally involved large amounts of money lost to the store.

AUTOMOBILE THEFT AND "JOYRIDING"

Automobiles occupy a central place in several kinds of crime. First, in "car-clouting," a frequently-encountered form of burglary and larceny, cars are broken into in parking lots and elsewhere and items of property are stolen from them. Car-clouting is a variant of semiprofessional predatory crime, in that it often involves considerable skill on the part of car-clouters, many of whom engage in this activity as a livelihood. Automobiles are also stolen by gangs of "car strippers" and car thieves, who either alter the identification markings and sell the stolen vehicles or who "strip" (dismantle) the cars and sell the parts obtained from them. Like car-clouting, this is a form of semiprofessional property crime. Finally, "joyriding" is still another version of car theft.

"Joyriding," in which the offenders steal automobiles to provide short-run recreation rather than to deprive the owner permanently of his or her property, is an extremely commonplace kind of illegality in the United States. In addition, joyriding spans juvenile delinquency and adult criminality. Joyriding car theft is often carried on by persons from about 13 to 20 years of age. Many of these individuals get apprehended and diverted into juvenile courts, thereby becoming "delinquents" in point of legal fact, whereas others are remanded to criminal courts and acquire the legal status of "criminal."

Leonard Savitz,[20] and Jerome Hall[21] have made detailed surveys of the existing information regarding car theft. In discussing joyriding car theft as distinguished from those automobile larcenies in which the car is "stripped" or permanently stolen, Savitz noted that many jurisdictions created special legislation to cover this form of behavior. Early efforts to prosecute joyriders under general larceny statutes were often unsuccessful because the offenders had not intended to deprive the owners of their automobiles permanently.[22] As a result, an offense usually labeled "Taking a Motor Vehicle Without the Owner's Permission" was invented to cover the activities of joyriders. Along a somewhat related line, Hall observed that some courts resorted to administrative procedures dealing with joyriders under a statute which, technically, did not apply to them, rather than under the relevant law covering theft of cars, to prevent these persons from being harshly punished for relatively minor criminal acts.[23]

The essays by Savitz and Hall indicated that the crime techniques or *modus operandi* of car thieves are varied; some employ technically simple tactics of lawbreaking, whereas others use more esoteric skills.[24] These authors also observed that about 90 percent of the vehicles reported stolen are ultimately recovered. usually undamaged, and usually within a short time interval.[25] Savitz also enumerated some major characteristics of car thieves indicated in available reports and studies.[26] Most of them are young males, usually under 20 years of age and single. Large cities have the highest rates of automobile theft, probably owing in part to anonymity and other features that provide opportunities for vehicles to be stolen easily and with slight risk.

pathways to predatory crime

There are many faces to predatory crime: houses are burglarized, persons are strong-armed or have their purses snatched on the subway, cars are stolen, "bad checks" are passed on unsuspecting retailers, items of personal property are stolen from hotel rooms by hotel prowlers, and so on, in a vast list of predatory acts. The miscreants responsible for these acts also vary markedly: some are skilled professionals, others blunder about at sporadic, low-paying crime, and many others engage in flirtations with criminality. Little wonder, then, that there are multiple pathways to predatory crime. We have already examined some of the theorizing and evidence on the etiological processes in professional theft, but the other patterns of predatory crime remain to be discussed.

PROFESSIONAL AND SEMIPROFESSIONAL CRIME

Descriptive data on the characteristics of professional and semiprofessional offenders are available in considerable quantity, including biographical and autobiographical reports concerning the social origins of offenders and their participation in crime.[27]

In an inquiry concerning armed robbery, Werner Einstadter studied several dozen paroled California robbers.[28] He maintained that professional armed robbers usually go about lawbreaking in transitory partnerships; they do not band together into diffuse and persisting criminal groups made up of criminal friends. Einstadter also noted that "viewed as a type, the individual careerist assumes the posture of a man whose round of life never quite seems to meet the standards of middle-class convention . . . . Typically, the careerist represents one who lives on the fringes, more a 'night' dweller than a 'day' dweller. In his circle of intimate acquaintances are the hustler, the bookie, the gambler, and the pimp; the bartender, the taxidriver, and the bellhop."[29] These findings were closely paralleled in a more recent study of armed robbers in a California prison.[30]

A number of detailed investigations of semiprofessional criminals have been carried out.[31] In one study, Norman Hayner tested a series of hunches regarding five hypothesized offender types, one of which was the "heavy."[32] Hayner examined the case records of inmates in Washington State institutions to determine if certain types, including "alcoholic forgers" and "heavies," do exist. The study identified "heavies" as prisoners over 25 years old who had been engaged in robbery or burglary as a crime pattern, so they were apparently semiprofessionals. Hayner discovered that these individuals had frequently attempted to escape from prison, exhibited antisocial personalities, and were defined as "right guys" by other inmates. The "heavies" had poor work records outside the institution, were often from families in which other members were delinquent or criminal, and were generally from lower socioeconomic status groups. As a result of this accumulation of unfavorable social characteristics, they were usually given long prison sentences.

The results of investigations by Clarence Schrag and his associates ran parallel to the findings of Hayner. Schrag reported the social characteristics of "antisocial" prisoners known as "right guys" in the argot of prison culture.[33] Antisocial inmates were recidivists who showed an evolving career pattern in law-breaking that began with truancy and casual theft during the adolescent period and developed into semiprofessional property criminality in adulthood. These prisoners showed a background of low socioeconomic status and associations with delinquent companions or criminalistic siblings. They often came from relatively warm, stable family backgrounds, which were generally criminogenic because of the involvement of family members in deviance.[34]

Roebuck conducted still another study that turned up compatible findings. He investigated the social backgrounds of a group of black robbers in the Washington, D.C., Reformatory by comparing these persons with inmates who had engaged in other kinds of criminality. The armed robbers were older than most of the other felons, had grown up in urban areas and in slum neighborhoods, had been inducted into delinquency early in their lives, and exhibited average intelligence ratings. Most had experienced dismal home conditions in which their families frequently depended on public assistance for support.[35]

Evidence on semiprofessional property offenders indicates that many of them show backgrounds of extensive involvement in delinquency, particularly in gang associations. But, not all adult semiprofessional offenders exhibit records as delinquent offenders, nor do most youngsters who engage in juvenile misconduct, within gangs or outside of them, advance on to become enmeshed in repetitive patterns of adult criminality. Most juvenile lawbreakers become disengaged from deviance and criminality by early adulthood, but some do not. The old saw that the delinquent of today will be the criminal of tomorrow is untrue. Stated differently, it would be an error to conclude that, because many adult semiprofessionals were delinquents earlier in life, most delinquents graduate into adult criminality.

Detailed data on careers in juvenile delinquency came from a comprehensive study in Philadelphia by Marvin Wolfgang, Robert Figlio, and Thorsten Sellin.[36] They obtained information on the delinquency histories, as measured by police contacts, of the cohort of boys born in 1945 who lived in Philadelphia at least between their tenth and eighteenth birthdays.

Wolfgang and associates reported that 35 percent of the 9,945 boys studied were involved with the police at least once to the extent that the contact had been officially recorded, while 65 percent had not been apprehended by the police. Black youngsters showed more police contacts than white boys, for 50.2 percent of the former and 28.6 of the latter were classified as offenders. Lower-socioeconomic-class members were more often involved in police action than were higher-income boys; 44.8 percent of the former and 26.5 percent of the latter had been in the hands of the police.

Examination of the offense patterns among the apprehended youths showed that 54 percent were repeaters, while 46 percent had been arrested only once. Recidivists were more frequently low-income youths, and black youngsters were disproportionately common in this group. The most salient portion of this study for the point being discussed here has to do with the activities of chronic offenders, that is, youngsters who had been involved in more than four violations. These boys made up only 18 percent of the total group of offenders but were responsible for over one-half of all known offenses. They were also most frequently involved in serious offenses. Moreover, the chronic offenders did not start out by committing petty offenses that eventually led them into more serious ones; rather, they generally began their delinquent involvement by engaging in relatively serious offenses.

Gang delinquency has been a subject of persistent interest to sociologists since the 1920s, so much so that only the outlines of the accumulated storehouse of theory and research evidence on delinquent gangs can be sketched here.[37] The empirical data on gangs includes the pioneering work of Frederic Thrasher, Clifford Shaw, Henry D. McKay, and others.[38] Thrasher examined the activities of 1,313 male gangs in Chicago and reported that juvenile gangs were most frequently encountered in deteriorated, working-class slum sections of the city. Paralleling Thrasher's work were the many reports of Shaw, McKay, and others. These included a series of ecological studies demonstrating that gang delinquency was concentrated in "delinquency areas" of the city, which were also slum neighborhoods characterized by high rates of social breakdown. They also contributed a number of detailed descriptions of delinquent behavior in urban gangs, indicating that most delinquent boys lacked personality pathologies and were the products of situations in which delinquent endeavors were initially learned as forms of hedonistic "fun." As they progressed through careers in delinquency, lawbreaking came to take on a more utilitarian form, so that many boys ultimately acquired the skills and criminal sophistication of semiprofessional offenders.

The study of delinquency was relatively dormant between the 1930s and the 1950s, but the publication in 1955 of Albert Cohen's *Delinquent Boys* triggered a torrent of renewed attention to delinquent activity in the form of theorizing and research inquiry.[39] Although the products of this criminological inquiry are not entirely clear or consistent, they do add up to some major conclusions about gang misconduct on the part of working-class youngsters:

1. Although delinquents are found throughout neighborhoods and communities in American society, organized group patterns of subcultural lawbreaking constituting a neighborhood tradition tend to be concentrated in urban working-class neighborhoods. These neighborhoods share a number of ecological characteristics, such as physical deterioration and blight, the presence of vice, and kindred conditions.

2. The most common form of subcultural misconduct is the "parent subculture" pattern of delinquency characterized by behavioral versatility rather than specialization. Subcultural gang delinquency varies somewhat between communities of different size or other characteristics, so that in some, offender gangs are small and loosely structured, while in others they are larger, more organized, and devoted to somewhat different kinds of lawbreaking.

3. Working-class boys become involved in subcultural misbehavior out of a variety of circumstances, but most of the causal influences center about social or economic deprivation experienced by lower-income citizens in metropolitan neighborhoods. While there is no single route to involvement in subcultural delinquency, a set of related circumstances stemming from the social-class structure conjoin to generate this behavior. Some gang offenders are responding to problems of perceived lack of opportunity and economic deprivation, others are more concerned about immediate status threats, still others are drawn into delinquency out of adjustment difficulties in school.

4. Subcultural offenders tend to be the products of lower-class families in which criminalistic members are sometimes present or in which relatively slight control over the behavior of the boys is exerted. Severe parent–child tension is not usually involved in these cases, but family factors of a less marked form do interact with social-class influences in subcultural delinquency.

5. Gang delinquents are not usually characterized by severe personality problems or emotional tensions, but they do exhibit antisocial attitudes, delinquent self-images, and certain other social-psychological characteristics which develop out of their involvement in delinquent subcultures.[40]

UNSKILLED PREDATORY CRIME AND NAÏVE CHECK FORGERY

Naïve check forgery is an extremely common form of predatory conduct usually directed at retail stores and other business concerns. "Bad checks" are frequent in business life and merchandisers expect a large volume of them. In turn, the merchandisers adopt pricing policies anticipating business losses from checks that "bounce" (as well as from shoplifting and pilferage by employees). Cases reported to the police represent only a fraction of the instances known to store personnel; moreover, other cases occur which go undetected even by business establishments. "Nice people" from moderate economic circumstances carry on a good many of these offenses. Not fitting the image of the slum "tough guy" probably has much to do with the infrequent referral of such persons to the police.

Unskilled predatory offenders ("one-time losers") are relatively naïve and unsophisticated persons who steal property from an individual or an organization such as a retail store or supermarket. Large numbers of individuals manage to find their way into isolated but sometimes serious instances of illegal conduct. Some culprits involved in this kind of criminality (e.g., a single burglary or theft) turn up in probation caseloads, and less frequently, in state prisons.

Why do they do it? Some etiological clues can be found in the theoretical conjectures of Edwin Lemert, some of which were touched upon in Chapter 9.[41] Two sources of deviant conduct he identified are particularly relevant to much of the criminal behavior under discussion. One has to do with value pluralism in the United States, in which groups holding one set of standards find they must conform to another, conflicting set of values. Insofar as these persons violate the alien standards, their actions come to be labeled deviant.[42] Lemert provided a number of illustrations of this form of deviance, including the case of "totin'" or petty theft by rural black migrants. Petty thievery is a not-uncommon kind of activity that is at least tolerated, if not actually supported, by value preferences in many rural areas in the United States. Thus, amateur or casual offenders may define isolated acts of larceny as "borrowing," so that such activities are fairly commonplace. Nonetheless, some of these persons are unlucky enough to be sternly dealt with in the correctional process and receive prison sentences for their actions.

The second etiological hypothesis that Lemert advanced centered about "risk taking," in which individuals get involved in deviant behavior as a result of embarking on a line of conduct having several potential outcomes, one of which is a deviant form.[43] This kind of nonconforming behavior cannot be linked to clear-cut motivational elements driving the actor, for the individual did not specifically intend to become involved in deviance at the beginning of the behavioral events. Commenting on the suicide behavior of residents of the island of Tikopia, Lemert argued: "This analysis of suicide suggests the more general possibility that there are many instances in which people do not elect deviant solutions to problems but instead initiate lines of behavior which, according to how circumstances unfold, may or may not become deviant."[44] In his research on naïve check forgery, he found a number of persons who were not motivated to pass bad checks but simply took chances that a check they authored might not be honored or that they might not be allowed to cover the check if it "bounced."[45]

Lemert's contentions regarding the risk-taking origins of deviance warn us against the automatic assumption that criminal conduct is always motivated, in the sense of being related to relatively long-standing attitudes and psychological concerns of the individual. All too frequently, criminal deviance is assumed to stem from "antisocial" orientations within the actor which are the product of some set of experiences that occurred much earlier in his or her life career. Although many kinds of criminality do show such a form, there are also many instances of situational risk-taking that emerge out of ongoing processes.

Likely examples of risk-taking criminality are abundant. One illustration is drunken driving in which the offender did not deliberately set out to become intoxicated. The majority of episodes in which individuals become drunk probably represent one of several possible outcomes of social drinking. At the beginning of the drinking activity, the prospect of becoming intoxicated was an eventuality the drinker least anticipated, so that drunkenness in this sense was unintentional. With the drunk driver, becoming intoxicated was an unplanned outcome of social drinking. In turn, the individual who drives while in a drunken condition does not intend to drive erratically and certainly does not plan to have an accident or injure anyone. However, when driving ability is impaired by alcohol, these can be the results if the driver is "unlucky," that is, if certain contingent events occur. Doubtless, most drivers perceive these risks, at least dimly, when they drive while intoxicated.

Unskilled property offenders also become involved in risk-taking. Data in probation-case files and elsewhere reveal that many of these persons get involved in petty acts of crime as part of a sequence of activities that were not initiated as criminalistic ventures. For example, Skid Row transients often find themselves in the hands of the police as a result of petty burglaries carried out after becoming markedly intoxicated in a drinking bout with alcoholic companions, or for falling into a drunken sleep in the bathtub of a cheap hotel, or for other ventures into risk situations. Other minor instances of theft are more a function of situational opportunities than of deep-seated motivational elements of the offenders. Many individuals may manage to suspend their normal feelings of condemnation toward crime and steal petty articles of property when the immediate situation appears conducive to such behavior, particularly when the victim is a relatively large and impersonal organization. The processes that operate have something in common with the activities of campers and picknickers who litter campgrounds with beer cans and rubbish in blatant disregard for fellow campers. These same individuals would probably hesitate to throw beer cans into the yards of neighbors in the residential areas where they live. They would also give verbal allegiance to the general principle that one should keep picnic grounds clean.

Some support for the characterization of one-time-loser property offenders comes from probation records which show that many probationers were involved in isolated, nonrecurrent acts of illegality. They also indicate that these individuals are quite conventional in appearance, without antisocial attitudes or criminogenic backgrounds. For example, Ralph England examined the records of 500 federal probation cases.[46] Most of these probationers were white, older, married men who had been sentenced for a variety of offenses, but nearly half had been convicted of liquor-law violations. The remainder had committed forgery, draft evasion, mail fraud, and assorted forms of theft. Most of them had records of law-abiding behavior prior to the offense, and 80 percent had remained free of recidivism in the five years after being released from probation. Few of them had received any significant amount of casework on probation, so their successful adjustment must be attributed to general lack of criminal orientation.[47]

In a report concerned with prison inmates, Clarence Schrag noted that prosocial "square Johns" were individuals who had been sentenced for various kinds of larceny.[48] They lacked serious records of criminality, they were not from particularly disordered or criminogenic backgrounds, and their actions were attributable to various kinds of situational stresses.

One detailed and revealing investigation of amateur check forgers was by Edwin Lemert.[49] His research investigated the theory that "naïve check forgery arises at a critical point in the process of social isolation, out of certain types of social situations, and is made possible by the closure or constriction of behavior alternatives subjectively held as available to the forger."[50] Lemert examined the case records of over 1,000 naïve forgers in the Los Angeles area and conducted interviews with a sample of these individuals. The subjects had little or no contact with criminal individuals, were nonviolent persons with a marked repugnance for forms of crime other than forgery, and appeared to be likable and attractive but impulsive individuals. The forgers were predominantly white males, older on the average than other probationers, and with higher intelligence ratings and better occupational status than other offenders.[51]

Lemert's hypothesis about social isolation as the prelude to forgery was borne out by his observations. Most of the check writers had been involved prior to their criminality in unemployment, gambling losses, alcoholic sprees, difficulties in military service, or estrangement from their families. Marital disruptions played a particularly critical role as an isolating experience, for about 40 percent of the forgers were divorced. In general, Lemert concluded that these various experiences tended to be progressive and mutually reinforcing, so the person caught up in them became more and more alienated from conventional social bonds.[52]

According to Lemert, the social experiences most of these persons got involved in immediately prior to check forgery were what he termed "certain dialectical forms of social behavior."[53] He meant that the individual usually embarked on a course of action or events having a clear beginning and end, so considerable impetus was built up to carry the activities through to their conclusion. An alcoholic "spree" is a case in point, in which initial involvement in drinking pressures the individual to continue until he has been intoxicated for a lengthy period of time. In the event that he prematurely exhausts his funds, considerable tension may arise, provoking him to seek some solution that will bring the action pattern to its terminal point.

Lemert argued that the forger found relief from this situational tension by a social-psychological process of "closure."[54] Check forgery was selected as a way to bring finality to the dialectical events. The choice of check writing came about in part because the individual was unaware of less deviant solutions; he felt he could not borrow money from anyone and could not employ other alternatives. Moreover, forgery is "in the culture," learned as part of becoming an adult, so no special skill was required to commit this act. It is also nonviolent and can be rationalized through such arguments as "You can't kill anyone with a fountain pen."

Other studies of naïve forgers revealed findings parallel to those of Lemert. Maurice Gauthier discovered that forgers in Kingston Penitentiary in Canada were older males of above-average education and from middle-class families.[55] He suggested that these offenders engaged in forgery as a technique for revealing inner tensions of the kind Lemert proposed. Irwin Berg's comparison of forgers and other inmates in Southern Michigan Penitentiary turned up similar results: the check offenders had higher intelligence ratings than the other inmates, were older than the other convicts, and were less criminally involved than the other felons.[56] John Gillin's report on Wisconsin criminals in the state prison noted that forgers were from middle-income backgrounds and were older and more intelligent than other felons.[57] Several case histories Gillin cited present a picture of check writing that meshed with the isolation and closure formulation. Finally, Norman Hayner contrasted professional or "con forgers" and naïve or "alcoholic forgers" with other prisoner types in the Washington State penal institutions. The naïve forgers turned out to have higher-than-average intelligence.[58] Many were from situations of social isolation; 45 percent were divorced. According to Hayner, alcoholic forgers were frequently "dependent" persons—a judgment he arrived at by examining case-record materials available on the prisoners.

AUTOMOBILE THEFT AND "JOYRIDING"

Some criminologists have constructed a profile of juvenile or young-adult joyriders as relatively well-adjusted boys who are on good terms with most of their peers, particularly fellow joyriders with whom they steal cars. They are frequently middle-class youths who have grown up in relatively stable family settings but with problems of adolescent masculine identity. Through riding around in stolen cars they are able to demonstrate to themselves and to social audiences that they are "tough guys," not "sissies." Further, boys who steal cars often show family backgrounds involving some mild degree of parent–child tension.[59]

Like some other descriptions of offenders, this one is too facile. The available research evidence indicates that car theft is related to a more mixed bag of causal factors than indicated by the sketch above.

William Wattenberg and James Balistrieri examined the detailed case records of over 200 white boys the Detroit police apprehended in 1948 for car theft and compared these youths with other white youngsters arrested for different delinquencies.[60] Black car thieves were not studied because they were infrequently encountered, at least by the police, even though blacks constituted a sizable portion of the Detroit population.

The major impression that emerged from the comparisons of car thieves with other delinquents centered about the "favored group" status of the former. Car thieves were from neighborhoods the police rated as "above average," from uncrowded single-family dwellings, from houses in good physical condition, and from racially homogeneous neighborhoods. They were also from families with only one employed parent. The car thieves were older boys on good terms with their peers. Although the automobile thieves were considered rambunctious gang members, the police frequently evaluated these youngsters as "responsive." Finally the parents' involvement in their son's recreation was judged to be "occasional" rather than "seldom" or "regular."[61] Wattenberg and Balistrieri interpreted this pattern of results as an indication that car thieves were the product of a permissive upbringing, which resulted in "other-directed" personality structure. These boys were thought to be easily drawn into peer-supported patterns of antisocial conduct; at the same time, they were unresponsive to larger social entities and their values.[62]

An investigation by Erwin Schepses involved boys in a New York-state training school.[63] Schepses compared 22 boys who were "pure" car thieves with records solely of vehicle theft with 59 "mixed" car thieves who had engaged in other delinquencies as well and 81 control-group cases of training-school wards charged with offenses other than automobile theft. He observed that, in most cases, joyriding was a group form of deviance, for most of the thieves had been apprehended with at least one other offender or "fall partner."[64]

Some other major results turned up in this inquiry. First, car thieves were more frequently white boys, rather than black or Puerto Rican, even though black car thieves were fairly common in the Warwick population. Car thieves were more intelligent and advanced in reading skills than were the other delinquent boys. They were also more commonly from comfortable economic circumstances than were the control youngsters. The "pure" automobile thieves were principally from unbroken homes, whereas the "mixed" car thieves and the control-group boys were from broken homes in over half the cases.[65] According to Schepses, the car thieves exhibited a wide variety of family constellations: some had passive fathers; some had authoritarian parents; others showed various other family backgrounds. In this view, theories alleging that a specific kind of nuclear, middle-class family pattern leads to joyriding is incorrect.

Martin Dosick provided some further evidence on car thieves, derived from a study of federal Dyer Act violators.[66] He hypothesized that car theft takes three general forms—joyriding by juveniles, along with "short-history" and "long-history" patterns of car theft among young adults. "Long-history" thieves engaged in a variety of criminal acts, were criminally sophisticated, and were enmeshed in delinquent subcultures. "Short-history" offenders had been less involved in criminality. In Dosick's view, the young-adult car thieves stole cars for "instrumental" reasons but for motives that differed between "short-history" and "long-history" offenders. "Long-history" thieves stole cars for various illegitimate and impulsive reasons; but "short-history" offenders stole cars as an illegitimate route to legitimate or conventional goals, such as a new job. Interviews and questionnaire responses on 200 Dyer Act violators generally confirmed these hypotheses. The "long-history" car thieves had stolen cars to display masculine daring and toughness or to obtain other short-run delinquent goals. The "short-history" offenders had taken cars to get to another area in search of a job or for other reasons of that kind. More were concerned about upward mobility and other middle-class goals than were the "long-history" cases. Dosick concluded: "My data, then, points to some men who stole cars as incidents in delinquent careers, and to other men who took cars to help solve the problem of educational and job-based transition into male adulthood."[67]

Several other studies of violators of federal auto-theft laws are available for examination. In one of these, a sample of auto offenders in federal institutions in 1964 was studied.[68] The researchers discovered that 49 percent of these lawbreakers had previously been convicted for auto theft, and 20 percent had stolen two or more cars in their last offense. The reasons for car theft were varied; 52 percent of the offenders had stolen cars for transportation, 32 percent had taken them for joyriding, and only 5 percent had stolen the auto to sell or strip it. However, 71 percent of the offenders under the age of 17 had taken cars for joyriding purposes.

Larry Karacki investigated a group of 632 federal offenders charged with auto theft and compared them with 369 prisoners who had committed other offenses.[69] The car thieves showed greater residential mobility than the other lawbreakers; 59.3 percent of them had moved three or more times in the previous five years. More auto thieves had been in military service or confinement prior to their offense than was true of the other inmates. More auto thieves had poor work records than did the other offenders. The institutional adjustments of car thieves were poorer, more of them having been involved in disciplinary incidents, escapes, transfers to other institutions, or close to maximum confinement. The auto thieves showed poorer postrelease records; 63.8 percent of them had violated parole in the two years after release, as contrasted to 46.3 percent of the other prisoners. Karacki concluded that car thieves are from more unfavorable backgrounds than most other offenders, a conclusion different from most of the claims made about auto thieves.

The observation that emerges most consistently from these studies is the "favored group" character of joyriding. However, these reports are not entirely consistent in this regard and are even less uniform on such matters as the ethnic backgrounds of car thieves. Most have little to say about specific contentions regarding family patterns in joyriding. Not much more can be said about car thieves until further studies are conducted on some of these hypothesized factors in car theft.

summary

This chapter has involved further exploration of causal themes that were introduced in Chapters 8 and 9. Chapter 8 argued that the question of psychological elements or factors in criminality remains debatable, with much more theorizing and research called for, directed at specific psychological patterns that may characterize particular offenders. Chapter 9 asserted that risk-taking processes and situational pressures in lawbreaking have not been given sufficient weight in most of the etiological arguments that have been advanced to date. These two themes were examined in connection with naïve forgery, car theft, and unskilled crime.

The growth of check forgery as a commonly encountered form of crime seems almost inevitable in modern societies, where monetary transactions frequently take place through checking accounts and personal checks. Indeed, convicted naïve check forgers represent a subgroup from a much larger population of citizens who engage in risk-taking involving personal checks. The apprehended and convicted forger frequently has written more worthless checks than citizens who have not been convicted of bad checks. But at the same time, many relatively law-abiding citizens have on occasion written checks against insufficient bank funds, hoping to get the bank to replenish their accounts before the checks "bounce." In many cases, the customer is charged a modest penalty by the bank for having written the NSF check, but the incident is then treated as an "accident" rather than as a criminal offense.

A more confused portrayal emerged regarding automobile theft. Some evidence, drawn principally from studies of juvenile car thieves, pointed to the "favored group" status of these individuals. However, some studies of young-adult car thieves provided findings that are not consistent with some of these contentions. Also, these latter inquiries turned up evidence indicating that the motivations that lie behind car theft are quite varied.

The lawbreakers considered in Chapter 12 tend to be those "bad guys" citizens have in mind when they discuss "the crime problem." Citizens also tend to be agitated about crimes of violence, to which our attention turns in the next chapter.

notes

[1]J. J. Tobias, *Crime and Industrial Society in the 19th Century* (London: B.T. Batsford, 1967).

[2]Peter Letkemann, *Crime as Work* (Englewood Cliffs, N.J.: Prentice-Hall, Inc., 1973).

[3]Everett Cherrington Hughes, *Men and Their Work* (New York: Free Press, 1958), p. 33. See Hughes's commentary, pp. 78–87, for some problems with the designation of criminality forms as professional in character.

[4]Herbert A. Bloch and Gilbert Geis, *Man, Crime, and Society*, 2nd ed. (New York: Random House, 1970), pp. 173–85; Walter Bromberg and Sylvan Keiser, "The Psychology of the Swindler," *American Journal of Psychiatry*, 94 (May 1938), 1441–58; Walter B. Gibson, *The Bunco Book* (Holyoke, Mass.: Sidney H. Radner, 1946); Richard L. Jenkins, *Breaking Patterns of Defeat* (Philadelphia: Lippincott, 1954), pp. 148–58; John C. R. McDonald, *Crime is a Business* (Stanford, Calif.: Stanford University Press, 1939); David W. Maurer, *The Big Con* (Indianapolis: Bobbs-Merrill, 1940); Maurer, *Whiz Mob* (New Haven, Conn.: College and University Press, 1964); Julian R. Roebuck and Ronald Johnson, "The 'Short Con' Man," *Crime and Delinquency*, 10 (July 1964), 235–48; Edwin M. Schur, "Sociological Analysis of Confidence Swindling," *Journal of Criminal Law, Criminology and Police Science*, 48 (September–October 1957), 296–304; Edwin H. Sutherland, *The Professional Thief* (Chicago: University of Chicago Press, 1937); Robert Louis Gasser, "The Confidence Game," *Federal Probation*, 27 (December 1963), 47–54.

[5]McDonald, *Crime Is a Business*.

[6]Maurer, *The Big Con*; Roebuck and Johnson, "The 'Short Con' Man."

[7]Sutherland, *The Professional Thief*, pp. 211–14; see also Gasser, "The Confidence Game." For some interesting commentary on Sutherland's observations on professional thieves, see Robert H. Vasoli and Dennis A. Terzola, "Sutherland's Professional Thief," *Criminology*, 12 (August 1974), 131–54; Don C. Gibbons, *The Criminological Enterprise* (Englewood Cliffs, N.J.: Prentice-Hall, Inc., 1979), pp. 48–51.

[8]Jenkins, *Breaking Patterns of Defeat*, pp. 148–58.

[9]Ibid., p. 150.

[10]At least one study has revealed that grifters do exhibit unique personality configurations. Julian Roebuck and Ronald Johnson reported that the "short con" men they examined were of above-average intelligence and that most of them exhibited the personality marks of the grifter suggested by Jenkins. See Roebuck and Johnson, "The 'Short Con' Man," pp. 238–41.

[11]Schur, "Sociological Analysis of Confidence Swindling."

[12]For one body of detailed evidence on these persons, see Joan Petersilia, Peter W. Greenwood, and Marvin L. Lavin, *Criminal Careers of Habitual Felons* (Washington, D.C.: Law Enforcement Assistance Administration, 1978).

[13]Everett DeBaun, "The Heist: The Theory and Practice of Armed Robbery," *Harper's*, 200 (Febuary 1950), 69–77; Quentin Reynolds, *I, Willie Sutton* (New York: Farrar, Straus & Giroux, 1953); John Bartlow Martin, *My Life in Crime* (New York: Harper & Row, Pub., 1952); Jack Black, "A Burglar Looks at Laws and Codes," *Harper's*, 160 (February 1930), 306–13; Black, *You Can't Win* (New York: Macmillan, 1926); Bruce Jackson, *A Thief's Primer* (New York: Macmillan, 1969); Harry King, *Box Man: A Professional Thief's Journey*, as told to and edited by Bill Chambliss (New York: Harper & Row, Pub., 1972).

[14]*Seattle Times*, January 11, 1957.

[15]DeBaun, "The Heist: The Theory and Practice of Armed Robbery"; see also Neal Shover, "The Social Organization of Burglary," *Social Problems*, 20 (Spring 1973), 499–514.

[16]Clayton A. Hartjen and Don C. Gibbons, "An Empirical Investigation of a Criminal Typology," *Sociology and Social Research*, 54 (October 1969), 56–62.

[17]Bloch and Geis, *Man, Crime, and Society*, p. 178.

[18]For evidence on aspects of professional forgery, see Edwin M. Lemert, "The Behavior of the Systematic Check Forger," *Social Problems*, 6 (Fall 1958), 141–49; David Maurer, "The Argot of Forgery," *American Speech*, 16 (December 1941), 243–50; Julius L. Sternitzky, *Forgery and Fictitious Checks* (Springfield, Ill.: Chas C Thomas 1955); Norman S. Hayner, "Characteristics of Five Offender Types," *American Sociological Review*, 26 (February 1961), 96–102.

[19]Unpublished study carried on by the author.

[20]Leonard D. Savitz, "Automobile Theft," *Journal of Criminal Law, Criminology and Police Science*, 50 (July–August 1959), 132–43. Several older studies of car thieves, not discussed in this book, are noted in Savitz's paper.

[21]Jerome Hall, *Theft, Law and Society*, 2nd ed. (Indianapolis: Bobbs-Merrill, 1952), pp. 233–88.

[22]Savitz, "Automobile Theft," p. 132.

[23]Hall, *Theft, Law and Society*, pp. 262–75.

[24]Savitz, "Automobile Theft," pp. 139–40; Hall, *Theft, Law and Society*, pp. 250–56.

[25]Savitz, "Automobile Theft," p. 133; Hall, *Theft, Law and Society*, pp. 240–45.

[26]Savitz, "Automobile Theft," pp. 133–35.

[27]See footnote 13. See also Donald MacKenzie, *Occupation: Thief* (Indianapolis: Bobbs-Merrill, 1955); Hutchins Hapgood, *Autobiography of a Thief* (New York: Fox, Duffield, 1930); John E. Conklin, *Robbery and the Criminal Justice System* (Philadelphia: Lippincott, 1972), pp. 59–78. Conklin presented a relatively crude typology of robbers: the professional robber, the opportunist robber, the addicted robber, and the alcoholic robber.

[28]Werner J. Einstadter, "The Social Organization of Armed Robbery," *Social Problems*, 17 (Summer 1969), 64–83; see also Shover, "The Social Organization of Burglary"; Letkemann, *Crime as Work*.

[29]Einstadter, "The Social Organization of Armed Robbery," p. 82.

[30]Petersilia, Greenwood, and Lavin, *Criminal Careers of Habitual Felons*.

[31]Two early studies are Sheldon Glueck and Eleanor Glueck, *500 Criminal Careers* (New York: Knopf, 1930); John L. Gillin, *The Wisconsin Prisoner* (Madison: University of Wisconsin Press, 1946).

[32]Hayner, "Characteristics of Five Offender Types."

[33]Clarence C. Schrag, "Some Foundations for a Theory of Correction," in *The Prison*, Donald R. Cressey, ed. (New York: Holt, Rinehart & Winston, 1961), pp. 346–56; Schrag, "A Preliminary Criminal Typology," *Pacific Sociological Review*, 4 (Spring 1961), 11–16.

[34]Julian B. Roebuck and Mervyn L. Cadwallader, "The Negro Armed Robber as a Criminal Type: The Construction and Application of a Typology," *Pacific Sociological Review*, 4 (Summer 1961), 21–26.

[35]Some other studies have also discovered offenders who exhibit relatively stable criminal careers. See Richard A. Peterson, David J. Pittman, and Patricia O'Neal, "Stabilities in Deviance: A Study of Assaultive and Non-Assaultive Offenders," *Journal of Criminal Law, Criminology and Police Science*, 53 (March 1962), 44–48; Harold S. Frum, "Adult Criminal Offense Trends Following Juvenile Delinquency," *Journal of Criminal Law, Criminology and Police Science*, 49 (May–June 1958), 29–49. Also see Thomas A. Reppetto, *Residential Crime* (Cambridge, Mass.: Ballinger Publishing Co., 1974).

[36]Marvin E. Wolfgang, Robert M. Figlio and Thorsten Sellin, *Delinquency in a Birth Cohort* (Chicago: University of Chicago Press, 1972).

[37]For a detailed review of this material, see Don C. Gibbons, *Delinquent Behavior*, 3rd ed. (Englewood Cliffs, N.J.: Prentice-Hall, Inc., 1981), pp. 153–90; Gibbons, *The Criminological Enterprise*, pp. 93–108.

[38]Frederic M. Thrasher, *The Gang*, abridged and with a new introduction by James F. Short, Jr. (Chicago: University of Chicago Press, 1963); Clifford Shaw, *The Jack Roller* (Chicago: University of Chicago Press, 1930); Shaw and Maurice E. Moore, *The Natural History of a Delinquent Career* (Philadelphia: A. Saifer, Publisher, 1951); Shaw, Henry D. McKay, and James F. McDonald, *Brothers in Crime* (Chicago: University of Chicago Press, 1938); Shaw and McKay, *Juvenile Delinquency in Urban Areas* (Chicago: University of Chicago Press, 1942); Shaw and McKay, *Social Factors in Juvenile Delinquency, Report on the Causes of Crime for the National Commission on Law Observance and Enforcement*, vol. 11 (Washington, D.C.: U.S. Government Printing Office, 1931).

[39]Albert K. Cohen, *Delinquent Boys* (New York: Free Press, 1955). For a summary of the work stimulated by Cohen's book, see Gibbons, *Delinquent Behavior*, pp. 160–90.

[40]Gibbons, *Delinquent Behavior*, p. 190.

[41]Edwin M. Lemert, *Human Deviance, Social Problems, and Social Control*, 2nd ed. (Englewood Cliffs, N.J.: Prentice-Hall, Inc., 1972), pp. 26–61.

[42]Ibid., pp. 64–66.

[43]Ibid., pp. 71–73.

[44]Ibid., p. 72.

[45]Ibid., p. 29.

[46]Ralph W. England, Jr., "A Study of Postprobation Recidivism Among Five Hundred Federal Offenders," *Federal Probation*, 19 (September 1955), 10–16; see also England, "What is Responsible for Satisfactory Probation and Postprobation Outcome?" *Journal of Criminal Law, Criminology and Police Science*, 47 (March–April 1957), 667–76; Albert Wahl and Daniel Glaser, "Pilot Time Study of the Federal Probation Officer's Job," *Federal Probation*, 27 (September 1963), 20–25.

[47]England, "What is Responsible for Satisfactory Probation and Post Probation Outcome?"

[48]Schrag, "A Preliminary Criminal Typology"; Schrag, "Some Foundations for a Theory of Correction"; see also Gillin, *The Wisconsin Prisoner*, passim.

[49]Edwin M. Lemert, "An Isolation and Closure Theory of Naïve Check Forgery," *Journal of Criminal Law, Criminology and Police Science*, 44 (September–October 1953), 296–307.

[50]Ibid., p. 298.

[51]Ibid., pp. 299–300.

[52]Ibid., pp. 301–14.

[53]Ibid., pp. 303–4.

[54]Ibid., pp. 304–5.

[55]Maurice Gauthier, "The Psychology of the Compulsive Forger," *Canadian Journal of Corrections*, 1 (July 1959), 62–69.

[56]Irwin A. Berg, "A Comparative Study of Forgery," *Journal of Applied Psychology*, 28 (June 1944), 232–38.

[57]John L. Gillin, *The Wisconsin Prisoner*, pp. 167–73.

[58]Hayner, "Characteristics of Five Offender Types," pp. 96–102. The hypothesis concerning dependency is worthy of exploration. Correctional workers often voice this claim about check forgers. The same argument turned up in Hayner's data. But, these reports could be artifacts of the belief systems of correctional persons rather than an accurate indicator of true characteristics of forgers. In other words, if correctional-treatment workers regard check writers as dependent individuals, they may report such observations in case documents, even though the forgers do not fit this characterization. A more carefully controlled kind of inquiry is needed to search out evidence on the psychological correlates of check-writing behavior. Lemert's study of dependency on the part of alcoholic individuals offers a model of the kind of investigation required. Edwin M. Lemert, "Dependency in Married Alcoholics," *Quarterly Journal of Studies on Alcohol*, 23 (December 1962), 590–609.

[59]For example, see Don C. Gibbons, "Problems of Causal Analysis in Criminology: A Case Illustration," *Journal of Research in Crime and Delinquency*, 3 (January 1966), 47–52. One British student of delinquency has also offered this masculinity hypothesis to account for car thieves he studied, holding that these boys were from families characterized by fathers who failed to serve as adequate role models. See T.C.N. Gibbens, "Car Thieves," *British Journal of Delinquency*, 8, (4:1958), 257–68.

[60]William W. Wattenberg and James Balistrieri, "Automobile Theft: A 'Favored-Group' Delinquency," *American Journal of Sociology*, 58 (May 1952), 575–79.

[61]Ibid., pp. 577–78.

[62]Ibid., pp. 578–79.

[63]Erwin Schepses, "Boys Who Steal Cars," *Federal Probation*, 25 (March 1961), 56–62; Schepses, "The Young Car Thief," *Journal of Criminal Law, Criminology and Police Science*, 50 (March–April 1960), 569.

[64]Schepses, "Boys Who Steal Cars," pp. 58–59.

[65]Ibid.

[66]Martin L. Dosick, "Statement for Presentation to the Subcommittee to Investigate Juvenile Delinquency, United States Senate, January 17, 1967," mimeographed.

[67]Ibid., p. 5.

[68]Federal Bureau of Prisons, "Auto Theft Offenders," 1964, mimeographed.

[69]Larry Karacki, "Youthful Auto Theft Offender Study," Federal Bureau of Prisons, 1966, unpublished.

homicides, assaults, and sex crimes

In this chapter, attention moves away from property crime and property offenders and toward murder, assaultive behavior, and a variety of sexual crimes. These forms of conduct appear to many laymen to be particularly bizarre, deviant, or unusual, as contrasted to the endeavors of thieves, robbers, burglars, or business offenders. To those uninformed about criminality, the taking of a human life, violent assault by one person on another, or coercion of a female into sexual intercourse appear extremely unusual events. The murderer, assaultist, or sexual offender is often presumed to be an individual with markedly idiosyncratic personal characteristics. In the public view, rapists must be "fiends" with pathological personalities, for how else can their actions be explained? Laymen often invoke an explanation of homicides emphasizing situations of extreme social stress as the mechanism triggering violent acts.

Murders and assaults actually depart markedly from the popular image of activities carried on by clever, scheming individuals and involving complex techniques by which persons are killed or assaulted. For every publicized case in which some person contrives a complicated and elaborate scheme for murder, countless other cases exist in which one person kills another on the spur of the moment and in dismal surroundings. From another perspective, if the facts were known to citizens, garden-variety homicides and assaults would appear strange and virtually inexplicable. In the eyes of the middle-class individual, homicides and assaults would seem to arise out of extremely trivial circumstances. The files of municipal police departments are filled with cases in which one person killed another over a slighting remark or a seemingly harmless, socially inappropriate action, such as a flirtatious gesture toward the murderer's spouse. Indeed, the mundane character of much assaultive conduct would bewilder individuals who live outside situations in which interpersonal violence is relatively commonplace.

the law of homicide and assault

In law, the term *homicide* is generic, referring to the killing of one person by another.[1] *Culpable* homicides, which result in criminal prosecution, are differentiated from *justifiable* homicides and *excusable* homicides. Justifiable homicide refers to killings performed as a result of legal demands, such as a police officer's shooting a fleeing suspect. In this instance, the homicide occurred while the officer was discharging his or her legal responsibility to pursue the criminal.

Justifiable homicide also occurs when jail or prison guards kill prisoners attempting to escape from confinement. Excusable homicide is the term for deaths that result accidentally from lawful acts performed by lawful means. The death of a child from medicine the parent administered in the course of an illness would be treated as excusable homicide.

Culpable homicides for which persons are held criminally responsible are normally differentiated in law into *murder* in the *first* or *second degrees* and *manslaughter*. These distinctions rest on degrees of *premeditation* and *malice aforethought*. Premeditation designates intent to violate the law formulated prior to the activity; in other words, a decision to commit a crime, planning the execution of it, and so on. Malice aforethought refers to the simple presence of intent to kill at the time of the act. For a person to be convicted of murder in the first degree, both premeditation and malice aforethought must be established. In second-degree murder, only malice aforethought must be proved. Statutes define manslaughter as culpable homicide in which neither premeditation nor malice aforethought are present. Manslaughter is unintended or unwitting homicide. Degrees of manslaughter are usually recognized in law; first-degree manslaughter designates that a prudent person could reasonably anticipate a fatal outcome to a set of behavioral events. The accidental death of a passenger in an automobile driven in a reckless manner by an intoxicated driver would be a case in point.

Although relatively clear distinctions among forms of homicide are drawn in law, these distinctions are often blurred in judicial practice. A host of conditions influence the decision to process a case of criminality as first- or second-degree murder or manslaughter, in addition to the similarity of the conduct to legal definition. Many homicides that could be prosecuted as first-degree murder are instead processed as second-degree murder or manslaughter. For instance, an individual may "cop a plea," that is, agree to plead guilty in return for reduction in the charge from second-degree murder to manslaughter. Accordingly, it would be an error to assume that court statistics on first- and second-degree murder and manslaughter correctly indicate the distribution of cases technically fitting the legal definition of these terms.

Assault in common law and statute law, both in the United States and in England, is usually defined as an attempt to commit a battery, which is the unlawful application of physical force to another person. Assaults can and frequently do culminate in two separate kinds of actions against the offender. The injured party can endeavor to obtain redress in civil action, and the assaulter is also liable to criminal-court prosecution for the criminal violation of law. Criminal laws usually distinguish degrees of assault. *Aggravated assault* involves such actions as assault with a deadly weapon or assault with intent to kill. Aggravated assault is a felony carrying more severe penalties than common or ordinary assault. The latter is a misdemeanor involving lesser punishments.

The persons who commit homicides or assaultive acts and the situations in which they engage in these are considerably more varied than the categories of murder, manslaughter, and assault recognized in statute law. As a consequence, any meaningful discussion of crimes against persons must concentrate on the major dimensions along which these vary. Students of homicide have made several attempts to provide taxonomies of murder or murderers. Manfred Guttmacher claimed that there are normal, sociopathic, alcoholic, and avenging murderers, as well as schizophrenic killers and those who are temporarily psychotic.[2] Still other murderers include homosexuals, passive-aggressive killers, and sadistic murderers. Doubtless, the population of killers includes each of these kinds of individuals, but Guttmacher's classification was too anecdotal and descriptive to be of much use in explanations of homicide behavior. Paralleling Guttmacher's scheme, W. Lindesay Neustatter used case histories to illustrate schizophrenic, hysteric, and mentally defective murderers.[3] Neustatter also argued that some killers are paranoiac, epileptic, or suffering from organic brain damage. Other murderers are sadistic, psychopathic, melancholic, or suffering from hypoglycemia. Much the same comment applies to Neustatter's scheme as to Guttmacher's, for both were relatively descriptive and anecdotal.[4]

four studies of homicide

Examination and comparison of four detailed studies of homicide may help provide a reasonably full understanding of homicide behavior. Although not strictly parallel in every detail, these investigations provide evidence on a number of points in common. The first study, by Marvin Wolfgang, involved information on all 588 criminal homicides known to the police which occurred in Philadelphia between 1948 and 1952.[5] Wolfgang's inquiry stands as the most comprehensive single examination of empirical evidence on homicide in the United States. The second piece of research, by Robert Bensing and Oliver Schroeder, concerned 462 homicides in Greater Cuyahoga County (Cleveland), Ohio, between 1947 and 1953.[6] Henry Bullock's examination of all cases of homicide in Houston between 1945 and 1949 is the third source of evidence,[7] and Alex Pokorny's replication of Wolfgang's Philadelphia work, analyzing Houston homicides between 1958 and 1961, is the final study.[8] The findings of all four investigations are considered in the following sections dealing with different aspects of violent behavior.

TEMPORAL AND ECOLOGICAL CHARACTERISTICS

In Philadelphia, homicides were found to occur most frequently on weekends: 66 percent occurred between Friday and Sunday, and 32 percent took place on a Saturday.[9] Bensing and Schroeder found that 62 percent of the homicides in Cleveland took place on the same three days,[10] and, similarly, Bullock reported that most homicides occur on weekends.[11] In both the Philadelphia and Cleveland cases these criminal events were most common between 8:00 P.M. and 2:00 A.M.[12] In both of these cases, the temporal fluctuation in violence was related to cycles of weekday labor and weekend leisure pursuits. Proximity of persons, increased use of alcohol, and so on, on weekends served to increase the potential for violent outbursts.

Homicides do not occur randomly throughout the urban community, for Bullock found that over 70 percent of those in Houston took place in 18 percent of the census tracts in the city.[13] Similarly, the Cleveland data showed that two-thirds of the crimes took place in 12 percent of the city.[14] Both studies located the urban centers of homicidal acts in predominantly black areas characterized by dense populations and overcrowding, physical deterioration, and other urban-slum conditions.

Wolfgang found that homicides were about evenly divided between the home and places outside the home, in terms of specific locale, which was also true of the Houston homicides investigated by Bullock and Pokorny.[15] Incidents of violence occurring outside of residences were mainly in streets adjacent to taverns or eating places.

MOTIVES, SITUATIONS, AND METHODS

The offender's private motives are always difficult to determine, particularly when police reports of motives are relied on instead of interviews with the culprits. Nonetheless, several of these studies enumerated the most commonly identified motives in police files and other official records and revealed a good deal about the social situations leading up to acts of violence. Records on the weapons employed in these behavioral episodes also provided useful information.

In Philadelphia, 37 percent of the offenses were attributed to altercations of one kind or another, whereas domestic quarrels accounted for 13 percent and jealousy for another 11 percent. The parties to the crime were close friends in 28 percent of the cases and family relatives in another quarter of the homicides.[16] Pokorny's evidence for Houston showed the same pattern, with the parties to homicide being close friends or family relations in most instances.[17] The Cleveland homicides were most frequently linked to petty quarrels, marital discord, and sexual disputes.[18] In each of these cases, the circumstances that appear to trigger homicides might well strike the outsider as petty.

These investigations of homicide were not in complete agreement on the methods of killing. In Wolfgang's data, stabbing was the leading technique, accounting for 39 percent of the homicides. Blacks were particularly likely to use knives, whereas white offenders more commonly beat their victims to death. Women most frequently employed cutting instruments, usually a kitchen knife.[19] In Cleveland, guns accounted for 55 percent of the homicides, whereas only 27 percent were accomplished with knives.[20]

RACIAL AND SEXUAL VARIATIONS

One of the most striking findings of all these inquiries was the high rate of homicide among blacks in American cities. Wolfgang found that 73 percent of the victims and 75 percent of the offenders in Philadelphia were blacks, although blacks made up only 18 percent of the 1950 population of that city. Homicides were also concentrated among males, for 76 percent of the victims and 82 percent of the offenders were males, although males made up only 48 percent of the population. Women were infrequently involved in homicide; although females represented only 18 percent of the offenders, they constituted 24 percent of the victims. *However, the racial concentration was more marked than the sexual one.* The rate of homicide for black males (41.7 offenses per 100,000 population) was many times greater than that for white males (3.4 homicides per 100,000 population). In addition, the homicide rate for black females (9.3 per 100,000 population) also exceeded that for white males. Racial lines were crossed in only 6 percent of the homicides, so blacks nearly all killed other blacks, and whites nearly all killed other whites.[21] The Cleveland homicides were distributed in the same fashion, for 76 percent of the offenders were black, although only 11 percent of the Cuyahoga County population was made up of blacks.[22] Pokorny reported that Houston blacks made up only 23 percent of the population of that city, but they contributed 63 percent of the offenders.[23]

AGE, SOCIAL CLASS, AND CRIMINAL BACKGROUNDS

These studies indicated that variations exist in the ages of offenders and victims. Wolfgang noted that the killers were generally younger than the victims; the majority of offenders were between 20 and 30 years of age, whereas the victims were on the average about five years older.[24] Bensing and Schroeder indicated that relatively young persons carried out most homicides, 72 percent of whom were between 21 and 45 years of age.[25]

The preceding material on the ecological distribution of homicides clearly indicated that this activity was most common among working-class groups. Both the Philadelphia and Cleveland studies confirmed these socioeconomic differentials; rates of homicide for lower-class individuals of all ethnic backgrounds exceeded those for persons of higher economic status.[26]

The Philadelphia material contained data on the criminal backgrounds of offenders and victims. Wolfgang indicated that 64 percent of the offenders and 47 percent of the victims had a record of prior offenses. Those with criminal backgrounds had usually been involved in earlier incidents of violence, for 66 percent had been implicated in crimes against persons.[27] Finally, Wolfgang noted that alcohol was present in 64 percent of the homicides and that both parties to the act had been drinking in 44 percent of the cases.[28]

One of the most important innovations in the study of homicide was Wolfgang's notion of "victim-precipitated homicide"—a term for acts of violence in which the victim initiated the fatal outburst by making the first menacing gesture or striking the first blow. Homicides often take place between persons who have been in social interaction with each other, but victim-precipitated killings involve more than prior interaction. In the victim-precipitated case, the victim induced his or her death through his or her own menacing actions. Wolfgang's examination of victim-precipitated homicides showed that these most commonly involved black victims and offenders, with the victim being male and the offender female. The victim was often the husband of the offender and was commonly stabbed in circumstances in which he had been drinking. Finally, the victim frequently had a prior record of assaultive conduct.[29]

subcultures of violence

According to Bullock's findings in Houston: "The basic ecological process of urban segregation centralizes people of like kind, throws them together at common institutions, occasions their association on levels of intimacy, and thereby paves the way for conflicts out of which homicides occur."[30] In other words, the urban community shows concentrations in particular areas of groups whose life styles are especially productive of homicides and assaultive acts. This is the subculture-of-violence thesis, in which the life circumstances of certain groups are claimed to trigger violence as a relatively commonplace outcome of social interaction.[31]

Subcultures of violence made up of groups quick to use force in interpersonal relations appear to be centralized in urban slum areas, which the preceding four studies indicated as the places where homicide rates are high. Frequently, these neighborhoods are populated by lower-income blacks and are residential ghettos. According to many sociologists, the grinding poverty, unstable community organization, and disorganized family life in such areas lead to the emergence of certain lower-class values or focal concerns.[32] Miller identified one of these as "trouble," which refers to suspicion of others and generalized anticipation of difficulty from police officers, welfare agencies, schools, and fellow citizens. Another focal concern is "excitement," which has to do with pursuit of hedonistic pleasures, particularly on weekends, to counteract the dullness of weekday pursuits. Persons with these motivations thrown together in close contact heighten the potential for violent incidents. The contention is that this subcultural situation goes far toward accounting for high rates of homicide among lower-class citizens. This argument makes it unnecessary to invoke notions of personality pathology to account for homicides.

One bit of evidence on this point came from a study by Leroy Schultz in St. Louis.[33] Schultz reviewed a series of investigations maintaining that blacks commonly carry weapons and that the arrest rates for weapons offenses are much higher among blacks than whites. He conducted interviews with 50 black offenders convicted of charges centering about possession of dangerous weapons. These violators offered a number of reasons for carrying guns—some did so to commit crimes; others did so to force payment of debts owed them. However, 70 percent declared that they carried weapons because they anticipated attack from others in their environment. Carrying a weapon was a defensive or anticipatory act. Schultz indicated: "This group voiced a chronic concern about being attacked and the need for self-defense and assumed automatically that others in their environment were also carrying weapons, or if not actually carrying weapons, 'acted as if they were.' "[34]

The violence-subculture argument has been utilized as an explanation of the consistently higher rates of homicide observed in Southern states than elsewhere in the United States. According to this line of contention, there is a regional subculture of violence found in the American South.[35] In addition, a number of persons have suggested that subcultures of violence elsewhere in the country have grown up, in considerable part, owing to the diffusion of Southern traditions of violence to other parts of the country through out-migration from Southern states to metropolitan communities elsewhere.[36]

some other studies

Several other studies of murder in the United States ought to be mentioned. One investigation, by John Gillin, involved inmates in a Wisconsin prison. Gillin observed that 44 percent of the murderers studied had committed their crime in connection with another offense, whereas 24 percent had killed in conjunction with an immediate quarrel, and another 32 percent had murdered someone with whom they had been carrying on a long-standing feud.[37] In addition, Gillin reported that the incarcerated killers were more frequently from rural areas than were the sex offenders or property criminals. More of them had contributed to the support of their families at an early age than had the other prisoners. More killers had foreign-born parents, more were from lower-income backgrounds, more had left school prematurely, and more had unsteady employment records than was the case with the other prisoners. Finally, the murderers had less frequently been involved in prior offenses than had the other convicts.[38] These findings added up to a picture of Wisconsin murderers as "square John" criminals, so although they were commonly detached and alienated individuals, they were also relatively conventional persons.

Another study of a group of imprisoned murderers, by Stuart Palmer, dealt with 51 offenders in New England penal institutions who were compared with their noncriminal siblings.[39] Palmer found that most of these murders were unplanned, shooting was the leading technique of homicide, and alcohol was not usually present. One difference between Palmer's data and that of the foregoing four studies is that the victims of these murderers were strangers or slight acquaintances in 67 percent of the cases. The murderers were persons with low educational attainment and low socioeconomic status.[40] Based on interviews with the mothers of the offenders, Palmer concluded that the killers had been subjected to uncommonly frequent frustrations in their lives, in contrast to their siblings. However, the observations of the mothers could be erroneous as they attempted to report retrospectively the experiences of their sons.

Harwin Voss and John Hepburn's study dealing with homicides in Chicago in 1965 was a replication of Wolfgang's research.[41] They found that nonwhites far exceeded whites in rates of homicide, occurrences of homicide were most frequent on weekends, most of them took place in the home, and alcohol was associated with them in over half the cases. Voss and Hepburn also observed that about one-third of the homicides were victim-precipitated. One point at which their data differed from that of Wolfgang was on the matter of methods of killing, in that about half the Chicago victims had been shot rather than stabbed.

homicide in other societies

Homicide occurs at markedly varying rates in different countries. In general, African societies have low homicide rates, as do many Asian nations and most European countries. The United States has comparatively large numbers of violent deaths, as do Sri Lanka (formerly Ceylon), Finland, and a number of other nations. Computations made in England between 1940 and 1949 of rates per 1,000,000 population give some indication of worldwide variations in homicide. England and Wales showed a rate of 4.0 and New Zealand a rate of 7.2, whereas in the United States rates varied from 13.6 in Massachusetts to 167.3 in Georgia. All of these cases suggest that something about the social structure of different nations influences their homicide rates.[42]

Although detailed data on homicide in other nations are not available in abundance, several revealing investigations have been conducted on this topic. Paul Bohannan reported on homicide in a number of African societies.[43] He noted that one of the forms of killing in Africa is nonculpable homicide in dangerous but legal institutions. Hunting with poisoned arrows falls into this category, for deaths frequently occur as a consequence of the risk in such activities. These nonculpable homicides have American parallels in such activities as auto racing, where the participants cause unintended deaths. A second form of nonculpable homicide is institutionalized killing, such as jural homicide (executions) or ritual killings. Finally, culpable homicides occur in African societies in which the offender is held criminally accountable.[44]

One of the most significant facts about African homicide centers about conflicting definitions of culpable and nonculpable homicide. Bohannan indicated that African tribes often defined thief killing, witch killing, and killing of adulterers as nonculpable acts. However, these were regarded as criminal actions in British law, which has been injected into African affairs. The conflict between tribal norms and Western law was reduced through compromises; hence, judges tended to be lenient in the sentences handed down to native killers. In some instances, the charge against the violator was reduced from murder to manslaughter. [45]

Another highly significant finding on African criminality was that homicide rates among natives were extremely low compared to rates for American blacks. The Philadelphia blacks in Wolfgang's study had a rate of 24.6 homicides per 100,000 population during the period between 1948 and 1952, whereas African tribes had rates of fewer than 12 homicides per 1,000,000 population. These African rates, among the lowest in the world, demolish effectively any hypotheses linking high homicide rates of American blacks to biological or racial factors. [46]

A third observation on African homicide was that the proportion of female offenders in the population of killers was even smaller than in the United States and other Western nations. However, in several African tribes, females made up 45 to 60 percent of the victims, whereas in the United States, women were homicide victims in only about one-quarter of the cases. [47]

Bohannan's material pointed to still another homicide variation from Western patterns. In the United States, when a family member is killed, the victim is likely to be a spouse; in Denmark, the victim is likely to be a child; but in African countries, a wide variety of different kinsmen are the victims of homicide. Clearly, this tendency has much to do with the extended family patterns more common in African nations than in Western ones. [48]

Homicide in Sri Lanka has received the attention of several investigators. Some years ago, Jacqueline Straus and Murray Straus observed that the relatively high rate of homicide in Sri Lanka was principally the result of killing among the lowland Sinhalese rather than among the Tamil group. Because they have experienced the most contact with European cultural influences, the Sinhalese lived in a less rigid class structure than the Tamil. According to these investigators, the looser social ties among the Sinhalese were responsible for their greater contribution to the homicide rate. [49]

In a more recent study of homicide in Sri Lanka, Arthur Wood examined and confirmed two hypotheses. [50] The first contended that homicide should be most common in the lowest ranks of an achieved-status system, particularly when members of these groups perceive themselves to be externally restrained from achieving their goals. Wood's second hypothesis was that homicide is more frequent among alienated, demoralized persons, who show reactions of hostility. Supporting evidence for both hypotheses was uncovered in this investigation.

Interpersonal relationships between victims and offenders in homicides have been the subject of two studies in Denmark and in India. Kaare Svalastoga observed that, in Danish homicides for the periods 1934–39 and 1946–51, family members were victims in 57 percent of the cases, friends and acquaintances were victims in 31 percent, and strangers were killed in only 12 percent of the homicides.[51] Along the same line, Edwin Driver noted that in Indian homicides the partners to the offense were usually kinsmen or close associates of the same sex, religion, or caste. Prior to the actual killing, the interactional partners had been caught up in situations of heightened enmity flowing out of sexual disputes, arguments about property, or kindred quarrels.[52]

In summary, although homicide is a universal form of crime, homicidal activities in different nations take on the coloration of the host social system.

patterns of aggression

A good deal of evidence points to two general forms of assaultive conduct. The first is situational or subcultural in character, in which individuals who reside in certain urban neighborhoods get involved in violence largely in response to the exacerbated tensions and disorder of their social situation. This kind of assaultive conduct bears a close similarity to the homicides occurring in subcultures of violence; indeed, both are the product of the same general social variables.

A second form of criminally aggressive behavior is psychogenic or individualistic in form, rather than subcultural. The evidence indicates that certain kinds of socialization experiences produce individuals with atypically hostile psychological orientations. These persons, often labeled by psychiatrists as "unsocialized aggressives," "psychopaths," or "sociopaths," find their way into the population of offenders as a result of attacks on others. Many commit property violations as well as assaultive acts, but in any event their conduct is marked by a violent and aggressive posture as a central feature of their personalities. These offenders are from a variety of social-class backgrounds, for the conditions that generate the offense are not class-linked.

SITUATIONAL AGGRESSION

An important study of assaultive conduct, by Richard Peterson, David Pittman, and Patricia O'Neal, concerned St. Louis police arrest cases.[53] These investigators determined that because most of the apprehended offenders had relatively stable patterns of deviance, individuals arrested for crimes of violence had rarely been involved in property crimes earlier in their careers. Conversely, most of the property offenders had avoided violence in their criminal careers. The assaultive offenders were from more seriously disrupted homes and, at the same time, had higher levels of generalized hostility than did the property criminals.

Another investigation of assaultive behavior, by David Pittman and William Handy, also centered in St. Louis.[54] The study tested Wolfgang's hypotheses to determine if assaults were similar to homicides. By and large, their observations about the morphology of assault closely paralleled Wolfgang's analyses of homicide. For example, 132 of the 241 aggravated-assault cases occurred between 6:00 P.M. Friday and 6:00 A.M. Monday, most taking place on Saturday. The assaults occurred in a variety of places; but 45 percent were on streets, whereas 38 percent transpired in homes. No seasonal variation in assaultive acts was observed. About one-half of the assaults involved knives; but physical force was more common among white assaultists, whereas black offenders used weapons. The victims reported many of the offenses to the police, and nearly all offenses were cleared by arrest. In only three cases was another crime involved.[55]

Most of Pittman and Handy's information duplicated that of Wolfgang. The majority of acts of violence occurred within an offender–victim dyad; most of the participants were similar in age; most of the parties to violence were "blue-collar" workers; interracial assaults were uncommon; and most of the offenders with criminal records had backgrounds of petty criminality. The majority of the assaults developed out of quarrels and arguments immediately prior to the violent outbursts.[56]

In another piece of evidence on assaultive offenders, Julian Roebuck and Ronald Johnson compared the social backgrounds of 40 black felons charged with assault and drunkenness with the backgrounds of 360 other prisoners.[57] The violent offenders had developed out of more rigid, fundamentalist family backgrounds and had stricter, more dominating fathers than the other inmates. But they also showed closer primary-group ties in childhood and adulthood than the other prisoners and were from less criminogenic social circumstances.

These investigations add up to a picture of assault carried on in relatively disorganized social settings by individuals who are not particularly bizarre or pathological in personality organization. For this reason, this kind of criminality can be called situational. For the most part, this material also confirms the argument about subcultures of violence.

"PSYCHOPATHIC" ASSAULT

A good deal of evidence indicates that a small band of violent and socially maladjusted individuals does exist in prison, and these individuals are designated in the inmate language system as "hard guys," "outlaws," "gorillas," "toughs," or some similar appellation. Sykes noted that inmates in a New Jersey state prison singled out "gorillas" as persons to be avoided, for such prisoners were quick to use coercion to extract favors from other convicts. Certain other individuals labeled "toughs" were also avoided because of their touchiness and willingness to employ physical violence in settling minor disputes.[58] Both of these argot roles or inmate types looked much like a within-prison variant of psychopathic assaultists. Much the same picture emerged from Clarence Schrag's studies, in which asocial prisoners called "outlaws" by their peers were reported. "Outlaws" had been imprisoned for a variety of offenses, but they had frequently employed violent and bizarre techniques of criminality. They exhibited records of excessive recidivism and were usually the product of backgrounds of early and severe parental and social rejection.[59] Donald Garrity observed that "outlaws" exhibited high rates of parole violation, which seemed little influenced by the amount of time spent in custody.[60] These reports were concerned with roughly the same kind of offender, so the different labels of "outlaw," "gorilla," "hard guy," and "tough" were apparently simply a reflection of regional variations in prison argot.

An abundance of data is available on the childhood social backgrounds of overly aggressive persons.[61] The specific socialization experiences such individuals have undergone vary considerably, but one recurrent thread throughout these case histories is early and severe parental rejection. For example, Jenkins examined numerous aggressive children, nearly all of whom had been abandoned by their parents or suffered some other severe form of rejection, including repeated physical assaults by their parents. As a consequence, they developed into relatively unsocialized individuals who engaged in myriad forms of aggression against human and animal targets.

Unfortunately, longitudinal studies that follow such persons from childhood through adult life are not available. Information is lacking about the effects of commitment to guidance clinics, training schools, reformatories, or kindred experiences. Nevertheless, these life events seem to intensify the hostile views of the offender so that he becomes cumulatively more aggressive and hostile as he encounters a variety of kinds of social rejection. Accordingly, the psychopathic assaultist is probably something more than the aggressive child grown up, for these career contingencies also influence his adult behavior.

the study of sexual behavior

Sociological analyses of criminality have not devoted equal attention to all forms of lawbreaking. Much work has been done on property crimes at the same time that little has been said about other illegality, particularly sexual misconduct. This relative inattention to sexual criminality reflects an assumption that this behavior is the result of causal factors of a different sort from those identified in social-structural explanations of property violations. Because it does not seem to fit conveniently within the usual frames of reference of the sociologist, sexual deviation has been systematically ignored.

Sociologists have done a fair amount of work on certain matters having to do with sexual behavior, but until recently they have had relatively little to say about sexual deviations of one kind or another.[62] This silence regarding patterns of deviant sexual activity can be linked to the lack of a socialization model concerning sexual development against which to measure departures from "normal" sexual socialization.[63]

Until recently, sociologists have ignored the developmental processes by which persons come to be homosexuals, exhibitionists, child molesters, or to engage in other forms of sexual conduct. One common tendency in the study of deviance and criminology has been to default on the etiological issues regarding sexual crimes by turning this matter over to psychiatrists.[64] For example, this kind of behavior is often attributed to "compulsions," which supposedly drive the deviant. Sex offenders are seen as persons whose actions are not rationally motivated, and hence they are thought to lie outside the purview of sociological commentary.[65] But, this interpretation is in error. Sexual conduct, deviant or otherwise, is learned behavior. As such it is no less sociological than most of the other phenomena with which we have been concerned.

sexual socialization

What have social psychologists had to say about sexual socialization in terms of a model of "normality" against which to contrast deviant sexual behavior and roles?

In a summary of the social-psychological state of interest in sexual issues, Irvin Child declared:

But while socialization variables are thus shown by elimination to have great importance as antecedents to adult sexual behavior, we do not yet have an adequate scientific basis for stating the exact relationships involved. Nor do we have as yet an adequate basis for judging the extent to which variations in adult sexual behavior are to be ascribed directly to variables in sexual socialization, and to what extent they are instead to be considered as indirect effects of variables originally pertinent to other systems of behavior.[66]

From what sources shall a conception of sexual learning be drawn? The most well-known approach to sexual development is in psychoanalytic theories.[67] These arguments stress the assumed role of instinctual sources of sexual motivation in behavior and include a number of claims about early life experiences and sexuality that are difficult or impossible to test scientifically. Accordingly, the search for directions regarding sexual socialization theory must be sought elsewhere. Some psychiatrists, such as Harry Stack Sullivan, have offered interpretations of sexual behavior that are rooted in learning theory and symbolic-interactional perspectives on human behavior.[68] Similarly, psychiatrists have conducted studies of sexual conduct that provide behavioral data for social-psychological interpretations; that is, these materials can be understood in interactional terms.[69]

Manford Kuhn has argued that sex acts, sexual objects, and sexual partners are *social objects* that have meaning to persons because social definitions have been assigned to them through language and communication. The physiology of humans does not explain their behavior, sexual or otherwise. Sexual roles are social; hence, although physiology sets limits on the role behavior, the learning process creates sexual motives, designates partners, and determines the kinds of behavior to be engaged in to reach sexual objectives.[70]

Kuhn's observations offer a starting point for the development of a social-psychological theory of sexual socialization and sex roles. Patterns of sexual behavior—sex roles—are learned.[71] A wide range of stimuli has the potential to call out sexual responses, so individuals could react, in theory at least, in ways they define as sexual (ejaculation and so on) to such varied stimuli as heterosexual intercourse, homosexual mouth, genital, or anal contacts, animal contacts, burglary of dwelling units, firesetting, and a plethora of seemingly nonsexual stimuli. Nearly all the potential sexual stimulus-response patterns are actually observed in any large population of adults. All the varied forms of sexual-role behavior are learned through some kind of socialization experience.[72]

Gagnon and Simon have offered some important observations regarding the learning of "sexual scripts" or frames of reference. Sexual scripts have two elements: interpersonal expectations, cues, etc., shared among individuals concerning sexuality, sexual responses, etc., and internal motivational patterns on the part of individuals.[73] According to Gagnon and Simon: "Scripts are involved in learning the meaning of internal states, organizing the sequences of specifically sexual acts, decoding novel situations, setting the limits on sexual responses, and linking meanings from nonsexual aspects of life to specifically sexual experience."[74]

One major observation is that an individual's relatively permanent sexual-role behavior is largely a function of his or her sexual self-concept. For example, evidence from the Kinsey studies showed that many males experience homosexual contacts at some point in their lives but do not adopt homosexuality as an adult preferred pattern of sexual adjustment.[75] On this same point, studies by David Ward and Gene Kassebaum and by Rose Giallombardo in two women's prisons indicated that a number of the prisoners became involved in a transitory pattern of homosexual activity, becoming known by other prisoners as "jail house turnouts."[76] Interestingly, most of these women continued to define themselves as heterosexual and apparently returned to heterosexual patterns of response on release from prison. In male prisons, similar homosexual liaisons occur among male inmates without leading to homosexuality as preferred sexual role outside of prison walls. Reiss's data on delinquent boys who "play the queers" indicated that these youths participated in homosexual mouth-genital contacts without adult heterosexual roles apparently being impaired.[77]

The central concern in accounts of sexual learning is not with how persons come to engage in certain forms of overt behavior, but rather with how they come to define themselves as "normal" (and subsequently engage in heterosexual acts). In the same way, inquiry should focus on how persons adopt role conceptions of themselves as "gay," "dykes," "sexually inadequate," and so on, and thereafter come to engage in various forms of deviant conduct.

In a general way, individuals usually appear to see themselves as "normal," heterosexual males or females out of a variety of sex-role experiences beginning early in life. Probably the most critical are those experiences that contribute to the development of a stable, *generalized* conception of self as male or female. That is, the specific sexual conception of self and the sexual response preferences that develop represent the relatively natural outgrowth of acquisition of a broad set of cultural definitions centering around gender roles.

The experiences involved in normal sexual socialization are those in which parents consistently deal with the child within the guidelines of culturally prescribed parent–child interactional norms. The clinical literature on sexual behavior indicates that an atmosphere of tolerance for forms of sexual experimentation, such as masturbation, and an open-minded parental attitude regarding sexual matters have important consequences for the individual's degree of sexual adjustment. The literature suggests that deviant sexual adjustment patterns are commonly the product of atypical socialization experiences in which the individual is dealt with in sexually inappropriate ways or fails to acquire an appropriate pattern of identification with the parents. This material shows that markedly unconventional, "seductive" parent–child experiences sometimes lead to markedly deviant sexual-role conceptions and behavior patterns.

Sexual learning is unduly complicated and dangerous in American society because of American sexual values that define sexuality as evil or "dirty" and not to be discussed openly. According to Gagnon, a pronounced lack of consensus regarding sexual behavior and sexual experiences exists in the United States. For the most part, value agreements concerning sexuality are evolved between such sexual pairs as husbands and wives largely in terms of subtle cues and gestures rather than explicit communicational dialogues. As a result of this secretive and unshared character to sexuality, parents are required to work out by themselves solutions to parent–child interactional concerns in the sexual area.[78] Because sexuality is a forbidden topic, parents normally fail to provide their children with a vocabulary for interpreting and integrating sexuality and allied matters, and widespread "nonlabeling" occurs. In turn, Gagnon held that "given this framework of repression and avoidance by parents, it is not surprising that the child gets the bulk of his sexual information, though not his attitudes, through peer relationships."[79]

The discussion so far suggests that early interactional experiences should be probed for clues regarding the plethora of sexual difficulties in which Americans are enmeshed. Such distortions of sexuality as frigidity might be traced to overly repressive parent–child experiences, and impotency or sexual fears are probably linked to identifiable interactional experiences. Some markedly atypical experiences, including seductive interaction, also probably contribute to the development of instances of violent sexual conduct in which the victim is mutilated, beaten, and otherwise abused by the offender. In brief, early interactional experiences condition the long-term sexual activity of the adult and lead to particular sexual self-notions that, in turn, result in adoption of some specific sexual role pattern.

Some forms of sexual behavior, particularly deviant ones, probably emerge out of adult life experiences. Moreover, in some cases, the person's sexual self-image is likely to have emerged *after* some initial, exploratory playing of a new sex role. For example, exhibitionism and child molesting are carried on by individuals who have gone through a conventional socialization experience and are "normal" in sexual orientation. But in later life certain of these persons undergo alterations in family relationships or other experiences, which culminate in self-concept changes toward notions of "inadequacy." Their behavior appears to be related to these relatively current experiences and cannot be traced back to initial sexual socialization.

Investigation of homosexual behavior might profit from attention to the risk-taking, processual conceptualization of the development of deviant careers advanced by Edwin Lemert.[80] Homosexual roles may sometimes grow out of situations in which tentative and exploratory flirtations with homosexual activities lead to social identification of the person as "gay." This altered social identity cuts the person off from reentry into the world of "normals," so he is prevented from reestablishing his heterosexual self-image. A mechanistic causal pattern could conceivably be operating here, instead of the commonly assumed genetic process in which early life experiences result in early sexual identities which then determine adult-role behavior.[81]

On the point of mechanistic or situational causation, Stanton Wheeler argued that a good deal of the behavior labeled as "normal" rape, in which force is employed in sexual intercourse but mutilation and other aberrant actions are absent, is carried on by "normal" individuals.[82] These instances of deviation often have arisen out of interaction in which the victim was initially a willing and voluntary participant in the actions. The activities of the two interactional partners become "rape" only at a later point, when the offender's sexual demands exceed the expectations of the "victim," as for example when he demands oral intercourse with the "victim." Some evidence hints that cases of "pedophilia" (child molesting) are carried on by relatively "normal" individuals who have come to develop feelings of sexual and interpersonal inadequacy out of relatively recent life events.[83] Deteriorated relationships between marital partners might contribute to genesis of this kind of behavior in several obvious ways. Finally, data on father–daughter incest contain indications that this activity is carried on by males with relatively conventional sexual orientations. Involvement in sexual behavior with inappropriate partners seems related to unavailability of more appropriate sexual partners, due to illness of the spouse, social and physical isolation of the family unit, and related factors. In some cases, seductive interaction between father and daughter may contribute to development of incestuous acts, as may covert collaboration of the wife in the relationship, as she encourages the father to refrain from sexual acts with her and ignores sexual contact between him and his daughter.

These broad outlines of a social-psychological perspective on sexual development and deviant sexual conduct are explored further in the remainder of this chapter.

The schizoid character of American social structure as it has to do with sexual conduct is readily apparent to any literate citizen in the United States. The major cultural heroes of American society include the Hollywood actress sex symbol who serves as an erotic object in the fantasies of millions of males. This society couples a kind of *Playboy* mentality and an emphasis on youthfulness, eroticism, and sexual attractiveness with laws that restrict sexual conduct to marriage. Even there, laws of various states attempt to regulate the forms of sexual activity in which marital partners may engage. In short, sexual behavior occupies a central place in American values, coexistent with puritanical sentiments which would severely circumscribe the citizen's opportunities to engage in sexual activity.

Criminal laws regarding sexual misbehavior are extremely common throughout the country. These laws endeavor to regulate the degree of consent in sexual acts, the nature of the sexual object, the nature of the act, or the setting in which the act occurs.[84] Wheeler argued that these statutes embody conflicting aims: some express the moral condemnation of the community, such as laws directed at homosexuals; others are concerned with sex acts viewed as socially harmful; and still others endeavor to control individuals thought to be psychopathological in personality organization.[85] The large number of laws directed at sexual behavior means that nearly all sexual acts other than specific forms of heterosexual intercourse in marriage are forbidden by law.

Of course, the fact that criminal laws are broadly defined does not mean that the majority of persons who violate them are dealt with as criminals. Quite the contrary, for a great many forbidden acts are voluntarily engaged in within situations of privacy and go unobserved and unreported. Laws against adultery and fornication would be cases in point, for it is doubtful that more than a negligible share of the adulterers and fornicators ever become subjected to the criminal law.

American sex laws are not without critics; it has been widely argued that these statutes improperly and unwisely extend the concern of criminal law to harmless matters of private morality, such as homosexual acts between consenting adults.[86] The critics would revise these prohibitions to narrow the kinds of behavior they proscribe to acts that are clearly harmful to society.[87] Sex laws in the individual states are also extremely inconsistent. For example, adultery laws vary both in definitions of adultery and in penalties associated with these acts; mutual masturbation is a criminal offense in some states and not in others; penalties for consensual homosexual acts range from fines or jail sentences to life imprisonment. The uniformity criminal law is presumed to contain is missing in the case of sex statutes.[88]

Existing laws defining sex offenders have several major implications for the study of causation. First, some kind of taxonomy of sexual offenses that will reduce the variety of criminal activities to an orderly set of patterns amenable to explanation is sorely needed. Second, an adequate formulation concerning sexual criminality will have to be sufficiently multifaceted and complex to explain extremely disparate kinds of behavior. Some forms of sexual criminality differ little or not at all from conventional patterns of sexual behavior, such as statutory rape, which involves consenting individuals both of whom are sexually although not chronologically mature. In that case, the explanatory problem is to account for social contingencies that result in some persons falling into the hands of the police rather than for personal idiosyncrasies of the offenders. At the polar extreme from this kind of illegality stand bizarre and violent sexual crimes. Because these actions are probably not carried on by individuals who are the product of normal sexual socialization, a strikingly different explanation of behavior must be uncovered.

Six types of offender behavior are singled out here: statutory rape, aggressive rape, violent sex offenses, nonviolent sex offenses (child molesting and exhibitionism), incest, and homosexuality.

Before turning to crime patterns, several major studies of sex offenders should be scrutinized.[89] A summary of these pieces of research should be useful in acquiring a sense of sex offenders in the aggregate.

studies of sex offenders

Three fairly old studies of apprehended sexual deviants collectively indicated that these persons had been convicted of a wide assortment of sex crimes. Additionally, many of them exhibited low socioeconomic status, poor social backgrounds, and relatively low intelligence.[90] However, it is not clear whether these are factors behind sexual offenses or, instead, variables that influence the likelihood of being socially processed as a sexual deviant.

Albert Ellis and Ralph Brancale examined a representative sample of sex offenders in New Jersey.[91] As a result of legislation passed in 1949 in that state, all persons charged with rape, sodomy, incest, lewdness, indecent exposure, dealing in obscene material, indecent communications to females, or carnal abuse were to be referred to the New Jersey Diagnostic Center.[92] This study reported on the characteristics of the first 300 persons sentenced to the center. These offenders were a mixed bag, for 20 percent had committed statutory rape, 17 percent had been involved in sex relations of other kinds with minors, 29 percent had engaged in exhibitionism, and 16 percent had been apprehended for homosexuality. Only 3 percent of the offenders had been involved in forcible rape, whereas incest cases made up only 4 percent of the group. Clearly, the majority of sex offenders who fell into the hands of the police and courts in New Jersey were relatively petty or nonviolent individuals.[93] In comparing the center commitments with inmates at the state prison, the former appeared to include many more relatively petty deviants, whereas the prison received the more disordered or violent individuals.

The Ellis and Brancale data led to two general conclusions. First, the vast majority of sex offenders were petty criminals who were relatively normal in personality structure. They did not fit the "sex fiend" image. Only about 5 percent of these offenders had used force in their crimes. Additionally, 78 percent were diagnosed as "normal," "mildly neurotic," or "severely neurotic," whereas only 3 percent were judged psychopathic. Over one-half of these violators were deemed to be sexually inhibited, with 72 percent of the exhibitionists and 66 percent of the child molesters being so classified. These findings do not support sex-fiend notions citizens in American society currently hold.[94]

The second major impression from this study was that apprehended sex offenders were socially disadvantaged individuals of generally low intelligence and economic position. It appeared that persons identified as sex offenders were often picked out of the population because of their social backgrounds rather than as a direct result of their criminality. In this sense, the case of apprehended sex offenders parallels that of property offenders, many of whom appear unluckier than other persons rather than distinctly more criminalistic than nonoffenders.

Another study, carried on in the 1950s in California, noted that felony sex crimes in 1952 constituted only 2.5 percent of all reported felonies in that state.[95] Of the 3,705 felony sex crimes in 1952, 1,941 were cases of forcible or statutory rape, whereas 1,764 were other kinds of sex offenses. Extreme force and violence were rare, even in felony crimes; hence, only 9 percent of the persons prosecuted in San Francisco on rape charges were convicted of forcible rape. The investigators reported that most of the sex offenses known to the police were petty misdemeanor offenses.[96] They concluded: "These data therefore show that the majority of all convicted sex offenders commit socially offensive but nondangerous acts, and the majority of all convictions occur at the level of misdemeanor."[97]

The most complex and detailed study of sex offenders was by the Kinsey-founded Institute for Sex Research, Inc.[98] The report of that investigation was nearly 1000 pages in length, representing a vast compendium of findings on sexual deviants. However, the study also demonstrated the relative paucity of results from inductive, fact-gathering inquiry. This work was not guided by theoretical propositions around which evidence was gathered. Instead, it endeavored to discover significant facts about sex offenders through examination of great amounts of descriptive information.

This study dealt with 1,356 convicted sex offenders, primarily from prisons in Indiana and California, who were interviewed during 1941–45 and 1953–55. These offenders were compared to 888 prison inmates convicted of nonsexual offenses and a control group of 477 noncriminal citizens.[99]

Because of the wide range of activities engaged in by the sex offenders, the researchers found they had to categorize the offenders and their actions in several major dimensions. The offenses were classified as homosexual or heterosexual actions in terms of the sex of the victim or coparticipant. In addition, sexual actions were divided into forced as opposed to consensual, and victims or coparticipants were categorized as children, minors (persons between 12 and 16 years of age), and adults. These dimensions yielded 12 possible types of behavior, but patterns of forced homosexual relations were excluded because they were rarely encountered among the offenders. Finally, the researchers sorted sex offenders into three additional incest types based on age of victim or coparticipant, as well as into two other categories, peepers and exhibitionists. In all, they singled out 14 types of sex misbehavior for study.[100]

The research strategy centered about examination of a number of kinds of experiences in the lives of each person involved in the 14 kinds of sexual activity. Facts on early life experiences, masturbation, sex dreams, heterosexual petting, premarital coitus, marital experiences, extramarital coitus and postmarital coitus, animal contacts, criminality of the offenders, and a number of other matters were reported. Although much of this factual and statistical material tended to obscure more than it revealed, some significant facets of sexual misconduct did emerge from this information. For example, almost none of the heterosexual offenders against children said they preferred young girls as sex objects, so their behavior appeared to be more the result of situational contingencies than pathological motivation.[101] Regarding heterosexual acts with minors or adults, the data indicated that the victim was frequently active in initiation of the sex behavior and that the offenders were fairly normal and conventional persons.[102] Also, those who used force in heterosexual offenses against adults were not markedly unconventional individuals, except for their willingness to use coercion in achieving sexual ends.[103] Finally, the investigators reported that exhibitionists and peepers were meek, sexually inadequate persons rather than sex fiends.[104]

patterns of sexual criminality

Clearly, sex offenses make up a mixed bag of criminal acts. But, six general groupings can be singled out, based upon the sexual acts and role of the victims in the behavior. Statutory rape and aggressive rape are similar in the sense that both involve relatively normal heterosexual conduct, but they differ in the degree of force and coercion employed in attaining sexual ends. These two kinds of offenses and offenders are fundamentally different from violent sexual assaults by persons who exhibit idiosyncratic and bizarre sexual motives centering about violence and cruelty. In turn, child molesting or exhibitionism differ from the preceding three types, both in terms of the behavior and in the characteristics of those who engage in them. Nonviolent offenders also vary from the others in the sense that the general public is likely to define them as perverted or in other ways markedly unusual. Their behavior is hard to identify with, either because the activity appears peculiar or the victims seem markedly inappropriate as sexual objects. Incest is a fifth kind of sexual deviancy that appears to be the product of a relatively specialized form of motivational process and background situation. Finally, male homosexuality is a sixth group; within this category important variations exist in sexual behavior, participation in homosexual subcultures, and so on. The six patterns are sufficiently homogeneous to warrant separate discussion.[105]

STATUTORY RAPE

Several of the studies discussed earlier contain evidence on the characteristics of statutory rape and statutory rapists. The investigation by Gebhard and others contained a number of relevant findings. The median age of men convicted of heterosexual offenses with minor partners (females between 12 and 16 years of age) was 25 years of age. Four-fifths of these individuals were first offenders; few were pathological persons. In most cases, the victim did not discourage the sexual activity and, in most cases, she failed to report the sexual behavior to anyone. Instead, a third party originated the complaint against the offender.[106]

Much the same picture emerged regarding offenders involved in heterosexual acts with adults. Because no unusual characteristics on the part of the offenders emerged from the data, the authors concluded: "One is left with the over-all impression of an uneducated, opportunistic, and basically goodhearted soul who takes his pleasure where he finds it and lets the future take care of itself."[107]

AGGRESSIVE OR FORCIBLE RAPE

During the past decade or so, forcible or aggressive rape has become the subject of much discussion, both by citizens generally and by sociologists. Forcible rape has become a major social concern in considerable part as a consequence of the women's movement of the 1970s and 1980s, which directed attention to sexism and the unequal treatment of women throughout many institutional areas in American society. According to many commentators, rape laws and their enforcement are striking illustrations of the pervasiveness of sexism in this society.

One incisive discussion of these matters was by Camille Le Grand, who analyzed American rape laws and their implementation in detail, arguing that these statutes were designed to protect male interests in women as sexual property, rather than to protect females from rape and its consequences.[108]

According to Le Grand, if rape laws were truly for the protection of women, they would extend to sexual assaults of husbands upon their wives and would prohibit violence and coercion in all sexual encounters. But in fact, husband–wife rape is a legal impossibility in nearly every state, within the current interpretation of rape laws. Le Grand noted that statutory-rape laws operate to protect the "market value" of virgins as potential brides. If existing rape laws were not sexist, they would allow young women under 18 years of age to decide for themselves whether to remain chaste or not, rather than forbidding them to engage in intercourse.

Le Grand's analysis also indicated that existing rape laws are designed less to protect women than to frighten and intimidate potential rapists and to suppress their activities. But once an incident of rape has occurred and the female victim becomes "damaged goods" in terms of sexual property, a variety of social and judicial processes go into operation to severely reduce the likelihood that the rapist will be apprehended, convicted, or incarcerated. Finally, the rape victim has often become transformed into the guilty party in the course of police interrogation or courtroom questioning, with questions centering about her previous sexual experiences or the extent of her interaction with the rapist prior to the sexual assault. These questions would be irrelevant and inadmissible in criminal proceedings that were focused upon full protection of the rights of women, including the unfettered right to decide whether or not to engage in sexual intercourse.

One of the salutary results of attacks such as Le Grand's on rape laws and their enforcement has been the rise of a number of programs in recent years created by police or prosecutors' offices and designed to bring about stricter enforcement of rape laws, as well as to reduce the trauma of rape victims.

Turning to rape behavior, aggressive rapists employ varying degrees of force to coerce a physically adult female into sexual activity. The amount of force varies, and, in addition, interpretations of the offender and the victim regarding the coercion involved in the event frequently differ. In most instances of aggressive rape, the sexual encounter centers around heterosexual genital intercourse, but occasionally, forcible rapists compel the victim to engage in other sex acts such as oral or anal intercourse.

Some relevant data regarding rape came from a study by Asher Pacht, Seymour Halleck, and John Ehrmann, who examined 1,605 offenders committed to the Wisconsin Department of Public Welfare for psychiatric diagnosis.[109] The Wisconsin Sex Crimes Law required a psychological investigation in all cases of rape, attempted rape, or indecent sex behavior with a child. Slightly less than half these offenders were judged to be "not deviated" in psychological makeup. Additionally, of the persons committed to prison, only 17 percent subsequently violated parole. These findings confirmed the picture of the aggressive rapist as a person without marked pathology.

The inquiry into sex offenses by Gebhard and others contained material on aggressive rapists. The heterosexual aggressors who had been involved with minors (females between 12 and 16 years of age) were relatively young men. Many were impulsive persons from relatively disorganized backgrounds. The heterosexual aggressors against adult females were relatively nondescript individuals who were unusual only in the sense that they had used force in sexual activities.[110]

The most ambitious study of rape to date was by Menachem Amir.[111] That investigation dealt with 646 cases of forcible rape in Philadelphia in 1958 and 1960 and examined the social backgrounds of the 646 victims of 1,292 offenders, as well as the circumstances surrounding the acts of forcible rape.

Amir's findings showed that most forcible rapes were intracial events rather than acts between persons of different racial background. Rapes were significantly more frequent among blacks than whites, for the rape rates were 12 times higher among black than white females. However, these observations should be treated with caution, for they may reflect differentials in crime reporting and law-enforcement practices as well as real racial variations in forcible rape.

Most forcible-rape offenders were between 15 and 25 years of age, and the majority of victims were also young women. Most offenders were unmarried, which was also true of the victims. However, Amir rejected a demographic-imbalance explanation of rape, for the sex ratio of unmarried persons in Philadelphia was not unbalanced. Most offenders and victims were from lower-income backgrounds, and many were unemployed. About half the rapists had prior records of criminality, and about a quarter of the victims had been in difficulties with the law or acquired tarnished reputations.[112]

Amir discovered no appreciable relationship between rape and season of the year. However, marked variations existed in forcible rapes by days of the week, for most occurred on the weekends, particularly on Saturday. The peak hours for rape were from 8:00 P.M. to 2:00 A.M. Alcohol appeared to be a factor in only about one-third of the cases.

Most rapists and their victims lived within the same general area of the community, and the acts of sexual assault occurred within this same neighborhood. About half the offenders and victims had been involved in a primary relationship with each other before the sexual assault, so these findings seriously undermined the stereotype of the wild-eyed rapist who assaults a total stranger.

The types of coercion or violence employed in the rape incidents were classified and tabulated. In 15 percent of the incidents, no force was used; in another 29 percent offenders were rough. Brutal beatings or choking accompanied forcible rapes in only about 30 percent of the cases. Here again, forcible rape departed from some of the public stereotypes about this behavior. Amir found that the victims were submissive and put up no resistance in over half the rape incidents. The rapists subjected the victims to "sexual humiliation" (fellatio, cunnilingus, or repeated intercourse) in only about a quarter of the cases. Multiple rape by two or more offenders was involved in 276 of the 646 rape cases.

According to Amir, 122 of the rapes were victim-precipitated, in that the victim deported herself in such a way as to encourage sexual assault. She had agreed to engage in intercourse but had later recanted, or she had acted in a sexually provocative manner. But, some disclaimers are in order regarding this observation. First, the characterization of rape incidents as victim-precipitated came out of police reports, some of which may have reflected male biases against rape victims. And more importantly, even if it could be demonstrated that a rape victim was involved in sexual interaction with the offender prior to the rape event, this fact is in no way a justification for rape. Women should be free to withdraw from sexual interaction at any point. Victim-precipitation is not a legitimizing basis for rape.

The strong suggestion emerged from Amir's research that forcible rape may be an occasional illegal outcome of situations in lower-class areas where casual and transitory sexual episodes are commonplace. Quite probably, a large number of the sexual liaisons that take place are not very different from the forcible rapes.

Richard Jenkins offered a set of theoretical contentions about rape and other sexual assaults in American society, which was congruent with the foregoing findings.[113] He maintained that the bulk of sexually assaultive conduct involves the use of fairly minor degrees of force by relatively normal persons. At the same time, he claimed that at the other end of the scale of violence, pathological actors engage in unprovoked sexual assaults of a bizarre and extraordinary kind. The following section deals with the last group.

Jenkins's central thesis was that themes or motives that join eroticism and cruelty are often learned in sexual socialization in American society. The results of this kind of socialization frequently show up in mildly sadistic acts, which do not become subject to official attention. If Jenkins is correct, we would expect marital partners to report such incidents fairly regularly. However, when these associations with sexuality occur in persons hostile to others, a potential rapist can be observed. According to Jenkins, the extreme example of hostility and sadistic orientations to sexual behavior can be recognized in so-called "lust murders." Jenkins contended that aggressive rapists are not a particularly unusual or aberrant group of individuals. He argued: "The difference between the law-abiding man and the rapist lies typically not in a difference of sex impulse but in a difference of inhibition and consideration for the personality of others."[114]

VIOLENT SEXUAL ASSAULT

Scattered among the offenders who engage in sex offenses against mature females is a group of lawbreakers referred to here as violent sex offenders. The actions they carry out against female victims are of such violence that homicides often result from their behavior. There is no denying that these offenders exist, for newspapers periodically report incidents of criminality fitting this characterization and case-history materials in prisons also turn up such persons. Some indication of the nature of this behavior can be obtained from a book by J. Paul de River, which contained a series of gruesome photographs of victims of these crimes but little else of reedeming value.[115]

There is a paucity of evidence on the causal backgrounds from which these offenders develop. The sex-offender studies examined previously are of little use as far as violent sexual offenders are concerned, for those investigations made no effort to separate out such lawbreakers for special attention.

However, some hints about these offenders worthy of attention can be offered. Violent sex offenders probably grow up in simultaneously seductive and repressive family environments. The developing person acquires out of this situation a basic heterosexual orientation centered about conventional erotic motives. A variety of sexually provocative overtures of the mother further arouses or stimulates this orientation. Case-history documents often note such experiences as the mother sleeping with the son or bathing with him long after he has become a physically mature young male. It would be surprising if the offender could repress completely any feelings of sexual arousal that emanate from these experiences. At the same time, the youth is prevented from overt demonstrations of arousal, partly because of the incest taboo that strongly forbids sexuality directed at the mother. The mother in many cases verbally treats sexual responsiveness as dirty, evil, and something not to be openly acknowledged. This interactive process may produce individuals who are carriers of combined themes of lust and aggression in pronounced form. Their hostility-charged sexual actions represent the extreme form of the erotic-aggressive syndrome described by Jenkins.

NONVIOLENT SEX OFFENSES

Probably the most abhorred sexual offender, in the eyes of both the general public and prison inmates, is that person who engages in exhibitionism or child molesting. These individuals are regarded as "perverts" because of involvement in sexual activities that depart strikingly from conventional heterosexual intercourse with adult partners. Even though the specific acts of lawbreaking in which they engage differ, both child molesters and exhibitionists share a good many characteristics in common.

For the most part, evidence concerning nonviolent sex offenders forms a consistent picture. However, Paul Gebhard and John Gagnon have presented some findings concerning male sex offenders against young children in which the subjects were relatively young adult males.[116] This finding was not consistent with other accounts, which reported that pedophiles are usually older men.

An investigation some years ago by Benjamin Apfelberg, Carl Sugar, and Arnold Pfeffer noted that child molesters were the oldest group among six different kinds of sex offenders held for psychiatric examination at Bellevue Hospital in New York. Exhibitionists showed inferiority feelings of a variety of kinds, including concerns about sexual adequacy.[117] The more recent work of Gebhard and others revealed that sex offenders against children infrequently had serious records of prior criminality and that those with previous involvement in lawbreaking had usually been involved in sex offenses. About 60 percent of the victims were known to the offenders before the sex acts had occurred.[118] This inquiry also uncovered evidence of heterosexual difficulties on the part of exhibitionists. These offenders were described as sexually inadequate; hence, their acts of exhibitionism served as affirmation of masculinity.[119] "Peeping Toms" also appeared to be inhibited individuals with inadequate heterosexual lives.[120] The New Jersey study discussed earlier also turned up evidence that exhibitionists and child molesters were sexually inhibited individuals rather than hypersexed "fiends."[121] Toobert and others subjected a large group of San Quentin Prison pedophiles to the Minnesota Multiphasic Personality Inventory, with the result that the child molesters appeared more distrustful, effeminate, and passive than the control-group prisoners.[122]

Charles McCaghy produced a study of child molesters, dealing with incarcerated molesters, as well as those on probation in two counties in Wisconsin.[123] His findings indicated that most of the offenders were unskilled or semiskilled workers. The average age of the molesters was 37.3, whereas that of the victims was 9.0. Over two-thirds of the molesters had been at least casually acquainted with the victims prior to the offense; in three-fourths of the cases the molester did not use overt coercion and restricted contact mainly to acts of genital manipulation.

Alex Gigeroff, J. W. Mohr, and R. E. Turner presented some summary observations about exhibitionists, which showed these individuals to be relatively young persons.[124] The average age of the exhibitionists they studied was about 25, with the peak period for this lawbreaking in the early to middle twenties. Because the social backgrounds of the offenders did not appear to be markedly unusual, these researchers argued that the behavior was a response to stress situations in the individual's personal and social relations rather than a manifestation of mental illness or impairment.

Nonviolent sex offenders occupy an outcast status among other prisoners in correctional institutions. Most convicts avoid social contacts with fellow prisoners known in the inmate argot as "dings." Many of these outcasts are assigned this outcast status because of their bizarre or unpredictable behavior. "Dings" who receive the special label of "rapos" are nonviolent sex offenders held in contempt by other prisoners because of the nature of their sexual crimes. One investigation of "rapos" by Walter Martin confirmed the commonplace assertion by inmates that nonviolent sex offenders are the major recruits into the prison religious program. Martin observed that "rapos" frequently verbalized religious sentiments in the institution and most frequently attended church.[125]

INCEST

Criminal statutes in the United States which define the offense of incest show a good deal of variation from state to state. Intercourse between father and daughter, mother and son, and brother and sister are prohibited everywhere; but some states extend the meaning of incest to sexual intercourse between first cousins. Brothers and sisters of half blood are sometimes included in incest legislation, as are fathers and adopted daughters. Other states do not prohibit sexual relations between these individuals, at the same time that some forbid such pairs of individuals to marry. These statutory variations are of little importance in one major respect, for, in practice, father–daughter incest is almost the sole form of forbidden sexual intercourse that results in prosecution as "incest." This is not to say that sexual intercourse never occurs between mothers and sons or between siblings. These acts occur but are rarely reported, unlike father–daughter incest. In the latter case, the mother often acts as complainant against the father. In other instances, the daughter becomes pregnant and is induced to identify her father as the person responsible for her pregnancy.

What does the evidence show regarding the dynamics of incest? Svend Reimer reported on a number of father–daughter incest cases in Sweden.[126] He indicated that incest occurred most frequently among agricultural laborers or other similarly disorganized groups of industrial workers. These persons generally came from broken homes or experienced early separation from their family because of tension in relationships with their parents. Entry into the labor market early in life restricted their educational attainment. As a consequence, their adult life showed frequent job changes and employment instability. Shortly preceding the incest episode, these persons had been involved in marked employment difficulties or other disruptions of social routine. Reimer contended that the offenders had been in situations of sexual frustration prior to occurrence of the crime, in that their wives had become incapacitated or had refused to engage in intercourse. Riemer held that incest was thus a result of indifference toward social responsibilities on the part of the actor along with extreme sexual frustration. The choice of a sexual partner outside of the family was limited; so although the offender had no special sexual interest in his daughter, she was the only sexual partner available to him.

A study of Illinois offenders by S. Kirson Weinberg involved predominantly father–daughter incest cases.[127] Weinberg argued that the offender's behavior was a manifestation of personal instability and retarded emotional development. According to Weinberg, incest offenders were of two general types. Some showed schizophrenic characteristics; they were involved in such ingrown family relationships that they had difficulty in relating effectively to persons outside of the family. The others exhibited "psychopathic" characteristics and had insufficiently internalized guilt and aversion toward sexual relations with family members. The latter individuals were involved in relatively disorganized family relationships in which effective social constraints against incest were absent. Weinberg pointed to social isolation and family disorganization as major precipitating factors in the onset of father–daughter incest. Other, more recent studies have confirmed this general picture.[128]

MALE HOMOSEXUALITY

Persons who engage in acts of sexual conduct with members of the same sex represent one of the most widely discussed groups of deviants in American society. There has been no shortage of commentary directed at homosexuals, ranging from objective analyses at one extreme to denunciatory attacks in moral terms at the other.[129] Until relatively recently, sociologists have paid little attention to homosexuality, so a major share of the literature is psychiatrically oriented and has been produced by psychiatrists.

The following sections focus exclusively on male homosexuality. This is not to say that female homosexuals are uncommon in the United States, for there is reason to believe that lesbians are about as numerous as male homosexuals. But nearly all arrests of individuals for homosexual conduct involve males. Although the police have considerable difficulty arresting males for homosexual acts, they would encounter even greater obstacles were they to attempt to round up a large number of lesbians. Homosexual acts among women are carried out in private places to which the police do not have access and so are less visible than acts of male homosexuality. Additionally, there is probably a general disbelief in the possibility of homosexuality among women, so agents of social control do not feel compelled to ferret out such persons. This situation is in contradistinction to male homosexuality, which the police go about detecting through a variety of techniques, such as vice-squad work by plainclothesmen who make themselves available for homosexual advances and then arrest the offender who makes such overtures.

Various hypotheses have been advanced to account for homosexual behavior. One school of thought contends that homosexuality is constitutional in nature, havings its base in physiological factors. This same line of argument often holds that homosexuals represent a fairly distinct personality type.[130] Edmund Bergler is an exponent of the view that homosexuality is always the result of a neurotic distortion of personality structure.[131] Persons who have advanced this contention have not offered much persuasive evidence in its support.

Another body of opinion asserts that homosexuality is the outcome of certain kinds of sexual socialization rather than the product of faulty biology. Abram Kardiner has stated that male homosexuality develops in family settings in which individuals develop incapacitating fears of females and other, related characteristics conducive to homosexual involvement.[132] Clara Thompson[133] and Donald Cory,[134] among others, have also enunciated this perspective.

The research of Bieber and others was in this genre.[135] It involved a sample of 106 homosexuals undergoing psychoanalytic treatment in metropolitan New York City, along with a sample of 100 control-group males. The data consisted of observations on these persons, which the psychiatrists treating them recorded on questionnaires.[136]

Bieber and his associates reported that most of these homosexual subjects were the product of peculiar family backgrounds. In particular, nearly 70 percent had been reared by "close-binding-intimate" (CBI) mothers who accorded them preferential treatment. These same mothers were overcontrolling in their dealings with their sons; many also behaved seductively toward their sons.[137] This family pattern also included a detached-hostile father as well as a close-binding mother. These investigators concluded that homosexuality is an adaptation to hidden but incapacitating fears of the opposite sex. In their view, homosexuality is a pathological alternative to heterosexuality.[138]

However, this study has not remained unscathed by criticism. Gagnon and Simon have argued that its theoretical framework was in error in equating homosexuality with femininity and passivity. It would be difficult to interpret many of the forms of sexual activity exhibited by homosexuals as "passive" or "feminine." Additionally, Gagnon and Simon pointed out that the data on family backgrounds were obtained from the homosexual patients rather than from their parents. The patients may have retrospectively assessed their earlier family experiences in ways designed to gain the approval of their therapists.[139]

Sociologists have voiced a good deal of skepticism about claims that equate homosexuality, psychological maladjustment, and distorted family interaction patterns. They have pointed out that much of the theorizing and research has proceeded in terms of implicit assumptions picturing the homosexual as a person dominated by his sexual patterns and preferences and generally ignoring his other social roles and activities. In much of the literature, the homosexual is portrayed as a person living a bizarre and idiosyncratic life. But in the view of Simon and Gagnon, this literature has grossly exaggerated the deviant component in the total behavior of persons who happen to be homosexual, presenting the deviant in a social landscape that has been stripped of everything but his deviant commitment. In their perspective on homosexuality, they contended that homosexuality is a heterogeneous category, representing many different sexual styles, and that homosexuals also occupy nonsexual roles. As in the case of heterosexuals, the particular forms of sexual activity in which homosexuals engage are quite varied and they also change over time, making it quite misleading to speak of homosexuality as though it is some uniform entity. Simon and Gagnon also argued that much more attention should be paid to the life cycle and career adjustments homosexuals go through after having become engaged in this line of sexual behavior, with less concern for the question of etiology.[140] They observed that:

It is necessary to move away from an obsessive concern with the sexuality of the individual, and attempt to see the homosexual in terms of the broader attachments that he must make to live in the world around him. Like the heterosexual, the homosexual must come to terms with the problems that are attendant upon being a member of society: he must find a place to work, learn to live with or without his family, be involved or apathetic in political life, find a group of friends to talk to and be with, fill his leisure time usefully or frivolously, handle all of the common and uncommon problems of impulse control and personal gratification, and in some manner socialize his sexual interests.[141]

Evelyn Hooker has provided some valuable data on homosexuals and their sexual patterns.[142] She observed that male homosexuals engage in varied and changeable forms of sexual activity, so that characterizations of such persons as "fellators," "insertees," "passive," or "active," oversimplify the real world.[143] Her most critical set of observations concerned the psychological adjustment of homosexuals. She showed that a group of 30 overt male homosexuals did not vary in psychological well-being from a sample of nonhomosexuals.[144] This finding was markedly at variance with the frequently stated opinion that homosexuals are neurotic or in some other way abnormal.

The introductory portion of this chapter suggested that acts of sexual deviation, including homosexuality, may sometimes be the product of situational causation. Some support for this argument came from Laud Humphries's study of men who patronize "tearooms" (public restrooms) to engage in impersonal homosexual acts.[145] Over half of the men Humphries observed were married and living with their wives. For many of them, involvement in acts of fellatio represented a quick, inexpensive, and impersonal alternative sexual outlet, additional to sexual intercourse with their wives. Most of the participants in these sexual acts refrained from sustained social intercourse with their sexual partners, to the point of avoiding even verbal communication with them. Humphries's data suggested that many of the participants in "tearoom" sex were without homosexual self-images.

The social world of homosexuals in American society has been the subject of fictional treatment[146] as well as objective scrutiny by social researchers including Donald Cory and John LeRoy[147] and James Reinhardt.[148] Maurice Leznoff and William Westley studied the homosexual community in a Canadian city and observed the existence of both "secret" and "overt" homosexuals.[149] Helmer's description of the homosexual subculture in New York City also pointed to the existence of organized social relations among homosexuals in that city.[150] These materials indicate that American cities include a group of homosexuals who frequent "gay bars," restaurants catering to "gay" individuals, and clothing stores that feature particular lines of apparel. The homosexuals who patronize these "gay" enterprises also restrict much of their social interaction to other homosexuals. Also, Reiss,[151] Raven,[152] and Ginsburg[153] have described the behavior patterns of "hustlers" who sell sexual services to homosexuals. However, some recent studies have also turned up evidence that the so-called "gay community" in American cities does not exist, rather, American urban "gays" are involved in a variety of life-styles, sexual patterns, and the like that are slurred over by those who speak of a single "gay community."[154]

summary

This chapter has endeavored to illuminate a number of questions concerning crimes against persons: homicides, assaults, and sexual offenses.

A central point of this chapter had to do with the relatively mundane character of violence in American society. Television and other mass media portrayals of vicious "mad dogs" and psychopathic killers, along with characterizations of murder as involving clever planning and the like, are wide of the mark. Most assaults and homicides are relatively unplanned, crude outbursts growing out of distortions in interpersonal relationships between marital partners or acquaintances. At the same time, the specific circumstances within which acts of violence occur tend to be quite diverse. Finally, much of the evidence pointed to the importance of situational elements in violence, in which these offenses stem from relatively spontaneous quarrels, arguments, or other interactional events, often involving persons who have been drinking. The research studies on assaults and homicides were also relatively consistent in underscoring the importance of subcultures of violence and victim-precipitation in accounting for violent behavior in American society.

Another major contention of this chapter was that traditional views of sex in American society, in which sexual conduct of all kinds was regarded as immoral or at least not a fit subject for public discussion, have impeded the development of an adequate social-psychological account of sexual learning and sexual socialization. As a consequence, we do not yet have an adequate benchmark or conceptualization regarding the learning of nondeviant patterns of sexual conduct against which to examine various forms of sexual deviance.

The studies of apprehended sexual offenders showed that most of these individuals are not "monsters," but rather, most of them have been involved in relatively mundane and nonviolent forms of sexual misconduct. Additionally, the evidence indicated that even many of the more exotic or seemingly bizarre forms of sexual criminality, such as father–daughter incest, turn out, upon further examination, to be amenable to explanation in sociological terms.

The patterns of sexual criminality examined in this chapter are quite varied, ranging from statutory rape to incest and violent sexual assaults. Statutory rape and forcible rape are forms of sexual misconduct that are not markedly different in character from noncriminal sexual intercourse. The persons who are involved in these kinds of activities do not usually turn out to be markedly different from individuals who refrain from rape.

Although laymen are quick to contend that violent sexual assaultists, nonviolent sexual offenders, incest offenders, and homosexuals are all driven by psychological disorders or emotional problems of relatively great severity, that view is not supported by much evidence, except in the case of violent sexual assaultists. Nonviolent sexual offenders and incest offenders are most frequently persons who respond in sexually inappropriate ways to stressful or unusual social circumstances, but they do not usually exhibit clear signs of mental pathology of some kind or another. Similarly, there is little firm evidence to support laymen notions about "sick" homosexuals.

This chapter concludes the examination of garden-variety crimes. In the next chapter, lawbreakers who are sequestered in corporate board rooms rather than roaming the streets are the subject of scrutiny.

notes

[1]For a discussion of homicide law, see Herbert A. Bloch and Gilbert Geis, *Man, Crime, and Society,* 2nd ed. (New York: Random House, 1970), pp. 222–24.
[2]Manfred S. Guttmacher, *The Mind of the Murderer* (New York: Farrar, Straus & Giroux, 1960), pp.

13–106; for another eclectic discussion of murder, see John M. MacDonald, *The Murderer and His Victim* (Springfield, Ill.: Chas C Thomas, 1961).

[3]W. Lindesay Neustatter, *The Mind of the Murderer* (New York: Philosophical Library, 1957).

[4]For a sophisticated attempt to delineate types of violence-prone persons, see Hans Toch, *Violent Men* (Chicago: Aldine, 1969). Also, for a useful study that focused upon offender–victim social-inter-action patterns in homicide, see James Boudouris, "A Classification of Homicides," *Criminology*, 11 (February 1974), 525–90. Boudouris studied all homicides in Detroit between 1926 and 1968 and developed a typology of 12 interactional patterns in homicide. The most frequent homicide type was the domestic relations one, involving husband–wife violence. Homicides involving friends or ac-quaintances were also frequently encountered, as were homicides growing out of criminal transac-tions. For a study of self-image patterns of violent offenders, along with observations on their defi-nitions of violent situations, see Lonnie H. Athens, *Violent Criminal Acts and Actors* (London: Routledge and Kegan Paul, 1980).

[5]Marvin E. Wolfgang, *Patterns of Criminal Homicide* (Philadelphia: University of Pennsylvania Press, 1958).

[6]Robert C. Bensing and Oliver Schroeder, Jr., *Homicide in an Urban Community* (Springfield, Ill.: Chas C Thomas, 1960).

[7]Henry A. Bullock, "Urban Homicide in Theory and Fact," *Journal of Criminal Law, Criminology and Police Science*, 45 (January–February 1955), 565–75.

[8]Alex D. Pokorny, "A Comparison of Homicides in Two Cities," *Journal of Criminal Law, Criminol-ogy and Police Science*, 56 (December 1965), 479–87; see also Pokorny, "Human Violence: A Com-parison of Homicide, Aggravated Assault, Suicide, and Attempted Suicide," *Journal of Criminal Law, Criminology and Police Science*, 56 (December 1965), 488–97.

[9]Wolfgang, *Patterns of Criminal Homicide*, pp. 96–119.

[10]Bensing and Schroeder, *Homicide in an Urban Community*, pp. 8–10.

[11]Bullock, "Urban Homicide in Theory and Fact," p. 566.

[12]Bensing and Schroeder, *Homicide in an Urban Community*, pp. 8–10; Wolfgang, *Patterns of Crim-inal Homicide*, pp. 96–119.

[13]Bullock, "Urban Homicide in Theory and Fact," pp. 567–69.

[14]Bensing and Schroeder, *Homicide in an Urban Community*, pp. 105–37.

[15]Wolfgang, *Patterns of Criminal Homicide*, pp. 120–33; Bullock, "Urban Homicide in Theory and Fact," pp. 570–75; Pokorny, "A Comparison of Homicides in Two Cities," pp. 481–82.

[16]Wolfgang, *Patterns of Criminal Homicide*, pp. 185–89, 203–21.

[17]Pokorny, "A Comparison of Homicides in Two Cities," p. 483.

[18]Bensing and Schroeder, *Homicide in an Urban Community*, pp. 72–77.

[19]Wolfgang, *Patterns of Criminal Homicide*, pp. 79–95.

[20]Bensing and Schroeder, *Homicide in an Urban Community*, p. 84.

[21]Wolfgang, *Patterns of Criminal Homicide*, pp. 31–35.

[22]Bensing and Schroeder, *Homicide in an Urban Community*, p. 41.

[23]Pokorny, "A Comparison of Homicides in Two Cities," pp. 480–81.

[24]Wolfgang, *Patterns of Criminal Homicide*, pp. 65–78.

[25]Bensing and Schroeder, *Homicide in an Urban Community*, pp. 70–71.

[26]Ibid., pp. 128–29; Wolfgang, *Patterns of Criminal Homicide*, pp. 36–39.

[27]Wolfgang, *Patterns of Criminal Homicide*, pp. 168–74.

[28]Ibid., pp. 134–67. On this point, see also MacDonald, *The Murderer and His Victim*, pp. 18–20. He summarized a series of studies which showed that a third or more of the offenders in homicide cases had been drinking prior to the act of violence.

[29]Wolfgang, *Patterns of Criminal Homicide*, pp. 264–65.

[30]Bullock, "Urban Homicide in Theory and Fact," p. 575.

[31]For a valuable discussion and resumé of the literture on this topic, see Frank E. Hartung. *Crime, Law and Society* (Detroit, Mich.: Wayne State University Press, 1965), pp. 136–66; see also Marvin E. Wolfgang and Franco Ferracuti, *The Subculture of Violence* (New York: Barnes and Noble, 1967).

[32]Miller has provided the richest description of these ingredients of lower-class life. See Walter B.

Miller, "Lower Class Culture as a Generating Milieu of Gang Delinquency," *Journal of Social Issues*, 14, (3:1958), 5–19; Miller, "Implications of Urban Lower Class Culture for Social Work," *Social Service Review*, 33 (September 1959), 219–36.

[33]Leroy G. Schultz, "Why the Negro Carries Weapons," *Journal of Criminal Law, Criminology and Police Science*, 53 (December 1962), 476–83.

[34]Ibid., p. 479.

[35]Raymond D. Gastil, "Homicide and a Regional Culture of Violence," *American Sociological Review*, 36 (June 1971), 412–27; Colin Loftin and Robert H. Hill, "Regional Subculture and Homicide: An Examination of the Gastil–Hackney Thesis," *American Sociological Review*, 39 (October 1974), 714–24; William G. Doerner, "A Regional Analysis of Homicide Rates in the United States," *Criminology*, 13 (May 1975), 90–101.

[36]John R. Hepburn, "Subcultures, Violence, and the Subculture of Violence: An Old Rut or a New Road? *Criminology*, 9 (May 1971), 87–98. For some negative evidence on the violence subculture argument, see Sandra J. Ball-Rokeach, "Values and Violence: A Test of the Subculture of Violence Thesis," *American Sociological Review*, 38 (December 1973), 736–49; but also see Stephen Magura, "Is There a Subculture of Violence?" *American Sociological Review*, 40 (December 1975), 831–35.

[37]John L. Gillin, *The Wisconsin Prisoner* (Madison: University of Wisconsin Press, 1946), pp. 56–60; see also Gillin, "Murder as a Sociological Phenomenon," *Annals of the American Academy of Political and Social Science*, 284 (November 1952), 20–25.

[38]Gillin, *The Wisconsin Prisoner*, pp. 9–11.

[39]Stuart Palmer, *A Study of Murder* (New York: Thomas Y. Crowell, 1960).

[40]Ibid., pp. 21–37.

[41]Harwin L. Voss and John R. Hepburn, "Patterns in Criminal Homicide in Chicago," *Journal of Criminal Law, Criminology and Police Science*, 59 (December 1968), 499–508.

[42]For an analysis of the high homicide rate in Finland, see Veli Verkko, *Homicides and Suicides in Finland and Their Dependence on National Character* (Copenhagen: G.E.C. Gads Forlag, 1951).

[43]Paul Bohannan, ed., *African Homicide and Suicide* (Princeton, N.J.: Princeton University Press, 1960).

[44]Ibid., pp. 230–34.

[45]Ibid., p. 233.

[46]Ibid., pp. 236–37.

[47]Ibid., pp. 237–39.

[48]Ibid., p. 242.

[49]Jacqueline H. Straus and Murray A. Straus, "Suicide, Homicide, and Social Structure in Ceylon," *American Journal of Sociology*, 58 (March 1953), 461–69.

[50]Arthur L. Wood, *Crime and Aggression in Changing Ceylon* (Philadelphia: Transactions of the American Philosophical Society, 1961); Wood, "A Socio-Structural Analysis of Murder, Suicide, and Economic Crime in Ceylon," *American Sociological Review*, 26 (October 1961), 744–53.

[51]Kaare Svalastoga. "Homicide and Social Contact in Denmark," *American Journal of Sociology*, 62 (July 1956), 37–41.

[52]Edwin D. Driver, "Interaction and Criminal Homicide in India," *Social Forces*, 40 (December 1961), 153–58.

[53]Richard A. Peterson, David J. Pittman, and Patricia O'Neal, "Stabilities in Deviance: A Study of Assaultive and Non-Assaultive Offenders," *Journal of Criminal Law, Criminology and Police Science*, 53 (March 1962), 44–48.

[54]David J. Pittman and William Handy, "Patterns in Criminal Aggravated Assault," *Journal of Criminal Law, Criminology and Police Science*, 53 (December 1964), 462–70.

[55]Ibid., pp. 463–67.

[56]Ibid., pp. 467–68.

[57]Julian Roebuck and Ronald Johnson, "The Negro Drinker and Assaulter as a Criminal Type," *Crime and Delinquency*, 8 (January 1962), 21–33.

[58]Gresham M. Sykes, *The Society of Captives* (Princeton, N.J.: Princeton University Press, 1958), pp. 84–108.

[59]Clarence Schrag, "Some Foundations for a Theory of Correction," in *The Prison*, Donald R. Cressey ed. (New York: Holt, Rinehart & Winston, 1961), pp. 346–56; Schrag, "A Preliminary Criminal Topology," *Pacific Sociological Review*, 4 (Spring 1961), 11–16.

[60]Donald L. Garrity, "The Prison as a Rehabilitation Agency," in *The Prison*, Cressey ed., pp. 375–78.

[61]R.L. Jenkins and Lester E. Hewitt, "Types of Personality Structure Encountered in Child Guidance Clinics," *American Journal of Orthopsychiatry*, 14 (January 1944), 84–94; Jenkins, *Breaking Patterns of Defeat* (Philadelphia: Lippincott, 1954), pp. 9–28; Albert J. Reiss, Jr., "Social Correlates of Psychological Types of Delinquency," *American Sociological Review*, 17 (December 1952), 710–18; John W. Kinch, "Self-Conceptions of Types of Delinquents," *Sociological Inquiry*, 32 (Spring 1962), 228–34; Fritz Redl and David Wineman, *The Aggressive Child* (New York: Free Press, 1960); Leonard Berkowitz, *Aggression* (New York: McGraw-Hill, 1962); Albert Bandura and Richard H. Walters, *Adolescent Aggression* (New York: The Ronald Press Co., 1959).

[62]This point has been made regarding homosexuality by Howard S. Becker, in his review of Hendrik M. Ruitenbeek, ed., *The Problem of Homosexuality in Modern Society* (New York: Dutton, 1963), in *American Journal of Sociology*, 70 (July 1964), 130.

[63]This same point (regarding homosexuality) has been made by Gagnon and Simon. See John H. Gagnon and William Simon, *Sexual Conduct* (Chicago: Aldine, 1973), p. 36. They contended that: ". . . the problem of finding out how some people become homosexual requires an adequate theory of how others become heterosexual; that is, one cannot explain homosexuality in one way and leave heterosexuality as a large residual category labeled 'all other.' Indeed, the explanation of homosexuality in this sense may await the explanation of the larger and more modal category of adjustment."

[64]One example of psychiatric analysis of sexual deviation is Anthony Storr, *Sexual Deviation* (Baltimore: Penguin Books, 1964).

[65]For an incisive analysis of the compulsive hypothesis, see Donald R. Cressey, "The Differential Association Theory and Compulsive Crimes," *Journal of Criminal Law, Criminology and Police Science*, 45 (May–June 1954), 29–40. Cressey noted that offenders to whom the label "compulsive" is attached, such as "kleptomaniacs," are motivated in the same way that other criminals are motivated. They select places in which to carry out their acts, plan their crimes in advance, and behave in other ways indicating deliberate, rational thought. Cressey suggested that application of the "compulsive crime" label most frequently occurs when the subject is not able to verbalize about his or her behavior in terms of current, popular, and sanctioned motives.

[66]Irvin L. Child, "Socialization," in *Handbook of Social Psychology*, vol. 2, Gardner Lindzey, ed. (Reading, Mass.: Addison-Wesley, 1954), p. 667.

[67]For examples of psychoanalytic theory applied to sex offenders, see Bernard Glueck, Sr., "Sex Offenses: A Clinical Approach," *Law and Contemporary Problems*, 25 (Spring 1960), 279–91; Clifford Allen, *A Textbook of Psychosexual Disorders* (London: Oxford University Press, 1962).

[68]Harry Stack Sullivan, *The Interpersonal Theory of Psychiatry* (New York: W. W. Norton & Co., 1953), pp. 263–96.

[69]Irving Bieber, Harvey J. Dain, Paul R. Dince, Marvin G. Drellich, Henry G. Grand, Ralph H. Gundlach, Malvina W. Kremer, Alfred H. Rifkin, Cornelia B. Wilbur, Toby B. Bieber, *Homosexuality* (New York: Basic Books, 1962).

[70]Manford H. Kuhn, "Kinsey's View of Human Behavior," *Social Problems*, 1 (April 1954), 123.

[71]For a general review of existing writings and research in the anthropology and sociology of sex, see Winston Ehrmann, "Social Determinants of Human Sexual Behavior," in *Determinants of Human Sexual Behavior*, George Winokur, ed. (Springfield, Ill.: Chas C Thomas, 1963), pp. 142–63.

[72]For one attempt to outline the stages of sexual development and learning, see Gagnon and Simon, *Sexual Conduct*, pp. 100–103. Also see Kenneth Plummer, *Sexual Stigma* (London: Routledge and Kegan Paul, 1975).

[73]Gagnon and Simon, *Sexual Conduct*, Chapter One, "The Social Origins of Sexual Development," pp. 1–26.

[74]Ibid., p. 19.

[75]Alfred C. Kinsey, Wardell B. Pomeroy, and Clyde E. Martin, *Sexual Behavior in the Human Male* (Philadelphia: Saunders, 1948); for a review and critique of the Kinsey studies see "Sexual Behavior in American Society," *Social Problems*, 1 (April 1954). This issue contains a series of papers centered around the Kinsey studies.

[76]David A. Ward and Gene G. Kassebaum, "Homosexuality: A Model of Adaptation in a Prison for Women," *Social Problems*, 12 (Fall 1964), 159–77; Ward and Kassebaum, *Women's Prison* (Chicago: Aldine, 1965); Rose Giallombardo, *Society of Women* (New York: John Wiley, 1966).

[77]Albert J. Reiss, Jr., "The Social Integration of Queers and Peers," *Social Problems*, 9 (Fall 1961), 102–20.

[78]John H. Gagnon, "Sexuality and Sexual Learning in the Child," *Psychiatry*, 28 (August 1965), 212–28; see also Daniel G. Brown and David B. Lynn, "Human Sexual Development: An Outline of Components and Concepts," *Journal of Marriage and the Family*, 28 (May 1966), 155–62; Clark E. Vincent, ed., *Human Sexuality in Medical Education and Practice* (Springfield, Ill.: Chas C Thomas, 1968).

[79]Gagnon, "Sexuality and Sexual Learning in the Child," p. 223.

[80]Edwin M. Lemert, *Human Deviance, Social Problems, and Social Control*, 2nd ed. (Englewood Cliffs, N.J.: Prentice-Hall, Inc., 1972), pp. 26–61.

[81]Laud Humphries, *Tearoom Trade* (Chicago: Aldine, 1970).

[82]Stanton Wheeler, "Sex Offenses: A Sociological Critique," *Law and Contemporary Problems*, 25 (Spring 1960), 258–78. Also see Lorne Gibson, Rick Linden, and Stuart Johnson, "A Situational Theory of Rape," *Canadian Journal of Criminology*, 22 (January 1980), 51–65.

[83]Saul Toobert, Kenwood F. Bartelme, and Eugene S. Jones, "Some Factors Related to Pedophilia," *International Journal of Social Psychiatry*, 4 (Spring 1959), 272–79.

[84]Wheeler, "Sex Offenses: A Sociological Critique," pp. 258–59.

[85]Ibid., pp. 299–61.

[86]Homosexual acts in private between consenting adults are legal in 23 states: Alabama, California, Colorado, Connecticut, Delaware, Hawaii, Illinois, Indiana, Iowa, Maine, Massachusetts, Nebraska, New Hampshire, New Jersey, New Mexico, North Dakota, Ohio, Oregon, South Dakota, Vermont, Washington, West Virginia, and Wyoming.

[87]Edwin M. Schur, *Crimes Without Victims* (Englewood Cliffs, N.J.: Prentice-Hall, Inc., 1965); Gilbert Geis, *Not the Law's Business?* (Rockville, Md.: National Institute of Mental Health, 1972).

[88]For an excellent summary of American laws, with emphasis on the variations in these laws, see Morris Ploscowe, "Sex Offenses: The American Legal Context," *Law and Contemporary Problems*, 25 (Spring 1960), 217–24; see also Karl M. Bowman and Bernice Engle, "A Psychiatric Evaluation of Laws of Homosexuality," *American Journal of Psychiatry*, 112 (February 1956), 577–83; Karl M. Bowman, "Review of Sex Legislation and Control of Sex Offenders in the United States of America," in *Final Report on California Sexual Deviation Research*, State of California, Department of Mental Hygiene (Sacramento: State of California, 1954), pp. 15–40; John Drzazga, *Sex Crimes* (Springfield, Ill.: Chas C Thomas, 1960).

[89]For a somewhat incoherent but rather complete summary of studies, see Benjamin Karpman, *The Sexual Offender and His Offenses* (New York: The Julian Press, 1954).

[90]Benjamin Apfelberg, Carl Sugar, and Arnold Z. Pfeffer, "A Psychiatric Study of 250 Sex Offenders," *American Journal of Psychiatry*, 100 (May 1964), 762–70; John L. Gillin, *The Wisconsin Prisoner* (Madison: University of Wisconsin Press, 1946), pp. 11–13, 88–131; Manfred S. Guttmacher, *Sex Offenses* (New York: W.W. Norton Co., 1951).

[91]Albert Ellis and Ralph Brancale, *The Psychology of Sex Offenders* (Springfield, Ill.: Chas C Thomas, 1956); for a summary of this study, see Brancale, Ellis, and Ruth R. Doorbar, "Psychiatric and Psychological Investigations of Convicted Sex Offenders: A Summary Report," *American Journal of Psychiatry*, 109 (July 1952), 17–21.

[92]Ellis and Brancale, *The Psychology of Sex Offenders*, pp. 11–12.

[93]Ibid., p. 31.

[94]Ibid., pp. 26–63.

[95]State of California, Department of Mental Hygiene, *Final Report on California Sexual Deviation Research*.

[96]Ibid., pp. 94–98.

[97]Ibid., p. 99.

[98]Paul H. Gebhard, John H. Gagnon, Wardell B. Pomeroy, and Cornelia V. Christenson, *Sex Offenders* (New York: Harper & Row, 1965).

[99]Ibid., pp. 27–53.

[100]Ibid., pp. 10–11.

[101]Ibid., p. 66.

[102]Ibid., pp. 83–102.

[103]Ibid., pp. 177–206.

[104]Ibid., pp. 358–99.

[105]Female prostitution and lesbianism are not considered in this chapter. For some useful discussions of these matters, see Gagnon and Simon, "Sexual Deviance in Contemporary America," in Gagnon and Simon, *Sexual Deviance*; see also Gagnon and Simon, *Sexual Conduct*.

[106]Gebhard, et al., *Sex Offenders*, pp. 83–105.

[107]Ibid., p. 132.

[108]Camille E. Le Grand, "Rape and Rape Laws: Sexism in Society and Law," *California Law Review*, 61 (May 1973), 919–41. Also see Susan Brownmiller, *Against Our Will: Men, Women, and Rape* (New York: Simon & Schuster, 1975). For a valuable collection of essays on rape, see Duncan Chappell, Robley Geis, and Gilbert Geis, eds., *Forcible Rape: The Crime, the Victim, and the Offender* (New York: Columbia University Press, 1977).

[109]Asher R. Pacht, Seymour L. Halleck, and John C. Ehrmann, "Diagnosis and Treatment of the Sexual Offender: A Nine-Year Study," *American Journal of Psychiatry*, 118 (March 1962), 802–8. Also see Ellis and Brancale, *The Psychology of Sex Offenders*, pp. 32–37.

[110]Gebhard et al., *Sex Offenders*, pp. 155–206.

[111]Menachem Amir, "Forcible Rape," *Federal Probation*, 31 (March 1967), 51–58; see also Amir, *Patterns in Forcible Rape* (Chicago: University of Chicago Press, 1971).

[112]Fairly parallel findings were reported for Denmark by Svalastoga. See Kaare Svalastoga, "Rape and Social Structure," *Pacific Sociological Review*, 5 (Spring 1962), 48–53.

[113]Richard L. Jenkins, "The Making of a Sex Offender," in *Criminology: A Book of Readings*, Clyde B. Vedder, Samuel Koenig, and Robert E. Clark, eds. (New York: The Dryden Press, 1953), pp. 293–300.

[114]Ibid., p. 295. One piece of evidence bearing on this claim that aggression and sexuality are often joined in American society came from a study of dating behavior on a college campus. Over half the girls interviewed said that they had been offended by sexual aggression directed at them in the previous year. The 162 females who were the targets of aggression reported 1,022 such episodes of gratuitous force, with nearly one-quarter of them claiming that their dates had tried to coerce them into sexual intercourse. See Clifford Kirkpatrick and Eugene Kanin, "Male Sex Aggression on a University Campus," *American Sociological Review*, 22 (February 1957), 52–58.

[115]J. Paul de River, *The Sexual Criminal*, 2nd ed. (Springfield, Ill.: Chas C Thomas, 1956).

[116]Paul H. Gebhard and John H. Gagnon, "Male Sex Offenders Against Very Young Children," *American Journal of Psychiatry*, 121 (December 1964), 576–80.

[117]Apfelberg, Sugar, and Pfeffer, "A Psychiatric Study of 250 Sex Offenders."

[118]Gebhard et al., *Sex Offenders*, pp. 54–82.

[119]Ibid., pp. 380–99.

[120]Ibid., pp. 358–79. Also see Bernard C. Glueck, Jr., "Psychodynamic Patterns in the Homosexual Sex Offender," *American Journal of Psychiatry*, 112 (February 1956), 584–90; see also N. K. Rickles, *Exhibitionism* (Philadelphia: Lippincott, 1950); Alex J. Arieff and David B. Rotman, "One Hundred Cases of Indecent Exposure," *Journal of Nervous and Mental Disease*, 96 (November 1942), 523–28.

[121]Ellis and Brancale, *The Psychology of Sex Offenders*, pp. 41–44.

[122]Toobert et al., "Some Factors Related to Pedophilia."

[123]Charles H. McCaghy, "Child Molesters: A Study of Their Careers as Deviants," in *Criminal Behavior Systems*, Marshall B. Clinard and Richard Quinney, eds. (New York: Holt, Rinehart & Winston, 1967), pp. 75–88.

[124]Alex K. Gigeroff, J. W. Mohr, and R. E. Turner, "Sex Offenders on Probation: The Exhibitionist," *Federal Probation*, 32 (September 1968), 18–21.

[125]Walter T. Martin, "The Religious Attitudes of the Prison Sex Offender" (Master's thesis, University of Washington, 1944).

[126]Svend Riemer, "A Research Note on Incest," *American Journal of Sociology*, 45 (January 1940), 566–75.

[127]S. Kirson Weinberg, *Incest Behavior* (New York: Citadel Press, 1955).

[128]Noel Lustig, John W. Dresser, Seth W. Spellman, and Thomas J. Murray, "Incest," *Archives of General Psychiatry*, 14 (January 1966), 31–40; Irving Kaufman, Alice L. Peck, and Consuelo K. Tagiuri, "The Family Constellation and Overt Incestuous Relations Between Father and Daughter," *American Journal of Orthopsychiatry*, 24 (April 1954), 266–77; Hector Cavallin, "Incestuous Fathers: A Clinical Report," *American Journal of Psychiatry*, 122 (April 1966), 1132–38; Karin C. Meiselman, *Incest* (San Francisco: Jossey-Bass, Publishers, 1978); Susan Forward and Craig Buck, *Betrayal of Innocence: Incest and Its Devastation* (New York: Penguin Books, 1979).

[129]Evidence on public views of homosexuality can be found in Russell A. Ward, "Typifications of Homosexuals," *Sociological Quarterly*, 20 (Summer 1979), 411–23; Ray C. Rist, Lee J. Haggerty, and Don C. Gibbons, "Public Perceptions of Sexual 'Deviance': A Study on the Interrelations of Knowledge and Values," *Western Sociological Review*, 5 (Summer 1974), 66–81.

[130]For example, see Herbert Greenspan and John D. Campbell, "The Homosexual as a Personality Type," *American Journal of Psychiatry*, 101 (March 1945), 682–89.

[131]Edmund Bergler, *Homosexuality: Disease or Way of Life?* (New York: Hill and Wang, 1956).

[132]Abram Kardiner, "The Flight from Masculinity," in *The Problem of Homosexuality in Modern Society*, Hendrik M. Ruitenbeek, ed. (New York: Dutton, 1963), pp. 17–39.

[133]Clara Thompson, "Changing Concepts of Homosexuality in Psychoanalysis," in Ruitenbeek, *The Problem of Homosexuality in Modern Society*, pp. 40–51.

[134]Donald Webster Cory, *The Homosexual in America* (New York: Greenberg, Publisher, 1951).

[135]Bieber, et al., *Homosexuality*.

[136]Ibid., pp. 21–29.

[137]Ibid., pp. 44–84.

[138]Ibid., pp. 303–19.

[139]Gagnon and Simon, *Sexual Conduct*, pp. 133–34.

[140]Simon and Gagnon, *Sexual Conduct*, pp. 129–75.

[141]Ibid., p. 142.

[142]Evelyn Hooker, "Male Homosexuality," in *Taboo Topics*, Norman L. Farberow, ed. (New York: Atherton Press, 1963), pp. 44–55; Hooker, "Male Homosexuals and Their Worlds," in *Sexual Inversion*, Judd Marmor, ed. (New York: Basic Books, 1965), pp. 83–107; Hooker, "An Empirical Study of Some Relations Between Sexual Patterns and Gender Identity in Male Homosexuals," in *Sex Research: New Developments*, John Money, ed. (New York: Holt, Rinehart & Winston, 1965), pp. 24–52; Hooker, "The Adjustment of the Male Overt Homosexual," *Journal of Projective Techniques*, 21 (March 1957), 18–31.

[143]Hooker, "An Empirical Study of Some Relations Between Sexual Patterns and Gender Identity in Male Homosexuals."

[144]Hooker, "The Adjustment of the Male Overt Homosexual."

[145]Humphries, *Tearoom Trade*.

[146]John Rechy, *City of Night* (New York: Grove Press, 1963); Hubert Selby, *Last Exit to Brooklyn* (New York: Grove Press, 1964).

[147]Donald Webster Cory and John P. LeRoy, *The Homosexual and His Society* (New York: Citadel Press, 1963).

[148]James M. Reinhardt, *Sex Perversions and Sex Crimes* (Springfield, Ill.: Chas C Thomas, 1957), pp. 17–77.

[149]Maurice Leznoff and William A. Westley, "The Homosexual Community," *Social Problems*, 3 (April 1956), 257–63.

[150]William J. Helmer, "New York's Middle-Class Homosexuals," *Harper's*, 266 (March 1963), 85–92.

[151]Albert J. Reiss, Jr., "The Social Integration of Queers and Peers," *Social Problems*, 9 (Fall 1961), 102–20.

[152]Simon Raven, "Boys Will Be Boys: The Male Prostitute in London," in Ruitenbeek, *The Problem of Homosexuality in Modern Society*, pp. 279–90.

[153]Kenneth N. Ginsburg, "The 'Meat-Rack': A Study of the Male Homosexual Prostitute," *American Journal of Psychotherapy*, 21 (April 1967), 170–85.

[154]Edward William Delph, *The Silent Community* (Beverly Hills, Calif.: Sage Publications, 1978); Kenneth E. Read, *Other Voices: The Style of a Male Homosexual Tavern* (Novato, Calif.: Chandler and Sharp Publishers, 1980); Alan P. Bell and Martin S. Weinberg, *Homosexualities* (New York: Simon and Schuster, 1978).

organizational and occupational crime

Imagine the case of a suburban resident named John Smith who returns home late in the evening from a weekend excursion, only to discover that the lock on the back door of his house has been broken. Imagine further than he discovers that his stereo is missing, as well as his wife's jewelry and the family silverware. What will Smith do now? In all probability he will call the police, for he senses that he is the victim of a burglary. The police will have no hesitation about arresting the apprehended stranger, for they recognize a burglar when they see one. When the offender is convicted of the crime, he will find the condemnation of the community directed at him, for he is clearly a criminal person. The same could be said of assault, rape, and various forms of property crime, and of the persons who do these things. Nearly all people consider such behavior as crime. These are usually crude, highly visible attacks on persons or private property carried on by offenders who are undistinguished in appearance and unknown to the victims. Laymen, lawyers, and criminologists rarely ask whether these are really crimes or whether the actors are really criminals. In legal theory, these crimes are *mala en se*, that is, behavioral deviations uniformly condemned in the community. Criminal laws regarding these activities are viewed as the formal expression of conduct definitions described "in the mores." Such crimes stand in contrast to those that are *mala prohibita*—technically illegal actions that do not offend basic moral values or common public sentiments.

Is this all there is to crime? Are the nondescript persons who carry out those crude actions the sum total of our criminals? What about respectable citizens who engage in antisocial or unethical conduct? What shall we say about "suede shoe" salesmen who use trickery and deceit to sell merchandise to unwary customers? What of violations of antitrust statutes, labor–management regulations, or related rules? Should criminologists be concerned with such things as fee-splitting by physicians or embezzlement of large sums of money by trusted employees? Perhaps a sociological conception of crime that focuses on socially harmful conduct should be developed.

Criminologists have had a good deal to say about activities of this kind. Most of them have lumped these offenses together as "white-collar crime," Edwin Sutherland's term for violations of laws designed to regulate conduct of business affairs. Used in this fashion, white-collar crime refers to illegal actions undertaken by individuals to contribute to the financial success of the organization. They violate the law *for* the firm, although they may also reap personal rewards and financial gain as well. However, the term has been loosely defined and indiscriminately employed since it was first introduced.[1] Even Sutherland failed to use it consistently. The label has often been attached to such actions as embezzlement, which bear little relationship to violations of regulatory provisions in business. Embezzlers are "enemies within" who surreptitiously steal the assets of the organization and make no contribution to the economic health of the business concern. Many other forms of conduct to which the term has been applied have even less in common with the original meaning of the concept.

Blanket application of a single term to unrelated kinds of activity will not do; neither will an attempt to analyze all forms of criminality under a single encompassing label, as though these activities had a good deal in common. Some distinctions must be made regarding unlike forms of behavior that occur in the business and corporate world. These disparate acts must be sorted into relatively homogeneous behavior units if causal progress is to be made.

The following pages examine several categories of criminality. The term *organizational crime* is reserved for violations of business regulations or occupational roles carried on as contributory to the business or occupational enterprise.[2] An offense will be said to be an organizational one insofar as it represents violation of a legal rule constructed to govern business affairs or occupational practice and insofar as the law violation took place as a part of the conduct of regular business or occupational activities. By this definition, misrepresentation in advertising is an organizational crime, embezzlement is not. Corporate crime is a major form of organizational crime, but there are other violations, not restricted to major corporations, that are also included in the general category. These offenses occur in small businesses and organizations. Organizational offenses are also distinguished from the common or conventional crimes of persons of comfortable economic circumstances. Murder, manslaughter, rape, or drunk driving by high-status individuals need no special label, and these lawbreakers are not discussed in this chapter. Embezzlement, in which employees are involved in stealing from the organization, is not organizational crime because it is not lawbreaking as a part of regular business practice. Finally, certain offenses, such as "ambulance chasing" by lawyers and other crimes engaged in by professional persons are singled out for attention. These are discussed as occupational "fringe" violations because they are frequently regarded with some condemnation within the professions in which they occur. Although these acts use professional skills, they are occupationally deviant and are often committed by marginal figures within the professional group. They are usually endeavors of individuals acting alone rather than organizational events involving a collection of fellow deviants.

organizational crime

ORGANIZATIONAL CRIME DEFINED

What is meant by organizational crimes? Laura Schrager and James F. Short have offered one definition: "*Organizational crimes are illegal acts of omission or commission of an individual or a group of individuals in a legitimate formal organization in accordance with the operative goals of the organization, which have serious physical or economic impact on employees, consumers or the general public"* (emphasis in the original).[3] A closely-parallel description has indicated that they involve:

criminal acts in which employees violate the law for the benefit of their employer (although the individual employee may benefit from these violations too). . . . The organizational crime category is comprised of violations of state and federal regulatory statutes. The violations are usually processed by such federal regulatory agencies as the Federal Trade Commission, the Securities and Exchange Commission, and the Attorney General's office. Informal or civil-court disposition of these cases is common, because of the difficulties of criminal prosecution. That is, partly because many of these activities are complex in character, it is often difficult to demonstrate that a clear-cut violation of law has occurred.

"Ignorance of the law" is not, in most cases, an important factor in these violations. That is, the offenders were involved in activities which they recognized as illegal or probably illegal. What does appear to be significant in these cases is a process in which business and corporate groups have come to define violations of regulatory statutes as acceptable or necessary conduct. Many of them acknowledge the moral superiority of regulatory provisions over prevailing business ethics, but legitimacy is withdrawn from these regulatory norms on the grounds that violation of such laws is necessary in order to survive in business, in order to regularize competition, and so on. In other words, it is likely that many business violators would prefer to conform to the law, but at the same time, they define the economic situation as demanding deviant conduct. If this line of argument is correct, explanations seeking to locate the genesis of organizational offenses in the backgrounds and personalities of the offenders would be misguided. Instead, these offenders are normal, conventional persons who come to learn definitions of the situation favorable to violation of law in the course of involvement in business or corporate organization.[4]

DEVELOPMENT OF THE CONCEPT

Relatively inarticulate observations about the criminality of respectable citizens, often accompanied by a good deal of moral indignation, have been made by many sociologists over the past 50 or 60 years. Recurrent reports in the mass media concerning criminality and unethical conduct by businessmen, professionals, and other high-status persons have also stimulated interest in this phenomenon. For example, many years ago *Reader's Digest* conducted an informal survey of illegal or questionable business tactics among auto repairmen, radio repairmen, and automobile mechanics, which turned up evidence of widespread "crookedness."[5] In the same way, a former retail furniture salesman has revealed some of the hazards the customer runs in patronizing "borax houses" selling inexpensive furniture.[6] However, Sutherland turned the behavioral deviations of high-status persons into an important sociological category which he termed "white-collar crime."[7]

Sutherland offered several accounts of what he meant by "white-collar crime." In one place, he declared: "White-collar crime may be defined approximately as a crime committed by a person of respectability and high status in the course of his occupation."[8] Elsewhere, he said: "The white collar criminal is defined as a person with high socioeconomic status who violates the laws designed to regulate his occupational activities."[9] The first of these definitions implied that embezzlers are included, while the second suggested that they should not be so designated. In yet another discussion, Sutherland mentioned "robber barons" and other rapacious early figures in American commerce and industry as white-collar criminals. He declared that Philip Musica, alias Donald F. Coster, who stole a huge sum of money from the McKesson-Robbins drug company while its president, was a white-collar criminal, as were other individuals of this ilk, such as Insull, Kruger, and Sinclair. In that essay, he also named abortions, fee-splitting, political graft, and embezzlement as forms of white-collar crime.[10]

Many persons who adopted Sutherland's term to their own uses showed an even more cavalier attitude toward precise definitions. No wonder critics of this concept warned that objective analysis of criminality could deteriorate into denunciatory comments by the criminologist directed at activities that offend his or her private sensibilities but have little or nothing in common with crime.[11] The term might be reduced to a pejorative one rather than a scientific concept.

Although it has been loosely defined, the concept has not been so recklessly employed in actual research studies. The several major investigations of organizational or white-collar crime have all directed attention at a body of violations of regulatory provisions designed to control business operations. It seems clear that these are the kinds of behavior to which Sutherland intended the term to apply. Accordingly, the concept should properly concern these forms of conduct and should exclude embezzlement and the like.

STUDIES OF ORGANIZATIONAL CRIME

Sutherland's research. Sutherland's investigation of the violations of corporations was once the best-known study of this kind.[12] He examined the corporate life histories of the 70 largest manufacturing, mining, and mercantile corporations in the United States, which had been in existence for an average of 45 years. He assembled the data on violations of regulations in the categories of restraint of trade, misrepresentation in advertising, infringement of patents, trademarks, and copyrights, unfair labor practices, rebates, financial fraud and trust violations, violations of wartime regulations, and certain miscellaneous offenses.

Sutherland argued that these were criminal activities because the regulations or rules they violate meet the two basic criteria of crimes: a legal description of acts as socially injurious, and legal provision of a penalty for violations.[13] Moreover, he noted that many of the regulatory statutes state explicitly that the forbidden acts are crimes or misdemeanors, and many of the laws have logical roots in the common law, so that false advertising is an extension of common-law fraud. Sutherland was forced to concede that the criminal status of certain of these activities was in question. In the instance of patent, trademark, and copyright infringements, federal statutes do not explicitly define some forms of infringement as crimes, nor do the laws provide criminal penalties, such as punitive damages. Sutherland admitted that of 222 decisions on infringements included in his data, 201 appeared not to constitute acts of criminality.[14]

The 70 corporations had been involved over their organizational lifetimes in 980 violations (including the aforementioned 201 infringement cases). The most criminal corporation had been implicated in 50 decisions, whereas the least criminal had been involved in a single decision. These organizations had an average of 14 adverse decisions in their careers.

Differential implementation of the law emerged most strikingly from the corporation records, in that only 158 (16 percent) of the 980 decisions had been reached in criminal courts. In other words, only 16 percent of these cases were crimes in the technical sense that they had been so labeled in a criminal tribunal. Of the rest, 425 had been reached in civil or equity courts, and 397 had been produced informally through commission orders or other procedures.[15] In Sutherland's view the use of civil or informal, rather than criminal, proceedings against business organizations was related to the high status of businessmen, the general trend away from harsh punishments, and relatively unorganized public resentment regarding these activities.[16]

Violations of wartime regulations. Two important investigations of violations of World War II rationing laws have been conducted. The first, by Marshall Clinard, dealt with black-market operations.[17] Like Sutherland, Clinard felt compelled to defend labeling as crime the violations of rationing and economic-control regulations imposed during the war. He argued that nearly all these rules defined the relevant behavior as offenses and allowed the use of criminal penalties in case of violations. However, the criminal status of certain behavioral forms Clinard studied was not clear, for example, civil-rule violations that were unintentional and to which criminal sanctions were not applied. Additionally, the criminal status was ambiguous in certain violations of administrative orders of governmental agencies, rather than statutory rules, which were handled under contempt proceedings.[18]

However one might label the activities Clinard studied, the rules violated were clearly required during wartime. He made a convincing case for the importance of these regulations in maintaining an equitable distribution of scarce goods and minimizing the long-term costs of the war.[19] He showed that violations of these regulations were so widespread that the war effort was jeopardized on more than one occasion. For example, during a nine-month period in 1944–45, counterfeit gasoline stamps involving 88 million gallons of gas were discovered, along with stamps for great quantities of rationed sugar and meat.[20] Price-ceiling violations, tie-in sales, and mislabeling and quality violations were similarly commonplace.

How can these violations be explained in the face of strong public support for price controls and rationing during wartime?[21] Who were the offenders? According to Clinard, the black-market violators were principally conventional businessmen, many of whom were carrying on forms of business conduct closely akin to tactics they had used prior to wartime and the imposition of controls. The major exception, in which conventional criminals were involved, was the counterfeiting of rationing stamps.[22] Clinard attributed these law violations to a combination of factors, one of which was the lenient penalties handed out for violations. These were not sufficient to act as a deterrent to illegality.[23] He also maintained that differential association among businessmen, in which group support was provided for hostile attitudes toward the regulations, was a major determinant of lawbreaking. He also believed that personality differences among businessmen must have played some part in their behavior, for some disobeyed the laws whereas others, similarly situated in the business world, did not.[24]

Another of the investigations was conducted by Frank Hartung and concerned violations of wartime regulations in the wholesale meat industry in Detroit.[25] Between 1942 and 1946, regulatory agencies in Detroit processed 122 cases of price violations and other illegal acts. Only two of the offenders had prior records of criminality, so these were predominantly acts of lawbreaking by respectable businessmen. The offenders paid $132,811 in damages and nearly $100,000 in fines; a few were given jail terms as well. A major conclusion was that there was a marked disparity between the generally lenient penalties invoked and the seriousness of the activities, measured in monetary terms and other ways as well.

ILLEGAL CORPORATE BEHAVIOR

Marshall Clinard and his associates completed in the late 1970s a very large study of corporate crime; although modeled somewhat after Sutherland's pioneering investigation, it is considerably more comprehensive in scope and more complex in design.[26] The research effort focused on the 582 largest corporations in the United States, of which 477 were manufacturing concerns, 18 wholesale organizations, 66 retail corporations, and 21 service organizations. The data consisted of detailed information from several sources concerning all enforcement actions taken against the corporations by 24 federal agencies in 1975 and 1976. The social and economic significance of corporate crime was clearly identified by Clinard and colleagues in the following observations:

". . . It is essential that one recognize the significance of the small frequencies of corporate cases and why they must be evaluated differently from statistics on ordinary crimes such as assault, burglary, or larceny. A single case of corporate law violation may involve millions or even billions of dollars of losses. The injuries caused by product defects or impure or dangerous drugs can involve thousands of persons in a single case. For example, in one case, the electrical price-fixing conspiracy of the 1960s, the losses amounted to over $2 billion, a sum far greater than the total losses from the 3 million burglaries in any given year. At the same time, the average loss from a larceny-theft is $165 and from a burglary $422, and the persons who commit these offenses may receive sentences of as much as five to ten years, or even longer. For the crimes committed by the large corporations the sole punishment often consists of warnings, consent orders, or comparatively small fines.[27]

Clinard and his associates reported that more than 60 percent of the large corporations had at least one enforcement action initiated against them in the two-year period. Of the manufacturing corporations, 300 had violated the law at least once, with an average of 4.8 actions against the violating organizations. Forty percent of the manufacturing corporations had been involved in repeated violations, with about one-fifth of them showing five or more offenses.

Clinard et al. argued that *"the world of the giant corporations does not necessarily require illegal behavior in order to compete successfully"* (emphasis in the original).[28] They based that claim on the fact that 40 percent of the corporations did not have a legal action taken against them in the two-year period. However, that conclusion seems weak, given the possibility that many of the 40 "noncriminal" corporations may have been involved in *undetected* violations or had legal actions taken against them in earlier years.

The offending corporations were responsible for a wide range of illegal acts, in part because of the proliferation of regulatory statutes in the past decades. With more laws come more crimes. These offenses fell into a number of broad groupings: environmental violations, financial violations, labor violations, manufacturing violations, unfair trade practices, water or air pollution, tax violations, and a number of other types of violations.

Although it might be supposed that smaller corporations are under greater pressure to violate the laws than are larger, more successful ones, Clinard et al. indicated that the largest corporations actually contributed a disproportionate share of the illegal acts.

Law violations were not distributed uniformly across all manufacturing groups, rather, motor-vehicle, drug, and oil-refining industries contributed nearly half of all violations and 40 percent of all serious or moderately serious infractions.

How were these offending corporations dealt with? The Clinard report indicated that the lenient, differential treatment reported by Sutherland continues to dominate in the enforcement of federal regulatory statutes. Warnings alone were issued by the 24 federal agencies in the majority of cases. In addition, in those instances where monetary penalties were imposed upon violating corporations, most of these were in the $1,000 range, with over 80 percent of them being for $5,000 or less. Only 16 corporation officials received sentences of imprisonment, almost always for very short sentences of a month or less.

Clinard and associates also endeavored to identify the characteristics of corporations that were predictive of law-abiding or illegal conduct. Financial strains due to unfavorable earnings and the like were to some degree implicated in corporate law violations, but the Clinard report also argued that variations in the corporate environment in terms of norms and attitudes toward unethical and illegal practices were also involved.

CONSUMER FRAUD

The principle of *caveat emptor,* or "Let the buyer beware," has always been dominant in merchandising relationships in the United States. Business tradition has always maintained that the customer should protect himself from the merchant. The evidence indicates that this tradition is still alive and that consumer fraud is endemic in the United States. For example, David Caplovitz directed a large-scale study of consumer practices in four low-income housing project areas in New York City.[29] He found that the poor do pay more, for, among other things, customers were often charged whatever the merchant thought he could obtain for his goods, with fixed prices being a rarity. Furthermore, the merchants often charged the poor exorbitant prices for inferior quality items and sold them used merchandise that was supposedly new. Although this activity was essentially unethical, much of it was also specifically illegal. Low-income citizens were frequently the victims of commercial crime directed at them by merchants and businessmen.

Other investigations all over the United States have turned up findings parallel to those of Caplovitz. Supermarkets, for example, have been observed charging higher prices to ghetto residents than to suburbanites for comparable items. Warren Magnuson and Jean Carper drew a large variety of these dismal facts together in a book documenting the widespread extent of consumer fraud in the United States.[30] For example, they reported on the large number of complaints that have been directed at a nationally franchised transmission-repair company for practices such as "lo-balling" in which a repair service was advertised at an extremely low price to lure a customer, and then the company gouged the unsuspecting person for unneeded repairs. The Magnuson and Carper book also documented the widespread selling of various unsafe products to American customers.

William Leonard and Marvin Weber provided still another report on consumer fraud.[31] In studying market pressures to which automobile manufacturers subject franchised new car dealers, these authors confirmed the widely voiced suspicion of citizens that car dealers conduct unethical and illegal sales practices. These practices included compelling customers to purchase unwanted accessories, gouging customers on repairs, and providing illegal finance charges.

In addition to the direct consequences of consumer fraud, the indirect ramifications of this criminality should be noted. Perhaps, because of their perceptions that businessmen often fail to observe proper standards of business conduct, many citizens show less allegiance to the law than they might otherwise. Although definitive evidence on this matter is lacking, it is possible to gather up an abundance of statements by articulate criminals and delinquents in which these individuals allude to the facts of business crime as one basis of their grievances against society.

A NOTE ON COMPUTER CRIME

Styles in crime wax and wane. Car theft did not exist before about 1900 because there were no automobiles to steal. Similarly, safe-cracking is a dying art, principally because businesses and other organizations now rarely keep large amounts of money in safes. By contrast, crime employing modern computers is a rapidly growing and major form of lawbreaking. With half-a-million computers now in operation in the United States, it is little wonder that some persons have found ways to utilize them for deviant purposes.

Some computer crimes, representing a new form of embezzlement, involve a computer technician or other employee who uses computers to steal money from his or her employer. A large number of computer crimes of this variety have occurred in banks in recent years. Money is stolen through what have been called "salami" methods, through which small amounts of money are sliced from large accounts, or by "trojan horse" methods, in which secret codes are hidden in someone else's computer program. According to recent estimates, the monetary losses due to computer-related crimes range from $100 to $300 million per year.[32]

Computers have also become implicated in corporate crimes. For example, Clinard and his associates provided some details on what is known as the "Equity Funding Case":

This fraud case, discovered in 1973, resulted in losses estimated at $2 billion, the victims being the company's insurance customers. Through fraudulent means the Equity Funding Corporation of America was made to appear one of the country's largest, most successful and fastest growing financial institutions in the world. The scheme, which was carried out by corporation management itself, inflated reported company earnings primarily by the use of computer and false bookkeeping; one operation, for example, involved 64,000 fictitious insurance policies out of 97,000 claimed to have been issued. The purpose of this operation was to secure funds to cover fraudulent activities elsewhere and which could have been created and concealed only by computers. At company direction, one computer specialist created fictitious insurance policies with a value of $430 million, with yearly premiums totaling $5.5 million.[33]

IS "ORGANIZATIONAL CRIME" CRIME?

Some persons would exclude the study of violations of regulatory statutes in business from criminological attention.[34] Paul Tappan has sometimes been identified as one of these abolitionists, although he disclaimed some of the views attributed to him. He criticized individuals who would study "unethical" or "immoral" behavior, much of it outside legal codes. He declared:

The author wishes to make it clear here, since there has been some misconstruction of his view in literature on the subject, that he believes white-collar crime, properly and precisely defined, to be not only a legitimate but an important phase of criminological inquiry. He deplores the loosely normative connotations that have been attached to the concept by some of Sutherland's interpreters, and he believes that they have resulted in some confusion so far as needed empirical research in this area is concerned.[35]

Robert Caldwell was another critic of Sutherland's white-collar crime concept. Several of his remarks were not entirely clear, but one did have merit. He pointed out that decisions of civil courts and administrative agencies are often arrived at by procedures that have less regard for strict due process than do criminal court proceedings. Consequently, some question exists as to whether the actions processed in these ways would have been declared criminal if they had been dealt with in a criminal court.[36] These remarks underscore the persistent ambiguity inherent in the phenomenon of white-collar crime, even when it is carefully defined.

One attack on the concept of white-collar crime was by Ernest Burgess, noted in Chapter 3. In a comment on Hartung's research, Burgess maintained that meat violations were not crimes because the offenders did not define themselves as criminals and the public did not regard them as criminals. Moreover, he held that because the mores did not support the regulations, little social condemnation was directed at the violators. Also, these were not crimes because great numbers of citizens were involved in them.[37] Burgess believed that these may have been criminal acts in legalistic but not in sociological terms, for: "A criminal is a person who regards himself as a criminal and is so regarded by society. He is the product of the criminal-making process."[38] Most of Burgess's factual contentions were highly questionable; for example, Hartung noted that many people did, in fact, support price controls in wartime.[39] Also, many of these offenders viewed themselves as implicated in wrongful and criminal conduct. But even if Burgess had been correct in these assertions, the general conception of crime and criminals he promoted must be rejected. Countless offenders in prison do not think of themselves as criminals, although some citizens regard them as criminals. Are they not criminals? What is the "criminal-making process" of which Burgess spoke? Probably the clearest example would be the judicial process through which lawbreakers get tagged as criminals! There is no single process through which law violators are manufactured.

SOME OTHER VIEWS

The ambiguities of business violations, differential treatment of these activities, and so on, are fundamental problems for criminological analysis. Donald Newman has argued that the problems of value conflicts, power relations, social control, and other matters revealed in white-collar crime should be a major research focus.[40] Vilhelm Aubert made much the same judgment, advising:

For purposes of theoretical analysis it is of prime importance to develop and apply concepts which preserve and emphasize the ambiguous nature of the white-collar crimes and not to "solve" the problem by classifying them as either "crimes" or "not crimes." Their controversial nature is exactly what makes them so interesting from a sociological point of view and what gives us a clue to important norm conflicts, clashing group interests, and maybe incipient social change.[41]

Aubert illustrated the kinds of research organizational crime demands. In one study of the attitudes of Norwegian businessmen toward regulatory statutes, he found that they held allegiance in principle to law-abiding conduct but that they also felt a commitment to the special norms of the business groups, which defined law violations of business regulations as acceptable behavior. In another case, he examined a new Norwegian law governing the working conditions of domestic help. He found that the law provided criminal sanctions but was practically unenforceable because of the private nature of the violations. The law was a legislative hybrid, designed to pacify several interest groups who were making divergent demands on the lawmakers.[42]

William Chambliss and Robert Seidman viewed the regulatory statutes defining organizational crime as dramatic illustrations of the validity of interest-group theories on the origins of laws.[43] They asserted:

It seems to be the case that two things characterize laws passed which superficially seem inimical to the best interests of the powerful. First, some laws are passed primarily as a token gesture to assuage some group that has the capacity to disrupt the ongoing processes of society. Secondly, laws which are passed under these conditions are rarely if ever enforced with the same vigor as characterizes the enforcement of those laws which are in the best interests of persons in positions of power.[44]

According to Chambliss and Seidman, contrary to common beliefs, the antitrust laws actually were designed to serve the interests of large companies and corporations, rather than to regulate them and curtail their excesses. These authors argued that the Sherman Antitrust Act was a legislative response to public outcry following the disclosure of the rapacious behavior of nineteenth-century "robber barons." This law was intended as a symbolic gesture to appease the public. Passage of this legislation gave the appearance that something was being done about corporate misbehavior, at the same time that its creators expected that the law would not be widely enforced.

Gilbert Geis has called for more attention to the analytical problems embodied in organizational crime.[45] Although he agreed that the concept of white-collar crime is valuable, Geis noted that a number of improvements in its application are in order. Separate studies of relatively homogeneous forms of business crime are urgently needed. Closer attention to internal variations would involve exploration of forms of corporate organization, patterns of corporate ethics, differential involvement of corporation officials in lawbreaking, and so on. The general theme was that criminologists have tended to make uncritical generalizations about the behavior of corporations as entities without sufficient awareness of variations in the internal workings of these organizations.[46]

Geis made much of the facts regarding the electrical-conspiracy case of 1961, for these revealed a good deal about the complex character of lawbreaking in corporate organizations.[47]

The electrical-conspiracy case was an antitrust criminal action taken by the federal government against 29 corporations and 45 corporation officials who had conspired to rig bids on electrical products and carry out other price-fixing schemes. The individual defendants were found guilty, a number were given jail terms, and the court fines totaled nearly 12 million dollars. General Electric received a $337,500 fine, and Westinghouse was fined $72,500. Additionally, these concerns were liable to civil actions by victims seeking recovery of the illegal profits.[48]

Richard Smith studied the workings of the conspiracy within General Electric. He indicated that the price fixing was not a new practice, for the circuit-breaker division of General Electric had been involved in price rigging for about 25 years before the criminal action was filed.[49] In his view, one condition that led to price fixing in that corporation was the decentralization inaugurated in 1950. The corporation was broken into 27 autonomous divisions made up of 110 small companies, thus reducing surveillance of the corporation from the top of the organizational hierarchy. A number of "collusionists" among the corporation executives looked on antitrust violations as illegal but necessary for economic survival, and therefore not unethical. Most of them engaged in conspiratorial tactics reluctantly but felt that the erratic features of the electrical business demanded violation of the law to stabilize the market. They were clearly aware of the illegal nature of their activities, for they took great precautions to conduct their conspiratorial affairs in secrecy and to disguise their activities. At the same time, other company officials refused to engage in price fixing, holding that such practices were clearly unethical. These observations undermined the picture of the corporation as a monolith of like-minded individuals.[50] Examples of corporation officials who were either ignorant of the conspiracy or refused to participate in it were also observed in other of the corporations.[51]

There is more to the explanation of price fixing in this case than the association of criminally inclined executives. Smith indicated that there were variations in the extent of lawbreaking in different parts of the corporation, as well as fluctuations in the degree of criminality within organizational units. During several periods of "white sale" waves of discounting prices, pressures to engage in price stabilization became particularly acute. The price-rigging conspiracies were revived at these times after they had been relatively dormant.[52]

In a final comment on this price-fixing case, Smith argued:

The problem for American business does not start and stop with the scofflaws of the electrical industry or with anti-trust. Much was made of the fact that G.E. operated under a system of disjointed authority, and this was one reason it got into trouble. A more significant factor, the disjointment of morals, is something for American executives to think about in all aspects of their relations with their companies, each other, and the community.[53]

THE ETHICS OF BUSINESSMEN

Some other evidence exists on the question of business ethics, corporate organization, and allied matters. Robert Lane studied patterns of labor-relations violations and misrepresentation cases in the New England shoe industry.[54] He examined the question of ignorance of the law as a factor of criminality. His findings suggested that this factor was not a major consideration, for shoe-manufacturing concerns with the largest employee groups were more involved in lawbreaking than those with fewer workers. This finding was the reverse of what we might expect if ignorance played a part in violations, in that large firms could avail themselves of more legal counsel and advice than small ones and should thus have been better able to maintain a law-abiding record.[55] Some support for a differential-association interpretation of law violations existed, for Lane observed that violation rates varied from community to community. Moreover, many of the individuals implicated in law violations also read materials hostile toward governmental regulations. Finally, illegality was more common in smaller manufacturing towns, where businessmen with antiregulatory attitudes might conceivably be in common contact with one another.[56] In another publication dealing at length with the attitudes and values of businessmen, Lane contended that an older business ideology involving such beliefs as the sacredness of private enterprise and the inalienable rights of industry has been undermined, without a newer ethical code taking complete form. Accordingly, hostility toward business regulations may be a transitional stage, to be succeeded by a revised ethical system.[57]

A study of the ethical standards of businessmen by Raymond Baumhart involved a sample of 1,700 executives in various business organizations in the United States.[58] These officials were given a detailed questionnaire having to do with ethical beliefs and practices in business. Although much of the behavior reported in that study had to do with activities and practices that were not clearly illegal, the responses shed considerable light on the question of antiregulatory attitudes of businessmen as a factor in organizational crime.

Most businessmen verbalized sentiments of general concern for ethical business behavior. Nearly all said that businessmen should be concerned with goals additional to profit making, and 85 percent declared that a manager who operates solely in terms of his stockholders' interest would be unethical. Only about 20 percent agreed with the principle of *caveat emptor*. Nearly all said that use of call girls as a business tactic or of padding of expense accounts would be clearly unethical.

However, many of these executives disagreed on the specifics of ethical or unethical conduct. Moreover, many of them professed a higher level of ethical aspiration and conduct for themselves than they were willing to concede for the average businessman. Baumhart argued that the judgments made about the probable behavior of other executives were probably closer to the actual conduct of affairs in business than were the claims these people made about themselves. In other words, executives may put forth an exaggerated picture of themselves, reporting on the kind of organizational official they would prefer to be rather than the kind they actually represent.[59]

These officials not only expressed cynicism about the ethical behavior of other organization executives, but many of them also asserted that unethical practices, many of which are also illegal, were widespread. Although the practices varied from one industry to another, the use of call girls, granting of gratuities, price violations, and dishonest advertising were among those often identified as common in industry.

The responses of the officials suggested that one major influence determining the degree of unethical behavior in organizations is the model of conduct set by those at the top of the executive pyramid. The behavior of company superiors was ranked as the most important variable for ethical or unethical conduct. Baumhart employed an "organization man" theory to interpret these results, arguing that organizations vary in the degree to which individual executives are in differential association with carriers of unethical beliefs or practices.[60] Interestingly, the majority of the persons studied argued that an industrywide ethical code would be desirable as a means of reducing unethical activities, but they favored systems of code enforcement without teeth, such as self-policing within the industry. Only about 4 percent of them thought that a government agency should have charge of enforcing a code of ethics.[61]

ORGANIZATIONAL CRIME AND PUBLIC OPINION

Some have argued that organizational crime is not really crime because the public does not regard it as criminality. However, certain studies of citizen opinion, particularly with regard to wartime rationing and price-control regulations, indicated that citizens supported these laws and condemned violations. Similarly, Newman examined laymen's views of violations of the Federal Food, Drug and Cosmetic Act of 1938.[62] In this investigation, a sample of citizens was asked to select the punishments thought appropriate in cases of product misbranding and food adulteration. Their selections were then compared to the penalties actually invoked in the cases studied. About 80 percent of the respondents felt that the penalties for these offenses should have been more severe than the ones levied. At the same time, the citizens favored sanctions that were less harsh than those used for such conventional crimes as burglary. In general, their penalty choices were within the range of punishments allowable in existing statutes. Thus, these citizens seemed generally satisfied with existing legislation, and their dissatisfaction was with the administration of the statutes.

embezzlement and embezzlers[63]

THE EXTENT OF EMBEZZLEMENT

The opening remarks of this chapter characterized embezzlers as enemies within who are engaged in financial subversion, rather than as organizational warriors who make positive contributions to the business firm or concern. They are furtive and secretive enemies, the extent of their surreptitious deviations almost impossible to identify with much accuracy. Instead, wildly divergent estimates of the total financial cost of employee pilfering and embezzlement have been advanced. Nevertheless, these employee thieves are clearly responsible for huge financial losses incurred by organizations.

One indication of the magnitude of this kind of crime has been provided by Norman Jaspan, who noted that in the 1950s, thefts and embezzlements by employees totaled more than $4,000,000 per day in the United States. He also indicated that bonded losses from thefts in 1946 amounted to $13,000,000, whereas in 1957 such losses totaled $35,000,000. The significance of these figures is that only about 10 percent of the private business firms in the United States were covered by theft insurance, so the total losses must have been greatly in excess of these figures.[64] Jaspan also observed that his own business-protective agency unearthed $60,000,000 of employee dishonesty in 1959 alone; again, this kind of deviant activity must be extensive indeed.[65] Jaspan's account on employees who steal was filled with case-history documents which seemed to show that dishonest workers were an extremely varied bag of individuals who steal out of a diverse set of motives.

Another statement on embezzlement and theft set the amount of employee larcenies at $500,000,000 in 1956, but also indicated that some experts regarded this figure as too low, contending that the losses from employee criminality were probably in excess of 1 billion dollars per year.[66] One expert has claimed that the total cost of this kind of crime is nearer 3 billion dollars than these lower estimates. To gauge the importance of these amounts, consider the FBI estimate that the total loss from burglaries, armed robberies, auto thefts, and incidents of pickpocket activity was only about $440,000,000 in 1956. Employees stole at least twice this amount from their employers. This same discussion noted that embezzlement is a crime of growing magnitude, for fidelity-insurance losses increased by about 250 percent between 1946 and 1956, although insurance in force grew only by about 70 percent. This article pointed out that bank losses through misappropriations of funds have been increasing steadily in recent decades. In 1951, the Federal Deposit Insurance Corporation had 608 reports of embezzlement in insured banks, involving 759 employees from various employee levels. These figures would be considerably higher at the present.

In her research on shoplifting, Mary Cameron found that 12 department stores in New York City set their losses from shoplifting and employee pilferage combined at 10 million dollars in 1951. She also noted that store protection agencies estimated that employee thefts made up three-fourths of all the "inventory shrinkage" stores suffered.[67] One writer argued that the increase in employee criminality is linked to the changing scale of modern societal organization, growing impersonality within organizations, and weakening of attitudes holding wealth sacred.[68] Whatever the causes, these findings indicate that respectable employees involved in stealing from their employers are legion.

CAUSES OF EMBEZZLEMENT

Embezzlement is an illegality that rarely results in criminal prosecution. Jerome Hall has suggested that only about 1 percent of the cases of trust violation are dealt with as criminal actions.[69] He enumerated a number of factors responsible for infrequent prosecution, one of which is the embezzler's deviation in appearance and demeanor from the stereotype of the "crook" or "bad guy." In addition, organizations fear adverse public reactions to "cold-hearted" companies that prosecute their employees. Management often feels some loyalty to the worker, particularly if he or she is an "old-timer." Along a similar line, the person's lawbreaking is often related to a dire emergency he or she faces, so the embezzler is often the beneficiary of sympathetic understanding. Still other factors include costs and uncertainty associated with prosecutions, as well as the difficulties of obtaining restitution. Finally, according to Hall, too much scrutiny of employee behavior may throw unwelcome investigative light into other dark corners and turn up evidence of petty sins by management.[70]

Several studies of embezzlers have been conducted, one of which was by Elizabeth Redden, who examined 7,629 cases from fidelity-insurance-company records and classified them into a half-dozen commonsensical categories, including such types as "the little-fellow embezzler," "the grab-and-run-embezzler," and so on.[71]

The most influential study of embezzlers was carried out by Donald Cressey.[72] He employed the method of analytic induction, in which hypotheses were formulated and then examined in application to a group of embezzlers. These hypotheses were rejected if found defective, until a hypothesis was discovered that accounted for the cases under study.[73] Although the research began as a study of embezzlement, it was quickly changed to an investigation of criminal violation of financial trust. Cressey discovered that some persons in his group of prisoners from Joliet Prison in Illinois, Chino in California, and the federal penitentiary at Terre Haute, Indiana, who were charged with embezzlement had actually been involved in such offenses as confidence swindles. For a subject to be included in the study as a violator of financial trust, he must have accepted a position of trust in good faith and then violated that trust by criminality.[74] Criminal violation of financial trust was not a category derived from statutory law, instead, it was composed of similar individuals who may have been formally charged with a variety of specific offenses.

Cressey rejected several initial formulations about the dynamics of trust violation, including one that violations occurred when employees learned that theft was defined as acceptable behavior within the organization. Another hypothesis that failed the test of evidence was that violations of trust took place when individuals experienced financial emergencies. Some offenders had encountered grave financial difficulties earlier but had not solved these by theft. The final generalization about embezzlement was: "Trusted persons become trust violators when they conceive of themselves as having a financial problem which is nonshareable, are aware that this problem can be secretly resolved by violation of the position of financial trust, and are able to apply to their own conduct in that situation verbalizations which enable them to adjust their conceptions of themselves as trusted persons with their conceptions as users of the entrusted funds or property."[75] The entire process was held to occur before trust violation took place.

Two major aspects of this process should be emphasized: the role of *nonshareable* problems in trust violation, and the development of justificatory rationalizations *in advance* of the deviant act. Cressey's concept of nonshareable problems was a label for a plethora of difficulties about which the actor could not communicate to others, so he could not resolve them by legitimate means. One kind of nonshareable problem was the sort of activity the layman calls "booze, bookies, and blondes," in which an individual got entangled in unconventional or discrediting experiences that had to be kept hidden from others. Many of Cressey's subjects had nonshareable problems involving attempts to "live up to one's position," including bank employees who felt compelled to affect life styles for which their incomes were not adequate. In general, most of the problems of the trust violators related to status-seeking or status-maintaining behaviors, which created financial problems for them.[76]

Cressey's analysis of the role of rationalizations in trust violation represented a major contribution to etiological understanding. His point was that these justificatory arguments must be developed *before* embezzlement can occur, which was markedly different from conventional views of rationalizations. He asserted:

The rationalizations which are used by trust violators are necessary and essential to criminal violation of trust. They are not merely *ex post facto* justifications for conduct which already has been enacted, but are pertinent and real "reasons" which the person has for acting. When the relationship between a personal nonshareable problem and the position of trust is perceived according to the bias induced by the presence of rationalization which makes trust violation in some way justified, trust violation results.[77]

The significance of this argument extends well beyond trust violation. The process wherein individuals develop rationalizations before they engage in deviance probably also occurs in other forms of lawbreaking. Gresham Sykes and

David Matza contended that juvenile delinquents contrive neutralizing beliefs allowing them to violate norms they uphold in principle. These techniques of neuturalization precede deviant activities rather than follow from them.[78]

Critics of Cressey's generalizations have stressed several points. Karl Schuessler complained that one can hardly imagine an adequate test of the argument, for a cross-section of the general population would have to be examined. In that way, it might be possible to determine whether all individuals who have nonshareable problems and appropriate rationalizations engage in trust violations.[79] Clinard also expressed disappointment with Cressey's research, arguing that some of Cressey's techniques were questionable. However, Clinard's major contention was that the behavioral sequence lacks predictive meaning. Occurrence of trust violation can only be predicted at the moment that the complete process has transpired. Clinard argued that other studies could perhaps discover particular personality configurations or social situations that are indicators of the onset of trust violation, and would be operative some time prior to trust violation.[80]

Another challenge to Cressey's formulation came from Gwynn Nettler.[81] He examined six major cases of embezzlement in Canada in the 1960s and concluded that desire and opportunity on the part of the embezzlers accounted for their crimes, rather than nonshareable financial problems. Nettler described this causal path in the following terms:

These five exceptions to Cressey's singular road to fraud are more clearly described as individuals who wanted things they could not afford and who were presented with (or who invented) ways of taking other people's money. Consistently there was desire—things one could do with the money. Consistently there was opportunity—ways to take the money with little apparent risk. There was, in one case, the 'other woman,' alcohol, and the races.[82]

Nettler's data indicated that there may be more than one route to embezzlement and that Cressey's account may have to be supplemented with other etiological generalizations. On this point, most of the commentary on embezzlement has emphasized the traits and characteristics of the violator. Little or no attention has been paid to situational contexts that may contribute to trust violation. However, one bit of material regarding the organization of a bank lends itself to speculation in this direction. Chris Argyris reported that one bank he studied went about hiring employees thought to be "the right type." These workers were passive, quiet, obedient, and careful individuals. Once employed, they avoided each other's conversation and remained on cordial but distant terms. These employees rarely communicated any complaints and opinions about the work situation to their superiors, and bank officials did not try to deal with human-relations problems in the bank.[83] Although this research had nothing directly to do with embezzlement, such a work situation could easily contribute to the nonshareable character of employee problems.

Another set of observations on this point had to do with the low rate of employee thefts among postal workers. Hall indicated that in 1951, only 531 workers were apprehended for mail theft and only 144 employees detected in embezzlement out of a work force of over a half-million employees. However, 569 of these 675 were prosecuted and convicted. Hall suggested that several factors operated to repress employee crimes, including the large number of postal inspectors, which maximized likelihood of detection, and the frequent prosecution of detected offenders, which deterred other potential thieves. On the positive side, postal employees had relatively high morale and identification with the postal service, which may have affected their behavior, too.[84] Any organization that desires to repress employee pilfering and embezzlement might pay close attention to these situational variables.[85]

Erwin Smigel's study of public attitudes toward stealing from organizations of varied size also has implications for embezzlement control. He discovered that most citizens said they disapproved of stealing from organizations of any size. But when forced to choose the organization from which they would steal with least reluctance, most said they would do so first from large business firms, then from governmental agencies, and from small businesses last. Apparently, two considerations influenced most of these persons: the risks of detection and the principle of least evil. They regarded stealing from large businesses as less reprehensible and less harmful than other thefts. Perhaps this willingness to steal from large businesses stemmed from views that regard such organizations as cold and impersonal.[86] At any rate, situational influences in employee theft are worthy of further exploration.

occupational "fringe" violations

Organizational crime is lawbreaking carried on in order to serve the interests of business organizations, while embezzlement is its polar opposite, involving enemies from within engaged in subverting the organization. Falling somewhere in between these forms are law violations of persons in which professional or occupational skills are centrally involved, but which are also viewed by professional colleagues as unacceptable forms of behavior. The term, *occupational fringe violations* can be applied to this form of criminality.

Occupational deviations have been little studied, particularly by sociologists. The professional person who commits these violations has not been subjected to much investigation, so little is known of the occupational career line that leads professionals into marginal activities. At the same time, it is well-known that violations of the law are not uncommon among many professional groups. For example, newspaper accounts often point to criminal acts by lawyers, including subornation (inducing persons to give perjured testimony), improper handling of the money of clients, and so on.

In one study of unethical and illegal activities by lawyers, Kenneth Reichstein investigated "ambulance chasing" (solicitation of cases) in personal-injury cases in Illinois.[87] He discovered that Chicago lawyers were not all in agreement in their opinions of personal-injury solicitation, even though Bar Association ethical canons and state law as well forbid such activity. Attorneys who worked in small firms or independently and served low-status clients looked on solicitation tolerantly, whereas lawyers from large, successful firms practicing corporation law viewed "ambulance chasing" unfavorably. Reichstein also indicated that lawyers who had been brought before the Illinois Supreme Court on disciplinary charges involving solicitation were dealt with relatively leniently. All of this suggests that the line between proper and improper behavior in the legal profession is a fuzzy one.

A second inquiry involving occupational deviations was that of Jack Ladinsky concerning legal careers among Detroit-area attorneys. Ladinsky pointed out that lawyers who engaged in "solo" work, as contrasted to group practice in a law firm, were usually sifted earlier in their careers into relatively poor law schools. They were barred from entry into high-prestige law schools because of ethnic considerations or other variables that influenced the selection process. These same "solo" lawyers did the "dirty work." The less desirable, poorer-paying legal tasks were allocated to them, such as criminal-court defense work, personal-injury cases, and parallel chores.[88] Some of these individuals might easily drift into unethical or illegal practices if their legal careers were to deteriorate, in that they were already vulnerable to occupational and financial ups and downs by virtue of their occupational detachment from the organized practice of law.

Richard Quinney's investigation of prescription violations among retail pharmacists identified another form of "fringe" criminality.[89] Quinney studied the extent and nature of prescription-law violations among druggists in Albany, New York. Twenty pharmacists detected in prescription violations were compared with another group of 60 druggists who had not been so involved.

Quinney pointed out that retail pharmacy combines elements of both a professional and a business pursuit, so the druggist should experience some degree of role strain as a consequence. He identified four role orientations among the pharmacists he studied: some saw themselves as professionals, some as businessmen, some as involved in both roles, and a few were indifferent to these matters. Prescription violations were significantly related to the role orientations of the druggists, in that 75 percent of the business-oriented persons had committed violations, whereas none of the professionally oriented persons had. Generally, the more professionally oriented the pharmacist, the lower the likelihood of occupational deviance. Quinney concluded that the professional orientation of the druggists provided internal social controls that constrained them from deviant activity, whereas these standards did not influence the business-oriented persons. Quinney suggested that role strains and deviant control might be found in other professions and occupations, such as dentistry, optometry, chiropody, osteopathy, real estate, and accounting, which combine elements of business and profession.

These observations do not exhaust the subject of occupational crime. For example, we will find in Chapter 18 that police officers in many police departments have used their authority in illegal ways, securing bribes, gratuities, and other illicit rewards from misuse of their positions. Similarly, college professors sometimes abuse their occupational positions by selling complimentary copies of textbooks to used-book dealers or engaging in other peccadilloes. The principal obstacle to further discussion of occupational crime is that criminologists have not been vigorous in uncovering these acts of illegality.

summary

This chapter examined several kinds of organizational and occupational crime. The discussion was intended as a corrective to those views holding that lawbreaking is restricted to crime in the streets carried on by lower-class persons. The evidence regarding the pervasive character of criminality and the interweaving of illegal conduct into the fabric of social and economic life demands abandoning the comforting notion that crime is restricted to only a relatively few daring "bad guys." The study of criminality turns out to be a major task in sociological inquiry, for lawbreaking is often a central feature of the day-to-day activities of citizens everywhere in American society.

Criminological formulations have often involved loosely defined concepts, which is certainly the case with the notion of white-collar crime. This term has frequently been used to cover a wide range of relatively disparate misconduct. This chapter differentiated three categories: organizational crime, which involves lawbreaking carried on as a part of business activities, embezzlement, and occupational "fringe" behavior.

Although these forms of criminality differ in many important ways, they are all similar in at least one respect. A major factor in the genesis of these activities is perceived financial strain or economic uncertainty on the part of the offenders.

The category of organizational crime is broad in scope, for it covers activities ranging from illegal forms of sharp business practices carried on by small business firms to antitrust violations and other crimes of corporations. But in all of these cases, it appears that those who engage in violations frequently see themselves as being driven into criminality in order to insure economic survival, regularize destructive competition, or to solve other economic pressures. The evidence also indicates that businessmen are often ambivalent about their criminal behavior, viewing it as wrong in principle at the same time that they excuse themselves from specific culpability.

Embezzlement is similarly a varied collection of activities, ranging from petty pilfering by workers to large-scale, complex thefts conducted through intricate manipulations of company financial records. Embezzlement is also a low-visibility offense in that employers are often loath to press for prosecution of employees who have been detected in thefts. Again, much of the evidence points to perceived economic stresses as pushing persons into embezzlement activities. The evidence also suggests much the same thing for occupational "fringe" violators—individuals who are marginal members of a profession and who employ professional skills in illegal ways.

In the next chapter, attention turns to another kind of organizational crime, namely, the activities of organized-crime networks, which include not only gangsters and alleged members of the Mafia, but also politicians, corrupt police officers, businessmen, and, finally, those law-abiding citizens who clamor for the services that are provided by organized crime.

notes

[1] The conceptual anarchy involved in applications of this term has been discussed by Geis. See Gilbert Geis, "Toward a Delineation of White-Collar Offenses," *Sociological Inquiry*, 32 (Spring 1962), 160–71. See also Geis and Robert F. Meier, eds., *White-Collar Criminal*, rev. ed. (New York: Free Press, 1977). This volume is a useful compilation of works on white-collar crime, including many of the studies and discussions cited in this chapter. For a detailed examination of white-collar crime, along with detailed comments on controversies surrounding this concept, see George B. Vold and Thomas J. Bernard, *Theoretical Criminology*, 2nd ed. (New York: Oxford University Press, 1979), pp. 359–78.

[2] For a detailed discussion of the concept of organizational crime, see Laura Shill Schrager and James F. Short, Jr., "Toward a Sociology of Organizational Crime," *Social Problems*, 25 (April 1978), 407–19.

[3] Ibid., pp. 411–12.

[4] Adapted from Gibbons, *Changing the Lawbreaker* (Englewood Cliffs, N.J.: Prentice-Hall, Inc., 1965), pp. 111–12.

[5] This survey was summarized in Herbert A. Bloch and Gilbert Geis, *Man, Crime, and Society*, 2nd ed. (New York: Random House, 1970), p. 315.

[6] Lee Nugent, "Here's How I Gyp You," *Saturday Evening Post* (June 29, 1957), pp. 25–76.

[7] Edwin H. Sutherland, "White Collar Criminality," *American Sociological Review*, 5 (February 1940), 1–12; Sutherland, "Crime and Business," *Annals of the American Academy of Political and Social Science*, 217 (September 1941), 112–18; Sutherland, "Is 'White Collar Crime' Crime?" *American Sociological Review*, 10 (April 1945), 132–39; Sutherland, "The White Collar Criminal," in *Encyclopedia of Criminology*, Vernon C. Branham and Samuel B. Kutash, eds. (New York: Philosophical Library, 1949), pp. 511–15; Sutherland, *White Collar Crime* (New York: The Dryden Press, 1949); Sutherland, "Crime of Corporations," in *The Sutherland Papers*, Albert Cohen, Alfred Lindesmith, and Karl Schuessler, eds. (Bloomington: Indiana University Press, 1956), pp. 78–96.

[8] Sutherland, *White Collar Crime*, p. 9.

[9] Sutherland, "The White Collar Criminal," p. 511.

[10] Sutherland, "White Collar Criminality."

[11] For a good résumé of the controversy surrounding this concept, see Frank E. Hartung, "A Critique of the Sociological Approach to Crime and Correction," *Law and Contemporary Problems*, 23 (Autumn 1958), 722–25.

[12] Sutherland, *White Collar Crime*.

[13] Sutherland, "Is 'White Collar Crime' Crime?"; Sutherland, "The White Collar Criminal," p. 511; Sutherland, *White Collar Crime*, pp. 29–55.

[14] Sutherland, *White Collar Crime*, pp. 36–38, 95.

[15] Ibid., pp. 22–25.

[16] Ibid., p. 46.

[17]Marshall B. Clinard, *The Black Market* (New York: Holt, Rinehart & Winston, 1952); Clinard, "Criminological Theories of Violations of Wartime Regulations," *American Sociological Review*, 11 (June 1946), 258–70.

[18]Clinard, *The Black Market*, pp. 226–63.

[19]Ibid., pp. 1–7.

[20]Ibid., pp. 28–50.

[21]Ibid., pp. 89–114.

[22]Ibid., pp. 156–63.

[23]Ibid., pp. 151–53.

[24]Ibid., pp. 285–389. See also Clinard, "Criminological Theories of Violations of Wartime Regulations," pp. 267–70. In this essay, Clinard indicated that the size of the firm was unrelated to rates of violation.

[25]Frank E. Hartung, "White-Collar Offenses in the Wholesale Meat Industry in Detroit," *American Journal of Sociology*, 56 (July 1950), 25–32.

[26]Marshall B. Clinard, Peter C. Yeager, Jeanne Brissette, David Petrashek, and Elizabeth Harries, *Illegal Corporate Behavior* (Washington, D.C.: Law Enforcement Assistance Administration, 1979). For a Canadian study of corporate crime, see Colin H. Goff and Charles E. Reasons, *Corporate Crime in Canada* (Scarborough Ont.: Prentice-Hall, Inc., 1978).

[27]Clinard, et al., *Illegal Corporate Behavior*, p. xix.

[28]Ibid., p. xix.

[29]David Caplovitz, *The Poor Pay More* (New York: Free Press, 1967).

[30]Warren G. Magnuson and Jean Carper, *The Dark Side of the Marketplace* (Englewood Cliffs, N.J.: Prentice-Hall, Inc., 1968).

[31]William N. Leonard and Marvin Glenn Weber, "Automakers and Dealers: A Study of Criminogenic Market Factors," *Law and Society Review*, 4 (February 1970), 407–24; also see Harvey A. Faberman, "A Criminogenic Market Structure: The Automobile Industry, *Sociological Quarterly*, 16 (August 1975), 438–57.

[32]*Portland Oregonian*, March 30, 1980. These data came from a large study of computer crime conducted by the Stanford Research Institute. See Stanford Research Institute, *Criminal Justice Resource Manual on Computer Crime* (Washington, D.C.: U.S. Government Printing Office, 1980); also see Donn B. Parker, *Crime by Computers* (New York: Scribner, 1976).

[33]Clinard, et al., *Illegal Corporate Behavior*, p. 15.

[34]For a good discussion of these criticisms, as well as rejoinders to them, see Donald R. Cressey, Foreword to 1961 edition of Sutherland, *White Collar Crime* (New York: Holt, Rinehart & Winston, 1961).

[35]Paul W. Tappan, *Crime, Justice and Correction* (New York: McGraw-Hill, 1960), p. 7.

[36]Robert G. Caldwell, "A Reexamination of the Concept of White-Collar Crime," *Federal Probation*, 22 (March 1958), 30–36.

[37]Ernest W. Burgess, "Comment," *American Journal of Sociology*, 56 (July 1950), 32–33; Hartung, "White-Collar Offenses"; Hartung, "Rejoinder," pp. 33–34; Burgess, "Concluding Comment," p. 34.

[38]Burgess, Concluding Comment."

[39]Hartung, "Rejoinder."

[40]Donald J. Newman, "White Collar Crime," *Law and Contemporary Problems*, 23 (Autumn 1958), 735–53.

[41]Vilhelm Aubert, "White-Collar Crime and Social Structure," *American Journal of Sociology*, 58 (November 1952), 266.

[42]Ibid., pp. 268–70.

[43]William J. Chambliss and Robert Seidman, *Law, Order, and Power* (Reading, Mass.: Addison-Wesley, 1971), pp. 65–68.

[44]Ibid., p. 65. For one contrary view arguing that this thesis is "curiously artificial," see Andrew Hopkins, "On the Sociology of Criminal Law," *Social Problems*, 22 (June 1975), 608–19. In Hopkins's view, the antitrust laws represent an instance in which the interests of groups hostile to business misbehavior won out.

45Geis, "Toward a Delineation of White-Collar Offenses." For more recent observations of this kind, see Schrager and Short, "Toward a Sociology of Organizational Crime."

46Geis, "Toward a Delineation of White-Collar Offenses," pp. 161–68. Another statement that took Sutherland to task for uncritical discussions of corporations as "criminal," as though they represented homogeneous entities, was Thomas I. Emerson, book review, *Yale Law Journal*, 59 (February 1950), 581–85.

47Richard Austin Smith, "The Incredible Electrical Conspiracy," Part I, *Fortune*, 63 (April 1961), 132–218; Part II, 63 (May 1961), 161–224. See also John Herling, *The Great Price Conspiracy: The Story of the Antitrust Violations in the Electrical Industry* (Washington, D.C.: Robert B. Luce, 1962).

48Smith, "The Incredible Electrical Conspiracy," Part I, pp. 132–34.

49Ibid., Part I, p. 137.

50Ibid., Part I, pp. 134–35.

51Geis, "Toward a Delineation of White-Collar Offenses," pp. 168–69.

52Smith, "The Incredible Electrical Conspiracy," Part I, pp. 132–218.

53Ibid., Part II, pp. 224.

54Robert E. Lane, "Why Business Men Violate the Law," *Journal of Criminal Law, Criminology and Police Science*, 44 (July–August 1953), 151–65. See this article for further data on the extent of white-collar offenses.

55Ibid., pp. 155–58.

56Ibid., pp. 158–61.

57Robert E. Lane, *The Regulation of Businessmen* (New Haven, Conn.: Yale University Press, 1954).

58Raymond C. Baumhart, "How Ethical are Businessmen?" *Harvard Business Review*, 39 (July–August 1961), 6–176.

59Ibid., pp. 16–19.

60Ibid., pp. 156–57.

61Ibid., pp. 166–72. Baumhart's study was replicated in 1976 by Brenner and Molander, who found much the same results as had Baumhart, except that their respondents voiced even greater cynicism about the ethics of other businessmen! See Steven N. Brenner and Earl A. Molander, "Is the Ethics of Business Changing?" *Harvard Business Review*, 55 (January–February 1977), 57–71. Also see L. Howard Silk and David Vogel, *Ethics and Profits: The Crisis of Confidence in American Business* (New York: Simon & Schuster, 1976).

62Donald J. Newman, "Public Attitudes Toward a Form of White Collar Crime," *Social Problems*, 4 (January 1957), 228–32.

63For a detailed bibliography of studies on embezzlement, see Donald R. Cressey, *Other People's Money* (New York: Free Press, 1953), pp. 159–66.

64Norman Jaspan with Hillel Black, *The Thief in the White Collar* (Philadelphia: Lippincott, 1960), p. 234.

65Ibid., p. 10.

66"Embezzlers, the Trusted Thieves," *Fortune*, 56 (November 1957), 142–88.

67Mary Owen Cameron, *The Booster and the Snitch* (New York: Free Press, 1964), pp. 9–11.

68David Cort, "The Embezzler," *The Nation*, 188 (April 18, 1959), 339–42.

69Jerome Hall, *Theft, Law and Society*, 2nd ed. (Indianapolis: Bobbs-Merrill, 1952), pp. 304–6.

70Ibid., pp. 306–12.

71Elizabeth Redden, "Embezzlement: A Study of One Kind of Criminal Behavior with Prediction Tables Based on Fidelity Insurance Records" (Ph.D. diss., University of Chicago, 1939).

72Cressey, *Other People's Money*.

73Ibid., pp. 13–17. For criticisms of this method, see Ralph H. Turner, "The Quest for Universals in Sociological Research," *American Sociological Review*, 18 (December 1953), 604–11; W. S. Robinson, "The Logical Structure of Analytic Induction," *American Sociological Review*, 16 (December 1961), 812–18.

74Cressey, *Other People's Money*, pp. 19–26.

[75]Ibid., p. 30.

[76]Ibid., pp. 33–76.

[77]Ibid., pp. 136–37.

[78]Gresham M. Sykes and David Matza, "Techniques of Neutralization: A Theory of Delinquency," *American Sociological Review*, 22 (December 1957), 664–70.

[79]Karl F. Schuessler, review of *Other People's Money, American Journal of Sociology*, 49 (May 1954), 604.

[80]Marshall B. Clinard, review of *Other People's Money, American Sociological Review*, 19 (June 1954), 362–63.

[81]Gwynn Nettler, "Embezzlement Without Problems," *British Journal of Criminology*, 14 (January 1974), 70–77.

[82]Ibid., p. 75.

[83]Chris Argyris, *Human Relations in a Bank*, Labor and Management Center, Reprint No. 21 (New Haven, Conn.: Yale University, 1954); Argyris, "Human Relations in a Bank," *Harvard Business Review*, 32 (September–October 1954), 63–72.

[84]Hall, *Theft, Law and Society*, pp. 326–30. For a discussion which indicated that postal workers have been involved in good deal of deviance which is not criminal in nature, see Dean Harper and Frederick Emmert, "Work Behavior in a Service Industry," *Social Forces*, 42 (December 1963), 216–25.

[85]For a technical discussion of methods of controlling embezzlement in business, see Albert E. Keller, *Embezzlement and Internal Control* (Washington, D.C.: Warner-Arms Publishing Co., 1946).

[86]Erwin O. Smigel, "Public Attitudes Toward Stealing as Related to the Size of the Victim Organization," *American Sociological Review*, 21 (June 1956), 320–27; see also Smigel and H. Laurence Ross, eds., *Crime Against Bureaucracy* (New York: Van Nostrand Reinhold 1970).

[87]Kenneth J. Reichstein, "Ambulance Chasing: A Case Study of Deviation and Control Within the Legal Profession," *Social Problems*, 13 (Summer 1965), 3–17.

[88]Jack Ladinsky, "Careers of Lawyers, Law Practice, and Legal Institutions," *American Sociological Review*, 28 (February 1963), 47–54; further evidence on this point is contained in Jerome E. Carlin, *Lawyers on Their Own* (New Brunswick, N.J.: Rutgers University Press, 1962). Carlin's study of 93 Chicago attorneys who were solo practitioners revealed that they were often compelled to engage in "dirty work" such as "fixing" cases, bribing officials, and so on. See also Arthur Lewis Wood, *Criminal Lawyer* (New Haven, Conn.: College and University Press, 1967).

[89]Earl R. Quinney, "Occupational Structure and Criminal Behavior: Prescription Violation by Retail Pharmacists," *Social Problems*, 11 (Fall 1963), 179–85.

organized
crime

The flamboyant cowboy gunfighter has frequently been alleged to be a unique cultural type, found only in the United States and symbolizing a variety of cultural values. Yet *vaqueros* and other kinds of cowboys are common in South America. A better candidate as a unique American type would be the gangsters engaged in racketeering or providing illicit services to the general public. Various authorities have pointed out that organized criminals embody major cultural values in their activities and scarcely differ from their fellow citizens with regard to the ends they pursue.[1] The gangster and the businessman are both engaged in single-minded pursuit of material success, so they differ primarily in terms of the services they render and the techniques they use.[2] Francis Ianni put this point well:

There is no organized crime "underworld." Rather, organized crime is an integral part of our cities. It is the result of an individualistic, predatory philosophy of success, the malaise of laissez-faire economic and political practice. Organized crime is that part of the business system operative in the illicit segment of American life. The degree and tenure of minority-group involvement in this business enterprise is basically a function of the social and cultural integration of the group into American society. At their first entrance into this society, immigrants and their children grasp at the immediate means of acquiring what the new world has to offer. As they are acculturated, their crimes become more American and in time merge into the area of marginal, legitimate business practice. Where one stops and the other begins is not always easy to see.[3]

The image of organized criminals or gangsters on television is of evil malefactors against whom the police are relatively powerless. These "bad guys" are pictured as involved in extortion, violence, and other crimes directed against an innocent public that is offended by such behavior but at the same time intimidated by these malevolent figures. Then, too, gangsters are presumed to be nefarious invaders to our shores who have infiltrated from southern Italy, where rule by Mafia bands of outlaws is a way of life. Like tarantulas that arrived on banana boats from South America, they brought evil with them.

This conception of organized crime has three fundamental flaws. First, gangsterism has normally involved collusion among criminals, police, and city officials. Cooperation rather than conflict among these groups has been commonplace, so the notion of society at war with gangsters is more of a caricature than anything else.[4]

Second, popular views of organized crime hold that this criminality exists *despite* the wishes of the public rather than *as a consequence* of citizen demands for illegal goods or services. Someone has to pay hoodlums to engage in union busting and similar violence; someone must be willing to purchase sexual intercourse for prostitution to succeed as a business; customers had to exist for illegal liquor for bootlegging to have flourished; and at least two persons are required in gambling, one of them a citizen who wishes to place a bet or draw a card. In short, organized crime exists to provide for the satisfaction of widely demanded, but legally prohibited, activities or products.

Daniel Bell has incisively identified the cultural roots of organized crime.[5] He argued:

Americans have had an extraordinary talent for compromise in politics and extremism in morality. The most shameless political deals (and "steals") have been rationalized as expedient and realistically necessary. Yet in no other country have there been such spectacular attempts to curb human appetites and brand them as illicit, and nowhere else such glaring failures. . . . Crime as a growing business was fed by the revenues from prostitution, liquor and gambling that a wideopen urban society encouraged and which a middle-class Protestant ethos tried to suppress with a ferocity unmatched in any other civilized country.[6]

His theme was echoed by Gus Tyler, who noted that American attempts to suppress immorality have provided the seed bed out of which organized crime has grown.[7] On this point, he indicated:

Our puritanism creates a whole range of illegal commodities and services, for which there is a widespread demand. Into the gap between what people want and what people can legally get leaps the underworld as purveyor and pimp, with gambling tables, narcotics, and women. Puritanism gives the underworld a monopoly on a market with an almost insatiable demand.[8]

Such commentary emphasizes the point that organized crime is not some kind of alien sickness afflicting an otherwise healthy social organism. Instead, organized criminality is as natural a part of society as various kinds of socially esteemed behavior. Three groups of citizens are bound together in the organized-crime complex: the criminals who engage in organized crime, the police and city officials with whom they are in collusive cooperation, and the citizens who purchase the services of racketeers, gamblers, and other related types.

Finally, the third flaw in the public's conception of organized crime is in the beliefs about the Sicilian roots of organized crime, the Italian ancestry of organized-crime figures, and the contemporary ties between Italian-American gangsters and their counterparts in Italy; these beliefs are, in fact, wildly inaccurate. Undeniably, Italian-Americans have played a major role in the rise of organized crime in this country. However, the majority of these Italian-Americans were native born, not immigrants. For example, Al Capone was born in Chicago, not Corleone or elsewhere in Sicily. While organized crime may not be an ethnic melting pot, persons of non-Italian ancestry have also been involved in it, for example, Jews, Irish, Germans, and other ethnic-group members. Currently, blacks and Puerto Ricans have begun to occupy important roles in organized crime. Finally, the evidence in support of claims that organized crime is international in scope with its command post in Italy is meager indeed.

the growth and development of organized crime

Although organized criminality has been in existence for a long time, passage of the Volstead Act (the Eighteenth Amendment) in 1919 was the primary reason for the pronounced growth of organized crime after 1920 in the United States.[9] During the 14 years of Prohibition in which consumption of alcohol was outlawed, gangsters such as Al Capone were prominent figures in every major American city. Those organized criminals in the 1920s and 1930s earned lucrative sums from bootlegging, labor racketeering such as strikebreaking, and prostitution.

Humbert Nelli produced a detailed historical analysis of the shift in the character of organized crime, dealing with the involvement of Italians and Italian-Americans in crime in Chicago between 1890 and 1920.[10] He indicated that the public furor regarding Italian criminality in the period before 1920 obscured a number of facets of that lawbreaking, including the fact that organized criminality by the Black Hand society was mainly directed at other immigrants *within* the Italian colony in Chicago. Various forms of extortion and other criminal practices within the Italian community provided the groundwork for the dominance of Italians in organized crime in Chicago after 1920. The decline of immigration after 1920 virtually put an end to criminal victimization of Italians, but the passage of Prohibition legislation presented vast new opportunities for gangsters. Many persons who had been involved in crime within the Italian community then moved into the mainstream of American gangsterism.

The organized crime of this period was noteworthy for its grossness, among other things. Prostitution was openly carried on in houses of prostitution within organized vice districts. Similarly, physical violence predominated in labor racketeering. Kenneth Allsop has indicated that during the 14 years of Prohibition, at least 700 gang murders occurred as a consequence of intergang conflicts.[11] Probably no period in American history exceeded this one in terms of violent lawlessness. The television and movie image of the Prohibition-era gangster in odd clothing, equipped with a submachine gun, racing through the streets in an open black touring car with machine gun blazing, is based on fact, even though other elements of this picture are not accurate.

Prostitution in American cities in early decades of this century provides an illustration of the symbiotic linkages between elements of the population involved in organized crime. Prostitution was almost exclusively conducted in segregated "red light" districts. These areas of the city, usually near the downtown section, were filled with houses of prostitution peopled by a madam and a collection of prostitutes. Clients either found their way there by themselves or were delivered to the vice district by taxicab drivers. The fact that prostitution was the major activity of the area was an open secret.

Prostitutes employed in houses turned their earnings over to the madam and were paid a share of their total earnings in wages. The police were involved in the regulation of this business rather than in its suppression. In return for tolerating the vice operations, and in payment for their actions in controlling unruly clients and other contingencies of this sort, the police extracted a sizable share of the proceeds from the persons operating the prostitution outlets. This payoff was then redistributed among various police officers, politicians, city officials, and other citizens.

Public attitudes were frequently tolerant during these years of organized prostitution in vice districts. Arguments were advanced on the positive social functions prostitution was alleged to perform. Prostitution was held to be a stimulant to business through attracting visitors to the city, or it was said to provide an outlet for sex deviants who would otherwise rape "decent" women. Reform campaigns would occasionally direct negative attention to prostitution, so a call for police suppression would sporadically be heard. On these occasions, conventional police practice was to stage token raids of houses of prostitution. A few days later, business would be back to normal, with prostitution running at full speed.

Part of the mythology of organized prostitution was that girls were forcibly abducted into sexual bondage by "White Slavers"; thus, the prostitute was seen as a female who had been physically coerced into a fate worse than death! The truth is that prostitutes usually engaged voluntarily in this activity. Most saw that work career as less obnoxious and more lucrative than the alternatives open to them, such as waitress or sales-clerk positions. Once involved in prostitution, the girls became caught up in an occupational pattern in which they were periodically moved from one community to another to provide variety to the customers of the houses.[12]

In a number of ways, organized crime mirrors the changes that have occurred in the host society. Take prostitution as an example. Although vice districts still exist in some American cities, prostitution has undergone radical changes in form. With the decline of political corruption in American cities, particularly since World War II, the police have suppressed organized prostitution in segregated vice districts. Prostitutes no longer work in large whorehouses with a dozen or so fellow employees. The new forms of prostitution involve individual women who "hustle" out of cocktail bars, other kinds of independent streetwalkers, or call girls who engage in sexual transactions involving relatively large amounts of money. Prostitution has also become a major source of income to be used for drug purchases by female addicts. This kind of prostitution is much less visible to the general public. Moreover, this form of vice activity does not depend on police collusion for its success. It creates some complicated law-enforcement problems for the police, which were not encountered in the days of organized vice districts.[13]

Daniel Bell has noted the changes in organized crime in the United States. He contended that as organized prostitution and industrial racketeering have declined, other forms of criminality have flourished. According to Bell, "in the last decade and a half, industrial racketeering has not offered much in the way of opportunity. *Like American capitalism itself, crime shifted its emphasis from production to consumption*" (emphasis in the original).[14] He argued that organized crime has become more "civilized" and technologically complex in recent decades. Wire-service betting on horseracing, with its telegraph communication of race results, network of bookies, and arrangements for "lay-off" betting, in which gamblers share the risks of financial losses, illustrates this transition nicely. Organized criminals have profited from the increasing subtlety of crime and have become more respectable figures.[15]

Bell argued that in the future organized crime will be less prominent as the social sources for it are eroded away. He asserted:

With the rationalization and absorption of some illicit activities into the structure of the economy, the passing of an older generation that had established a hegemony over crime, the general rise of minority groups to social position, and the break-up of the urban boss system, the pattern of crime we have discussed is passing as well. Crime, of course, remains as long as passion and the desire for gain remain. But big, organized city crime, as we have known it for the past seventy-five years, was based on more than these universal motives. It was based on certain characteristics of the American economy, American ethnic groups, and American politics. The changes in all these areas mean that it too, in the form we have known it, is at an end.[16]

In this passage Bell sounded the death knell for labor racketeering, extortion, prostitution, and certain other kinds of organized crime. However, the newer forms of organized lawbreaking, particularly gambling, narcotics traffic, and loan sharking, are likely to be with us for a long time. Bell's forecast seems less valid for these kinds of organized criminality.

Evidence regarding organized crime has been uncovered in greatest detail by two investigative committees of the United States Senate. The first of these was the Committee to Investigate Crime in Interstate Commerce, commonly known as the Kefauver Committee and chaired by the late Senator Estes Kefauver. This group, investigating organized crime in the late 1940s, found widespread evidence of gambling and other forms of racketeering in a number of American cities.[17] More recently, the Select Committee on Improper Activities in the Labor or Management Field, often designated as the McClellan Committee and led by Senator John L. McClellan, turned up a vast amount of information about corrupt practices in American labor unions. This committee uncovered a large number of instances in which gangsters and racketeers were influential in the conduct of union affairs.[18]

The most recent survey of organized crime in the United States was presented in the report of The President's Commission on Law Enforcement and Administration of Justice.[19] The commission indicated that estimates of the amount of money spent on illegal gambling in the United States ranged from $7 billion to $50 billion per year. Loan sharking was alleged to be a widespread form of organized crime, although no figures were offered regarding the profits involved. Narcotics traffic was held to result in $21 million in profits per year to importers and distributors of drugs. The commission also claimed that organized criminals had reinvested much of their money in legitimate businesses indirectly controlled by gangsters. Finally, labor racketeering was said to remain an important form of organized crime. According to the commission, organized crime exists in all sections of the United States, in small cities as well as in large ones.[20]

mafia: myth or reality?

One of the most widely held notions among the mass audience in the United States is that organized crime is under the control of a national and international criminal conspiracy, ruled from Sicily and known as the Mafia. According to this view, Italian-American criminals such as Frank Costello, Albert Anastasia, and Joey Adonis are linked to "Lucky" Luciano and other members of the Mafia hierarchy in Sicily. The Kefauver Committee gave great credence to this hypothesis. On the basis of testimony before his committee, Senator Kefauver contended: "*A nationwide crime syndicate does exist in the United States of America, despite the protestations of a strangely assorted company of criminals, self-serving politicians, plain blind fools, and others who may be honestly misguided, that there is no such combine*" (emphasis in the original).[21] Kefauver's discussion of this claim was unconvincing, for he went on to indicate that the nationwide syndicate was elusive and furtive. Nonetheless, he continued by asserting: "*Behind the local mobs which make up the national crime syndicate is a shadowy, international criminal organization known as the Mafia, so fantastic that most Americans find it hard to believe it really exists*" (emphasis in the original).[22]

Supporters of the Mafia interpretation of organized crime make much of a supposed summit meeting of gangsters held in 1957, in which 58 persons from all over the United States converged on the Apalachin, New York, residence of Joseph Barbara, a wealthy beverage distributor. These individuals all drove expensive automobiles, carried extraordinarily large sums of money on their persons, had extensive criminal records, and were of Italian extraction. They explained their presence at the small village of Apalachin as guests at a barbecue. Twenty of these persons were subsequently convicted in a federal court in 1959 of conspiring to obstruct justice by lying about the purpose of their meeting. However, in 1960 an appellate court overturned this conviction on the grounds that the federal government had failed to prove that any improper conduct had taken place at that meeting. Although their tale about attending a barbecue sounded implausible, it may have nonetheless been true. After all, gangsters are not indifferent to family, ethnic, and friendship ties, which often provide the justification for social get-togethers on the part of conventional citizens. At any rate, this affair was sufficiently ambiguous to be interpreted either as support for the Mafia argument or as contrary to that contention.

That the Mafia existed as a quasi-political organization in certain parts of Sicily is not debated, for a number of investigators have thrown light on that phenomenon.[23] At issue is the claim advanced by such persons as Harry Anslinger, former Director of the Federal Bureau of Narcotics, that an international Mafia controls the traffic in narcotics, gambling, and other forms of organized crime in America. Edward Allen,[24] Frederic Sondern,[25] and Ed Reid[26] have also stridently enunciated this view of the Mafia and organized crime.

The report of The President's Commission on Law Enforcement and Administration of Justice contained a modified version of the Mafia argument, which is probably somewhat closer to the truth. This description portrayed the system of organized crime as made up of a number of loosely coordinated regional syndicates. According to the commission, organized crime in America has the following features:

Today the core of organized crime in the United States consists of 24 groups operating as criminal cartels in large cities across the Nation. Their membership is exclusively Italian, they are in frequent communication with each other, and their smooth functioning is insured by a national body of overseers. To date, only the Federal Bureau of Investigation has been able to document fully the national scope of these groups, and FBI intelligence indicates that the organization as a whole has changed its name from the Mafia to La Cosa Nostra. . . .

In individual cities, the local core group may also be known as the "outfit," the "syndicate," or the "mob." These 24 groups work with and control other racket groups, whose leaders are of various ethnic derivations. In addition, the thousands of employees who perform the street-level functions of organized crime's gambling, usury, and other illegal activities represent a cross section of the Nation's population groups. . . .

The highest ruling body of the 24 families is the "commission." This body serves as a combination legislature, supreme court, board of directors, and arbitration board; its principal functions are judicial. Family members look to the commission as the ultimate authority on organizational and jurisdictional disputes. It is composed of the bosses of the Nation's most powerful families but has authority over all 24. The composition of the commission varies from 9 to 12 men. According to current information, there are presently 9 families represented, 5 from New York City and 1 each from Philadelphia, Buffalo, Detroit, and Chicago. The commission is not a representative legislative assembly or an elected judicial body. Members of this council do not regard each other as equals. Those with long tenure on the commission and those who head large families, or possess unusual wealth, exercise greater authority and receive utmost respect. The balance of power on this nationwide council rests with the leaders of New York's 5 families. They have always served on the commission and consider New York as at least the unofficial headquarters of the entire organization.[27]

Robert Anderson's discussion of the changing character of organized crime presented a similar view of the Mafia or Cosa Nostra:

The Mafia as a traditional type of formal organization has disappeared in America. Modern criminals refer to its successor as *Cosa Nostra*, "Our Thing." The Cosa Nostra is a lineal descendant of the Mafia, but it is a different kind of organization. Its goals are much broader as it exploits modern cities and an industrialized nation. The real and fictive kinship ties of the Old Mafia still operate among fellow Sicilians and Italians, but these ties now coexist with bureaucratic ones. The Cosa Nostra operates above all in new and different terms. The new type of organization includes elaboration of the hierarchy of authority; the specialization and departmentalization of activities; new and more pragmatic, but still unwritten, rules; and a more developed impartiality. In America, the traditional Mafia has evolved into a relatively complex organization which perpetuates selected features of the older peasant organization but subordinates them to the requirements of a bureaucracy.[28]

Still another description of the contemporary structure of the Cosa Nostra came from Donald R. Cressey, who prepared the report on organized crime for The President's Commission on Law Enforcement and Administration of Justice. He contended:

1. A nationwide alliance of at least twenty-four tightly knit "families" of criminals exists in the United States. (Because the "families" are fictive, in the sense that the members are not all relatives, it is necessary to refer to them in quotation marks.)
2. The members of these "families" are all Italians and Sicilians, or of Italian and Sicilian descent, and those on the Eastern Seaboard, especially, call the entire system "Cosa Nostra." Each participant thinks of himself as a "member" of a specific "family" and of Cosa Nostra (or some equivalent term).
3. The names, criminal records, and principal criminal activities of about five thousand of the participants have been assembled.
4. The persons occupying key positions in the skeletal structure of each "family"—consisting of positions for boss, underboss, lieutenants, (also called "captains"), counselor, and for low-ranking members called "soldiers" or "button men"—are well known to law-enforcement officials having access to informants. Names of persons who permanently or temporarily occupy other positions, such as "buffer," "money mover," "enforcer," and "executioner," also are well known.
5. The "families" are linked to each other, and to non–Cosa Nostra syndicates, by understandings, agreements, and "treaties," and by mutual deference to a "Commission" made up of the leaders of the most powerful of the "families."
6. The boss of each "family" directs the activities, especially the illegal activities, of the members of his "family."
7. The members of this organization control all but a tiny part of the illegal gambling in the United States. They are the principal loan sharks. They are the principal importers and wholesalers of narcotics. They have infiltrated certain labor unions, where they extort money from employers and, at the same time, cheat the members of the union. The members have a virtual monopoly on some legitimate enterprises, such as cigarette vending machines and juke boxes, and they own a wide variety of retail firms, restaurants and bars, hotels, trucking companies, food companies, linen-supply houses, garbage collection routes, and factories. Until recently, they owned a large proportion of Las Vegas. They own several state legislators and federal congressmen and other officials in the legislative, executive, and judicial branches of government at the local, state, and federal levels. Some governmental officials (including judges) are considered, and consider themselves, members.
8. The information about the Commission, the "families," and the activities of members has come from detailed reports made by a wide variety of police observers, informants, wire taps, and electronic bugs.[29]

In spite of its widespread popularity, there are many who remain unconvinced of the accuracy of the Mafia hypothesis.[30] For example, Joseph Albini argued that the claims about a national commission in charge of a criminal conspiracy are defective, for they attribute more formal structure to organized crime than actually exists.[31] Similarly, Dwight Smith claimed that "mafia" stands for a state of mind or attitude on the part of Italian-Americans that is a part of their Italian heritage, involving family loyalty and similar values, rather than representing a highly organized criminal hierarchy of the kind described by Cressey and others.[32] Other skeptics, such as Gordon Hawkins, have noted that the evidence on which the Mafia argument is based, such as the testimony of a relatively petty gangster, Joseph Valachi, was of dubious character.[33] Ianni asserted that the conspiratorial theory involved in Mafia claims is a comforting myth through which public attention is diverted away from the complex social linkages between organized crime and respectable society. He contended that: "Like the alleged Communist conspiracy which preceded it, and the Black power and youth rebellions which are succeeding it in public interest, the '*Mafia* conspiracy' requires a *Mafia* organization."[34]

Those who argue against the Mafia theory agree that Italian-Americans have been inordinately frequent among organized criminals in the United States. However, they maintain that organized crime consists of a number of loosely coordinated regional syndicates in the United States rather than a single network of criminal associations. They are highly skeptical of the accuracy of The President's Commission description of an all-powerful commission. Furthermore, critics of the Mafia hypothesis suggest that organized crime and participation of Italian-Americans in it is an indigenous feature of American life. Daniel Bell, one of these disbelievers, argued that heavy involvement of Italians in organized crime must be seen as a consequence of the late arrival of Italian immigrants into the United States.[35] Most of them came to this country after the beginning of the present century and found many of the routes to upward mobility and wealth closed to them. Many of these individuals turned to what Bell termed "a queer ladder of mobility," such as bootlegging; others found their way into relatively unconventional occupations, which offered the promise of success, such as boxing; and still others entered urban politics. The latter were frequently aided by the criminals, who provided financial support for Italian political hopefuls. As a result of these developments, a number of Italian-Americans did rise to positions of political importance in city government, at the same time that others became prominent in criminal mobs and gambling. Within the Italian-American community, gangsters and mobsters were viewed with a good deal of respect and admiration, for their careers represented success, even though by somewhat unconventional means.[36] All of this is a far cry from a nationwide conspiracy controlled from Sicilian soil. Moreover, as Bell noted, this interlocking structure of Italian politicians and criminals is probably on the wane with the assimilation of Italian-Americans into more conventional opportunity structures.

Giovanni Schiavo is another student of the Mafia who contended that those who have put forth this argument regarding American organized crime are de-luded.[37] He argued that the Mafia did exist in Sicily but virtually disappeared after 1927 when the Italian dictator, Mussolini, forcibly disbanded it. Moreover, Schiavo argued that no evidence supports the existence of either an American or an international Mafia in control of organized crime.

What is to be made of these divergent claims about the Mafia or Cosa Nostra? Some authorities contend that there is a nationwide crime syndicate or conglomerate in operation, directed by a corporationlike commission. Others maintain that organized crime consists of local or regional criminal power structures linked together only tenuously by informal ties. These persons deny the validity of claims about a single crime establishment called the Mafia or Cosa Nostra. A major problem in adjudicating between these opposing contentions is that the data on which students of organized crime draw have been restricted mainly to reports on criminal activities rather than analyses of organizational patterns in crime.[38] In other words, claims about the existence of the Mafia usually consist of inferences from reports on criminality, rather than direct field observations of organized crime. However, there are some reports on the organizational structure of crime groups in specific cities which throw considerable light upon the Mafia controversy.

organized crime in American cities

The most detailed field study on organized crime yet conducted was that of Francis Ianni, dealing mainly with the Lupollo family in New York City and also with the Passalaqua family organization in Bayonne, New Jersey, and the DeMaio group in East Harlem. All of these were pseudonyms for criminal organizations.[39] Ianni's analysis was directed at identification of: (1) the ways in which Italian-American criminal structures have been rooted in characteristics of social life in southern Italy, and (2) the effects of American values and social patterns in modifying those characteristics. Ianni asserted that: "Italian involvement in organized crime (in the United States) has been molded by a unique combination of Italian and American cultural values and social conditions."[40]

According to Ianni, in order to understand the behavior of Italian-American crime families, one must begin with the social values that predominated in southern Italy, involving primacy of the family, juxtaposition of Church and state, and stress upon personal honor over statutory law. Ianni argued that in southern Italy, the family is *the* social structure of real importance, with family relationships extending to all blood relatives and relatives by marriage. Although the members of these expanded families do not all live together under one roof, they nonetheless constitute a version of the extended-family pattern. The social life of southern Italian communities revolves around familism and family honor. The southern Italian has traditionally been highly suspicious of the remote central government at the same time that he has distrusted the Catholic Church, so that for him, his family has been his world.

Ianni also had much to say about the nature of Mafia patterns in southern Italy. He argued that: ". . . *Mafia* is a generic form of social organization which developed in the south of Italy under some very particular social and cultural conditions. It is impossible to understand the Lupollo family as an organized crime group unless you first understand what 'family' and *Mafia* really mean to them."[41] In southern Italy, *mafia* refers to two distinct phenomena: "mafia" which is a state of mind, and "Mafia" which denotes a small number of criminal bands. The spirit of mafia requires that every man seek protection for himself and his family members in his own way.

Ianni asserted that there has never been a single, unified Mafia organization in Sicily, hence it could not have been exported to the United States as the organizing framework for criminal activities. What was diffused to this country was the mafia state of mind, but Italian-American participation in organized crime cannot be attributed wholly to a mafia ethos, in view of the fact that their domination over organized criminality did not develop until the 1930s, long after the waves of immigration of Italians to the United States had occurred. What was required for the development of Italian-American hegemony was stress on familism, the spirit of mafia, *and* opportunities in crime that were created by the Volstead Act prohibiting the sale and consumption of alcohol. Bootlegging was the door through which Al Capone and other second-generation Italian-Americans entered into the crime business, eventually wresting control of it from the Jewish and Irish-American elements.

Ianni's detailed account of the Lupollo family in New York indicated that it grew out of the modestly scaled crime activities of Guiseppe Lupollo, who immigrated to the United States from Sicily in 1902. As the Lupollo family group grew in this country, it came to include members of other Italian families added through marriage. The Lupollo criminal organization was a family business, in which all of the important leadership and authority positions in it were filled by members of the family. The organizational rules of the family business consisted of the following:

The family operates as a social unit with social organization and business functions merged.

All leadership positions, down to "middle-management" level, are assigned on the basis of kinship.

The higher the position in the organization, the closer the kinship relationship.

Leadership positions are assigned to a central group of family members, all of whom have close consanguineal or affinal relationships.

Members of this leadership group are assigned to either legal or illegal enterprises, but not to both.

Transfer of monies from illegal to legal and back into illegal activities takes place through individuals, and is part of the close-kin organization of the family.[42]

Ianni conceded that there are other criminal-family organizations in organized crime, including the Passalaqua and DeMaio groups included in his study. He argued, however, that the Lupollo crime business operated independently of any national commission ruling over all organized crime in the United States. He declared that: "The Lupollos do maintain contacts with other reputed *Cosa Nostra* families in the New York area and in other parts of the country. There is no question, however, that as far as the Lupollo family is concerned membership in the organizational hierarchy is determined by blood and marriage and is not an option for outsiders."[43]

This discussion has already noted the arguments of Bell and others regarding organized crime as a "queer ladder of opportunity" which Italian-Americans have utilized to gain entry into the mainstream of American life. Ianni reported that the Lupollo family business became increasingly concentrated on legitimate activities in its later decades, so that in the fourth generation, only four of twenty-seven male family members were involved in criminal activities, with the rest being engaged in medicine, law, education, or private business. He predicted that Italian-Americans, like the Irish and Jews before them, ultimately will move out of crime entirely and into legitimate enterprises, with their place in criminal organizations being taken by blacks, Puerto Ricans, and Cubans.[44]

In a subsequent study growing out of his investigation of the Lupollo organization, Ianni probed into ethnic succession of blacks and Hispanic-Americans in organized crime in Harlem, Brooklyn, and Paterson, New Jersey.[45] He contended that members of these groups are gaining increased control over lower-echelon levels of organized crime in these communities. However, rather than being integrated around familism, activities among these individuals were structured around networks, that is, collectivities of unrelated individuals drawn together in criminality. These networks have been created out of bonding relationships of various kinds, including childhood friendships, recruitment of juveniles into crime by adult offenders, prison ties, adult friendships, and kinship links between two or more persons. Ianni speculated that full-scale ethnic succession of blacks and Hispanic-Americans in organized crime will require that they gain control over criminal activities outside the ghetto, which they have not yet managed to accomplish. Further, some organizing principle parallel to Italian-American kinship links which will bring a number of independent criminal networks together into a larger structure will have to be found, along with greater access to political power and opportunities to corrupt public officials. In short, there is an uncertain criminal future for these groups.

Another report on organized crime which paralleled Ianni's description of the Lupollo family in a number of ways was Gardiner's study of "Wincanton," which was a fictitious name for an East Coast city.[46] In Wincanton, a crime syndicate operated by a Jewish head, Irv Stern, controlled organized prostitution and, later in its career, gambling operations in that city. The Stern organization survived through extensive corruption of police administrators and politicians which was deliberately brought about and nourished by the criminal syndicate. Indeed, as in other cities where organized crime exists, collusion of the police and city officials is required if crime is to continue. But, of greatest significance for the arguments in this chapter was the observation by Gardiner that no evidence existed to show that the Stern organization was dominated by or intimately tied to any out-of-state or national crime commission.

Finally, William Chambliss's study of organized crime in "Rainfall West," a fictitious name for Seattle, contributed to clarification of this question of a national crime commission.[47] The organized-crime syndicate in Seattle was in control of gambling, distribution of pornographic materials, prostitution, and certain other forms of crime. Chambliss indicated that the police, in collusion with the organized-crime elements, managed the contradictions between citizen demands for vice and demands for vice suppression by adopting tolerance policies and by segregating vice activities ecologically, containing them in slum areas where citizens were least likely to protest against them. Chambliss also identified a "crime cabal" in the Seattle area, made up of politicians, corrupted police officers, and certain business interests, all of whom were joined together in collusion with those who managed the criminal activities. But, as in Gardiner's report on Wincanton, few links of this cabal to a nationwide crime commission were apparent.

The most reasonable conclusion from these studies is that the burden of proof rests with those who maintain that there is a national crime commission which exerts control over local or regional organized-crime operations, for the accounts provided by Ianni, Gardiner, and Chambliss do not square with those contentions about a national Mafia or Cosa Nostra.

gambling in the United States

The discussion earlier in this chapter suggested that gambling and other forms of consumptive activity have emerged as prominent contemporary forms of organized crime in America.

Although facts regarding the extent of gambling are difficult to ascertain, all the available estimates indicate that gambling is big business.[48] For example, Kefauver suggested that over 50 million adult Americans gamble in some way or another and spend $30 billion per year in this activity. Of this sum, $6 billion represented the profit to syndicates and gambling entrepreneurs. This figure was greater than the annual profits of all the largest industrial enterprises combined in the United States.[49] Fred Cook offered a similar staggering estimate of the profits in gambling; he asserted that this activity nets $10 billion per year in profits to those who control gambling.[50]

What accounts for the involvement of hordes of Americans in gambling? On a general level, Herbert Bloch argued that gambling of various kinds meets deep-seated human needs.[51] Among other things, it introduces an element of hope into lives otherwise filled with failure and despair. The chance of winning through gambling offers working-class persons an opportunity to demonstrate mastery over their lives. Furthermore, Bloch contended that gambling finds a particularly tolerant audience in the United States, for it is little different in principle from socially approved forms of risk-taking and tampering with fate, such as stock-market speculation.

Irving Zola made some concrete observations regarding the social functions of gambling.[52] He studied horse race betting in a lower-class bar and discovered that this behavior represented a method by which the working-class person could gain some recognition by "beating the system" and demonstrating that one's fate is not solely a matter of luck. The horse players who had highest status among their peers were those who at least occasionally won and employed betting systems, handicapping techniques, and so on.

Gambling serves other social functions as well. The persistence and popularity of "numbers" or "policy" gambling in urban areas is due in part to the fact that it operates as a kind of welfare aid. Although the numbers player has a slight likelihood of winning a wager placed on some number in a drawing of some sort, when he or she does occasionally win, the earnings allow the purchase of goods and services he or she could not otherwise obtain. Policy winnings make possible hedonistic pleasures that could not be obtained through legitimate welfare services provided by local or state government. Thus, numbers profits make the difference between dull monotony and an occasional moment of novelty and pleasure. Local residents of urban slum areas have relatively enthusiastic views of policy gambling.[53]

In their detailed examination of the numbers racket in Chicago's "Black Belt" area, St. Clair Drake and Horace Cayton indicated that it was one of the major businesses in that neighborhood, providing employment for many local residents. Their analysis documented the linkages between organized crime and the police. Chicago blacks prominent in numbers enjoyed high status as "race leaders" and "race heroes" in the community.[54]

In locales where the playing of numbers is commonplace, it is often bound up with magical practices and other elaborations. George McCall has shown that numbers and hoodoo religion are intertwined in black communities, so the players' choices of numbers on which to bet are made in terms of superstitions, religious omens, and so on.[55]

These observations about gambling suggest that it is likely to persist as one of the more enduring forms of organized crime in America. In an affluent society which at the same time produces a marked sense of alienation in many citizens, gambling will continue as an outlet for numerous frustrations and hostilities.[56]

the drug business

Organized-crime syndicates have often been accused of corrupting citizens through the purveying of gambling, pornography, or drugs. In all of these cases, citizens are seen as being seduced or lured into degradation by malevolent organized-crime figures.

Something is out of whack with laymen's perceptions of the drug problem. William Simon and John Gagnon, among others, have pointed out that ours is a drug age or culture, in which the majority of citizens use one kind of drug or another—stimulants, tranquilizers, or other chemical substance—to face the demands of modern living.[57] Accordingly, it is not just the "grass" smoker or opiate user who represents the drug user; instead, these are but two relatively uncommon forms of a much wider drug problem that the criminal-justice system has singled out for attention. Table 16 indicates the range of drugs Americans use in addition to alcohol.

A few words of explanation are in order concerning Table 16. *Drug use* should be distinguished from *drug addiction*, for the latter is a special case of the former. Drug addiction involves three elements: overpowering compulsion to take a drug, tolerance or the development of a need for increased dosages of the drug over time, and psychic dependence on it. Marijuana is not an addicting drug, whereas opiates are markedly addicting in character. Individuals engage in sporadic smoking of marijuana without developing any pronounced craving for the drug or tolerance to it. Opiate users, on the other hand, exhibit compulsive use of the drug, tolerance, and also exhibit an *abstinence syndrome*. That is, persons who have become involved in continued use of opiates invariably experience physiological distress involving tearing of the eyes, cramps, tenseness, sweating, and other physical responses when they withdraw from opiate use.

The use of opiates—that is, opium derivatives (morphine, heroin, and codeine)—as well as of cocaine, marijuana, and other drugs has not always been illegal. Some authorities have pointed out that nineteenth-century America was a "dope fiend's paradise," in that physicians openly dispensed opiates, drug stores sold them over the counter without prescriptions, and they could be obtained from general stores, grocery stores, and mail-order houses as well. Most of the opium was imported, but some was grown in the Southern states during the Civil War.[58]

Doubtless, there are a number of reasons behind the rise of "drug fiend" stereotypes, in which users of marijuana, opiates, or other drugs have become the target of hostile public attitudes and efforts to criminalize behavior through the passage of laws proscribing the use of these substances. Howard Becker identified the Federal Narcotics Bureau, acting in the role of *moral entrepreneur*, as a major force in promulgating hostile views of addicts.[59] Federal and state narcotics-enforcement personnel have been the principal source from which these definitions of the seriousness of drug use and the drug addict have derived, so these groups have contributed heavily to current attitudes.

The history of legislation against opiates is instructive.[60] The first major piece of legislation concerning opiates was the Pure Food and Drug Act of 1906, which required that medicines containing opium derivatives be so labeled. That act also had the consequence of protecting addicts from impure drugs.

The 1906 act was followed by the Harrison Narcotic Act of 1914, which cut

table 16 classification of psychoactive drugs, with medically addictive properties and examples of each type[a]

drug effects[b]	opiate narcotics	stimulants	minor tranquilizers (sedative hypnotics and depressants)	major tranquilizers	antidepressants	hallucinogenic (psychotogenic or "mind expanding")	cannabis
Physical dependence	+	–	+		–		–
Tolerance	+	+	+	–	–	+	– ?
Psychological dependence	+	+	+	–	–		+
Examples of each drug type	Heroin Morphine Meperidine (demerol) Methadone (dolophine) Hydromorphine (dilaudid) Codeine Paregoric	Cocaine Amphetamine (dexedrine, benzedrine) Metham-phetamine (methedrine)	Barbiturate (pentobarbital, phenobarbital, amytal, seconal) Glutethamide (doriden) Meprobamate (equanil, miltown) Chlordiazepoxide (librium) Chloral hydrate Peraldehyde Alcohol	Phenothiazines (thorazine, mellaril, stelazine)	Imipramine (tofranil) Amitriptyline (elavil)	LSD STP DMT Mescaline (peyote) Psilocybin Morning glory seeds	Marijuana Hashish

[a]From Donald D. Pet and John C. Ball, "Marijuana Smoking in the United States," *Federal Probation*, 32 (September 1968), 8–15.
[b]In considering the medically addictive properties of each drug type, "–" represents slight or no effect; "+" that the property is present; and "?" that the effect is not clearly established.

off the legal supply of opiates to addicts. Interestingly, the apparent intent of the act was to regulate the flow of drugs by imposing a tax on persons who produced, imported, or in other ways dealt with opium and cocaine. The act explicitly exempted physicians from registration and taxation, requiring them only to keep records of drugs dispensed "in the course of his professional practice only." However, this phrase was interpreted by enforcement agents and the courts as prohibiting physicians from prescribing opiates for the purpose of maintaining addicts in their addiction. Denied was the claim that addiction was a disease, and addicts were not regarded as medical patients. The end result, apparently quite unintended by the 1914 Congress, was that drug addiction became criminalized, opiate addicts became defined as criminals, the legal sources of opiates dried up, and organized crime moved into the business of importing and supplying illicit heroin.

Estimates of the extent of drug use or the profits from the illegal traffic in drugs are relatively easy to come by but difficult to give much credence. Consider the obstacles faced by anyone who would attempt to accurately identify all heroin addicts in this country. Even so, various estimates of the magnitude of this phenomenon have been made. John Clausen contended that there are probably between 100,000 and 200,000 opiate users in the United States, concentrated in metropolitan areas within New York, Illinois, and California, with others gathered in Washington, D.C., Detroit, St. Louis, Dallas, and a few other metropolitan areas.[61] Another estimate put the number of heroin users in the early 1970s at between 400,000 and 600,000 persons.[62]

Parenthetically, popular public opinion sterotypes opiate addicts as wild-eyed fiends from the criminal underworld. However, a relatively large number of physicians and other medical personnel also are narcotic addicts. Charles Winick claimed that the addiction rate among doctors is 1 in 100 physicians, compared to a rate of 1 in 3,000 in the general population. He studied nearly a hundred doctors who had been drug addicts and attributed their addiction to a number of factors, one of which was relatively easy access to narcotics.[63]

Regarding the heroin business, Cressey indicated that one congressional investigatory committee estimated that drug addicts in the United States spend about $350 million per year for heroin.[64] Even if that estimate is inaccurate, it is clear enough that drug trafficking is big business. Cressey and others have also outlined the nature of this importing-distributing-wholesaling-retailing business in opiates and the central role of organized crime in it.[65]

What can be said about heroin users themselves? In the years since passage of the Harrison Act, certain major shifts have occurred in the social characteristics of addicts. In earlier decades, only about 10 percent of the addicts at the U.S. Public Health Service Hospital, Lexington, Kentucky, which treats drug users, were blacks, whereas in recent years about two-fifths of the addict patients have been blacks. Although two or three decades ago only about 10 percent of the addicts were under 25 years of age, in recent years over one-third of them were under 25 years of age.

Present-day heroin addicts come from certain urban social areas in largest numbers. These neighborhoods show a concentration of indices of social breakdown—high crime and delinquency rates, high rates of prostitution and illegitimacy, high infant mortality, and large numbers of broken homes. They are also areas of marked population density, with a great deal of population turnover among the heterogeneous groups who live there.

One major study that documented the wretched character of the neighborhoods from which addicts come was carried out by Isidor Chein and others in New York City.[66] Their evidence showed that, in addition to the social and physical deterioration characteristic of these areas, two cultural themes pervaded the social life of high-delinquency–high-addiction neighborhoods. The residents commonly exhibited negative perspectives on life along with a deep-seated sense of futility.[67]

summary

This chapter has examined organized crime, a form of lawbreaking which Americans often pretend does not exist. Public attention is much more often addressed to garden-variety street crimes, burglaries, and the like, than at criminal business enterprises. At other times, organized crime has captured the interest of Americans, frequently in the form of glorified portrayals encountered in the *Godfather* movies, based on the novel by Mario Puzo,[68] or in Gay Talese's *Honor Thy Father*, an account of the real-life Bonanno crime family which characterized the members of this group along lines of middle-class conventionality.[69]

The basic facts regarding the widespread character of organized crime in America and of the financial returns from syndicated lawbreaking are not in question. In addition, nearly all would identify the Prohibition era as the time when organized crime grew to prominence in this country. However, claims regarding the existence of an international Mafia crime cartel or of a nationwide criminal conspiracy administered by a central crime commission, are matters of considerable controversy.

Those who are skeptical of the accounts of a national Mafia or Cosa Nostra organization often have suggested that these contentions serve to deflect attention away from the extent to which organized crime is bound up with the conventional social order. Organized crime is an illegal business, providing illicit services that are in wide demand. Also, organized crime is nourished through the corruption and connivance of politicians, the police, and others. In short, organized crime cannot be accounted for by simplistic claims about the insidious activities of Italian-American or other ethnic "enemies within."

The empirical studies of organized-crime groups in American cities examined in this chapter support the characterization of organized crime as: (1) local or regional in form, and (2) constituting a criminal business in which criminals, governmental officials, business interests, and the local police are all implicated.

A parallel point can be made about the use of illegal drugs in the United States. This chapter indicated some of the ways in which the use of illegal drugs arises out of widespread use of chemical substances of one kind or another in this country. In this sense, if the criminal addict is a fiend, we must be a nation of drug fiends.

notes

[1]One general discussion of organized crime in America, drawing upon much of the literature on organized crime, is Frederic D. Homer, *Guns and Garlic* (West Lafayette, Ind.: Purdue University Press, 1974).

[2]Alfred R. Lindesmith, "Organized Crime," *Annals of the American Academy of Political and Social Science*, 217 (September 1941), 119–27.

[3]Francis A. J. Ianni with Elizabeth Reuss-Ianni, *A Family Business* (New York: Russell Sage Foundation, 1972), p. 61.

[4]For some commentary on this matter, see Robert K. Merton, *Social Theory and Social Structure*, rev. ed. (New York: Free Press, 1957), pp. 72–82.

[5]Daniel Bell, "Crime as an American Way of Life," *Antioch Review*, 13 (June 1953), 131–54.

[6]Ibid., p. 132.

[7]Gus Tyler, ed., *Organized Crime in America* (Ann Arbor: University of Michigan Press, 1962). Also see Thomas C. Shelling, "Economic Analysis and Organized Crime," in *The Crime Establishment*, John E. Conklin, ed. (Englewood Cliffs, N.J.: Prentice-Hall, Inc., 1973), pp. 75–103.

[8]Ibid, p. 48.

[9]For a history of organized crime, see Bell, "Crime as an American Way of Life"; Herbert A. Bloch and Gilbert Geis, *Man, Crime, and Society*, 2nd ed. (New York: Random House, 1970), pp. 194–97.

[10]Humbert S. Nelli, "Italians and Crime in Chicago: The Formative Years, 1890–1920," *American Journal of Sociology*, 74 (January 1969), 373–91. Also see Nelli, *The Business of Crime* (New York: Oxford University Press, 1976). This same point was made by Ianni and Ianni, *A Family Business*, pp. 48–54.

[11]Kenneth Allsop, *The Bootleggers and Their Era* (Garden City, N.Y.: Doubleday, 1961), p. 14; see also Alson J. Smith, *Syndicate City* (Chicago: Henry Regnery & Co., 1954).

[12]For a description of this operation on the west coast, see Robert Y. Thornton, "Organized Crime in the Field of Prostitution," *Journal of Criminal Law, Criminology and Police Science*, 46 (March–April 1956), 775–79.

[13]See Jerome H. Skolnick, *Justice Without Trial* (New York: John Wiley, 1966), pp. 96–111.

[14]Bell, "Crime as an American Way of Life," p. 152.

[15]Geis has also remarked on the decline of violence as a style among organized criminals. Gilbert Geis, "Violence and Organized Crime," *Annals of The American Academy of Political and Social Science*, 364 (March 1966), 86–95.

[16]Bell, "Crime as an American Way of Life," p. 154.

[17]Estes Kefauver, *Crime in America* (Garden City, N.Y.: Doubleday, 1951); see also Morris Ploscowe, ed., *Organized Crime and Law Enforcement*, two vols. (New York: The Grosby Press, 1952).

[18]Robert F. Kennedy, *The Enemy Within* (New York: Harper & Row, Pub., 1960).

[19]The President's Commission on Law Enforcement and Administration of Justice, *The Challenge of Crime in a Free Society* (Washington, D.C.: U.S. Government Printing Office, 1967), pp. 187–209.

[20]Ibid., pp. 188–91.

[21]Kefauver, *Crime in America*, p. 12.

[22]Ibid., p. 14.

[23]For accounts of the Sicilian Mafia, see Norman Lewis, *The Honored Society* (New York: Putnam's 1964); Giovanni Schiavo, *The Truth About the Mafia* (New York: Vigo Press, 1962); Ianni and Ianni, *A Family Business;* Nelli, *The Business of Crime*.

[24]Edward J. Allen, *Merchants of Menace—The Mafia* (Springfield, Ill.: Chas C Thomas, 1962).

[25]Frederic Sondern, Jr., *Brotherhood of Evil: The Mafia* (New York: Farrar, Straus & Giroux, 1959).

[26]Ed Reid, *Mafia* (New York: Random House, 1952).

[27]The President's Commission on Law Enforcement and Administration of Justice, *The Challenge of Crime in a Free Society*, pp. 192–95.

[28]Robert T. Anderson, "From Mafia to Cosa Nostra," *American Journal of Sociology*, 71 (November 1965), 10.

[29]Donald R. Cressey *Theft of the Nation* (New York: Harper & Row, Pub., 1969), pp. x–xi. Copyright © 1969 by Donald R. Cressey. Reprinted by permission of Harper & Row Publishers, Inc. See also Cressey, *Criminal Organization* (New York: Harper & Row, Pub., 1972). In this book, Cressey discussed the Mafia hypothesis. In addition, he presented a typology of forms of criminal organization, of which the alleged national crime alliance managed by a commission is the most complex pattern.

[30]For incisive, detailed discussions of the arguments and evidence concerning a nationwide Mafia, see Ianni and Ianni, *A Family Business*, pp. 1–14; Conklin, *The Crime Establishment*, pp. 1–24.

[31]Joseph L. Albini, *The American Mafia: Genesis of a Legend* (Englewood Cliffs, N.J.: Prentice-Hall, Inc., 1971).

[32]Dwight C. Smith, Jr., *The Mafia Myth* (New York: Basic Books, 1975).

[33]Gordon Hawkins, "God and the Mafia," *The Public Interest*, 14 (Winter 1969), 24–51. Hawkins drew attention to such curious logic as instances where denials by organized crime figures that a Mafia exists were taken as strong evidence for its existence.

[34]Ianni and Ianni, *A Family Business*, p. 110.

[35]Bell, "Crime as an American Way of Life."

[36]Cf. Nelli, who asserted: "At the time when 'American' Italians were arriving at maturity only to find economic advancement made difficult (but not impossible) by inadequate education, social and ethnic background, lack of political connections, a new field of endeavor appeared, requiring as qualifications only ambition, ruthlessness, and loyalty." Nelli, "Italians and Crime in Chicago," p. 389.

[37]Shiavo, *The Truth About the Mafia*.

[38]Ianni and Ianni, *A Family Business*, pp. 1–14.

[39]Ibid.

[40]Ibid., p. 43.

[41]Ibid., p. 15.

[42]Ibid., p. 106.

[43]Ibid., p. 134.

[44]Ibid., pp. 192–94.

[45]Francis A. J. Ianni, *Black Mafia* (New York: Simon & Schuster, 1974).

[46]John A. Gardiner, *The Politics of Corruption: Organized Crime in an American City* (New York: Russell Sage Foundation, 1970); Gardiner, "Wincanton: The Politics of Corruption," in The President's Commission on Law Enforcement and Administration of Justice, *Task Force Report: Organized Crime* (Washington, D.C.: U.S. Government Printing Office, 1967), pp. 61–79.

[47]William J. Chambliss, "Vice, Corruption, Bureaucracy, and Power." *Wisconsin Law Review*, 4 (1971), 1130–55. Also see Chambliss, *On the Take* (Bloomington, Ind.: Indiana University Press, 1978).

[48]For a useful review of materials on gambling, see Robert D. Herman, *Gambling* (New York: Harper & Row, Pub. 1967); for analyses of gambling in Nevada where it is legal, see Wallace Turner, *Gambler's Money* (Boston: Houghton Mifflin Company, 1965); Jerome H. Skolnick, *House of Cards* (Boston: Little, Brown, 1980).

[49]Herbert A. Bloch, "The Dilemma of American Gambling: Crime or Pastime?" in *Crime in America*, Bloch, ed., (New York: Philosophical Library, 1961), p. 335.

[50]Fred J. Cook, "Gambling, Inc.," *The Nation*, 191 (October 22, 1960). This special issue of *The Nation* was devoted to a lengthy and revealing essay on American gambling by Cook.

[51]Bloch, "The Dilemma of American Gambling."

[52]Irving Kenneth Zola, "Observations on Gambling in a Lower-Class Setting," in *The Other Side*, Howard S. Becker, ed., (New York: Free Press, 1964), pp. 247–60.

[53]For a detailed account of the numbers racket, see St. Clair Drake and Horace R. Cayton, *Black Metropolis* (New York: Harcourt Brace Jovanovich, 1945), pp. 470–94.

[54]Ibid.

[55]George J. McCall, "Symbiosis: The Case of Hoodoo and the Numbers Racket," in Becker, *The Other Side*, pp. 51–66.

[56]For one case illustration of this point, see William Barry Furlong, "Out in the Bleachers, Where the Action Is," *Harper's*, 233 (July 1966), 49–53.

[57]William Simon and John H. Gagnon, "Children of the Drug Age," *Saturday Review*, 51 (September 21, 1968), 60–78.

[58]Edward M. Brecher and the editors of *Consumer Reports*, *Licit and Illicit Drugs* (Boston: Little, Brown, 1972), pp. 3–7. See this entire volume for a detailed compendium of information on licit and illicit drugs in the United States.

[59]Howard S. Becker, *Outsiders* (New York: Free Press, 1963), pp. 121–46. See also Troy Duster, *The Legislation of Morality* (New York: Free Press, 1970), pp. 3–28.

[60]Brecher, *Licit and Illicit Drugs*, pp. 47–55.

[61]John A. Clausen, "Drug Use," in *Contemporary Social Problems*, 3rd ed., Robert K. Merton and Robert A. Nisbet, eds. (New York: Harcourt Brace Jovanovich, 1970), p. 205.

[62]Marshall B. Clinard, *Sociology of Deviant Behavior*, 4th ed. (New York: Holt, Rinehart & Winston, 1974), p. 401.

[63]Charles Winick, "Physician Narcotic Addicts," *Social Problems*, 9 (Fall 1961), 174–86.

[64]Cressey, *Theft of the Nation*, p. 91.

[65]Ibid., pp. 91–95; Edward A. Preble and John J. Casey, Jr., "Taking Care of Business—The Heroin User's Life on the Street," *International Journal of the Addictions*, 4 (March 1969): 7.

[66]Isidor Chein, Donald L. Gerard, Robert S. Lee, and Eva Rosenfeld, *The Road to H* (New York: Basic Books, 1964), pp. 47–77.

[67]Ibid., pp. 78–108.

[68]Mario Puzo, *The Godfather* (New York: Fawcett Publications, 1969).

[69]Gay Talese, *Honor Thy Father* (New York: World Publishing Co., 1971).

"vice"
and
folk
crime

Occasionally, in preceding chapters on garden-variety, white-collar, and organized crime, discussions have been interrupted by brief asides about "folk crime," "victimless crimes," and other relatively invisible, petty, but common kinds of lawbreaking in American society. The general observation has been offered a number of times that much of the crime in modern societies is mundane and unexciting stuff but is behavior in which many citizens engage. The time has now come to give these latter forms of criminality more systematic and detailed attention.

Some indication of the extent of relatively petty and socially less visible crime can be gained from FBI statistics, which, in Table 17, estimate the total arrests for a number of specific crimes in the United States in 1979.

The data in Table 17 show that large numbers of arrests are made each year for marijuana use and various crimes involving alcohol, as well as for a number of other forms of lawbreaking, many of which appear to be relatively petty and inconsequential. Parenthetically, FBI estimates indicate that while arrests for drug use of various kinds increased by roughly 25 percent between 1970 and 1979, arrests for drunkenness dropped by 46 percent, while disorderly conduct arrests declined by roughly 4.5 percent and vagrancy arrests shrunk by 66 percent.[1] These figures are related to relatively recent court decisions that prohibit the arrest of chronic alcoholics for public drunkenness, as well as certain other law-enforcement developments.

These lifeless statistics from FBI and other police-agency sources on arrests and crimes known to the police can be supplemented by journalistic and qualitative accounts revealing widespread lawbreaking that usually goes undetected. Vandalism is a case in point, for reports on vandalism make it abundantly clear that large numbers of relatively law-abiding citizens apparently consider such acts not to be serious in nature.[2] Along the same line, supermarkets are plagued by shoppers who take expensive shopping carts away from the stores, later abandoning them to rust in vacant lots, ditches, and so on. These same supermarkets have found it increasingly necessary to contrive various devices designed to deter shoppers from stealing razor blades, small canned goods, and various other small items from the store shelves. Such theft is crime, whether it is regarded as such by the perpetrators or not. Finally, although detailed statistics are impossible to come by, there is convincing evidence that many service employees such as waitresses and hotel bellhops fail to report tip income, in violation of tax regulations. These activities are so difficult to detect that the guilty parties are able to engage in them with impunity.

crime in the hinterland

Few contemporary Americans lead the bucolic existence that is believed to have characterized life in this nation before the turn of the century. As the country has grown in size and complexity, particularly in the second half of the twentieth century, the sharp division between urban and rural American has become blurred. Then, too, as many commentators have pointed out, the mass media, particularly television, have further homogenized the cultural life of the nation.

However, rural and small-town life has not disappeared entirely, nor have the differences between large metropolitan areas and the hinterland entirely vanished. One indication of the persistence of these differences is found in crime rates for metropolitan areas, smaller cities, and rural areas. Comparative rates for major crimes in 1979 are shown in Table 18. Crime rates for smaller cities and rural areas were generally lower than those for standard metropolitan areas, with particularly low rates in rural areas being recorded for robbery, burglary, larceny, car theft, and assault.[3] This abstract data can also be brought to life through anecdotal evidence, studies of crime in a few rural or hinterland areas, and other materials of that kind.

One bit of anecdotal data on crime in the hinterland can be found in the "Police Log" column of a weekly newspaper published in a relatively rural county on the Washington-state coast. That log is comprised of incident reports from police in the two small towns in that county as well as the county sheriff's office. A sampling of these items includes the following:

A citizen called and stated that there was a drunk man laying on the street at the corner of Lake and Myrtle Streets. Officer found the subject at the corner and returned him home.
One double-bladed axe with a yellow head valued at $15 and two splitting mauls valued at $20 each were reported stolen from Bill Cutting's garage October 25 between 8 A.M. and 3 P.M. The garage is located at the south end of Myrtle Street.
The Shelburne Inn of Seaview reported that a restaurant guest had left the business without paying his bill and was last seen heading toward Ilwaco.
Alan Goulter complained that there were people picking mushroons in his field.

These reports of crimes, mostly petty in nature, were sprinkled in with other items having to do with peace-keeping activities of the local police in which law violations were not involved. Indeed, incidents such as those following were more frequently reported by the police than were arrests:

Dick Murfin of Seaview reported that approximately 7 to 8 cows belonging to Mrs. Christner were out on Butts Road.
The upper Naselle area experienced a power outage.[4]

table 17   total estimated arrests, United States, 1979[a]

offense	number
Drug-abuse violations	558,500
Opium or cocaine and their derivatives	(68,100)
Marijuana	(391,600)
Synthetic or manufactured narcotics	(18,400)
Other dangerous nonnarcotic drugs	(80,400)
Gambling	54,800
Offenses against family	57,400
Driving under the influence	1,324,800
Liquor laws	416,200
Drunkenness	1,172,700
Disorderly conduct	765,500
Vagrancy	37,200
All other offenses (except traffic)	1,716,600

[a]Federal Bureau of Investigation, U.S.Department of Justice, *Crime in the United States: Uniform Crime Reports, 1979* (Washington, D.C.: U.S.Government Printing Office, 1980), p. 188.

table 18   crime rates, metropolitan areas, other cities, and rural areas, 1979[a] (rates per 100,000 population)

	total	murder, nonnegligent manslaughter	forcible rape	robbery	aggravated assault	burglary	larceny–theft	motor-vehicle theft
U.S. Total	5,521.5	9.7	34.5	212.1	279.1	1,499.1	2,988.4	498.5
Standard metropolitan areas	6,313.1	10.9	41.1	276.2	312.5	1,708.8	3,353.1	610.6
Other cities	4,948.6	5.7	18.3	57.9	248.0	1,134.4	3,218.0	266.3
Rural areas	2,167.5	7.4	15.1	22.1	142.8	770.8	1,072.2	137.1

[a]Federal Bureau of Investigation, *Crime in the United States: Uniform Crime Reports, 1979*), p.38.

One study of criminality in the hinterland was conducted by the author in three relatively rural adjacent counties in Oregon.[5] Approximately 75 to 150 miles east of Portland, the three counties had a diversified economic base, but in all three fruit growing and other forms of agriculture were predominant features of their economy. One of the counties had a population of about 22,000 in 1970, while the other two had 14,000 and 2,400 residents. The largest city in the three counties had a 1970 population of 12,000.

The police agencies in these three counties included a state-police contingent with general law-enforcement powers, city police in two communities, and sheriff's departments in all three counties. The court system involved: two justice-of-the-peace courts which handled traffic cases and petty misdemeanors; three municipal courts dealing with violations of city ordinances; two district courts handling traffic cases, along with petty and more serious misdemeanors; and one circuit court handling felony cases.

The two city police departments dealt principally with traffic violations, particularly parking tickets. Most of the arrests in the two towns were for relatively petty forms of lawbreaking, such as drunkenness and traffic violations of one kind or another. Those arrested persons who appeared in municipal court and were convicted were given fines, or jail terms if unable to pay fines, in most cases.

What part did the sheriff's departments in the three counties play in the law-enforcement picture? Investigators such as T. C. Esselstyn have noted that the role of county sheriff is often a peace-keeping one, rather than a law-enforcement job.[6] The sheriffs in these three counties were heavily involved in maintaining public order, rather than in apprehending dangerous criminals.

One sheriff did not maintain regular statistical records, while in another sheriff's office, most of the cases handled were for traffic violations and other relatively petty matters. The third department enumerated "complaints received" rather than arrests, with such entries as the following: "beer parties," "bikes, cycles, and Hondas," "dynamite," "hippies," "late fisherman," and "disturbances." Peace-keeping operations apparently loomed large in the workload of these agencies.

The two justice-of-the-peace courts, presided over by untrained laymen, did a large-scale business in traffic cases of one kind of another, including violations of various highway commercial-vehicles weight-and-load restrictions detected by the state weighmaster at a weigh station on a nearby interstate highway.

In 1969, the two district courts processed approximately 4,500 traffic cases, along with a much smaller number of game-law and boating violations, as well as petty offenses involving drunkenness or drinking-related activities. Serious criminality was infrequently encountered in the three counties, for in 1969 only 44 felony cases were processed through the circuit court. Eleven of these involved illegal possession of salmon and were ultimately dismissed.

In summary, in this relatively rural, three-county region of Oregon, petty lawbreaking was fairly commonplace, but major crimes were infrequent. What significance, if any, should be attached to these findings?

Two things can be said about these results. First, they point to the existence of a correctional backwater where large numbers of petty offenders receive little in the way of modern correctional assistance. Felony offenders get sent off to state prison, while the petty offenders receive fines or jail sentences. Sentence serving in the jails of the area was "doing time" in its grimmest form.

A second point is that few of the lawbreakers in the hinterland were career criminals who had acquired antisocial attitudes out of some long-term learning process. Risk-taking and situational factors go far toward accounting for this activity.[7]

Some similar observations about hinterland crime were made by Simon Dinitz, who conducted an in-depth study of a west-central Ohio town with 11,250 residents, located in a county of 30,000 population.[8] According to Dinitz, life in that small town resembled the peaceful and tranquil existence which many citizens of modern America apparently find appealing (but which others might regard as excruciatingly dull). At any rate, citizens of the town, dubbed "Lincoln" by Dinitz, commonly left their cars and houses unlocked while unattended, took few other precautions against criminals, and voiced little fear of crime in the community.

The crime and delinquency data gathered up by Dinitz largely confirmed citizens' views. Slightly over a hundred felony offenses, made up largely of burglaries, larcenies, and auto thefts, were reported to the city police in 1969. Crimes against the person were extremely rare. Relatively few of the felonies were cleared by arrest, thus misdemeanors made up most of the police arrests, with over three-fourths of them involving "offenses involving booze and boisterousness."[9]

According to Dinitz, when interviewed, many of the citizens of Lincoln alluded to "hanky panky" such as gambling, illicit sex, and other vices in which they believed many of their neighbors to be involved. But at the same time, when asked what they considered the major crime problem in Lincoln, many residents asserted that there was little or no crime in the town.

The citizens of Lincoln were relatively unconcerned about serious crime, largely because it was rare there. However, Dinitz also indicated that the residents were greatly concerned about "the drug pushers, murderers, hippies, protesters, long-hairs, freaks, demonstrators, rioters, and communists 'out there.' "[10] According to Dinitz, many of them were fearful that their peaceful existence was soon to be upset by an invasion of criminals and other deviants from urban America. The residents had a gut-level fear that the highly prized small-town life style was in danger of being destroyed, a premonition with which Dinitz agreed.

Some other indicators of the extent of crime in the hinterland can be drawn from the many studies of self-reported or "hidden" delinquency that have been carried out over the past three decades.[11] For example, in one of these Robert Dentler and Lawrence Monroe quizzed young adolescents in three locales—a suburban area, a rural nonfarm community, and a rural town in Kansas—about their involvement in delinquency.[12] Most of them reported engaging in petty delinquent acts, with those in the rural town being least frequently involved in misconduct. A number of these self-report studies have turned up parallel findings, with petty lawbreaking being least frequent among rural, hinterland youngsters.

Thus far in this discussion the lower rates of crime observed in rural areas have been emphasized along with the less serious nature of much of the criminality occurring there, as contrasted to crime in major cities. But, the other side of the coin also warrants mention, namely, that Table 18 does indicate that lawbreaking is not unheard of in rural areas. Homicide rates are fairly similar for rural and other areas. Although rape, robbery, assault, burglary, larceny, and car theft occur less frequently in rural communities, a considerable number of them do take place there. It would be a mistake to suppose that rural areas are totally free from serious acts of criminality. Finally, although sociologists have not given much attention to rural lawbreaking, there are plausible reasons to suspect that the fears of the citizens of Lincoln, reported by Dinitz, may reflect the growing frequency of criminality in rural areas throughout the United States.

folk crime

The observations to this point have indicated that criminality is less often encountered in rural and nonmetropolitan areas of the United States and also that much of the lawbreaking that is observed is relatively mundane activity that does not exact enormous social or economic costs from its victims. But, equally important, much of the lawbreaking that takes place in metropolitan areas also constitutes what H. Laurence Ross termed *folk crime*.[13]

Folk crimes are violations of laws enacted to solve problems arising out of the increased complexity and division of labor in modern societies. Traffic-law violations, chiseling on unemployment compensation, and violations of business and commercial regulations are examples of folk crime. Most of these offenses provoke mild social responses and involve only a low degree of social stigma. The persons who engage in them are often from middle- or upper-class groups. Folk crimes are often dealt with outside of the criminal courts, through traffic-violation bureaus, bail forfeiture, and administrative hearings.

The notion of folk crimes is sociological, not legalistic, thus the dividing line between folk and nonfolk crime is not entirely clear. However, an investigation in a large California probation department by Hartjen and Gibbons turned up a very large number of probationers who were involved in petty, transitory, socially innocuous offenses of the kind designated by Ross as folk crimes.[14] For example, many of these persons had been convicted of "failure to provide," which meant they had disregarded a court order from a divorce hearing that had directed them to provide child-support money to their exspouses. .

Another indication of the widespread existence of folk crime emerged from data of the Oregon state police which showed that, in 1969, they issued 2,928 warnings and made 10,738 arrests for fish-and-game-law violations, while the offenders in these cases paid nearly $200,000 in fines.[15] Although "chumming" for fish, hunting without a license, poaching deer, and so forth are not what citizens usually have in mind when they talk about the crime problem, this sort of activity is a significant form of lawbreaking, resulting in a considerable amount of police and court work.

This chapter has already alluded to some other offenses fitting the folk-crime description, including weight and load violations by trucking firms and waitresses and bellhops failing to report tip income to the state and federal taxing agencies.

If criminologists were to direct more attention to the search for other folk crimes, it it likely that myriad forms and massive amounts of it would come to light. For example, it is certainly not only bellhops and waitresses who withhold payment of state and federal taxes. A number of other professionals (e.g., college professors) are in a position to cheat on their taxes, for many of them earn sizable amounts of outside income from book publishers, consulting tasks, and kindred sources which can be hidden and not reported.

Criminologists and other sociologists not infrequently encounter other bits of information which suggest that folk crime is widespread. For example, some light is shed on folk crime in the pages of *Consumer Reports*, in which a variety of unethical and/or illegal practices on the part of automobile dealers, automobile repair shops, and various other business agencies have been reported.

One form of criminality that may straddle the borderland between folk and nonfolk crime is sex crime in subways, particularly in New York City. Recently, investigators have reported that "frottage," that is, genital rubbing, and genital exhibitionism, have become commonly encountered subway crimes in New York.[16] Frottage is often accomplished in crowded subway cars, where a sexual assailant bumps and rubs against a female victim and also subjects her to unwelcomed groping and fondling; exhibitionists expose their genitals to female strangers. Not uncommonly, these offenders engage in both offenses.

One would be ill-advised to invoke psychiatric hypotheses concerning this activity, attributing it to compulsions or other psychological aberrations. The offenders in these cases exhibited a good deal of planning and foresight, choosing times of the day in which the likelihood of being apprehended was lowest. Many also had developed some complicated sexual rituals and techniques employed in their crimes. Then, too, many of these persons showed prior records for violent offenses, which runs counter to psychiatric arguments that characterize these offenders as passive persons.

Contrary to popular wisdom that links such sexual offenses to middle-aged or older white males, these subway offenders were predominately under the age of 40. About half of them were married, and the majority were employed. Nearly 80 percent of the offenders who had been arrested were blacks or Hispanics.

Doubtless, most if not all of those women who are accosted by subway sex offenders are upset by the experience, thus these are not entirely innocuous crimes. However, the victims are more likely to regard the assailants as "creeps" than they are to view them as fiends who pose a real danger to them.

Parenthetically, another result of lawbreaking exists in New York subways that ought to be mentioned in any discussion of folk crimes, namely, the graffiti which covers subway cars there. For some years, New York City youths have been at work filling nearly every available blank space inside subway cars with scrawls from ink marking-pens and spray paint, as well as covering the exteriors of many cars with multicolored designs and graffiti. Although this subway activity is an instance of vandalism, it can also be viewed as a modern form of folk art. Most of the graffiti and painting on subway cars is abstract and decorative, rather than consisting of four-letter words or hostile remarks. Popular wisdom has it that the offender–folk artists who engage in this activity are youths from deprived backgrounds who are attempting to express their individuality and give some meaning to their lives. But whatever the explanation, it seems unlikely that it is to be found within the theories that criminologists usually offer for criminality.

"vices" and "crimes without victims"

Personal "vices" and victimless crimes are lawbreaking acts that are widely regarded as harmful only to the person or persons involved in them, if indeed they are harmful at all. Those who speak of "crimes without victims" have identified homosexuality, drug addiction, and, prior to its legalization, abortion as major exemplars of this category,[17] while others have added prostitution and gambling to this list.[18] A broad interpretation would extend this notion to the pornography business and public drunkenness as well.

A number of critics of laws directed at personal vices and victimless crimes have argued that, because these crimes lack victims and cause no other social harm, the laws prohibiting them ought to be expunged.[19] Thus, such activities would no longer be the law's business, even though the previously forbidden acts might well continue to take place. Another argument for decriminalization of these activities is that because most of them take place between consenting adults, as in the case of homosexuality, or between customers and suppliers of forbidden but sought-after substances or services, the laws related to them are virtually unenforceable, however desirable it might be to suppress the behavior. Because many of the illegal acts take place in private and no complainants come forth to report them, the police are virtually powerless to enforce the law unless they become involved in entrapment or other questionable detection tactics.

There is some evidence indicating that much of the general public agrees with proposals to abolish some victimless crimes by expunging the laws related to them.[20] At the same time, a major stumbling block to decriminalization is the widespread controversy among citizens—and sometimes among criminologists— regarding the extent to which particular activities are truly victimless.

Consider the case of abortion laws.[21] Prior to 1973 abortions were illegal in nearly every state except when absolutely necessary to preserve the life of the mother. However, in part due to the growing public support for liberalized abortion laws, the Supreme Court ruled in *Roe* vs. *Wade* that laws forbidding abortions are unconstitutional and that states may not regulate the conditions under which abortions can be performed by physicians within the first three months of pregnancy. However, various "right to life" groups have continued to agitate for a return to the older, restrictive antiabortion laws. Further, a 1977 Supreme Court decision ruled that neither the states nor the federal government are required to pay for elective abortions for persons who cannot afford them. The end result has been that in most states abortions are not state-funded, thus they are mainly available only to those who can pay for them.

The victimless status of other crimes is also at issue.[22] Many persons are of the opinion that prostitution should be legalized, but there are others who see a variety of social harms that are implicated in commercial sexual transactions. Similarly, many citizens regard marijuana smoking as a harmless personal habit and have gone about using marijuana on a regular basis. Even so, testimony is offered from time to time by physicians and other medical researchers, law-enforcement agents, and other citizens, holding that marijuana is harmful in some way and that its use should continue to be illegal. Then, too, while consensual acts of homosexuality among adult males, carried on in private, are now legal in 23 states, persons can be and still are arrested for public lewdness and solicitation. A number of large and highly vocal groups continue to resist the gay-rights movement and press for criminal sanctions against homosexuality. And, some medical practitioners and public-health workers point to the high rates of gonorrhea and syphilis among male homosexuals as indicating that their activities are not entirely harmless.[23]

Elsewhere in this book we have already touched upon certain victimless crimes and the social controversy swirling around them. Chapter 13 contained a discussion of male homosexuality, while Chapter 15 devoted attention to opiate use and the drug business operated by organized-crime figures. A few additional remarks are in order concerning other victimless crimes.

MARIJUANA USE

How many people smoke marijuana in the United States? Answers to questions about the extent of drug use are notoriously unreliable. Some authorities have offered the estimate that 50 million Americans have experimented with marijuana, but it is difficult to place much faith in that figure. Data on the extent of marijuana use rapidly become outdated, due to the rapid spread of marijuana use in the United States. On this point, the National Institute of Drug Abuse of the U.S. Department of Health and Human Services has indicated that, between 1962 and 1980, the proportion of persons 18 to 25 years of age who have used marijuana increased from 4 to 68 percent. Also, the 1979 National Survey on Drug Abuse, conducted by the same agency, reported that between 1972 and 1979 experience with marijuana and cocaine doubled among 12 to 17 year olds and among those over 25 years of age.[24]

As the population of "dopers" smoking marijuana has expanded, with more and more middle-class persons taking up marijuana, proposals to decriminalize this activity have also increased in popularity. At present, eight states have the most liberal marijuana laws, having made possession of small amounts of marijuana punishable only by a small fine; they are, Alaska, California, Colorado, Ohio, Oregon, Maine, Minnesota, and Mississippi.[25] However, marijuana use has not been completely decriminalized, in that it cannot be freely purchased without penalty, as can tobacco cigarettes anywhere in the United States. For example, in Oregon possession of less than one ounce of marijuana is a violation, punishable by a maximum fine of $100.

PROSTITUTION[26]

According to the familiar claim, female prostitution is "the world's oldest profession." Prostitution has existed for centuries nearly everywhere in the world. FBI statistics have indicated that 85,900 prostitution arrests were made by the police in the United States in 1977.[27] One frequently cited estimate is that somewhere between 100,000 and 500,000 women are involved in the prostitution business in this country, which nets $173 billion to those who operate prostitution or are employed in it.[28]

The arguments that have been offered in support of decriminalization of prostitution stress the inelastic demand for sexual services, resulting in strong pressures for its continuation. Among those who support prostitution are, of course, the customers, but it is also favored by businessmen who believe it attracts visitors to their cities and results in increased profits. Additionally, laws against prostitution are difficult if not impossible to enforce without discriminating against certain groups of prostitutes, such as streetwalkers, getting the police involved in the use of "decoys" and other practices of that kind.

"SKID ROAD" ALCOHOLISM[29]

No statistics are required to demonstrate that drinking of alcoholic beverages is extremely widespread in the United States. One indication of the ubiquity of alcohol use came from Harold Mulford's study involving a nationwide sample of persons over 21 years of age.[30] Nearly three-fourths of these persons reported themselves as drinkers, which translates to more than 80 million adult Americans who consume alcoholic beverages. Of these drinkers, 11 percent said they were "heavy drinkers." and 10 percent admitted that they had experienced difficulties in managing their drinking behavior.

Drinking behavior is of interest to criminologists for several reasons, but the most important is that arrests for drunkenness are extremely common in the United States. In 1979, 1,172,700 arrests for drunkenness were reported to the FBI.[31] "Skid Road" alcoholics, who make up many of these arrests, represent garden-variety offenders constituting a major class of lawbreakers. They also are involved in a sizable portion of the arrests for vagrancy and disorderly conduct.

The report of The President's Commission on Law Enforcement and the Administration of Justice contained information about drunkenness arrests in the United States. The commission indicated that not only were arrests for drunkenness and allied offenses exceedingly common, many offenders were chronic repeaters, turning up repeatedly in arrest statistics over an extended period of time. The commission also noted that communities varied markedly in their arrest policies for drunkenness. In a comparison of Washington, D.C., St. Louis, and Atlanta, widely discrepant figures emerged regarding the percentage that drunk arrests constituted of total arrests. In Washington, 76.5 percent of all arrests in 1965 were for drunkenness, disorderly conduct, and vagrancy, whereas in Atlanta 76.7 percent of the total arrests were for these reasons. In St. Louis, on the other hand—which had a tolerant policy toward drunks—only 18.9 percent of all arrests were for these offenses.[32]

Among alcoholics, it is the denizens of "Skid Road" who are of most concern to criminologists. In the folklore of American society, these individuals are sometimes thought to be similar to middle-class alcoholics. They are seen as persons who have experienced a fall from grace from which they eventually drifted to the "Skid Road" area and drinking as a life career. According to this romanticized version of "Skid Road" alcoholism, numerous exprofessors, exlawyers, and other persons of that sort are to be found on "Skid Road." But in fact, rather than being persons who gradually drifted into social degradation because of drinking, most "Skid Roaders" came from humble backgrounds and have been isolated from conventional patterns of social life and strong social ties for most of their adult lives.

One study of "Skid Roaders" was by David Pittman and C. Wayne Gordon, who gathered detailed data on 187 chronic-police-case inebriates in the Monroe County Penitentiary in Rochester, New York.[33] The sociocultural profile of these persons indicated that they were older than males in the general population, with a mean of 47.7 years of age. A high percentage of the inebriates were blacks, whereas Irish and English made up the largest nationality groups. Nearly 60 percent of the alcoholics had been married at some time, but almost none were living with their wives at the time of the study. These offenders were from disadvantaged social backgrounds, for 70 percent had not gone beyond grammar school, whereas 68 percent were unskilled workers. The majority of these individuals showed backgrounds of great residential instability. Most of them had been arrested many times, so they had a mean number of 16.5 arrests.[34]

Pittman and Gordon reported that the alcoholics were products of early family-life situations marked by inadequate socialization. According to these investigators, "Skid Roaders" were ill-equipped by virtue of their backgrounds to embark on stable adult lives.[35] As a result, most of them had experienced unsatisfactory marriages and had failed in their occupational endeavors.[36] Many of them then became caught up in "Skid Road" life, and a number of them had been institutionalized for lengthy periods of their lives. On "Skid Road" they turned to daily wine drinking, often with small groups of other alcoholics.[37]

A third report compared workhouse inmates incarcerated for drunkenness with a group of alcoholic patients in a volunteer clinic. The workhouse inmates were "Skid Roaders" who differed markedly from the volunteer patients, for the former were either unmarried or divorced, had begun drinking early in their lives, and had been isolated from conventional social ties for a long time.[38]

Additional studies of "Skid Road" alcoholics and other "Skid Road" residents have been conducted in Minneapolis,[39] Philadelphia,[40] Chicago,[41] New York,[42] San Francisco,[43] and Seattle.[44] These reports included findings that support the sketch of "Skid Roaders" in this book.

The social life of "Skid Road" has also been the subject of sociological attention. Joan Jackson and Ralph Connor have investigated this matter in Seattle, where they reported that two groups of residents populated "Skid Road": nonalcoholics and alcoholics. The alcoholic group was further divided into types recognized in the argot of the drinkers as "bums," "characters," "winos," "rubby-dubs," and "lushes." "Bums" and "characters" violated group norms about drinking or exhibited bizarre forms of behavior. "Winos" and "lushes," on the other hand, banded together in social groups devoted to drinking and forms of mutual aid.[45] W. Jack Peterson and Milton Maxwell have also analyzed the social life of "Skid Road" and have shown that many alcoholic residents were involved in a rich, although deviant, interactional network of social ties.[46] Jacqueline Wiseman's study revealed many details of life on "Skid Road," many of the alcoholics she studied were involved in a recurrent pattern of incarceration in a county jail, commitment to a state mental hospital, and residency in a Salvation Army facility.[47] James Spradley's study also provided a number of insights into the relationships between "Skid Roaders" and the police, courts, and jails.[48]

It is also true that different "Skid Roads" have different characteristics, reflecting in part at least the nature of the communities in which they are located. For example, a study of the Anchorage, Alaska, "Skid Road" showed the population to be roughly half Indian and half non-Indian, contrary to the expectation that an overwhelming majority would be Native Alaskans.[49] That study also indicated that the unemployed-derelict stereotype of the population of "Skid Road" was not totally accurate, for a significant number of "Skid Roaders" interviewed, both males and females, were either employed or employable and between jobs.

In their comparative analysis of the life styles of residents of an affluent area, a low-income area, and the Bowery in New York City, Bahr and Caplow convincingly demonstrated that the distinctive life style of the "Skid Road" resident is not due to alcohol consumption alone.[50] As they indicated: "We have tried to identify the characteristics which distinguish poor men, in skid row or out of it, from richer men, and have repeatedly found that the latter differences are greater than the former."[51] At another point, they noted: "Many of the factors conventionally identified as explaining the problems of skid row men prove on closer analysis to be generally characteristic of lives in poverty, although the skid row man *is* distinctive in his extraordinarily low occupational status and his extreme poverty" (emphasis in the original).[52]

Until recently, "Skid Roaders" have been arrested for "public drunkenness," sent off to jail or, much less frequently, to a detoxification center where they are "dried out" or detoxified, and then later released back to "Skid Road"; there, most of them quickly get rearrested and reenter the revolving door of the criminal-justice system. However, in 1966, two decisions reached in federal appeals courts, *Driver* v. *Hinnant* and *Easter* v. *District of Columbia*, declared that chronic alcoholics cannot be found guilty of public intoxication because alcoholism is a disease. Alcoholics were held to be compulsively driven to drinking, thus their drinking is not a voluntary act and they lack criminal intent. The thrust of these decisions was to get chronic-drunkenness cases out of the criminal-justice machinery and into some kind of treatment program.

These decisions led to the expectation that the Supreme Court would similarly find that alcoholics are incapable of refraining from drinking due to the disease of alcoholism and thus that they cannot be arrested for an illness which causes their behavior. Based upon this anticipation, a number of states and municipalities initiated steps toward providing detoxification facilities for the public inebriate to replace the usual police drunk tank. Even though in *Powell* v. *Texas* (1968) the Supreme Court did not so find, momentum for the decriminalization of public intoxication had begun to develop.[53]

A major force toward such a decriminalization has been provided by the National Institute on Alcohol and Alcoholism. Those states which adopt key elements of the Uniform Alcoholism and Intoxication Treatment Act—including the crucial element forbidding political subdivisions from passing ordinances making intoxication, in and of itself, a crime—qualify for incentive grants designed to allow State Alcoholism Authorities, also part of the Uniform Act, to apply for funds to facilitate the nonjudicial handling of public inebriates. This program has been the major force behind the decriminalization of public intoxication in 29 states and Puerto Rico as of 1979. In those jurisdictions, the "Skid Road" dweller remains subject to police attention, but he or she is no longer subject to arrest for any charge in which public drinking or drunkenness is the key element.

However, as the data presented earlier indicated, large numbers of persons, including "Skid Roaders," continue to be arrested for public drunkenness because public intoxication has not been decriminalized in many states. Large numbers of drunks continue to be dealt with through the criminal-justice apparatus.

Researchers have investigated the impact of court decisions on the processing of public inebriates. In one study, trends in public-drunkenness arrests in Minneapolis and Washington, D.C., prior to and following the decriminalization decisions of the federal courts were examined.[54] In both cities, significant declines in the number of public inebriates handled by the police took place. However, in Washington, the police simply left large numbers of drunks on the streets, while in Minneapolis, public-health agencies absorbed many inebriates into treatment and rehabilitation programs.

summary

This chapter has examined a number of kinds of behavior that many citizens regard as noncriminal in spite of the fact that they are prohibited by criminal law. Criminologists have invented the categories of "folk crime" and "crimes without victims" to cover these socially invisible, often relatively petty kinds of criminality. The data in this chapter made it clear that these criminal activities are widespread, although less frequently encountered in the hinterland than in metropolitan areas. Given the fact that many of these forms of lawbreaking appear to be relatively harmless personal vices, it is little wonder that some observers have come to the conclusion that they should not be the law's business. Indeed, decriminalization of some of them is already underway. Finally, this chapter indicated that efforts to remove particular activities from the purview of the criminal law do not always turn out the way reformers intended.

notes

[1]Federal Bureau of Investigation, U.S. Department of Justice, *Crime in the United States: Uniform Crime Reports, 1979* (Washington, D.C.: U.S. Government Printing Office, 1980), p. 191.

[2]Joseph W. Bennett, *Vandals Wild* (Portland, Ore.: Bennett Publishing Co., 1969); Colin Ward, ed., *Vandalism* (New York: Van Nostrand Reinhold, 1973). On this point, reports of the Oregon Fish and Wildlife Commission make frequent mention of "inappropriate hunter behavior," by which is meant such things as shooting powerline insulators, water towers, and farmer's cattle. These offenses are usually the work of ostensibly law-abiding citizens.

[3]Some detailed data on historical trends in rural and urban crime can be found in Claude S. Fischer, "The Spread of Violent Crime from City to Countryside, 1955 to 1975," *Rural Sociology*, 45 (Fall 1980), 416–34; Darrell J. Steffensmeier and Charlene Jordan, "Changing Patterns of Female Crime in Rural America, 1962–75," *Rural Sociology*, 43 (Spring 1978), 87–102.

[4]*Chinook Observer*, November 1, 1979.

[5]Don C. Gibbons, "Crime in the Hinterland," *Criminology*, 10 (August 1972), 177–90.

[6]T. C. Esselstyn, "The Social Role of the County Sheriff," *Journal of Criminal Law, Criminology and Police Science*, 44 (July–August 1953), 177–84.

[7]Regarding law violations of this kind, Edwin Lemert has argued that they have been "normalized" by truckers and trucking companies. He reported that fines for violations of weight regulations for trucks in northern California were accepted by drivers and companies as a necessary cost of doing business. Whether or not to comply with the regulations was decided in individual cases through an economic calculus; thus the cost of a fine might be outweighed by the extra cost that would be involved if freight were moved in two trips rather than one overloaded trip. Edwin M. Lemert, *Human Deviance, Social Problems, and Social Control*, 2nd ed. (Englewood Cliffs, N.J.: Prentice-Hall, Inc., 1972), p. 38.

[8]Simon Dinitz, "Progress, Crime, and the Folk Ethic: Portrait of a Small Town," *Criminology*, 11 (May 1973), 3–21.

[9]Ibid., p. 10.

[10]Ibid., p. 17.

[11]The studies of "hidden" delinquency are reviewed in Don C. Gibbons, *Delinquent Behavior*, 3rd ed. (Englewood Cliffs, N.J.: Prentice-Hall, Inc., 1981), pp. 37–49.

[12]Robert A. Dentler and Lawrence J. Monroe, "Social Correlates of Early Adolescent Theft," *American Sociological Review*, 26 (October 1961), 33–43.

[13]H. Laurence Ross, "Traffic Law Violation: A Folk Crime," *Social Problems*, 9 (Winter 1960–1961), 231–41.

[14]Clayton A. Hartjen and Don C. Gibbons, "An Empirical Investigation of a Criminal Typology," *Sociology and Social Research*, 54 (October 1969), 56–62.

[15]Gibbons, "Crime in the Hinterland," p. 178.

[16]Anne Beller, Sanford Garelik, and Sydney Cooper, "Sex Crimes in the Subway," *Criminology*, 18 (May 1980), 35–52. For a report on another form of folk crime by railway commuters, see Paul H. Noguchi, "Law, Custom, and Morality in Japan: The Culture of Cheating on the Japanese National Railways," *Anthropological Quarterly*, 52 (July 1979), 165–77.

[17]Edwin M. Schur, *Crimes Without Victims* (Englewood Cliffs, N.J.; Prentice-Hall, Inc., 1965).

[18]Gilbert Geis, *Not the Law's Business?* (Rockville, Md.: National Institute of Mental Health, 1972).

[19]Geis, *Not the Law's Business?*; Herbert L. Packer, *The Limits of the Criminal Sanction* (Stanford, Cal.: Stanford University Press, 1972).

[20]Elizabeth A. Rooney and Don C. Gibbons, "Social Reactions to 'Crimes Without Victims,' " *Social Problems*, 13 (Spring 1966), 400–10; Ray C. Rist, Lee J. Haggerty, and Don C. Gibbons, "Public Perceptions of Sexual 'Deviance' ": A Study on the Interrelations of Knowledge and Values," *Western Sociological Review*, 5 (Summer 1974), 66–81.

[21]Abortion legislation is discussed in detail in Charles H. McCaghy, *Crime in American Society* (New York: Macmillan, 1980), pp. 322–26.

[22]Edwin M. Schur and Hugo Adam Bedau, *Victimless Crimes* (Englewood Cliffs, N.J.: Prentice-Hall, Inc., 1974).

[23]Franklyn N. Judson, Kenneth G. Miller, and Thomas R. Schaffnit, "Screening for Gonorrhea and Syphilis in the Gay Baths–Denver, Colorado," *American Journal of Public Health*, 67 (August 1977), 740–42.

[24]U.S. Department of Health and Human Services, *ADAMHA News*, VI (July 1980), 1–6.

[25]Peter Wickman and Phillip Whitten, *Criminology* (Lexington, Mass.: D. C. Heath, 1980), p. 385.

[26]For detailed discussions of prostitution, see Geis, *Not the Law's Business?*, pp. 173–221; Sheila Balkan, Ronald J. Berger, and Janet Schmidt, *Crime and Deviance in America: A Critical Approach* (New York: Wadsworth, 1980), pp. 254–61.

[27]Federal Bureau of Investigation, *Crime in the United States*, p. 172.

[28]Charles Winick and Paul M. Kinsie, *The Lively Commerce: Prostitution in the United States* (Chicago: Quadrangle Books, 1971).

[29]In the literature on alcoholism, the male-vagrant area of a city is referred to as both "Skid Road" and "Skid Row." The label "Skid Road" originated in Seattle and preceded the term "Skid Row." As used initially, "Skid Road" had reference to logging roads constructed of small logs laid side by side, over which larger logs were "skidded" to a loading area. The term was applied to the area of homeless men and transients because a good many of the residents of that area were heavy-drinking unmarried loggers.

[30]Harold A. Mulford, "Drinking and Deviant Drinking, U.S.A., 1963," *Quarterly Journal of Studies on Alcohol*, 25 (December 1964), 634–50.

[31]Federal Bureau of Investigation, *Crime in the United States*, p. 188. In fact, the evidence suggests that many of the persons arrested for drunkenness are not legally intoxicated. A considerable number of persons are picked up for other reasons but then charged with being drunk. See Raymond T. Nimmer, *Two Million Unnecessary Arrests* (Chicago: American Bar Foundation, 1971), p. 160.

[32]The President's Commission on Law Enforcement and Administration of Justice, *The Challenge of Crime in a Free Society* (Washington, D.C.: U.S. Government Printing Office, 1967), pp. 233–37.

[33]David J. Pittman and C. Wayne Gordon, *Revolving Door* (New York: Free Press, 1958).

[34]Ibid., pp. 16–58.

[35]Ibid., pp. 78–93.

[36]Ibid., pp. 109–24.

[37]Ibid., pp. 59–77.

[38]Francis E. Feeney, Dorothee F. Mindlin, Verna H. Minear, and Eleanor E. Short, "The Challenge of the Skid Row Alcoholic," *Quarterly Journal of Studies on Alcohol*, 16 (December 1955), 645–67.

[39]Theodore Caplow, Keith Lovald, and Samuel Wallace, *A General Report on the Problem of Relocating the Population of the Lower Loop Redevelopment Area* (Minneapolis: Minneapolis Housing and Redevelopment Authority, 1958); Lovald, "From Hobohemia to Skid Row" (Ph.D. diss., University of Minnesota, 1960); Wallace, *Skid Row as a Way of Life* (Totowa, N.J.: Bedminster Press, 1965).

[40]Leonard Blumberg, Irving Shandler, and Thomas E. Shipley, Jr., *Relocation Services to Skid Row Men* (Philadelphia: Greater Philadelphia Movement and Redevelopment Authority of the City of Philadelphia, 1966).

[41]Donald Bogue, *Skid Row in American Cities* (Chicago: University of Chicago Press, 1963).

[42]Howard M. Bahr, *Homelessness and Disaffiliation* (New York: Bureau of Applied Social Research, Columbia University, 1968); Bahr, *Skid Row* (New York: Oxford University Press, 1973).

[43]Jacqueline P. Wiseman, *Stations of the Lost* (Englewood Cliffs, N.J.: Prentice-Hall, Inc., 1970).

[44]James P. Spradley, *You Owe Yourself a Drunk* (Boston: Little, Brown, 1970).

[45]Joan K. Jackson and Ralph Connor, "The Skid Road Alcoholic," *Quarterly Journal of Studies on Alcohol*, 14 (September 1953), 468–86.

[46]W. Jack Peterson and Milton A. Maxwell, "The Skid Road 'Wino,' " *Social Problems*, 5 (Spring 1958), 308–16.

[47]Wiseman, *Stations of the Lost*, passim.

[48]Spradley, *You Owe Yourself a Drunk*, passim.

[49]S. E. Hobfoll, D. Kelso, and W. J. Peterson, "The Anchorage Skid Row," *Journal of Studies on Alcohol*, 41 (January 1980), 94–99.

[50]Howard M. Bahr and Theodore Caplow, *Old Men Drunk and Sober* (New York: New York University Press, 1973).

[51]Ibid., p. 304.

[52]Ibid., p. 305.

[53]Frank Grad, "Legal Control of Drinking, Public Drunkenness, and Alcoholism Treatment," in *Drinking: Alcohol in American Society—Issues and Current Research*, John A. Ewing and Beatrice A. Rouse, eds. (Chicago: Nelson–Hall, 1978), pp. 307–36.

[54]David E. Aaronson, C. Thomas Dienes, and Michael C. Musheno, "Changing the Public Drunkenness Laws: The Impact of Decriminalization," *Law and Society Review*, 12 (Spring 1978), 407–36.

women, crime, and the criminal justice system

The world of crime is a man's world, judging from discussions of it in criminology textbooks. It is easy to demonstrate that criminology books have generally given short shrift to the subject of women and crime, which is a reflection of the paucity of theoretical or research materials in criminology that attend specifically to female criminality. This lack of attention to lawbreaking on the part of women is in part a reflection of official statistics indicating that crime is a predominantly male phenomenon, but it probably reveals a more general lack of interest in the activities of women as well. In short, sexism and discriminatory attitudes relegating women to positions of social inferiority have much to do with the concentration of criminological scrutiny upon male offenders.

One indication of textbook inattention to female criminality is that the first two editions of this book contained only a brief discussion of female shoplifters and a few other, isolated references to the participation of women in crime. It is probably no accident that the fullest textbook treatment of women and crime was authored by a female criminologist, Mabel Elliott.[1] Her book, published in 1952, contained two chapters on female criminality, but in the 30 succeeding years, others did not follow her lead. For example, Donald Taft and Ralph England made virtually no mention of female lawbreaking.[2] while Sutherland and Cressey[3] and Haskell and Yablonsky[4] devoted only a few pages to this subject. Some other works in which female crime was generally overlooked include those by Walter C. Reckless,[5] Richard Knudten,[6] Richard Quinney,[7] and Gresham Sykes.[8]

the study of female crime and delinquency

Although female crime has been passed over quickly in criminological texts, this subject has not been entirely overlooked. On the contrary, criminological interest in women offenders can be traced back as far as Lombroso, and in addition, there has been a recent revival of interest directed at women lawbreakers.[9]

Dorie Klein has summarized much of the theoretical literature on female crime that has been produced in past decades, with particular attention directed at the writings of Cesare Lombroso, W. I. Thomas, Sigmund Freud, Kingsley Davis, and Otto Pollak.[10] According to Klein, the shared assumptions running through the works of these persons included the proposition that female crime was the result of *physiological* or *psychological* characteristics of *individuals,* with little or no recognition being given to the importance of social-structural forces. These physiological or psychological traits and characteristics of women offenders were usually viewed as pathological distortions or departures from the normal, inherent nature of women. Females were seen as biologically predisposed toward passivity and other "ladylike" characteristics, such that aggressiveness was viewed as a violation of their true nature. The crime-control proposals that flowed from these assumptions centered about techniques of individual counseling and the like, through which errant women could be drawn back into "proper" feminine behavior.

Klein judged these older formulations about female criminality to be sexist and moralistic, for she contended that they were consistent with general societal attitudes toward women which defined them as psychologically and biologically inferior to men, which identified patterns of passive femininity as the "natural" character of females, and which regarded any departures from these expectations as indicators of pathology. Such views equated social deviance on the part of women with biological or psychological aberrance and overlooked the possibility that lawbreaking was no less normal for females than for males. Summing them up, Klein asserted that:

These assumptions of universal, biological/psychological characteristics, of individual responsibility for crime, of the necessity for maintaining social harmony, and of the benevolence of the state link different theories along a continuum, transcending political labels and minor divergences. The road from Lombroso to the present is surprisingly straight.[11]

One of the earliest of these biological-psychological theories was that of Lombroso, framed in terms of the concept of atavism examined in Chapter 2. Lombroso reported that his researches turned up fewer indications among women of atavism in the form of biological anomalies, supporting his belief that women were organically conservative. He noted "the conservative tendency of women in all questions of social order," and claimed that this was "a conservatism of which the primary cause is to be sought in the immobility of the ovule compared with the zoosperm."[12] This argument was designed to account for the lesser involvement of women in criminality and also for those females who did exhibit atavistic features and who were involved in crimes. For example, Lombroso explained female prostitution by arguing that women were originally given to sexual promiscuity and that modern-day female prostitutes are biological throwbacks to this earlier female type.

Freud was another early figure who offered a physiological explanation of female criminality, holding that lawbreaking represents a perversion of, or rebellion against, the biologically natural female role.[13] Freud interpreted crime among women, career aspirations on their part, and kindred activities as evidence of a masculinity complex. He maintained that all females experience some degree of penis envy and jealousy of males, but normal women ultimately manage to accept and internalize societal definitions of femininity centered about a single-minded interest in motherhood. Normal women also exhibit feminine traits of passivity, masochism, and narcissism. In all of this, Freud engaged in implicit condemnation of all departures from cultural stereotypes of the proper role of women, holding that it was natural for females to behave according to these narrow expectations.

Critics of Freudian interpretations of female crime have scored them on at least two counts. First, these arguments were defective as explanations of the genesis of female criminality for they contained erroneous assumptions about biological characteristics of women and they also failed to take cognizance of social-structural factors in criminal etiology.[14] Additionally, Klein and others have charged that these views were sexist in character, for they supported and reinforced those social arrangements which relegated women to child-bearing and domestic worker roles.

Simon, Klein, Smart, and others have identified these problems of defective assumptions about women and female crime in the writings of W. I. Thomas,[15] Kingsley Davis,[16] and Otto Pollak. W. I. Thomas offered an explanation for the delinquency of young females which characterized them as engaging in departures from lines of conduct that are biologically and psychologically normal for women. Kingsley Davis, on the other hand, presented a functionalist interpretation of prostitution, arguing that it arises in circumstances where demands for sexual novelty cannot be supplied within the framework of marriage and/or where some males are cut off from access to sexual partners because they are unmarried, ugly, deformed, or at a sexually competitive disadvantage in some other respect. Commercial prostitution arises as a black market in sex. The problem with this theory, according to Klein and Simon, is that it lent support to the sexist thesis that the only proper role for women was that of child bearer and housewife.

Otto Pollak's work ought to be singled out for special attention.[17] Drawing upon an array of data and reports of variable quality, he advanced the markedly unconventional claim that women are actually as criminal as men. He asserted that the lower rates of detected crime among females are not due to lesser participation in lawbreaking on their part; instead, the crimes they commit are less likely to be detected. Also, according to Pollak, when those crimes are detected, they are less likely to be reported to the authorities. Moreover, when crimes of women are reported, the offenders have a better chance than men of avoiding arrest or conviction because of a lenient double standard that is applied to them.

Pollak maintained that women are able to engage in widespread hidden crime, frequently involving murder of spouses by poisoning, assaults, offenses against children, and abortions, because of their greater skill at deceit and cunning behavior, acquired through sexual socialization. Although Pollak placed most emphasis upon the surreptitious and cunning crime techniques of women offenders which reflect the patterns of differential socialization they have undergone, he also suggested that biological factors, including lesser physical strength on the part of women, as well as psychological concomitants of menstruation, pregnancy, and menopause, enter into the etiology of female crime. His own summary of this thesis argued:

> In summary, then, we are forced into the conclusion that the amount of female crime has been greatly underestimated by traditional opinion. At least in our culture, women are particularly protected against the detection of criminal behavior on the one hand and exposed to a wealth of irritations, temptations, and opportunities which may lead them to criminal behavior on the other. Therefore, meaningful differentials between male and female crime must be looked for, not in any appreciable and validly demonstrable difference in crime volume, but in the ways in which women commit their crimes and in the causes of their criminal behavior. They must be looked for in the interplay between biological and cultural determinants which distinguishes this behavior from that of man. In short, the criminality of women reflects their biological nature in a given cultural setting.[18]

Returning to the criticisms of these varied contentions by Lombroso, Freud, Thomas, Davis, Pollak, and others, Rita James Simon argued that all of them are defective because of their sexist and erroneous presuppositions about normal traits of women or natural social roles to which females ought to be assigned, principally those centering around motherhood and housewifery:

> Inevitably, in both Freudian and functionalist perspectives, analyses that may start out as descriptive soon take on prescriptive, or value-laden tones; and actors who deviate from the "normal" modes are characterized as maladjusted and dangerous to themselves and to the stability of the social system.[19]

These complaints by Klein and Simon about the deficiencies of theories on female crime were well founded. Also, one should not suppose that these erroneous notions have disappeared. For example, these questionable assumptions about biological and psychological traits of normal women and criminal females ran through a series of articles in a criminology journal[20] dealing with female offenders. In one case, Mazie Rappaport opined that most women offenders are psychological misfits,[21] while psychiatrist Fabian Rouke offered some contentious conjectures about the symbolic motivation that may lie behind shoplifting on the part of women.[22] Nowhere in Rouke's commentary was there any awareness of the possibility that the motivations arising from economic precariousness and perceived financial strain that characterize much larceny carried on by men may also explain thefts by females.

So much for past efforts to account for female crime. Let us turn to contemporary efforts to comprehend female criminality, including books by Adler[23] and Simon.[24] First, let us examine the available statistical data regarding crime rates of men and women, trends in female crime, and related matters. Second, let us look in more detail at the evidence on certain specific forms of crime carried on by women, particularly amateur shoplifting.[25] Third, we need to scrutinize the theories that have been advanced to account for patterns and trends of lawbreaking among women. Finally, this chapter will devote some attention to sex discrimination in the processing of female offenders through the juvenile- and adult-justice systems. Some have argued that the official crime-control machinery shows leniency toward women, while others have suggested that this social apparatus sometimes processes females more harshly than it does males.

crime patterns and crime trends

ADULT CRIME

At first glance, the statistics on arrests of men and women in the United States bear out the observation at the beginning of this chapter, to wit, that males have a monopoly on crime. Table 19 identifies the proportions of males and females arrested for various crimes in this country in 1979, indicating that, overall, males were responsible for 84.3 percent of all arrests, while women accounted for only 15.7 percent of the arrests. Table 19 also indicates that females were differentially involved in specific forms of crime, so that they accounted for two-thirds of the prostitution arrests, but only 6.3 percent of the burglaries, 8.9 percent of the auto thefts, and 7.4 percent of the robberies.

However, Table 19 does not tell the whole story, for it does not reveal anything about trends in criminality of men and women over the past decade or so. Table 20 presents arrest figures for 1974 for males and females, along with percentage change figures for these offenses between 1960 and 1974.

Perusal of Table 20 indicates that between 1960 and 1974, the rates of crime among women climbed much more sharply than those for men for such crimes as robbery, burglary, larceny, car theft, forgery, fraud and embezzlement, as well as for weapons offenses and common assaults. The central significance of these trends is that these offenses for which women showed the most pronounced increases were for the most part criminal activities that had been dominated by males in the past.[26] On this point, Rita Simon noted that the proportion of women among persons arrested for all crimes increased from 10.8 percent in 1953 to 16.1 percent in 1974, while the proportion arrested for index offenses (except rape) changed from 9.4 percent in 1953 to 19.0 percent in 1974. The rise in index crimes on the part of women was due to their increased involvement in more property offenses, for females arrested for serious crimes of violence made up 11.9 percent of the total arrests in 1953 and 11.0 percent in 1974. Additionally, most of the change in women's rate of property crime was due to their greater involvement in larceny, rather than burglary, robbery, or auto theft.[27]

This apparent movement of females toward parity with males in terms of incidence of crime, along with the shift of women into offense patterns that have traditionally been men's crimes, was interpreted by Simon[28] as reflecting the breakdown of patterns of sexual inequality. Increased labor force participation of women and other developments in the direction of sexual equality have expanded the crime opportunities and pressures toward lawbreaking among women. She also predicted that as these trends accelerate, crime patterns and rates among women will come to approximate those of men even more closely.

The statistical trends highlighted in Table 20 and in Simon's book are relatively clear. However, what is not so clear is the extent to which the movement toward sexual equality has occurred. In the same way, the question of how pronounced this trend will become in future decades and the rate at which it will proceed is still moot. For example, Simon examined the evidence regarding demographic trends and changes in labor-force participation on the part of women.[29] She argued that as labor-force participation increases, opportunities to engage in criminality should expand for women as well. In particular, financial and white-collar offenses ought to become more common on the part of women,

table 19   arrests by sex, 1979[a]

offense charged	percentage male	percentage female
Total	84.3	15.7
Murder and nonnegligent manslaughter	86.3	13.7
Forcible rape	99.2	0.8
Robbery	92.6	7.4
Aggravated assault	87.6	12.4
Burglary—breaking and entering	93.7	6.3
Larceny—theft	69.7	30.3
Motor-vehicle theft	91.1	8.9
Other assaults	86.4	13.6
Arson	88.7	11.3
Forgery and counterfeiting	69.1	30.9
Fraud	59.6	40.4
Embezzlement	74.7	25.3
Stolen property: buying, receiving, etc.	89.3	10.7
Vandalism	91.6	8.4
Weapons: carrying, possessing, etc.	92.6	7.4
Prostitution and commercial vice	32.5	67.5
Sex offenses (except forcible rape and prostitution)	92.2	7.8
Narcotic drug laws	86.5	13.5
Gambling	90.5	9.5
Offenses against family and children	90.1	9.9
Driving under the influence	91.3	8.7
Liquor laws	85.3	14.7
Drunkenness	92.7	7.3
Disorderly conduct	84.6	15.4
Vagrancy	77.5	22.5
All other offenses (except traffic)	85.2	14.8
Curfew- and loitering-law violations	78.0	22.0
Runaway	41.6	58.4

[a]Federal Bureau of Investigation, U.S. Department of Justice, *Crime in the United States: Uniform Crime Reports, 1979* (Washington, D.C.: U.S. Government Printing Office, 1980), p. 199. Arrest figures based on reports from 11,758 police agencies, representing an estimated 1979 population of 204,622,000.

at the same time that female violence should decrease, owing to the weakening of their feelings of frustration, powerlessness, and victimization. Much of the data presented in Table 20 is consistent with these forecasts.

Simon also provided data showing the labor-force participation by women increased by about 40 percent between 1948 and 1971. More women are delaying marriage, more are completing college, more are having fewer children, and

table 20   arrests by sex, 1974, and arrest trends, 1960–1974[a]

offense charged	males		females	
	arrests 1974	percent change 1960–1974	arrests 1974	percent change 1960–1974
Criminal homicide				
(a) murder and non-negligent man-slaughter	6,917	137.7	1,247	116.1
(b) manslaughter by negligence	872	−18.7	132	29.4
Forcible rape	10,546	108.5	—	—
Robbery	65,214	172.5	5,059	305.7
Aggravated assault	79,126	130.6	13,414	133.7
Burglary—breaking and entering	175,689	106.2	10,212	245.9
Larceny—theft	262,949	121.1	124,838	404.0
Motor-vehicle theft	59,038	45.9	4,109	161.6
Other assaults	127,597	60.7	23,837	144.9
Forgery and counter-feiting	16,864	27.5	7,025	166.7
Fraud and embezzlement	32,090	54.0	15,856	331.9
Stolen property: buying, receiving, etc.	40,451	531.5	4,639	767.1
Weapons: carrying, possessing, etc.	60,245	193.5	5,672	390.7
Prostitution and commercialized vice	9,232	75.3	26,393	89.9
Sex offenses (except forcible rape and prostitution)	24,464	−6.1	1,706	−61.8
Narcotic drug laws	204,313	831.8	34,646	860.5
Gambling	25,807	−67.9	2,411	−65.1
Offenses against family and children	13,542	−47.9	1,973	−13.0
Driving under the influence	251,765	160.3	21,276	249.2
Liquor laws	68,796	38.3	12,783	49.1
Drunkenness	484,256	−42.8	36,413	−50.9
Disordery conduct	188,711	−16.6	75,902	121.9
Vagrancy	14,722	−79.4	2,655	−60.0
All other offenses (except traffic)	442,133	74.9	110,789	149.6

[a]Federal Bureau of Investigation, U.S. Department of Justice, *Crime in the United States: Uniform Crime Reports, 1974* (Washington, D.C.: U.S. Government Printing Office, 1975), p. 184. Arrest figures based on reports from 1,824 police agencies, representing an estimated 1974 population of 69,222,000.

more are turning up in the labor force. However, the other side of the coin is that involvement of women in managerial or other work roles that have been monopolized by men in the past has *not* increased significantly, so that Simon concluded: "One can find little evidence in these statistics for a major shift in the occupational patterns of American women."[30] This continuing uncertainty about the pace at which the movement toward sexual equality will proceed makes precise forecasts about the criminality of women in coming decades impossible. Even so, it seems clear enough that permanent changes are occurring in the lawbreaking endeavors of American women.

Freda Adler has developed a detailed but controversial version of this thesis regarding trends in female criminality. She argued that a growing trend toward female assertiveness, manifested most clearly in the contemporary women's movement in the United States but revealed in other ways as well, has led to consequences that are already showing up in crime statistics. According to Adler, women are moving out of traditional crimes, such as prostitution and shoplifting into grand larceny, embezzlement, robbery, and crimes of violence, such that their participation in these offenses has increased much more markedly than has men's in recent years. Adler also asserted that juvenile females have been turning to forms of delinquency that were formerly the exclusive province of males, so that drinking, gang fights, and other assaultive activities are becoming more common. Finally, she contended that the breakdown of sexual inequality lies behind the increased involvement of women in various forms of drug use.

Adler claimed that organized prostitution is on the wane, with prostitution now shifting to call-girl activities, part-time participation by housewives, and other forms of individual entrepreneurship in commercial sex.[31] Furthermore, prostitutes have risen in social esteem, according to Adler:

> Most prostitutes have risen in social esteem for the same reason that women in general have . . . Let us review them: 1) Promiscuity has not lessened but increased; however, it has lost much of its stigma and is no longer considered shameful. 2) The earnings of part-timers and semi-professional housewives contribute to familial goals. 3) The bachelor women, call girls, and housewives, each in different ways, combine other roles with prostitution.[32]

Adler's central argument in *Sisters in Crime* centered around the rise of "the new woman criminal."[33] Adler's theory was that the women's liberation movement has been moving men and women toward androgynous sex roles in which traditional sex-role distinctions are being blurred. Women have become more competitive with males both in criminal and noncriminal activities, with the result that crime rates among women are rising more rapidly than crime rates among men. Finally, Adler claimed that women have begun to engage in masculine, aggressive, collective forms of lawbreaking that were largely restricted to males in the past.

The available data do not lend much support to this argument concerning the rise of the new female criminal. For example, the statistics examined by Simon did indicate that criminal behavior among women has increased in the past two or three decades, however, most of the change in crime was due to increased involvement in property crimes, principally larceny, rather than burglary, robbery, or auto theft—traditional male crimes. Furthermore, Simon found little evidence that women offenders have become more involved in assaults and other violent offenses.

Darrell Steffensmeier's analysis of changes in crime rates from 1960 to 1975 provided parallel findings.[34] These data showed that participation in property crimes on the part of women did increase during this period, but it was only in theft, fraud, and embezzlement that women's rates rose markedly faster than those of men. Steffensmeier also emphasized that although rates for some offenses have increased fairly dramatically for women, large absolute differences in recorded criminality between men and women are still observed. For example, women's rates for burglary and car theft increased during this period, so that the gap between men and women in terms of participation in these offenses narrowed somewhat. But, females continued to be so infrequently involved in those crimes that their increased involvement made little dent in the overall pattern of male-female participation in them. Steffensmeier's analysis also undermined the argument that the women's movement has led to pronounced increases in female crime in that he showed that the changes in the direction of higher rates of crime for women began in the early 1960s, before the women's movement would have begun to have had some impact upon lawbreaking. In summary, the world of criminality is still largely a man's domain. Steffensmeier concluded that "the new female criminal" is a social fiction rather than an emergent problem of large proportions.

Much the same picture emerges when victimization data rather than police arrests are considered. Michael Hindelang examined a number of victimization surveys carried on between 1972 and 1976.[35] He found that victim reports on rape, robbery, assault, and personal larceny, as well as household crimes of burglary, larceny, and auto theft, paralleled arrest data. Male involvement in these crimes was proportionately much greater than was participation by women. In general, no systematic changes in the proportionate involvement of women were found for the period between 1972 and 1976. Hindelang also indicated that the chivalry hypothesis, arguing that male victims of female offenders are loath to report these crimes to the police, was not supported by the victimization data.

JUVENILE DELINQUENCY

One portion of Adler's analysis of the alleged explosion of crime among women centered on female juvenile offenders.[36] She argued that while the ratio of male to female delinquents was about fifty to one in the early 1900s, currently it is about five to one, which indicates that female lawbreaking is increasing very rapidly. She also claimed that the women's rights movement is heavily implicated in the rise of female delinquency. Adler offered some anecdotal evidence which appeared to show that much female lawbreaking has already become masculinized, in that many female delinquents have become involved in aggressive activities, gang offenses, and in other conduct that was formerly the exclusive province of males. Finally, she asserted that as the movement toward sexual equality continues, the gap between male and female rates of youthful criminality will continue to narrow. Adler concluded that: "Female delinquency today is a serious problem not only because of its capacity for social disruption but because it often leads to future adult criminality. Although it is not a new problem, it is far more prevalent and has undergone ominous qualitative changes in recent years."[37]

But Adler's argument is unconvincing. For one thing, a few dramatic case histories do not demonstrate the hypothesis that female delinquency is changing markedly. Then, too, the claim that the women's movement has created a wave of female delinquency is less than persuasive in that the ratio of male to female delinquents in the juvenile courts has changed relatively slightly since the early 1950s. It would be difficult to argue that the movement for sexual equality was underway in the 1950s.[38]

causation of female lawbreaking

The major outlines of prevailing sociological theories regarding the causation of female crime have already been identified in an oblique fashion in the commentary on the claims of Adler, Simon, and others, about trends toward sexual equality. Recent sociological opinion has been virtually unanimous in attributing low crime rates among women to differential sexual socialization and the separation of adult social roles characteristic of males and females in our society. Sociological formulations have employed those same factors to account for the particular forms of lawbreaking in which women do engage.

One version of sociological theorizing about the etiology of female crime has been presented by Dale Hoffman-Bustamente,[39] who argued that women's crimes are the result of five major factors: differential sex role expectations, sex differences in socialization patterns and application of social control, differential opportunities to engage in crime, differential access to criminal subcultures and careers, and sex differences built into crime categories. She argued:

When we look at crimes in which female arrest rates are well below their average for all crimes, we again find a close relationship to sex roles. Women tend not to be arrested for crimes that require stereotyped male behavior, *i.e.*, robbery, burglary. When they are arrested on such charges, it appears that they have played secondary, supportive roles. Even in crimes where women are more frequently arrested, their involvement in the offense is closely tied to the female sex role. Where women are often sole perpetrators, *i.e.*, homicide, shoplifting, the close ties are still evident. Where the crime requires behavior that is consistent with expected female roles, women appear to make up a large number of the petty criminals (forgery, fraud, embezzlement, prostitution, vagrancy, curfew, and runaway). Thus, women seem to commit crimes in roles auxiliary to men, in keeping with their sex roles and for lesser returns, often making them more vulnerable to arrest. In addition, those acts for which women have received adequate training in the normal process of growing up, *i.e.*, forgery, are more likely to have high rates of women arrestees. Those for which more masculine skills and techniques are required, *i.e.*, auto theft, will likely show a lower than expected rate of female participation.

In addition to these characteristics of female arrestees and their techniques of committing the various offenses, the rates are definitely affected by the ways in which the category boundaries are drawn. For example, the general term theft encompasses the offense categories of robbery, burglary, larceny, auto theft, forgery and counterfeiting, fraud and embezzlement. Indeed, when the arrest rates for all these offenses are combined, women's arrest rate is much closer to the female average for all crimes. This also appears true in the area of sex offenses, when we combine rates of arrest for rape, prostitution and other sex offenses. Thus, there seems to be a tendency in the law itself to classify offenses in ways that correspond to sex role differences. This principle operates even more obviously when we compare major and other crimes. Those classified as major, with the exception of theft, are typically ones that require active independence on the part of the offender and the use or threat of violence.[40]

Parallel versions of this perspective have been offered by other scholars. Anthony Harris has provided an account of male and female involvement in deviance which stressed the social "type scripts" or culturally widespread sex-role expectations in modern societies as important determinants of levels of deviance, including lawbreaking, among men and women.[41] Some indication of the nature of his argument can be gained from the following passage:

Put simply, dominant typifications about what kinds of actors "do" criminal behavior—typifications which have served dominant male interests and have been held by both sexes—have played a crucial role in, on the one hand, keeping sociologists from seeing the sex variable in criminal deviance, and on the other, keeping men in crime and women out of it.[42]

Sociological arguments about the causation of female delinquency are parallel to those for crime on the part of adult women. Low rates of official delinquency among young females have been linked to the more restrictive social roles in which they are involved and to the greater control and surveillance exercised over them by parents and other adult figures.[43] In addition, delinquent misconduct on the part of females is frequently held to be due to "under the roof culture" in the form of family tensions of one kind or another. Stated another way, the misbehavior of juvenile females is thought to reflect parent-child conflicts which impel them into delinquent involvement taking the form of affection seeking among juvenile boys. In turn, these young women get referred to juvenile court, often by their parents, and often because someone supposes that they have become involved in sexual activities or are in danger of engaging in promiscuous conduct.

Although this "under the roof culture" formulation is the most frequently encountered one in the literature on female delinquency, it is not the sole account of etiology that has been offered. Instead, sociological discussions of female lawbreaking are often more eclectic, providing room for other factors of possible causal significance, such as excessive weight or other physical problems,[44] self-concept deficiencies and perceptions of lack of opportunity,[45] and various other factors.[46]

As interest in female crime and delinquency increases, we are likely to see theoretical and research directions develop, similar to those that have been pursued in the study of crime among males. That is, it is likely that criminologists will conclude that there is little theoretical mileage to be found in broad formulations about female delinquents or criminals *en masse*, and that instead, more attention will need to be directed at specific patterns of lawbreaking among women. One case in point can be found in the material that has already accumulated on amateur shoplifting, an activity in which women apparently are markedly overrepresented.

PATTERNS OF SHOPLIFTING

Shoplifting is a low-visibility offense which rarely becomes a matter of public knowledge. Shoplifters are infrequently observed in the act, so those who become known to the victim store or business concern represent only a fraction of those actually involved in stealing from it. Individuals who shoplift are most likely to be apprehended in stores that employ private police or protective personnel. Other factors that condition the likelihood of shoplifters being detected include variations in the operating procedures of store detectives, racial biases of protective officers which lead them to scrutinize more closely the movements of blacks in the stores, reluctance to confront "respectable" people with accusations of criminality, and special attention to juveniles who are thought to be particularly theft prone.[47]

Known shoplifters constitute a minority of all thieves who direct their activities at retail stores. In addition, most offenders known to store personnel are not reported to the police, so officially labeled shoplifters represent an even smaller sample of all store thieves. Shoplifters who become publicly identified as criminals through court proceedings are in no sense representative of known thieves or of all shoplifters.

How much shoplifting takes place in the United States? How much money is lost to store thieves? A variety of estimates have been advanced, not all in agreement. However, they all indicate that shoplifting is a far from inconsequential kind of lawbreaking. For example, one specialist has claimed that shoplifters stole $247,000,000 of merchandise from drug and department stores, grocery stores, and variety stores in the United States in 1948.[48] Another has contended that 12 department stores in New York City suffered over $10,000,000 in shoplifter losses in 1951, and still another authority argued that each year shoplifters take over $1,700,000,000 from retailers in the United States.[49] A final estimate of the magnitude of shoplifting is derived from a report of the National Commission on Food Marketing, established by Congress. That commission set the annual cost of shoplifting at $300,000,000 per year, or 2 percent of total sales. The commission survey profiled the average shoplifter as betweeen 18 and 30 years of age, stealing predominantly on Thursday, Friday, or Saturday, between 3:00 P.M. and 6:00 P.M. and stealing about $3.75 worth of goods. The commission urged that all shoplifters except pregnant women, senile aged, and "kleptomaniacs" be prosecuted.[50]

According to store protective agents, most losses are inflicted on stores by amateur shoplifters or "snitches," rather than by professional "boosters," although the average amount stolen is larger in cases of professional shoplifting than in amateur stealing.[51] In general, criminal skills used by professionals exceed those of "snitches," although the latter often show some degree of sophistication in their criminality. Many use "bad bags" (well-worn shopping bags issued by the victim store), are equipped with scissors or razor blades for snipping price tags from stolen merchandise, sometimes carry lists of items they intend to steal, and often plan their offenses in advance.[52]

An important parenthetical note is that even though it is commonplace, shoplifting makes a relatively small contribution to the total losses suffered by stores. Protection agencies estimate that about 75 percent of all pilferage in stores is the work of employees rather than customer thieves.[53]

Mary Owen Cameron conducted a study of shoplifters involving analysis of records on a sample of shoplifters apprended in a Chicago department store between 1943 and 1950, along with a sample of women charged with petty larceny and shoplifting in Chicago courts between 1948 and 1950.[54] She discovered that shoplifters in "Lakeside Company" were generally apprehended for relatively small thefts averaging about six dollars, juveniles stole amounts of merchandise of lesser value than did adults, and male shoplifters were caught with fewer stolen items in their possession than was true of women. About one-fifth of the apprehended adult thieves were men. The much higher number of shoplifting women is attributable to most department store customers being women, as well as to women stealing more items than men and thus running a greater risk of being observed.[55]

Cameron's findings from "Lakeside Company" indicated that shoplifters were a cross-section of the Chicago population in terms of socioeconomic status, although they were of somewhat lower status than the overall customer group in the store. Black shoplifters were found in about the same proportions as in the Chicago population, but black shoplifters were much more likely to be reported to the police. Moreover, black offenders convicted in court tende to receive stiffer penalties than did white shoplifters.[56]

Cameron's results made abundantly clear that officially recognized shoplifters made up only a small part of all store thieves. She indicated that between

1943 and 1949 the Chicago Police Department tallied an average of 633 women per year charged with larceny of all kinds. At the same time, "Lakeside Company" apprehended about 400 women each year for shoplifting, although only about 10 percent were turned over to the police. Thus, Cameron declared: "One department store, in other words, *arrested* for shoplifting about 60 percent of the total number of women per year as were officially charged with all types of larceny (including shoplifting) in the entire city of Chicago" (emphasis in the original).[57]

Many factors were involved in the decision to prosecute, such as refusal of the suspected thief to confess and difficulties of getting speedy court action at any particular time. Stores were more likely to report black offenders to the police as well as to turn over professional "boosters" to the authorities. The result of these decisions was that court cases of store thieves were ecologically concentrated in areas with high crime rates and low socioeconomic status, although the total group of known thieves was not so distributed.[58] Shoplifting was a prominent example of differential law enforcement, with official rates of shoplifting bearing little relationship to the true distribution of such behavior.

Cameron effectively demolished hypotheses about shoplifting which would explain this behavior as a result of psychiatric disturbances, compulsiveness, or "kleptomania." The contention that store theft is a compulsive psychiatric aberration was inconsistent with her evidence that most shoplifters stopped stealing after getting caught, even though they had engaged in repeated acts of criminality up to that point.[59] "Kleptomania" turned out to be nothing more than a social label that was hung on "nice people" who stole and withheld from "bad people" who were simply "crooks"! The label was a social identity akin to that of "sick alcoholic," which is accorded the middle-class drinker and denied the Skid Road "drunk." Cameron's interpretation of her findings was that amateur female shoplifters were women who stole items their limited budgets would not allow them to buy without depriving other family members. These women had no self-conception as thieves and offered a variety of rationalizations to explain their deviance. When apprehended by store detectives, they were forced to acknowledge that they were thieves. These women were without any in-group support for their stealing, so they had no way of buffering themselves against social condemnation. Consequently, they refrained from further shoplifting because they could not accommodate themselves to a revised self-definition as a thief.[60]

The most important single conclusion from Cameron's data had to do with the observation that normal, respectable people can and do engage in systematic criminality. As Howard Becker has suggested, these findings call into question notions that use middle-class morality as an explanation for conformity of middle-status individuals. A deeply introjected set of values probably guides the conduct of fewer respectable citizens than is sometimes supposed. Instead of being kept on a consistent course of conformity by an internal gyroscope of ethical standards, many reinterpret values to fit particular situations and invoke rationalizations that allow them to deviate under certain circumstances. Their law-abiding conduct may frequently be a result of fear of being caught and punished rather than of deeply held values of upright conduct.[61]

In a report on department-store shoplifting, Gerald Robin[62] examined data on 1,584 persons apprehended for shoplifting in three of the five largest department stores in Philadelphia in 1958. Most of his findings ran parallel to those of Cameron; for example, he discovered that the stores were both cautious and informal in their handling of detected thieves. Juvenile thieves were almost never turned over to the authorities for official action, and only about one-fourth of the adult shoplifters were prosecuted.[63] Individual thefts that were detected usually involved relatively small losses, about half of them of merchandise valued at less than $10. Juveniles were responsible for smaller losses than were adult thieves.[64] However, these two studies did differ in some respects. Robin noted that nearly half the shoplifters in the Philadelphia stores were black, although blacks made up considerably less of the total city population. Women thieves outnumbered male shoplifters, but not so strikingly as in Cameron's materials. Juvenile thieves constituted about 60 percent of all shoplifters; thus they were more frequent than in Cameron's data.[65]

One major observation that emerged both from Robin's and Cameron's research was that juvenile shoplifting was most commonly *group* activity, whereas adult thieves usually engaged in surreptitious and individualistic thievery.[66] Among juveniles, many of the youngsters were aiders or abettors who acted as lookouts for their peers. Cameron suggested that adult thieves were probably often persons who engaged in group stealing as adolescents and learned their crime skills in that setting; in other words, the juvenile thieves of of today become the adult shoplifters of tomorrow. This may be a dubious hypothesis, for juvenile theft could be a peer-supported kind of conduct developing out of some temporally circumscribed influences of a youth culture and terminated as youngsters move out of this age period. At any rate, the hypothesis needs more study, for its accuracy is presently indeterminate.

Robin indicated that a major factor influencing the decision to prosecute cases of shoplifting was size of theft, so few individuals who pilfered less than $20 worth of merchandise were reported to the police, but nearly all of those who stole items valued at over $60 were prosecuted.[67]

Robin's observations also undermined contentions that psychological aberrations or compulsions drive amateur shoplifters to steal. He showed that thefts were markedly more common during October, November, and December than they were at any other time of the year.[68] If compulsions impel individuals toward thievery, rates of stealing should be much the same the year round, for compulsions should not wax and wane with the seasons. Clearly, these fluctuations had more to do with seasonal budgetary strains and seasonal enticements to theft in the way of holiday merchandise on prominent display than with psychological tensions. Along the same line, Robin cited an instance of a power failure in Chicago's Loop area in which, during the 30 minutes of darkness, thousands of dollars of merchandise was stolen.[69] Finally, he noted that a study of 698 "food lifters" in Chicago supermarkets in 1951 showed that nearly all were ordinary citizens, mainly housewives who had enough money to pay for the stolen items found in their custody.[70] These bits of evidence support Cameron's argument that amateur shoplifters stole to stretch their budgets, doing so deliberately and rationally, after conjuring up rationalizations that allowed them to continue to think of themselves as honest, law-abiding citizens. These thieves stole when they evaluated the elements of immediate situations to be most conducive to success.

Paula Newberg conducted an investigation of shoplifting in national food-chain stores in the Chicago area.[71] She reported that the company estimated its losses through shoplifting and employee theft at over $2,500,000 out of a net profit of $25,000,000 in 1958. Newberg also found that the individual stores in the chain had different rates of shoplifting, produced by differing actions on the part of store personnel toward shoplifters. That is, in some food stores, employees dealt with shoplifters differently from other stores.

George Won and George Yamamoto examined shoplifting in Honolulu, dealing with the social characteristics of about 500 persons who had been apprehended for shoplifting in a major supermarket chain.[72] The major finding of their inquiry centered about the middle-class social status of the thieves, for these lawbreakers were numerically and proportionately middle class in background. Here again, the data indicate that shoplifting is often a criminal act carried on by respectable people.

sexism in criminal-justice processes

Sociological inattention to female offenders has extended to the processing of women through the law enforcement and correctional machinery. The implicit assumption has been that female criminality is relatively uncommon and unimportant and that females receive benign handling within the criminal-justice system.

However, the women's movement of the 1970s directed attention to sexism and unequal treatment of women throughout many institutional areas of American society. One consequence of the drive for women's rights and equality has been closer scrutiny of discriminatory treatment of women within the criminal-justice apparatus. Evidence of unequal and harsher responses directed at females is not hard to find.

Chapter 13 discussed one case in point in which Camille LeGrand argued that American rape laws are designed to protect male interests in women as sexual property, rather than to protect females from rape and its consequences.[73] If rape laws were truly for the protection of women, they would extend to sexual assaults of husbands upon their wives and would prohibit violence and coercion in all sexual encounters between men and women.

LeGrand's analysis also indicated that rape laws are designed less to protect women than to frighten and intimidate potential rapists and to suppress their activities. Once a rape has occurred and the female victim has become damaged goods in terms of sexual property, a variety of social and judicial processes go into operation that severely reduce the likelihood that the rapist will be apprehended, convicted, or incarcerated. Finally, the rape victim often becomes transformed into the guilty party in the course of police interrogation or courtroom questioning that raises questions about her previous sexual experiences or the extent of her interaction with the rapist prior to the sexual assault.

Sexism operates in other parts of the crime-control system as well. For example, Sarah Gold reported that in New York State, the New York Family Court Act specifies that females can be declared to be "Persons in Need of Supervision" and held by the court up to the age 18, while the same act extends that control only to boys under 16.[74] The act also provides that females can be retained under court supervision to an older age than can males. Other states vary in terms of the maximum ages of court control over male and female delinquents.

Meda Chesney-Lind argued that female delinquents are the victims of sexist discrimination in other parts of the juvenile-justice system.[75] Among other things, she pointed out that many states have allowed the incarceration of female delinquents for status offenses such as ungovernability or waywardness at the same time that they provide that males can only be sent to training schools for offenses that constitute crimes when carried out by adults. Further, Chesney-Lind noted that status offenses are disproportionately involved in the case of females referred to juvenile court or sent to training schools, in that hidden-delinquency studies show that females not infrequently also admit to acts of theft and other nonstatus offenses. She commented: "The findings of these studies indicate that official court statistics probably underestimate the volume of female delinquency while overestimating its sexual character."[76] In short, the screening processes ignore certain kinds of misbehavior, while at the same time they catch up many young women for relatively petty misconduct and for status offenses. Males who engage in these same activities are ignored by the police or other persons within the juvenile-justice apparatus. An oversolicitous concern for the sexual morality of young women appears to underlie this heightened sensitivity to female status offenses. In short, the authorities are most likely to take action against young females who are suspected of being involved in sexual misconduct or in danger of becoming entangled in sexual experimentation. Since the same close scrutiny is not maintained over males, it can be argued that the police and the juvenile court are involved in sexual discrimination.

Chesney-Lind also maintained that juvenile courts discriminate against juvenile females by handing out harsher dispositions to them than to males, even though the latter are more frequently involved in serious violations of the personal or property rights of others. Then, too, she presented findings from a study in Honolulu that indicated that juvenile detention was used quite frequently in relatively petty cases of female delinquency but not in similar male instances. She also observed that females are subjected to pelvic examinations and vaginal smears in many juvenile jurisdictions, even though such practices raise grave questions about infringement upon the civil rights of juvenile women.[77] These practices grow out of the operating premises of court personnel holding that most delinquent females are involved in sexual misconduct, regardless of the specific charges that brought them to court attention. In turn, court workers apparently feel obliged to confirm these suspicions by subjecting young women to interrogations, pelvic examinations, and vaginal smears.

Chesney-Lind saw sexual discrimination operating against female offenders at a variety of points in the juvenile-enforcement and correctional systems. Her summary judgment held that:

If parents are unwilling or unable to control their daughter's behavior, our society believes, the court can and should. As a consequence, the labels of "incorrigible," "ungovernable," and "runaway" permit the same abuses that characterize the labels of "sick" or "insane." That is, saving or protecting girls often justifies treating them more severely than boys who break the law. Thus the courts' commitment to the sexual double standard and the subordinate status of women results in a clear violation of the civil rights of young women. Punishment in the name of protection is much like bombing a village to save it from the enemy.[78]

Parallel observations about discriminatory handling of female offenders have been offered by Kristine Olson Rogers.[79] After conducting an investigation of institutional practices at a Connecticut state training school for juvenile females, she concluded that the institution was devoted to a correctional regimen designed to prepare young women to reenter the community as nineteenth-century domestics. Little effort was expended on programs that would more adequately equip the young women released from it to deal with the variety of social adjustment problems they are likely to encounter in modern society.

Rogers also presented data indicating that nearly three-fourths of the female wards were in the Connecticut institution for status offenses, while only 18 percent of male training school inmates in that state had been sentenced for those activities. Alarmingly, although the young women were involved in less serious offenses than was true of the males, they received longer sentences. According to Rogers, these differential sentences arose because the staff members of the boys' school were eager to return males to the community, while at the female training school, the "staff often insists that a girl finish an academic term even though her behavior would warrant release, or they may fear 'summer temptations' if a girl is released over the summer with nothing to 'keep her occupied,' or they may keep a girl through a pregnancy and for two months afterward until she is 'medically cleared.' "[80]

Chesney-Lind and Rogers agreed that juvenile courts discriminate against female offenders by imposing a sexual double standard upon them and by reacting in an overly harsh manner when young women are suspected of sexual involvement. In turn, these court actions reflect broader societal concerns about the sexual activities of minor females and at the same time pay relatively slight heed to sexual misconduct on the part of juvenile males. Finally, young females are often detained by the court or sent off to the training school because no readily available and more desirable alternative placement is available in the community. It is frequently difficult to demonstrate that these correctional responses and actions are beneficial to the young women involved.

Discriminatory treatment of women occurs in the adult-justice machinery as well. Stuart Nagel and Lenore Weitzman indicated that, on the one hand, paternalism and favoritism toward females results in fewer of them being placed in pretrial detention than males, with fewer being convicted in court, and fewer receiving severe sentences for offenses comparable to those committed by males.[81] On the other hand, women in court are less likely to have an attorney, less likely to receive a preliminary hearing, and less likely to receive a jury trial. Accordingly, there is reason to suspect that women may be deprived of due process and be at greater risk in the court system even though that system seems to accord them more lenient handling.

Sexual discrimination in the criminal-justice system also turned up in Linda Singer's review of correctional programs for women in the United States.[82] She reported that although correctional facilities for women varied widely from one jurisdiction to another, most of them were in worse condition than state facilities for men. The social experiences encountered by women inmates were decidedly negative ones, with the rules of conduct in women's prisons being more restrictive than in men's prisons, even though most of the former are medium or minimum-security institutions. Treatment programs for female prisoners were usually nonexistent or markedly inadequate. Female prisoners were often excluded from training programs, work-release and halfway-house experiences, and furloughs. Singer contended that the class-action suits that have resulted in some easing of the severity of incarceration in men's prisons in recent years have had little impact upon penal institutions for women.

summary

The veil of indifference that has covered the subject of female criminality for many decades has recently been lifted. We are now witnessing a pronounced growth of interest in female lawbreaking and responses to it, which is part of the broader concern that has been stimulated by the women's movement, the push for sexual equality, and related trends.

Most of the theorizing about female crime in the early writings of social scientists and others was shot through with broad cultural assumptions about alleged psychobiological traits of women that served to justify sexual discrimination against them. Women were said to be naturally destined to maternal roles and were regarded as intellectually inferior to men. Those who rebelled against these views of the proper place of women or who engaged in deviant conduct were held to be involved in pathological departures from normality.

The pioneers in American criminology were often "male chauvinist pigs" by modern definitions, but we need to remember that male chauvinism was to be found everywhere when those early figures were writing on female criminality.[83]

Contemporary accounts of the etiology of female crime stress the patterns of differential sexual socialization which females experience, through which they acquire those culturally preferred patterns of feminity and the like. These arguments also center about the restricted social roles which women are allowed to occupy in modern society, social roles which curtail their opportunities to engage in lawbreaking. This argument has been offered both as an explanation for low rates of recognized crime on the part of women, and also as a causal interpretation of the forms of criminal misconduct in which they do engage.

The social position of women is undergoing modification, although the extent of change and the rate at which sexual equality is proceeding are matters about which a good deal of uncertainty still exists. A number of theorists, such as Adler, Simon, and others, have contended that as these broad shifts in male-female definitions and roles accelerate, we shall witness pronounced changes in the extent and character of female criminality. The lawbreaking of women will come to parallel more closely the criminality of males, both in extent, incidence, and form. Indeed, the statistical evidence at hand suggests that the movement toward equality in crime is already underway. Finally, it seems likely that some of the forms of sexual discrimination against females that now characterize the operations of the justice system will also diminish as the trend toward greater sexual equality continues.

notes

[1]Mabel A. Elliott, *Crime in Modern Society* (New York: Harper & Brothers, 1952). The first of the two chapters in Elliott's book presented a review of theories on female crime, including a sex-role formulation to account for low rates of official crime among women. Elliott also discussed statistics on crime, war and its effects upon female lawbreaking, the characteristics of incarcerated females, and a number of sociodemographic characteristics of women offenders. The second of the chapters consisted of discussion of anecdotal, case history accounts of prostitutes, women gangsters, and other "types" of female offenders.

[2]Donald R. Taft and Ralph W. England, Jr., *Criminology*, 4th ed. (New York: Macmillan, 1964).

[3]Edwin H. Sutherland and Donald R. Cressey, *Criminology*, 10th ed. (Philadelphia: Lippincott, 1978).

[4]Martin R. Haskell and Lewis Yablonsky, *Criminology: Crime and Criminality* (Chicago: Rand McNally, 1974).

[5]Walter C. Reckless, *The Crime Problem*, 4th ed. (New York: Prentice-Hall, Inc., 1967). Interestingly, Chapter 8 of Reckless's book was devoted to "Female Involvement" and discussed a number of theories of female criminality, along with data on male and female prisoners and male and female delinquents. But the fifth edition of this book, published in 1973, dropped this chapter and replaced it with a narrower one dealing with prostitution.

[6]Richard D. Knudten, *Crime in a Complex Society* (Homewood, Ill.: The Dorsey Press, 1970). Chapter 8 of this book dealt with "special forms of female criminality," i.e., abortion and prostitution.

[7]Richard Quinney, *Criminology* (Boston: Little, Brown, 1975).

[8]Gresham M. Sykes, *Criminology* (New York: Harcourt Brace Jovanovich, 1978).

[9]Some examples of recent commentary on criminality of women would include: "Women, Crime, and Criminology," special issue, *Issues in Criminology*, 8 (Fall 1973); Rita James Simon, *Women and Crime* (Lexington, Mass.: D.C.Heath & Co., 1975); Freda Adler, *Sisters in Crime* (New York: McGraw-Hill, 1975); Freda Adler and Rita James Simon, eds., *The Criminology of Deviant Women* (Boston: Houghton Mifflin Co., 1978).

[10]Dorie Klein, "The Etiology of Female Crime: A Review of the Literature," *Issues in Criminology*, 8 (Fall 1973), 3–30. For a more detailed, sophisticated critique of the writings of Lombroso, Thomas, Pollak, and others on female crime, see Carol Smart, *Women, Crime, and Criminology: A Feminist Critique* (London: Routledge & Kegan Paul, 1977). Also see Joy Pollack, "Early Theories of Female Criminality," in Lee H. Bowker, ed., *Women, Crime, and the Criminal Justice System* (Lexington, Mass.: Lexington Books, 1978), pp. 25–55.

[11]Dorie Klein, "The Etiology of Female Crime," pp. 6–7. Simon also has drawn attention to the single-minded simplicity of most theoretical statements that have been offered on female criminality. See Simon, *Women and Crime*, pp. 2–9. See also Adler, *Sisters in Crime*, p. 9.

[12]Cesare Lombroso, *The Female Offender* (Englewood Cliffs, N.J.: Prentice-Hall, Inc. 1903).

[13]For summaries and criticisms of Freud's views, see Klein, "The Etiology of Female Crime"; Simon, *Women and Crime*, pp. 2–9.

[14]Adler put this matter well, asserting that: "It is not man's penis that a woman strives for but his power . . ." Adler, *Sisters in Crime*, p. 9. More generally, she argued that most commentators on female crime have incorrectly reasoned backwards from the observation that women use different crime techniques than men, or that they engage in different forms of lawbreaking, to the conclusion that they must also have basically different motivation and goals.

[15]W. I. Thomas, *The Unadjusted Girl* (Boston: Little, Brown, 1923).

[16]Kingsley Davis, "The Sociology of Prostitution," *American Sociological Review*, 2 (October 1937), 744–55.

[17]Otto Pollak, *The Criminality of Women* (Philadelphia: University of Pennsylvania Press, 1950). Although Pollak's book did not receive widespread notice or positive acclaim when it appeared, it is the case that his analysis was quite sensitive and sophisticated. Summaries of his book have often portrayed Pollak in a poor light, with critics drawing attention to the relatively low quality of the statistical evidence on which his argument rested and to other problems with his analysis. For example, see Elliott, *Crime in Modern Society*, pp. 199–200. However, a careful reading of Pollak's book suggests that it was a more thoughtful work than some descriptions of it imply. Among other things, Pollak (pp. 58–76) anticipated the recent theorizing of Adler, *Sisters in Crime*, and Simon, *Women and Crime*, regarding rising crime rates among women as a result of sexual emancipation.

[18]Pollak, *The Criminality of Women*, p. 161.

[19]Simon, *Women and Crime*, p. 4.

[20]*NPPA Journal*, 3 (January 1957), "The Female Offender." One essay in this collection did present a useful summary of much of the literature on female crime that had accumulated up to about 1956. See Walter C. Reckless, "Female Criminality," *NPPA Journal*, 3 (January 1957), 1–6.

[21]Mazie F. Rappaport, "The Psychology of the Female Offender," *NPPA Journal*, 3 (January 1957), 7–12.

[22]Fabian L. Rouke, "Shoplifting: Its Symbolic Motivation," *NPPA Journal*, 3 (January 1957), 54–58.

[23]Adler, *Sisters in Crime*.

[24]Simon, *Women and Crime*.

[25]F.B.I. statistics showing crime rates for males and females in the United States have already been examined in Chapter 4. Also, Chapter 13 reported on several investigations of homicide which indicated that both black males and females exceed white males and females in rates of homicide.

[26]Arrest trends for males and females are reviewed at greater length in Simon, *Women and Crime*, pp. 33–47; Darrell J. Steffensmeier, "Crime and the Contemporary Woman: An Analysis of Changing Levels of Female Property Crime, 1960–75," *Social Forces*, 57 (December 1978), 566–84.

[27]Simon, *Women and Crime*, p. 35.

[28]Ibid., p. 1.

[29]Ibid., Chapter 3.

[30]Ibid., p. 26.

[31]Adler, *Sisters in Crime*, pp. 55–83.

[32]Ibid., p. 81.

[33]Ibid., passim.

[34]Steffensmeier, "Crime and the Contemporary Woman".

[35]Michael J. Hindelang, "Sex Differences in Criminal Activity," *Social Problems*, 27 (December 1979), 143–56.

[36]Adler, *Sisters in Crime*, pp. 85–110.

[37]Ibid., p. 108.

[38]Data on female delinquency are presented in detail in Don C. Gibbons, *Delinquent Behavior*, 3rd ed. (Englewood Cliffs, N.J.: Prentice-Hall, Inc., 1981), pp. 224–32.

[39]Dale Hoffman-Bustamente, "The Nature of Female Criminality," *Issues in Criminology*, 8 (Fall 1973), 117–36. For another detailed argument about female crime, see Smart, *Women, Crime, and Criminology*.

[40]Ibid., pp. 131–32.

[41]Anthony R. Harris, "Sex and Theories of Deviance: Toward a Functional Theory of Deviant Type-Scripts," *American Sociological Review*, 42 (February 1977), 3–16; also see John Hagan, John H. Simpson, and A. R. Gillis, "The Sexual Stratification of Social Control: A Gender-Based Perspective on Crime and Delinquency," *British Journal of Sociology*, 30 (March 1979), 25–38.

[42]Harris, "Sex and Theories of Deviance," p. 15.

[43]A number of theories of female delinquency, along with a number of pieces of research on female juvenile delinquency, are reviewed in Gibbons, *Delinquent Behavior*, pp. 236–48.

[44]John Cowie, Valerie Cowie, and Eliot Slater, *Delinquency in Girls* (London: Heinemann, 1968).

[45]Susan K. Datesman, Frank R. Scarpitti, and Richard M. Stephenson, "Female Delinquency: An Application of Self and Opportunity Theories," *Journal of Research in Crime and Delinquency*, 12 (July 1975), 107–23; Stephen A. Cernkovich and Peggy C. Giordano, "Delinquency, Opportunity, and Gender," *Journal of Criminal Law and Criminology*, 70 (Summer 1979), 145–51.

[46]See Gisela Konopka, *The Adolescent Girl in Conflict* (Englewood Cliffs, N.J.: Prentice-Hall, Inc., 1966); Clyde Vedder and Dora Somerville, *The Delinquent Girl* (Springfield, Ill.: Chas C Thomas, 1970).

[47]Mary Owen Cameron, *The Booster and the Snitch* (New York: Free Press, 1964); Loren E. Edwards, *Shoplifting and Shrinkage Protection for Stores* (Springfield, Ill.: Chas C Thomas, 1958); Gerald D. Robin, "The American Customer: Shopper or Shoplifter?" *Police* (January–February 1964); Robin, "Patterns of Department Store Shoplifting," *Crime and Delinquency*, 9 (April 1963), 163–72.

[48]Robin, "The American Customer: Shopper of Shoplifter?"

[49]Cameron, *The Booster and the Snitch*, pp. 9–15.

[50]National Council on Crime and Delinquency, *NCCD News*, 45 (March–April 1966).

[51]Cameron, *The Booster and the Snitch*, p. 56.

[52]Ibid., pp. 58–60, 70–84.

[53]Ibid., pp. 11–15.

[54]Ibid., pp. 24–38.

[55]Ibid., pp. 70–88.

[56]Ibid., pp. 91–96, 136–44.

[57]Ibid., p. 123.

[58]Ibid., pp. 132–33.

[59]Ibid., pp. 115–17, 154–57; the psychiatric theme concerning shoplifting is expressed in Rouke, "Shoplifting: Its Symbolic Motivation."

[60]Cameron, *The Booster and the Snitch*, pp. 159–70.

[61]Howard S. Becker, review of Cameron, *The Booster and the Snitch*, *American Journal of Sociology*, 70 (March 1965), 635–36.

[62]Robin, "Patterns of Department Store Shoplifting."

[63]Ibid., pp. 169–70.

[64]Ibid., pp. 167–69.

[65]Ibid., p. 166.

[66]Ibid., p. 170. Cameron, *The Booster and the Snitch*, pp. 101–4.

[67]Robin, "Patterns of Department Store Shoplifting," pp. 169–70.

[68]Ibid., pp. 170–71.

[69]Robin, "The American Customer: Shopper or Shoplifter?"

[70]Ibid.

[71]Paula Newberg, "A Study in Deviance: Shoplifting," *International Journal of Comparative Sociology*, 9 (June 1968), 132–36.

[72]George Won and George Yamamoto, "Social Structure and Deviant Behavior: A Study of Shoplifting," *Sociology and Social Research*, 53 (October 1968), 44–55.

[73]Camille E. Le Grand, "Rape and Rape Laws: Sexism in Society and Law," *California Law Review*, 61 (May 1973), 919–41.

[74]Sarah Gold, "Equal Protection for Juvenile Girls in Need of Supervision in New York State," *New York Law Forum*, 17 (2:1971), 570–98.

[75]Meda Chesney-Lind, "Juvenile Delinquency: The Sexualization of Female Crime," *Psychology Today*, 8 (July 1974), 43–46; Chesney-Lind, "Judicial Enforcement of the Female Sex Role: The Family Court and the Female Delinquent," *Issues in Criminology*, 8 (Fall 1973), 51–69.

[76]Chesney-Lind, "Juvenile Delinquency." See also Kristine Olson Rogers, " 'For Her Own Protection . . .': Conditions of Incarceration for Female Juvenile Offenders in the State of Connecticut," *Law and Society Review*, 7 (Winter 1972), 223–46.

[77]Chesney-Lind, "Juvenile Delinquency," pp. 45–46.

[78]Ibid., p. 46.

[79]Rogers, "For Her Own Protection."

[80]Ibid., p. 227.

[81]Stuart S. Nagel and Lenore J. Weitzman, "Women as Litigants," *The Hastings Law Journal*, 23 (November 1971), 171–98.

[82]Linda R. Singer, "Women and the Correctional Process," *American Criminal Law Review*, 11 (2:1973), 295–308. For a somewhat different view, see Ralph R. Arditi, Frederick Goldberg, Jr., M. Martha Hartle, John H. Peters, and William R. Phelps, "The Sexual Segregation of American Prisons," *Yale Law Journal*, 82 (May 1973), 1229–73. These authors looked at various dimensions of prison programs for males and females and concluded (p. 1244): "In sum, male and female inmates face markedly different prison experiences: neither has an exclusive claim to 'better' treatment."

[83]I have made this point about the early writings of Maurice F. Parmelee, who produced the first criminology textbook in this country: Maurice F. Parmelee, *Criminology* (New York: Macmillan, 1918). See Don C. Gibbons, "Say, Whatever Became of Maurice Parmelee, Anyway?" *Sociological Quarterly*, 15 (Summer 1974), 405–16.

becoming
a "criminal":
the police

Where do criminals come from? The citizen, the psychiatrist, and the sociologist have usually given roughly similar answers to this question. Depending on one's theoretical preferences, lawbreakers have been seen as willfully deciding to violate the law, as driven into deviance by urges from deep within the psyche, or as impelled toward criminality by adverse social circumstances. These views assign police agencies a minor role in crime causation. The police are thought of as reacting *after* crime has broken out but playing no part in the causes of criminality.

Police organizations deserve much more attention than they have traditionally received, if for no other reason than their omnipresent character in modern life. Formalized police agencies have grown rapidly in size and number from their beginnings in the 1800s. Police agencies were initially restricted to nighttime activity carried on by citizen volunteers but eventually gave way to organized, full-time police systems. The London metropolitan police force was created in 1829, and the first day and night police force in the United States originated in New York City in 1844. From this beginning, police agencies in the United States have grown to approximately 700,000 people working for approximately 19,500 county or municipal police agencies that spend more than 11 billion dollars per year.[1]

We challenge the notion that the police exercise a minor influence on criminality and that their role is restricted to responding to law violation. Of those individuals who become involved in actions forbidden in criminal law, some become officially designated as criminals, whereas others remain as covert or hidden deviants. The experience of police apprehension may be an important causal one in that offenders who fall into the hands of the police may have difficulty withdrawing from criminal careers. Being singled out publicly as a criminal may cut the individual off from nondeviant pathways. Indeed, this factor may be more important in criminal recidivism than many of the variables to which criminologists have usually attended. If so, study of the police ought to be elevated to major status in criminological inquiry.

How do some violators fall into the hands of the police while others remain undetected? Complaints of misbehavior against persons originate from a variety of sources, but usually the police officer effects an arrest of a wrongdoer. The private citizen's authority to arrest individuals is rarely invoked. Still, let us be clear on one point. The urban police are usually engaged in *reactive* rather than *proactive* police work. Somewhere in the neighborhood of 90 percent of police contacts with citizens are in response to calls initiated by citizens, rather than the result of the police drumming up business through detection of offenses. Drawing on data from studies in several American cities, Albert Reiss observed that: "Our observational studies of police activity in high-crime-rate areas of three cities show that 87 percent of all patrol mobilizations were initiated by citizens. Officers initiated (both in the field and on view) only 13 percent. Thus, it becomes apparent that citizens exercise considerable control over police patrol work through their discretionary decisions to call the police."[2]

Law-enforcement officials remain unaware of a vast amount of offender behavior occurring in modern societies because this activity is not reported to them. Prostitutes and their clients, addicts and drug peddlers, and kindred souls frequently manage to avoid the scrutiny of the police, for their behavior involves no victim who complains to the police. In addition, much criminality reported to the police fails to result in apprehension of the lawbreakers, largely because of the obstacles to efficient police work inherent in modern societies. That is, many burglaries, robberies, and so on, go unsolved because the criminals are highly mobile in their operations and skilled in the practice of crime. The police have few tools with which to deal with this kind of criminality. Much crime known to the police is handled in informal and discretionary ways as, for example, when the authorities wink at gambling or minor traffic offenses. In other cases, law-enforcement officials deal out warnings and admonitions instead of arresting offenders. Finally, some individuals known to the police are arrested and started on their way through the legal machinery that tags them as criminals.

We should know a good deal about the activities of police agencies, the contingencies that determine whether offenses become known to the police, and the variables that influence the differential handling of cases of which the police are informed. But until recently, social scientists have paid little attention to police agencies. Several reasons account for this lack of attention, but the major one is the problem of rapport involved in efforts to study law-enforcement agencies. Police officers are frequently the targets of public hostility, and they return these feelings. A sociologist would get an especially cold reception in many police stations, for he or she would be suspected of having a major interest in exposing the police to further public condemnation.

For such reasons, much of the sociological commentary on the police has dealt with relations of police agencies to the host society, including such factors as public hostility toward them. Relatively few investigations have studied the internal workings of police systems. However, in recent years a number of sophisticated and revealing studies of police agencies have been carried out by sociologists.[3]

Much commentary on law-enforcement agencies has dealt with city police systems primarily because they are responsible for the largest portion of arrests in the United States. However, we should note that a large number of different police agencies characterize American society.

One local police organization is the sheriff system found in nearly every county in the United States. County sheriff departments in metropolitan areas are often quite large, for these departments are responsible for law enforcement in all unincorporated parts of the county. The sheriff system is an anomaly: the sheriff is an elected official who usually comes to office without any special training in police work. The job of sheriff involves rapid turnover of personnel because the incumbent is often defeated when he runs for reelection. In some sheriff's departments, the deputy officers obtain their positions as political favors. For such reasons, sheriff's departments have been particularly vulnerable to corrupt practices.[4]

Federal police represent another major group of law-enforcement personnel in the United States. The most famous federal agency is, of course, the Federal Bureau of Investigation. However, there are eight national police organizations in all, including the Bureau of Narcotics, the Secret Service, and Post Office inspectors.

Still another collection of law-enforcement groups is found at the state level. The best known state policing agency is identified variously as the State Police, or the State Highway Patrol. The latter are sometimes restricted to enforcement of motor-vehicle laws, where state police usually have more general law-enforcement powers. In addition, most states also have state narcotics bureaus, tax-enforcement organizations, game wardens, liquor inspectors, and other police groups.

Private police of various kinds represent a final form of police organization. Suburban shopping centers frequently employ police officers paid by the merchants, although the agent has certain law-enforcement powers. Store detectives and hotel protective personnel constitute another kind of private police.

The following pages deal primarily with municipal police systems and comment on the relations of these police agencies to the host society. We shall look at police structures as social organizations, showing how the structural features of the society in which the police operate tend to determine the central dimensions of law-enforcement practice. This view differs from the layman's, which often interprets police activity in terms of assumed stupidity or venality on the part of policemen. We agree with Skolnick, who held:

It is rarely recognized that the conduct of police may be related in a fundamental way to the character and goals of the institution itself—the duties police are called upon to perform, associated with the assumptions of the system of legal justice—and that it may not be men who are good or bad, so much as the premises and design of the system in which they find themselves.[5]

This chapter is not concerned with police administration, that is, operating standards and procedures for efficient, professional police work.[6] Rather, the focus of this chapter is upon the social reality of police work as it actually occurs.

the police and society

PUBLIC HOSTILITY TOWARD THE POLICE

Police officers have been the targets of negative responses from citizens from nearly the beginnings of organized law enforcement.[7] In the United States, the idea of individual liberty and freedom from external interference has always been a central theme. Accordingly, in the eyes of many people, the less the police intrude into their affairs, the better.

In American history, another source as well has fed antagonistic views of the police. Urban law-enforcement agencies have frequently been linked with organized criminals and corrupt city officials in the operation of vice. In this arrangement, city police have often operated as regulators of prostitution, gambling, and other forbidden activities and have shared in the division of spoils from these enterprises. Although prostitution and gambling depend for their support on the public, this fact has not prevented a good many citizens from venting their indignation on the police, particularly on the occasion of recurrent exposés of police corruption reported in urban newspapers.

A third source of citizen dissatisfaction with law-enforcement agencies has grown from police use of various illegal or questionable enforcement procedures, including the use of excessive physical force in effecting arrests. Other instances of illegal police behavior include gratuitous use of force in mob control as well as cases of entrapment. These incidents have encouraged the spread of public notions that the police department is a haven for incompetents and sadists. Whether or not they square with the facts, such images have contributed to the low esteem in which police officers are held in this society.

Another aspect of public hostility concerns the antagonism of the police toward the citizenry. American law-enforcement agencies have often assumed many characteristics of a secret society. They have adopted the posture that they are besieged by enemies of all kinds, including most members of the general public. As a consequence, they have closed ranks to prevent disclosure of any information about their internal workings.[8] At the same time, they have gone to great lengths to protect even the most deviant and lawless officer on the force. The tension between the police and the society that employs them is evident in the former's response to efforts to create civilian review boards to police the police. Such suggestions have frequently been violently opposed by the department in question.

Some evidence is at hand concerning public hostility toward the police. Research indicates that citizens' views of law-enforcement workers are probably more negative in the United States than in many other nations. Yet at the same time, the majority of American citizens voice supportive attitudes toward the police, so public hostility is perhaps not as great as is sometimes assumed. For example, James Q. Wilson has discussed some national-opinion-survey data on this question.[9] These findings indicated that black citizens had less positive views of the police than did whites, whereas higher-income blacks were more critical of the police than were lower-income blacks. At the same time, over three-fourths of the whites and over 60 percent of the black respondents at all social-class levels believed that the police were doing a "very good" or "pretty good" job of protecting people in their neighborhoods. Charles McCaghy, Irving Allen, and J. David Colfax reported similar results in a 1966 study in Hartford, Connecticut,[10] as also did Charles Thomas and Jeffrey Hyman in an investigation in the Norfolk metropolitan area.[11] McCaghy, Allen, and Colfax indicated that two-thirds of the persons surveyed were satisfied with the police, although black citizens were less enthusiastic about the police than were white citizens. Thomas and Hyman found general support for the police, except among young persons, blacks, and inner-city residents. Frank Furstenberg and Charles Wellford found that most citizens who called the police in Baltimore were relatively satisfied with the police response, although black citizens were less pleased than whites.[12] Finally, Paul Smith and Richard Hawkins conducted an investigation of citizens' attitudes in Seattle, finding that three-fourths of the respondents had favorable views of the police.[13] However, the majority of nonwhite citizens in their sample viewed the police negatively. Further, negative opinions were not related to fear of crime, nor did those persons who were acquainted with police officers have more favorable views of them.

LIMITATIONS ON POLICE POWERS

Citizens often demand that law-enforcement agents attempt to bring about near total repression of criminality, or at the very least they are charged with the responsibility of apprehending all lawbreakers reported to them. At the same time, the police labor under various restraints in the way of rules of arrest, evidence, and so on, which render this task almost impossible to accomplish. For example, an officer who arrested an individual detained for a misdemeanor by a citizen would be guilty of illegal arrest and could be sued by the person arrested, if the officer did not observe the misdemeanor being committed. Law-enforcement agencies are placed in a situation of great strain in that they are given a mandate to promote social order at the same time that they are circumscribed by a variety of restraints on police practice. Modern societies are a far cry from police states, in which the police have such virtually unlimited powers that technical efficiency is the only limit on their tactics. Skolnick has discussed the inherent conflict between the goals of social order and rule of law to be observed by police officers.[14] He noted:

The police in democratic society are required to maintain order and to do so under the rule of law. As functionaries charged with maintaining order, they are part of the bureaucracy. The ideology of democratic bureaucracy emphasizes initiative rather than disciplined adherence to rules and regulations. By contrast, the rule of law emphasizes the rights of individual citizens and constraints upon the initiative of legal officials. This tension between the operational consequences of ideas of order, efficiency, and initiative, on the one hand, and legality, on the other, constitutes the principal problem of police as a democratic legal organization (emphasis in the original).[15]

Skolnick observed that another ingredient in the conflict between social order and rule of law derives from the varied conceptions of order in modern society. Some persons would applaud the police for harassing transients, homosexuals, or some other group, but other individuals contend that these matters are not the business of the police.[16]

According to Skolnick, the police bitterly resent the legal restrictions imposed on them. They see themselves as craftsmen, skilled in the work of crime detection and law enforcement. They view the world in probabilistic terms and contend that when their observations lead them to suspect someone of wrongdoing, they are nearly always correct in their suspicions. From this perspective, they often regard procedural rules as obstacles that prevent the officer from doing his or her job to the extent of the officer's capabilities.[17]

The case for police restraints to prevent infringement of civil rights has been stated many times. In 1928, Justice Oliver Wendell Holmes, Jr., declared: "We have to choose, and for my part, I think it is less evil that some criminals should escape than that the government should play an ignoble part."

The citizen in American society enjoys freedom from improper police actions through the guarantees of the Bill of Rights, specifically the first eight amendments, which protect the citizen from illegal searches, from being compelled to testify against himself or herself, and so on. However, throughout United States history, the Supreme Court has been reluctant to extend the protections of the Bill of Rights beyond federal cases. For decades, the police in various states felt themselves to be under no obligation to desist from searches without warrants or the use of other indefensible tactics.

Police work in city police departments has included the third degree, that is, the use of force to coerce confessions from suspects. Police officers have engaged in searches without warrants, interrogated suspects for unduly long periods of time, and employed a variety of other expedient techniques, such as the use of informants, to make arrests. Thus, historically, the police have promoted social order by circumventing or ignoring the procedural rules that supposedly control their activities.[18]

Over the past several decades, the police have come under greater pressure to conform to the rule of law. The Supreme Court, in a series of decisions extending over this period, moved to sharpen the conflict over social order versus rule of law. Herbert Packer has summarized these Supreme Court changes.:

The choice, basically, is between what I have termed the Crime Control and the Due Process models. The Crime Control model sees the efficient expeditious and reliable screening and disposition of persons suspected of crime as the central value to be served by the criminal process. The Due Process model sees that function as limited by and subordinate to the maintenance of the dignity and autonomy of the individual. The Crime Control model is administrative and managerial; the Due Process model is adversary and judicial. The Crime Control model may be analogized to an assembly line, the Due Process model to an obstacle course.

What we have at work today is a situation in which the criminal process as it actually operates in the large majority of cases probably approximates fairly closely the dictates of the Crime Control model. The real-world criminal process tends to be far more administrative and managerial than it does adversary and judicial. Yet, the officially prescribed norms for the criminal process, as laid down primarily by the Supreme Court, are rapidly providing a view that looks more and more like the Due Process model. The development, with which everyone here is intimately familiar, has been in the direction of "judicializing" each stage of the criminal process, of enhancing the capacity of the accused to challenge the operation of the process, and of equalizing the capacity of all persons to avail themselves of the opportunity for challenge so created.[19]

The older "hands-off" policy of the Supreme Court, as concerned with local-police abridgment of constitutional guarantees, was exemplified in the *Wolf* decision handed down in 1949. In that case, the court exempted the states from the exclusionary rule disallowing use of evidence obtained through illegal search or seizure. The court voiced reluctance to intrude into a situation of long standing, in which state courts had been accepting evidence obtained illegally.

One of the first signs of court movement toward what Packer called the Due Process model came in the 1947 *Adamson* case. In that appeal, the court debated the question of whether the states are bound by the provisions of the Fifth Amendment concerning the right of the accused to remain silent and to refuse to testify against himself. Although four of the justices took the affirmative view in this case, the five-man majority ruled that the states would violate due process only by action that "shocks the conscience." In 1952, in the case of *Mallory*, the court ruled that a person under arrest in a federal case must be taken without unnecessary delay before a federal commissioner to be apprised of his or her rights to silence and legal counsel. Then in 1961, the *Mapp* decision ordered the states to enforce the Fourth Amendment guarantee against unreasonable search and seizure. The exclusionary rule was thus extended to the states, compelling the police to have valid search warrants before seizing evidence.

The *Gideon* decision of 1963 represented another landmark case in which the court extended the Sixth Amendment guarantee of legal counsel to all serious crimes. This decision meant that an indigent accused will be said to have been deprived of a fair trial unless that person has been provided with adequate legal assistance.

The most controversial actions of the Supreme Court have occurred in the past two decades, beginning with the *Escobedo* decision in 1964,[20] in which the court voided a murder confession because the accused person had been prevented from seeing his lawyer, who was present in the police station house. Since the *Escobedo* case, decisions in a series of other cases, including *Miranda*, have mandated that the police inform any person whom they detain or take into custody of his or her right to remain silent.

A great deal of heated controversy and bitter comment have surrounded these decisions. Supporters of these court actions have argued that all the decisions merely extend protections to accused individuals which have been standard in England for a long time. Moreover, these persons have contended that the rulings will have the salutary effect of correcting laziness among policemen. These rulings make it difficult for them to depend solely on confessions to obtain convictions and force them to work harder at building a strong framework of evidence obtained through diligent detective work to support accusations against suspects. Opponents of these actions have argued that these rulings against interrogation further tie the hands of the police, who have already been rendered relatively powerless by court rulings at the very time that crime is increasing dramatically.

Many angry words have been exchanged in this controversy, but little real evidence has been assembled. However, Theodore Souris has reported one instance that indicated that the post-*Escobedo* period has not been one of law-enforcement breakdown.[21] Souris observed that the Detroit police reported that in 1961 they obtained confessions in 60.8 percent of the criminal cases in that city, and they deemed these confessions essential to conviction in 13.1 percent of the cases. In 1965, the Detroit police claimed that they obtained confessions in 58 percent of the offenses, 11 percent of which were critical in leading to conviction.

Another study of the impact of court rulings on police practice was conducted in New Haven, Connecticut.[22] This research dealt with the *Miranda* ruling, which requires the police to inform the suspect in clear terms that he or she has the right to remain silent and the right to legal counsel, which will be provided the suspect if he or she cannot afford a lawyer. Observers were stationed at the police station. The results showed that although the student observers were present, the police advised only 25 of 118 suspects of their rights. Interestingly, the detectives obtained a greater percentage of confessions from those who were given thorough warnings. Apparently, the police were being careful to warn fully those individuals accused of serious crimes, after which they questioned them vigorously. The researchers concluded that the *Miranda* ruling had altered police practices in New Haven only slightly.

An inquiry in Washington, D.C., concerning the *Miranda* rule provided related findings.[23] That investigation found that the police in that city often failed to properly advise suspects of their rights. Nonetheless, nearly half of those warned of their rights made incriminating statements anyway. Also, only 1,262 of 15,430 persons arrested for serious crimes during the year of the study requested the volunteer attorneys available to them. In both New Haven and Washington, D.C., the investigators found that *Miranda* warnings were delivered to suspects in a wooden, unsympathetic manner so that many individuals were probably dissuaded from taking advantage of their rights.

Finally, Neal Milner's study, dealing with four Wisconsin communities of under 200,000 population, provided evidence on compliance with the *Miranda* rule.[24] He ranked the police departments in these cities in terms of professionalism and found that police attitudes were most positive toward legal rights of suspects in the most professional department. However, the actual interrogation practices of the police were similar in all four cities.

Supreme Court decisions in the past several decades have been in the direction of further protection of the rights of individuals in juvenile-court proceedings, court sentencing, postconviction handling of offenders, and other areas of the criminal-justice machinery.[25] Without doubt, controversy will continue regarding these decisions. Whatever the end result of Supreme Court decisions, the police will continue to face the dilemma of contradictory expectations. They will be held responsible for the repression of crime at the same time that they are expected to behave with scrupulous attention to individual rights. The solution of this problem will come only when we recognize that both these goals cannot be realized. If we are to have police agencies that respect individual rights, we shall have to become reconciled to the situation in which a good many persons escape the law-enforcement machinery.

THE POLICE AND DISCRETIONARY ACTION[26]

Although police chiefs often publicly assert that their departments enforce all laws equally, the fact is that police everywhere go about selective enforcement of criminal laws. This discretionary and selective enforcement is of two kinds. In one case, the police do not attend to certain statutes at all. In many localities, they ignore archaic laws designed for earlier social conditions. In other cases, the police do not enforce certain laws, even though the conditions these statutes attempt to regulate do exist in the community. Rules against various forms of gambling represent a case in point, for in many areas the police have evolved tolerance policies that allow such statutes to be violated with impunity. The second general form of discretionary police activity centers about the differential application of laws to different individuals. That is, the police often apprehend some, but not all, persons whom they observe violating some statute, or in the more frequent case, who have been reported to them by some irate citizen.

The usual defense for discretionary actions is that total enforcement would almost immediately bring the judicial machinery to a halt, jails and prisons would overflow, and chaos would result. The argument has also been advanced that judicious enforcement of laws is needed to keep petty offenders out of the legal machinery at the same time that intractable lawbreakers receive intensive attention and handling. According to this view, selective law enforcement, rather than legal intervention applied indiscriminately, best serves the interests of society. However, the problem comes when efforts are made to implement basic policies of police discretion. The danger is that what begins as selective enforcement might degenerate into discriminatory law enforcement.

What principles guide the police in exercising discretionary powers? According to Banton, the police are attuned to notions of popular morality. They endeavor to take official action in cases where even the people who suffer from this intervention will be compelled to concede that the police are morally right in their activity. In short, Banton argued that police officers are much like other citizens in certain ways and are sensitive to many widely held cultural values.[27]

Joseph Goldstein has provided one of the most incisive discussions of the problems inherent in use of police discretion.[28] He noted that selective enforcement represents low-visibility interaction between individual officers and various citizens. The exercise of discretion is not guided by clear policy directives, nor is it subject to administrative scrutiny. For such reasons, selective enforcement can easily deteriorate into police abuse and discriminatory conduct. In Goldstein's view, an impartial civilian body should scrutinize the decisions as to which laws should be enforced. In that way, discretionary conduct would become more visible and might result in selective law enforcement that would then become a subject for open public dialogue.

A body of information is at hand regarding the exercise of police discretion in dealing with juvenile offenders.[29] One report of delinquency cases in Washington, D.C., showed that only a fraction of the cases known to the police and other public agencies resulted in juvenile-court referral.[30] Also, the percentages of juveniles referred to the court varied from one offense to another. Most known thieves ended up in the court, whereas almost none of the truancy cases were handled in that way.

Nathan Goldman conducted an investigation of juvenile arrests in Allegheny County, Pennsylvania, in a small mill town, an industrial center, a trade center, and an upper-class residential area.[31] The data indicated that two-thirds of the apprehended juveniles were released without court referral, although 91 percent of the auto thieves were taken to court and only 11 percent of the mischief cases were reported. A major differential in police reporting was that 65 percent of the black offenders were taken to court, in marked contrast to 34 percent of the white juveniles so handled.[32]

Goldman also found that males and females were reported to the court in about the same proportions, but referrals increased with the age of offenders.[33] Somewhat surprisingly, the upper-class residential area had the highest arrest rate of the four communities. But the communities with the lowest arrest rates, "Trade City" and "Steel City," had the highest proportion of arrests for serious offenses. Citizens and police in "Trade City" and "Steel City" generally ignored complaints leading to juvenile arrests in the upper-class area and the mill town. In short, the police in the latter communities apparently found themselves engaged in more serious business than responding to juvenile peccadilloes.[34]

Goldman gathered interview material from the police regarding the factors influencing their decisions. The officers were attentive to the seriousness of offenses. They were also affected by their views of the juvenile court; those who thought the court had harmful effects on youths referred few of them. They also emphasized the demeanor of the juveniles; they were more likely to refer surly or defiant youths than polite, contrite youngsters.[35]

Irving Piliavin and Scott Briar turned up findings similar to those of Goldman.[36] These investigators studied the behavior of police officers in a large California city and reported that discretion was widely used in police dealings with juveniles. Most of the youngsters apprehended for serious forms of lawbreaking were subsequently referred to the court. However, the less serious cases were differentially reported; some youngsters were turned loose with admonitions to behave themselves, whereas others were taken to court. Officers made such discretionary decisions in terms of the demeanor of the youngsters. Those who were members of gangs, who were blacks, who dressed like "cats," or who were flippant ended up in juvenile hall.

Theodore Ferdinand and Elmer Luchterhand also found evidence of differential handling of black and white delinquents in a study carried on in "Easton," an eastern city of 150,000 population, 30 percent of which was black.[37] The black offenders who got into the hands of the police in that community were more likely than the white youths to be referred to the juvenile court. However, Ferdinand and Luchterhand did *not* attribute this higher rate of referral for black juveniles to involvement in more serious offenses or to age differences between them and white youths. Instead, they concluded that black juveniles in all offense groupings were more frequently referred to court than white youngsters and, in addition, that black juveniles who were referred to court were less aggressive and antisocial than the white court referrals. Ferdinand and Luchterhand asserted that at least some of the differential reporting of black youths to juvenile court was due to racial prejudice on the part of police officers so that they were more harsh with black delinquents than white ones.[38]

James Wilson provided a different focus on discretion in juvenile police work.[39] Wilson looked at two relatively large cities: "Western City" had a professionalized police department, whereas "Eastern City" showed a fraternal law-enforcement agency. Western City selected its recruits impartially, practiced consistent law enforcement, and had a formal, bureaucratic organizational structure. Eastern City had officers recruited entirely from among local residents, practiced differential law enforcement, showed considerable graft, and commonly had informal and fraternal relations in its operation.[40]

The juvenile bureaus of the two departments differed on a number of points. In Eastern City, the police were moralistic in outlook, holding that faulty personal or family morality produced delinquents. They verbalized restrictive and punitive attitudes toward offenders. In Western City, the officers were less moralistic and more therapeutic in their opinions. Somewhat surprisingly, in view of these differences, the Western City police processed a larger proportion of its city's juvenile population than did the Eastern City police.[41] Also, a larger share of those contacted were arrested in Western City than in the other community. These results suggested professionalization of police departments leads to more formal handling of offenders and stricter enforcement of the law.

These studies have to do with discretionary activities concerning juvenile offenders. We could assemble a large amount of impressionistic data suggesting that the police commonly engage in selective law enforcement with adults as well. One piece of evidence on this point came from Skolnick's study.[42] He indicated that the Oakland officers made discretionary decisions in their traffic-warrant enforcement operation. Some offenders who had traffic fines outstanding were arrested for nonpayment, and other individuals were allowed to remain at liberty while they arranged to pay these fines. Proportionately more blacks than whites were arrested instead of being dealt with more leniently, but not because of racial factors per se. According to Skolnick, the police were about as biased in their attitudes toward blacks as citizens generally, customarily referring to blacks in uncomplimentary terms and showing other prejudicial attitudes. However, the reason they arrested more blacks was that these persons were more likely to be unemployed, so they had difficulty in satisfactorily settling their affairs with the warrant bureau. Skolnick maintained that the police managed to keep their antiblack sentiments from intruding on their work in warrant-bureau operations, even though these prejudices did enter into other aspects of police relations with minority-group members.

Differential law enforcement was found in John Gardiner's study of the enforcement of moving traffic regulations in four Massachusetts cities.[43] He noted that in the larger communities surrounding Boston, the rates for traffic tickets handed out during 1964 varied from 12 to 158 citations per 1,000 motor vehicles.[44] Traffic citations were issued in markedly different numbers in the four cities he studied, even though actual traffic offenses seemed to be equally distributed in these communities. Gardiner maintained that these variations in traffic-law enforcement resulted in considerable part from departmental policy, particularly as defined by the police chief or other policy-setting agency. In some cities, traffic enforcement was viewed as a residual police function, whereas in others it was seen as a major form of police business.

James Wilson's investigation of eight separate police agencies also contained a good deal of information on differential law enforcement.[45] He observed that the arrest rates for moving traffic violations ranged from 11.4 to 247.7 per 1,000 population in the cities he studied.[46] Enforcement of laws concerning vice and other criminal matters also varied in the eight communities. Wilson contended that police agencies often exhibited one of several styles of police activity and organization. Those police organizations that pursued the watchman style emphasized maintenance of public order and made few arrests. Police agencies structured on the legalistic style handled most complaints as matters of law enforcement and produced a high arrest rate. Organizations that followed a service style intervened frequently into complaints and behavioral episodes that came to their attention but handled relatively few cases formally.[47] Wilson summarized differential enforcement thus:

How frequently the police intervene in a situation, and whether they intervene by making an arrest, will depend in part on the number and seriousness of the demands the city places on them. Second, some police behavior will be affected by the tastes, interests, and styles of the police administrator. Finally, the administrator's views of both particular problems and the general level and vigor of enforcement may be influenced, intentionally or unintentionally, by local politics.[48]

The foregoing evidence suggests some major dimensions involved in selective law enforcement. However, one aspect that needs further study is the process by which officers learn to practice discretion in law enforcement. The police are not empowered to enforce laws selectively so that this feature of law enforcement is not usually articulated in the formal socialization of recruits in police academies. Instead, the rookie patrolman probably acquires norms governing discretion through informal socialization in a squad car, in which an older, more experienced officer relates "the facts of life."

THE POLICE AND PEACE KEEPING

Many citizens think of the police in stereotyped images that portray their main business as the pursuit of violent and dangerous criminals. Actually, the police officer's job resembles many other occupations in that much of the work is tedious, routine, and unglamorous. The routine character of police work in American society stems from the delegation of a great many responsibilities as peace officers in addition to tasks of crime detection and repression. That is, American police are held responsible for the maintenance of orderly social life. They spend much of their time patrolling "Skid Road" to make certain that the vagrants remain out of the vision of other citizens. They give over time to regulating the flow of traffic throughout the city, supervising the movements of pedestrians, and taking care of a host of other regulatory functions that have come to them by default. In many cities, the police are responsible for all licensing functions. They are usually the persons appealed to when a citizen perceives that someone he or she associates with has begun to act "crazy"; thus, the police routinely process referrals to psychiatric wards of county hospitals. The police handle myriad other chores, most of which are relatively distinct from crime repression or prevention.

A study by Elaine Cumming, Ian Cumming, and Laura Edell[49] documented the extent of peace officer activities of the police. In recording calls coming into the complaint desk of an American city, they found that over half of the calls dealt with appeals for assistance or support on personal or interpersonal problems rather than with criminal matters. Their data suggested that although citizens may not always admire policemen, the police are the first persons who come to mind when members of the general public are casting about for someone to rescue them from the complexities of urban life.

The Cumming and associates findings are not atypical ones that applied only to the city they studied. For example, in Portland, Oregon, the police deal with a large number of peace-keeping incidents, including what they term "Stand by for Move Out," by which they refer to cases in which they remain on the premises while wives who have been fighting with their spouses move out from their place of residence. The police task is to prevent the husband from harassing or assaulting his wife. Similarly, Robert Lilly conducted a study, in a relatively small Kentucky city, in which he found that during a four-month period the police received over 18,000 calls from citizens, with about 60 percent of them being requests for information, 12 percent having to do with traffic matters, and only a very small number centering around crime-related matters.[50]

Some further insight into the peace-keeping roles of American policemen came from a study of law-enforcement practices on "Skid Road."[51] Egon Bittner reported that patrolmen assigned to this section of the city saw themselves not as law officers but rather as mainly concerned with keeping order. They received few explicit directives from their superiors as to how they were to keep the peace. Thus, as craftsmen, they contrived their own techniques and procedures.

"Skid Road" officers sought to accumulate a rich supply of information on area residents and such community operations as flophouses and missions. As they went about their peace keeping, they were relatively unconcerned with strict notions of culpability and evidential standards. Instead, they tended to ignore fine distinctions between offenders and victims, and acted toward "Skid Road" denizens as though all were lawbreakers. Moreover, policemen made arrests informally, even though they could arrest persons for illegal acts. In short, decisions to use force or to refrain from coercion, to arrest or not to arrest, and other choices were made with an eye toward maintenance of order. Their behavior was less a response to lawbreaking than it was to the aim of peace keeping.

Bittner also provided data concerning order-keeping endeavors of policemen concerned with the mentally ill.[52] Urban law-enforcement persons are routinely involved in large numbers of cases contending that someone is mentally ill. The officer in these cases must act the role of quasi-psychiatrist; he or she must decide whether to make an emergency apprehension of a person to be held for psychiatric examination. Bittner suggested that emergency apprehensions were most common in instances of attempted suicide, extreme agitation, or serious disorientation on the part of the person. On the other hand, informal dispositions of complaints occurred most often when the officer found someone who would take charge of the disturbed individual.

The principal problem in making the police serve as a jack-of-all-trades organization is that budgets have often failed to increase at the same rate as additions to responsibilities. As a result, the police in various municipalities frequently engage in chronic appeals to the city government for more funds and personnel. The addition of peace-maintenance tasks to the traditional responsibilities of the police further complicates their law-enforcement activities. Critics who would have them make large numbers of arrests often fail to take into account both the procedural restrictions and the manpower limitations under which the police function.

Few citizens would probably challenge the contention that the Federal Bureau of Investigation is a relatively efficient, professional police force from which offenders rarely escape, or the contrasting claim that inefficiency, laxness, and poor performance mark city police forces.[53] Nevertheless, much of this highly flattering picture of the FBI is a carefully constructed myth.[54] But let us assume that municipal police do solve fewer crimes than do federal police, even though the disparity in performance may not be as great as sometimes thought. Such an assumption is probably a correct one. How are we to account for this difference? One possible explanation is that the FBI recruits intelligent agents, whereas the city police attract dullards and incompetents. However, a more likely hypothesis is that the kinds of criminality with which these agencies deal and the circumstances surrounding them play a major role in police practice. In short, the municipal police may be faced with offenders who are less "catchable" than those the federal authorities encounter.

Arthur Stinchcombe has discussed some structural conditions influencing police practice.[55] He pointed out that private places can be distinguished from public ones. The police do not have access to the former without warrants, although they can freely enter public settings. Some crimes normally occur in private places, whereas others usually take place in public ones. Some crimes involve violence, whereas others are free from violence. Following these distinctions, Stinchcombe identified a number of different patterns of criminality, along with their law-enforcement consequences. For example, coercion in private life, such as wife-beating, occurs in private places. Although these cases are usually reported to the police, they infrequently result in convictions. The complainants tend to be reluctant to testify against the accused persons. Wives who have been beaten do not wish to have their spouses prosecuted, for fear this action will bring about a permanent rupture in their marriage.

Another form of criminality centers about illegitimate businesses such as prostitution, gambling, and traffic in drugs. Some of these activities occur in public places, whereas others take place in private situations. In either event, these offenses are victimless because they have to do with illicit commodities that are widely desired. The participants are motivated to keep their conduct secret from the police, so there is no one to act as a complainant. As a result, the police must drum up their own business by means of undercover agents, informants, and other techniques which they do not employ in other kinds of criminality.

Still another general form of lawbreaking has to do with criminal invasion of private places, for example, burglary. This kind of crime is usually reported to the police, but it infrequently results in apprehension of the responsible parties. These offenses are carried on with stealth; providing few clues for the police, the culprits are highly mobile and exceedingly difficult to intercept. Finally, disorders and nuisances in public places are forms of criminality that the police can easily observe and the courts can successfully process.

The foregoing analysis suggests that the large number of crimes unsolved by the city police stems from the difficulty of observing or solving many of these offenses. The federal law-enforcement business more commonly involves such criminal actions as tax evasion, in which incriminating evidence against offenders is easily gathered through perusal of tax records or kindred enforcement techniques.

POLICE CORRUPTION

The police are often involved in misbehavior of various kinds, only some of which qualifies as corruption. The use of wiretaps, police brutality, fabrication of evidence, entrapment of prostitutes and other alleged offenders, and "cooping" (sleeping on duty and avoiding routine patrol responsibilities) are all forms of police misconduct additional to corruption. The sense of police corruption is captured in citizen allegations that officers are "on the take" or "on the pad," in other words, that they are involved in taking bribes. One student of police corruption, Lawrence Sherman, offered the following definition: "A public official is corrupt if he accepts money or moneys worth for doing something that he is under a duty to do anyway, that he is under a duty not to do, or to exercise a legitimate discretion for improper reasons."[56]

It should come as no surprise to hear that police corruption has been endemic in this country for as long as metropolitan police have existed. Police corruption has also been a recurrent phenomenon in county sheriff's departments.[57]

Julian Roebuck and Thomas Barker have provided a typology of eight forms of police corruption, indicating the different patterns it assumes.[58] They listed corruption of authority, kickbacks, opportunist theft, and shake-downs among these forms. Additionally, corruption involves protection of illegal activities, "the fix," involvement in direct criminal activities, and internal payoffs.

The most common explanation for corruption advanced by police administrators and city officials is the rotten-apple hypothesis, attributing police misbehavior to the work of a few, isolated, aberrant officers in an otherwise honest department. This contention is a parallel of those notions often entertained by members of the general public which explain police brutality as the work of sadists who have somehow managed to slip by the psychiatric screening they underwent when being hired, or which account for malfeasance by prison guards in terms of individual defects thought to characterize a few guards. Although it may be the case that police corruption is sometimes the work of a few "bad apples," such explanations fail to give appropriate weight to organizational or institutional factors that are implicated in police misconduct.

Sherman outlined a typology of corrupt police departments which endeavored to deal with the individual and organizational dimensions of corruption.[59]

One type of corrupt department involves "rotten apples" and "rotten pockets," in which only a few, isolated police officers or small groups of officers accept bribes within departments that are for the most part honest ones. Pockets of corruption are sometimes found in such places as vice bureaus where bribes are most likely to be offered to officers and where police are under pressure by various community groups to overlook certain forms of vice, particularly prostitution.

A second type of corrupt department, according to Sherman, is one involved in pervasive but unorganized corruption. In these police agencies, large numbers of officers take bribes but they are not joined together to form networks of corruption. Also, the bribes are most frequently tendered by individual offenders and citizens, rather than by organized criminal syndicates.

The third form of police corruption, and one that is quite familiar to Americans, is pervasive organized corruption. According to Sherman: "Type III police departments are pervasively corrupt, with corruption organized in a hierarchical, authoritarian fashion. The corruption extends beyond the police department to the high (local) criminal justice and political officials, and revolves around the vice operations of a local crime syndicate.[60]

Sherman also gave attention to a series of factors that contribute to police corruption.[61] He enumerated a number of constant factors omnipresent in police agencies throughout the nation that tend to encourage corruption, with special emphasis upon the discretionary role of the police in deciding whether to arrest someone or not. Additionally, corruption is abetted by the low visibility of police work and by the secret-society character of police organizations.[62] Individual police officers and police administrators all tend to emphasize loyalty to fellow police officers, even to the point of covering up knowledge of lawbreaking within the department.

In many of the commentaries on police corruption, particularly in the United States, attention has focused upon certain laws designed to legislate morality as being a constant, core factor in corruption. These laws generate corruption, so the argument goes, by prohibiting services or goods that are in wide demand among members of the public, for example, prostitution, gambling, and liquor. Police corruption has been encouraged by the tendency of legislatures to overextend the reach of the criminal law to these kinds of activities, thereby creating many of the opportunities for bribes that are offered to policemen.

However, Sherman pointed out that the scope of these laws and the demands for the services they provide are not constant, even within the United States. His analysis identified 14 propositions or hypotheses regarding variable factors that influence the amount of corruption found in particular communities.[63] These were divided into four groups having to do with variations in community structure, organizational differences among police departments, differences in demands for vice, and finally, variations in the nature of corruption controls in communities and police departments.

In identifying community variations, Sherman suggested that large urban communities differ from smaller towns and rural communities in community solidarity and related characteristics which exert considerable influence upon police corruption. Additionally, some police administrators and agencies are much more punishment-oriented than are others and are much more likely to endeavor to ferret out corrupt police officers and punish them severely. Police departments also vary in terms of public reputation for integrity and other organizational dynamics which influence the level of corruption in departments. Communities also differ from each other in the extent of legal prohibitions against various vices and/or in citizens' demands for these forbidden services. Bribes are least frequent in those communities where such demands are relatively uncommon. Finally, some police departments employ vigorous investigative procedures designed to uncover instances of corrupt conduct, while other agencies make no effort to uncover corruption. In the former instances, police misconduct is likely to be deterred by the officers' perceptions that they run a high risk of being detected, apprehended, and punished.

social organization of the police

Modern sociological inquiry often centers upon the study of complex social organizations such as industrial settings, welfare agencies, educational institutions, correctional facilities, and a number of other kinds of organizational structures. Police departments have also been subjected to organizational analysis. Let us examine some of the major findings from this work.

THE SOCIAL ROLE OF POLICE OFFICERS

The notion that a person's occupation influences his or her personality and social life is familiar to sociologists. The varied conditions under which persons earn a living in complex societies heavily influence their general perspectives on life and their modes of social participation. On this point, Skolnick has sketched some features of the police officer's "working personality."[64] According to Skolnick, the elements of danger and authority, which are central to police work, lead law-enforcement persons to develop certain common personality characteristics. One of these is suspiciousness; another is conservatism. Police officers come to be especially attentive to unusual situations, for the unpredictable is also likely to be dangerous. The police are defenders of the status quo, so they come to prefer stability and lack of rapid social change. The dangerous aspects of their work and their task of compelling others to obey laws, many of which are unpopular with citizens, give rise to police solidarity and social isolation from others. Skolnick presented evidence to show that the police he studied were involved in more off-the-job interaction with one another than most other occupational groups.

The thrust of Skolnick's observations, Banton's parallel report on American police,[65] and other studies of police organizations is that there is indeed a "cop mentality," as claimed by laymen. Equally important, these studies indicate that the nature of the job produces the personality elements, rather than the other way around.

POLICE BUREAUCRACIES

Metropolitan police organizations are complex bureaucracies or formal organizations. A variety of specific organizational tables or patterns describe how the police divide up tasks, but in every case a formal and highly complex division of labor characterizes these systems.[66] Most police departments are under administrative supervision of a police commission, which is supposed to police the police, but the control exercised through this device is often minimal. In most cases, the real power and leadership of the department emanates from the office of the Chief of Police.

Police bureaucracies usually involve a group of deputy chiefs immediately under the control of the chief. These persons are responsible for the major divisions of the departmental organization, patrol supervision, crime prevention, juvenile services, traffic management, detective services, and other major tasks of the police force. They are housed in a Hall of Justice or other headquarters located in the city center and are held responsible for the citywide supervision of the police force. Also located downtown are police workers who perform such staff functions as planning and research, the detectives whose work takes them throughout the city, crime prevention personnel, and clerical workers. These headquarters personnel are arranged into a vertical hierarchy of ranks so that some are captains, others lieutenants, sergeants, or patrol officers.

City departments are further segmented through the precinct pattern of operation. Most large municipalities are divided into police districts or precincts, with district police stations out of which the patrol officers operate. These stations are organized in hierarchical fashion, headed by a captain assisted by lieutenants and sergeants.

One feature of police activity about which relatively little is known concerns occupational mobility within departments. City police organizations are usually included within a civil-service system; entry into the department is by means of standardized recruiting procedures, testing, and other regularized practices. Civil-service regulations govern advancement from the rank of patrol officer upward, with standard examinations used for selection of sergeants and more advanced ranks. This aspect of occupational mobility in police departments is the familiar one of bureaucratic progression through stages of the occupational system.

The determinants of job assignments within the department are much less evident. Nearly all officers start as patrol officers, but some move into coveted police jobs, such as detective assignments. These jobs often put the incumbents in line for advancement into the administrative hierarchy. Other police officers remain in precinct patrol work and never rise beyond the rank of sergeant in the system. Finally, some officers receive distasteful assignments, such as fixed-post jobs directing traffic at downtown street intersections. Civil-service procedures do not govern an officer's assignments. Individual police officers account for assignment practices through a variety of informal processes, which they sum up by such expressions as "clout" and "juice." These terms refer to interpersonal influence resulting in desirable assignments for certain officers. There are several forms of "clout"; in different departments: ethnic background, kinship ties to high officials, a record of having made a number of dramatic "big pinches," or other variables contribute to "juice."[67]

Without doubt, informal factors are implicated in mobility patterns in police departments, just as these considerations often appear in other bureaucratic organizations. The formal organization in which explicit rules govern all events does not exist, except in the abstract formulations of sociologists.

Another observation about police bureaucracies has to do with ecological peculiarities in these organizations. Many formal organizations are located in one place, such as a college, a prison, or a factory. Visual surveillance makes easier control of individuals. But the police organization is scattered about the community in headquarters and precinct stations. The largest single group of employees is that of the patrol officers, most of whom are in patrol cars and not in the station house at all. These conditions make it difficult for police officials to conduct systematic evaluations of job performance of the workers, except through such devices as recording the number of official arrests. The ecological structure of police work also creates difficulties in the way of control over deviant workers. Many deviant acts in which police officers sometimes engage, such as drinking on the job, are extremely difficult for administrators to observe. The spatial peculiarities of police systems probably go some way toward explaining the persistence of corrupt practices in the face of reform efforts occurring on the occasion of police scandals.[68]

POLICE VIOLENCE

One of the chronic complaints against police officers in American cities has dealt with gratuitous use of force. The observation has repeatedly been made that the police have engaged in the use of force to extract confessions from suspects. Additionally, innumerable cases have come to light in which the police have assaulted suspects or physically abused other citizens. In the past several decades, much criticism of the police over illegal use of violence in civil-rights demonstrations, racial disturbances, political demonstrations, and campus unrest has been voiced. Although some charges may have been exaggerated, there is little doubt law-enforcement officers have often used force in their dealings with citizens in which the violence clearly exceeded the demands of the situation.[69]

William Westley made a pioneering study of police use of violence.[70] He argued that the police lean to the view that any technique helpful in making arrests is acceptable so that force is justified on expedient grounds. In particular, police values uphold the use of force if it contributes to the making of "good pinches," that is, arrests in well-publicized and serious criminal cases. Along the same line, many police officers regard violence as particularly useful in handling such cases as sex offenses, where prosecutions are difficult to obtain. They argue that application of a beating to a sex offender operates as a deterrent to future episodes of such conduct on his part.

Westley asked a number of officers in a city department to indicate the circumstances they deemed appropriate for violent techniques. The largest number of responses centered about the use of force to obtain respect from hostile or defiant persons. Over one-third of the officers said that they regarded force as appropriate in these cases.

Westley's research was done some years ago. Accordingly, we might wonder what the situation is with respect to police abuse of citizens. In 1967, a task force of The President's Commission on Law Enforcement and Administration of Justice reported that brutality, intimidation, and dishonesty remain as common features in many American police departments. As a consequence, police relations with minority groups were at explosive levels in a number of cities, including Washington, Baltimore, Detroit, Newark, St. Louis, New Orleans, Atlanta, Memphis, Chicago, Cleveland, Philadelphia, and Cincinnati.[71]

What form does police abuse take? The National Advisory Commission on Civil Disorder (Kerner Commission) noted in its 1968 report that many ghetto residents in American cities believed that the police frequently use tactics of violence in their dealings with citizens.[72] At the same time, the President's Commission on Law Enforcement surveys indicated that abusive physical force was much less commonly encountered than was harassment and verbal abuse of citizens by the police.[73] James Wilson provided this summary:

Observations of police behavior by researchers hired by the President's Commission also suggest that unnecessary force occurs in but a tiny fraction of police–citizen contacts, that discourtesy is more common, and—most important—that such incidents seem to be provoked more by *class* than racial differences and by unconventional or bizarre behavior on the part of the suspect (emphasis in the original).[74]

In contrast, some studies, such as the one by Paul Chevigny in New York City, have shown that police abuses, including violence and brutality, continue to be widespread enough to cause considerable alarm.[75] Then, too, from one standpoint, *any* abuse of citizens by law-enforcement agencies should be cause for concern, in that isolated instances of undue force can touch off citizen protests and disorder as well as undermine public confidence in the police.

How are the police to be brought under control so that they refrain from abusive conduct directed at citizens? Chevigny aptly summarized one major impediment to efforts to police the police:

The police themselves are the most formidable obstacle to redress for police abuses. An arrest, together with the necessary testimony, is used to cover almost all street-corner abuses. The testimony is usually effective in covering the abuse for perfectly natural reasons—for example, because there is no one in court to contradict it except another policeman, and he will not do so. The graded structure for advancement in the Police Department, together with its tradition of hostility to outsiders, tends to create almost complete solidarity up the police chain of command. This protects any individual officer from criticism, even by people higher up in the chain, and it reinforces the effectiveness of cover charges and other obstacles to redress, simply because substantially all policemen share similar values and because they are forbidden by their code to betray one another's mistakes.[76]

The Kerner Commission recommended a number of steps to reduce police violence and abusive conduct in the ghetto and to improve citizen perceptions of the police.[77] These included strategies for getting superior police officers assigned to urban ghettos, along with the creation of a specialized agency, independent of the police, to handle, investigate, and make recommendations on citizen complaints. In short, the commission opted for improved personnel and civilian review boards to police the police.[78]

summary

This chapter has directed attention to a number of facets of the police in modern societies. We noted that police agencies have expanded markedly since the creation of the London metropolitan police in 1829, such that American society is now characterized by a wide variety of police organizations, including city police departments, county sheriffs, several federal police agencies, and a number of private police structures.

The basic police mandate is to catch criminals. However, modern police agencies manage to apprehend only a small number of offenders even when crimes are reported to them. Further, the police engage in reactive rather than proactive police work, in which they respond to reports of crime from citizens rather than detecting offenses on their own initiative.

The low degree of efficiency of the police in apprehending lawbreakers is due to a number of factors. For one, the simple fact is that American society has an abundance of criminals but relatively few police officers. Then, too, the police are charged with a number of responsibilities other than pursuit of criminals which consume some of the time they might otherwise devote to the solution of crimes. Third, much crime takes place in private places to which the police do not have access, or it is conducted surreptitiously by highly mobile offenders, rendering the detection task extremely difficult. A fourth factor of major significance centers about the due-process strictures imposed upon the police. Packer and others have noted that Supreme Court decisions have established limitations on the police such that they are frequently not able to employ crime-solving techniques that might be recommended on efficiency grounds, such as unlimited search and seizure procedures, the "third degree," protracted interrogation of suspects, and the like. Even though the police sometimes find ways to circumvent these restrictions, these rules do affect their ability to apprehend alleged criminals.

Although the police make arrests in only a fraction of the cases in which felonies and other serious crimes are reported to them, they also exercise a good deal of discretion in dealing with those citizens they encounter in acts of lawbreaking. A number of studies of police discretion indicate that offense seriousness is the major determinant of the police officer's decision as to whether to arrest the individual involved. However, some research findings point to discriminatory law enforcement on the part of the police, in which characteristics of the alleged offender, such as racial background or economic status, also loom as important in the decisions of the officer.

Although it certainly cannot be said that the police are revered figures in the United States, the evidence considered in this chapter showed a mixed picture with regard to citizen hostility toward the police. Much of the antagonism toward the police that is observed from time to time arises out of police corruption, the use of illegal violence by the police, or racial hostility expressed by police officers.

A major concern of this chapter has been how police action starts offenders on their way toward becoming criminals. But this is only half the story. We also need to examine the workings of the legal machinery as it takes arrested persons and turns out various products from this human material. This is the topic of Chapter 19, where we shall consider what happens to different individuals apprehended by the police.

notes

[1]Timothy J. Flanagan, Michael J. Hindelang, and Michael R. Gottfredson, eds., *Sourcebook of Criminal Justice Statistics, 1979* (Washington, D.C.: Law Enforcement Assistance Administration, 1980), pp. 3–25.

[2]Albert J. Reiss, Jr., *The Police and the Public* (New Haven, Conn.: Yale University Press, 1971), p. 11. On this point, a complex experiment in Kansas City, Mo., cast considerable doubt upon the traditional police view that intensified police patrol in urban neighborhoods will decrease opportunities for crime and increase the arrest rates for reported crimes. See George L. Kelling, Tony Pate, Duane Dieckman, and Charles E. Brown, *The Kansas City Preventive Parole Experiment: A Summary Report* (Washington, D.C.: Police Foundation, 1974). The authors of this report indicated that (p.v.): "Three controlled levels of routine preventive patrol were used in the experimental areas. One area, termed 'reactive,' received no preventive patrol. Officers entered the area only in response to citizen calls for assistance. This in effect substantially reduced police visibility in the area. In the second area, called 'proactive,' police visibility was increased two to three times its usual level. In the third area, termed 'control,' the normal level of patrol was maintained. Analysis of the data gathered revealed that the three areas experienced no significant differences in the level of crime, citizens' attitudes toward police services, citizens' fear of crime, police response time, or citizens' satisfaction with police response time." For further elaboration of these matters, see James

P. Levine, "The Ineffectiveness of Adding Police to Prevent Crime," *Public Policy*, 23 (Fall 1975), 523–45. Also see Charles A. Wellford, "Crime and the Police." *Criminology*, 12 (August 1974), 195–213. In this study, Wellford conducted a multivariate analysis of the 21 largest urban centers in the United States (except New York City). He found that the rates of police officers-per 1,000 citizens and the municipal police budgets were not markedly correlated with crime rates or police clearance rates in the cities. Instead, crime rates were mainly accounted for in terms of socioeconomic variations among the cities.

[3]Michael Banton, *The Policeman in the Community* (New York: Basic Books, 1964); Jerome H. Skolnick, *Justice Without Trial* (New York: John Wiley, 1966); James Q. Wilson, *Varieties of Police Behavior* (Cambridge, Mass.: Harvard University Press, 1968); Reiss, *The Police and the Public*; Arthur Niederhoffer, *Behind the Shield* (Garden City, N.Y.: Doubleday, 1967); Jonathan Rubenstein, *City Police* (New York: Farrar, Straus & Giroux, 1973). Several useful collections of essays on the police are Niederhoffer and Abraham S. Blumberg, eds., *The Ambivalent Force: Perspectives on the Police* (Lexington, Mass.: Ginn 1970); David J. Bordua, ed., *The Police: Six Sociological Essays* (New York: John Wiley 1967); Anthony Platt and Lynn Cooper, eds., *Policing America* (Englewood Cliffs, N.J.: Prentice-Hall, Inc., 1974); Jerome H. Skolnick and Thomas C. Gray, eds., *Police in America* (Boston: Little, Brown, 1975); Peter K. Manning and John Van Maanen, eds., *Policing: A View from the Street* (Santa Monica, Cal.: Goodyear Publishing Co., 1978); Richard J. Lundman, ed., *Policing: A Sociological Perspective* (New York: Oxford University Press, 1980).

[4]One study of the sheriff system is T. C. Esselstyn, "The Social Role of the County Sheriff," *Journal of Criminal Law, Criminology and Police Science*, 44 (July–August 1953), 177–84. These claims about the deficiencies of sheriff's departments are probably in need of qualification, in light of the fact that in many larger counties sheriffs or Directors of Public Safety are now appointed by the local government. Also, a number of sheriff departments have made significant moves in the direction of professionalization and improvement of agency operations.

[5]Skolnick, *Justice Without Trial*, pp. 4–5.

[6]O. W. Wilson and Roy C. McLaren, *Police Administration*, 2nd ed. (New York: McGraw-Hill, 1972); George D. Eastman and Esther M. Eastman, eds., *Municipal Police Administration* (Washington, D.C.: International City Management Association, 1969).

[7]Data regarding the occupational prestige rating of policework and a variety of other occupations can be found in Robert W. Hodge, Paul M. Siegel, and Peter H. Rossi, "Occupational Prestige in the United States: 1925–1963," *American Journal of Sociology*, 70 (November 1964), 286–302. Police perceptions of citizen hostility are discussed in Skolnick, *Justice Without Trial*, pp. 42–70.

[8]One study of police deviancy and the secret society character of police organization is Ellwyn R. Stoddard, "The Informal 'Code' of Police Deviancy: A Group Approach to 'Blue-Coat Crime,'" *Journal of Criminal Law, Criminology and Police Science*, 59 (June 1968), 201–13. Stoddard noted that the police in a Texas city were "on the take" and involved in other extralegal activities, but police department norms discouraged individual officers from reporting this behavior to their superiors or to outsiders. Also see Reiss, *The Police and the Public*, pp. 121–72.

[9]James Q. Wilson, *Varieties of Police Behavior*, p. 28.

[10]Charles H. McCaghy, Irving L. Allen, and J. David Colfax, "Public Attitudes Toward City Police in a Middle-Sized Northern City," *Criminologica*, 6 (May 1968), 14–22.

[11]Charles W. Thomas and Jeffrey M. Hyman, "Perceptions of Crime, Fear of Victimization, and Public Perceptions of Police Performance," *Journal of Police Science and Adminstration*, 5 (September 1977), 305–17.

[12]Frank F. Furstenberg, Jr. and Charles Wellford, "Calling the Police: The Evaluation of Police Service," *Law and Society Review*, 7 (Spring 1973), 382–406.

[13]Paul E. Smith and Richard O. Hawkins, "Victimization, Types of Citizen-Police Contacts, and Attitudes Toward the Police," *Law and Society Review*, 8 (Fall 1973), 135–52.

[14]Skolnick, *Justice Without Trial*, pp. 1–22.

[15]Ibid., p. 6.

[16]Ibid., pp. 10–12.

[17]Ibid., pp. 182–203.

[18]For a discussion of how police employ informants in detective work and of the reciprocity between the police and the informants, see ibid., pp. 122–38. The use of informants is *not* an illegal police procedure. Moreover, most policemen argue that informants are vital to successful law enforcement. For a report on narcotics-enforcement patterns and the use of informants, see Skolnick's discussion, ibid., pp. 139–63. He noted that unlike routine narcotics work or "good pinches," "big cases" provide the police with the conditions under which constitutional standards of legality can best be met. For example, officers do not labor under the same time pressures in "big cases" as they do in others. Other data on detective work can be found in William B. Sanders, *Detective Work* (New York: Free Press, 1977); Peter Greenwood and Joan Petersilia, *The Criminal Investigation Process* (Santa Monica: Rand Corporation, 1975).

[19]Herbert L. Packer, "The Courts, The Police, and the Rest of Us," *Journal of Criminal Law, Criminology and Police Science*, 57 (September 1966), 239; see this entire issue for a series of papers presenting discrepant views of the correctness and significance of these decisions. Also on the Crime Control model, see Packer, *The Limits of the Criminal Sanction* (Stanford, Calif.: Stanford University Press, 1968), pp. 149–246; Abraham S. Blumberg, "Criminal Justice in America," in *Crime and Justice in American Society*, Jack D. Douglas, ed., (Indianapolis: Bobbs-Merrill, 1971), pp. 45–78.

[20]The court decisions are summarized in Niederhoffer, *Behind the Shield*, pp. 161–74.

[21]Theodore Souris, "Stop and Frisk or Arrest and Search—The Use and Misuse of Euphemisms," *Journal of Criminal Law, Criminology and Police Science*, 57 (September 1966), 251–64.

[22]"Interrogation in New Haven," *Yale Law Journal*, 76 (July 1967), 1521–1648.

[23]Richard J. Medalie, Leonard Zeitz, and Paul Alexander, "Custodial Police Interrogation in Our Nation's Capital: The Attempt to Implement Miranda," *Michigan Law Review*, 66 (May 1968), 1347–1422.

[24]Neal Milner, "Comparative Analysis of Patterns of Compliance with Supreme Court Decisions: 'Miranda' and the Police in Four Communities," *Law ,and Society Review*, 5 (August 1970), 119–34.

[25]However, the due process decisions of the Supreme Court have tended toward a more conservative direction in recent years, following appointment of several conservative justices to the Court by former President Nixon.

[26]For a detailed discussion of arrest procedures used by the police, along with reports on police discretionary behavior, drawn from a study of police in Kansas, Michigan, and Wisconsin, see Wayne LaFave, *Arrest, The Decision to Take a Suspect into Custody* (Boston: Little, Brown, 1965). For a summary of the factors involved in police decision making, along with a review of evidence on this topic, see Harold E. Pepinsky, "Police Decision-Making," in *Decision-Making in the Criminal Justice System: Review and Essays*, Don M. Gottfredson, ed. (Rockville, Md.: National Institute of Mental Health, 1975), pp. 21–52.

[27]Banton, *The Policeman in the Community*, pp. 127–55.

[28]Joseph Goldstein, "Police Discretion Not to Invoke the Criminal Process: Low Visibility Decisions in the Administration of Criminal Justice," *Yale Law Journal*, 69 (March 1960), 543–94.

[29]Evidence concerning differential law enforcement and juveniles is summarized in Don C. Gibbons, *Delinquent Behavior*, 3rd ed. (Englewood Cliffs, N.J.: Prentice-Hall, Inc., 1981) pp. 58–75.

[30]Edward E. Schwartz, "A Community Experiment in the Measurement of Juvenile Delinquency," *National Probation Association Yearbook, 1945* (New York: National Probation Association, 1945), pp. 157–81.

[31]Nathan Goldman, *The Differential Selection of Juvenile Offenders for Court Appearance* (New York: National Council on Crime and Delinquency, 1963).

[32]Ibid., pp. 35–47. This matter of differentials in handling racial groups was fairly complex in character. Goldman indicated that the referral rate was about the same for white and black youths involved in serious offenses. But blacks apprehended for minor delinquencies were much more likely to be taken to juvenile court than were their white counterparts. Sidney Axelrad made much the same observation concerning black and white training school wards. The black males were younger and less delinquent and had been placed on probation fewer times than the white youths. Axelrad argued that these actions were taken against the black youths because of their deprived social backgrounds rather than as a result of prejudicial attitudes on the part of the police and court officials. See Sidney Axelrad, "Negro and White Male Institutionalized Delinquents," *American Journal of Sociology*, 57 (May 1952), 569–74.

[33]Goldman, *Differential Selection of Juvenile Offenders*, pp. 44–47.

[34]Ibid., pp. 48–92.

[35]Ibid., pp. 93–124.

[36]Irving Piliavin and Scott Briar, "Police Encounters with Juveniles," *American Journal of Sociology*, 70 (September 1964), 206–14.

[37]Theodore N. Ferdinand and Elmer G. Luchterhand, "Inner-City Youth, the Police, the Juvenile Court, and Justice," *Social Problems*, 17 (Spring 1970), 510–27.

[38]Another study purporting to show police discrimination against black delinquents was Terence P. Thornberry, "Race, Socioeconomic Status and Sentencing in the Juvenile Justice System," *Journal of Criminal Law and Criminology*, 64 (March 1973),90–98. But, for criticisms of the methodology in Thornberry's research investigation, see Charles Wellford, "Labelling Theory and Criminology: An Assessment," *Social Problems*, 22 (Fall 1975), 332–45.

[39]James Q. Wilson, "The Police and the Delinquent in Two Cities," in *Controlling Delinquents*, Stanton Wheeler, ed. (New York: John Wiley, 1968), pp. 9–30.

[40]Ibid., pp. 10–14.

[41]Ibid., pp. 14–19. Some contrary evidence, in which professional and community attachment characteristics of police agencies were *not* related to rates at which those agencies diverted juveniles out of official handling can be found in Richard A. Sundeen, Jr., "Police Professionalization and Community Attachments and Diversion of Juveniles," *Criminology*, 11 (February 1974), 570–80.

[42]Skolnick, *Justice Without Trial*, pp. 71–90.

[43]John A. Gardiner, *Traffic and the Police* (Cambridge, Mass.: Harvard University Press, 1969).

[44]Ibid., p. 11.

[45]Wilson, *Varieties of Police Behavior*.

[46]Ibid., p. 95.

[47]Ibid., pp. 140–226.

[48]Ibid., p. 83.

[49]Elaine Cumming, Ian Cumming, and Laura Edell, "Policeman as Philosopher, Guide and Friend," *Social Problems*, 12 (Winter 1965), 276–86.

[50]J. Robert Lilly, "What Are the Police Now Doing?" *Journal of Police Science and Administration*, 6 (January 1978), 51–60.

[51]Egon Bittner, "The Police in Skid-Row: A Study of Peace Keeping," *American Sociological Review*, 32 (October 1967), 699–715.

[52]Egon Bittner, "Police Discretion in Emergency Apprehension of Mentally Ill Persons," *Social Problems*, 14 (Winter 1967), 278–92.

[53]This view is seen in Don Whitehead, *The FBI Story* (New York: Random House, 1965).

[54]Fred J. Cook, *The FBI Nobody Knows* (New York: Macmillan, 1964). Much of the luster has gone from the FBI's image following revelations growing out of the Watergate scandal, in which it was revealed that the agency was involved in a number of forms of highly questionable conduct and that it had not managed to remain free from political influence. The Watergate disclosures also did much to tarnish the image of J. Edgar Hoover, showing him to be a considerably different person than portrayed in the heroic characterizations of him that were common prior to the Watergate scandal.

[55]Arthur L. Stinchcombe, "Institutions of Privacy in the Determination of Police Administrative Practice," *Americal Journal of Sociology*, 69 (September 1963), 150–60.

[56]Lawrence W. Sherman, ed., *Police Corruption* (Garden City, N.Y.: Anchor Press, 1974), p. 6. Sherman's book contains a brief but very useful sociological theory of police corruption (pp. 1–39).

[57]Journalistic accounts of police corruption are contained in Albert Deutsch, *The Trouble with Cops* (London: ARCO Publishers, Ltd., 1955); Ralph Lee Smith, *The Tarnished Badge* (New York: Thomas Y. Crowell, 1965).

[58]Julian B. Roebuck and Thomas Barker, "A Typology of Police Corruption," *Social Problems*, 21, (3:1974), 423–37.

[59]Sherman, *Police Corruption*, pp. 6–12.

[60]Ibid., p. 10. For one detailed analysis of pervasive organized corruption, involving the Seattle

police department in a local "crime cabal" which included the police, city officials, criminal-justice authorities, businessmen, and organized criminals, see William J. Chambliss, "Vice, Corruption, Bureaucracy, and Power," *Wisconsin Law Review* (1971), 1150–73; also see John A. Gardiner, with the assistance of David J. Olson, "Wincanton: The Politics of Corruption," in *Crime and the Legal Process*, William J. Chambliss, ed. (New York: McGraw-Hill, 1969), pp. 103–35.

[61]Sherman, *Police Corruption*, pp. 12–14.

[62]Stoddard, "The Informal 'Code' of Police Deviancy."

[63]Sherman, *Police Corruption*, pp. 14–30.

[64]Skolnick, *Justice Without Trial*, pp. 42–70.

[65]Banton, *The Policeman in the Community*, pp. 110–26.

[66]For a detailed discussion of police organizational patterns, see Wilson and McLaren, *Police Administration*.

[67]One study of ethnic factors in police organizations is James Q. Wilson, "Generational and Ethnic Differences Among Career Police Officers," *American Journal of Sociology*, 69 (March 1964), 522–28.

[68]For a discussion of police control systems, see David J. Bordua and Albert J. Reiss, Jr., "Command, Control, and Charisma: Reflections on Police Bureaucracy," *American Journal of Sociology*, 72 (July 1966), 68–76.

[69]Widespread and collective use of violence by the police is amply documented in Rodney Stark *Police Riots* (New York: Wadsworth, 1972).

[70]William A. Westley, "Violence and the Police," *American Journal of Sociology*, 59 (July 1953), 34–41.

[71]The President's Commission on Law Enforcement and Administration of Justice, *Task Force Report: The Police*, pp. 144–207. Also see the studies on public views of the police discussed earlier in this chapter.

[72]*Report of the National Advisory Commission on Civil Disorders* (New York: Bantam, 1968), pp. 299–322.

[73]These data are summarized in James Q. Wilson, *Varieties of Police Behavior*, pp. 34–38; see also Reiss. *The Police and the Public*, pp. 121–72; Reiss, "Police Brutality—Answers to Key Questions," *Trans-action*, 5 (July–August 1968), 15–16. One point that is sometimes slurred over in these observations is that they deal principally with police abuse in *routine* police–citizen encounters. While it is probably the case that the police do not usually behave in an excessively abusive manner in these routine encounters, they may well engage in occasional, highly violent activities directed at minority-group members, particularly blacks. Stated differently, the observations noted in these sources do not speak to the issue of police harassment of Black Muslims, Black Panthers, and other groups.

[74]Ibid., p. 46.

[75]Paul Chevigny, *Police Power* (New York: Vintage Books, 1969).

[76]Ibid., pp. 248–49. See also Stoddard, "The Informal 'Code' of Police Deviancy."

[77]*Report of the National Advisory Commission on Civil Disorders*, pp. 299–322.

[78]Racial hostility on the part of the police has been observed *within* police departments as well, in the form of discrimination against black officers, departmental resistance toward hiring black officers, and the like. For some analyses of these matters, see William M. Kephart, *Racial Factors in Urban Law Enforcement* (Philadelphia: University of Pennsylvania Press, 1957); Nicholas Alex, *Black in Blue* (Englewood Cliffs, N.J.: Prentice-Hall, Inc., 1969); Paul Jacobs, "The Los Angeles Police," *Atlantic*, 218 (December 1966), 95–101.

becoming a "criminal": from arrest to trial

This chapter traces out what can happen to a person identified as an accused or a suspect. In Chapter 18, we saw that the police dispose informally of a great many cases they learn about, exercising discretion in moving persons into the official legal machinery. What happens to those individuals whom the police start on their way through this processing? What happens when citizens take complaints to a district attorney? We shall begin with a brief examination of the major elements of state and federal legal systems. A more detailed look at the workings of various parts of these systems will follow this discussion.

elements of the legal system

STATE SYSTEMS

The chief legal officer in state criminal systems is the county prosecuting attorney (district attorney). This elected official, along with deputy prosecutors in larger counties, is responsible for representing the state in criminal actions against accused individuals. The prosecutor's adversaries, whose task is to represent and defend the accused, are criminal attorneys hired by the accused, lawyers provided the indigent by a legal-aid society, or legal counsel supplied through a public defender's office. Other functionaries in the legal system maintain the county jail or lockup in which persons awaiting trial are held. Certain private citizens are systematically involved in the handling of persons caught up in this machinery. The chief group of these is the bail bondsmen who arrange bail for accused individuals.

The state courts, which constitute the central component of the legal operation, are diverse in character throughout the United States.[1] Nonetheless, there is a general pattern of court structure involving two basic forms—trial courts and appellate courts. Trial courts are, in turn, divided into several levels.

Trial courts include inferior courts, which are variously termed justice-of-the-peace courts or municipal courts. In urban areas, elected officials who are full-time, qualified judges with legal training preside over these courts. These magistrates hold hearings in municipal courts and other courtlike surroundings. In rural areas, on the other hand, relatively unqualified magistrates are more likely to control the municipal courts. These hearings are frequently conducted in out-of-the-ordinary circumstances. The business of inferior courts centers about the processing of minor civil cases, adjudication of such minor criminal cases as misdemeanor charges and traffic violations, and preliminary hearings regarding serious criminal cases.

The higher trial courts in the various states are usually organized on a county basis. These courts deal with serious felony cases and are variously called circuit courts, superior courts, county courts, or district courts. In some states, these courts have general jurisdiction, hearing criminal, civil, matrimonial, and probate matters. In other states, the courts are fragmented so that each handles only one of these matters.[2]

Appellate courts on the state level are usually called supreme courts. These courts mainly hear appeals, in which they review the proceedings of trial courts to determine whether errors have occurred in the trial of an individual that would require reversal of judgment or a new trial. Appellate courts also have the responsibility of scrutinizing the constitutionality of new legislation.

THE FEDERAL SYSTEM[3]

The legal officers and courts of the federal government have jurisdiction over offenders who commit ordinary crimes on federal reservations or against federal instrumentalities. Thus, although no federal law prohibits murder, homicides occurring on military posts or similar places fall within federal-court jurisdiction. However, the largest group of lawbreakers with whom the federal machinery is concerned is that of persons who violate federal laws.

Although the federal criminal code runs to almost 2,500 sections, federal concern with criminality is considerably narrower than that of the individual states. The federal criminal code grows out of the legislative powers accorded Congress,[4] which is empowered to regulate interstate and foreign commerce, establish post offices, declare war, maintain order, and organize armed forces. Congress also has jurisdiction over counterfeiting and piracy, naturalization procedures, and rules on bankruptcy, patents, and copyrights. Finally, Congress is authorized to make all laws necessary and proper to executing its powers. Federal criminal law centers about these matters; for example, the Mann Act deals with interstate traffic in prostitution, and the Dyer Act is directed at transportation of stolen vehicles across state lines.

The federal-court system consists of three kinds of courts: district courts, courts of appeals, and the Supreme Court. The 97 district courts are trial courts with control over federal offenses in all or part of a single state. The 11 appellate courts receive appeals from district courts and from federal administrative agencies. Lastly, the Supreme Court takes up questions of constitutionality.

We should not suppose that state and federal courts have an equal share of the criminal workload. Although there are about 550 federal judges, New York State alone has eight times that number of state magistrates. Even when we exclude justices of the peace from this comparison, New York judges are still twice as numerous as their federal counterparts.[5]

processing the suspect through the legal machinery[6]

Let us examine the flow of business through the state courts, for this pattern is closely paralleled in federal courts. The criminal-processing machinery is usually set in motion by the arrest of an individual by the police, who take him or her into custody. However, in some cases a preliminary investigation by the district attorney or the grand jury leads to a formal accusation against an individual, followed by issuance of a warrant for his or her arrest. Embezzlement is an offense for which preliminary investigation is commonly carried on prior to arrest. A third means of entry into this system is through citizen complaints to the prosecuting attorney. Common cases of this type are bad checks and other improper business conduct, nonsupport and other domestic quarrels, borderline offenses against the person, such as negligent homicide, and obscene literature and other borderline offenses against morality. Many cases in this latter group are dealt with informally by the prosecutor and are not moved farther along. For example, district attorneys often endeavor to settle bad-check complaints without prosecution by sending letters to the offender with the direction that financial affairs with the complaining citizen be settled. If the check forger complies, the district attorney then terminates the case.[7]

After the police have apprehended an individual he or she is supposed to be taken almost immediately before a magistrate of an inferior court. In the instance of petty misdemeanor offenses, a police officer or private citizen makes a formal accusation called a *complaint* against the person. These petty cases are normally dealt with quite swiftly, usually through a plea of guilty, which the accused individual enters. In felony charges, appearance before a magistrate is for the purpose of setting bail and arranging for a *preliminary hearing*. This hearing, also before a magistrate, is an inquiry to determine whether there is "probable cause," that is, enough evidence against an individual to warrant holding him or her for prosecution. Normally, only the prosecutor presents evidence at a preliminary hearing, and then only the minimum necessary to establish probable cause. If the preliminary hearing results in the judgment that probable cause has been demonstrated, a formal accusation is made against the accused. In about half the states, a *grand jury* made up of citizens chosen by judges hears testimony in secret and draws up a formal accusation called an *indictment*; in other states, the prosecutor formulates the accusation, called an *information*, without going through grand-jury hearings. The general trend in the United States in recent decades has been to bypass the grand jury. For example, in California, less than 10 percent of the felony cases proceed through the grand jury.[8]

When a preliminary hearing has resulted in holding an accused individual for prosecution, the suspect has reached a critical juncture in his or her travel through the machinery. At this point, the prosecutor may offer a "deal" so that if the accused agrees to plead guilty, a plea to a reduced charge will be allowed. The offender is given an opportunity to "cop out" to a "knocked-down" charge. If the accused agrees to this arrangement, an indictment will be drawn up alleging that he or she committed a different and less serious offense than the one for which the person was originally apprehended.

The next step in the criminal process in felony cases is *arraignment*, which takes place in the court empowered to try the case. At arraignment, the accused is read the indictment, or information, and asked how he or she pleads to the charge. If the plea is guilty, which occurs in three-fourths or more of the cases, the judge will then hand down a sentence. If the accused pleads not guilty, he or she will be held for trial before a judge or a *petit jury* (trial jury). The usual outcome of a trial is that the accused is found guilty, eventually receiving a sentence from the judge. The end product ground out by this machinery is a legal entity, the criminal, who becomes, among other things, a statistic in crime reports. He or she also becomes a target for correctional activities, which attempt to change him or her from a criminal to a reformed offender.

The criminal-justice system goes into operation at the point that crimes occur, for these events set the police to work. From that point onward, a large number of subsequent actions and dispositions are made of criminal cases. Figure 6 shows a general view of the parts of the legal machinery in terms of the flow of cases through that apparatus.

Figure 6 outlines the elements of the criminal-justice system and of the juvenile system as well. On the whole, the juvenile-justice structure follows the form of the criminal system but has tended toward informality and less concern for due process than the criminal courts. However, recent thinking has moved in the direction of modifications in juvenile justice designed to restore due process to accused juveniles. Thus, in some places, attorneys have been provided to charged juveniles, more attention has been paid to due process for youths, and court proceedings have become more legalistic.[9]

some problems of criminal courts

Reports of The President's Commission on Law Enforcement and Administration of Justice made it abundantly clear that many American courts fall far short of ideal in operation. Lower or inferior courts in particular turn out to be inferior in a number of ways.[10] According to the commission, many lower courts are nearly swamped with impressively large workloads. They are staffed by ill-trained personnel. Little or no screening or investigation of cases occurs. Assembly-line justice is dispensed to the misdemeanants who appear there. The com-

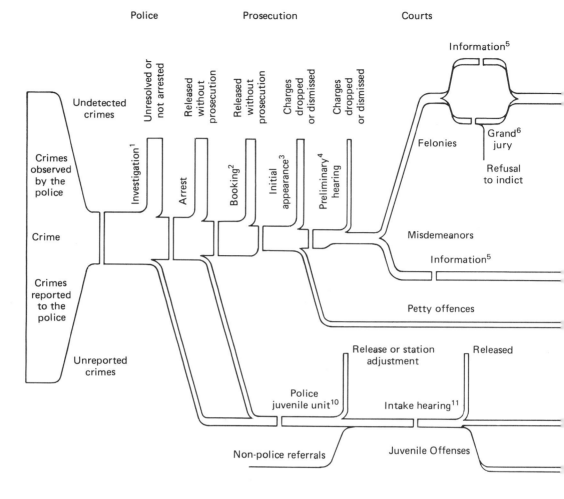

Police   Prosecution   Courts

Crimes observed by the police

Crime

Crimes reported to the police

Undetected crimes

Unreported crimes

Unresolved or not arrested

Released without prosecution

Released without prosecution

Charges dropped or dismissed

Charges dropped or dismissed

Investigation[1]

Arrest

Booking[2]

Initial appearance[3]

Preliminary[4] hearing

Information[5]

Grand[6] jury

Refusal to indict

Felonies

Misdemeanors

Information[5]

Petty offences

Release or station adjustment

Released

Police juvenile unit[10]

Intake hearing[11]

Non-police referrals

Juvenile Offenses

1 May continue until trial.

2 Administrative record of arrest first stage at which temporary release on bail may be available.

3 Before magistrate, commissioner, or justice of peace, formal notice of charge, advice of rights, Budget Summary trials for party offenses usually conducted here without further processing.

4 Preliminary testing of evidence against defendant. Charge may be reduced. No separate preliminary hearing for misdemeanors in some systems.

5 Charge filed by prosecutor on basis of information submitted by police or citizens. Alternative to grand jury indictment often used in felonies, almost always in misdemeanors.

6 Reviews whether government evidence sufficient to justify trial. Some states have no grand jury system, others seldom use it.

figure 6 *A General View of the Criminal-Justice System. This chart presents a simple yet comprehensive view of the movement of cases through the criminal-justice system. Procedures in individual jurisdictions may vary from the pattern shown here. The differing weights of line, indicating the relative volumes of*

430

Corrections

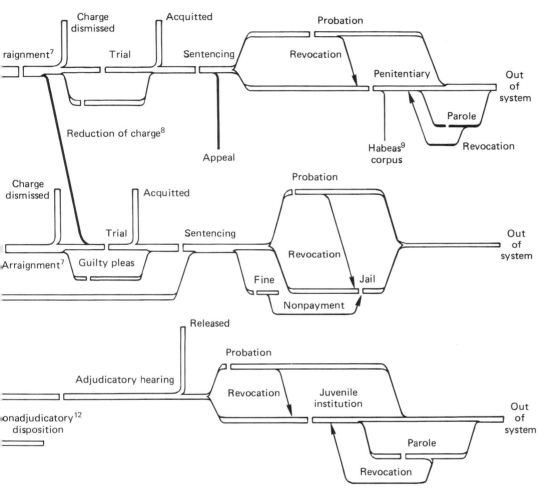

7 Appearance for plea. Defendent elects trial by judge or jury. If available counsel for indigent usually appointed here in felonies. Often not at all in other cases.

8 Charge may be reduced at any time prior to trial in return for plea of guilty or for other reasons.

9 Challenge on constitutional grounds to legality of detention. May be sought at any point in process.

10 Police often hold informal hearings, dismiss or adjust many cases without further processing.

11 Probation officer decides desirability of further court action.

12 Welfare agency, social services, counseling, medical care, etc., for cases where judicatory handling not needed.

cases disposed of at various points in the system, are only suggestive because no nationwide data of this sort exist. **source:** *This chart is taken from pp. 8–9 of The President's Commission on Law Enforcement and Administration of Justice,* The Challenge of Crime in a Free Society *(Washington, D.C.: U.S. Government Printing Office, 1967).*

mission indicated that in justice-of-the-peace courts in three states the justice still receives payment only when he or she convicts and collects the fee from the defendant, a practice the United States Supreme Court ruled unconstitutional 40 years ago![11]

INDIVIDUAL JUSTICE VERSUS BUREAUCRATIC PROCESSING

A rising chorus of opinion holds that in the American criminal-justice system the accused rarely receives justice of any kind. Instead, he or she is processed through the bureaucratic machinery with relatively little concern for his or her rights. The criminal-justice machinery is portrayed as a gigantic operation paying lip service to the ideals of individual justice but dominated in fact by the pressure to meet production workloads in the way of people handled and moved through the system. Those who staff this bureaucracy—judges, prosecutors, defense attorneys, bail bondsmen, sheriffs, probation officers, and others—are often involved in tacit bargains and arrangements of one kind or another, designed to push the accused individual from one stage to another in the operation. Throughout this process, the rights and interests of the alleged offender are secondary to the needs of the machinery.

One of the most incisive commentators of this persuasion is Abraham Blumberg, a criminologist and former defense attorney. He contended that the role of criminal lawyer has a good deal in common with that of the criminal con man, in that the criminal lawyer is a double agent serving the interests of the court more than those of his or her client.[12] The lawyer, according to Blumberg, enters into deals with the prosecutor, agreeing to persuade the client to plead guilty. In turn, the courts often cooperate with criminal lawyers by arranging for continuances so that the attorney can collect the fee due from the client. These linkages are not part of the common stereotype of the defense attorney, vigorously endeavoring to gain his or her client's freedom by whatever trick or stratagem that can be devised. On the issue of individual rights and the bureaucratic pressure to get cases dealt with, Blumberg argued:

To meet production requirements in our criminal courts, a tenuous resolution of the dilemma has emerged: a variety of bureaucratically ordained and controlled shortcuts, deviations, and outright violations of the rules are employed by all court personnel, ranging from lawyers and prosecutors to probation officers and judges. Fearfully anticipating criticism on ethical as well as legal grounds, all the significant participants in the court's structure are bound into an organized system of complicity. The rhetoric of official rules governing the behavior of police, prosecutors, judges, and probation officers is not a reliable guide to their actual behavior, which consists of patterned, covert, and informal evasions of due process in order to meet production requirements.[13]

Blumberg's arguments concerning the lack of individual justice in criminal courts were based on his investigations in New York State. George Cole reported the same pattern of relationships in the King County (Seattle), Washington Prosecutor's Office.[14] He argued that the various participants in the system were bound together in a pattern of symbiotic relationships:

> The legal system may be viewed as a set of interorganizational exchange relationships analogous to what Long has called a community game. The participants in the legal system (game) share a common territorial field and collaborate for different and particular ends. They interact on a continuing basis as their responsibilities demand contact with other participants in the process. Thus, the need for the cooperation of other participants can have a bearing on the decision to prosecute. A decision not to prosecute a narcotics offender may be a move to pressure the United States Attorney's Office to cooperate on another case. It is obvious that bargaining occurs not only between the major actors in a case—the prosecutor and the defense attorney—but also between the clientele groups that are influential in structuring the actions of the prosecuting attorney.[15]

Cole observed that many of the decisions reached within the justice system had little to do with guilt or innocence, individual rights, and the like. The prosecutor dropped some cases where the evidence pointed strongly to the suspect, and in other instances took to court flimsy cases to quiet public agitation. Then, too, the prosecutor adjusted the flow of cases into court to respond to prison overcrowding and other factors of that kind. Concerning defense attorneys, Cole noted that most of these individuals were not specialists in criminal law but did take some criminal cases along with divorce actions, probate work, and other kinds of legal problems. All of them retained close ties to the prosecutor's office to engage in plea bargaining, which was perhaps the most important single action they performed for their clients.[16]

Clearly, the judicial portion of the criminal-justice system falls short of dispensing swift and fair justice to persons accused of criminal acts.[17] Moreover, the postconviction part of this machinery also leaves much to be desired. Although the purpose of prisons, probation services, and other correctional experiences is to treat and rehabilitate, time serving and punishment remain in most parts of the nation. Let us continue this chapter by examining some of the criminal court system in more detail.

BAIL

One of the concerns in preliminary hearings has to do with the setting of bail. Bail is a sum of money, determined by the judge, which the accused must post to guarantee his or her appearance in court at a later date. The individual either produces his or her own money as bail or obtains it from a bail bondsman at a high rate of interest. If he or she is not allowed bail or cannot obtain bail funds, the person must then remain in jail until his or her trial. In a good many cases he or she may languish in a lockup for a number of months before the trial takes place.

The bail practices of American courts have received a great deal of negative commentary.[18] The bail set at preliminary hearings is often unreasonably high. An investigation of the accused person's financial status, social stability, or other factors might lead to a low bail figure being set, but such inquiry is rarely held. A second complaint is that the ultimate decision on whether an accused awaits trial in jail rather than in the community rests with a private citizen, the bail bondsman, rather than with a court functionary. Finally, bail practices are vulnerable to criticism on the grounds that persons held in jail unnecessarily suffer severe handicaps as a result. They do not have easy access to lawyers, their entrance into the court in the company of a guard may bias their case with a jury, and, in the event of acquittal, they have undergone incarceration without being guilty of a crime.

Caleb Foote has reported two studies of the operation of the bail process.[19] These investigations took place in Philadelphia in 1953 and in New York City in 1957. Foote's findings indicated that many defendants were unable to furnish bail even when the amount set was nominal. In Philadelphia, almost one-half of the accused individuals could not post bail and were detained from 50 to 100 days before trial.[20] Furthermore, as the amount of bail increased beyond $1,000, decidedly fewer persons managed to secure pretrial release. Foote noted that bail was usually set at such a high figure in serious felony cases that most defendants could not obtain bail. Although some 10 to 20 percent of those defendants confined in jail before trial were not convicted, on the whole, jailed defendants were more likely to be convicted and also received more severe sentences than counterparts freed on bail. Finally, these studies indicated that bail was often used for purposes other than to ensure the defendant's court appearance. For example, persons accused of attacks on police officers either were not offered bail or had an excessive bail figure set in their cases.

One response to these criticisms of bail procedures has taken the form of efforts to have defendants released on their own recognizance, that is, without posting bail. One of these efforts was the Manhattan Bail Project, started in 1961 in New York City.[21] A group of New York University law students interviewed indigent defendants and in many cases were able to secure their release on own recognizance pending trial. The unnecessary character of bail in many cases was apparent in the finding that only 3 of the 275 persons released on their own recognizance on the basis of information provided by the bail project failed to appear in court.[22]

A parallel project was conducted in a United States district court in Michigan, where about 72 percent of the defendants were released on their own recognizance. No difference was observed in absconding by bonded and non-bonded persons. Only 12 of 12,400 defendants failed to appear in court.[23] In recent years, a number of other such projects designed to obtain pretrial release for indigent accused persons have been conducted in widely separated parts of the United States.[24]

"plea copping": pleading guilty for considerations[25]

Many citizens probably carry around a view of the legal machinery based on movie and television portrayals. This picture characterizes the legal process as usually culminating in a jury trial of the accused person, who has pleaded not guilty. In fact, most criminal cases end with guilty pleas by offenders, so trials are the exception rather than the rule. Jerome Skolnick reported that 86 percent of the cases in federal courts between 1960 and 1963 were settled by guilty pleas, whereas such pleas were only slightly less frequent in state courts.[26]

Donald Newman conducted a detailed study of guilty pleas in felony cases in a Wisconsin county and found that over 90 percent of the offenders had been sentenced on a guilty plea, although about a third of them had originally entered pleas of not guilty.[27] In nearly every case, the offense to which an offender plead guilty was lesser than or different from the original charge or charges.

The incentive to the prosecutor for accepting a guilty plea is readily apparent, for this arrangement allows the state to avoid a costly and lengthy court trial. But what does the accused receive in exchange for a guilty plea? Newman indicated four kinds of bargains offered the offender. Some had reduced charges placed against them. About half the offenders received a deal in the form of a reduction in sentence for pleading guilty. A third group got concurrent sentences rather than separate ones for each offense committed. Finally, some suspects had some charges dropped in exchange for a guilty plea.

David Sudnow provided further detail on guilty pleas and allied matters in an investigation carried on in a public defender's office in a metropolitan community in California.[28] The job of the public defender, an employee of the county, is to defend indigent accused persons in criminal trials. The public-defender system has grown as a replacement for legal-aid societies and as a device to ensure that low-income persons will not be deprived of legal counsel.

Sudnow's discussion included the distinction between "necessarily-included-lesser-offenses" and "situationally-included-lesser-offenses." Assault is an example of the first category. It must occur prior to battery in that assault refers to menacing gestures, such as verbal threats, and battery consists of carrying out the threats. Similarly, second-degree homicide is necessarily included in first-degree murder because the latter involves premeditation along with all the other ingredients of second-degree homicide. Situationally included offenses usually occur with another law violation, even though the one is not incorporated in the other in the criminal statutes. Drunkenness as an accompaniment of vehicular homicides illustrates this category.

At first glance, one might suppose that most reduced charges against offenders would involve necessarily included or situationally included lesser offenses. But this apparently was not the case, at least in the situation that Sudnow observed. Instead, both the prosecutor and the public defender acted out their roles with a shared conception of "normal crimes." For example, both perceived that most rapes grow out of flirtations between persons who have been drinking and have engaged in sexual byplay. These generalizations about the way offenses usually occur constitute a classification of "normal crimes."

In the court studied by Sudnow, when they bargained about a "normal crime," the prosecutor and public defender cast about for a reduced charge that met the ends of justice and provided an incentive to the accused to plead guilty. Quite often the offense they eventually settled on was neither situationally nor necessarily included in the crime with which the person was originally charged. Sudnow noted that both the prosecutor and the public defender tried to obtain a guilty plea wherever possible so as to avoid a trial. But each party was concerned that the defendant "receive his due" in the way of a penalty. The reduced charge had to be of such a nature that the offender would plead guilty to it, but it also had to be a sentence the person "deserved."[29]

The day-to-day operations of the public-defender system and the prosecutor's office departed markedly from the image of the combative struggle between the state and the counsel for the accused. Sudnow observed that the public defender viewed his interests as close to those of the prosecutor—to move offenders in an orderly fashion through the legal machinery. The public defender assumed that the persons he served were guilty. His interviews with his clients were designed to determine whether the person's offense was a "normal" one so that they could reach a bargain with the prosecutor. In most "normal" cases, the public defender persuaded the accused individuals to plead guilty. However, the prosecutor did not solicit or accept guilty pleas from those lawbreakers who had engaged in crimes that were atypical and not "normal."

trial by jury[30]

The right to jury trial is Constitutionally guaranteed in all states in cases of serious crimes and in some states for minor crimes, although the Constitution is silent on the question of jury size and on the issue of whether unanimous verdicts are necessary for conviction. Also, while a jury trial can be waived in favor of trial before a judge, relatively few defendants exercise this option.

The trial jury (or *petit jury*) is drawn from a larger panel of potential jurors previously selected for jury duty by a jury commissioner or court clerk. In principle, jury duty is an obligation of all citizens who meet some minimal qualifications, such as citizenship and literacy. Conversely, blacks or other groups of persons are not supposed to be excluded from jury duty, for juries are intended to be representative of the larger community. A specific jury is assembled out of a panel of potential jurors through a *voire dire* selection process in which both the prosecutor and defense attorney participate. Both are allowed to challenge for cause prospective jurors thought to be unfit for jury duty. Potential jurors are challenged on such grounds as being related to the defendant or having already formed an opinion of the guilt or innocence of the accused. The presiding judge excuses these persons from jury duty. In addition, potential jurors are the target of *peremptory challenges*. Both the prosecutor and defense attorney have a limited number of these challenges, for which no reason has to be stated.

After the completion of jury selection, the prosecutor makes an opening statement, outlines the evidence he or she expects to introduce against the accused, and usually the defense presents opening remarks as well. Following these statements, the prosecutor presents the state's evidence, and the defense attorney cross-examines witnesses. When the prosecution has completed its case, the accused may make a motion for acquittal on the grounds of insufficient evidence. If the judge deems the evidence sufficient to proceed, the defense then has its opportunity to present evidence to undermine the state's case. After presenting the case for the accused, the defense may move for a directed verdict of acquittal by the judge.

If the judge does not direct a verdict of acquittal, the trial moves to final arguments to the jury by both sides. The judge gives instructions to the jury, and the jury retires behind closed doors for secret deliberations. If the jury brings in a verdict of not guilty, the case is closed forever. But if the accused is found guilty, his or her attorney may move for a new trial, arguing that the trial proceedings erred at some point. If the judge does not grant this motion, the defendant is sentenced and becomes the legal entity, a criminal.

In common law, juries have consisted of twelve persons and unanimous decisions have been required in order to convict persons. However, in *Williams* v. *Florida* (1970) the Supreme Court ruled that six-person juries are acceptable in felony cases. A number of states had already introduced smaller juries in misdemeanor cases prior to this court decision. By the mid 1970s, 31 states allowed juries of less than twelve persons, while in Oregon and Connecticut, six-person juries are now allowed in all cases except those involving capital punishment. Further, the Supreme Court ruled in *Johnson* v. *Louisiana* (1972) that nonunanimous jury decisions are allowable. Currently in Oregon, persons can be convicted if ten of the twelve jurors decide against the individual, except in capital cases.[31]

the juvenile court

This book is concerned with adult criminality rather than with juvenile delinquency. That is, our analysis concentrates on the criminal courts and persons processed through them rather than on juvenile courts and juvenile delinquents. At the same time, however, many of the individuals who get caught up in the criminal-justice machinery are youthful violators. Many criminal offenders begin their lawbreaking activities as juveniles and first appear in juvenile courts. A survey of the criminal-justice machinery in American society cannot entirely ignore the juvenile-court system. Let us briefly mention the juvenile-justice system sketched in Figure 6.

The American juvenile court grew out of a series of developments in the 1800s designed to mitigate the severity of punishment handed out to juveniles.[32] The first juvenile court was created in Cook County, Illinois, in 1899, and within ten years, 20 states had created juvenile court laws; by 1945, court legislation had been extended to all the states.

The motives of those who sponsored the juvenile-court movement were mixed, but generally their intent was to create a structure that would minister to the needs of children, treating them rather than punishing them. Omnibus juvenile-delinquency statutes were created in all the states, giving the court jurisdiction over juveniles who were wayward, ungovernable, and the like, as well as over those who had violated criminal laws.[33] A new language and special procedures for juvenile justice were concocted. A petition, rather than an information or an indictment, is filed alleging that a juvenile is a delinquent. The youngster is housed in juvenile hall rather than in jail, and he or she is adjudicated rather than convicted. Finally, he or she is supposed to be treated according to individual need rather than being punished for lawbreaking.

Much commentary in the past has centered on the failure of the states to implement juvenile-court philosophy by providing adequate probation personnel, diagnostic and psychiatric services, and other arrangements that would allow the court to carry out its rehabilitative mandate. In short, criticism of the court has centered on "bread and butter" issues, noting that these organizations represent inadequately fabricated social machinery.[34]

Although there has been much dialogue on the juvenile court, studies of the actual operations of these tribunals have been relatively few in number. However, a collection of investigations dealing with the factors in police referral of youths to the court is now available.[35]

Aaron Cicourel has studied the workings of the juvenile court and strongly suggested that the court often inadvertently pressures youthful offenders in the direction of more rather than less deviance.[36] Robert Emerson examined a juvenile court in a northern United States metropolitan area.[37] His book presented a relatively dismal view of the court, observing that it was deficient in resources and that it provided assembly-line handling of offenders rather than individualized treatment. Finally, Frank Scarpitti and Richard Stephenson examined the flow of 1,200 cases within a juvenile court in a large Eastern county.[38] Their data indicated that judicial sorting of delinquents into those who receive probation, institutional commitment, or some other disposition was not capricious. Instead, most of these decisions revolved around assessments of delinquency risk so that the most socially disadvantaged delinquent, and psychologically atypical boys got sent off to training schools.[39]

The pendulum of opinion has begun to swing back from early criticisms of the court for not treating juveniles to warnings against overuse of the court machinery. A number of jurists, sociologists, and others have questioned whether the court can ever manage to serve in a *parens patriae* or guardian role on a grand scale, diverting misbehaving youths into law-abiding pathways.[40]

Those who have expressed this kind of cynical realism have contended that the juvenile court can never be more than a crude social apparatus. On this point, Edwin Lemert remarked:

Neither the Spartan gymnasium, nor the Russian creches, nor the Israeli kibbutz nurseries, nor scientifically run children's homes have been found to successfully duplicate the sociopsychological mystique which nurtures children into stable adults. Explicit recognition of this might very well preface the juvenile court codes and statutes of the land. At the same time it might be well to delete entirely from such laws pious injunctions that "care, custody and discipline of children under the control of the juvenile court shall approximate that which they would receive from their parents" which taken literally becomes meaningless either as ideal or reality. Neither the modern state nor an harassed juvenile court judge is a father; a halfway house is not a home; a reformatory cell is not a teenager's bedroom; a juvenile hall counselor is not a dutch uncle; a cottage matron is not a mother. This does not mean that the people referred to should not be or are not kindly and dedicated, but rather that they are first and foremost members of organizations, enforcers of superimposed rules. Where conflicts arise between the interests of a youth and those of the organization to which these functionaries are bureaucratically responsible there is no pattern of action which can predict that they will observe an order of value satisfaction favorable to the youth's interest.[41]

The critics of the court have not advocated that we abandon it but have argued that we should entertain only modest expectations for it.[42] We should not expect the court to rehabilitate all those wards who proceed through it. Then, too, the critics have argued that we should discard omnibus provisions or status-offender categories in delinquency laws and at the same time make due-process standards for court processing more stringent.

These criticisms of the court have not gone unnoticed. Thus, in California in 1961, a number of revisions of juvenile-court laws were enacted, providing for closer adherence to standards of due process.[43] More recently, the United States Supreme Court handed down several rulings requiring individual courts to conform more closely to standards of due process. The 1967 decision in *Kent v. United States* ruled that when youths are being considered for transfer or remand to an adult court, they are entitled to a hearing, assistance of legal counsel, access to records, and statement of the judge's reasons for waiving juvenile-court jurisdiction.

Another 1967 Supreme Court decision was *In re Gault*, in which a youth was sent off to a training school after an extremely informal court hearing. In this case, the court ruled that juveniles must be provided with notice of charges, legal counsel, right of confrontation and cross-examination of witnesses, and protection against self-incrimination. These are among the rights enjoyed by adults in criminal courts.

A recent Supreme Court decision was *In re Winship* in 1970, holding that proof beyond a reasonable doubt, which the due-process clause requires in criminal trials, is among the essentials of due process and fair treatment required during the adjudicatory stage when a juvenile is charged with an act that would constitute a crime if committed by an adult. This standard replaced the preponderance-of-evidence rule (used in most juvenile courts in the past), requiring a quantum of proof similar to that required in civil-court actions. As a result of the *Winship* decision, courts cannot easily exercise wardship over juveniles.[44]

We saw in Chapter 18 that Supreme Court rulings regarding due process for adults in the hands of the police are sometimes ignored or circumvented in practice. We might also wonder about the pace at which these rulings of the court have spread to the individual courts.

Some evidence on this point came from Lemert's inquiry into the implementation of 1961 changes in California juvenile-court procedures.[45] The new law required split hearings, with the court jurisdictional part being conducted separately from the dispositional portion. Four years later in 1965, Lemert discovered that two-thirds of the judges were still reading social-investigation reports on youths prior to the adjudicatory hearing. The development of bifurcated hearings was designed to eliminate that practice. Then, too, Lemert found that the use of legal counsel varied widely from county to county, even though by law juveniles were guaranteed lawyers.

Several studies have been produced on the *Gault* ruling and its implementation. Charles Reasons observed that in Franklin County (Columbus), Ohio, the number of lawyers in court and dismissals of cases increased in the post-*Gault* period, whereas the number of cases reaching adjudication declined.[46] Obviously, the *Gault* ruling had some consequences for court practice in Ohio. On the other hand, Norman Lefstein, Vaughn Stapleton, and Lee Teitelbaum's study in three large Eastern cities indicated that the extent of full compliance with due-process requirements in the courts in these three cities was relatively slight.[47] Court officials often failed to advise juveniles of their rights or did so in a wooden fashion that tended to dissuade many youths from asserting their rights.

Data are not available concerning implementation of the *Winship* decision. However, the foregoing material indicates that although recent Supreme Court rulings may not be fully implemented overnight, in the long run they promise to bring about drastic reforms in juvenile-court procedure.

summary

This chapter has been concerned with the extent to which the legal processing of offenders, court structure, and jury activities as described in formal theory match up with the workings of these people-processing structures in real life. We began with textbook descriptions of legal processing, starting with the arrest of an individual, through a preliminary hearing, the drawing up of an information or indictment, arraignment, appearance in a trial court, and a jury decision.

It became apparent quite quickly that this formalized description breaks down in the real world. For example, complaints about injustice in bail practices have been endemic, with many persons noting that bail is often set at excessively high limits and that many individuals who do not need to be kept in jail pending trial are nonetheless unable to secure release because of their inability to post bail. Criminal courts are plagued with problems of overload, being called upon to process many more individuals than can be dealt with through jury trials. A major response to the problems of overload has been widespread use of negotiated pleas of guilty ("plea copping"), through which accused persons are disposed of much more quickly and routinely. The picture that emerged from studies of the criminal-court machinery and supporting operations is one in which bureaucratic emphasis upon routinization of people-processing has won out over the ideal of providing maximum legal protections to all accused persons.

The discussion of the juvenile court came to parallel conclusions. These tribunals have not achieved the goals set for them by those who were the architects of the juvenile-court movement. Juvenile courts have failed to provide the rehabilitative services they were intended to offer, at the same time that they have frequently run roughshod over the legal rights of accused youths. A good deal of disillusionment has set in regarding the juvenile court, reflected in Supreme Court decisions which have restored a good many due-process protections to juveniles. Recent agitation for policies of diversion, in which many youngsters would be turned away from court without legal action being taken against them, is another indication of a decline of faith in the efficacy of juvenile courts.

This chapter concludes our overview of the workings of the parts of the law-enforcement machinery through which individuals come to be tagged as criminals or delinquents. In the next chapter, we turn to the processing of offenders in the postconviction stages of the criminal-justice machinery.

notes

[1]Delmar Karlen, *The Citizen in Court* (New York: Holt, Rinehart & Winston, 1964), pp. 3–7. For detailed information on state courts, including variations in court organization from one state to another, see Law Enforcement Assistance Administration, *National Survey of Court Organization* (Washington, D.C.: U.S. Department of Justice, Law Enforcement Assistance Administration, 1973).

[2]The backgrounds and activities of judges in the United States have received relatively little research attention. For two studies of the sort needed, see Shirley D. McCune and Daniel L. Skoler, "Juvenile Court Judges in the United States, Part I: A National Profile," *Crime and Delinquency*, 11 (April 1965), 121–131; Regis H. Walther and Shirley D. McCune, "Juvenile Court Judges in the United States, Part II: Working Styles and Characteristics," *Crime and Delinquency*, 11 (October 1965), 384–93.

[3]Karlen, *The Citizen in Court*, pp. 14–23.

[4]Ibid., pp. 7–8.

[5]Ibid., pp. 23–35.

[6]Ibid., pp. 38–57; see also The President's Commission on Law Enforcement and Administration of Justice, *Task Force Report: The Courts* (Washington, D.C.: U.S. Government Printing Office, 1967); John Kaplan, *Criminal Justice: Introductory Cases and Materials* (Mineola, N.Y.: The Foundation Press, 1973); Donald J. Newman, *Introduction to Criminal Justice* (Philadelphia: Lippincott, 1975).

[7]Frank W. Miller and Frank J. Remington, "Procedures Before Trial," *Annals of the American Academy of Political and Social Science*, 339 (January 1962), 111–24.

[8]Herbert A. Bloch and Gilbert Geis, *Man, Crime, and Society*, 2nd ed. (New York: Random House, 1970), p. 419.

[9]Due-process developments in juvenile courts are discussed in Don C. Gibbons, *Delinquent Behavior*, 3rd ed. (Englewood Cliffs, N.J.: Prentice-Hall, Inc., 1981), pp. 85–88.

[10]The President's Commission on Law Enforcement and Administration of Justice, *Task Force Report*, pp. 29–36.

[11]Ibid., p. 34.

[12]Abraham S. Blumberg, "Criminal Justice in America" in *Crime and Justice in America*, Jack D. Douglas, ed. (Indianapolis: Bobbs-Merrill, 1971), pp. 45–78; Blumberg, *Criminal Justice* (Chicago: Quadrangle Books, 1967); Blumberg, "Lawyers with Convictions," *Trans-action*, 4 (July–August 1967), 18–24.

[13]Blumberg, "Criminal Justice in America," p. 51.

[14]George F. Cole, "The Decision to Prosecute," *Law and Society Review*, 4 (February 1970), 331–43.

[15]Ibid., p. 332.

[16]Ibid., pp. 338–43. Other studies of criminal lawyers include Jack Ladinsky, "Careers of Lawyers, Law Practice, and Legal Institutions," *American Sociological Review*, 28 (February 1963), 47–54; Jerome E. Carlin, *Lawyers on Their Own* (New Brunswick, N.J.: Rutgers University Press, 1962); Arthur Lewis Wood, *Criminal Lawyer* (New Haven, Conn.: College and University Press, 1967).

[17]Another study supporting this conclusion is Maureen Mileski, "Courtroom Encounters: An Observational Study of a Lower Criminal Court," *Law and Society Review*, 5 (May 1971); 473–538. Mileski conducted an observational study of a lower court in a middle-sized Eastern city, finding assembly-line justice to be characteristic of that court. Defendants frequently failed to be properly apprised of their right to legal counsel. Legal representation was rare, and defense lawyers acted as part of the court system rather than solely as advocates of accused persons. Defense attorneys usually endeavored to obtain leniency for their clients rather than their acquittal of charges. About 85 percent of all accused individuals entered guilty pleas; hence the court was involved in sentencing, not fact finding, for the most part. For another, fairly parallel research report, see David W. Neubauer, *Criminal Justice in Middle America* (Morristown, N.J.: General Learning Press, 1974).

[18]Ronald Goldfarb, *Ransom: A Critique of the American Bail System* (New York: Harper & Row, Pub., 1965); Charles Ares and Herbert Sturz, "Bail and the Indigent Accused," *Crime and Delinquency*, 8 (January 1962), 12–20.

[19]Caleb Foote, "The Bail System and Equal Justice," *Federal Probation*, 23 (September 1959), 43–48.

[20]Caleb Foote, "Compelling Appearance in Court: Administration of Bail in Philadelphia," *University of Pennsylvania Law Review*, 102 (June 1954), 1031–79.

[21]Ares and Sturz, "Bail and the Indigent Accused"; see also Frederic Suffet, "Bail Setting: A Study of Courtroom Interaction," *Crime and Delinquency*, 12 (October 1966), 318–31.

[22]Herbert Sturz, "An Alternative to the Bail System," *Federal Probation*, 26 (December 1962), 49–53.

[23]Talbot Smith, "A New Approach to the Bail Practice," *Federal Probation*, 21 (March 1965), 3–6.

[24]For a summary of these projects, see Dorothy C. Tompkins, *Bail in the United States, A Bibliography* (Berkeley, Calif.: Institute of Governmental Studies, 1964).

[25]For a detailed analysis of the pros and cons of plea bargaining, see Arthur Rosett and Donald R. Cressey, *Justice by Consent* (Philadelphia: Lippincott, 1976).

[26]Jerome H. Skolnick, *Justice Without Trial* (New York: John Wiley, 1966), pp. 12–15; see also the President's Commission on Law Enforcement and Administration of Justice, *Task Force Report*, p. 9. The commission report indicated that negotiated pleas of guilty were responsible for convictions in between 66 and 96 percent of the cases in a sample of different state jurisdictions for which information was available.

[27]Donald J. Newman, "Pleading Guilty for Considerations: A Study of Bargain Justice," *Journal of Criminal Law, Criminology and Police Science*, 46 (March–April 1956), 780–90.

[28]David Sudnow, "Normal Crimes: Sociological Features of the Penal Code in a Public Defender Office," *Social Problems*, 12 (Winter 1965), 255–76.

[29]In a parallel study in Portland, Farr found that most persons plead guilty to offenses closely related to those with which they were originally charged. Thus, that study failed to support Sudnow's account of plea negotiation. See Kathryn A. Farr, *Negotiating the Guilty Plea: A Study of the Process*

of Felony Case Disposition in One Urban Court System (Ph.D. diss., Portland State University, 1979).

[30]For a detailed discussion of the American jury system, see Gerald D. Robin, *Introduction to the Criminal Justice System* (New York: Harper and Row, Pub., 1980), pp. 265–87.

[31]For detailed evidence on jury behavior and jury decisions, see Harry Kalven, Jr. and Hans Zeisel, *The American Jury* (Boston: Little, Brown, 1966); Fred L. Strodtbeck, Rita M. James, and Charles Hawkins, "Social Status in Jury Deliberations," *American Sociological Review*, 22 (December 1957), 713–19; Rita M. James, "Status and Competence of Jurors," *American Journal of Sociology*, 64 (May 1959), 565–66; Rita James Simon, "Jurors' Evaluation of Expert Psychiatric Testimony," in *The Sociology of Law*, Simon, ed. (San Francisco: Chandler Publishing Co., 1968), pp. 314–28; Simon and Linda Mahan, "Quantifying Burdens of Proof: A View from the Bench, the Jury, and the Classroom," *Law and Society Review*, 5 (February 1971), 319–30.

[32]The origins of the juvenile court are discussed in ibid., pp. 75–80.

[33]Delinquency laws are discussed in Gibbons, *Delinquent Behavior*, pp. 17–23.

[34]Juvenile courts in operation are discussed in ibid., pp. 81–93.

[35]See ibid., Chapter 3, pp. 58–73.

[36]Aaron V. Cicourel, *The Social Organization of Juvenile Justice* (New York: John Wiley, 1968).

[37]Robert M. Emerson, *Judging Delinquents* (Chicago: Aldine, 1969).

[38]Frank R. Scarpitti and Richard M. Stephenson, "Juvenile Court Dispositions: Factors in the Decision-Making Process," *Crime and Delinquency*, 17 (April 1971), 142–51.

[39]For a collection of reports on juvenile-court operations, including the working styles of judges and probation officers, see Peter G. Garabedian and Don C. Gibbons, eds., *Becoming Delinquent* (Chicago: Aldine, 1970).

[40]Edwin M. Lemert, "The Juvenile Court—Quest and Realities," in the President's Commission on Law Enforcement and Administration of Justice, *Task Force Report: Juvenile Delinquency and Youth Crime* (Washington, D.C.: U.S. Government Printing Office, 1967), pp. 91–105.

[41]Ibid., p. 92.

[42]A good deal of the critical commentary on juvenile courts has advocated alternatives to the court such as Youth Services Bureaus and diversion programs. For commentary on the development of Youth Services Bureau and diversion programs and of some of the problems of these agencies, see Gibbons, *Delinquent Behavior*, pp. 336–48. Also see Edwin M. Lemert, *Instead of Court: Diversion in Juvenile Justice* (Rockville, Md.: National Institute of Mental Health, 1971); Donald R. Cressey and Robert A. McDermott, *Diversion from the Juvenile Justice System* (Washington, D.C.: U.S. Government Printing Office, 1974); Delbert S. Elliott, *Diversion—A Study of Alternative Processing Practices* (Washington, D.C.: Department of Health, Education and Welfare, 1974); Robert M. Carter and Malcolm W. Klein, eds., *Back on the Street* (Englewood Cliffs, N.J.: Prentice-Hall, Inc., 1976).

[43]For a detailed discussion of these developments, see Edwin M. Lemert, *Social Action and Legal Change: Revolution Within the Juvenile Court* (Chicago: Aldine, 1970).

[44]Three additional Supreme Court rulings handed down in 1978 and 1979 also dealt with due process in the juvenile-court system. In *Fare* v. *Michael C.*, the Court ruled that the police can interrogate juveniles when no attorney is present but where a probation officer is present. *Swisher* v. *Brady* held that judges may reverse a decision of a court referee without holding a new hearing, while *Smith* v. *Daily Mail Publishing Co.* ruled that newspapers may publish the name of a juvenile arrested for murder, along with an account of the case.

[45]Lemert, "The Juvenile Court—Quest and Realities."

[46]Charles E. Reasons, "*Gault*: Procedural Change and Substantive Effect," *Crime and Delinquency*, 16 (April 1970), 163–71.

[47]Norman Lefstein, Vaughn Stapleton, and Lee Teitelbaum, "In Search of Juvenile Justice: *Gault* and its Implementation," *Law and Society Review*, 3 (May 1969), 491–562; see also David Duffee and Larry Siegel, "The Organization Man: Legal Counsel in the Juvenile Court," *Criminal Law Bulletin*, 7 (July–August 1971), 544–53. In a study in a New York county, these investigators found that offenders represented by lawyers in a juvenile court received more severe dispositions than those unrepresented by legal counsel. Apparently, the juvenile court in question was careful to obtain lawyers for those offenders who were regarded as in need of incarceration. In these cases, legal counsel shielded the judge from criticisms of the decision to incarcerate.

variations in correctional dispositions

TWENTY

This chapter is concerned with an overview of the various dispositions that can be made of lawbreakers who have been convicted in a criminal court. The chapter is divided into two parts, the first dealing with the ways criminals have been disposed of in earlier historical periods, the second having to do with contemporary correctional proceedings. The remaining chapters of the book take up various facets of current correctional procedures in greater detail.

a brief history of correctional practices

During the long, complex history of correctional actions against criminals, all manner of reactions have been employed at one time or another. Offenders have been subjected to death or torture, social humiliation such as the pillories and stocks, banishment and transportation, imprisonment, and financial penalties. Responses toward lawbreakers were originally retributive, compelling the criminal to make amends in some way. Later, restraint and punishment became the principal form of reaction to deviants, and this approach is still dominant in Western societies and elsewhere in the world. During the present century, a rehabilitative philosophy emerged, maintaining that some form of corrective action should be taken against criminals to deflect them from deviant pathways. However, support for treatment efforts directed at lawbreakers has weakened in recent years, with many persons calling for a return to punitive or retributive responses to criminals.

Large-scale societal devices and procedures for dealing with criminals are of recent origin. For example, the United States prison system, in which over 250,000 adults are incarcerated at any one time, developed within the past 100 years. The entire world population numbered only about 450 million in 1650, although it exceeds 3 billion at present. Thus, until the last several centuries, individual societies were generally small and characterized by uncodified and informal techniques of social control. In this sense, the history of corrections extends only over the past several centuries.

Some formalized legal codes and state-administered procedures of justice can be uncovered in ancient times. The earliest known system of laws was the Code of Hammurabi, developed by King Hammurabi of Babylon in the eighteenth century B.C. This code was exceedingly complicated, designed to regulate a wide variety of human affairs. Concerning crime, the ruling principle was the retributive *lex talionis*, or "an eye for an eye, a tooth for a tooth." Death was a frequently employed means of dealing with lawbreakers, as was mutilation and monetary compensation. Mosaic law and the legal codes of the Roman Empire are other cases of formalized legal codes and criminal proceedings in antiquity.

In small, preliterate societies, both past and present, secular offenses not thought to offend the spirits were handled as private wrongs. These acts were usually left to family or clan groups to settle as they saw fit, commonly by means of retaliatory blood feuds.[1] For example, the Germanic conquerors of Rome were organized into tribal groups in which retaliation by victims was seen as a hereditary right that the offended family could exercise if it so chose. In this system of private vengeance, society played a secondary role. Eventually, pecuniary compensation replaced blood feuds. At the beginning of the Christian era, the Teutonic tribes of Northwest Europe took vengeful retaliation on offenders by extracting monetary compensation. Still, the injuries for which persons were forced to make compensation were regarded as private matters. The Germanic groups recognized only a limited number of tribal crimes, as contrasted to private wrongs. In the same way, until about the twelfth century, England was divided into shires presided over by sheriffs who assisted in obtaining compensation from violators to be paid to injured parties.

The emergence of criminal codes and a system of punishment in England has already been discussed in Chapter 4.

During the twelfth century, the crown gradually assumed control over administration of justice, so compensation began to be paid to the king rather than to the wronged party. As the crown intruded into the regulation of these matters, a system of punishment slowly began to emerge. Punishment involves pain or suffering produced by design and inflicted on a member of a group by that group or society in its corporate capacity. Punishment is directed at persons viewed as having wronged the group as well as the victim. As we shall see, punitive policies developed and flourished well before the emergence of a clear-cut philosophy of punishment that rationalized this posture toward offenders.

The forms of punishment most common in Europe in the Middle Ages and in the period up to the nineteenth century involved corporal punishment or banishment; imprisonment is a relatively recent invention. European jails in the Middle Ages were places for the confinement of prisoners awaiting trial or punishment, rather than custodial institutions in which punishment was meted out. These jails were frequently maintained in castle towers and similar locations, managed by private citizens, and were wretched places in which persons of both sexes and all ages were indiscriminately thrown together. In the sixteenth and seventeenth centuries, offenders were often sentenced to labor in the galleys, but this was more an expedient for providing laborers in the ships than a conscious effort to contrive a kind of imprisonment.

Houses of correction established in England in the 1500s, were forerunners of imprisonment as a form of punishment. A house of correction known as Bridewell, opened in London in 1557, was used for incarceration of vagrants and other idle persons. This was a congregate institution, as were other English houses of correction, so the inmates were not maintained in separate cells. Those vagrants, unemployed persons, orphans, and other individuals kept therein were put to work at various kinds of labor, and their services were frequently contracted out to private citizens. Such institutions were constructed in some number on the European continent in the 1600s and 1700s. The most famous of these was a workhouse at Ghent, Belgium, opened in 1773. That institution featured individual cells and certain other characteristics to become common in modern prisons. Some other prototypes of modern correctional institutions were found in Italy in the 1700s. However, prisons and penitentiaries in which offenders are incarcerated for extended periods of time and subjected to various punitive or corrective measures did not become widespread until the nineteenth century.

At various points in human history, banishment was a technique for dealing with malefactors. Between 1597 and 1776, England transported as many as 100,000 criminals to America. After England was compelled to discontinue sending offenders to America, criminals were banished to Australia; from 1787 to 1875, over 135,000 lawbreakers were disposed of in that manner.[2] Many of these criminals eventually became influential citizens in Australia and, along with other Australians, were ultimately successful in forcing England to discontinue the policy of transportation. France and other nations have also banished offenders to other lands and penal colonies at various times in the past.

Capital punishment was another procedure for handling offenders and was widely used in Europe in past centuries. For example, England had only about 17 capital crimes in the early 1400s; but by 1688 the number of capital offenses had increased to 50, and by 1780, 350 separate crimes carried the death penalty. Between 1327 and 1509, 6 statutes were enacted which carried the death penalty; between 1509 and 1660, 30 more capital crimes were defined; and from 1660 to 1819, 187 additional capital offenses were created. Moreover, creation of new capital offenses at an accelerated pace during the eighteenth century was not an empty ritual, for large numbers of executions were carried out in accordance with this legislation. Many of these executions were of persons convicted of property crimes, so these penalties were grossly severe by contemporary standards. Life was cheap, and society had little hesitation in spending that of criminals.[3] The excesses of this period eventually ran their course, for by 1830 the number of capital offenses had been reduced to only 17.

Punitive responses to offenders grew in advance of tightly reasoned philosophies of punishment. The first full-blown argument in defense of punishment was found in the classical school of thought that developed out of the writings of Locke, Hume, Voltaire, Montesquieu, Rousseau, and others.[4] The most prominent classical theorist was the Italian nobleman Cesare Bonesana, Marchese de Beccaria (1738–1794), while others involved in this school of thought were Blackstone, Eden, and Romilly in England. Beccaria's book, *An Essay on Crimes and Punishment*, written in 1764, criticized widespread abuses and inequities in prevailing legal practices. He was disturbed by the secret accusations, inadequate defense of accused persons, arbitrary and capricious exercise of powers by judges, and barbarous penalties common in the Europe of his time.

The classical position on punishment viewed men as rational animals who deliberately and willfully chose the courses of action they pursued. According to this view, the ruling principle by which men oriented their behavior was *hedonism*, or pursuit of pleasure and avoidance of pain. Criminals were individuals who made a conscious choice to behave in a lawbreaking manner but could be coerced into conformity. Nondeviant behavior was to be obtained through application of a finely calculated measure of suffering; the offender would make a hedonistic decision to refrain from crime in the future. Beccaria endeavored to introduce order into the punitive system and to modify the situation in which offenders were frequently punished in a harsh and violent fashion well beyond the quantity of suffering required to tip the hedonistic balance toward law-abiding conduct. He was also concerned about ending the practices through which many more fortunate law violators escaped punishment altogether. Many of Beccaria's suggestions for reform of punishment were embodied in the French Penal Code of 1791 as well as in the revisions of correctional practice in nineteenth-century England.[5]

The initial reforms in criminal law that grew out of classical arguments made little provision for discretionary handling of lawbreakers. The French Penal Code of 1791 ignored individual differences among criminals and treated adults and minors, intelligent persons and mentally defectives, sane persons and psychotics, as all equally competent to stand trial. All were held equally responsible for their criminality. Subsequent revisions in punitive theory, usually identified as neoclassical reforms, granted judges some freedom to modify sentences on the basis of extenuating circumstances. Neoclassical reforms also made exception in correctional practices for children and incompetents. By and large, underlying behavioral presumptions of contemporary criminal laws and procedures are the same as those in neoclassical thought. Additionally, the penalty structure built into criminal codes in Western societies has remained relatively unmodified in the past century. Such developments as probation and parole have introduced a measure of variability into correctional practice without making any fundamental changes in neoclassical punitive philosophy.

Another distinct philosophy of punishment arose in the latter part of the nineteenth century in the positivist school of thought associated with Lombroso, Ferri, Garofalo, and others. Lombroso's views have already been noted in Chapter 2. He and his followers believed that a multiplicity of factors cause criminality. The positivist position denied that offenders were responsible for their deeds, thus claiming that a punitive posture toward them is unjustified. Instead, lawbreakers were to be treated if they were treatable; but those who could not be reclaimed from criminality were to be segregated from their fellow men.

Modern criminology is positivist, in the sense that criminologists contend that criminality can and should be studied by the methods of science. Contemporary criminology is also positivist in that some version of behavioral determinism is contained within the theoretical assumptions of most criminologists. Positivism has been involved in correctional methods as well, but to a lesser extent; rehabilitative endeavors that have grown up have been allied with behaviorist conceptions of criminality. Most correctional workers involved in treatment activities have been followers of a positivist perspective on criminality. However, it would be a mistake to suppose that the "new penology," which endeavors to rehabilitate offenders rather than punish them, has been much in evidence in the United States and elsewhere.[6]

Returning to historical developments in correctional practice, we should note that penitentiaries are an American invention that arose in the early years of American history.[7] The forerunner of the modern prison was the Walnut Street Jail opened in Philadelphia in 1776, under the urging of Pennsylvania Quakers. This institution was followed by the Pennsylvania Prison at Cherry Hill, opened in 1829. These penitentiaries operated on the *solitary system.* The Pennsylvania-system prisons, as they are often called, were characterized by a distinct architecture intended to isolate prisoners from one another. Inmates were kept in single cells in which they took their meals, engaged in individual forms of labor, exercised, and contemplated the error of their ways. This prison program and architecture attracted a good deal of attention from European observers. Many were persuaded that this system would reform prisoners, and as a result a number of solitary institutions were created in Europe.

However, the Pennsylvania system had a major competitor in the United States, Auburn Prison in New York was opened in 1819, followed a few years later by Sing Sing Prison in the same state. These institutions provided the architectural model for nearly all penitentiaries and reformatories constructed in the United States until the last several decades. The Auburn–Sing Sing system was sometimes referred to as a *silent system.* These prisons were walled institutions in which inmates were incarcerated in cells in multitiered cell blocks. The prisoners worked together and took their meals in a common dining room. Nearly total silence among convicts was maintained within a repressive regime featuring striped uniforms, lock-step marching, and severe punishment for violations of rules.

Advocates of the Auburn–Sing Sing prison model won out in the United States. In the period from the 1830s to World War II, nearly all prisons and reformatories constructed in this country were based on the same general physical-plant design. These places are surrounded by high walls on which guard towers are placed at various points, they include a number of multitiered cell houses with inside cells housing one or more prisoners, and they have dining halls and work areas in which inmates are handled in congregate fashion. Most of these institutions had additions made in relatively haphazard fashion, with new cell houses or other buildings occasionally built within the original walled area to alleviate the pressures of a growing inmate population. As a consequence, these foreboding-looking penal institutions are actually difficult places in which to maintain close security over prisoners, and escapes from them are fairly common.

The rapid growth of prisons in this country was indicated in a publication of the American Correctional Association.[8] That report showed that, of the 90 state penal institutions for males in the United States in 1957, 15 were constructed before 1850, and 52 were opened before 1900. Only 16 institutions were built between 1930 and 1957. Many of these facilities are large, for 48 of the 90 institutions had inmate populations exceeding 1,000. Eighteen of the penal facilities held over 2,000 inmates; of these, San Quentin Prison in California, Joliet-Stateville Prison in Illinois, and Southern Michigan Prison at Jackson each held over 4,000 prisoners.

Over the decades since the beginnings of imprisonment in the United States, institutions gradually became less severe and more humane places, at least in terms of improved diets provided inmates and other changes of that sort. The lock-step, rules of silence, physical punishments for rule infractions, isolation of recalcitrant prisoners in "the hole," strict limits on visiting privileges of inmates, and so on, have been abandoned or eased. These changes in prison life represent humanitarian reforms designed to lessen the pains of imprisonment.[9] Prisoners in contemporary prisons listen to radios in their cells and see movies regularly; they are also permitted visitors each month, are fed well, and receive good medical and dental care. In these ways, doing time has been made less painful. However, little has been done to relieve the psychological pains of imprisonment, which inevitably accompany the experience of doing time.[10]

There have been several other major developments in correctional practices that should be noted. Probation has become a widely used technique for handling juvenile offenders and many relatively petty adult criminals. Probation originated with the work of a Boston shoemaker, John Augustus, who interceded with the courts to take on the informal supervision of offenders in that city in the middle of the nineteenth century. Probation ultimately became a state-sponsored program with passage of enabling legislation in Massachusetts in 1878. In the past century, probation services have become standard in all states and in the federal correctional system. Parole programs also became commonplace in the United States within the last century; until recently about 95 percent of all adult offenders sentenced to institutions have been eventually released on parole, under supervision. However, a number of states have moved in recent years either to abolish parole in favor of fixed or determinate sentences or to place limitations upon the powers of parole boards.

Innovations continue to be attempted in correctional work. For example, halfway houses to which parolees are released from prisons have been suggested as a device for curbing parole failure. Along a somewhat related line are work-release programs developed in county jails, in which prisoners work at conventional jobs during the day and return to the jail at night. Still other innovations can be found in private correctional endeavors such as Synanon, a residential treatment facility for drug addicts. These activities are the subject of extended discussion in later chapters, where attention turns to contemporary correctional programs.

punishment: some general considerations

What does it mean to punish criminals? Sutherland and Cressey have offered the following definition of the ingredients of punishment as a form of social control: "Two essential ideas are contained in the concept of punishment as an instrument of public justice. First, it is deliberately inflicted by officials of the state upon one who is regarded as subject to the laws of the state . . . . Second, punishment involves pain or suffering produced by design and justified by some value that the suffering is assumed to have."[11]

What purposes does the infliction of suffering on lawbreakers serve? Paul Tappan offered an incisive summary of the purposes of punishment. He noted that punishment is designed to achieve the goal of *retribution* or *social retaliation* against the offender.[12] Punishment also involves *incapacitation*, which prevents the violator from misbehaving during the time he or she is being punished. Additionally, punishment is supposed to have a *deterrent* effect, both on the lawbreaker and on potential misbehavers. *Individual* or *specific* deterrence may be achieved by intimidation of the person, frightening him or her against further misbehavior, or it may be effected through reformation, in which the lawbreaker changes his or her deviant sentiments. *General deterrence* results from the warning offered to potential criminals by the example of punishment directed at a specific wrongdoer.

Tappan warned against the misleading supposition that the retributive function of punishment is disappearing. Instead, he argued that retribution has been and continues to be a major ingredient of penal law and correctional systems. Thus, he contended that "it appears likely that the effects of a retributive legal and moral tradition will persist for a long time, though mixed increasingly with other purposes of correctional treatment."[13]

deterrence: general and specific

The subject of deterrence is an extraordinarily important, extraordinarily complex, and until recently, a virtually ignored subject.[14] We can do little more than touch upon some of the highlights of this complex matter. As we have already noted, specific and general deterrence are major goals which punishment is supposed to achieve. Specifically defined, to *deter* means "to turn aside, discourage, or prevent from acting (as by fear)."[15] The term *deterrence* is often employed to designate punishment in the form of threats directed at offenders or potential offenders so as to frighten them into law-abiding conduct. However, we need to keep in mind that treatment is another form which punishment takes, in which the offender suffers the pain of loss of liberty, accompanied by efforts directed at changing his or her attitudes and perspectives so that he or she will no longer be motivated to engage in lawbreaking. Treatment is imposed upon unwilling subjects who are defined by the criminal law as wrongdoers. It is viewed by most of them as punitive and unpleasant, so that arguments that characterize treatment as something distinct from punishment are misleading.

We need to be reminded of the punitive nature and deterrent aims of treatment, particularly given the clamoring for a return to deterrence that has developed in the United States in recent years. A number of persons have begun to voice the conclusion that treatment ventures have failed to stem the tide of crime. Thus, they argue, we need to turn away from the rehabilitation model in corrections toward deterrence policies, in which severe punishments would be administered swiftly and certainly to apprehended lawbreakers.[16] A number of these essays have implied that treatment is something distinct from and in opposition to punishment.

What do the sizable recidivism rates, to be examined later in this book, mean? What conclusions can we draw from the fact that the correctional system fails to prevent many of the offenders it processes from further involvement in criminality? One naïve conclusion is that punishment is a failure, both as a specific and a general deterrent. But as Tappan cautioned: "A complete failure of legal prevention cannot be inferred from the serious crimes committed by a small percentage of the population any more than its success by the law obedience of the great preponderance of men."[17]

Tappan's view of the evidence was that punishment does achieve a significant level of general deterrence. He argued that punishment may bring about deterrence through the fear of unpleasant consequences it instills in potential lawbreakers, but it may also operate to strengthen the public moral code, bringing about deterrence through inhibition of wayward impulses and formation of conformist habits.[18]

The issue of general deterrence has often been posed in terms of half-truths, such that some have argued the case against deterrence in terms of the specific experience of the death penalty. Homicide rates are higher in the United States than in many other nations where the death penalty does not exist; therefore, it is argued, punishment of any kind fails to deter. But special conditions surrounding homicide make it a form of criminality least amenable to deterrence.

Another defective argument points to the Prohibition experience as evidence that people cannot be deterred from activities in which they are motivated to engage. In truth, all that the Prohibition episode demonstrated was that a highly unpopular law, lacking support even from many of the persons who sponsored and enacted it, and enforced by only a handful of police officers, was consequently disobeyed by large numbers of persons. Similarly, the oft-repeated allegation that prisons must be abject failures since three-fourths or more of the persons who go through them are subsequently imprisoned again is in actuality a myth. Daniel Glaser has presented a body of factual evidence indicating that this claim is simply untrue, and that markedly fewer individuals are actually returned to prison.[19] Moreover, many of these parole failures are returned to prison for failure to obey parole rules, rather than because they have committed new felonies.[20]

Any comprehensive and adequate discussion of the deterrent effects of punishment would have to examine the effects of different kinds of punishment on the diverse forms of crime, as well as the various kinds of persons who may be potential lawbreakers. Specific penalties may deter some kinds of criminality and potential lawbreakers, whereas punishment may have little influence upon other kinds of misbehavior. Then, too, the effectiveness of punishment may vary with its *celerity, certainty*, and *severity*. Celerity refers to the swiftness with which punishment is administered, while certainty and severity are self-evident. Punitive sanctions, no matter what their severity, probably are most effective when they are relatively certain in application.[21] The empirical study of sanctions as curbs to lawbreaking has hardly begun; until recently this subject has been restricted principally to philosophers and others of a speculative mind.[22] Doubtless, one obstacle to such research has been the enormous complexity of the phenomena to be investigated. Franklin Zimring provided some idea of the range of considerations that must be kept in mind in the study of deterrence.[23] He drew attention to a number of important distinctions, such as that between *partial* deterrence and *marginal* deterrence. The former refers to threats or punishment that reduce the magnitude of the threatened or punished behavior but without curbing it entirely. Zimring argued that a number of partial deterrents may curtail lawbreaking. Marginal deterrence is the degree to which some specific punishment reduces the rate of illegal behavior below that produced by some lesser penalty. For example, marginal deterrence is in operation in the instance of prison sentences that reduce the rate of reinvolvement in criminality from that brought about by placing offenders on probation.

Zimring's analysis also identified a number of different ways threats of punishment may operate as deterrents. He further suggested that research on the deterrent impact of sanctions will have to accommodate various forms of punishment. Perhaps punishments of one degree of severity have quite different effects on lawbreakers than do sanctions of lesser or greater severity. Finally, the study of deterrence must consider the variations among lawbreakers. No wonder, then, the study of deterrence is so difficult.

SOME STUDIES OF PUNISHMENT AND DETERRENCE[24]

In a study on a Midwestern university campus, William Chambliss found a significant reduction in parking violations after an increase in the severity and certainty of penalties.[25] In another investigation, Jack Gibbs calculated indexes of the certainty and severity of punishment for homicide in the United States. He found evidence that homicide was least frequent where apprehension was relatively certain and where prison sentences were severe.[26]

Charles Tittle's study of crime rates and punishment paralleled that of Gibbs, but it dealt with a series of criminal offenses.[27] Tittle found strong and consistent negative relationships between certainty of punishment and crime rates for different states, as measured in terms of the ratio between felony admissions to state prisons and the total crimes known to the police in different states. Those states with the lowest crime rates had a proportionately larger number of incarcerated persons. On the other hand, severity of punishment bore no marked relationship to crime rates. Tittle's findings led him to conclude that measures to improve the efficiency of police work probably would have significant effects on crime rates, but that increasing the severity of punishment would be of limited effectiveness.[28]

Most deterrence studies have utilized crime rates and have correlated these with various indices of the certainty and severity of punishment, with inferences then being drawn about the ways in which individuals perceive the threat of punishment.[29] However, relatively few studies have endeavored to "get inside the heads" of persons, so to speak, in order to gather direct evidence on how punishment is perceived by offenders and potential offenders. This is the key problem for investigation, for in the last analysis, successful deterrence hinges upon individuals coming to perceive that they run a real risk of being punished if they engage in lawbreaking.[30]

There are some investigations upon which we can draw for instructive findings on this point. Separate studies conducted in California in the 1960s by Don Gibbons[31] and by a private research firm for the State Assembly Committee on Criminal Procedure[32] indicated that few citizens had detailed and accurate knowledge of the workings of the criminal-justice system or of the penalties provided in state criminal statutes. Interestingly, in the latter inquiry, which dealt with knowledge about the maximum penalties for six serious crimes including robbery, rape, and auto theft, the prison inmates who also were quizzed were most well informed, but substantial proportions of them (15 to 50 percent on individual offense questions) were unaware of the specific penalty provided by law.[33] Some parallel observations have been offered by Leonard Goodman, Trudy Miller, and Paul De Forrest, drawn from their research on perceptions of punishment held by offenders.[34] They reported that most of the offenders either did not perceive the risk of punishment as very likely in their case, or if they did acknowledge that criminality carries with it considerable risk of being punished, they downplayed the possibility that they themselves would be apprehended or punished.[35]

The most judicious conclusions to be drawn from the investigations to date on the deterrent effects of criminal sanctions are the following. First, virtually nothing is known about the impact of celerity or swiftness of punishment upon offenders or potential miscreants, although a plausible argument could be constructed, drawn in part out of social learning theory, to the effect that the more closely punishment follows an act of deviance the less the likelihood that such an act will be repeated. Second, most of the research suggests that certainty of punishment is a more important consideration in the minds of actual or potential lawbreakers than is severity, particularly when a severe punishment is viewed by the person as unlikely to be visited upon him. Third, a few studies have produced findings that indicate that many persons are relatively uninformed about the nature and severity of criminal penalties, which is probably a major factor accounting for the failure of punitive actions to deter persons from criminality. Finally, almost nothing is known about the extent to which perceptions of economic hardship, feelings of relative deprivation, or other attitudes and sentiments outweigh the perceived risk of punishment in the minds of many individuals.

THE RETURN TO PUNISHMENT

Over the past hundred years, humanitarian reforms in the punishment of offenders have taken place and treatment or rehabilitation has been grafted on to the punitive aims of the correctional machinery, although humanitarianism and treatment have not replaced punishment. Chapter 22 will discuss the development and implementation of treatment programs in American prisons and in other parts of the correctional machinery in detail. Looking ahead, we will find that a number of studies have been completed in the past several decades, apparently indicating that treatment has been a failure. According to contemporary critics of rehabilitation ventures, these programs have not deflected individuals away from careers in crime nor prevented potential lawbreakers from becoming involved in criminality.

The pessimism concerning rehabilitative ventures, coupled with growing fears about an apparent, dramatic increase in lawbreaking in America, have resulted in considerable clamoring among the general public, some members of the legal profession and the criminal-justice system, legislators, and some criminal-justice scholars for an end to various treatment programs and a return to a more straightforward system that hands out fixed and relatively severe doses of punishment to offenders.

Exemplifying this movement toward the restoration of punishment as the central goal of the juvenile- and adult-justice systems are the career-criminal specialists in the prosecutor's office who press for vigorous prosecution of persons regarded as career criminals and who attempt to secure long prison sentences for such individuals. The restoration of the death penalty, to be examined later in this chapter, is another development in this direction.

Another example of the return to punishment can be found in the Juvenile Justice Act, passed in Washington State in 1977, which explicitly defined punishment of offenders and protection of the general public as major aims of the juvenile-justice system in that state. In that statute, a relatively fixed set of punishments was enacted into law. Adjudicated delinquents are sorted out as minor, medium, or serious offenders on the basis of age and prior delinquent record. The juvenile-justice system act requires that nearly all serious offenders be sent to training schools, with the length of incarceration being determined largely by statute. Middle and minor offenders also receive sentences of fines or are required to perform community services that are spelled out in the juvenile-justice act.[36]

A final and extremely significant development in the direction of greater stress on punishment is found in the case of parole and indeterminate sentences.[37] Until recently, some form of indefinite sentences and parole was found in all states in this country. Under this general arrangement, persons were sentenced to serve indefinite or indeterminate periods of time in prison, with only an upper limit specified by statute. Accordingly, inmates serving sentences for the identical offenses sometimes spent markedly different periods of time in prison, with the prison term being determined by a parole board or other paroling agency. After release from prison, the parolee was obliged to continue serving his or her sentence while under supervision by a parole officer in the community. Finally, failure to obey the directives of the parole agent often resulted in the parolee being returned to prison as a parole violator. This body of practices grew up as part of the movement toward rehabilitation of offenders. According to the rationale for parole, the purpose of imprisonment is to cure offenders, hence they ought to be released when they have been rehabilitated, rather than serving some fixed period of time in prison.

The theory and practice of parole were widely applauded and accepted until recently. However, parole has come under attack in the past decade or so, with its opponents arguing that it is inherently unfair, discriminatory, oppressive, capricious, unethical, and unworkable. These critics have argued that we ought to abolish indeterminate sentencing and parole in favor of fixed prison terms for specific offenses.

A number of states, including California, Maine, and Indiana have abolished parole, while in some others, such as Oregon, a parole system has been developed which severely circumscribes the powers of the parole board to hand out disparate sentences to persons who have committed similar offenses.

Although recent changes in parole practices have reduced the discretionary powers of parole boards, making it more difficult for them to imprison persons convicted of similar crimes for markedly varied time periods, it would be a mistake to assume that changes in parole will completely remove the discretionary powers of criminal-justice-system decision makers. In California, much freedom to vary the sentences handed out to convicted offenders is still enjoyed by prosecutors and judges, so that the abolition of parole has meant only that those persons who get sent to prison will now receive relatively uniform prison sentences for similar crimes.[38] Indeed, the experiences to date in California suggest that discretionary decision making will be extremely difficult to eliminate, owing to the size of the offender population, lack of resources for dealing with them, and various other factors that impinge upon the criminal-justice system. As a result, it is likely that as punitive policies receive greater public support, some individuals will come to be the targets of these policies, at the same time that other persons will be diverted out of the criminal-justice system or will receive less punitive handling.

variations in contemporary dispositions[39]

Criminals in the United States and other Western societies are disposed of in one of several major ways.[40] A few who have committed felonies are executed, but most felons are imprisoned or placed on probation. Those guilty of lesser crimes are put on probation, fined, or sentenced to relatively short terms in jail. Although the major outlines of criminal handling are clear, the details are not so apparent, particularly because detailed and accurate statistical data on the flow of cases through the correctional machinery are often difficult to obtain.

The enormous size of the correctional workload in the United States is revealed in figures of the President's Commission on Law Enforcement and Administration of Justice. Table 21 shows data the commission obtained in a nationwide survey of the correctional caseload. The offenders in institutions were in jails, reformatories, penitentiaries, and other custodial facilities. Individuals listed in the community were offenders on probation or parole.

Correctional work represents a major employment category, as Table 21 indicates. However, we should not suppose that the 121,000 persons employed in this activity in 1965 were principally involved in rehabilitation and treatment. Only 24,000—or 20 percent of the correctional workers—were engaged in some treatment capacity in institutions or the community. The time of the remaining 80 percent was taken up with custodial or maintenance tasks.[41]

More recent figures on correctional dispositions and the correctional workload show that on June 30, 1975, 46,980 juveniles were incarcerated in public juvenile detention and correctional facilities. Of this number, 34,255 were in long-term facilities, including training schools, ranches, forest camps, farms, and halfway houses, while the remainder were in short-term facilities such as detention centers and diagnostic facilities. Persons under probation supervision on September 1, 1976 numbered 923,064 adults and 328,854 juveniles. Finally, the

table 21   some national characteristics of corrections, 1965[a]

	average daily population of offenders	total operating costs	average cost of offender per year	number of employees in corrections	number of employees treating offenders
Juvenile corrections					
Institutions	62,773	$ 226,809,600	$3613	31,687	5,621
Community	285,431	93,613,400	328	9,633	7,706
Adult felon corrections					
Institutions	221,597	435,594,500	1966	51,866	3,220
Community	369,897	73,251,900	198	6,352	5,081
Misdemeanant corrections					
Institutions	141,303	147,794,200	1046	19,195	501
Community	201,385	28,682,900	142	2,430	1,944
Total	1,282,386	$1,005,746,500	—	121,163	24,073

[a]The President's Commission on Law Enforcement and Administration of Justice, *The Challenge of Crime in a Free Society* (Washington, D.C.: U.S. Government Printing Office, 1967), p. 161.

number of individuals in state and federal prisons and reformatories on December 31, 1977 was 278,141.[42]

Some additional comments are in order regarding imprisonment as a correctional practice. Although most American citizens go through their lives without ever seeing the inside of a correctional institution, incarceration befalls more persons in the United States than in most other nations. The imprisonment rate in this country is about 115 persons out of each 100,000 population. In other words, each year about this number of individuals serves time in penal institutions. When the number of persons serving time is calculated to include individuals sentenced to jails, the rate of imprisonment increases to about 180 persons per 100,000. By contrast, the imprisonment rate in England and Wales is 65 persons and in Japan 89 persons per 100,000 population.[43]

Some marked changes have occurred over the past several decades in the United States in the use of imprisonment. The population of incarcerated persons was about 130,000 in 1945, rising to about 225,000 by 1960. The number of imprisoned individuals then began to decline, so that between 1967 and 1973, prison populations numbered about 200,000 inmates. However, since 1973, the trend has been one in which larger numbers of persons are imprisoned each year. The 1973 prison population was 204,211, increasing to 218,205 in 1974 and 278,141 in 1977. These changes are directly related to the broader shift toward increased punitiveness noted earlier.

Although incarceration is more widely used in the United States than in most other nations, it is not employed uniformly from one state to another. Figure 7 shows the rates of incarceration for the various states in 1977. That figure suggests that variations in rates of imprisonment probably have less to do with crime levels in specific states than they do with broader variations in social influences that characterize different states and regions in the United States.

CAPITAL PUNISHMENT[44]

Although the death penalty is not widely used, it has been employed more frequently in the United States than elsewhere. For example, 632 persons were executed in England and Wales between 1900 and 1940, while between 1930 and 1960, 3,724 executions were held in the United States. Even though the United States is much larger than England and Wales, the relative number of executions was still far greater, in the former. Of these executions, 3,225 were in cases of murder, 434 were for rape, 23 for armed robbery, 18 for kidnapping, 11 for burglary, and 13 for other crimes. Only 31 of these executions were for federal offenses, and only 31 involved women.

There have been some pronounced patterns in capital punishment in the United States. Of the 3,724 executions between 1930 and 1960, nonwhites were executed in 50 percent of the murders, 90 percent of the rapes, and 46 percent of the other offenses. One of the principal arguments against capital punishment

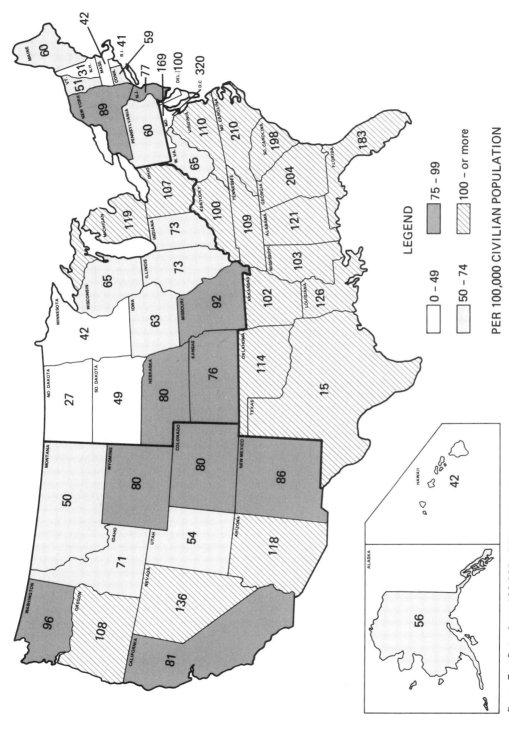

figure 7   Rate (per 100,000 civilian population) of sentenced prisoners incarcerated in state institutions, by jurisdiction, on Dec. 31, 1977 *Source: U.S. Department of Justice, Law Enforcement Assistance Administration. Prisoners in State and Federal Institutions on December 31, 1977. (Washington, D.C., U.S. Government Printing Office, 1979), p. 4.*

LEGEND

PER 100,000 CIVILIAN POPULATION

| 0 – 49 | 50 – 74 | 75 – 99 | 100 – or more |

is that it is highly discriminatory, so that offenders from lower-income backgrounds and disadvantaged ethnic groups have been most likely to be executed. Capital punishment was also more common in some sections of the country than in others—60 percent of the executions occurred in the 17 Southern states. All but two of the executions for rape and all burglary executions took place in Southern states. Only one execution occurred between 1940 and 1960 in New Hampshire, although Georgia executed 358 individuals. These figures partially reflect regional variations in occurrence of capital offenses, but the Southern states also showed a greater willingness to snuff out the lives of criminals.

One trend in capital punishment in the United States prior to 1972, when it was declared to be unconstitutional by the Supreme Court, was toward a reduced number of executions. Table 22, which shows the number of persons executed in individual years since 1952, indicates that capital punishment was infrequently employed in recent decades. In the period from 1930 to 1934, the average annual number of executions in this country was 155, whereas in the 1956–1960 period, the yearly average was 57, and between 1962 and 1966, the average was 18.

There are many arguments against capital punishment, including the ethical position that it is morally wrong. Opponents of the death penalty have stressed its inequitable features, pointing to the large proportion of lower-class and non-white individuals executed. In addition, abolitionists have noted that execution is irrevocable and cannot be undone once it is carried out. Doubtless, there have been cases of persons wrongfully convicted and executed.

Enemies of the death penalty contend that the major argument for its use, its presumed deterrent effect, is erroneous. If capital punishment reduced the occurrence of capital offenses, its impact should be observed in comparisons of crime rates. Instead, statistical studies show that yearly homicide rates have been about the same for contiguous states that are socially and economically similar, even though the death penalty has been used in one state and not in another. The long-term trends in homicide rates have been similar in adjoining states even though some have used capital punishment and others have not. In

table 22 executions, united states, 1952–1971

year	number of executions	year	number of executions
1952	88	1962	47
1953	62	1963	21
1954	82	1964	15
1955	76	1965	7
1956	65	1966	1
1957	65	1967	0
1958	48	1968	0
1959	49	1969	0
1960	57	1970	0
1961	42	1971	0

cases where the death penalty has been introduced, abolished, or reintroduced in a state, the homicide rate has not fluctuated as proponents of capital punishment suggest it should. Finally, the rates of homicide involving police officers are no higher in states without capital punishment than in states with the death penalty.

Capital punishment was declared unconstitutional by the U.S. Supreme Court in 1972.[45] In *Furman* v. *Georgia*, the Court ruled that the death penalty violated the Eighth Amendment prohibition against cruel and unusual punishment, because there were no limits on the discretionary use of the death penalty and it was discriminatory, excessive, haphazard, and capricious in operation. The effect of this ruling was to invalidate existing state statutes allowing the death penalty and also to suspend executions of persons already convicted under those statutes.

In most states where the death penalty existed in 1972, the response was to turn to revising the law, either by making the death penalty mandatory in the case of certain crimes, or by establishing guided-discretion standards which explicitly identified the circumstances in which the death penalty could be handed down—but not requiring that it be imposed on all persons coming within those guidelines. However, the Supreme Court failed to uphold the revised laws which called for a mandatory death penalty, ruling that they, too, violate the Eighth Amendment by removing all traces of necessary discretion from the sentencing process. On the other hand, in *Gregg* v. *Georgia* (1976) the Court declared that the death penalty per se does not constitute cruel and unusual punishment. It upheld as constitutional the Georgia statute (and those of other states following similar procedures) in which a bifurcated trial procedure is used in capital cases. In this system, the guilt of the accused is first determined, following which the jury then arrives at a sentence decision. In the Georgia statute, persons can be given the death penalty for murder if it involved at least one of ten aggravating circumstances outlined in the statute. In effect, the Court asserted that this guided discretion effectively guards against the capricious and discriminatory application of the death penalty.

Since 1976, less than a half dozen persons have been executed in the United States. However, it appears likely that a return to a sizeable number of executions per year may well take place in this country in the years ahead.

summary

This chapter has been concerned with the different events that occur after offenders have been convicted or adjudicated in the courts. In the next chapter, we shall examine the social workings of the agencies and institutions to which these individuals are consigned. We shall discover that most of these agencies and institutions operate in ways not accurately described in organizational charts stating the purposes or workings of these structures. In particular, we shall find that prisons and other correctional institutions often constitute social communities at cross-purposes with their official aims.

notes

[1] For a discussion of regulation of private feuding by the larger society, see E. Adamson Hoebel, *The Law of Primitive Man* (Cambridge, Mass.: Harvard University Press, 1954).

[2] Harry Elmer Barnes and Negley K. Teeters, *New Horizons in Criminology*, 3rd ed. (Englewood Cliffs, N.J.: Prentice-Hall, Inc., 1959), pp. 294–305.

[3] For some penetrating historical analyses of these developments, see Douglas Hay, Peter Linebaugh, John G. Rule, E. P. Thompson, and Cal Winslow, *Albion's Fatal Tree: Crime and Society in Eighteenth-Century England* (New York: Pantheon Books, 1975); E. P. Thompson, *Whigs and Hunters: The Origin of the Black Act* (New York: Pantheon Books, 1975).

[4] For a summary of classical, neoclassical, and positivist views on punishment, see George B. Vold and Thomas Bernard, *Theoretical Criminology*, 2nd ed. (New York: Oxford University Press, 1979), pp. 18–74. The rise of classical views is discussed briefly in Barnes and Teeters, *New Horizons in Criminology*, pp. 322–27, and in detail in Leon Radzinowicz, *A History of English Criminal Law and its Administration from 1750*, 3 vols. (New York: Macmillan, 1948–1957).

[5] Radzinowicz, *A History of English Criminal Law*.

[6] The undeveloped state of a treatment-oriented correctional practice is discussed in Don C. Gibbons, *Changing the Lawbreaker* (Englewood Cliffs, N.J.: Prentice-Hall, Inc., 1965), pp. 190–96.

[7] Brief discussions of the historical origins of American prisons can be found in Barnes and Teeters, *New Horizons in Criminology*, pp. 328–47. A more detailed essay is David J. Rothman, *The Discovery of the Asylum* (Boston: Little, Brown, 1971).

[8] American Correctional Association, *State and National Correctional Institutions of the United States of America, Canada, England and Scotland* (New York: American Correctional Association, 1957). Minimum security institutions and farms were not counted in these tabulations.

[9] On the rise of humanitarianism, see Gibbons, *Changing the Lawbreaker*, pp. 130–34.

[10] Gresham M. Sykes, *The Society of Captives* (Princeton, N.J.: Princeton University Press, 1958), pp. 63–83.

[11] Edwin H. Sutherland and Donald R. Cressey, *Criminology*, 10th ed. (Philadelphia: Lippincott, 1978), p. 304.

[12] Paul W. Tappan, *Crime, Justice and Correction* (New York: McGraw-Hill, 1960), pp. 241–61.

[13] Ibid., p. 242.

[14] The complex nature of the deterrence question has been indicated in detail in Jack P. Gibbs, *Crime, Punishment, and Deterrence* (New York: Elsevier/North-Holland, 1975). Indeed, the central thrust of Gibbs's book was that the phenomenon of deterrence is so much bound up with other factors and with other consequences of punishment as to be almost beyond empirical examination. At the very least, his discussion indicated that almost nothing can be asserted unequivocally about deterrence on the basis of the evidence at hand from research studies.

[15] *Webster's New Collegiate Dictionary* (Springfield, Mass.: Merriam, 1971), p. 226.

[16] One well-known statement of this thesis was James Q. Wilson, *Thinking About Crime* (New York: Basic Books, 1975). In fairness to Wilson, it should be noted that his emphasis was more upon the gains to be derived from incapacitating increased numbers of offenders and from increasing the certainty and swiftness of punishment than it was upon maximizing the severity of punitive sanctions. For some trenchant criticisms of these views, see Jerome H. Skolnick, "Are More Jails the Answer?" *Dissent* (Winter 1976), 95–97.

[17] Tappan, *Crime, Justice, and Correction*, p. 246.

[18] Ibid., pp. 248–49.

[19]Daniel Glaser, *The Effectiveness of a Prison and Parole System* (Indianapolis: Bobbs-Merrill, 1964), pp. 13–35. Observers have sometimes concluded that most inmates become recidivists or repeaters from observing an offender population in prison at one point in time. On any particular day, the prison population does contain a large proportion of inmates who have been incarcerated a number of times previously. At the same time, a large number of persons proceed through the institution over time and do not subsequently return. Unless we take some kind of census outside of the prison, or unless we follow a cohort of newly admitted prisoners for an extended period of time, we are likely to overlook the prisoners who do not return to the prison for a second time. Nonetheless, the successes are at least as frequent as are the cases of those who keep coming back through the revolving door of the penitentiary.

[20]David F. Greenberg, "The Incapacitative Effect of Imprisonment: Some Estimates," *Law and Society Review*, 9 (Summer 1975), 541–80.

[21]Tappan, *Crime, Justice, and Correction*, pp. 251–53.

[22]For excellent sociological essays dealing with many of the issues here, see Alexander L. Clark and Jack P. Gibbs, "Social Control: A Reformulation," *Social Problems*, 12 (Spring 1965), 398–415; Gibbs, "Sanctions," *Social Problems*, 14 (Fall 1966), 147–59; Gibbs, *Crime, Punishment, and Deterrence*.

[23]Franklin E. Zimring, *Perspectives on Deterrence* (Washington, D.C.: National Institute of Mental Health, 1971). See also Gibbs, *Crime, Punishment, and Deterrence*.

[24]For summaries of this research, see Gibbs, *Crime, Punishment, and Deterrence*; Charles W. Thomas and J. Sherwood Williams, eds., *The Deterrent Effect of Sanctions: A Selected Bibliography*, Metropolitan Criminal Justice Center, College of William and Mary, 1975; Charles R. Tittle and Charles H. Logan, "Sanctions and Deviance: Evidence and Remaining Questions," *Law and Society Review*, 7 (Spring 1973), 371–92; Tittle, "Punishment and Deterrence of Deviance," in *The Economics of Crime and Punishment*, Simon Rottenberg, ed. (Washington, D.C.: American Enterprise Institute for Public Policy Research, 1973), pp. 85–102; Franklin Zimring and Gordon J. Hawkins, *Deterrence: The Legal Threat in Crime Control* (Chicago: University of Chicago Press, 1973).

[25]William J. Chambliss, "The Deterrent Influence of Punishment," *Crime and Delinquency*, 12 (January 1966), 70–75.

[26]Jack P. Gibbs, "Crime, Punishment, and Deterrence," *Southwestern Social Science Quarterly*, 28 (March 1968), 515–30.

[27]Charles R. Tittle, "Crime Rates and Legal Sanctions," *Social Problems*, 16 (Spring 1969), 409–23.

[28]Another study, reporting results generally consistent with those of Gibbs and Tittle, was Theodore G. Chiricos and Gordon P. Waldo, "Punishment and Crime: An Examination of Some Empirical Evidence," *Social Problems*, 18 (Fall 1970), 200–17.

[29]One illustrative case involving speculation about perceptions of the risks of punishment was James P. Levine, "The Ineffectiveness of Adding Police to Prevent Crime," *Public Policy*, 23 (Fall 1975), 523–45.

[30]Geerken and Gove presented a theoretical explication of some of the dimensions of this research problem in an argument which conceptualized deterrence in terms of communication processes. Their analysis indicated some of the factors that enter into communications systems which effectively convey the deterrent message to individuals. See Michael R. Geerken and Walter R. Gove, "Deterrence: Some Theoretical Considerations," *Law and Society Review*, 9 (Spring 1975), 497–513. For evidence on this issue, see Jack P. Gibbs and Maynard Erickson, "Conceptions of Criminal and Delinquent Acts," *Deviant Behavior*, 1 (October 1979), 71–100; Kirk R. Williams, Gibbs, and Erickson, "Public Knowledge of Statutory Penalties: The Extent and Basis of Accurate Perception," *Pacific Sociological Review*, 23 (January 1980), 105–28; Harold G. Grasmick and George J. Bryjak, "The Deterrent Effect of Perceived Certainty of Punishment," *Social Forces*, 59 (December 1980), 471–91

[31]Don C. Gibbons, "Who Knows What About Correction?" *Crime and Delinquency*, 9 (April 1963), 137–44.

[32]Assembly Committee on Criminal Procedure, *Deterrent Effects of Criminal Sanctions* (Sacramento: California State Legislature, 1968); see also Joint Commission on Correctional Manpower and Training, *The Public Looks at Crime and Corrections* (Washington, D.C.: Joint Commission on Correctional Manpower and Training, 1968); Peter Rossi, Emily Waite, Christine Bose, and Richard Berk, "The Seriousness of Crimes: Normative Structure and Individual Differences," *American Sociological Review*, 39 (April 1974), 224–37.

[33]Assembly Committee on Criminal Procedure, *Deterrent Effects of Criminal Sanctions*, p. 13.

[34]Leonard H. Goodman, Trudy Miller, and Paul De Forrest, *A Study of the Deterrent Value of Crime Prevention Measures as Perceived by Criminal Offenders* (Washington, D.C.: Bureau of Social Research, 1966).

[35]In one other study that was somewhat similar to the Goodman, Miller and De Forrest investigation, the researchers quizzed a sample of college students about theft behavior and marijuana use. Certainty of punishment appeared to have the greatest impact in deterring these individuals from involvement or continuation in these activities. See Gordon P. Waldo and Theodore G. Chiricos, "Perceived Penal Sanction and Self-Reported Criminality: A Neglected Approach to Deterrence Research," *Social Problems*, 19 (Spring 1972), 522–40.

[36]These developments are discussed in H. Ted Rubin, "Retain the Juvenile Court? Legislative Developments, Reform Directions, and the Call for Abolition," *Crime and Delinquency*, 25 (July 1979), 271–98; Michael S. Serrill, "Police Write a New Law on Juvenile Crime," *Police Magazine*, 2 (September 1979), 47–52.

[37]Parole practices and criticisms of parole are discussed in Gerald D. Robin, *Introduction to the Criminal Justice System* (New York: Harper and Row, Pub., 1980), pp. 374–77.

[38]Sheldon L. Messinger and Phillip D. Johnson, "California's Determinate Sentence Statute: History and Issues," in *Determinate Sentencing: Reform or Regression?* National Institute of Law Enforcement and Criminal Justice (Washington, D.C.: Law Enforcement Assistance Administration, 1978), pp. 13–88.

[39]For a valuable survey of correctional dispositions in the United States, see The President's Commission on Law Enforcement and Administration of Justice, *The Challenge of Crime in a Free Society* (Washington, D.C.: U.S. Government Printing Office, 1967), pp. 159–85; see also The President's Commission on Law Enforcement and Administration of Justice, *Task Force Report: Corrections* (Washington, D.C.: U.S. Government Printing Office, 1967). For detailed data on correctional dispositions, numbers of persons in various correctional agencies and facilities, and related matters, see Timothy J. Flanagan, Michael J. Hindelang, and Michael R. Gottfredson, eds., *Sourcebook of Criminal Justice Statistics, 1979* (Washington, D.C.: Law Enforcement Assistance Administration, 1980).

[40]Contemporary correctional practices outside the United States are surveyed in John P. Conrad, *Crime and Its Correction* (Berkeley: University of California Press, 1967).

[41]The President's Commission on Law Enforcement, *The Challenge of Crime*, p. 162.

[42]Flanagan, Hindelang, and Gottfredson, *Sourcebook of Criminal Justice Statistics*, pp. 600–633.

[43]Herbert A. Bloch and Gilbert Geis, *Man, Crime, and Society* (New York: Random House, 1970). p. 465.

[44]A useful sourcebook on capital punishment is Thorsten Sellin, ed., *Capital Punishment*, (New York: Harper & Row, Pub., 1967).

correctional
social
organization

As societies have grown in size and complexity, particularly in the past few centuries, relatively permanent organizational structures have been invented for dealing with lawbreakers. Some of these, such as prisons, are physically separated from the societies they serve, whereas others, such as police agencies or probation organizations, exist within the community and impinge more directly on the activities of citizens. In either case, these law-enforcement and correctional devices represent prominent social forms in modern societies.

In the past several decades, sociologists have begun to subject these structures to scrutiny, so that at present a large and growing literature exists on the sociology of correctional organizations.[1] This body of sociological work has attempted to discover the social processes and patterns characteristic of correctional organizations. The sociologist approaches prisons and other custodial institutions as particular cases of "total institutions" or as a subtype of the larger class of formal, complex organizations.[2]

Analysis of the social workings of legal and correctional agencies encompasses a wide variety of organizations, not all of which are discussed in this chapter. Inquiries into the social structure of the police represent one case of the sociology of correctional organizations, but Chapter 18 has already dealt with the police. Studies of social values and attitudes regarding crime have been reported in Chapter 4,[3] and the question of social stigma resulting from legal handling has also been examined earlier.[4] This chapter is devoted to sociological aspects of prisons, training schools, and other custodial institutions, as well as probation and parole agencies.

Sociologists have not subjected all the various correctional devices in modern society to equal research treatment: jails and certain police systems have generally been ignored. We shall note various gaps and deficiencies in the literature on correctional social organization at various points in this chapter.

prison social organization

In a number of ways, prisons are unlike any other kind of institution or organization in modern society. They are foreign to the experience of most citizens, for few individuals other than prisoners and their keepers ever see the inside of a prison. Although life in a penal institution can be described to persons who have not been in one, such a description can hardly portray all the atmosphere of the place. It fails to capture the noises of clanging cell doors, the mean, harsh flavor of institutional living, even in the most humane penitentiary, and many other elements that make life in the penal institution unique as a human experience. Nonetheless, the following pages provide some glimpses of social life behind prison walls, beginning with an examination of similarities and variations among prisons.[5]

PRISON SIMILARITIES AND VARIATIONS

One characteristic all prisons share is that they are places where one group of persons devote their attention to managing a group of captives. Prisoners do not enter penitentiaries voluntarily; they are forcibly brought there and restrained by prison workers whose main product is social order among inmates. Prisons are also similar in the sense that inmates who enter them are relatively alike; hence, prisons everywhere work with much the same raw material. Most reformatories and penitentiaries in the United States are walled institutions with inside cell blocks and other features of the Auburn–Sing Sing physical plant. Most inmates depart from penal facilities through parole or outright release before serving the maximum sentence imposed on them. Finally, prisons are devoted to the same general functions—administering some punishment to lawbreakers while keeping them securely in custody, and with certain other aims.

Some important differences among penal institutions probably condition the kind of social structure that grows in them. For one, prisons vary considerably in size of physical plant and inmate population. As noted in Chapter 20, American prisons range in size from some holding several hundred inmates to several with over 4,000 inmates.

Although the Auburn–Sing Sing style of architecture is the most commonly encountered in the United States, some penal institutions have been constructed along different lines. A major variant in physical design is the so-called telephone-pole physical plan, in which all the institutional buildings are connected to one central corridor. This architectural style evolved relatively recently and has provided the model for most of the newer institutions in this country. One major advantage of this physical plant is that control over inmates does not demand the inordinate amount of time and energy devoted to that task in the older Auburn–Sing Sing kind of prison, with its hodgepodge of poorly designed and poorly located structures.

Penal institutions also vary in the financial resources they can call on for implementation of their programs. For example, in some states, guards receive extremely low wages; in some other states, correctional officers are paid fairly reasonable salaries. Another variation among prisons has to do with the kind of administrative organization within which they are placed. In some states, a Department of Corrections or similar agency exercises continued jurisdiction over the individual institutions and usually provides a degree of stability to the correctional program. In other areas, prisons are autonomous operations subjected to the ups and downs of political interference.[6]

Custodial institutions show some differences in the kinds of inmates with which they deal. Reformatories usually handle relatively young prisoners, most of them under 25 years of age, whereas prisons and penitentiaries hold an older, more mature offender population. Institutions with youthful populations are often subjected to more violent and erratic behavior by inmates than are those places with an older convict population. Certain states, such as California, have established diversified institutions, each holding a relatively uniform group of prisoners. The institution at Chino holds minimum-security inmates, while San Quentin and Folsom prisons are restricted to more dangerous, criminally mature offenders. In many states with a smaller total population of prisoners, one prison handles the entire varied mixture of felons.

Penal institutions mirror various features of the societies in which they are found. Accordingly, the student of prison life might expect to find variations in these places from one country to another. Indeed, studies of European prisons have turned up discrepancies between them and American institutions largely along a violence dimension, with American prisons being the most dangerous places.[7] Similarly, Donald Cressey and Witold Krassowski have identified some features of Soviet labor camps not found in American institutions.[8]

PRISONS AND THE HOST SOCIETY

Prisons are sometimes seen as "total institutions" in which all of the prisoner's life events occur. This label implies that penal facilities exist in isolation from the society they serve, but such a view is not entirely accurate. Most of the day-to-day concerns of prisoners center about life inside the walls, and they are painfully aware that they have been isolated from other citizens. Yet convicts are not completely cut off from contact with the outside world. Visitors and tours frequently pass through the institution. Inmates listen to radios, read newspapers, and watch TV, so that they do not lose complete contact with the world outside the prison. They sometimes seize on such devices as riots and disturbances to dramatize their complaints against the institution to an audience in the free community.

Prisons are less than total in another sense, since the persons who run these places are restrained by interests outside the institution. What kinds of restraints operate on prison administrators? Citizens generally know little about prisons. One study of public knowledge about correctional practices in California indicated that most citizens were unaware of the bases on which persons are committed to prisons. They were also ignorant of the number, variety, or character of penal institutions in that state. Most laymen knew that executions took place by means of gas at San Quentin Prison, but they showed little awareness of most other facets of the correctional program.[9]

Although laymen do not appear to have any sustained or informed interest in penitentiaries, it would be a mistake to suppose that the public plays no part in the program of prisons. Various community groups interested in penal operations function as pressure groups that influence institutional programs. For example, social-worker associations pressure the prison to establish therapy programs, and various industry and labor organizations attempt to force the institution to curtail manufacture of goods that compete with products of private industry. We cannot understand such prison phenomena as the widespread idleness in American institutions without taking into account the activities of outside pressure groups, which have forced institutions to restrict their production to states-use goods, that is, items to be used by other state institutions.

The interest groups that intrude into prison policies are a mixed collection that often press for conflicting ends. Correctional administrators can sometimes manage the disruptive potential of these claims on the system because much of the activity of these groups is intermittent. Administrators sometimes deal with interest groups by "giving" one institution to one group and another to a different pressure group. In other words, treatment is stressed in one facility to reduce agitation from welfare workers, whereas a repressive regime is established in a second prison to satisfy proponents of punitive themes.[10]

PRISON PROGRAMS

A brief sketch of the workings of the prison would include the following elements. The prison is nominally under the control of an administrator, usually called a warden or superintendent, who is assisted by one or more associate wardens responsible for the custodial or treatment programs of the institution. The custodial staff is by far the largest group of employees, composed of a captain of the guards and a number of lieutenants, along with the guards. The latter are sometimes called correctional officers by administrators and are usually termed "bulls" or "screws" by the inmates.

A second group of prison employees consists of a business manager along with various clerical persons and bookkeepers. These individuals manage the flow of goods and supplies into and out of the prison community.

The third group of workers in the modern prison is made up of individuals presumed to be working at the rehabilitation of the prisoners. Most prisons have some kind of classification office that gathers detailed facts about newly arrived prisoners. This information is then used in making custodial assignments and other program decisions about inmates. Institutions also maintain a school program and a number of teachers who attempt to continue the education of some of the convicts. Vocational training is often found in modern penal facilities, so some prisoners learn typewriter repair or other skills of that kind. However, the bulk of the inmates work during the day in various prison industries that have no vocational consequences for them. Prisoners assist in kitchen duties, make clothing or shoes for other state institutions, manufacture road signs and license plates, or engage in other kinds of prison labor. Supervisory employees are responsible for these activities, along with guards who also maintain surveillance of the inmates during the day. The institution employs social workers to engage in various kinds of counseling activity with the convicts.

Correctional administrators often distribute descriptions of their prisons that imply orderly, efficient, coherent systems in which the various facets of correctional activity converge on the inmate to convert him or her into a law-abiding citizen. But how accurate is the official description of the prison? The evidence on the social workings of penal organizations indicates that the official view of penal operations is more fiction than fact.

PRISON SOCIAL STRUCTURE

The description of prison organization that follows should be viewed as most descriptive of maximum-security prisons for male prisoners and as more or less accurate for institutions that vary in the ways suggested in the preceding pages.

Members of the general public have often thought of prisons as autocratic.[11] Custodial officers *give orders* and inmates *obey* them. Prisoners are totally managed persons whose opportunities for self-direction and independent action are almost completely circumscribed. Penal institutions are monoliths with a singularity of purpose in which all responsibilities of members of the system are clearly and specifically defined. Prisons are well-oiled, smooth-running, people-punishing, and people-changing social machines. In this view, all prison employees, from the warden down to the guards, agree on their tasks of maintaining, disciplining, and sometimes treating inmates. Prisons are frequently believed to be models of autocratic and rational bureaucratic structures.

This image is greatly distorted, for prisons depart markedly from this monolithic model. Cressey has devoted a good deal of attention to the organizational cross-currents built into modern prisons.[12] He pointed out that as basic concepts of prison purposes and institutional management have changed, new activities have been added to the institutional operation but without being integrated with the earlier forms of administrative structure. Accordingly, nearly all modern penal facilities have three administrative hierarchies, relatively independent of one another, and devoted to keeping, serving, and using inmates. In other words, prisons have a number of employees who maintain custody over prisoners, another group which supervises inmates in their work activities, and a third collection of workers who endeavor to rehabilitate the prisoners.[13] In many institutions, that part of the system supposedly devoted to treatment is a small segment of the organization, but at least a token effort to develop a rehabilitative program has been made in many penal institutions. Cressey also noted that in the general shift in the past century, away from the view that persons are sent to prison *for* punishment to the perspective that imprisonment alone is punishment enough, "mere incarceration" has not been consistently defined. Over the decades, prisons have vacillated from repressive regimes to periods in which they have been loosely run and less punitive and harsh. Still, most contemporary prisons continue to place prisoners in some degree of physical discomfort, so "mere incarceration" refers to a mean existence unrelieved by many of the pleasures and diversions of normal living.[14]

Cressey has summarized the contradictory mandate under which modern prisons operate:

. . . at present there are three popular and sanctioned reactions to crime in contemporary American society. One is hostility, with insistence that the criminal be made to suffer in prison, whether the suffering is physical or psychological. Another reaction is one of humanitarian concern that the punishments in prisons not be too harsh, severe, cruel, or inhuman. A third is inquiry designed to secure comprehension of the social and psychological processes in criminal behavior, so that control can be based on knowledge.[15]

The responsibility of the prison to maintain secure custody over prisoners, so they cannot escape, and at the same time to refrain from brutalizing them creates grave difficulties for the institution. The prisoners are not in the institution voluntarily and do not grant legitimacy to the official norms of the organization. The situation of prisoners is different from that of a military autocracy, for in the latter case most members of the system have internalized the authority of the rules, even though somewhat grudgingly. Most are motivated to conform to military regulations and procedures, even though they may regard conformity as personally unpleasant. The same cannot be said for many (but not all) prison inmates.

Autocratic rule over hostile and uncooperative inmates could theoretically be obtained at a price. Prisoners could be isolated, physically abused and coerced, and put under continual and pervasive surveillance. In theory, they could be maintained under conditions of marked anomie and demoralization. However, these possibilities do not actually exist, for prison officials are expected to deal with their charges in a humane fashion. They are obligated to minimize the physical and social isolation of inmates, rather than maximize it, and are forbidden to abuse physically or coerce prisoners. These are real limitations, for institutions do come under periodic scrutiny by the outside world. In addition, constant surveillance of prisoners by correctional officers to detect rule violations is impossible for two reasons: most prisons are not constructed in such a way as to allow continual supervision and observation of convicts, and not enough observers are available. Although guards make up the largest single class of employee, the prisoners greatly outnumber them.[16]

In theory, officers are expected to maintain social distance from prisoners and give orders inmates are presumed to obey because they are powerless to do otherwise. But prison guards do not have techniques of physical coercion available to obtain compliance from defiant prisoners. Moreover, even if it were legitimized, physical force as a technique for managing convicts would be self-defeating in the long run. Because of the disproportionate number of inmates to guards, extensive use of force would produce convict reprisals, uprisings, and other negative consequences.

One technique contrived for control of uncooperative prisoners has been to urge them to put themselves into voluntary isolation from other convicts, to "do your own time," and pursue incentives and privileges as rewards for conformity. In turn, if an inmate violates rules, he loses privileges.[17] However, this mechanism has severe limitations. Deprivation of privileges has little effect within the harsh environment of institutions because the prisoners are already severely deprived. They are cut off from sexual relations and many kinds of freedom of action as to choice of clothing, companionship, and so on. To be denied the privilege of attending a movie tends not to be viewed as a severe loss. Prisoners have redefined such incentives as reduction of the inmate's sentence for good behavior as rights rather than rewards, so the administration tends to tamper with "good time" credits only in extreme cases. Furthermore, they are accorded to the inmate at the start of his sentence rather than at points in his instutitional career as rewards for appropriate institutional conduct. Thus, they do not operate as important incentives and are normally awarded routinely to nearly all inmates except those who have had extremely troublesome and violent institutional careers.

The modern prison must find some way of maintaining order without extreme physical coercion and manipulation of meaningful rewards for conformity. The solution of this problem of how to keep the peace with and among uncooperative inmates takes the form of corruption of authority in many prisons.[18] Corruption of authority assumes several forms. One form refers to liaisons, relationships, "deals," and other informal *sub rosa* ties, which develop between inmates and administrators and are not defined as legitimate or proper within the formal definitions of prison procedures. Penal administrators and prisoner elites enter into informal relationships that provide special privileges to these leaders. In turn, they take over the job of coercing other inmates into minimally disruptive behavior. As Richard Korn and Lloyd McCorkle have indicated, "far from systematically attempting to undermine the inmate hierarchy, the institution generally gives it covert support and recognition by assigning better jobs and quarters to its high-status members providing they are 'good inmates.' In this and other ways the institution buys peace with the system by avoiding battle with it."[19] Being a good inmate in this context means refraining from direct assaults on the administrative system. It does *not* mean "doing your own time," for elites interfere with other inmates, control them, and demand special privileges and favors from less powerful prisoners. They are covertly aided in these activities by the prison administration, which pretends not to see this interaction among the convicts.

A second form of corruption of authority extends to inmate–guard relationships generally, in which correctional officers obtain a measure of cooperation and obedience from inmates by discretionary action in which they overlook some conduct infractions. In turn, in a *quid pro quo* relationship, inmates are expected to create a minimum of visible trouble for the officers. In other words, guards persuade convicts to behave by allowing them to deviate from rules in certain situations. This form of authority corruption stems from several factors. Correctional officers are not immune from general pressures to be "good guys." They probably find it difficult to associate with inmates on extremely distant and aloof terms, for they quickly discover that prisoners are ordinary humans and not monsters. More important, discretionary actions represent the easiest way for guards to keep inmate disorder at a minimum. The officer without a club of some sort must persuade and cajole. Discretionary action represents the carrot by which he obtains a modicum of conformity to major rules and regulations.

In the public view, the job of correctional officer is fit for simpletons who need only follow explicit orders. In reality, it is probably one of the more difficult occupational tasks in American society. The job demands a high order of skill in manipulating and managing men. The officer must use discretion but at the same time must be alert to the dangers of being drawn into situations where he buys cooperation from prisoners at too great a price. He must avoid being lured into *sub rosa* relationships in which he takes contraband into or out of the institution or performs other illicit services for inmates. The guard must use discretion up to a point, but he risks being manipulated by convicts into discretionary actions beyond the tolerance point of his superiors. If he uses too much discretionary judgment, he may be fired or punished in some other way. To complicate his situation further, appropriate action must be worked out by each officer, for the most part unguided by advice and instruction from anyone else. Cressey has suggested that in prisons of either custodial or therapeutic orientation, the guard's superiors are not able to give him explicit directions as to precisely how he is to function in his discretionary role.[20]

For such reasons, prisons might be more accurately defined as partially disorganized rather than as model autocracies. They exhibit less than complete organizational consensus among employees and show defective communication patterns. Orders are supposed to move down a chain of command to guards, where they are implemented, and information on which decisions are made moves up the command line. But distortions often occur in message flow, particularly in the feedback of explanations behind orders to such low-ranking members as custodial officers. Consequently, prisons frequently show a degree of guard alienation from the institutional program.[21] Officers either do not understand the bases on which decisions and orders are formulated or disagree with these directives. This lack of internal consensus among employees regarding goals of the system is found in prisons of various kinds but is particularly severe in treatment-oriented prisons, where the guards are often more similar to the inmates than they are to the higher administrators. Because they view therapy operations as a threat to sound custody, they are in accord, although for different reasons, with the prisoners' negative definitions of treatment programs.

The problems of prisons discussed to this point seem generic to treatment and custodial institutions alike. But some additional difficulties are found in therapy-oriented prisons.[22]

The rehabilitative function has never been widely adopted or implemented in many American prisons. Commenting on the situation in the 1960s, Alfred Schnur noted that it does not make much sense to ask whether the "New Penology" oriented around rehabilitation was a success, for the "New Penology" existed for the most part mainly in textbooks.[23] Schnur pointed out that, around 1958, about 27,000 persons were employed in state and federal penal facilities to manage some 165,000 inmates—a ratio of one employee for every six prisoners. Few of these employees were assigned to treatment activities; most were custodial officers. Moreover, only a small proportion of the persons designated as treatment personnel were actually involved in therapy activities. According to Schnur, "more people, however, are employed to shuffle papers than to implement the new penology."[24] For example, only 23 psychiatrists were available full-time to treat 165,000 inmates, so the ratio of prisoners to psychiatrists was 7,026 to 1. If each convict received the same amount of psychiatric help, each would get 82 seconds of therapy per month.

In a similar study of 47 state correctional systems in the early 1960s, Elmer Johnson[25] found that persons with master of social work degrees were employed in only 14 states. Eighteen states indicated that no social workers were employed in their programs. Additionally, in the remaining states, the social-worker occupational category was defined so broadly as to include persons who did not have training in social-work practice and techniques. The definition of social work was stretched to include a variety of institutional activities not conventionally thought of as social work.

Although the rehabilitative function has not been developed in detail in many states, particularly in the South, treatment programs of some considerable degree of complexity were inaugurated in many states in the 1950s and 1960s, with California leading the way in these ventures.

Addition of the treatment role has introduced views into the institution to the effect that a coercive, restrictive social climate is unfavorable to therapy. Prisoners need opportunities to ventilate hostility, work out new patterns of adjustment, and so on. Prisons came to be regarded as serving ends similar to those presumed to characterize mental hospitals, with guards enjoined to be receptive, passive, and relaxed. Significantly, this new view was not usually shared by all members of the employee group. Such notions were frequently brought into the institution by top administrators who then attempted to impose them on the custodial force. However, a large segment of the guard group was made up of veterans of the old order who had served for many years under a straightforward custodial system. These officers have been supported by the force of tradition in their belief that the old ways are better, and they tended to be unreceptive to rehabilitative declarations by recently arrived administrators. Nonetheless, correctional institutions attempting transformation into treatment-oriented systems have exhibited a more relaxed, less coercive social climate than the more traditional penal facilities. Although there are serious questions regarding the extent to which prisons can be converted into therapeutic communities, efforts to do so have weakened the authoritarian order of the institutions and disrupted relations among employees.

The most usual outcome of introduction of treatment into an institution has been an uneasy marriage of custodial and therapeutic activities, and security considerations have often prevailed in the operation of the organization.[26] In other cases, the rehabilitative goal has pervaded many facets of the prison in the face of resistance by some employee holdouts. The specific pattern that has emerged has probably depended mainly on how the treatment function was brought into the prison. If it was introduced by hiring middle-level employees such as social workers but was not supported by the warden and his aides, the common consequence has been that in practice it merely has served custodial ends. Psychiatrists have been used in such institutions to "cool out" threatening inmates rather than to conduct therapy. In the same way, the treatment recommendations of other workers have been subordinated to custodial decisions. The custodial force has controlled communication within the organizations, so the therapists have been kept ignorant of, and removed from, the important operations of the prison. They have been reduced to a form of prison window dressing.[27]

The outcome of the custody–treatment quarrel has differed when the warden and other top-level administrators have introduced rehabilitation as an end or given allegiance to this goal. In this case, treatment workers have been more influential in the operation of the institution and have made important policy decisions. But again, the situation has tended to be an uneasy one in which functional harmony has been less than complete. No clear format for an effective therapy program operating within the limits of necessary security provisions has yet been devised. Treatment-oriented penitentiaries have lacked unambiguous definitions of the specific manner in which rehabilitative agents are to operate. As a consequence, many of these employees have seen themselves as rescuers, helpers, and protectors of inmates rather than as rehabilitators. The worker who has identified his task as helping inmates has sometimes come to see his job as protecting convicts from the custodial force. He has seen himself as a mediator between offenders and guards rather than as a co-worker with the correctional officer. This kind of role performance probably aggravates the treatment–custody conflict in prisons. It has been argued that the therapy agent who views his task as rescuing and helping inmates plays into the hands of the prisoners. He lends covert support to that group's attempts to "reject the rejectors" or deflect blame away from themselves.[28]

The treatment-oriented prison creates special difficulties for the guard force. Not only have correctional officers been told to maintain order without being given clear instructions as to how they are to accomplish this goal, they have also been told to behave in ways that contribute to therapy. As Cressey noted:

It is clear that in treatment-oriented prisons, directions to guards regarding their relationships with inmates are likely to be confusing and contradictory. There are to be no rules to enforce, but the guard is to enforce "understandings" to the extent necessary for the prison to achieve the minimum degree of orderliness it needs. There is to be no punishment, but guards are to report nonconformists to a central board for hearings, during the course of which punishments are ordered, in the name of justice. Guards are to "relax" but they are not to relax "too much."[29]

Correctional officers in the treatment prison have been pulled at from several different sides, so they are "damned if they do, and damned if they don't." Such a state of affairs could hardly add to the attractiveness of this occupation.

As is evident from the discussion thus far, administrations of most prisons do not present a united front to the inmate group. Points of ambiguity exist within the organizations, conflicts between different administrative groups lie barely hidden and sometimes blossom into open interorganizational conflict, and other difficulties characterize prisons. Little has been said so far about the inmate group. What is the nature of social life among male prisoners in maximum-security prisons?[30]

THE INMATE SOCIAL SYSTEM

One common but exaggerated view of convicts is that they are a unified group in opposition to the administrative regime. In the layman's view, inmates are a collectivity of "wild beasts" from whom the guards have much to fear, continually engaged in attempts to escape and carrying on a variety of violent activities among themselves. Something of this same conception of the inmate group can sometimes be found in the sociological literature as well. Gresham Sykes and Sheldon Messinger have described an inmate code of normative prescriptions said to exist in all prisons.[31] By implication, allegiance to this code characterizes most convicts. The code consists of conduct definitions centering around directives to refrain from interfering with inmate interests, avoid quarrels and conflicts with other prisoners or go "no rap" with one's fellow convicts, and so on. The code defines the model convict, from the inmates' perspective, in terms that contrast markedly with the staff version of the good inmate. Prisoners are expected to cooperate with one another in overt and covert defiance of institutional expectations.

Several hypotheses have been advanced to account for this code. Sykes and Messinger maintained that the most likely explanation was functional, in which the code serves to reduce the "pains of imprisonment" in custodial institutions.[32] These pains of incarceration include deprivations of liberty, goods and services, heterosexual relations, and autonomy, which offenders experience as psychologically painful. According to these authors, "as a population of prisoners moves in the direction of solidarity, as demanded by the inmate code, the pains of imprisonment become less severe."[33] McCorkle and Korn advanced a compatible thesis. They held that the code and prisoner solidarity in opposition to the authorities permit the inmate to "reject his rejectors" instead of himself.[34] That is, convicts are supported by their peers in a set of definitions and attitudes, which maintain that society is at fault for their criminality, so they are not forced to turn blame inward, to themselves. Cloward has advanced much the same argument.[35]

There is no question that an inmate code exists in prisons and that psychological pains accompany incarceration. But such a code may not be solely the product of pressures of confinement.[36] It is conceivable that it exists in prisons in part because some prisoners bring it into the institution from the outside. Several pieces of evidence support a diffusion interpretation of inmate norms. Stanton Wheeler has shown that role conflict and discrepancies in role expectations between inmates and administrators are less than complete.[37] He found that prisoners had different expectations regarding the behavior of other inmates than did guards, but some offenders had similar views to those of correctional officers who approved of violations of inmate definitions. Wheeler also suggested that some of the conflict between prisoners and authorities was more apparent than real. His data showed that prisoners judged other inmates to be more hostile to treatment and other institutional activities than they were in fact. This discrepancy between private sentiments and estimates of group views was related to the greater visibility of the most antisocial persons in the prison. Individual prisoners gauged the degree of antiadministration sentiment among other offenders from observation of a biased sample of the total inmate group.

Wheeler contributed other evidence supporting a diffusion interpretation of the inmate code. His findings from a number of Scandinavian prisons showed that the pains of imprisonment were found in these places, but there was no clear parallel to the inmate code or prisoner solidarity observed in American institutions.[38] Wheeler's interpretation of these results was that most prisoners in Scandinavian institutions enter from a society with a lower incidence of antiauthoritarian attitudes than the United States. Conversely, in American prisons, many offenders bring into the institution antisocial attitudes that are widespread among lower-class groups.[39]

Observations regarding social types or argot roles in prisons also support diffusion hypotheses regarding the inmate code.[40] Schrag has shown that a pattern of four inmate roles oriented around certain focal issues exists in the prison community. These role patterns are identified in the argot of inmates by such labels as "square John," "right guy," "outlaw," "ding," "rapo," and "politician." Similarly, Sykes's report on the New Jersey state prison indicated that the inmates recognized the existence of different behavioral roles in their midst and employed argot labels such as "center man," "hipster," "gorilla," "real man," and "ball buster" to designate these inmate patterns. Apparently, basic patterns of inmate adjustment arise in prison, so although the inmate terminology varies from one prison to another, the patterns are similar.

According to Schrag, prosocial inmates ("square Johns") consistently defined role requirements in terms of the legitimate norms of the civilian community of law-abiding citizens, whereas antisocial inmates ("right guys") perceived role requirements in terms of the norms of prisoner society. The latter were loyal to other convicts and engaged in minimal contact with prison officials. Pseudosocial prisoners ("politicians") shifted their allegiance between legitimate norms and prisoner standards and engaged in interaction with both inmates and administrators. Asocial inmates ("outlaws") were rebels against both legitimate norms and prescriptions and the standards of inmate society.

Schrag summarized a series of studies demonstrating that these role patterns were of primary importance in understanding inmate behavior within prisons. Among other observations, he noted that each role was the product of a relatively distinct constellation of background experiences. Prosocial offenders were usually involved in crimes of violence or naïve property offenses. Their behavior was the product of situational stress rather than long-term conditions of family instability or other kinds of disorganization. On the other hand, antisocial inmates were highly recidivistic, frequently involved in crime careers at an early age, and usually from urban, slum-area backgrounds. They were gang delinquents grown up. Pseudosocial inmates engaged in sophisticated and subtle property crimes involving manipulation of other persons rather than coercion and violence. They developed out of relatively stable and comfortable economic backgrounds. Asocial prisoners were involved in violent, bizarre forms of crime and closely resembled descriptions of sociopaths. In most cases, such individuals seemed to be the product of backgrounds of early and severe parental rejection.

In addition to differences in social background, Schrag reported other correlates of these role patterns. Social participation within the institution varied among these different types, as did the inmates' responses to such prison experiences as treatment programs or punishment. For example, prosocial inmates associated differentially with other prosocial prisoners and engaged in frequent contacts with staff members. Prosocial convicts also made considerable use of various treatment programs in the prison, in contrast to other types who shunned such activities.[41]

The important point regarding social types, the inmate code, and the functional and diffusionist arguments is that many prisoners engage in antiadministration, proinmate code activity, while others cooperate with the authorities, uphold conventional norms, and reject the inmate code. Antisocial inmates are usually from lower-class backgrounds with long prior records and previous institutional commitments, whereas "square Johns" often show no prior criminal pattern or history of previous incarceration. If the pains of imprisonment lead to emergence of a prisoner code and allegiance to the code, how are prosocial "square Johns" to be explained? Certainly the situational first-offender criminal would be the most traumatized by prison, whereas the recidivism-prone, crime-wise, working-class prisoner would be less likely to experience a prison sentence as severe social rejection. The diffusionist view is that allegiance to an inmate code is the continuation, inside the walls, of a pattern of rejection of the rejectors, which originated at a much earlier point in their careers. In many cases, the point of origin probably lies in early experiences with the police, juvenile courts, and so on. Elements of the inmate code represent institutional manifestations of hostility to the police and other attitudes widespread in lower-class society. The first offender experiences the pains of imprisonment and societal rejection, but his preprison experiences and involvement in prosocial reference groups outside the walls serve to insulate him from developing any serious loyalty to the inmate code. In addition, insofar as he is a novice in crime, the situational first offender is likely to be rebuffed in any attempt to play the role of real criminal among the antisocial inmates in the prison.

Another effort to unravel the threads of prison social life has been made by John Irwin and Donald Cressey, who suggested that some elements of institutional culture are indigenous to penal facilities, whereas other facets of prison life are examples of "latent culture" brought in from outside the walls.[42] They suggested that the penitentiary is made up of three subcultures: a "prison culture," a "criminal subculture," and a "legitimate" or conventional system. Some prisoners, oriented toward "making out" *inside* the institution, often have spent most of their lives in custodial facilities. They participate in conniving and other antiadministration interaction, endeavor to obtain "bonaroos" (special clothing) and other material goods, and are members of a "convict" subculture. "Thieves," are members of the "criminal" subculture oriented toward the society of lawbreakers *outside* the prison. They exhibit toughness, courage, and so on; these values are not indigeneous to the institution but are widespread in general society. "Thieves" remain aloof from participation in the conniving and machinations of convicts, for they prefer to "do their own time" and "go no rap" with other prisoners. The latter term prefers to deliberate noninvolvement with criminal peers in the situation. Members of the legitimate subculture, "do-rights", or "square Johns," remain outside the groups of antisocial prisoners.

This analysis by Irwin and Cressey, as well as much of the other material previously discussed, stressed the diffusionist view that the prison life that emerges among inmates is significantly influenced by characteristics these individuals import into the institution. There is evidence supporting this argument in observations on women's prisons.[43]

WOMEN'S PRISONS

Few sociological investigations of women's prisons have taken place.[44] One reason for the lack of attention to women's institutions is that, in many states, no prison for females exists autonomous from the state prison because of the small number of incarcerated females.[45]

Two studies of women's prisons have reported quite similar findings. One investigation concerned the Federal Reformatory at Alderson, West Virginia,[46] and the other had to do with the state prison for women at Frontera, California.[47]

Rose Giallombardo's research in the federal facility turned up evidence that role problems and administrative conflicts similar to those noted for men's institutions occur in women's prisons.[48] Many workers were hostile to the therapy program introduced a short time earlier. The correctional officers were held to ambiguous role requirements, for they were charged with the responsibility of carrying out counseling without the requisite knowledge for the task. Giallombardo indicated:

In the new program, with its emphasis on freedom and understanding, the correctional officers were to counsel and to use friendliness and firmness to secure compliance from the inmates. This meant that they had to accept some expressions of aggressive behavior which might be distasteful to them. Their confusion was further intensified because they were expected to control some forms of aggression by suppression just as they had in the earlier program.[49]

Although therapeutic notions had gained entry into the institution and created problems for many workers, the rehabilitation program had not yet become the primary institutional activity. Maintenance and custodial concerns continued to be central to organizational operations.[50]

Both studies of women's prisons provided information on the pains of inprisonment in such places.[51] Prisoners in both institutions felt loss of liberty and autonomy. Most Alderson inmates were from places quite distant from the prison, so they rarely received visitors. The Frontera women were particularly troubled by the forced separation from their families, in that 68 percent were mothers and 59 percent had minor children.[52] Inmates in both places felt markedly deprived of various material goods that make life tolerable in free society, but this feeling was particularly strong in the federal facility. In that reformatory, prisoners were dressed in shabby, ill-fitting prison clothing, including brown or white panties cut in the pattern of men's boxer shorts.[53] Although the women prisoners in these two places did not feel physically threatened by other inmates, they did find life in a one-sex society disagreeable. At Alderson, the inmates complained of the "bitchiness" of other prisoners, contending that most of them were untrustworthy, predatory, and prone to "penitentiary darby," that is, involvement in malicious gossip. The women in Frontera had relatively little allegiance to an inmate code of loyalty among prisoners.[54]

One other pain of imprisonment in these two women's prisons was deprivation of heterosexual relations. These psychological problems of imprisonment influenced the social life among female felons, but the last was particularly critical to an understanding of inmate life.

A large number of inmate social types were observed at Alderson, including "snitchs," "inmate cops," "squares," "jive bitches," and "homeys."[55] The first involved women who interfered with the lives of other prisoners, "squares" were prosocial inmates, "jive bitches" were troublemakers, and the last type consisted of women from the same geographical area. "Connects" were inmate connivers, "boosters" were women who stole food and other goods, and "pinners" were lookouts who assisted in illicit activities among other prisoners.

The most significant grouping of inmates in both prisons centered about homosexual activities. David Ward and Gene Kassebaum estimated that about half the prisoners had been involved in at least one homosexual episode during their stay at Frontera.[56] In both places, "lesbians" or "true" homosexuals were distinguished from "penitentiary turnouts" ("jailhouse turnouts" in Frontera).[57] True homosexuals had been involved in homosexual activity prior to incarceration. Both studies suggested that patterns of sexual activity made up a variety of social-sexual roles, but the basic division was between "butches" or "stud broads" and "femmes." "Butches" were masculine-appearing women who were the active or aggressive partners in sexual activity, whereas "femmes" played a passive role in sexual episodes. More true homosexuals took the "stud broad" role than did the "jailhouse turnouts," but some of the latter engaged in "butch" behavior.[58]

Both investigations indicated that prison homosexuality on the part of "jailhouse turnouts" was a transitory pattern of adjustment to prison life that was usually discontinued on release. The investigators contended that disruptions of conventional sex roles attendant on a prison commitment led most women to involvement in a sexual-affectional paired relationship that buffered them against the pains of prison life. However, the difficulties of prison life for women arise out of the sex-role definition of women in American society. As Giallombardo pointed out:

The deprivations of imprisonment may provide necessary conditions for the emergence of an inmate system, but our findings clearly indicate that the deprivations of imprisonment are in themselves not sufficient to account for the form that the inmate social structure assumes in the male and female prison communities. Rather, general features of American society with respect to the cultural definition and content of male and female roles are brought into the prison setting and function to determine the direction and focus of the inmate cultural systems.[59]

A third study of a women's prison was Esther Heffernan's investigation of the now-closed District of Columbia Reformatory at Occoquan, Virginia.[60] This prison held about 170 inmates, of whom about 100 were felony cases. According to Heffernan, the behavior of women prisoners fell into three patterns: those inmates who were involved in the "square" system, those who were in "the life," and those who engaged in the "cool" style. The square offenders had been convicted for homicides or kindred offenses and were similar to "square Johns" in male prisons. Inmates who were in "the life" had been sentenced for narcotics use, prostitution, shoplifting, petty theft, or some combination of these offenses. These prisoners were habitual, petty criminals. Finally, those who were engaged in the "cool" style were professional criminals. Heffernan's account of the social relations characteristic of these three inmate groups portrayed them as relatively similar to the criminal, convict, and legitimate subcultures of men's prisons, described by Irwin and Cressey. Additionally, Heffernan described pseudo-family and homosexual arrangements among prisoners in Occoquan which appeared to be closely parallel to the relational patterns noted in Alderson and Frontera.

PRISON SOCIAL CHANGE

From the early 1800s to the present, American prisons have gradually been modified from extremely repressive, punitive institutions to relatively humane places. Some prisons have adopted treatment programs as well. The changes wrought in prison life had drifted with the tide of broad trends in American life. These alterations have occurred over an extended time period, so reform leaders would be difficult to identify at any specific time. Much of the history of penal change has also been cyclical. Humanitarian developments have been repudiated only to be followed by further humanitarian modifications. This ebb and flow of changes in prison systems has followed closely the shifting fortunes of state political parties.

However, it is possible to single out some instances of deliberate or planned correctional social change, the most prominent case being in California.[61] Starting in the 1940s, an orderly and planned series of major improvements was made in the penal system in that state. These modifications produced a correctional system generally acknowledged to be the most progressive, treatment-oriented one in the United States.

Planned correctional social change, insofar as it has occurred at all, has taken place unobtrusively. In the past three decades, public attention has focused on prison riots and disturbances, which were particularly prominent in the early 1950s. These cases of prisoner insurgency have been viewed as attempts by the captives to obtain penal reforms. Although disturbances have not always produced modifications in correctional practices, they have had that result in at least some instances.

The wave of prison riots in this country began in 1952, with major uprisings in the Southern Michigan Prison at Jackson and the New Jersey State Prison at Trenton,[62] followed by riots in Idaho, Illinois, Kentucky, Louisiana, Massachusetts, New Mexico, North Carolina, Utah, Ohio, California, Oregon, and Washington, among other states.

A kind of *morphology of prison riots* was common to these incidents—most of them followed the same general pattern. Prison revolts were preceded by extended periods of uneasiness and tension, often described by prisoners and employees in such expressions as "The joint is 'hot'; it's going to 'blow up.'" Some event, such as a rumor that the guards had beaten an inmate, sparked these tensions, which in turn touched off widespread destruction of property, seizure of hostages, and occasionally assaults on staff members and convicts. After some days of internal disorder in the prison, inmate leaders made demands for correctional reforms, including better food, improved medical care, segregation of sex offenders, and modifications in sentencing and parole practices. The offenders who stepped forward to act as leaders and spokesmen were frequently from the "outlaw" group of violent and asocial persons, and the "right guys" remained in the background.[63] Moreover, many of the prisoners' grievances appeared to be invented after the riot rather than before it.[64] Negotiations between convicts and state officials usually resulted in promises of improvements in the penal program, at which point the inmates returned to their cells and the riot ended. On some occasions, the state eventually prosecuted the leaders, and the correctional authorities repudiated their agreements.

What was responsible for the wave of rioting in prisons in the early 1950s? The American Prison Association analyzed these disturbances, alleging that they were due to such evils as inadequate financial support for prison programs, inadequate and untrained staffs, widespread idleness, a shortage of well-trained leadership, overcrowding of prisoners in institutions of excessive size, and poor sentencing and parole practices.[65] These factors closely paralleled the inmates' grievances. Certain prison uprisings, particularly those in the southern United States, did seem to fit this explanation. For example, a series of protest actions occurred at the Lousiana prison at Angola in 1951, culminating in the slashing of heel tendons by several dozen prisoners. A subsequent inquiry into conditions in that institution turned up evidence of severe abuses against inmates which closely fitted the aforementioned list. The public outcry following these disclosures resulted in construction of a new prison in that state.[66]

A number of authorities have criticized this intolerable-conditions argument as an explanation of all riots. Ohlin noted that conditions were generally worse in many states where riots had not taken place, whereas the prisons that had suffered disturbances had begun to move in the direction of improved penal practices.[67]

The alternative view of the 1950s prison riots was a disequilibrium one, in which disturbances were said to stem from disruptions in the stability of inmate–administration relations in institutions. Maurice Floch and Frank Hartung offered this explanation for collective riots, which they distinguished from uprisings due to brutal conditions.[68] They asserted that protests and incidents grew out of the nature of the maximum-security prison, with its overcrowding and other features along with the aggregation of the heterogeneous mixture of prisoners, and from the destruction of the semiofficial pattern of informal inmate self-government that occurred when a new reform administration took over. When reform came to the "con-run" institution, authorities endeavored to "tighten up" the organization by removing prisoners from positions of power and influence. These moves overlooked the fact that the inmate leaders had been a stabilizing force in the prison, enforcing order among other prisoners in exchange for privileges from the administrators. As a result of their fall from power, the leaders turned their attention to subversive ends. They stirred up dissatisfaction among other convicts, which smoldered until finally triggered by some dramatic incident. These leaders then emerged during and after the riot as the champions of mistreated prisoners, so they appeared to be revolutionaries striving for a better way of life. But the leaders were really seeking a return to the older ways of life, rather than penological reforms.

Ohlin offered some similar hypotheses regarding prison unrest, but he also contended that these disturbances were most common in penitentiaries where reform efforts were only embryonic.[69] Prisons where progressive aims had been translated into programs of education and therapy experienced fewer incidents than places where tightening of security and removal of inmate leaders from influential positions represented the major reforms achieved. Ohlin also maintained that disturbances were fairly common in institutions characterized by decentralization of authority, for in these institutions, cooperation between administrative units in the prison had broken down. These conditions produced disruptions in the established expectation system which controlled relations between staff and inmates. Channels for airing grievances were closed off, leading to increased disciplinary incidents. Efforts on the part of the authorities to repress such incidents by increasing controls over prisoners then led to heightened tension among staff and inmates. The end product of this circular build-up of tension was often a prison riot. Such events seemed to have touched off an insurrection in the Oahu Prison.[70]

Prison uprisings continued in the 1960s, but less frequently than in the previous decade. In the early 1970s, however, prison riots, disturbances, and turmoil sprang up again. During 1970 and 1971, dramatic prison incidents occurred in New York jails, Stateville-Joliet Prison in Illinois, and several other places. One well-publicized case of prison violence involved an alleged escape attempt in San Quentin Prison, California, by George Jackson, a black prisoner and one of the "Soledad Brothers" charged with murdering a guard in another California prison. However, the most violent instances of prison disorder took place in 1971 at Attica State Prison in New York, where 43 inmates and hostages were killed during police efforts to regain control of the institution following a prisoner strike and revolt,[71] and in the New Mexico State Prison in February 1980, where 35 inmates were killed by other prisoners in a 36-hour rampage.

What are the causes behind these recent instances of prison disorder? Can we expect more of these outbreaks in the decades ahead?

To begin with, these new episodes are not the same as the wave of prison riots that swept the United States in the 1950s. John Pallas and Bob Barber offered a persuasive analysis of the changes in prison disturbances and turmoil since the 1950s.[72] Their thesis was that prison disorders mirror and reflect the social changes and conflicts in the general society. They contended that prison episodes fall into three historical patterns: the riots of the 1950s centering on intolerable living conditions; conflicts surrounding the recruiting activities of Black Muslims in prison in the 1960s; and revolutionary upheavals in the late 1960s and early 1970s.

Pallas and Barber were somewhat off the mark in characterizing the riots of the 1950's as "spontaneous uprisings against intolerable living conditions."[73] Many of those disturbances occurred in prisons where improvements in living conditions had begun to take place. However, they were correct in describing these riots as unplanned and uncoordinated, led by white inmates, and concerned principally with gaining improvements and changes in internal conditions of prisons. They were also accurate in portraying these riots as consistent with liberal reform movements, in which the inmates were challenging the *abuse* of power by prison officials rather than the basic legitimacy of the social order. Pallas and Barber noted that the civil-rights movement of the 1950s and prison disturbances were both expressions of the same liberal, reform impulse, in which the participants assumed that the legitimate system would respond to their appeals. They argued that:

The tenor of the demands and political thrust of these riots and strikes was consistent with that of the general forms of challenge to American society which occurred in the 1950s and early 1960s. Likewise, the officials of the state used essentially the same means of containing and suppressing prison revolts as they did for the larger Civil Rights movements.[74]

In the 1960s, prison problems became centered largely upon the activities of Black Muslims behind walls. The Black Muslim movement emphasized the creation of a separate black nation in this country and was buttressed ideologically by separatist religious beliefs. The Black Muslims saw prisons as a source of new recruits and went about proselytizing there, as well as advancing demands for the right to hold religious meetings in prison, to purchase the Koran, and to have Muslim visitors from outside. All of this was viewed as extremely threatening by prison administrators, for the Muslim movement stressed inmate solidarity and undermined traditional control techniques employed by the keepers, in which prisoners were urged to "do your own time." The administrative response to the Muslim movement was to try to break up the organization through transferring leaders from one prison to another, to place Muslims in isolation, to harass them in other ways, and to disseminate a misleading description of them as violent "crazies" to the general public. Although the Muslim movement in prisons declined in the 1960s, it did leave its mark upon many penitentiaries in the form of heightened inmate awareness of the importance of prisoner organization.

According to Pallas and Barber, increasing numbers of inmates in the late 1960s and early 1970s came to entertain revolutionary sentiments, in which they asserted that meaningful reforms in the American system are impossible. Convict intellectuals presented forceful and articulate versions of the theme that American society is racist, with racism being an ideology employed by the ruling class to divide and oppress underdogs. Further, blacks are virtually compelled to respond to the strains of American life by engaging in criminality; the urban police are embarked on policies of genocide, as witnessed by armed attacks on Muslims and Black Panthers; the criminal-justice machinery is grossly discriminatory and unfair in its handling of black offenders; and blacks are incarcerated in prisons as political prisoners, held captive by their oppressors not for being lawbreakers, but for being black.[75] Additionally, many black prisoners in California and elsewhere began to claim that parole policies and the indeterminate sentence were used as instruments to hold them in prison for excessive lengths of time. Pallas and Barber argued that this growing militancy and racial unity among prisoners must be viewed in the light of the broader trends in American society, in which increased numbers of citizens everywhere came to question the legitimacy of the political order and the morality of the political-economic system.

The movement toward a radical ideology among prisoners, along with racial conciliation and increased organization among prisoners, called forth administrative responses designed to disrupt these developments. Prisoner leaders were transferred to other institutions, correctional workers attempted to foment racial incidents and conflicts among inmates, and other tactics of that kind were employed. All of these measures were related to awareness on the part of the prison administrators that the movement of inmates toward greater solidarity and increased militancy posed a much more profound challenge to the maintenance of penal institutions than did the riots of the 1950s. Speaking of the demands of the Attica prisoners, Pallas and Barber pointed out that:

Negotiations around the demands soon came down to the issues of amnesty and the resignation of the warden. These demands focus the political nature of the revolt. If granted, they would have established the precedent that prisoners have a right to participation (if not control) in the process of choosing who rules them, and that they have a right to rebel without fear of punishment. Both prisoners and officials knew that these issues were at stake and that the implications went far beyond Attica.[76]

According to Pallas and Barber, such contentions about racial injustice have become widespread among black prisoners. If true, this fact poses great problems for prison administrators. Prison order rests on the consent of the governed, just as it does in the outside society. Historically, most inmates served their time passively, without attempting to escape from the penitentiary. Most of them agreed in principle with the view that criminality is "bad" and that criminals deserve to be punished; hence, they believed that they should suffer stoically while in prison.

Now, however, American prisons are being used to "warehouse" growing proportions of black offenders. About 85 percent of the Attica prisoners were blacks or Puerto Ricans; while California institutions are heavily populated with black inmates, as are many other state prisons. The stage now seems set for more violence and disorder in prisons, centering around the grievances of blacks and the efforts of the authorities to maintain order.

There is no question that racial cleavages among prisoners have become central in the day-to-day activities of American prisons. For example, James Jacobs has reported on the emerging prison culture in Stateville Penitentiary in Illinois.[77] He indicated that most of the inmate behavior in that prison now centers about street-gang ties and activities brought into the prison from Chicago slums. Three large black gangs dominate the prison group, along with one Latin gang. Jacobs maintained that these gangs have established solidarity within the walls, posing major threats to the prison administration.

On this same point, Leo Carroll has provided a detailed account of life in a prison in the eastern United States, where conflicts between guards, black prisoners, and other convicts loomed large.[78] Similarly, Theodore Davidson has produced a detailed report on the growing militancy among Chicano prisoners in California institutions.[79] Finally, John Irwin has argued that a situation of *ordered segmentation* has grown up in American prisons; an uneasy peace has been struck between white prisoners—many of whom belong to neo-Nazi groups—black convicts, and Chicano prisoners.[80] However, according to Irwin that peace is fragile, interrupted from time to time by interracial outbursts and other breaches and continually threatening to come apart entirely. In Irwin's view, far-reaching changes in the structure of prisons are required if the potential for massive and widespread turmoil is to be avoided in the years ahead.

training school social organization

This book is primarily concerned with adult lawbreaking. For this reason, our commentary on the social workings of correctional agencies centers on adult institutions and organizations. However, we should mention the social structure of training schools, if only because many adult lawbreakers begin their institutional experiences in these places. We shall briefly sketch the traditional form of social organization in state training schools.[81]

Most state training schools have smaller populations than do prisons. In many states, the boys' schools handle a few hundred boys or less, and the girls' schools are even smaller. The administrative staffs of juvenile facilities are also usually smaller than in adult institutions. Training schools normally show a physical structure quite different from that of prisons and reformatories. They are usually unwalled institutions made up of a number of dormitory buildings euphemistically called cottages. Groups of several dozen or more juveniles, or wards as they are often called, inhabit these dormitories, and much of the social life of the institution goes on within these structures. Training schools also include an assortment of other buildings. Juvenile institutions more closely resemble residential academies or schools than prisons, although many of them appear more rundown and deteriorated. Escapes, or rambles, as they are often called, are frequent from training schools, partly because of the ease of escape from such places.

Although at one time, the superintendent of the training school was often the product of the political spoils system, such as as an ex–county sheriff or similar person to whom a political debt was owed, training-school administrators are now most often social workers or other trained child-welfare workers. The rest of the staff is usually divided into two general groups. The first includes work supervisors, teachers, and sometimes social caseworkers, who deal with the inmates during the day. Also included in this group are the kitchen personnel, clerks, and similar workers. The second group of employees is made up of cottage supervisors or cottage parents who manage the wards at night and during those times of the day when the inmates are not involved in some formal program. The cottage workers have the greatest amount of interaction with the wards and the most difficult experiences with them. They are responsible for prevention of runaways and other disturbances of the institutional routine.

Training schools in the past have usually operated a minimal-treatment program. Most inmates have been placed in a school program or some kind of vocational or other work experience. Occasionally, they have received individual therapy from a social caseworker, but this has been a relatively infrequent event.

The overriding concern in juvenile institutions has revolved around prevention of escapes and large-scale disturbances. Staff members regard runaway behavior as serious, for even though most fugitives are quickly apprehended and normally do not create any incidents in the surrounding community, the community reacts negatively to escapes. Consequently, a juvenile institution that acquires a reputation for frequent escapes usually receives a good deal of hostile, highly vocal criticism. In turn, employees define runaways as extremely serious.

Juvenile facilities share certain structural shortcomings with their adult counterparts. In both places, uncooperative individuals must be restrained in some way, but a number of potentially effective control techniques are not available to the authorities. Although the training-school personnel can keep their charges in line by occasional beatings and other kinds of physical coercion, they must be circumspect in the use of force. Word may get out to the community if beatings become a regular part of the school's disciplinary program. Cottage parents who use physical aggression as a main technique of control are also in danger of reprisals. The worker may be physically able to intimidate any individual ward but may not emerge the victor in a fight with a half-dozen or more inmates. This is not to say that corporal punishment is never used in juvenile institutions. Coercion beyond the official rules is employed, but it tends to be relatively mild and is used to supplement other control devices.[82]

The tactic commonly employed to deal with uncooperative boys parallels the arrangements in adult prisons. The institutional staff enters into tacit bargains with certain inmate leaders in the dormitories. These older, physically mature, sophisticated juveniles coerce other, weaker youths into docile behavior. In addition to keeping order and preventing rambles, these toughs often use their power to force other inmates into homosexual practices, obtain money from them, and victimize them in other ways.

As these remarks suggest, a prisoner social system exists in juvenile institutions. An inmate code characterizes most training schools. This is a juvenile parallel of that found in prisons, centering around the same antisocial norms as the adult counterpart, and antiadministration and antitreatment in content. It prescribes "playing it cool" as model behavior for wards, who are expected to do their time as pleasantly as possible without entering into meaningful relationships with staff members.

Inmate role types also exist in juvenile institutions. These types tend to be relatively simple, based on differences in physical prowess and criminal sophistication. Two major role types emerge in training schools: "toughs" or "dukes" and "punks." The former have been in the institution for a relatively long time, have extensive delinquency records, and are physically superior to other inmates. The second group is made up of boys who are physically immature and are often less-sophisticated offenders.

Gordon Barker and W. Thomas Adams described the social structure of a boys' training school in Colorado.[83] They reported rigid interactional and communication barriers between inmates and staff members, along with a pervasive spirit of authoritarianism in which the offenders did not identify with the values and goals of the staff. The authors also noted the existence of a status order among the inmates, structured around displays of physical toughness and victimization of peers. They speculated that this system was the result, at least in part, of widespread insecurities among delinquent boys regarding masculinity.

Howard Polsky has provided a detailed description of the social structure among inmates through a study of the boys residing in a cottage within a private correctional institution.[84] He reported a diamond-shaped status system in which a few boys had high or low rank among their peers, with the largest group falling into a middle-range. Polsky argued that this system was independent of the particular youths who filled it in any particular period, for it persisted relatively unaltered over time, even though cottage residents entered and left the system. Departure of a leader, for example, produced competition, conflict, and jockeying among inmate aspirants for the position, followed by reestablishment of equilibrium. According to Polsky, the status types in the cottage included "toughs" and "con artists" at the apex of the order, "quiet types" in the middle, and "bushboys" and "scapegoats" at the bottom of the system. The latter were subjected to unrelenting physical and psychological attacks by those higher in the order. Probably the most significant of Polsky's observations was that the institutional staff abetted the inmate system:

Thus, the theme of aggression with all its authoritarian overtones is structurally configurated in the cottage. Under its roof the cottage parents join the older boys in scapegoating the defenseless low-status boys—the sneaks, punks, and the sick. The latter "deserve" the beatings because of *their* provocativeness and "unfitness." The unwritten compact of cottage parents and toughs makes it unbearable for the "deviants" because they are blamed for everything.[85]

An examination of a training school in California indicated that even in that state, where treatment goals had been emphasized in state institutions for several decades, training schools placed primary emphasis on regimentation of youngsters in the interests of controlling them.[86] Therapeutic activities were subordinated to custodial ends. As a part of this study, Fisher observed the social structure among inmates.[87] He found that both the wards and supervisors ranked and victimized certain boys; moreover, the low-ranked boys in the eyes of the officials were also the low-status inmates in the ward hierarchy. Staff workers often interpreted disruptive behavior by low-status boys as evidence of psychological maladjustment rather than as flowing out of the social structure and interactional patterns among offenders. Low-ranked, victimized inmates were defined as "mess-ups," implying that they willfully engaged in disapproved behavior out of psychological tensions. Instead of attempting to undermine the inmate system, authorities reacted to boys in its terms, so institutional rewards were differentially accorded to boys with high status among their peers.

Some attention has been given to problems that develop in training schools when rehabilitation is introduced as a major goal. George Weber pointed to a number of areas in which conflict arises between professional and nonprofessional personnel.[88] One major problem he identified, also noted by Ohlin,[89] centered around the role difficulties that develop for cottage workers. Their authority position is often reduced or undermined with the introduction of treatment goals. They are likely to feel that their prestige has been lowered with the entry of professional personnel into the program. Role redefinition also occurs, and the cottage worker is expected to run a quiet and well-disciplined dormitory and to contribute to therapy. But because the cottage worker is not given clear instructions on how to accomplish these ends, he or she experiences much the same role dilemma noted for prison guards. Weber and others have suggested that a number of negative consequences develop when rehabilitation is introduced into previously custodial institutions.[90] Staff cooperation is reduced and replaced by conflicts between professional and custodial personnel, defensive reactions develop among cottage workers, and other difficulties arise. Inmates manipulate these conflicts to their own ends by playing competing groups against each other.

The most ambitious research on training schools to date compared six juvenile institutions.[91] These training schools varied in size, several being small institutions and others having inmate populations of well over a hundred boys. Some were private institutions; others were state schools. These facilities also varied in terms of program, ranging from institutions favoring obedience and strict conformity to treatment-oriented, milieu operations. The researchers supposed that variations in size might influence the social structure of the institutions, as would the different auspices under which these places operated. State schools should be under greater pressure from the general public. Finally, the investigators hypothesized that the treatment-oriented schools would be more conflict ridden than the strictly custodial places.

The findings supported most of these contentions. Among other things, the institutions varied in terms of the leadership styles of their executives. The staff members exhibited different perspectives on delinquents, the workers in custodial schools viewing boys as more willful than did employees in treatment institutions. Marked variations in the level of staff conflict existed from school to school, with greatest staff conflict in the rehabilitation-oriented institution in which a high degree of staff *interdependence* existed. That is, in the milieu treatment school, staff members representing different segments of the school program were in frequent communication with one another and were involved in much joint decision making.

probation and parole organization

Parole and probation agencies can justifiably be discussed together, even though they differ in some important ways. The major dissimilarity is that parole involves more serious, criminalistic offenders than does probation; the former handles persons processed through institutions, whereas the latter does not. Penal commitment represents the harshest penalty outside of capital punishment, so it tends to be used with the most difficult and intractable law violators, whereas probation is commonly reserved for persons lacking in criminalistic orientation. Even though parole and probation differ in this respect, both deal with offenders in the community and have organizational features in common.[92]

THE STRUCTURE OF PAROLE AND PROBATION

Parole programs in the United States were developed out of changes in criminal laws, which established indeterminate sentences for offenses within the limits of minimum and maximum statutory penalties. Although criminal codes have varied from one state to another, they have the same general structure. They have allowed for alternative penalties for convicted offenders, so that individuals can be placed on probation or committed to institutions. The maximum periods of incarceration have been specified in statutes, but prisoners have been released at various points prior to expiration of their maximum sentences. Paroling authorities have determined when inmates should be released from the penitentiary, to serve the remainder of their sentence under supervision in the community. However, as noted in Chapter 20, the discretionary powers of parole boards have been curbed or eliminated entirely in a number of states in recent years.

The paroling function has been structured in different ways in the various states. In some, *ex officio* boards made up of government officials have served as the paroling agency; individuals who have major governmental responsibilities elsewhere made release decisions on the side. The more common arrangement, particularly in the larger states, has involved an agency called the Board of Prison Terms and Paroles, Adult Authority, or some similar label. In some states operating under this pattern, the board has had two functions. It has acted as a quasi-judicial board, setting release dates for prisoners, and it also has administered the parole supervision organization.

In theory, decisions to release or not to release an inmate are based on such criteria as his or her behavioral change and favorable prognosis for success on parole.[93] In fact, the decisions have not been made in this fashion. For one thing, parole boards have been limited in the degree to which they could determine release dates by statutory minimum sentences, which require that persons convicted of certain crimes spend no less than some specific period in prison. Boards have frequently set minimum sentences near the beginning of the prisoner's stay in the institution, so they have been determined before a sufficient period of time has elapsed to estimate the person's response to therapy. In addition, parole boards have often been made up of members ill-trained to estimate the rehabilitative prospects for inmates. Indeed, the knowledge on which such decisions must be based is not at hand, so no paroling authority, however assembled, could make accurate judgments. Finally, boards have had to contend with factors other than the needs of the prisoners. In particular, they have been sensitive to public pressure, which has demanded that certain offenders be kept in prison for long periods of time. The decision to release a sex offender who will return to a small community from which he was convicted has frequently been more contingent on the level of community tolerance than on the offender's needs. The prisoner has been paroled if the board has judged such a decision will provoke a slight amount of "heat."[94]

For such reasons, parole decisions have been intuitive and based on a mixture of considerations: the type of offense, the offender's needs, and the general public's reactions. They have not been as individualized as parole theory would lead one to suppose. Instead, paroling agencies have developed informal precedents, and prison terms handed out for various offenses have averaged out to a fairly specific figure, such as three years, with little variation around that average.

Variations also exist in the structure of probation services. In some states, probation is attached to parole services, and probation is sometimes shunted aside because of the heavy work demands of parole. As a consequence, few offenders are placed on probation. In a number of states, such as California, probation is county operated, with individual probation services in the various counties. Each of these is autonomous and managed by county supervisors or commissioners.

One variation between probation and parole, in addition to patterns of placement within governmental systems, has to do with involvement of probation officers in selection of offenders to be placed under their control. Parole agents receive their clients from the institution, without any option to select or reject in terms of some set of eligibility criteria. But in both adult- and juvenile-probation services, the workers play a major role in the selection process. In juvenile operations, they compile information about youths undergoing court hearings. This collection of data, called the social investigation, is a principal source of evidence on which adjudication and disposition of cases is based. Similarly, in adult probation, convicted offenders are referred to probation agents for presentence investigation. The presentence report prepared by the officer becomes, in turn, a major consideration in disposition of the case. This report normally includes the officer's sentence recommendations, which the judge customarily follows in his or her decision.

ON BEING A PROBATION OR PAROLE OFFICER

Much of the literature on probation and parole implies that workers in these operations are highly trained professionals who administer intensive and valuable therapy to correctional clients. But several time-and-motion studies of probation officers have shown that they are harried by clerical tasks and huge caseloads, which have prevented them from rendering much professional help. For example, Lewis Diana investigated the kind and amount of assistance given to juvenile probationers in the Allegheny County (Pittsburgh), Pennsylvania, juvenile court.[95] He found that the average number of contacts between probationers and probation officers was about five within a 16-month period. Moreover, these meetings were for the most part quite superficial, only about 14 percent of the wards receiving any sort of casework treatment. Diana also found an inverse relationship between frequency of probation contacts and later criminality: offenders who had the least interaction with officers were less recidivistic than boys who had received more frequent assistance. These findings probably indicate that many juveniles placed on probation are not seriously delinquent, need little supervision from probation agents, and turn out to be "self-correctors." Accordingly, the officer tends to work with more serious offenders, ignoring the low-risk cases in his or her caseload.

Another study by Ralph England turned up similar findings. He reported that a group of adult probationers had a recidivism rate of only 17.7 percent but that this low rate was unrelated to treatment.[96] Most offenders received only routine surveillance and superficial help from the probation officers. England attributed the generally high success rates to the fact that most of the persons placed on probation were essentially prosocial and not in need of intensive resocialization.

Gertrude Hengerer's study of several juvenile-probation departments suggested that most of what goes on in probation is something other than treatment.[97] The workers examined in that study spent most of their time writing reports, driving from one place to another, and similar operations. They had large caseloads and little time to provide therapy to their wards.

Lloyd Ohlin, Herman Piven, and Donnell Pappenfort[98] have examined the role dilemmas of probation and parole officers. These authors indicated that probation and parole services have traditionally been assigned a number of not entirely compatible functions. Probationers and parolees were supposed to be supervised, assisted, and treated, but at the same time officers have been expected to collect fines, protect society in various ways, and perform other tasks having little to do with helping offenders. These agents have had to contend with persistent suspicion and hostility directed at them and their charges by the police and other groups in the community. Because of this antagonism, agencies often have come to be as much concerned about shielding the organization from criticism as they have been about protecting clients. Thus, officers have spent some of their time giving speeches to citizen groups in which they have argued for the merits of their services, agitated for greater financial support, and defended their agencies against charges of softness, coddling, and so on.

Several other consequences have followed from the uneasy status of probation and parole in the public eye. First, the public relations orientations that have developed have frequently meant that occupational mobility in these agencies has been more dependent on public relations talents than on technical competency. Second, two main kinds of workers, punitive and protective agents, have developed. The former have carried guns, regarded themselves as law-enforcement officers rather than rehabilitative agents, have not been trained in social work, and have defined their responsibilities as principally those of protecting society. They attempted to coerce their charges into appropriate behavior, and punished noncooperative cases by revoking their parole or probation status. The protective agents have sometimes had training in corrections and regard themselves as responsible for treatment, but have vacillated back and forth from protecting the public to helping clients.

Additional problems have cropped up in parole-probation agencies following the recruitment of large numbers of welfare workers into these systems. The officer who has been trained in social work and entered these fields expecting to protect clients and to treat them as in other welfare settings has come prepared to apply generic principles of social work in this setting. However, the officer soon has found that such training has not covered the difficulties he or she has encountered with treatment in corrections. Social-work education has not been much concerned with the special problems of dealing with captive, hostile persons. These subjects differ markedly from the conventional volunteer clients who seek help. The probation-parole social worker also has found that his or her training has not equipped the officer to deal with authority problems and has not prepared him or her to function within the special structure of corrections as both a representative of the punitive social-control system and as a helper. In addition, the agent has discovered that he or she lacks the knowledge to understand different client types or deal effectively with them.

The agent trained in social work has also discovered discrepancies between probation-parole settings and traditional images of the welfare agency. For one, the rules of client supervision, such as those forbidding probationers or parolees from using alcohol, differentiated correctional settings from noncorrectional ones. Other rules have restrained the kinds of decisions workers can make, and the needs of the client have frequently been subordinated to these demands. These agency rules and procedures have forced the agent to act in ways that depart from the conventional picture of his or her professional role.

According to Ohlin and his associates, the outcomes of inadequate educational preparation and the discrepancies encountered between correctional and conventional welfare agencies have been varied in form. Some workers have solved these dilemmas by getting out of correctional or social work entirely. Others have stayed in probation-parole, but with different styles of work adjustment. Those in relatively autonomous systems have deported themselves in a fashion close enough to their notion of the welfare-worker role to preserve a social-worker identity. In most restrictive settings, the agent has tried to evade demands regarded as unprofessional, such as collection of fines, and thereby retain a social-worker role conception. Some workers have become reconciled to the pecularities of restrictive correctional settings and have redefined their role as a special type of social worker. They have gradually lost interest in, or contact with, the general social-welfare literature and social-worker organizations.

Existing studies lend support to this picture of the probation–parole agent and his or her occupational problems. In one of these, nearly 400 probation officers from various parts of the United States filled out a questionnaire on tasks they felt to be appropriate or inappropriate.[99] Most qualified as professionals, in that 88 percent possessed bachelor's degrees, while 16 percent had completed master's degrees. Most of these officers agreed that referral services and counseling activities were appropriate probation responsibilities. But these same agents demonstrated a good deal of disagreement and confusion about various law-enforcement and supervisory actions. Some felt that officers should assist sheriffs in arresting an absconding probationer; some thought they should make surprise home visits or contact the probationer's employer to check on work behavior, or engage in other surveillance activities. Some officers felt obliged to order probationers to pay their bills, refrain from hanging around poolrooms, or even go to church or marry their pregnant girl friends. At the same time, many of the workers regarded these as inappropriate responsibilities. Nonetheless, supervisory actions in which an offender is coerced into a line of conduct are often required of probation officers, even though they may regard these actions as alien to their helping role.[100]

summary

This chapter has given the reader a glimpse of the workings of the criminal-justice machinery as it goes about processing offenders. Much of the chapter focused upon the world of imprisonment, for relatively few citizens have an accurate understanding of what is involved in being "in the joint." Instead, most of us gain our erroneous impressions from the mass media, such that we come to view prisons either as institutions populated by happy-go-lucky convicts enjoying the jocular give and take with kindly guards or as extraordinarily grim places managed by assorted sadists and moronic figures. The truth of prison life is somewhere in between these extremes. Penal institutions are characterized by omnipresent danger from other prisoners, monotonous living, and a variety of other pains of imprisonment. Those who administer these organizations are relatively ordinary men and women who have been called upon to preside over structures with massive contradictions and problems built into them, making them exceedingly difficult to manage under the best of circumstances.

In the last analysis, maintenance of prison order rests upon at least grudging cooperation of the prisoners. Wardens and guards do not have total power which they can exercise over convicts by brutalizing them; instead, internal order is managed through some blend of manipulation of prisoners, corruption of authority, and tacit cooperation by inmates. The recent gestures on the part of incarcerated offenders, in the direction of challenges to the legitimacy of the prison, do not augur well for peaceful relations between prisoners and keepers in coming decades.

This chapter also indicated that contrary to public beliefs that view prisons as alien structures outside the mainstream of American society, life in these places is influenced and colored by the host society. The functions and tasks of penal institutions are determined by forces in the free world. Then, too, the adaptive responses inmates make to the pains and stresses of institutional living arise out of their preprison experiences.

This chapter raised serious doubts about the prospects for prisoner rehabilitation carried on inside prison walls. Treatment runs counter to the maintenance of security over inmates, such that the rehabilitative goal often receives short shrift. In addition, the penal institution is an unlikely place in which to endeavor to provide offenders with the skills and resources through which they might refrain from criminality. Many criminologists have come to the opinion that prisons can probably never be more than relatively benign social warehouses in which to incapacitate lawbreakers for relatively short periods of time.

This chapter contained similarly pessimistic observations about the prospects for rehabilitation in juvenile training schools or in probation and parole settings. This commentary has suggested a fairly dismal outlook for therapeutic endeavors in corrections, for agencies that press in this direction become beset by all kinds of difficulties. However, rehabilitation and the results of treatment to date have only been addressed tangentially to this point. In the next chapter, we shall consider a more direct and detailed study of people-changing activities that might be directed at lawbreakers.

notes

[1]For an anthology containing a generous sample of this material, see Lawrence E. Hazelrigg, ed., *Prison Within Society* (Garden City, N.Y.: Doubleday, 1968).

[2]For a discussion of the characteristics of "total institutions," see Erving Goffman, "On the Characteristics of Total Institutions: The Inmate World," and "On the Characteristics of Total Institutions: Staff-Inmate Relations," in *The Prison*, Donald R. Cressey, ed. (New York: Holt, Rinehart & Winston, 1961), pp. 15–106.

[3]For data on citizen views of corrections, see Joint Commission on Correctional Manpower and Training, *The Public Looks at Crime and Corrections* (Washington, D.C.: Joint Commission on Correctional Manpower and Training, 1968); Don C. Gibbons, "Who Knows What About Correction?" *Crime and Delinquency*, 9 (April 1963), 137–44.

[4]Richard D. Schwartz and Jerome H. Skolnick, "Two Studies of Legal Stigma," in *The Other Side*, Howard S. Becker, ed. (New York: Free Press, 1964), pp. 103–17.

[5]One of the best reports on the flavor of prison life is contained in a prison novel. See Malcolm Braly, *On the Yard* (Boston: Little, Brown, 1967). See also John Irwin, *The Felon* (Englewood Cliffs, N.J.: Prentice-Hall, Inc., 1970), for a lucid sociological analysis of prison life as experienced by the felon. Both Braly and Irwin are exfelons, which probably accounts in part for the persuasiveness of their accounts. For a detailed research report on the problems encountered by prisoners in their attempts to minimize the difficulties of "doing time" in prison, see Hans Toch, *Living in Prison* (New York: Free Press, 1977).

[6]For an analysis of variations in state political structure within which prisons operate, see Richard A. Berk and Peter H. Rossi, *Prison Reform and State Elites* (Cambridge, Mass.: Ballinger, 1977).

[7]Terrence and Pauline Morris, *Pentonville* (London: Routledge & Kegan Paul, 1963); Hugh J. Klare, *Anatomy of Prison* (New York: Penguin, 1962); Thomas Mathiesen, *The Defenses of the Weak—A Sociological Study of a Norwegian Correctional Institution* (London: Tavistock Publications, 1965).

[8]Donald R. Cressey and Witold Krassowski, "Inmate Organization and Anomie in American Prisons and Soviet Labor Camps," *Social Problems*, 5 (Winter 1957–58), 217–30.

[9]Gibbons, "Who Knows What About Correction?"

[10]For a discussion of correctional interest groups, see Donald R. Cressey, "Prison Organizations," in *Handbook of Organizations*, James G. March, ed. (Chicago: Rand McNally, 1965), pp. 1030–32.

[11]For an analysis of prisons as autocracies, see Norman A. Polansky, "The Prison as an Autocracy," *Journal of Criminal Law and Criminology*, 33 (May–June 1942), 16–22.

[12]Cressey, "Prison Organizations," pp. 1023–70.

[13]Ibid., p. 1024.

[14]Ibid., pp. 1026–30.

[15]Ibid., pp. 1029–30.

[16]For one incisive commentary on the limits of "total power" in prisons, see Gresham M. Sykes, *The Society of Captives* (Princeton, N.J.: Princeton University Press, 1958), pp. 40–62; Sykes, "The Corruption of Authority and Rehabilitation," *Social Forces*, 34 (March 1956), 257–62; Clarence Schrag, "Some Foundations for a Theory of Correction," in Cressey, *The Prison*, pp. 338–39.

[17]Richard A. Cloward, "Social Control in the Prison," in Cloward, Donald R. Cressey, George H. Grosser, Richard McCleery, Lloyd E. Ohlin, Gresham M. Sykes, and Sheldon L. Messinger, *Theoretical Studies in Social Organization of the Prison* (New York: Social Science Research Council, 1960), pp. 20–48.

[18]Sykes, *The Society of Captives*, pp. 52–62.

[19]Richard Korn and Lloyd W. McCorkle, "Resocialization Within Walls," *Annals of the American Academy of Political and Social Science*, 293 (May 1954), 91.

[20]Cressey, "Contradictory Directives in Complex Organizations: The Case of the Prison," *Administrative Science Quarterly*, 4 (June 1959), pp. 1–19.

[21]Schrag, "Some Foundations for a Theory of Correction," pp. 336–38.

[22]Organizational differences between punitive-oriented and treatment-oriented prisons are discussed at length in Cressey, "Prison Organizations," pp. 1033–54; see also Johan Galtung, "The Social Functions of a Prison," *Social Problems*, 6 (Fall 1958), 127–40; Galtung, "Prison: The Organization of Dilemma," in Cressey, *The Prison*, p. 107–45.

[23]Alfred C. Schnur, "The New Penology: Fact or Fiction?" *Journal of Criminal Law, Criminology and Police Science*, 49 (November–December 1958), 331–34; for some evidence suggesting that the "New Penology" has not been fully implemented in England either, see Terrence Morris, "In the Nick," and Alan Little, "The Borstal Boys," *The Twentieth Century* (London), 170 (Winter 1962), 22–34, 35–42.

[24]Schnur, "The New Penology: Fact or Fiction?" 332.

[25]Elmer H. Johnson, "The Present Level of Social Work in Prisons," *Crime and Delinquency*, 9 (July 1963), pp. 290–96.

[26]Donald R. Cressey, "Limitations on Organization of Treatment in the Modern Prison," in Cloward, et. al., *Theoretical Studies in Social Organization of the Prison*, pp. 78–110.

[27]Harvey Powelson and Reinhard Bendix, "Psychiatry in Prison," *Psychiatry*, 14 (February 1951), pp. 73–86.

[28]Korn and McCorkle, "Resocialization Within Walls," pp. 88–89.

[29]Cressey, "Prison Organizations," p. 1058.

[30]Public views on prison life tend to be stereotypical in the extreme. One common notion about prisons is that homosexuality is the major fact of prisoner life, with homosexual conduct being rampant in men's prisons. In fact, other prisoner values and interests tend to be more important than this one. For an analysis of prison homosexuality, see John H. Gagnon and William Simon, "The Social Meaning of Prison Homosexuality," *Federal Probation*, 32 (March 1968), pp. 23–29. Also see Daniel Lockwood, *Prison Sexual Violence* (New York: Elsevier/North-Holland, 1980).

[31]Gresham M. Sykes and Sheldon L. Messinger, "The Inmate Social System," in Cloward et al., *Theoretical Studies in Social Organization of the Prison*, pp. 5–19.

[32]Ibid.

[33]Ibid., p. 16.

[34]Korn and McCorkle, "Resocialization Within Walls," pp. 88–89.

[35]Cloward, "Social Control in the Prison."

[36]For evidence in support of the functionalist thesis, see Charles R. Tittle and Drollene P. Tittle, "Social Organization of Prisoners: An Empirical Test," *Social Forces*, 43 (December 1964), 216–21. This investigation was conducted in the U.S. Public Health Service Hospital, which held drug addicts. See also Ronald L. Akers, Norman S. Hayner, and Werner Gruninger, "Homosexual and Drug Behavior in Prison: A Test of the Functional and Importation Models of the Inmate System," *Social Problems*, 21, (3: 1974), 410–22. In a study of seven prisons which varied in terms of program stress upon custody or treatment goals, these authors found that homosexuality and drug use were most frequently reported by inmates in the custodially oriented prisons. The only social background variable that was related to drug use or homosexuality was age, with the youngest inmates reporting most contact with homosexual patterns. Younger inmates in custodial prisons were most likely to be engaged in homosexual activities.

[37]Stanton Wheeler, "Role Conflict in Correctional Communities," in Cressey, *The Prison*, pp. 229–59.

[38]Wheeler, "The Comparative Analysis of Prison Social Structure," paper read at meetings of the American Sociological Association, September 1962.

[39]See also Mathieson, *The Defenses of the Weak*. Mathieson reported that in the Norwegian prison he studied, censoriousness on the part of inmates replaced peer-group solidarity. Censoriousness referred to complaining behavior, apparently not unlike the phenomenon of "bitching" in the military services in the United States.

[40]Schrag, "Some Foundations for a Theory of Correction," pp. 309–57; Schrag, "A Preliminary Criminal Typology," *Pacific Sociological Review*, 4 (Spring 1961), 11–16; Sykes, *The Society of Captives*, pp. 84–108. Regarding offender role types in prison, the reader might do well to reexamine the detailed commentary in Chapter 10 which indicated that, although inmate social types do exist in prison, many convicts are not easily classified in any of these role-type categories, while other prisoners do not fit within the social role scheme at all. On this point, see Robert G. Leger, "Research Findings and Theory as a Function of Operationalization of Variables: A Comparison of Four Techniques for the Construct, 'Inmate Type,' " *Sociology and Social Research*, 63 (January 1979), 346–65.

[41]One of the studies Schrag drew on in this discussion of role types was by Garabedian in a maximum-security prison in a Western state. See Peter G. Garabedian, "Social Roles in a Correctional Community," *Journal of Criminal Law, Criminology and Police Science*, 55 (September 1964), 338–47; Garabedian, "Social Roles and Processes of Socialization in the Prison Community," *Social Problems*, 11 (Fall 1963), 139–52.

[42]John Irwin and Donald R. Cressey, "Thieves, Convicts and the Inmate Culture," *Social Problems*, 10 (Fall 1962), 142–55; see also Julian Roebuck, "A Critique of 'Thieves, Convicts and the Inmate Culture," *Social Problems*, 11 (Fall 1963), 193–200.

[43]Another investigation which lent support to the importational or diffusion argument is Charles W. Thomas and Samuel C. Foster, "Prisonization in the Inmate Contraculture," *Social Problems*, 20 (Fall 1972), 229–39.

[44]One early study is Ida Harper, "The Role of the 'Fringer' in a State Prison for Women," *Social Forces*, 31 (October 1952), 53–60.

[45]One useful source of descriptive material on women's prisons is Kathryn W. Burkhart, *Women in Prison* (New York: Doubleday, 1973). Ms. Burkhart, a journalist, visited 21 state prisons for women and interviewed about 900 prisoners. Her report documented the pains of imprisonment experienced by the inmates, particularly those centering around deprivation of contact with spouses, children, and other kin.

[46]Rose Giallombardo, *Society of Women* (New York: John Wiley, 1966).

[47]David A. Ward and Gene G. Kassebaum, *Women's Prison* (Chicago: Aldine, 1965).

[48]Giallombardo, *Society of Women*, pp. 39–56.

[49]Ibid., pp. 47–48.

[50]Ibid., pp. 57–91.

[51]Ibid., pp. 92–104; Ward and Kassebaum, *Women's Prison*, pp. 1–29.

[52]Ward and Kassebaum, *Women's Prison*, pp. 14–16.

[53]Giallombardo, *Society of Women*, pp. 95–98.

[54]Ward and Kassebaum, *Women's Prison*, pp. 30–55.

[55]Giallombardo, *Society of Women*, pp. 105–32; "snitchs" were also common in Frontera. See Ward and Kassebaum, *Women's Prison*, pp. 32–37.

[56]Ward and Kassebaum, *Women's Prison*, p. 92.

[57]Ibid., pp. 95–98; Giallombardo, *Society of Women*, pp. 105–32.

[58]Ward and Kassebaum, *Women's Prison*, p. 104.

[59]Giallombardo, *Society of Women*, p. 187.

[60]Esther Heffernan, *Making it in Prison: The Square, the Cool, and the Life* (New York: John Wiley, 1972).

[61]For a history of correctional change in California, see Joseph W. Eaton, *Stone Walls Do Not a Prison Make* (Springfield, Ill.: Chas C Thomas, 1962).

[62]For details of the Michigan riot, see John Bartlow Martin, *Break Down the Walls* (New York: Ballantine, 1954); for a popular treatment of the New Jersey disturbances, see Peg McGraw and Walter McGraw, *Assignment: Prison Riots* (New York: Holt, Rinehart & Winston, 1954).

[63]Maurice Floch and Frank E. Hartung, "A Social-Psychological Analysis of Prison Riots: An Hypothesis," *Journal of Criminal Law, Criminology and Police Science*, 47 (May–June 1956), 55.

[64]Lloyd E. Ohlin, *Sociology and the Field of Corrections* (New York: Russell Sage Foundation, 1956), pp. 23–24.

[65]Committee on Riots, *Prison Riots and Disturbances* (New York: American Prison Association, 1953).

[66]Reed Cozart, "What Has Happened to 'America's Worst Prison'?" *Federal Probation*, 19 (December 1955), 32–38.

[67]Ohlin, *Sociology and the Field of Corrections*, p. 23.

[68]Floch and Hartung, "A Social-Psychological Analysis of Prison Riots," pp. 51–57.

[69]Ohlin, *Sociology and the Field of Corrections*, p. 24.

[70]Richard McCleery, "The Governmental Process and Informal Social Control," in Cressey, *The Prison*, pp. 149–98; see also Sykes, *The Society of Captives*, pp. 109–29.

[71]The events surrounding the negotiations between prisoners and state officials, the attempts to retake control of Attica, and other features of the Attica riot were reported in detail by journalist Tom Wicker, who was one of the outside negotiators who endeavored to bring about a nonviolent solution to the disturbance. See Tom Wicker, *A Time to Die* (New York: Quadrangle/New York Times Book Co., 1975).

[72]John Pallas and Bob Barber, "From Riot to Revolution," in *Criminal Justice in America*, Richard

Quinney, ed. (Boston: Little, Brown, 1974), pp. 340–55; see also Frank Browning, "Organizing Behind Bars," *Ramparts*, February 1972, pp. 40–45.

[73]Pallas and Barber, "From Riot to Revolution," pp. 342–43.

[74]Ibid., p. 343.

[75]Eldridge Cleaver, *Soul on Ice* (New York: McGraw-Hill, 1968); George Jackson, *Soledad Brother* (New York: Bantam, 1970).

[76]Pallas and Barber, "From Riot to Revolution," p. 352. Also see Wicker, *A Time to Die*.

[77]James B. Jacobs, "Street Gangs Behind Bars," *Social Problems*, 21, (3: 1974), 395–409. Also see Jacobs, "Stratification and Conflict Among Prison Inmates," *Journal of Criminal Law and Criminology*, 66 (December 1975), 476–82.

[78]Leo Carroll, *Hacks, Blacks, and Cons—Race Relations in a Maximum Security Prison* (Lexington, Mass.: Lexington Books, 1974).

[79]Theodore R. Davidson, *Chicano Prisoners: The Key to San Quentin* (New York: Holt, Rinehart & Winston, 1974).

[80]John Irwin, *Prisons in Turmoil* (Boston: Little, Brown, 1980).

[81]Training schools for girls and detention facilities have gone relatively unstudied. For one study of a private training school for girls, see Raymond J. Adamek and Edward Z. Dager, "Social Structure, Identification and Change in a Treatment-Oriented Institution," *American Sociological Review*, 33 (December 1968), 931–44. See also Kristine Olson Rogers, " 'For Her Own Protection . . .': Conditions of Incarceration for Female Juvenile Offenders in the State of Connecticut," *Law and Society Review*, 7 (Winter 1972), 223–46.

[82]Sethard Fisher, "Social Organization in a Correctional Residence," *Pacific Sociological Review*, 4 (Fall 1961), 88.

[83]Gordon H. Barker and W. Thomas Adams, "The Social Structure of a Correctional Institution," *Journal of Criminal Law, Criminology and Police Science*, 49 (January–February 1959), 417–22.

[84]Howard W. Polsky, "Changing Delinquent Subcultures: A Social-Psychological Approach," *Social Work*, 4 (October 1959), 3–15; Polsky, *Cottage Six* (New York: Russell Sage Foundation, 1962).

[85]Polsky, *Cottage Six*, p. 133.

[86]Carl F. Jesness, *The Fricot Ranch Study* (Sacramento: State of California, Department of the Youth Authority, 1965), pp. 8–17. A generous portion of this report appears in Don C. Gibbons, *Delinquent Behavior*, 3rd ed. (Englewood Cliffs, N.J.: Prentice-Hall, Inc., 1981, pp. 304–13; Peter G. Garabedian and Gibbons, eds., *Becoming Delinquent* (Chicago: Aldine, 1970), pp. 226–37.

[87]Fisher, "Social Organization in a Correctional Residence," pp. 87–93.

[88]George H. Weber, "Conflicts Between Professional and Non-Professional Personnel in Institutional Delinquency Treatment," *Journal of Criminal Law, Criminology and Police Science*, 48 (May–June 1957), 26–43; see also Weber, "Emotional and Defensive Reactions of Cottage Parents," in Cressey, *The Prison*, pp. 189–228.

[89]Lloyd E. Ohlin, "The Reduction of Role-Conflict in Institutional Staff," *Children*, 5 (March–April 1958), 65–69.

[90]Weber, "Emotional and Defensive Reactions of Cottage Parents"; Mayer N. Zald, "Power Balance and Staff Conflict in Correctional Institutions," *Administrative Science Quarterly*, 7 (June 1962), 22–49.

[91]David Street, Robert D. Vinter, and Charles Perrow, *Organization for Treatment* (New York: Free Press, 1966).

[92]For a study on juvenile parole, see William R. Arnold, *Juveniles on Parole* (New York: Random House, 1970).

[93]One study of parole board decision making is Don M. Gottfredson and Kelley B. Ballard, Jr., "Differences in Decisions Associated with Decision Makers," *Journal of Research in Crime and Delinquency* 3 (July 1966), 112–19.

[94]For a harsh view of the California paroling agency, the Adult Authority, see Assembly Committee on Criminal Procedure, *Deterrent Effects of Criminal Sanctions* (Sacramento: California State Assembly, 1968). That study indicated that the paroling agency had been increasing the length of prison sentences over the years without any effect on recidivism rates. Parole decisions were made in terms of intuitive hunches. On occasion, allegations of crimes the parole candidate may have been involved

in were considered, as well as other questionable kinds of information, in the decision to parole or not to parole the person. For another discussion of the injustices of parole, see Jessica Mitford, *Kind and Usual Punishment* (New York: Knopf, 1973).

[95]Lewis Diana, "Is Casework in Probation Necessary?" *Focus*, 34 (January 1955), 1–8.

[96]Ralph W. England, Jr., "What is Responsible for Satisfactory Probation and Postprobation Outcome?", *Journal of Criminal Law, Criminology and Police Science*, 47 (March–April 1957), 667–76; see also England, "A Study of Postprobation Recidivism Among 500 Federal Offenders," *Federal Probation*, 19 (September 1955), 10–16. See also a more recent report that presented similar findings regarding federal probation work: Albert Wahl and Daniel Glaser, "Pilot Time Study of the Federal Probation Officer's Job," *Federal Probation*, 27 (September 1963), 20–25.

[97]Gertrude M. Hengerer, "Organizing Probation Services," *National Probation and Parole Association Yearbook*, 1953, pp. 45–59.

[98]Lloyd E. Ohlin, Herman Piven, and Donnell M. Pappenfort, "Major Dilemmas of the Social Worker in Probation and Parole," *NPPA Journal*, 2 (July 1956), 211–25.

[99]Dale E. Van Laningham, Merlin Taber, and Rita Dimants, "How Adult Probation Officers View Their Job Responsibilities," *Crime and Delinquency*, 12 (April 1966), 97–108.

[100]Seymour Z. Gross, "Biographical Characteristics of Juvenile Probation Officers," *Crime and Delinquency*, 12 (April 1966), 109–16.

treatment programs and results

The rehabilitative philosophy regarding handling of lawbreakers is a relatively recent development. Throughout most of history, offenders have been made to suffer so that society might extract retribution from them or potential law violators might be deterred. The notion that punishment might also prevent recurrence of deviant behavior by the person being punished, because of his or her desire to avoid pain, has also been around for some time. But the view that the correctional processes should strive to reform, resocialize, modify, or remake the criminal so that he or she will refrain from further lawbreaking is of recent origin.

As this chapter unfolds, we shall see that there has been considerable criminological enthusiasm for correctional treatment in the past. Sociologists have often been in the forefront of the rehabilitation movement, agitating for more professional treatment workers, expansion of parole and other services, and improvements in the treatment theory on which correctional ventures are based.[1] However, in the past two decades, a good deal of pessimism has developed regarding the prospects for correctional treatment. Disillusionment with the treatment goal has been expressed by a large number of observers of the contemporary scene, including many criminologists who had earlier been supporters of rehabilitation efforts.[2] This chapter takes up the rise of the rehabilitation movement and also examines a small sampling of treatment programs. The latter portion of the chapter turns to the research evaluations of treatment ventures which have led many to question whether correctional treatment might be an illusory goal.

The therapeutic perspective is a late development, and a number of indications of its immaturity can be found. For one thing, the treatment point of view has often been little more than a broad orientation to offenders, stressing that something positive should be done to miscreants. Correctional therapy programs have often been based on vague assumptions about the causes of lawbreaking. Finally, rehabilitation has been talked about a good deal more than it has been implemented in practice.

The contemporary student of criminology might look back on earlier practices as barbaric or senseless. But, at any point in time, the things done to offenders made sense because they were buttressed by images of man that rationalized the practices. Also, they arose out of broad social and economic conditions prevailing in earlier times. When life was mean and harsh, early death from natural causes a common occurrence, and life expectancy short, societies had little hesitation in putting deviants to death. The classical views of punishment in the late 1700s were predicated on a conception of men as willful hedonists; hence, criminals were seen as individuals who had made deliberate decisions to be bad. Such persons could be deflected from criminality by judicious application of some kind of pain. The classical picture of the willful law violator has lingered on and lies behind endeavors to correct criminality by processing offenders through regimented programs involving work training or allied activities. Defenders of these programs maintain that when criminals are forced to conform to rules or are compelled to work regularly, they learn good habits, and these experiences will carry over to their lives outside penal institutions.

Aside from the neoclassical ideas about criminality, two markedly different images of lawbreakers have served as the underpinnings of modern-day treatment proposals and practices. One has held that offenders are psychologically "sick" persons who need the services of a psychiatrist, whereas the other has argued that law violators are no less normal than citizens generally. A number of tactics have been contrived around these two perspectives, some of which are noted below.[3]

the development of treatment

In Chapter 20, we saw that humanitarian gestures made toward offenders during the past century have modified the conditions of punishment. Prisoners are now incarcerated under more relaxed and humane conditions than was once the case. In most modern prisons, inmates are well fed, their medical needs are served, they are allowed visitors, receive an unlimited number of letters, and so on. Youths in training schools are usually protected from severe abuse by staff members or other wards, go into the community to engage in athletic events, are allowed home visits from the school, and so on. These developments, and many others as well, are examples of humanitarian reforms. Offenders are still dealt with in overly harsh ways, so humanitarianism could go still further. However, humanitarianism has often been confused with treatment, rather than being defended on its own terms. Not infrequently, citizens and correctional workers have assumed that enlightened processing of lawbreakers must have therapeutic consequences. But the hope that good food and other forms of humane handling will cause deviants to mend their ways is naïve, for these actions are not directed at the factors that have drawn individuals into criminality. Treatment has to do with specific efforts designed to modify social and psychological characteristics of persons, rather than with humane handling of them.

The confusion about what is and is not treatment has extended to other programs, in addition to those developed to relieve the grimness of correctional experiences. Most modern institutions provide a variety of school activities and vocational-training operations for inmates. These are sometimes pointed to as treatment in contrast to other operations identified as custodial. However, these services, which have been created to implement the growing emphasis on re-habilitation as a correctional goal, represent adjuncts to treatment.

Endeavors such as education or vocational training are different from humanitarian acts, but they are not treatment programs. For example, the rationale behind inmate classification programs has involved more than simply an interest in reducing the severity of serving time. The justification has been that thorough investigation of the inmate's background is a prerequisite for effective treatment and custodial decisions. As a consequence, well-developed classification programs have collected a mass of information about newly arrived prisoners, which has been presented in a document called the Admission Summary. This record has been the basis for various institutional decisions made about these persons. Classification activities have produced diagnoses and recommendations about what should be done with the prisoner, whereas implementation of the therapy recommendations constitutes treatment.

Other programs, such as vocational or educational training, religious activities, recreational participation, or prerelease planning, are adjuncts to treatment because none deals directly with some therapy problem of the prisoner. Vocational experiences may improve the rehabilitation potential of the offender subjected to them, but they are likely to have some impact only when accompanied by some kind of direct resocialization work.

What kinds of treatment theories have grown up in corrections?[4] Rehabilitative theory has been heavily larded with psychogenic contentions picturing the offender as psychologically disturbed or "sick." In this view, the criminal is a parallel of the neurotic or psychotic individual, except his or her personality pathology is expressed in an illegal fashion. This perspective has seen offenders as analogous to machines wired in a defective manner. The therapeutic corollary has been that lawbreakers need to be rewired by a psychiatrist or some other psychiatric technician who can delve inside their psyches.

This approach to law violators, which divides the world into "bad guys" who are "sick," and "good guys" (correctional workers and other citizens) who are emotionally healthy, has been dominant in the rehabilitative theories with which correctional agents have operated.[5] The view remains vigorously alive, even though evidence examined in Chapter 8 and succeeding chapters indicated that the large majority of law-violating deviants are relatively well socialized and normal.

Rehabilitation theories based upon sociological evidence on the causation of delinquency and crime have been much less frequently encountered. The treatment implications of sociological theories and findings have usually remained implicit and have rarely turned up in correctional practice.[6] Also, the rehabilitation literature on which correctional practice has been based has frequently failed to acknowledge variations among types of lawbreakers. Offenders constitute a mixed collection of individuals. Although many criminals and delinquents are normal, they are not all alike in attitudinal or self-image terms. Different tactics of therapy may be in order for these various patterns. Some persons fit the psychiatric picture of the abnormal offender, so psychotherapeutic activities may be called for in these cases. In summary, much of the treatment theory now in existence is based on overly simplified assumptions about law violators.

the nature of treatment[7]

Treatment consists of some explicit activity designed to alter or remove conditions operating on offenders which are responsible for their behavior. What is the nature of these conditions to which therapy is directed? Criminal and delinquent activities are often a function of *definitions of the situation*, which refer to individuals' self-concepts and attitudes toward criminality and other matters, that is, the belief systems and interpretive frameworks by which they make sense out of sensory perceptions and direct their behavior. If offenders are to be directed toward law-abiding behavior, certain aspects of their self-images, attitudes, and beliefs must be modified.

Consider an example or two of offender perceptions. Donald Cressey's research on financial-trust violation indicated that individuals engage in embezzlement when they define themselves as having nonshareable problems and *after* they have managed to construct a set of justificatory arguments or rationalizations for trust violation.[8] Similarly, many property offenders are involved in criminality, at least in part, because they think of themselves as having little opportunity to earn money in conventional ways and because they regard themselves as victims of a corrupt society.

Some further observations can be made about the definitions of the situation expressed by offenders. Some criminalistic definitions are common within certain social-class groups, others are restricted to the members of such smaller collectivities as peer groups, and some are novel views held by isolated individuals. Definitions of the situation also vary along a time dimension; some are acquired early in life from socialization experiences and remain with the individual throughout his or her lifetime, whereas others are of extremely short duration. Some interpretive beliefs arise out of specific interactional events and have an extremely short life span.

Some definitions of the situation are more difficult to modify than others. In extreme examples, certain definitions are so central a part of the personality of the person as to be unchangeable. The beliefs of overly aggressive offenders that other persons are basically mean and untrustworthy are extremely difficult to alter. At the other extreme, some definitions are of recent origin, not firmly held, and as a consequence rather easily modified. "One-time losers" are individuals with temporary definitions favorable to criminality.

Offenders are characterized by various patterns of definitions rather than a uniform set of attitudes and beliefs, which separates them from noncriminals or nondelinquents. Because definitions vary, as do the experiences producing them, no single kind of therapy activity can be expected to accomplish the rehabilitative task.

There is an important caveat in order regarding this discussion of interpretive frameworks on the part of offenders. Situational pressures and contingencies are also important factors in many instances of criminality. We ought not to suppose that all lawbreakers are carriers of firmly held criminalistic definitions of the situation which need modification through treatment. Additionally, situational contingencies and stresses may have much to do with whether offenders who have undergone some program of therapy manage to refrain from further lawbreaking. Thus, the treatment task ought not to be viewed as centering solely upon efforts to change some attitudinal characteristics of offenders. On this point, Glaser has noted that successful postrelease adjustment on the part of prisoners is heavily influenced by the extent to which they manage to secure relatively rewarding jobs and establish meaningful postprison social relationships.[9]

variations in treatment tactics[10]

The various treatment procedures for dealing with law violators can be lumped into two major categories: psychotherapies and environmental therapies. The first group of strategies proceed from psychogenic assumptions that because offenders are emotionally troubled to some degree, their psyches must be altered. In general, psychotherapeutic approaches center about the individual, with less concern for his or her group affiliations or social circumstances.

Environmental-treatment activities operate from a different perspective. They assume that lawbreakers are relatively normal individuals who exhibit antisocial conduct definitions related to their interactional experiences and social relations. Consequently, environmental tactics are directed at groups of deviants rather than at individuals.

These major categories of treatment involve a number of subtypes. Let us take a glance at some of these variations.

PSYCHOTHERAPIES

Depth psychotherapy has often been advocated as an appropriate strategy for treatment of criminals. Law violators have often been regarded as persons whose behavior is a function of cognitive elements buried deep within the "inner layers of personality." These deep-seated tensions are dimly perceived by the individual, or may be unperceived by him or her but can be made apparent by a skilled psychiatrist. Once the individual becomes aware of the bases of his or her behavior, the way is opened for behavioral change. This intensive individual therapy has widely been urged for mentally disordered individuals. It has been portrayed in countless movies and television plays.

Group psychotherapy is closely parallel to individual depth psychotherapy. The major difference between the two is that in group psychotherapy, a therapist endeavors to bring about insight and catharsis on the part of a number of patients who meet together, whereas depth psychotherapy goes on in pairs made up of a patient and a therapist. Although individual and group psychotherapy have frequently been suggested as ideal tactics for use in correctional treatment, they are rarely used in fact, primarily because of the great shortage of trained psychotherapists in correction.

Client-centered therapy is a tactic used quite regularly with offenders.[11] This kind of counseling is predicated on a picture of clients as persons who have problems of social adjustment. However, they are seen as normal individuals who can be aided toward working out their social difficulties in a relatively short time without intensive, probing psychotherapy. As a general set of procedures of dealing with persons in trouble, probation officers and other correctional employees use client-centered therapy with their clients. This kind of treatment is similar to reality therapy, which psychiatrist William Glasser advocated.[12] These procedures have been used in correctional practice when probation officers have tried to get check forgers to adopt nondeviant solutions to their problems, or attempted to persuade delinquents to adopt new perspectives on work, the police, and so on.

Behavior modification is another intervention tactic that ought to be mentioned. Behavior modification and token-economy programs do not fit exactly into either the psychotherapy or environmental-program categories, although they are closer to the former than the latter. Behavior modification represents an attempt to rid offenders of deviant and undesirable behavior patterns through the use of social-learning principles.[13] The emphasis in behavior modification is upon encouragement of positive *behaviors* and extinction of undesirable ones, with less concern for attitude change and other social–psychological goals. Behavior-modification strategems center about providing rewards to offenders for exhibiting desirable behaviors, along with withholding rewards for disapproved activities. Token-economy programs are a specific form of behavior modification, in which institutions are structured around tangible reward systems that are employed in order to induce conformity and positive behavior.

ENVIRONMENTAL PROGRAMS: GROUP THERAPY

One prominent trend in the fields of mental health and corrections since World War II has been the rise of group forms of treatment. The suggestion has been voiced from a number of quarters that group treatment offers more promise in rehabilitation of deviants than does individual therapy. Much of the commentary on group endeavors has implied that this is a single form of therapy, even though it has variously been labeled group psychotherapy, group therapy, guided-group interaction, or group counseling.

Two distinct kinds of therapy involve the "group" label. *The first, group psychotherapy, is essentially individual therapy in a group setting, whereas the second is "group" therapy in the true sense and is designed to change groups, not individuals.* The aims of these two programs differ, the role of the therapist differs, the group activities differ, and still other contrasts can be identified.[14]

Cressey has identified the principles underlying group therapy:

1. If criminals are to be changed, they must be assimilated into groups which emphasize values conducive to law-abiding behavior and, concurrently, alienated from groups emphasizing values conducive to criminality. . . .

2. The more relevant the common purpose of the group to the reformation of criminals, the greater will be its influence on the criminal members' attitudes and values. . . .

3. The more cohesive the group, the greater the members' readiness to influence others and the more relevant the problem of conformity to group norms. . . .

4. Both reformers and those to be reformed must achieve status within the group by exhibition of "pro-reform" or anticriminal values and behavior patterns. . . .

5. The most effective mechanism for exerting group pressure on members will be found in groups so organized that criminals are induced to join with noncriminals for the purposes of changing other criminals. . . .

6. When an entire group is the target of change, as in a prison or among delinquent gangs, strong pressure for change can be achieved by convincing the members of the need for change, thus making the group itself the source of pressure for change.[15]

The principles of group therapy have been involved in a number of correctional programs. For example, Alcoholics Anonymous is a voluntary program devoted to rehabilitation of alcoholics, which operates in ways parallel to those outlined by Cressey. Alcoholic individuals join groups of exalcoholics as a way of refraining from drinking. These groups strive to get new members to take on new norms against drinking, both by exerting group pressure and by rewarding them with group approval. As he or she continues in this interaction, the exalcoholic is eventually expected to lend his or her support to new recruits in their efforts to stay sober. As he or she succeeds in these efforts, his or her self-image as a reformed drunk is strengthened and reinforced.

Group-therapy programs have also been tried in a number of institutional settings. In some of these institutions, the professional-treatment agents have conducted group-treatment sessions with inmates, oriented along group-relations lines. A variant of group treatment called group counseling has been suggested as a useful way of mobilizing resources of the institution in the rehabilitative task by using lay persons, such as guards, as therapists.[16]

The task of treating prisoners effectively through group methods within the confines of a custodial institution is fraught with problems. Inmates often put on a sham performance by pretending that they have acquired new perspectives and attitudes from the group interaction. Many employees have shown antagonistic feelings toward these rehabilitative ventures, for they have feared that the freedom allowed prisoners might undermine the security of the institution. Finally, the correctional administrator has had a difficult time finding meaningful rewards to bestow on individuals who seem to have truly changed in their orientations toward criminality. The warden cannot release inmates when he regards their prognosis as favorable to law-abiding adjustment; the prisoners must wait for the decisions of a parole board. For such reasons, group-treatment programs subjected to research evaluation have not achieved dramatic results.

ENVIRONMENTAL PROGRAMS: MILIEU MANAGEMENT

Milieu management is a form of treatment not too different from group therapy; indeed, the latter is often included as part of the former. Milieu programs usually have gone on in institutions where efforts have been made to coordinate all parts of the operation to the goal of rehabilitation. The developers of milieu programs have tried to construct therapeutic communities that provide opportunities for inmates to experiment with law-abiding social living. Similarly, milieu-treatment institutions have tried to ensure that all events which occur to the prisoners will be therapeutic. In a conventional prison, such an operation might take the form of group therapy augmented with regularized work experiences. The guards would also be dissuaded from expressing views that psychiatrists are "head shrinkers" or "bug doctors" and the caseworkers immature "college boys," and from other acts that might have a negative effect on treatment.

The Highfields Project in New Jersey was a clear example of milieu management.[17] The delinquent subjects were placed in a small institution of two dozen boys, where they were subjected to a treatment diet of guided group interaction in the evenings. In addition, these youths were given opportunities to work for pay during the daytime at a nearby mental institution. They were not compelled to work and could be fired it they did not perform adequately. The developers of this system regarded delinquent boys as normal youngsters with antisocial attitudes and delinquent self-images. The boys tended to belittle the importance of conventional work careers and regarded other conforming behavior patterns scornfully. The entire program of guided group interaction, along with the related work experiences and peer interaction, was directed toward pressuring the delinquents toward new perspectives and improved work skills.

Milieu therapy can also be seen in an experimental treatment program at Fricot Ranch, a training school for boys in California.[18] One of the cottages in that institution was singled out as the target of an intensive milieu effort. A series of coordinated experiences running throughout the day was established to obtain behavioral change on the part of the wards.[19]

ENVIRONMENTAL PROGRAMS: ENVIRONMENTAL CHANGE[20]

This last form of treatment attempts to change various features of natural social environments, such as urban community areas. Environmental modification has been designed to bring about improvements in community social organization, so it is not as individual-centered as other therapeutic endeavors. Environmental operations have frequently been pointed at social agencies and noncriminals as well as offenders. Yet their ultimate aim has been to modify the antisocial sentiments of citizens and thereby reduce rates of criminality.

Most environmental change efforts have been oriented toward prevention— geared toward curtailing budding delinquent careers before they get under way. Rehabilitation of persons already known to be law violators has been a secondary goal of these efforts. Most cases of environmental change have had to do with delinquency rather than with adult criminality.

Consider some examples of environmental change. One of the earliest was the Chicago Area Project.[21] The goals and assumptions of that project, which operated in certain Chicago working-class, high-delinquency neighborhoods, were as follows:

The Chicago Area Project operates on the assumption that much of the delinquency in slum areas is to be attributed to lack of neighborhood cohesiveness and to the consequent lack of concern on the part of many residents about the welfare of children. The Project strives to counteract this situation through encouraging local self-help enterprises through which a sense of neighborliness and mutual responsibility will develop. It is expected that delinquency will decline as youngsters become better integrated into community life and thereby influenced by the values of conventional society rather than by those of the underworld.[22]

The Chicago Area Project operated on the theory that delinquency and criminality in working-class neighborhoods stemmed from the unavailability of conventional routes to American success goals and was thus a response to economic and social frustration. The area project also presumed that lower-income areas were to a degree disorganized, in that they were characterized by value conflicts and lack of social cohesion. Criminal persons existed side by side with law-abiding citizens, and many social ties united the deviants with the conformists. The area project attempted to bring about neighborhood cohesiveness through establishment of a neighborhood center, staffed principally by local leaders. Thus, the Chicago Area Project tried to develop an antidelinquency society in slum neighborhoods to reduce pressures toward delinquency and criminality.

The most ambitious program of environmental change has been the multimillion dollar Mobilization of Youth operation in a lower-east-side neighborhood in New York City.[23] The basis for the undertaking was Cloward and Ohlin's opportunity-structures theory.[24] They contended that working-class, subcultural delinquency is the product of disjunction between the goals of lower-class youths and their opportunities to achieve these goals through legitimate or conventional pursuits. Mobilization for Youth involved 30 separate programs in the four major areas of work, education, community, and group services. All these were pointed at the task of opening up or increasing the law-abiding opportunities for success and achievement in slum neighborhoods. For example, a Youth Service Corps provided employment for unemployed, out-of-school youths, and a Youth Jobs Center served as an employment office and tried to find permanent jobs for youngsters. Several devices were conjured up for improving school performance of the youths, while efforts were also made to strengthen the existing community social agencies.

The precise results of this program are unknown.[25] Moreover, given the many components included in this operation, it would be exceedingly difficult to untangle the specific contribution, if any, that each part made to an end result, such as reduced rates of deviant behavior. At least one critic of Mobilization for Youth suggested that such undertakings can produce only slight results unless major changes are made in the general employment structure of American society. In other words, these programs are involved in preparing persons for conventional jobs which are either relatively unrewarding or, in many cases, nonexistent.[26]

types of treatment and types of offenders

Most literature on treatment contains singular treatment prescriptions. Group therapy or some other form of handling has been recommended for all offenders as though they all exhibit much the same problem for rehabilitative action. However, what may be called for is "different strokes for different folks," that is, different types of law violators may require different kinds of attention.

According to the differential-treatment argument, the population of lawbreakers is made up of groups of individuals who differ in criminal activities and developmental backgrounds. Many criminal or delinquent persons are well socialized but have acquired subcultural standards that emphasize hostility toward the police or other antisocial perspectives. Others such as naïve check forgers or joyriders, are relatively stable and conventional and not members of deviant subcultures but have adopted illegal problem-solving techniques. Finally, several kinds of offenders, such as violent sex offenders or psychopathic assaultists, are relatively aberrant individuals. The different types require different kinds of treatment.[27]

The most ambitious attempt in the direction of differential treatment has been conducted in California, where the Community Treatment Project studied the use of community-based treatment as an alternative to incarceration of relatively serious delinquents in institutions.[28] The research subjects were sorted into nine diagnostic types, classified in terms of levels of interpersonal maturity. Interpersonal-maturity-levels theory was examined in Chapter 8. The youngsters were designated as asocial aggressives, asocial passives, immature conformists, cultural conformists, manipulators, acting-out neurotics, anxious neurotics, cultural identifiers, or as exhibiting situational-emotional reactions. Different techniques for therapeutic management of each of these nine patterns were employed.

What are the legal and ethical boundaries beyond which we should not go in efforts to punish and treat lawbreakers? Who deserves to be punished? How much punishment do they deserve?

Some years ago, a physician who served in an informal advisory role to former President Nixon proposed a program of massive preventive intervention in which six-year-olds would be subjected to psychiatric screening; those thought to be potential lawbreakers would be carted off for some kind of preventive therapy. The behavioral knowledge this proposal implied does not exist, however, so predelinquents cannot be picked out from among potential nondelinquents with any degree of accuracy.[29] But what if it did exist? What if social engineering were so well developed that potential deviants could be identified at any early age? Does it follow automatically that in a democratic society we are warranted in doing something to them to deflect them from deviance? Many persons would recoil from this proposal and would raise violent objections to it.

The proposal for prediction and treatment of potential delinquents at age six is an outrageous one, sufficiently so that nearly every rational person would reject it. However, most legal and ethical issues in correctional treatment are a good deal more subtle than this one and a good deal more difficult to address. These issues center on the following problems: the extent to which the penal sanction should be used at all, the limits to the degree of punishment to be dealt out to the lawbreaker, and the restrictions to be imposed on coercive application of treatment to offenders. Additionally, the question of due process for lawbreakers after they have been convicted of crimes is an important one, as is the matter of how far we should be permitted to go in using human subjects against their will in correctional experiments. Finally, some prickly problems develop around such things as electronic-surveillance procedures that might be used to gain therapeutic or deterrent effects.[30]

First, take the question of the limits of the penal sanction. To what kinds of misconduct should criminal penalties be applied? The superficial answer is that they should be handed out to individuals who engage in antisocial acts. But that answer will not do, for few people agree on what is or is not antisocial behavior. Is homosexuality carried on in private by two consenting adults antisocial? Is a poker game among friends, or an act of prostitution, a criminal, antisocial act?

Herbert Packer has provided a set of criteria for the imposition of the criminal sanction:

1. The conduct is prominent in most people's view of socially threatening behavior, and is not condoned by any significant segment of society.
2. Subjecting it to the criminal sanction is not inconsistent with the goals of punishment.
3. Suppressing it will not inhibit socially desirable conduct.
4. It may be dealt with through even-handed and nondiscriminatory enforcement.

5. Controlling it through the criminal process will not expose that process to severe qualitative or quantitative strains.

6. There are no reasonable alternatives to the criminal sanction for dealing with it.[31]

Let us assume that some agreement exists on the forms of misconduct that are dangerous and antisocial and therefore should be controlled by criminal legislation and punishment. At that point, we must face the question of how much punishment or suffering we may legitimately inflict on offenders. This question is *not* principally one of efficiency, that is, of how much punishment is required for specific deterrence. Instead, the initial and fundamental issue is one of *justice* and *humanity:* what degree of punishment does the offender *deserve?* For example, suppose hard evidence were available, showing that most conventional property offenders will refrain from further lawbreaking if they are made to undergo a prison experience of social isolation for five years, but they do not respond well to alternative forms of punishment. If so, should isolation be supported on pragmatic grounds that it "gets the job done"? Perhaps, but many people would contend that five years of social isolation goes beyond the limits of just punishment, that it subjects the offender to pain out of proportion to the gravity of his or her crime. That this question is an ethical rather than an empirical one in no way reduces the need of criminologists as well as citizens to consider it. Adopting a stance of ethical neutrality would put sociologists in the position of tacitly supporting the status quo and whatever ethical stance happens to be fashionable among the general public.

Unrestrained advocacy of questionable treatment measures has often cropped up in the writings of psychiatrists, as they have urged preventive detention of some lawbreakers, psychiatric therapy for others, early identification of potential offenders, and other, related tactics. Karl Menninger placed unwarranted faith in the effectiveness of psychiatric counseling, along with a willingness to intervene drastically in the lives of offenders under the guise of treatment and without much in the way of due-process safeguards.[32] Menninger's recommendations stand in marked contrast to the writings of Thomas Szasz, who has warned of the potential tyranny of psychiatrists as they go about depriving persons of their liberty, subjecting them to therapy, and tinkering with them in other ways in the name of mental-health treatment.[33]

Nicholas Kittrie is another critic who has warned of the excesses that are inherent in the spread of rehabilitation notions.[34] Kittrie directed attention to the process of divestment in the criminal law, in which various forms of conduct, including youth crime, drug addiction, alcoholism, and other activities have been shunted off to programs of civil commitment or other therapeutic programs and are no longer dealt with through traditional criminal sanctions. Kittrie indicated that these developments are all manifestations of the rise of what he called the "therapeutic state." This term was employed to designate that viewpoint which regards criminals and other deviants not as bad persons who need to be punished, but as "sick" individuals who are unable to control their behavior and who need the benevolent intervention of psychiatrists and other therapists who will cure them. But in all of this, those persons who have been brought under control of the therapeutic state have often suffered markedly more than if they had simply been dealt with as bad persons. They have not received effective therapy, and they have often been deprived of elementary protections of due process, in the name of treatment.

More specifically, David Sternberg has offered a number of cautionary observations about prison group psychotherapy, contending that the involuntary assignment of prisoners to this kind of treatment raises some prickly ethical questions about justice and equitable punishment.[35] Along the same line, one might question whether the scientific trade-off in the way of increased knowledge is sufficient justification for programs such as the Community Treatment Project in California, in which delinquent wards were randomly assigned to a state training school or were released outright to parole in the community from a reception center, after having spent only a few days in incarceration.[36] One cannot argue that these are nearly equivalent forms of response to offenders; those who end up at the training school stand to experience considerably more unpleasantness than those who are randomly selected for parole. In summary, we need to ask how far we should be permitted to go in experimenting with offenders or in probing about in the psyches of convicts, particularly in view of the fact that the outcome of these tinkering activities is pretty much a mystery.

The concern for procedural safeguards which the Supreme Court has shown in the areas of police work and court operations has been extended to correctional decision making in recent years. Although prisoners and other offenders do not enjoy complete protection against the capricious and arbitrary exercise of power by correctional officials acting in the name of treatment, correctional decision makers are increasingly being controlled by legal strictures. These restrictions compel them to provide specific grounds for the actions they take against offenders, demand that they provide legal advice and right of appeal to accused persons, and require them to operate with considerable regard for due process at other points in the correctional experience.[37] For example, in the *Mempa* v. *Rhay* decision in 1967 and the *Gagnon* v. *Scarpelli* decision in 1973, the Supreme Court held that probationers have the right to legal counsel at probation revocation hearings or when a suspended prison sentence is to be reimposed. Similarly, in *Arciniega* v. *Freeman* in 1971, the Court ruled that parolees cannot have their parole revoked merely for incidental association with other exconvicts in a work setting, while in *Morrisey* v. *Brewer* in 1972, the Court ruled that parole boards cannot revoke the paroles of offenders without providing them with a revocation hearing and protections of due process.

Along somewhat similar lines, Gilbert Geis has devoted careful attention to the ethical and legal issues in experimental programs. He argued that restrictions must be imposed against wholesale experimentation with involuntary clients in correction and that beyond certain boundaries the search for correctional answers is not permissible.[38]

Let us close this brief examination of ethical questions with a look at electronic-rehabilitation and -surveillance measures. Ralph Schwitzgebel has discussed the use of modern electronic technology in corrections.[39] He indicated that devices are available through which the activities of parolees and other correctional wards could be electronically monitored so that they could be kept under continuous surveillance. Schwitzgebel indicated that these gadgets might be used in a variety of ways: "Thus, for example, if a parolee who had previously been very inconsistent in his work patterns was at work on time he might be sent a signal from the parole officer that meant: 'You're doing well,' or that he would receive a bonus. On the other hand, if it appeared that the parolee was in a high crime rate area at two o'clock in the morning, he might be sent a signal reminding him to return home."[40]

Doubtless, the use of mechanical and electronic gadgetry could do more to curtail some forms of criminality than is currently possible through conventional means of rehabilitation. Markedly increasing the illumination intensity of street lights in urban areas might do more to curb strong-armed robbery than nearly any other strategy available to us. Much more attention should be given to the development of improved automobile locks to deter car theft, television-monitoring systems to discourage shoplifting, and other mechanical deterrents of this kind. Electronic surveillance of parolees through sensors and similar devices falls into this general category of technological measures to alleviate the crime problem.

However, there is a difference between the question: "Can it be done?" and the query: "Should it be done?" Schwitzgebel was *not* a Dr. Strangelove, conjuring up some kind of Orwellian "Big Brother" system for totally removing the individual citizen's privacy so that no one would be safe from the eyes or ears of the electronic monitor. Quite the contrary, he was aware that although some things are technologically possible, they should not be used because of the potential harm that might result. The danger was not that Schwitzgebel would engage in unconscionable excursions into the privacy of offenders, but that less-restrained individuals may seize on the electronic parole officer as a panacea, unleashing all manner of excesses in their haste to cure the crime problem. From much past history in corrections, we have learned that many people who have used treatment recommendations have not always shown the restraint and ethical sensitivity demonstrated by the originators of the ideas.

the impact of correctional treatment

What happens to individuals after they are placed on probation? Do they continue to engage in criminality? What are the effects of a penal commitment? Do offenders refrain from further lawbreaking after they have been given therapeutic attention in an institution? For example, does group counseling improve the chances of an inmate's succeeding on parole?

Answers to questions of this kind must be tentative and partial, given the paucity of good evidence on the effects of correctional practices. Correctional agencies have rarely gathered adequate statistics on the posttreatment careers of persons whom they process. Definitive data dealing with the effects of specific kinds of correctional intervention have been even more uncommon.[41]

There are various reasons for the scarcity of empirical studies of the effects of correctional actions, not the least of which is lack of financial support, which prevents research on a sustained basis. Also, in view of the lack of therapeutic activities in the past, concern for evidence about programs has been premature until relatively recently. Evaluative research has not always been enthusiastically supported, so even supporters of treatment sometimes have had ambivalent feelings about this kind of investigation. The problem with careful and objective research is that it sometimes turns up unpalatable findings! Few correctional managers wish to court the possibility that research will uncover evidence that their program is a failure, for one's job may be in jeopardy from such findings, or one's ego bruised.

PROBATION

Adult-probation departments generally show results in which three-fourths or more of the probationers are successes, in that they apparently refrain from further criminality. At the same time, studies of probation departments have indicated that little or no counseling occurs, so the high success rates must be explained some other way.[42] Probation departments select prosocial, "square John" kinds of offenders for placement at the same time that they divert more troublesome lawbreakers toward prisons. These prosocial individuals are self-correctors who deter themselves from repeated criminality.

JUVENILE INSTITUTIONS[43]

The efficiency of training schools in arresting progress of deviant careers is largely conjectural, in that careful follow-up studies of these places are hard to find. However, the results of one study carried out in California were not encouraging and surely do not lead to much confidence in the operations of training schools in other states.[44] In this research, 4,000 delinquent wards discharged from the Youth Authority in 1953 and 1958 were examined. Less than 20 percent of the female wards acquired any sort of criminal record in the five-year follow-up period after discharge. The boys followed quite different paths. About 22 percent of the males wards had been discharged from Youth Authority custody as a result of being sent to prison. Another 22 percent were sentenced to prison within five years after discharge, and another 26 percent received one or more nonprison sentences (fines, jail, and/or probation). Thus, only 30 percent of the boys managed to remain free from detected criminality.

What is the meaning of statistics showing that most wards released from training schools become reinvolved in misconduct? Are these institutions directly responsible for recidivism? Not necessarily, for the juveniles who are paroled from training schools might have continued in criminality even if they had been dealt with in some form of community treatment. In other words, parole failures may be attributable mainly to the characteristics and experiences wards bring with them to the training school rather than to the effects of the institution itself.[45]

The Community Treatment Project in California provided data bearing on this issue.[46] In that experimental effort, youths who would normally be sent to training schools were instead dealt with in the community. Two kinds of intervention were involved. In one kind, differential-treatment units consisting of a supervisor, treatment agents, and a work supervisor counseled wards who had been sorted into diagnostic types. In the second kind of intervention, guided-group-interaction units administered group treatment to offenders. Youths in the community-treatment experimental groups were matched with institutionalized control-group subjects. Wards were randomly assigned either to community treatment or to the training school.

The findings on this project initially seemed to indicate that community treatment was more effective than institutionalization, in that the experimental subjects had a lower parole violation rate than the control subjects. However, we should not be too quick to accept these results as an indictment of training schools. Paul Lerman pointed out that the parole-violation figures were misleading. The community-treated youths actually committed more violations in the parole period than did the control cases. Although the parole agents observed more lawbreaking on the part of the community-treated parolees, the agents took action more frequently against the control subjects. The percentages of offenders who had their paroles revoked for offenses of low or medium seriousness were considerably higher for the control cases than for the experimentals. Lerman concluded that the behavior of the parole agents of the two groups differed, producing the different parole-violation figures.[47]

PRISONS

Most studies of populations of offenders in adult institutions have shown that large numbers of these persons have previously been in trouble with the authorities. Furthermore, these surveys have noted that incarcerated offenders often shown prior records of institutionalization. These figures fail to indicate the proportion of prison inmates who succeed on parole. That prisoners have often been in custody before does not necessarily mean that most inmates fail on parole. Instead, many of them may succeed on release at the same time that a group of chronic failures flow into, out of, and back into the penitentiary.

One indication of postrelease adjustments made by inmates is shown in Table 23, reporting on parole outcomes for a sample of persons released from state prisons in 1976.[48] As Table 23 indicates, only 13.4 percent of the males and 6.7 percent of the females were returned to prison within the first year on parole. Moreover, most of those who were sent back to prison had not committed new major crimes, instead, they were recommitted for technical violations of parole rules.

table 23   parole outcomes in first year after release for inmates paroled in 1976, by sex

	Males	Females
Discharged	16.9	19.6
Continued on parole	64.9	68.6
Absconded	4.2	4.9
Returned to prison	13.4	6.7
no violation	(0.4)	(0.4)
no new convictions and not in lieu of prosecution	(4.8)	(3.3)
new minor or lesser conviction(s) or in lieu of prosecution	(1.2)	(0.7)
in lieu of prosecution for new major offense(s)	(1.0)	(0.5)
recommitted to prison with new major conviction	(6.0)	(1.8)
Died	0.6	0.2

Daniel Glaser's survey of the federal prison system also indicated that prisoners frequently made adequate parole adjustments.[49] Glaser noted that the notion is frequently expressed that two-thirds of those who are imprisoned subsequently returned to prison. However, Glaser reviewed a collection of surveys indicating that only about one-third of the parolees from state institutions are returned to penitentiaries within five years after release.

Glaser identified some major variables associated with parole success or failure. Younger prisoners most often violated parole. Parolees who had been confined in juvenile institutions, left home at an early age, or had records of repeated property crime most commonly failed on parole.[50]

Glaser's investigation showed that inmates did not violently dislike treatment personnel in institutions but did not accord them much respect or positive feelings. Thus, the therapeutic impact of treatment on convicts may be slight.[51] Glaser also suggested that training in vocational skills was less important as an influence on parole behavior than habituation of inmates to regularity in employment. Finally, Glaser noted that positive effects of prisons did not necessarily produce good behavior by offenders on parole. Rather, the most successful releasee was able to assume a conventional social role outside the prison *despite* having been imprisoned. Thus, he remarked:

This half-century's most promising correctional development for alleviating post-release problems of prisoners consists of the counseling centers in metropolitan areas to which prisoners scheduled for release are transferred some months before their release date, and from which they regularly go forth to enter the job market and to develop correctionally acceptable post-prison social relationships, before they are released on a regular parole or any other type of release from prison.[52]

DOES TREATMENT WORK?[53]

The evidence examined to this point has suggested that whatever results of various dispositions such as probation or imprisonment, these outcomes are explained more by the background characteristics of the offenders who succeed or fail in these structures than by the therapeutic actions directed at them. For example, the Community Treatment Project turned up negative findings indicating that community treatment in small caseloads was no more effective than incarceration of offenders.

Unfortunately for advocates of correctional treatment, there is additional evidence regarding the negligible impact of therapeutic intervention upon lawbreakers. For example, the findings from the Highfields Project alluded to earlier did *not* support the hypothesis that small-group milieu treatment was more effective than incarceration in a state training school. Similarly, while the data from the Fricot Ranch study mentioned earlier indicated that, when compared with conventional institutional handling, the experimental treatment retarded the speed at which parolees became reinvolved in delinquency, it did not significantly reduce the number who eventually got into further trouble.[54] A massive experiment in group counseling conducted at the California Men's Colony, San Luis Obispo showed no parole-outcome differences among those who received group counseling in small groups, counseling in large groups, or regular institutional processing.[55]

One pessimistic review of correctional treatment endeavors was presented by Walter Bailey, who examined 100 studies of correctional outcome published between 1940 and 1960.[56] He noted that about two-thirds of the programs were based on a "sick" model of the offender, who was in need of psychotherapeutic handling. From these studies, Bailey concluded:

Since positive results were indicated in roughly one-half of the total sample of 100 reports analyzed, the problem of interpretation is not unrelated to that of determining "whether the cup is half empty or half full." But, when one recalls that these results, in terms of success or failure of the treatment used, are based upon the conclusions of the authors of the reports, themselves, then the implications of these findings regarding the effectiveness of correctional treatment become rather discouraging. A critical evaluation of the actual design and the specific research procedures described in each instance would substantially decrease the relative frequency of successful outcomes based upon reliably valid evidence. *Therefore, it seems quite clear that, on the sample of outcome reports with all of its limitations, evidence supporting the efficacy of correctional treatment is slight, inconsistent, and of questionable reliability* (emphasis added).[57]

Another of these negative assessments of correctional treatment was an examination by Robison and Smith of about a dozen projects carried on in California.[58] They utilized the studies in order to gauge the extent to which different posttreatment outcomes might have been produced by sentencing persons to probation rather than imprisonment, by varying the length of the period of incarceration, by different forms of treatment in the institution, by variations in the intensity of probation or parole supervision, or by releasing persons to parole as contrasted to discharging them outright from prison. Robison and Smith asserted that any variations in outcomes observed for these different dispositions were the consequence either of initial differences among the types of offenders processed by community agencies or institutions, or the result of variations in the agency policies, rather than being attributable to treatment impact. For example, the seemingly more positive impact of the Community Treatment Project was a reflection of more lenient revocation policies on the part of parole agents supervising the experimental group cases.

One conclusion of Robison and Smith is well worth reporting here. Speaking to the question of long prison sentences as a means of curtailing crime, they stated:

It is difficult to escape the conclusion that the act of incarcerating a person at all will impair whatever potential he has for crime-free future adjustment and that, regardless of which "treatments" are administered while he is in prison, the longer he is kept there the more he will deteriorate and the more likely it is that he will recidivate. In any event, it seems almost certain that releasing men from prison earlier than is now customary in California would not increase recidivism.[59]

The most ambitious and devastating of these surveys of results from correctional intervention was by Douglas Lipton, Robert Martinson, and Judith Wilks,[60] who examined 231 treatment projects that had been conducted between 1945 and 1967. The rehabilitation endeavors were categorized in terms of the treatment methods employed, such as milieu therapy, parole supervision, medical treatment, individual counseling, group therapy, and so on. Treatment outcomes were similarly examined in a number of different ways, including recidivism, personality and attitude change, and community adjustment. The central conclusion from this massive scrutiny of treatment ventures was that: *"with few and isolated exceptions, the rehabilitative efforts that have been reported so far have had no appreciable effect on recidivism"* (emphasis in the original).[61]

Martinson conceded that these dismal results *might* merely mean that the therapy that has been provided to offenders in these past experiments was not intensive enough, so that if more high-powered and intensive treatment had been administered, positive results would have been produced. But, he did not favor that interpretation, arguing instead that:

It may be, on the other hand, that there is a more radical flaw in our present strategies—that education at its best, or that psychotherapy at its best, cannot overcome, or even appreciably reduce, the powerful tendency for offenders to continue in criminal behavior. Our present treatment programs are based on a theory of crime as a "disease"—that is to say, as something foreign and abnormal in the individual which can presumably be cured. This theory may well be flawed, in that it overlooks—indeed, denies—both the normality of crime in society and the personal normality of a very large proportion of offenders, criminals who are merely responding to facts and conditions of our society.[62]

Other voices have been raised in this chorus of pessimism about correctional intervention.[63] At the same time, some continue to see a ray of hope for correctional treatment contained within these generally negative studies. Supporters of correctional treatment have taken up the "different strokes for different folks" view, arguing that treatment has been ineffective because of the poor match that has been made between particular offenders and specific kinds of treatment. For example, Charles Shireman, Katherine Mann, Charles Larsen, and Thomas

Young reviewed a dozen studies of treatment within correctional institutions.[64] They concluded that certain forms of institutional therapy may produce results sufficiently powerful to carry over into the postrelease period. More specifically, they argued that short-term milieu therapy coupled with a situation of high staff morale showed promise for some offenders. Similarly, they found some indication in the 12 projects that intensive milieu treatment directed at younger boys, group counseling of young first offenders, certain kinds of individual psychiatric therapy given to younger adolescents, and provision of plastic surgery to selected cases all were associated with positive treatment results.

Daniel Glaser examined a number of correctional treatment studies and presented a similar argument that certain programs appeared to work for certain kinds of offenders.[65] In both the PICO (Pilot Intensive Counseling Organization) project in a California prison, involving intensive counseling administered to inmates,[66] and in the Community Treatment Project, some evidence pointed to the positive impact of counseling upon offenders classified as "conflicted," "neurotic," or "amenable" to treatment. Finally, Ted Palmer claimed that Martinson's report on the effectiveness of correctional intervention contained some supporting evidence for the argument that certain specific tactics of treatment were associated with significant posttreatment results.[67] Palmer's own conclusion was that: "Rather than ask, 'What works—for offenders as a whole?' we must increasingly ask, 'Which methods work best for *which* types of offenders, and under *what* conditions or in what types of setting?' " (emphasis in the original).[68]

THE FUTURE OF TREATMENT

It would be comforting for the supporters of the treatment goal in corrections to take refuge in arguments that the failure of treatment has only been a failure of *implementation*, such that the ideal remains valid and intact. But, that claim is difficult to sustain in the light of the fact that many of the experiments reviewed by Martinson and others were relatively intensive ones in which a relatively heavy measure of treatment was provided to the offenders in the experimental groups. Accordingly, we need to be wary of these arguments which explain away the paucity of positive results, for they may constitute what Cressey has termed a vocabulary of adjustment that allows us to avoid confronting the harsh reality that correctional intervention as currently operated is, in fact, lacking in impact.[69]

As we move toward the last decade of the twentieth century, it is not clear what the final result will be of the current dialogue on correctional intervention. However, it seems probable that efforts to rehabilitate offenders will continue for some time, if for no other reason than inertia. There have been several decades of development of the treatment goal, resulting in generous amounts of public funds being expended on correctional intervention and the creation of a massive correctional bureaucracy. Once in operation, it is difficult to bring this machinery to a halt.

If treatment efforts are to continue, these are going to have to be informed by the best available criminological knowledge. Treatment endeavors of the future also are going to require that more effort be focused upon *posttreatment contingencies*, such as possession of a meaningful job, availability of advanced educational opportunities, and the like, which play a major part in success or failure. Intervention activities in coming decades will probably be less involved with psychiatric tinkering and other forms of resocialization of lawbreakers and more concerned with increasing the offender's "stake in conformity." However, provision of meaningful occupational opportunities and kindred efforts are much easier to identify than to accomplish, particularly at a time when the economic health of the nation seems to be moving toward a relatively permanent state of debilitation.

It is also probable that there will be further movement away from enforced therapy and toward a justice model in corrections, in which offenders will gain other protections against the arbitrary exercise of power by correctional decision makers. There have already been some significant modifications, through Supreme Court decisions, of what Fred Cohen identified as the benevolent-purpose doctrine.[70] According to Cohen, the benevolent-purpose doctrine involves the following:

> The operating principle that emerges from use of the benevolent purpose doctrine, then, is that the goals of corrections can best be obtained by the preservation of maximum discretion on the part of judicial and correctional authorities. Discretion, in turn, is maximized by the reduction or elimination of procedural "obstacles"; minimizing the role of the offender or his representative in the decision-making processes; and the maintenance of a statutory framework that is so broad that virtually any decisions can be smuggled through the mythical borders of legislative intent.[71]

The benevolent-purpose doctrine probably will give way in other regards as well. For example, there has been agitation in recent years for movement toward voluntary treatment in prisons, along with greater attention to prisoner rights.[72] Along this same line, parole boards and parole systems currently are under attack nearly everywhere in the United States. Critics of parole have argued that the basic assumption of parole is erroneous: to wit, that it is possible for quasi-judicial parole boards to individualize prison sentences and select prison terms that are of optimal length for achieving successful treatment of the offender. Parole critics would abandon indeterminate-sentencing laws in favor of "flat time" or fixed sentences that would be defined by statutes. Moreover, Chapter 20 indicated that a number of states have already moved legislatively to abolish parole or to impose statutory strictures upon parole systems.

Those who would agitate for continuation of the rehabilitation goal will also have to contend with opponents who are now voicing recommendations that correctional responses should center more heavily upon deterrence or incapacitation of offenders in order to bring about crime reduction.[73]

summary

Until the latter part of the nineteenth century, the processing of criminals everywhere in the world embodied motives of revenge, retaliation, and punishment. However, from the early 1900s to the 1960s in the United States, treatment of criminals as a major correctional goal seemed to be an idea whose time had come. Now, in recent years, a gray fog of pessimism about treatment has descended over the correctional enterprise. It now appears that rehabilitation is an idea whose time has gone!

Although treatment has existed for over a century, articulation of that goal into a coherent body of thought is a relatively recent development. During much of the earlier history of the rehabilitation movement, treatment was often confused with humanitarianism or related activities. In the last several decades, however, rehabilitation theory matured, often taking the form of detailed formulations about specific types of intervention to be directed at specific kinds of lawbreakers.

The benevolent-purpose doctrine has been one of the less desirable companions of the criminal-rehabilitation movement. Offenders have been deprived of the elementary protections of due process and subjected to relatively arbitrary and oftentimes excessive dispositions in the name of treatment. The benevolent-purpose doctrine has held that because the things that are done to lawbreakers are "for their own good," little or no concern need be paid to providing them with fair hearings and procedural safeguards.

The benevolent-purpose doctrine and the rehabilitation movement of which it is a part have been attacked by those who have pointed to the failure of treatment projects and experiments to produce tangible evidence of positive impact upon offenders. New voices are now being heard, additional to those of probation officers, caseworkers, and other people-changers. Advocates of deterrence, incapacitation, and other correctional goals have begun to press for those goals largely to replace the therapeutic aims. It is far from clear how the current controversy and turmoil revolving around the different correctional goals of rehabilitation, deterrence, incapacitation, and revenge will ultimately be resolved. But one thing is obvious: major shifts are going to occur in the system of criminal justice responses to lawbreakers in the next several decades.

notes

[1] One detailed example is Don C. Gibbons, *Changing the Lawbreaker* (Englewood Cliffs, N.J.: Prentice-Hall, Inc., 1965).

[2] One prominent recent example is James Q. Wilson, *Thinking About Crime* (New York: Basic Books, 1975); see also Jerome H. Skolnick, "Are More Jails the Answer?" *Dissent* (Winter 1976), 95–97.

[3] The discussion of treatment in this chapter is an abbreviated version of the analysis of treatment theory and therapeutic programs found in Gibbons, *Changing the Lawbreaker.* Also see Gibbons,

"Punish the Criminal or Rehabilitate the Offender? The Current Debate," in *Current Perspectives on Criminal Behavior*, 2nd ed., Abraham S. Blumberg, ed. (New York: Knopf, 1981), pp. 364–81.

[4]Gibbons, *Changing the Lawbreaker*, pp. 6–12.

[5]See Stanton Wheeler, "The Social Sources of Criminology," *Sociological Inquiry*, 32 (Spring 1962), 139–59, for a discussion of some of the reasons why sociological theories have played an insignificant part in most correctional programs.

[6]Daniel Glaser has endeavored to spell out, in considerable detail, the treatment implications of sociological knowledge on criminal etiology. See Daniel Glaser, *Strategic Criminal Justice Planning* (Rockville, Md.: National Institute of Mental Health, 1975); Glaser, *Adult Crime and Social Policy* (Englewood Cliffs, N.J.: Prentice-Hall, Inc., 1972). Also see Gibbons, *Changing the Lawbreaker*.

[7]The matters discussed in this section are analyzed in greater detail in Gibbons, *Changing the Lawbreaker*, pp. 136–43.

[8]Donald R. Cressey, *Other People's Money* (New York: Free Press, 1953).

[9]Daniel Glaser, *The Effectiveness of a Prison and Parole System* (Indianapolis: Bobbs-Merrill, 1964), p. 511.

[10]Variations in treatment procedures are discussed at greater length in Gibbons, *Changing the Lawbreaker*, pp. 142–88. For another explication of the elements of different forms of intervention, see LaMar T. Empey and Steven G. Lubeck, *The Silverlake Experiment* (Chicago: Aldine, 1971), pp. 74–98.

[11]Carl R. Rogers, *Client-Centered Therapy* (Boston: Houghton Mifflin Co., 1951).

[12]William Glasser, *Reality Therapy* (New York: Harper & Row, Pub., 1965).

[13]Behavior modification has been described in Robert J. Wicks, *Correctional Psychology* (San Francisco: Canfield Press, 1974), pp. 55–74. Wicks discussed several programs employing behavior-modification principles, including the Robert F. Kennedy Youth Center in Morgantown, West Virginia. He also noted some criticisms of behavior modification, including the claim that this form of intervention deals only with symptoms and not with underlying causes. A closely related criticism has been that token economies and other relatively mechanistic programs cannot alter the underlying causes of negative behavior. In addition, critics have argued that behavior modification fails to bring about lasting changes in behavior, so that while wards show positive behavior in an institutional setting, these changes are not likely to persist upon release from the institution.

[14]Donald R. Cressey, "Contradictory Theories in Correctional Group Therapy Programs," *Federal Probation* 18 (June 1954), 20–26. See also Dogan K. Akman, Andre Normandeau, and Marvin E. Wolfgang, "The Group Treatment Literature in Correctional Institutions: An International Bibliography, 1945–1969," *Journal of Criminal Law, Criminology and Police Science*, 59 (March 1968), 41–56.

[15]Donald R. Cressey, "Changing Criminals: The Application of the Theory of Differential Association," *American Journal of Sociology*, 61 (September 1955), 118–19.

[16]Norman Fenton, *An Introduction to Group Counseling in State Correctional Service* (New York: The American Correctional Association, 1958); Fenton, ed., *Explorations in the Use of Group Counseling in the County Correctional Program* (Palo Alto, Calif.: Pacific Books, 1962).

[17]Lloyd W. McCorkle, Albert Elias, and F. Lovell Bixby, *The Highfields Story* (New York: Holt, Rinehart & Winston, 1958).

[18]Carl F. Jesness, *The Fricot Ranch Study* (Sacramento: State of California, Department of Youth Authority, 1965).

[19]Korn and McCorkle have developed another version of milieu management as a prescription for converting penal institutions into treatment milieus. Their program involved systematic frustration of the inmate in his attempts to "beat the system" by manipulating officials. The offender is prevented from developing exploitative techniques by which he can do "easy time." The program was designed to bring prisoners to the ultimate realization that they had much to gain by living within conventional rules, first in the prison and later in the free community. See Richard R. Korn and Lloyd W. McCorkle, *Criminology and Penology* (New York: Holt, Rinehart & Winston, 1959), pp. 540–52.

[20]Environmental-change programs are discussed in more detail in Don C. Gibbons, *Delinquent Behavior*, 3rd ed. (Englewood Cliffs, N.J.: Prentice-Hall, Inc., 1981), pp. 357–61.

[21]Solomon Kobrin, "The Chicago Area Project—A 25-Year Assessment," *Annals of The American Academy of Political and Social Science*, 322 (March 1959), 19–29; Helen L. Witmer and Edith Tufts, *The Effectiveness of Delinquency Prevention Programs*, U.S. Children's Bureau Publication no. 350 (Washington, D.C.: U.S. Government Printing Office, 1954).

[22]Witmer and Tufts, *The Effectiveness of Delinquency Prevention Programs*, p. 11. For a parallel effort, see Walter B. Miller, "The Impact of a 'Total Community' Delinquency Control Project," *Social Problems*, 10 (Fall 1962), 168–91.

[23]*A Proposal for the Prevention and Control of Delinquency by Expanding Opportunities* (New York: Mobilization for Youth, 1961); see also *A Report on Juvenile Delinquency* (Washington, D.C.: Hearings of the Subcommittee on Appropriations, 1960), pp. 113–16.

[24]Richard A. Cloward and Lloyd E. Ohlin, *Delinquency and Opportunity* (New York: Free Press, 1960).

[25]The evaluative literature on this project includes George A. Brager and Francis P. Purcell, eds., *Community Action Against Poverty* (New Haven: College and Universities Press, 1967); Harold H. Weissman, ed., *Individual and Group Services in the Mobilization for Youth Experience* (New York: Association Press, 1969); Weissman, ed., *Justice and the Law* (New York: Association Press, 1969); Weissman, ed., *Community Development in the Mobilization for Youth Experience* (New York: Association Press, 1969); Richard A. Cloward, "Index of Research Studies," in Weissman, *Justice and the Law*, pp. 205–13.

[26]Robert Arnold, "Mobilization for Youth: Patchwork or Solution?" *Dissent*, 11 (Summer 1964), 347–54. For another pessimistic report on this kind of program, see James C. Hackler, "Boys, Blisters, and Behavior: The Impact of a Work Program in an Urban Central Area," *Journal of Research in Crime and Delinquency*, 3 (July 1966), 155–64.

[27]Gibbons, *Changing the Lawbreaker*, pp. 228–82. See also, Glaser, *Adult Crime and Social Policy*; Margaret Q. Warren, "Intervention with Juvenile Delinquents," in *Pursuing Justice for the Child*, Margaret K. Rosenheim, ed. (Chicago: University of Chicago Press, 1976), pp. 176–204.

[28]This project was reported in Ted Palmer, "The Youth Authority's Community Treatment Project," *Federal Probation*, 38 (March 1974), 3–14. For critical comments on the maturity-levels theory and the treatment project, see Don C. Gibbons, "Differential Treatment of Delinquents and Interpersonal Maturity Levels Theory: A Critique," *Social Service Review*, 44 (March 1970), 22–33; Paul Lerman, "Evaluative Studies of Institutions for Delinquents: Implications for Research and Social Policy," *Social Work*, 13 (July 1968), 55–64; Lerman, *Community Treatment and Social Control* (Chicago: University of Chicago Press, 1975). Lerman's analysis indicated that community treatment was no more successful than institutionalization. Also, the community-treated wards actually spent considerable time in detention, hence this was not truly a community-intervention venture.

[29]See Jackson Toby, "Early Identification and Intensive Treatment of Predelinquents: A Negative View," *Social Work*, 6 (July 1961), 3–13.

[30]For one detailed discussion of these questions, see R. Kirkland Schwitzgebel, *Legal Aspects of the Enforced Treatment of Offenders* (Rockville, Md.: National Institute of Mental Health, 1979).

[31]Herbert L. Packer, *The Limits of the Criminal Sanction* (Stanford, Calif.: Stanford University Press, 1968), p. 296.

[32]Karl Menninger, *The Crime of Punishment* (New York: Viking, 1968).

[33]Thomas S. Szasz, *Ideology and Insanity* (New York: Doubleday, 1970); Szasz, *Law, Liberty, and Psychiatry* (New York: Macmillan, 1963): Szasz, *The Myth of Mental Illness* (New York: Hoeber-Harper, 1961).

[34]Nicholas N. Kittrie, *The Right to be Different* (Baltimore: The Johns Hopkins Press, 1971).

[35]David Sternberg, "Legal Frontiers in Prison Group Psychotherapy," *Journal of Criminal Law, Criminology and Police Science*, 56 (December 1966), 446–69.

[36]Palmer, "The Youth Authority's Community Treatment Project." It ought to be noted that the delinquent wards who were released on parole would presumably have been sent to the training school had there been no experimental project, as would those youths who actually were incarcerated. Accordingly, it was not the case that youngsters were given forms of intervention "in the name of science" that were more severe than customary-penalties. This point probably mitigates at least some of the concern about arbitrary and unusual treatment that might be voiced regarding this project.

[37]Court decisions and legal rights of convicted offenders are discussed in detail in Leonard Orland, *Justice, Punishment, and Treatment* (New York: Free Press, 1973); Gerald D. Robin, *Introduction to the Criminal Justice System* (New York: Harper & Row, Pub., 1980), pp. 383–417.

[38]Gilbert Geis, "Ethical and Legal Issues in Experimentation with Offender Populations," in Joint Commission on Correctional Manpower and Training, *Research in Correctional Rehabilitation* (Washington, D.C.: Joint Commission on Correctional Manpower and Training, 1967), pp. 34–41.

[39]Ralph K. Schwitzgebel, "Issues in the Use of an Electronic Rehabilitation System with Chronic Recidivists," *Law and Society Review*, 3 (May 1969), 597–611; see also Bernard Beck, "Commentary," 611–14.

[40]Schwitzgebel, "Issues in the Use of an Electronic Rehabilitation System," p. 603.

[41]The problems encountered in correctional evaluation research have been discussed in Leslie T. Wilkins, *The Evaluation of Penal Measures* (New York: Random House, 1969); Daniel Glaser, *Routinizing Evaluation: Getting Feedback on the Effectiveness of Crime and Delinquency Programs* (Rockville, Md.: National Institute of Mental Health, 1973); Stuart Adams, *Evaluative Research in Corrections: A Practical Guide* (Washington, D.C. National Institute of Law Enforcement and Criminal Justice, Law Enforcement Assistance Administration, 1975); Don C. Gibbons, Barry D. Lebowitz, and Gerald F. Blake, "Program Evaluation in Correction," *Crime and Delinquency*, 22 (July 1976), 390–21; Malcolm W. Klein and Katherine S. Teilmann, eds., *Handbook of Criminal Justice Evaluation* (Beverly Hills, Calif.: Sage Publications, 1980).

[42]See Ralph W. England, Jr., "What is Responsible for Satisfactory Probation and Post-Probation Outcome?" *Journal of Criminal Law, Criminology and Police Science*, 47 (March–April), 667–76; England, "A Study of Postprobation Recidivism Among 500 Federal Offenders," *Federal Probation*, 19 (September 1955), 10–16.

[43]For a more detailed discussion of the impact of training schools, see Gibbons, *Delinquent Behavior*, pp. 316–22.

[44]Carolyn B. Jamison, Bertram M. Johnson, and Evelyn S. Guttmann, *An Analysis of Post-Discharge Criminal Behavior* (Sacramento: State of California, Department of the Youth Authority, 1966).

[45]Most of the available evidence suggests that training schools have a benign influence on delinquents, as far as attitude change is concerned. Juvenile wards do not adopt more positive attitudes while in the institution, and they do not acquire markedly more antisocial sentiments. This evidence is reviewed in Gibbons, *Delinquent Behavior*, pp. 320–22.

[46]Department of the Youth Authority, *The Status of Current Research in the California Youth Authority* (Sacramento: State of California, 1966), pp. 22–27. See also Palmer, "The Youth Authority's Community Treatment Project."

[47]Lerman, "Evaluative Studies of Institutions for Delinquents," pp. 22–27.

[48]Timothy J. Flanagan, Michael J. Hindelang, and Michael R. Gottfredson, eds., *Sourcebook of Criminal Justice Statistics, 1979* (Washington, D.C.: Law Enforcement Assistance Administration, 1980), p. 666; see also David F. Greenberg, "The Incapacitative Effect of Imprisonment: Some Estimates," *Law and Society Review*, 9 (Summer 1975), 541–80. Greenberg indicated that only 12 percent of the 5,910 men released from prison on parole in California in 1967 were returned to prison with a new felony commitment within two years.

[49]Glaser, *The Effectiveness of a Prison and Parole System*, pp. 13–35. For a discussion of factors which explain the persistence of the erroneous view that most persons who are released from prison fail on parole, see Charles R. Tittle, "Prisons and Rehabilitation: The Inevitability of Disfavor," *Social Problems* 21 (3: 1974), 385–95.

[50]Glaser, *The Effectiveness of a Prison and Parole System*, pp. 36–53.

[51]Ibid., pp. 134–39.

[52]Ibid., p. 511. Also see Richard A. Berk, Kenneth J. Lenihan, and Peter H. Rossi, "Crime and Poverty: Some Experimental Evidence from Ex-Offenders," *American Sociological Review*, 45 (October 1980), 766–86.

[53]Some of the obstacles involved in measurement of rehabilitation and treatment effects are identified in Tittle, "Prisons and Rehabilitation: The Inevitability of Disfavor".

[54]These results are discussed in Gibbons, *Delinquent Behavior*, pp. 323–28, 348–55.

[55]Gene Kassebaum, David A. Ward, and Daniel Wilner, *Prison Treatment and Parole Survival* (New

York: John Wiley, 1971). An earlier experimental study of psychotherapy took place in California with the Intensive Treatment Program at San Quentin and Chino prisons. That operation involved treatment groups that received intensive individual and group psychotherapy, along with control groups processed through the regular institutional program. Results of the program showed no important differences in parole adjustment between the treated and untreated prisoners. See California Department of Corrections, *Second Annual Report, Intensive Treatment Program* (Sacramento: State of California, Department of Corrections, 1958).

[56]Walter C. Bailey, "An Evaluation of 100 Studies of Correctional Outcome," *Journal of Criminal Law, Criminology and Police Science*, 57 (June 1966), 153–60.

[57]Ibid., p. 158.

[58]James Robison and Gerald Smith, "The Effectiveness of Correctional Programs," *Crime and Delinquency*, 17 (January 1971), 67–80.

[59]Ibid., p. 72.

[60]Douglas Lipton, Robert Martinson, and Judith Wilks, *The Effectiveness of Correctional Treatment—A Survey of Treatment Evaluation Studies* (Springfield, Mass.: Praeger Publishers, 1975); Martinson, "What Works?—Questions and Answers about Prison Reform," *The Public Interest*, 35 (Spring 1974), 22–54. Similar findings have also been reported in David F. Greenberg, "The Correctional Effects of Corrections," in *Corrections and Punishment*, Greenberg, ed. (Beverly Hills, Calif.: Sage Publications, 1977), pp. 111–48.

[61]Martinson, "What Works?," p. 25.

[62]Ibid., p. 49. For parallel conclusions, see Stanton Wheeler, "Socialization in Correctional Institutions," in *Handbook of Socialization Theory and Research*, David A. Goslin, ed. (Chicago: Rand McNally, 1969), pp. 1005–23.

[63]For example, see David A. Ward, "Evaluative Research for Corrections," in *Prisoners in America*, Lloyd E. Ohlin, ed. (Englewood Cliffs, N.J.: Prentice-Hall, Inc., 1973), pp. 184–203; Don C. Gibbons and Gerald F. Blake, Jr., "Evaluating the Impact of Juvenile Diversion Programs," *Crime and Delinquency*, 22 (October 1976), 411–20. Gibbons and Blake reviewed a dozen juvenile-diversion projects and reported that most of them were deficient in terms of research design. Also, little evidence of greater success attributable to diversion as opposed to more conventional processing of youthful offenders could be found in these projects.

[64]Charles H. Shireman, Katherine Baird Mann, Charles Larsen, and Thomas Young, "Findings from Experiments in Treatment in the Correctional Institution," *Social Service Review*, 46 (March 1972), 38–59. Other advocates of differential treatment include Warren, "Intervention with Juvenile Delinquents."

[65]Glaser, *Strategic Criminal Justice Planning*, pp. 92–94.

[66]Stuart Adams, "The PICO Project," in *The Sociology of Punishment and Correction*, Norman Johnston, Leonard Savitz, and Marvin E. Wolfgang, eds. 2nd ed. (New York: John Wiley, 1970), pp. 548–61.

[67]Ted Palmer, "Martinson Revisited," *Journal of Research in Crime and Delinquency*, 12 (July 1975), 133–52. See also Charles H. Logan, "Evaluation Research in Crime and Delinquency: A Reappraisal," *Journal of Criminal Law, Criminology and Police Science*, 63 (September 1972), 378–87.

[68]Ibid., p. 152.

[69]Donald R. Cressey, "The Nature and Effectiveness of Correctional Techniques," *Law and Contemporary Problems*, 23 (August 1958), 754–77.

[70]Fred Cohen, *The Legal Challenge to Corrections* (Washington, D.C.: Joint Commission on Correctional Manpower and Training, 1969).

[71]Ibid., p. 29.

[72]Norval Morris, *The Future of Imprisonment* (Chicago: University of Chicago Press, 1974); David Fogel, *We Are the Living Proof* (Cincinnati: W. H. Anderson Co., 1976).

[73]For example, see Wilson, *Thinking About Crime*.

crime in america: the uncertain future

In a message to Congress on February 6, 1967, President Lyndon B. Johnson declared war on crime in the United States, proposing the enactment of a measure titled the Safe Streets and Crime Control Act of 1967. The subsequent offensive against garden-variety lawbreaking became obscured by the tumultuous events of the decade that followed. Johnson declined to run for another term as president, largely because of his growing unpopularity stemming from the marked acceleration of the American role in the Vietnam war which occurred during his term in office. The student protests and the growing disenchantment of other citizens with the war, which had much to do with Johnson's decision not to be a candidate for reelection, continued in the presidency of Richard M. Nixon. In turn, Nixon and his aides responded to these events, which they perceived as threatening, by creation of the Huston plan calling for illegal counter-intelligence activities against dissidents. That plan resulted in "the Plumbers," our nation's first private police agency within the executive branch of government. These activities, many of which were criminal in nature, ultimately came to light after the arrest of the Watergate burglars and finally produced Nixon's resignation and flight from office in disgrace in August 1974. The Watergate disclosures and other revelations regarding the pervasive, insidious illegal acts by the FBI and the Central Intelligence Agency pointed to massive corruption of the democratic system by the very governmental leaders and agencies who were entrusted with its preservation.

This mass of scandal and corruption that surfaced in the 1970s involved a list of crimes by persons in high places in those years so lengthy as to dull one's sensibilities. In October 1973, Vice President Agnew resigned from office after pleading *nolo contendere* to bribery and other criminal charges. His resignation was followed by trials of a number of key presidential aides who were convicted of assorted offenses related to the Watergate conspiracy and who were later sent to prison. The media were filled with accounts of corporate bribes and illegal campaign contributions by Lockheed, Exxon, Gulf, Mobil, Northrop, United Brands, and other corporate giants. Evidence emerged of CIA complicity in attempts to murder leaders of foreign countries, as well as in domestic spying on citizens. The FBI was shown to have acted as an *agent provocateur*, inciting racial incidents and student disorders. Responsible citizens began to take seriously claims that the FBI may have also been directed involved in the assassination of Martin Luther King, conjectures which once were advanced only by members of a "lunatic fringe." Conspiratorial theories which speculated that the

Martin Luther King assassination may have been tied to the murders of John Kennedy and Robert Kennedy, with all three being the work of a group of conspirators, rather than crazed assassins acting alone, attracted some support. This dreary list of facts and plausible speculation is almost endless. Moreover, there were many who suspected that only the tip of the iceberg was revealed, that even more staggering cases of corruption, malfeasance, and criminality remain undetected.

One thing is clear enough: the Nixon administration wallowed in political corruption and governmental illegality on an unprecedented scale. The Teapot Dome scandal of the Harding administration or the petty graft associated with the Truman presidency shrink to insignificance when compared with all of the misconduct that is summed up as "the Watergate scandal."

The Watergate revelations and the reports of CIA intrigue, assassination plots, FBI misconduct, and the like, provided powerful ammunition to radical criminologists, with their vivid claims about the machinations of a ruling class, widespread oppression of persons in foreign lands, domestic repression, and related manifestations of the degeneracy of corporate capitalism.[1] The discussion of radical theorizing in Chapter 7 scored much of this work on the grounds of theoretical shallowness. At the same time, the Watergate disclosures and other reports of governmental and corporate criminality indicated that there is more than a slight measure of truth to the sweeping generalizations of radical criminologists.

Then, too, there is a ring of plausibility to conjectures about a general decline of citizen allegiance to the law which may have resulted from the Watergate era. According to this line of argument, the spectacle of pervasive criminality by corporations, governmental agencies, and political leaders has produced growing cynicism and scorn for the law on the part of the general public. The granting of a pardon to Nixon dramatized the double standard on which the criminal-justice machinery operates, severely punishing the powerless while allowing the powerful to carry on their misdeeds with impunity. Many have claimed that the Watergate scandal, corporate bribes, and assorted other crimes by the powerful have eroded citizen confidence in the government and produced widespread cynicism among members of the general public. In turn, this growing alienation of citizens from their government may lead to the breakdown of law and order and to marked increases in lawbreaking at all levels in American society.[2]

A contrary view regarding the long-term consequences of the Watergate case and the efforts of governmental officials to subvert the democratic system has been advanced by some. Perhaps these disclosures will ultimately have salutary consequences in the way of renewed efforts on the part of both the legislative and executive branches of the government to regain control over governmental officials, the CIA, the FBI, and over corporate activities. In turn, the predicted decline of public confidence in the government and growing disrespect for the law may be less marked than previously forecast.

Unequivocal predictions about the impact of the events of the 1970s on crime levels in the future would be premature. It is too early to tell precisely what effect these dramatic episodes in American history will have upon lawbreaking in the decades ahead.

During the recent past, public concern about the political crimes of the Nixon presidency has diminished at the same time that citizens have become increasingly concerned about the jarring ups and downs experienced by the American economy, runaway inflation, the drastically increased costs of OPEC oil, and a host of other economic ills that have plagued this country. In the view of many, the American economy is out of control, with neither major political party able to stem the tide of economic deterioration. The American dream may be vanishing due to balance-of-payment deficits, uncontrolled oil prices, rampant inflation, and other insoluble economic ills besetting us.

What do these gloomy assessments of the present and the future have to do with criminality? What are the implications of these broad economic, political, and social trends for lawbreaking in the United States in the decades ahead? These are questions for which there are no clear answers, but it is possible to provide some tentative, informed guesses about the future of lawbreaking and responses to it in American society.

the future of crime

How should we go about efforts to peer into the future, so as to anticipate the nature and extent of the crime problem in the next few decades and beyond? In a recent attempt at crime forecasting, Gresham Sykes remarked:

Despite the elaboration of jargon in futurology and the development of specialized statistical techniques, the basic approaches to social forecasting remain few in number and of uncertain worth. Extrapolations from trends in the past, intuitive descriptions of things to come, and predictions based on theories of stability or change in the underlying causal variables constitute the major methods, and none can be accepted as a sure guide.[3]

Let us first look at statistical extrapolation as a forecasting guide. We have seen that most garden-variety lawbreaking, particularly predatory offenses, is carried on by relatively young males. Although the population growth rate of the nation has slowed in recent years, it has not stopped entirely, and young adult males will continue to constitute a sizable part of the expanding total population. For example, in Oregon in 1970, 20- to 29-year-old males made up 6.9 percent of the total population of 2,091,385, while it has been estimated that this group will compose 9.2 percent of the state population of over 2,800,000 in 1985. Males in this age group will increase from 144,300 in 1970 to over 260,000 in 1985, almost assuring that property-crime rates in that state will remain as high as in 1970.

A similar prediction emerged when FBI arrest data were applied to national-population forecasts for the year 2050.[4] Table 24 indicates the number of arrests that would be observed in 2050 if 1974 arrest rates were to continue unchanged.

The problem with this kind of forecasting is that it rests upon the *ceteris paribus* ("other things being equal") assumption. For these predictions to be meaningful, the assumption must be made that the underlying forces which determine crime levels will remain constant, with only the size of the population changing over the forecast period. Or, if statistical forecasts are regarded as baseline estimates against which to gauge future changes in crime levels, considerable knowledge about lawbreaking and its determinants is required so that the baseline figures can be appropriately modified. But, the plain fact is that these underlying factors accounting for current crime rates and patterns are not well understood. As a result extrapolations are often misleading, in that they imply a level of precision in social forecasting well beyond that of which sociologists and criminologists are capable.

In his venture into crime forecasting, Gresham Sykes opted for predictions drawn from existing sociological theories and research evidence concerning crime causation, rather than statistical manipulations. This strategy yields relatively fuzzy predictions, but ones which are probably more realistic than those produced by statistical extrapolation from present rates of lawbreaking.

Although Sykes attributed some of the apparent dramatic 1960s and 1970s crime rise to increased reporting of lawbreaking, he also concluded that criminality reached a critical level in this period. Moreover, he observed that the proportion of 18- to 44-year-olds in the general population will be larger in 1990 than in 1975, as well as increasing in absolute numbers, so that continued high levels of illegal activity are probable, in that these persons contribute most heavily to garden-variety crime.

CONVENTIONAL CRIME

Sykes based his conjectures about the future of crime in the United States upon the body of criminological theory that has been reviewed in the pages of this book. He indicated that garden-variety or conventional crime, particularly of a

table 24   arrests, 1974, and predicted arrests, 2050

offense	arrests, 1974	predicted arrests, 2050
Total	2,164,100	2,344,789
Homicide	20,200	34,045
Forcible rape	26,380	31,152
Robbery	148,720	159,714
Aggravated assault	234,060	265,949
Burglary	516,000	506,230
Larceny	1,056,300	1,125,353
Auto theft	158,600	222,346

predatory variety, flourishes in substandard, deteriorated, inner-city neighborhoods within metropolitan areas. Many lines of criminological theorizing converge in the form of arguments over the criminogenic influences thought to operate upon persons at the bottom of the socioeconomic ladder, who tend to collect in these areas of social disorganization and breakdown. Also, criminological theory assigns much importance to racial discrimination and barriers to economic mobility which confront black citizens in American cities, making them particularly vulnerable to crime-inducing influences. In short, criminological theory argues that many persons are driven into lawbreaking because of economic pressures, accompanied by lack of positive family and community ties.[5] Sykes also noted that crimes of violence as well as predatory offenses are most frequent in deteriorated, inner-city areas within major cities. He interpreted this pattern as reflecting the concentration of subcultural patterns of violence in these neighborhoods.

A gloomy view of the future flows from these criminological observations. According to Sykes, poverty and unemployment are likely to continue or even increase in inner-city neighborhoods, the physical deterioration of urban areas is not likely to be halted, and other social and economic conditions are likely to become exacerbated, leading to higher levels of crime. He declared: "In short, the problem of a large mass of alienated people, trapped at the bottom of the socioeconomic ladder in cities where traditional social ties have disintegrated, is likely to grow worse. The likely result is higher rates of crime, such as homicide, assault, robbery, rape, and larceny, that have long been associated with urban poverty."[6]

There is a body of supporting evidence upon which Sykes's predictions are based. For example, some years ago, Daniel Glaser and Kent Rice pointed out that criminality among adults between 18 and 35 years of age is most frequent during periods of widespread unemployment.[7] Along the same line, James Levine reported that the correlation coefficient between robbery rates and the number of out-of-school and unemployed males in the 16- to 21-year-old category in the 26 largest cities in the country in 1970 was 0.67.[8] In much the same way, Llad Phillips, Harold Votey, and Darold Maxwell have indicated that property-crime rates are strongly correlated in inverse fashion with labor-force participation on the part of 18- to 19-year-old males.[9] In other words, youths who are employed or who are unemployed but seeking a job show lower crime rates than do those youths who have given up the search for a job. In short, these studies have reported relatively consistent findings regarding the impact of poverty and unemployment on crime rates.

Crime rates for a variety of offenses are higher for blacks than for whites, apparently because of the particularly disadvantaged position of blacks in terms of employment and economic status. The basic fact of severe economic inequality suffered by blacks in the United States surely does not require detailed proof. But as one indicator, consider Table 25, showing the percentage distribution of income for white and nonwhite families in 1970.

These reports regarding linkages between race, unemployment, and crime would not be so ominous if one could see evidence that these criminogenic conditions are likely to be reduced in the next few years. Some observers have argued that there were substantial black economic gains in the 1960s, thus offering some hope for the future.[10] However, Wayne Villemez and Alan Row examined a number of the studies on which those claims are based and concluded that most of the apparent narrowing of the gap between black and white income was an illusion produced by research methodology.[11] They indicated that although there has been some relative increase in affluence for a small portion of blacks, most blacks continue to show significantly lower incomes, with no narrowing of the white–black disparity. For example, the median income for employed white males in the United States in 1970 was approximately $9,000, while the figure for blacks was only $5,900. This income gap becomes even more pronounced when the higher proportion of unemployed blacks is acknowledged, and when, in addition, account is taken of the fact that the entire income distribution from highest to lowest income status shows blacks to be disadvantaged when compared to whites.

It would be well to acknowledge, as did Sykes, that the linkages between economic factors such as poverty, underemployment and unemployment, and the like are neither simple nor entirely clear.[12] Among other things, property crimes are not committed solely by persons from lower socioeconomic levels, nor is it true that unemployed individuals usually turn to crime. Instead, some persons who find themselves in positions of severe economic disadvantage are likely to become alienated from conventional behavior and engage in lawbreaking, while many others continue to behave in noncriminal ways. Additionally, there are multiple routes to criminality, some of them traveled by persons from favored social and economic backgrounds. For the latter, greed rather than need may have much to do with explaining their misconduct. It is these complex mixtures of etiological influences which render the task of crime prediction so difficult. As Sykes put it:

table 25 distribution of white and nonwhite family income, 1970[a]

income group	percent	
	white	nonwhite
Under $3000	7.5	20.1
$3000–$4000	9.5	17.0
$5000–$6999	11.3	16.4
$7000–$9999	20.1	18.2
$10,000–$14,999	27.9	17.3
$15,000 and over	23.7	10.9
Median income	$10,236	$6,516

[a]Charles H. Anderson, *The Political Economy of Social Class* (Englewood Cliffs, N.J.: Prentice-Hall, Inc. 1974), p. 93.

Since the correlations between economic factors and the intervening or accompanying variables are undoubtedly imperfect, and the latter are imperfectly correlated with crime, the relationships between economic factors and crime are not apt to be strong and consistent. The task of trying to estimate the future impact of economic variables on criminal behavior must be approached with some caution.[13]

Sykes's cautious predictions about continued high crime levels in urban, inner-city, lower-socioeconomic-status areas were joined to other, tentative estimates regarding economic changes and lawbreaking. Because of major alterations in the American economy in the past several decades, "we face the prospect of a social order that will be chronically unable to create sufficient places in the world of work for both the most and least educated."[14] A situation of zero economic growth in the United States could mean that newer and broader forms of poverty will arise, impelling increased numbers of persons from diverse backgrounds toward criminality.[15]

Sykes also examined a group of criminological arguments centered around family patterns, noting that, in the early part of the century, family disorganization was assigned a major causal role in delinquency and adult criminality.[16] In more recent decades, the family has been downplayed as a major force in lawbreaking, although parent–child interaction patterns are given rather heavy stress, at least implicitly, in social-control explanations of juvenile delinquency.[17] Sykes observed that American family patterns have changed considerably since World War II, with a marked increase in the incidence of divorce, growing proportions of married women employed outside the home, and increased illegitimacy. At the same time, the impact, if any, of these changes upon criminality is not clear. According to Sykes, "It cannot be concluded, therefore, that future changes along these lines will lead to a serious disruption of the socialization process, causing in turn an increase in delinquent or criminal behavior, although it is possible that future research will show such linkages."[18]

In Sykes's view, changes in the American family may well result in increases in adult criminality rather than juvenile delinquency. As more women enter the labor force and gain access to criminal opportunities that have in the past been restricted to males, rising female crime rates may be observed. Increasing crime rates among women and the factors that account for them were examined in detail in Chapter 17, where we saw that, to date, the move toward sexual parity in crime has been less marked than some have claimed. Nonetheless, it seems clear that as the occupational roles of men and women become more alike in the future, so too will their rates of participation in criminality.

UNCONVENTIONAL CRIME

Although much of Sykes's attention was on garden-variety crime, he also endeavored to forecast future levels of unconventional crime, principally white-collar crime, political crime, and political corruption.[19] Because white-collar crime has been most frequent among giant corporations, it is reasonable to suspect it will increase as the trend toward megabusinesses, conglomerates, and multinational corporations continues. He noted other factors as well that may lead to increased business involvement in white-collar crime, including pressures to violate tax regulations. Then, too, as more government regulations are promulgated to control businesses, increased law violation will almost inevitably result from that fact alone.

Embezzlement, computer thefts, and a variety of other illegal activities of employees directed at the property of their employers may also become even more commonplace, according to Sykes, as respect for private property diminishes. The impersonality of large firms allows employees to rationalize their thefts as being victimless and harmless because they can deny that they are stealing from anyone in particular.

Sykes was on the mark in indicating that predictions about political crime in the future are exceedingly hazardous, largely because so little effort has been expended on analysis of this form of lawbreaking. As he noted: "Analysis in this field has tended to remain at the level of description and post hoc interpretation."[20] Indeed, the category of political crime has rarely been clearly defined. In his discussion, Sykes defined political crime as lawbreaking centered on political goals and involving: (1) illegal efforts to change the political structure, (2) attempts to seize power, (3) refusals to obey the law, or (4) failure to enforce the law (as in the case of political favoritism and the like). The Watergate affair, activities of the Symbionese Liberation Army, or crimes by the Ku Klux Klan come to mind as illustrative cases.

Sykes was careful to hedge his predictions about political crime in coming decades, but he did argue that the political calm of the late 1970s and early 1980s may well be disrupted by new forms of political protest and acts of political crime in the years ahead. For example, a prolonged depression might touch off widespread civil disturbances, particularly because of pervasive alienation of citizens from their government which is already said to exist. Also, small groups of terrorists may continue to crop up, carrying out skyjackings, assassinations, kidnappings, and other acts that will alarm the general public. The possibilities for political crimes in the future, as outlined by Sykes, are numerous enough to provoke a good deal of concern.

Sykes also offered little comfort to those who have been concerned about the lawlessness on the part of the FBI, CIA, and other governmental agencies that turned up in the 1970s. He argued that, although many citizens deplore these abuses of power, they may nonetheless continue to view them with ambivalence, believing that wiretapping, clandestine operations, and the like are necessary evils. Many persons may be persuaded that this kind of "dirty work" is required if the Mafia is to be pursued, domestic radicals are to be ferreted out and prosecuted, or necessary international intrigue is to be accomplished. If so, certain crime-control agencies may continue to operate "out of control," engaging in various abuses of citizens here and abroad.

What about political corruption? Will it also increase in the years ahead? Unfortunately, Sykes offered little hope for the dimunition of this kind of law-breaking. Rather than decreasing, it is likely to increase both at the local and state level.

Life in the United States is likely to become a good deal more unpleasant in the twenty-first century, with lawbreaking touching the lives of markedly more citizens and in relatively traumatic ways, if many of Sykes's forecasts are accurate. Regrettably, it is hard to find strong counterevidence which would lead to more positive or optimistic predictions about crime in the future. What, then, is to be done about the diminished future which appears to be threatening us? In particular, what can be done to deal with crime, reducing its occurrence or turning more lawbreakers away from careers in crime?

responding to crime

Criminologists and other observers of the American scene do not entertain a single vision of the future. Some persons, such as Daniel Glaser, have projected a relatively optimistic view of crime and American society in the decades ahead. Glaser conjectured that over the next decade or so the offender population will come to include more whites and more affluent citizens, owing to welfare reforms and economic-opportunity programs that will reduce poverty and economic precariousness.[21] Glaser also asserted that revolution is impossible in this country because the politically and economically powerfully respond to the legitimate grievances of less-advantaged citizens by orderly reforms:

In countries such as the United States and Sweden for example, firmly institutionalized election procedures make the government frequently subject to peaceful change that reflects shifts in the public's political preferences. As the inclusion process accelerated, liberals win control of the government whenever there is much pressure for change, and long before radicals have enough support to gain power through either electoral or revolutionary methods. When liberals introduce reforms, the revolutionary movements lose support. Thus, whenever radicalism begins to gain support it is likely to accelerate reforms benefitting those to whom its potential appeal is greatest, but the reforms are enacted by liberal rather than radical governments.

The foregoing discussion implies that revolution is impossible in the United States. Before any revolutionary cause obtains sufficient popular support to have any prospect of gaining power the policies that gave it support are championed effectively in the elected government, since competing candidates win or lose on the basis of their appeal to the populace. Thus any particular issue that the polls indicate much of the public endorses is also endorsed by many candidates and elected officials.[22]

There is considerable room for argument about the extent to which liberal reforms have occurred in the past in response to public agitation. There are a number of analysts who offer a less sanguine view of the past than did Glaser. And, even if Glaser was correct about liberal reform being relatively prominent in the history of the country, he may well have been considerably off the mark in projecting these trends into the future. His conjectures rest upon a very shaky implicit assumption that economic expansion and growth will continue to characterize the United States.

James Q. Wilson foresaw a somewhat different state of affairs regarding criminality.[23] The general tone of his observations on crime was that we ought to entertain relatively modest hopes as far as crime reduction goes. He would shift emphasis to deterrence efforts designed to increase the risks of apprehension, but he would also give some attention to employment opportunities through which offenders might develop a stake in conformity. Accordingly, at one point he recommended that: "the benefits of work and the costs of crime must be increased simultaneously; to increase one but not the other makes sense only if one assumes that young people are irrational."[24] Wilson's position, which might be termed pragmatic or hardheaded liberalism, did not call for massive changes in the social and economic order.

Some analysts have concluded that anything short of drastic alterations in the economic structure of the nation will have little effect upon lawbreaking. Ronald Chester reviewed a body of theory and research evidence on property crime and concluded that this activity grows out of perceptions of relative deprivation on the part of offenders.[25] In turn, he argued that the sting of relative deprivation cannot be reduced unless a more equitable distribution of income is achieved. He suggested legislation to limit the transfer of wealth from generation to generation through inheritance laws. Needless to say, those who now benefit from the existing arrangements are not likely to look favorably upon such proposals for income redistribution. Congressional action along this line, or legislation designed to make massive shifts in the income-tax burden by closing off tax loopholes and advantages now enjoyed by the more affluent, seem unlikely. Rather, it is more likely that offenders will continue to effect income redistribution through robberies, burglaries, and the like.

We have already observed at a number of points in this book that radical criminologists contend that economic revolution is required if crime is to be eradicated in the United States. For example, Richard Quinney has stated that position well:

Is there an alternative to the future? Certainly the liberal reform solutions are not the answer; they lead only to further repression and open the way for the neofascist state. Only a vision that goes beyond reform of the capitalistic system can provide us with a humane existence and a world free of the authoritarian state. Crime control in modern America is a crucial indication of the world that could come to be under present images and theories of society and human nature. Only with a critical philosophy of our present condition can we suggest a way out of our possible future.[26]

There is more than a little truth in the claims of Gordon and other radical theorists who have argued that conventional crime grows out of economic precariousness engendered by the economic system of monopolistic capitalism.[27]

Moreover, the key to crime reduction does lie in eradication of the root causes of criminality, rather than through target-hardening or tinkering with known offenders.

But, wholesale attacks upon the social and economic bases of criminality are likely to be even more difficult to mount in the future than they have been in the past. There is growing evidence that American society has reached the apogee of its economic affluence, with economic instability or stagnation destined to become a more-or-less continual characteristic of this nature in the future. The human prospect is likely to become increasingly more dreary in this country.[28]

American corporate capitalism has been expansionist, depending upon foreign sources of raw materials to be converted into finished goods and upon foreign markets in which to sell those goods at a considerable profit. Historically, the partnership between the corporate, industrialized United States and the Third World countries has been a highly unequal one in which one partner was exploited in the interests of profit making for the other. American corporations and the national economy thrived upon the domination and exploitation of the world's resources and markets, through which economic expansion and profit making have been sustained.[29] Ours has been an expanding economy with much of this expansion coming at the expense of the underdeveloped nations. But, that situation is changing, as indicated by the emergence of the Organization of Petroleum Exporting Countries (OPEC), wars against colonial or neocolonial powers in various parts of the world, and other indicators of shifts in the structure of the international economy. On this same point, the United States has begun to experience international trade deficits in recent years, as American products have been priced out of world markets because of inflated prices which put them at a disadvantage to the industrial output of countries such as Japan or West Germany.

Economists of various stripes have begun to warn that the national economy is moving toward a situation of increasingly wild swings between inflation and recession, accompanied by widespread and chronic unemployment, with the state endeavoring to control these shifts by alternately heating up or cooling off the economy through taxation, governmental spending, and regulation of interest rates. Some sense of this pattern is indicated by Anderson:

Picking up the cycle at an arbitrary point, say in the early sixties, we find a situation of overproduction and underutilization (recession) being stimulated by deficit government spending. Given the widespread unemployment and correspondingly weak labor position together with the flow of government monies, corporate profits sharply expanded. But continued spending and accumulation cut unemployment and strengthened the wage position of labor, particularly upon the escalation of war spending after 1965. With an unpopular war being paid for out of deficit instead of taxation, wage pressures from higher employment levels increasing, and military as opposed to consumer goods being produced from the deficit spending, the pendulum swung in the late sixties toward sharp inflation. . . . Now came time for a reversal of strategies: cut federal spending, raise unemployment, weaken labor, and thus attempt to control the inflation previously set in motion by the attempt to overcome stagnation at home and revolution abroad.[30]

This is not the place for an extended discussion of the current problems of the American economy. At this writing, some of the ugly facts are readily apparent. The nation is simultaneously in a period of inflation and recession, with high interest rates, deficit spending, and unemployment rates at their highest level since the Depression period of the 1930s. Moreover, even the most optimistic politicians and economists are willing to forecast only modest reductions in unemployment and economic instability over the next few years. The liberal slogan of full employment is taken seriously or verbalized by almost no one. It seems palpably the case that hard times are upon us. Although it is unlikely that the nation is about to suffer a swift and complete economic catastrophe, it is equally unlikely that the current situation will turn out to be only a short-lived and isolated economic aberration. And, if these observations are accurate, crime will surely continue to be "an American way of life."

notes

[1]For example, see Richard Quinney, *Critique of Legal Order* (Boston: Little, Brown, 1974), passim.

[2]One study of the Watergate episode found evidence of loss of confidence in the executive branch of the government and in political leaders generally to some extent, but this loss of confidence did not extend to the political system as a whole. Further, disillusionment was most pronounced among Nixon supporters. See Roger G. Dunham and Armand L. Mauss, "Waves from Watergate: Evidence Concerning the Impact of the Watergate Scandal Upon Political Legitimacy and Social Control," *Pacific Sociological Review*, 19 (October 1976), 469–90.

[3]Gresham M. Sykes, *The Future of Crime* (Rockville, Md.: National Institute of Mental Health, 1980), pp. 1–2.

[4]R. Kelly Hancock and Don C. Gibbons, "The Future of Crime in American Society," paper presented at the Pacific Sociological Association meetings, Victoria, Canada, April 1975.

[5]Sykes, *The Future of Crime*, pp. 10–14.

[6]Ibid., p. 15.

[7]Daniel Glaser and Kent Rice, "Crime, Age, and Employment," *American Sociological Review*, 24 (October 1959), 679–86.

[8]James P. Levine, "The Ineffectiveness of Adding Police to Prevent Crime," *Public Policy*, 4 (Fall 1975), 136.

[9]Llad Phillips, Harold L. Votey, Jr., and Darold Maxwell, "Crime, Youth, and the Labor Market," *Journal of Political Economy* (May–June 1972), 491–503.

[10]For a review of much of the evidence on economic and social inequality, see William J. Chambliss and Thomas E. Ryther, *Sociology* (New York: McGraw-Hill, 1975), pp. 350–86.

[11]Wayne J. Villemez and Alan R. Row, "Black Economic Gains in the Sixties: A Methodological Critique and Reassessment," *Social Forces*, 54 (September 1975), 181–93; see also Charles H. Anderson, *The Political Economy of Social Class* (Englewood Cliffs, N.J.: Prentice-Hall, Inc., 1974), pp. 76–115; Sidney Willhelm, *Who Needs the Negro?* (Cambridge: Schenkman, 1970); Edna Bonacich, "Advanced Capitalism and Black/White Race Relations in the United States: A Split Labor Market Interpretation," *American Sociological Review*, 41 (February 1976), 34–51.

[12]Sykes, *The Future of Crime*, pp. 26–35.

[13]Ibid., p. 30.

[14]Ibid., p. 32.

[15]For example, for a discussion of one potential new form of poverty, see Walter F. Abbott, "Commentary: When Will Academicians Enter the Ranks of the Working Poor?" *Academe*, 66 (October 1980): 349–53.

[16]Sykes, *The Future of Crime*, pp. 19–26.

[17]Travis Hirschi, *Causes of Delinquency* (Berkeley: University of California Press, 1969).

[18]Sykes, *The Future of Crime*, p. 23.

[19]Ibid., pp. 44–62.

[20]Ibid., p. 50.

[21]Daniel Glaser, "Changes in Corrections During the Next 20 Years," in American Justice Institute, *Future of Criminal Justice Personnel: Position Papers* (Sacramento: American Justice Institute, 1972).

[22]Glaser, *Strategic Criminal Justice Planning* (Rockville, Md.: National Institute of Mental Health, 1975), pp. 22–23.

[23]James Q. Wilson, *Thinking About Crime* (New York: Basic Books, 1975), pp. 198–209. See also Edward C. Banfield, *The Unheavenly City Revisited* (Boston: Little. Brown, 1974), pp. 179–210.

[24]Wilson, *Thinking About Crime*, p. 202.

[25]C. Ronald Chester, "Relative Deprivation as a Cause of Property Crime," *Crime and Delinquency*, 22 (January 1976), 17–30; see also Jackson Toby, "The Prospects for Reducing Delinquency Rates in Industrial Societies," *Federal Probation*, 27 (December 1963), 23–25.

[26]Richard Quinney, *Criminology* (Boston: Little, Brown, 1975), p. 301.

[27]David M. Gordon, "Class and the Economics of Crime," *Review of Radical Political Economics*, 3 (Summer 1971), 51–75.

[28]Robert L. Heilbroner, *An Inquiry into the Human Prospect* (New York: W. W. Norton & Co., Inc., 1974).

[29]Anderson, *The Political Economy of Social Class*, pp. 234–81; Harry Magdoff, *The Age of Imperialism* (New York: Monthly Review Press, 1969); Paul M. Sweezy and Magdoff, *The Dynamics of U.S. Capitalism* (New York: Monthly Review Press, 1972).

[30]Anderson, *The Political Economy of Social Class*, pp. 243–44.

author
index

Cohen, Fred, 523, 528
Cole, George F., 432, 433, 442
Cole, Stephen, 129
Coleman, James, 150, 210
Colfax, J.David, 402, 421
Conger, John Janeway, 172, 179, 186
Conklin, John E., 13, 221, 230, 231, 234, 236, 266, 353, 354
Connor, Ralph, 368, 372
Connor, Walter D., 152
Conrad, Earl, 130
Cook, Fred J., 347, 355, 423
Cooley, Charles Horton, 149
Cooper, Lynn, 421
Cooper, Sydney, 371
Cort, David, 332
Cortés, Juan B., 30
Cory, Donald Webster, 297, 299, 306
Coser, Lewis A., 128
Cottrell, Leonard S., Jr., 48
Couzens, Michael, 107
Cowie, John, 395
Cowie, Valerie, 395
Cozart, Reed, 499
Cressey, Donald R., 29, 30, 32, 36, 39, 47, 48, 54, 75, 79, 82, 86, 107, 122, 123, 130, 170, 175, 185, 187, 199, 200, 207, 211, 212, 213, 235, 240, 244, 267, 303, 324, 325, 326, 331, 332, 342, 343, 351, 354, 355, 374, 393, 442, 443, 451, 462, 468, 470, 471, 476, 479, 481, 496, 497, 498, 499, 500, 506, 509, 522, 525, 528
Cumming, Elaine, 410, 423
Cumming, Ian, 410, 423

d

Dager, Edward Z., 500
Dahl, Robert, 151
Dain, Harvey J., 303
Dalgard, Odd Steffen, 183
Danziger, Sheldon, 152
Datesman, Susan K., 213, 395
Davenport, C.B., 30
Davidson, Theodore R., 487, 500
Davis, John A., 130
Davis, Kingsley, 374, 376, 377, 394
Davis, Nanette J., 191, 210
De Baun, Everett, 252, 266
De Fleur, Melvin, 201, 212
De Forrest, Paul, 454, 464
Delph, Edward William, 307

Demerath, Nicholas J., 120, 129
Dentler, Robert A., 108, 362, 371
de River, J.Paul, 293, 305
Deutsch, Albert, 423
Diana, Lewis, 493, 501
Dieckman, Duane, 420
Dienes, C.Thomas, 372
Dimants, Rita, 501
Dince, Paul R., 303
Dinitz, Simon, 170, 185, 187, 235, 361, 362, 371
Doerner, William G., 302
Doleschal, Eugene, 150
Domhoff, William G., 145, 151
Doorbar, Ruth S., 304
Dosick, Martin, 262, 263, 268
Douglas, Jack D., 107, 129, 210, 422, 442
Drake, St.Clair, 348, 355
Drellich, Marvin G., 303
Dresser, John W., 306
Driver, Edward D., 234, 279, 302
Drzazga, John, 304
Dugdale, Richard L., 30
Dunham, H.Warren, 166, 184
Dunham, Roger G., 541
Durkheim, Emile, 33, 112, 113, 114, 128, 129
Duster, Troy, 81, 355

e

Eastman, Esther M., 421
Eastman, George D., 421
Eaton, Joseph W., 61, 79, 129, 499
Edell, Laura, 410, 423
Edgerton, Robert B., 81, 129, 211, 234
Edwards, Loren E., 395
Ehrmann, John C., 291, 305
Ehrmann, Winston, 303
Einstader, Werner J., 255, 266
Elias, Albert, 525
Elliott, Delbert S., 443
Elliott, Mabel, 374, 393, 394
Ellis, Albert, 287, 288, 304, 305
Emerson, Robert M., 438, 443
Emerson, Thomas I., 332
Emmert, Frederick, 333
Empey, LaMar T., 108, 525
England, Ralph W., Jr., 30, 122, 130, 260, 267, 374, 393, 493, 501, 527
Engle, Bernice, 304
Erickson, Maynard L., 13, 81, 108, 150, 210, 463

Erickson, M.H., 166, 184
Erikson, Kai T., 48, 210
Esselstyn, T.C., 360, 370, 421
Estabrook, A.H., 30
Ewing, John A., 372
Eysenck, Hans J., 158, 159, 183
Eysenck, Sybil B.G., 159, 183

f

Faberman, Harvey A., 331
Falla, P.S., 152
Faris, Elsworth, 120
Faris, Robert E.L., 119, 120, 129, 130, 185
Farr, Kathryn A., 442
Feeney, Francis E., 372
Fenton, Norman, 525
Ferdinand, Theodore N., 124, 130, 234, 408, 423
Ferracuti, Franco, 156, 183, 301
Ferri, Enrico, 19, 21, 29
Field, Mark G., 152
Figlio, Robert M., 257, 267
Filstead, William J., 210
Fischer, Claude S., 370
Fisher, Sethard, 186, 234, 490, 500
Fishman, Mark, 12
Flanagan, Timothy J., 5, 13, 81, 96, 97, 99, 101, 108, 420, 464, 527
Floch, Maurice, 483, 499
Fogel, David, 528
Foote, Caleb, 434, 442
Forrest, A.R., 159, 183
Forward, Susan, 306
Foster, Samuel C., 499
Fox, Richard G., 160, 162, 183, 184
Freidson, Eliot, 210
Freud, Sigmund, 166, 184, 374, 375, 376, 377
Friedlander, Kate, 165, 168, 185
Frum, Harold S., 267
Furlong, William Barry, 355
Furstenberg, Frank F., Jr., 402, 421

g

Gagnon, John H., 203, 212, 283, 284, 294, 298, 303, 304, 305, 306, 349, 355, 498
Gall, Franz Joseph, 22
Galliher, John F., 150
Galtung, Johan, 497
Garabedian, Peter G., 13, 128, 230, 235, 443, 498, 500

Gardiner, John A., 346, 347, 354, 409, 423, 424
Garelik, Sanford, 371
Garner, Roberta Ash, 145, 151
Garofalo, Raffaele, 21, 29
Garrity, Donald L., 281, 303
Gasser, Robert Louis, 265, 266
Gastil, Raymond D., 302
Gatti, Florence M., 30
Gauthier, Maurice, 262, 268
Gebhard, Paul, 290, 291, 294, 304, 305
Geer, Blanche, 235
Geerken, Michael R., 463
Geis, Gilbert, 13, 74, 79, 82, 206, 213, 253, 265, 266, 300, 304, 305, 319, 320, 330, 332, 353, 371, 442, 515, 527
Geis, Robley, 305
Gerard, Donald L., 355
Gerver, Israel, 211
Giallombardo, Rose, 283, 479, 480, 481, 499
Gibbens, T.C.N., 268
Gibbons, Don C., 13, 14, 28, 47, 48, 73, 79, 80, 81, 82, 108, 128, 129, 149, 151, 182, 184, 185, 186, 210, 211, 212, 213, 233, 234, 235, 236, 266, 267, 268, 306, 330, 362, 370, 371, 395, 396, 422, 442, 443, 454, 462, 463, 497, 500, 524, 525, 526, 527, 528, 541
Gibbs, Jack P., 13, 81, 150, 210, 453, 462, 463
Gibson, Evelyn, 233
Gibson, Lorne, 213, 304
Gibson, Walter B., 265
Gigeroff, Alex K., 295, 305
Gillin, John L., 48, 262, 267, 268, 276, 302, 304
Gillis, A.R., 395
Ginsburg, Kenneth N., 299, 307
Giordano, Peggy C., 395
Glaser, Daniel, 30, 79, 183, 212, 220, 221, 234, 267, 463, 501, 507, 519, 522, 525, 526, 527, 528, 538, 541, 542
Glasser, William, 525
Glickman, Sylvia, 186, 234
Glueck, Bernard, Sr., 165, 184, 303
Glueck, Bernard C., Jr., 305
Glueck, Eleanor, 30, 156, 165, 171, 179, 183, 185, 207, 208, 213, 267
Glueck, Sheldon, 30, 156, 165, 171, 179, 183, 185, 207, 208, 213, 267
Goddard, Henry H., 25, 30
Goff, Colin H., 331
Goffman, Erving, 496
Gold, Martin, 108
Gold, Sarah, 390, 396
Goldberg, Frederick, Jr., 396

Goldfarb, Ronald, 442
Goldhamer, Herbert, 130
Goldman, Nathan, 124, 130, 407, 408, 422, 423
Goldstein, Joseph, 407, 422
Goode, Erich, 210
Goodenough, Donald R., 184
Goodman, Leonard, 454, 464
Gordon, C. Wayne, 367, 368, 372
Gordon, David M., 136, 141, 142, 150, 539, 542
Gordon, Robert, 162, 184
Goring, Charles, 21, 29
Goslin, David A., 528
Gottfredson, Don M., 422, 500
Gottfredson, Michael R., 5, 13, 81, 96, 97, 99, 101, 108, 420, 464, 527
Gough, Harrison, 174, 175, 176, 177, 178, 179, 186, 187
Gould, Leroy C., 87, 107, 108, 204, 212
Gove, Walter R., 211, 463
Grad, Frank, 372
Grand, Henry G., 303
Grasmick, Harold G., 463
Gray, Thomas C., 421
Green, Edward, 93, 108
Greenberg, David F., 80, 146, 150, 151, 152, 463, 527, 528
Greenspan, Herbert, 306
Greenwood, Peter W., 236, 266, 422
Griswold, Manzer J., 213
Gross, Seymour Z., 501
Grosser, George H., 497
Gruninger, Werner, 498
Guerry, A. M., 18, 19
Gundlach, Ralph H., 29, 303
Gusfield, Joseph R., 69, 87
Guttmacher, Manfred S., 272, 300, 304
Guttmann, Evelyn S., 527

h

Hackler, James C., 526
Hagan, John, 81, 152, 395
Haggerty, Lee J., 306, 371
Hakeem, Michael, 170, 171, 185, 187
Hall, Calvin S., 184
Hall, Jerome, 8, 13, 65, 66, 79, 80, 254, 255, 266, 324, 327, 332, 333
Halleck, Seymour L., 184, 291, 305
Hancock, R. Kelly, 541
Handy, William, 279, 280, 302
Hannum, Thomas E., 186
Hapgood, Hutchins, 266

Harper, Dean, 333
Harper, Ida, 499
Harries, Elizabeth, 331
Harries, Keith D., 29
Harring, Sidney L., 152
Harris, Anthony R., 384, 395
Hart, H., 186
Hartjen, Clayton A., 13, 79, 82, 231, 236, 266, 362, 371
Hartl, Emil M., 29, 30
Hartle, M. Martha, 396
Hartmann, Richard, 150
Hartung, Frank E., 76, 82, 301, 314, 318, 330, 331, 483, 499
Haskell, Martin R., 374, 393
Hathaway, Starke, 172, 185, 186
Hawkins, Charles, 443
Hawkins, Gordon J., 343, 354, 463
Hawkins, Richard O., 78, 402, 421
Hay, Douglas, 13, 80, 462
Hayner, Norman S., 256, 262, 266, 267, 268, 498
Hazelrigg, Lawrence E., 496
Healy, William, 165, 170, 185
Heffernan, Esther, 481, 499
Heilbroner, Robert L., 542
Helmer, William J., 299, 306
Henderson, Charles Richmond, 128
Hengerer, Gertrude, 493, 501
Hepburn, John R., 150, 152, 277, 302
Herling, John, 332
Herman, Robert D., 354
Hewitt, John P., 13
Hewitt, Lester E., 165, 179, 186, 213, 234, 303
Heyman, Doris S., 186
Hill, Robert H., 302
Hills, Stuart L., 80, 133, 150
Hindelang, Michael J., 5, 13, 81, 96, 97, 99, 101, 108, 109, 162, 183, 184, 187, 382, 395, 420, 464, 527
Hippchen, Leonard, 157, 183
Hirschhorn, Kurt, 184
Hirschi, Travis, 109, 128, 162, 184, 542
Hirst, Paul Q., 144, 151
Hobfoll, S. E., 372
Hodge, Robert W., 421
Hoebel, E. Adamson, 51, 79, 462
Hoghughi, M. S., 159, 183
Hollingshead, August B., 184
Homer, Frederic D., 353
Hooker, Evelyn, 298, 306
Hooton, Earnest A., 21, 22, 29, 154
Hopkins, Andrew, 152, 331

Lebowitz, Barry D., 527
Lee, Robert S., 355
Lefstein, Norman, 440, 443
Leger, Robert G., 230, 235, 498
Le Grand, Camille, 290, 291, 305, 389, 390, 396
Lekschas, John, 150
Lemert, Edwin M., 117, 129, 130, 181, 187, 192, 193, 194, 195, 204, 210, 211, 212, 222, 223, 234, 235, 259, 261, 262, 266, 267, 268, 285, 304, 371, 439, 443
Lenihan, Kenneth J., 527
Lentz, William P., 73, 82
Leon, Jeffrey, 81
Leonard, William, 316, 331
Lerman, Paul, 518, 526, 527
Le Roy, John P., 299, 306
Letkemann, Peter, 265, 266
Levin, Yale, 18, 28
Levine, James P., 152, 421, 463, 541
Lewis, Norman, 354
Leznoff, Maurice, 299, 306
Liazos, Alexander, 48
Liebow, Elliot, 212
Lilly, J.Robert, 411, 423
Linden, Rick, 213, 304
Lindesmith, Alfred, 18, 28, 149, 211, 212, 330, 353
Lindner, Robert M., 185
Lindzey, Gardner, 184
Linebaugh, Peter, 13, 80, 462
Lipton, Douglas, 521, 528
Lipton, Harry R., 186
Little, Alan, 497
Llewellyn, Karl, 51, 79
Lockwood, Daniel, 498
Lofland, John, 205, 210, 213
Loftin, Colin, 302
Logan, Charles H., 463, 528
Lombroso, Cesare, 18, 20, 21, 22, 29, 154, 374, 375, 377, 394, 448
Lottier, Stuart, 29
Lovald, Keith, 372
Lubeck, Steven G., 525
Luchterhand, Elmer G., 124, 130, 408, 423
Lundman, Richard J., 421
Lunsteen, Claes, 184
Lustig, Noel, 306
Lynn, David B., 304

m

McCaghy, Charles, 230, 236, 295, 305, 371, 402, 421

McCall, George J., 348, 355
McCartney, James L., 150
McCleery, Richard, 497, 499
McClintock, F.H., 233
McCord, Joan, 186, 187
McCord, William, 186, 187
McCorkle, Lloyd W., 182, 472, 477, 497, 498, 525
McCune, Shirley D., 441
McDermott, Eugene, 29, 30
McDermott, Robert A., 443
McDonald, James F., 267
McDonald, John C.R., 265
McDonald, John M., 301
McGraw, Peg, 499
McGraw, Walter, 499
McIntyre, Jennie, 13
McKay, Henry D., 34, 35, 48, 144, 208, 213, 257, 267
McKenna, James, 231, 232, 236
McKenzie, Donald, 266
McKinney, John C., 129, 149, 210
McLaren, Roy C., 421, 424
Magdoff, Harry, 542
Magnuson, Warren G., 13, 316, 331
Magura, Stephen, 302
Mahan, Linda, 443
Mankoff, Milton, 210
Mann, Katherine Baird, 521, 528
Manning, Peter K., 63, 80, 146, 150, 151, 210, 421
March, James G., 497
Marmor, Judd, 306
Marshall, Andrew W., 130
Martin, Clyde E., 303
Martin, John Bartlow, 266, 499
Martin, Walter T., 295, 305
Martinson, Robert, 521, 528
Marx, Karl, 26, 132, 135, 136, 137, 138, 139, 140, 141, 142, 143, 144, 146, 148
Mathieson, Thomas, 497, 498
Matza, David, 44, 48, 210, 326, 333
Maurer, David W., 265, 266
Mauss, Armand L., 541
Mawson, A.R., 129
Maxwell, Darold, 152, 541
Maxwell, Milton A., 368, 372
Mead, Geoege Herbert, 128
Medalie, Richard J., 422
Mednick, Sarnoff A., 157, 158, 183, 184
Megargee, Edwin I., 186
Meier, Robert F., 13, 143, 144, 151, 183, 330
Meiselman, Karin C., 306
Mennel, Robert M., 81

subject
index